PATENT
TRADEMARK
AND COPYRIGHT
LAWS

June 2015 Edition

Intellectual Property Titles from Bloomberg BNA

Anatomy of a Patent Case

Biotechnology and the Federal Circuit

Constructing and Deconstructing Patents

Copyright Law Deskbook

Drafting Patent License Agreements

Drafting Patents for Litigation and Licensing

Electronic and Software Patents: Law and Practice

Global Patent Litigation: How and Where to Win

Harmon on Patents: Black-Letter Law and Commentary

Intellectual Property Law in Cyberspace

Intellectual Property, Software, and Information Licensing: Law and Practice

Intellectual Property Taxation: Transaction and Litigation Issues

Intellectual Property Technology Transfer

International Patent Litigation: A Country-by-Country Analysis

Patents and the Federal Circuit

Patent Law and Practice

Patent Infringement Remedies

Patent Litigation Strategies Handbook

Patent Prosecution: Law, Practice, and Procedure

Patent, Trademark, and Copyright Laws

Pharmaceutical Patent Law

Post-Grant Patent Practice

Products Comparison Manual for Trademark Users

Secondary Trademark Infringement

Trademark Dilution: Federal, State, and International Law

Trademark Infringement Remedies

Trademark Litigation Practice

PATENT
TRADEMARK
AND COPYRIGHT
LAWS

June 2015 Edition

Current through May 15, 2015

Edited by
Jeffrey M. Samuels

Professor Emeritus
University of Akron School of Law

formerly

David L. Brennan Professor of Law and Director,
Center for Intellectual Property Law and Technology
University of Akron School of Law

Assistant Commissioner for Trademarks
U.S. Patent and Trademark Office

and
Managing Editor
BNA's Patent, Trademark, and Copyright Journal

Bloomberg BNA

Arlington, VA

1801 S. Bell St., Arlington, VA 22202-4501

Library of Congress Catalog Number: 84-644547
ISBN 978-1-61746-651-9
International Standard Serial Number: 0741-1219
Printed in the United States of America

Published by Bloomberg BNA

Summary Contents

Preface

Patent, Trademark, and Copyright Laws includes Title 35 (Patents), Title 17 (Copyrights), and Chapters 22, 63, and 107 of Title 15 (Trademarks, Technology Innovation, and Protection of Intellectual Property Rights) of the United States Code. It also includes miscellaneous sections of the United States Code and treaties relating to intellectual property.

This edition of the book updates the patent statute to reflect the changes set forth in Title 1 of the "Patent Law Treaties Implementation Act of 2012" (Pub. L. 112-211) relating to the Hague Agreement Concerning International Registration of Industrial Designs, which took effect on May 13, 2015. This edition also updates the copyright statute to incorporate those changes regarding the satellite compulsory license set forth in the "STELA Reauthorization Act of 2014" (Pub. L. 113-200), which was signed into law on December 4, 2014. Also included in this edition are the provisions of Pub. L. 113-227, signed into law on December 16, 2014, which establish the Law School Clinic Certification Program of the United States Patent and Trademark Office.

The Fiscal Year 2015 appropriations for the United States Patent and Trademark Office and the Copyright Office, as set forth in the "Consolidated and Further Appropriations Act, 2015," Pub. L. 113-235, which was signed into law on December 16, 2014, are also included in this edition, as are the terms of Section 540 of that Act, which prohibits the National Telecommunications and Information Administration from expending funds during Fiscal Year 2015 to relinquish responsibility with respect to Internet domain name system functions.

The CD-ROM that accompanies this edition includes the patent reform proposals set forth in H.R. 9, the "Innovation Act" as introduced on February 5, 2015, S. 632, the "STRONG Patents Act of 2015," as introduced on March 3, 2015, and S. 1137, the "PATENT Act," as introduced on April 29, 2015. The CD-ROM also includes the text of H.R. 2045, the "Targeting Rogue and Opaque Letters (TROL) Act," as introduced on April 28, 2015.

Jeffrey M. Samuels
Sausalito, CA
May 15, 2015

Detailed Contents
UNITED STATES CODE
TITLE 35—PATENTS

PART I—UNITED STATES PATENT AND TRADEMARK OFFICE

CHAPTER 1—ESTABLISHMENT, OFFICERS AND EMPLOYEES, FUNCTIONS

CHAPTER 2—PROCEEDINGS IN THE PATENT AND TRADEMARK OFFICE

CHAPTER 3—PRACTICE BEFORE PATENT AND TRADEMARK OFFICE

CHAPTER 4—PATENT FEES; FUNDING; SEARCH SYSTEMS

PART II—PATENTABILITY OF INVENTIONS AND
GRANT OF PATENTS

CHAPTER 10—PATENTABILITY OF INVENTIONS

CHAPTER 11—APPLICATION FOR PATENT

CHAPTER 12—EXAMINATION OF APPLICATION

CHAPTER 13—REVIEW OF PATENT AND TRADEMARK OFFICE DECISION

CHAPTER 14—ISSUE OF PATENT

CHAPTER 15—PLANT PATENTS

CHAPTER 16—DESIGNS

CHAPTER 17—SECRECY OF CERTAIN INVENTIONS AND FILING
APPLICATIONS IN FOREIGN COUNTRY

CHAPTER 18—PATENT RIGHTS IN INVENTIONS MADE WITH
FEDERAL ASSISTANCE

PART III—PATENTS AND PROTECTION OF PATENT RIGHTS

CHAPTER 25—AMENDMENT AND CORRECTION OF PATENTS

CHAPTER 26—OWNERSHIP AND ASSIGNMENT

CHAPTER 27—GOVERNMENT INTERESTS IN PATENTS

CHAPTER 28—INFRINGEMENT OF PATENTS

CHAPTER 29—REMEDIES FOR INFRINGEMENT OF PATENT,
AND OTHER ACTIONS

CHAPTER 30—PRIOR ART CITATIONS TO OFFICE AND
EX PARTE REEXAMINATION OF PATENTS

CHAPTER 31 — INTER PARTES REVIEW

[CHAPTER 31 — OPTIONAL INTER PARTES REEXAMINATION PROCEDURES

CHAPTER 32 — POST-GRANT REVIEW

PART IV — PATENT COOPERATION TREATY

CHAPTER 35 — DEFINITIONS

[CHAPTER 36 — INTERNATIONAL STAGE

CHAPTER 37 — NATIONAL STAGE

CHAPTER 38 — INTERNATIONAL DESIGN APPLICATIONS

UNCODIFIED PROVISIONS OF THE AMERICA INVENTS ACT

Detailed Contents

UNITED STATES CODE

TITLE 15, CHAPTER 22—TRADEMARKS

SUBCHAPTER I — THE PRINCIPAL REGISTER

SUBCHAPTER II — THE SUPPLEMENTAL REGISTER

SUBCHAPTER III — GENERAL PROVISIONS

SUBCHAPTER IV—THE MADRID PROTOCOL

Uncodified Lanham Act Provisions

Subchapter 2 — Cybersquatting Protection

Detailed Contents

UNITED STATES CODE

TITLE 15, CHAPTER 63—TECHNOLOGY INNOVATION

Detailed Contents

UNITED STATES CODE

TITLE 17—COPYRIGHTS

CHAPTER 2—COPYRIGHT OWNERSHIP AND TRANSFER

CHAPTER 3—DURATION OF COPYRIGHT

CHAPTER 4—COPYRIGHT NOTICE, DEPOSIT, AND REGISTRATION

CHAPTER 5—COPYRIGHT INFRINGEMENT AND REMEDIES

CHAPTER 6—IMPORTATION, AND EXPORTATION

CHAPTER 7—COPYRIGHT OFFICE

CHAPTER 8—COPYRIGHT ARBITRATION ROYALTY PANELS

CHAPTER 9—PROTECTION OF SEMICONDUCTOR CHIP PRODUCTS

CHAPTER 10—DIGITAL AUDIO RECORDING DEVICES AND MEDIA

SUBCHAPTER A—DEFINITIONS

SUBCHAPTER B—COPYING CONTROLS

SUBCHAPTER C—ROYALTY PAYMENTS

SUBCHAPTER D—PROHIBITION ON CERTAIN INFRINGEMENT ACTIONS, REMEDIES,
AND ARBITRATION

CHAPTER 11—SOUND RECORDINGS AND MUSIC VIDEOS

CHAPTER 12—COPYRIGHT PROTECTION AND MANAGEMENT SYSTEMS

CHAPTER 13—PROTECTION OF ORIGINAL DESIGNS

UNCODIFIED COPYRIGHT-RELATED PROVISIONS

Detailed Contents

OTHER STATUTES

Note.—Some sections, or portions of sections, or other titles of the United States Code, of the District of Columbia Code, and of the Canal Zone Code, relating to patents, trademarks, copyrights, trade secrets, or to the Patent and Trademark Office and the Copyright Office, are reprinted or noted here for convenience. This collection does not purport to be complete.

Detailed Contents

INTERNATIONAL TREATIES AND AGREEMENTS

FINDING LIST BY U.S.C. SECTION

POPULAR NAMES OF SELECTED STATUTES

America Invents Act
Pub. L. 112-29; Sept. 16, 2011; 35 U.S.C. §1 et seq.; 15 U.S.C. §1071;
28 U.S.C. §§1295, 1338, 1454

American Inventors Protection Act of 1999
Pub. L. 106-113; Nov. 29, 1999; 35 U.S.C. §1 et seq.

Anticounterfeiting Consumer Protection Act
Pub. L. 104-153; July 2, 1996; 15 U.S.C. §§1116, 1117(c)

Anticybersquatting Consumer Protection Act
Pub. L. 106-113; Nov. 29, 1999; 15 U.S.C. §1125(d)

Audio Home Recording Act of 1992
Pub. L. 102-563; Oct. 28, 1992; 17 U.S.C. §1001 et seq.

Bayh-Dole Act
Pub. L. 96-517; Dec. 12, 1980; 35 U.S.C. §§200-212

Berne Convention Implementation Act of 1988
Pub. L. 100-568; Oct. 31, 1988; 17 U.S.C. §101 et seq.

Computer Maintenance Competition Assurance Act
Pub. L. 105-304; Oct. 28, 1998; 17 U.S.C. §117.

Computer Software Rental Amendments Act of 1990
Pub. L. 101-650; Title VIII, Dec. 1, 1990; 17 U.S.C. §§101, 109

Copyright Act of 1976
Pub. L. 94-553; Oct. 19, 1976; 17 U.S.C. §101 et seq.

Copyright Amendments Act of 1992
Pub. L. 102-307; June 26, 1992; 17 U.S.C. §§101, 109

Copyright Fees and Technical Amendments Act of 1989
Pub. L. 101-318; July 3, 1990; 17 U.S.C. §§101, 109

Copyright Remedy Clarification Act
Pub. L. 101-553; Nov. 15, 1990; 17 U.S.C. §511

Copyright Renewal Act of 1992
Pub. L. 102-307, Title I; June 26, 1992; 17 U.S.C. §§304, 408, 409, 708

Copyright Royalty Tribunal Reform Act of 1993
Pub. L. 103-198; Dec. 17, 1993; 17 U.S.C. §801 et seq.

Digital Millennium Copyright Act
Pub. L. 105-304; Oct. 28, 1998; 17 U.S.C. §101 et seq.

Digital Performance Right in Sound Recordings Act of 1995
 Pub. L. 104-39; Nov. 1, 1995; 17 U.S.C. §§114, 115
Digital Theft Deterrence and Copyright Damages Improvement Act of 1999
 Pub. L. 106-160; Dec. 9, 1999, 17 U.S.C. §504(c)
Economic Espionage Act of 1996
 Pub. L. 104-294; Oct. 11, 1996; 18 U.S.C. §1831 et seq.
Fairness in Music Licensing Act of 1998
 Pub. L. 105-298; Oct. 27, 1998; 17 U.S.C. §§110,512.
Family Entertainment and Copyright Act of 2005
 Pub. L. 109-9; April 27, 2005; 18 U.S.C. §2319B, 15 U.S.C. §1114, 17 U.S.C.
 §§110, 408, and 506
Federal Trademark Dilution Act of 1995
 Pub. L. 104-98; Jan. 15, 1996; 15 U.S.C. §§1125, 1127
First Inventor Defense Act of 1999
 Pub. L. 106-113; Nov. 29, 1999; 35 U.S.C. §273
Intellectual Property and High Technology Technical Amendments
 Pub. L. 107-273; Nov. 2, 2002; 35 U.S.C. §1, et seq.
Intellectual Property Protection and Courts Amendments Act of 2004
 Pub. L. 108-482; Dec. 23, 2004; 18 U.S.C. §2318, 15 U.S.C. §1117, §17 U.S.C. 504
Inventors' Rights Act of 1999
 Pub. L. 106-113; Nov. 29, 1999; 35 U.S.C. §297
Madrid Protocol Implementation Act
 Pub. L. 107-273; Nov. 2, 2002; 15 U.S.C., Title XII
Medicare Prescription Drug, Improvement, and Modernization Act of 2003
 Pub. L. 108-173; Dec. 8, 2003; 21 U.S.C. §355
National Technology Transfer and Advancement Act
 Pub. L. 104-113; Mar. 7, 1996; 15 U.S.C. §3701 et seq.
No Electronic Theft Act
 Pub. L. 105-147; Dec. 16, 1997; 17 U.S.C. §506, 18 U.S.C. §§2319, 2319A, 2320
North American Free Trade Agreement Implementation Act
 Pub. L. 103-182; Dec. 8, 1993; 35 U.S.C. §102, 15 U.S.C. §§1052(e), (f), 17 U.S.C.
 §104A
Online Copyright Infringement Liability Limitation Act
 Pub. L. 105-304; Oct. 28, 1998; 17 U.S.C. §512
Optional Inter Partes Reexamination Procedure Act
 Pub. L. 106-113; Nov. 29, 1999, 35 U.S.C. §§311-318
Patent Act of 1952
 ch. 950, 66 Stat. 792; July 19, 1952; 35 U.S.C. §1 et seq.

Patent and Trademark Office Efficiency Act
Pub. L. 106-113; Nov. 29, 1999; 35 U.S.C. §1 et seq.
Patent Law Amendments Act of 1984
Pub. L. 98-622; Nov. 8, 1984; 35 U.S.C. §1 et seq.
Patent Law Foreign Filing Amendments Act of 1988
Pub. L. 100-418, Title IX, Subtitle B, §9101; Aug. 23, 1988; 35 U.S.C. §184 et seq.
Patent Law Treaties Implementation Act of 2012
Pub. L. 112-211, Dec. 18, 2012; 35 U.S.C. §1 et seq.
Plant Patent Amendments Act of 1998
Pub. L. 105-289; Oct. 27, 1998; 35 U.S.C. §63.
Pro IP Act of 2008
Pub. L. 110-403; Oct. 13, 2008; 15 U.S.C §§1116, 1117; 17 U.S.C §§109, 111, 115, 119, 122, 411, 412, 503, 506, 509, 601, 602; 18 U.S.C. §§1834, 2318, 2319A, 2319B, 2320, 2323
Process Patent Amendments Act of 1988
Pub. L. 100-418; Title IX, Subtitle A, Aug. 23, 1988; 35 U.S.C. §§271, 287
Satellite Home Viewer Act of 1988
Pub. L. 100-667; Title II, Nov. 16, 1988; 17 U.S.C. §119
Satellite Home Viewer Act of 1994
Pub. L. 103-369; Oct. 18, 1994; 17 U.S.C. §119
Satellite Home Viewer Improvement Act of 1999
Pub. L. 106-113; Nov. 29, 1999; 17 U.S.C. §§119, 122.
Satellite Television Extension and Localism Act of 2010
Pub. L. 111-175; May 27, 2010; 17 U.S.C. §§111, 119, 122
Semiconductor Chip Protection Act of 1984
Pub. L. 98-620; Title III, Nov. 8, 1984; 17 U.S.C. §901
Semiconductor International Protection Extension Act of 1991
Pub. L. 102-64; June 28, 1991; 17 U.S.C. §901
Small Webcaster Settlement Act of 2002
Pub. L. 107-321, Dec. 4, 2002, 17 U.S.C. §114
Sonny Bono Copyright Term Extension Act
Pub. L. 105-298; Oct. 27, 1998; 17 U.S.C. §101 et seq.
Stevenson-Wydler Technology Innovation Act of 1980
Pub. L. 96-480; Oct. 21, 1980; 15 U.S.C. §3701 et seq.
Stop Counterfeiting in Manufactured Goods Act
Pub. L. 109-181, Mar. 16, 2006; 18 U.S.C. §2320
Technology, Education, and Copyright Harmonization Act of 2002
Pub. L. 107-273, Nov. 2, 2002; 17 U.S.C. §110

Technology Transfer Commercialization Act of 2000
  Pub. L. 106-404; Nov. 1, 2000; 35 U.S.C. §200 et seq.
Trademark (Lanham) Act of 1946
  ch. 540, 60 Stat. 427; July 5, 1946; 15 U.S.C. §1051 et seq.
Trademark Amendments Act of 1999
  Pub. L. 106-43; Aug. 5, 1999; 15 U.S.C. §§1052, 1122, 1125
Trademark Clarification Act of 1984
  Pub. L. 98-620; Title I, Nov. 8, 1984; 15 U.S.C. §1064
Trademark Counterfeiting Act of 1984
  Pub. L. 98-473, Title II, ch. XV, Oct. 12, 1984, 18 U.S.C. §2320
Trademark Dilution Revision Act of 2006
  Pub. L. 109-312, Oct. 9, 2006; 15 U.S.C. §1125(c)
Trademark Law Revision Act of 1988
  Pub. L. 100-667; Title 1, Nov. 16, 1988; 15 U.S.C. §1051 et seq.
Trademark Law Treaty Implementation Act
  Pub. L. 105-298, Oct. 27, 1998; 15 U.S.C. §1051 et seq.
Trademark Remedy Clarification Act
  Pub. L. 102-542; Oct. 27, 1992; 15 U.S.C. §1122
Trademark Technical and Conforming Amendment Act of 2010
  Pub. L. 111-146; Mar. 17, 2010; 15 U.S.C. §§1057, 1058, 1065, 1071, 1141k
Unlocking Consumer Choice and Wireless Competition Act
  Pub. L. 113-144; Aug. 1, 2014, uncodified (follows 17 U.S.C. §1332)
Uruguay Round Agreements Act
  Pub. L. 103-465; Dec. 8, 1994; 35 U.S.C. §§104, 111, 154, 271, 15 U.S.C. §§1052(a),
  1127, 17 U.S.C. §§104A, 1101 et seq.
Vessel Hull Design Protection Act
  Pub. L. 105-304; Oct. 28, 1998; 17 U.S.C. §§1301-1332
Vessel Hull Design Protection Amendments of 2008
  Pub. L. 110-434; Oct. 16, 2008; 17 U.S.C. §1301
Webcaster Settlement Act of 2008
  Pub. L. 110-435; Oct. 16, 2008; 17 U.S.C. §114(f)
Webcaster Settlement Act of 2009
  Pub. L. 111-36; June 30, 2009; 17 U.S.C. §114(f)
WIPO Copyright and Performances and Phonograms Treaties Implementation Act of
1998
  Pub. L. 105-304; Oct. 28, 1998; 17 U.S.C. §§1201-1205
Work Made For Hire and Copyright Corrections Act of 2000
  Pub. L. 106-379; Oct. 27, 2000; 17 U.S.C. §101 et seq.

The Constitutional Provisions

ART. 1, SEC. 8, CL. 3. The Congress shall have power . . . To regulate commerce with foreign nations, and among the several states, and with the Indian tribes.

ART. 1, SEC. 8, CL. 8. The Congress shall have power . . . To promote the progress of science and useful arts, by securing for limited times to authors and inventors the exclusive right to their respective writings and discoveries.

Part 1

PATENTS

UNITED STATES CODE

TITLE 35—PATENTS

UNITED STATES CODE

TITLE 35 — PATENTS

PART I — UNITED STATES PATENT AND TRADEMARK OFFICE

CHAPTER 1 — ESTABLISHMENT, OFFICERS AND EMPLOYEES, FUNCTIONS

§ 1   Establishment

(a) *Establishment.* — The United States Patent and Trademark Office is established as an agency of the United States, within the Department of Commerce. In carrying out its functions, the United States Patent and Trademark Office shall be subject to the policy direction of the Secretary of Commerce, but otherwise shall retain responsibility for decisions regarding the management and administration of its operations and shall exercise independent control of its budget allocations and expenditures, personnel decisions and processes, procurements, and other administrative and management functions in accordance with this title and applicable provisions of law. Those operations designed to grant and issue patents and those operations which are designed to facilitate the registration of trademarks shall be treated as separate operating units within the Office.

(b) *Offices.* — The United States Patent and Trademark Office shall maintain its principal office in the metropolitan Washington, D.C., area, for the service of process and papers and for the purpose of carrying out its functions. The United States Patent and Trademark Office shall be deemed, for purposes of venue in civil actions, to be a resident of the district in which its principal office is located, except where jurisdiction is otherwise provided by law. The United States Patent and Trademark Office may establish satellite offices in such other places in the United States as it considers necessary and appropriate in the conduct of its business.

(c) *Reference.* — For purposes of this title, the United States Patent and Trademark Office shall also be referred to as the "Office" and the "Patent and Trademark Office".

(July 19, 1952, ch. 950, §1, 66 Stat. 792; Jan. 2, 1975, Pub. L. 93-596, §1, 88 Stat. 1949; Nov. 29, 1999, Pub. L. 106-113, §4711, 113 Stat. 1501A-572.)

§ 2   Powers and duties

(a) *In general.* — The United States Patent and Trademark Office, subject to the policy direction of the Secretary of Commerce —

(1) shall be responsible for the granting and issuing of patents and the registration of trademarks; and

(2) shall be responsible for disseminating to the public information with respect to patents and trademarks.

(b) *Specific powers.* — The Office —

(1) shall adopt and use a seal of the Office, which shall be judicially noticed and with which letters patent, certificates of trademark registrations, and papers issued by the Office shall be authenticated;

(2) may establish regulations, not inconsistent with law, which —

(A) shall govern the conduct of proceedings in the Office;

(B) shall be made in accordance with section 553 of title 5;

(C) shall facilitate and expedite the processing of patent applications, particularly those which can be filed, stored, processed, searched, and retrieved electronically, subject to the provisions of section 122 relating to the confidential status of applications;

(D) may govern the recognition and conduct of agents, attorneys, or other persons representing applicants or other parties before the Office, and may require them, before being recognized as representatives of applicants or other persons, to show that they are of good moral character and reputation and are possessed of the necessary qualifications to render to applicants or other persons valuable service, advice, and assistance in the presentation or prosecution of their applications or other business before the Office;

(E) shall recognize the public interest in continuing to safeguard broad access to the United States patent system through the reduced fee structure for small entities under section 41(h)(1);

(F) provide for the development of a performance-based process that includes quantitative and qualitative measures and standards for evaluating cost-effectiveness and is consistent with the principles of impartiality and competitiveness; and

(G) may, subject to any conditions prescribed by the Director and at the request of the patent applicant, provide for prioritization of examination of applications for products, processes, or technologies that are important to the national economy or national competitiveness without recovering the aggregate extra cost of providing such prioritization, notwithstanding section 41 or any other provision of law;

(3) may acquire, construct, purchase, lease, hold, manage, operate, improve, alter, and renovate any real, personal, or mixed property, or any interest therein, as it considers necessary to carry out its functions;

(4)(A) may make such purchases, contracts for the construction, maintenance, or management and operation of facilities, and contracts for supplies or services, without regard to the provisions of subtitle I and chapter 33 of title 40, division C (except sections 3302, 3501(b), 3509, 3906, 4710, and 4711) of subtitle I of title 41, and the Stewart B. McKinney Homeless Assistance Act (42 U.S.C. 11301 et seq.); and

(B) may enter into and perform such purchases and contracts for printing services, including the process of composition, platemaking, presswork, silk screen processes, binding, microform, and the products of such processes, as it considers necessary to carry out the functions of the Office, without regard to sections 501 through 517 and 1101 through 1123 of title 44;

(5) may use, with their consent, services, equipment, personnel, and facilities of other departments, agencies, and instrumentalities of the Federal Government, on a reimbursable basis, and cooperate with such other departments, agencies, and instrumentalities in the establishment and use of services, equipment, and facilities of the Office;

(6) may, when the Director determines that it is practicable, efficient, and cost-effective to do so, use, with the consent of the United States and the agency, instrumentality, Patent and Trademark Office, or international organization concerned, the services, records, facilities, or personnel of any State or local government agency or instrumentality or foreign patent and trademark office or international organization to perform functions on its behalf;

(7) may retain and use all of its revenues and receipts, including revenues from the sale, lease, or disposal of any real, personal, or mixed property, or any interest therein, of the Office;

(8) shall advise the President, through the Secretary of Commerce, on national and certain international intellectual property policy issues;

(9) shall advise Federal departments and agencies on matters of intellectual property policy in the United States and intellectual property protection in other countries;

(10) shall provide guidance, as appropriate, with respect to proposals by agencies to assist foreign governments and international intergovernmental organizations on matters of intellectual property protection;

(11) may conduct programs, studies, or exchanges of items or services regarding domestic and international intellectual property law and the effectiveness of intellectual property protection domestically and throughout the world, and the Office is authorized to expend funds to cover the subsistence expenses and travel-related expenses, including per diem, lodging costs, and transportation costs, of persons attending such programs who are not federal employees;

(12)(A) shall advise the Secretary of Commerce on programs and studies relating to intellectual property policy that are conducted, or authorized to be conducted, cooperatively with foreign intellectual property offices and international intergovernmental organizations; and

(B) may conduct programs and studies described in subparagraph (A); and

(13)(A) in coordination with the Department of State, may conduct programs and studies cooperatively with foreign intellectual property offices and international intergovernmental organizations; and

(B) with the concurrence of the Secretary of State, may authorize the transfer of not to exceed $100,000 in any year to the Department of State for the purpose of making special payments to international intergovernmental organizations for studies and programs for advancing international cooperation concerning patents, trademarks, and other matters.

(c) *Clarification of specific powers.* — (1) The special payments under subsection (b)(13)(B) shall be in addition to any other payments or contributions to international organizations described in subsection (b)(13)(B) and shall not be subject to any limitations imposed by law on the amounts of such other payments or contributions by the United States Government.

(2) Nothing in subsection (b) shall derogate from the duties of the Secretary of State or from the duties of the United States Trade Representative as set forth in section 141 of the Trade Act of 1974 (19 U.S.C. 2171).

(3) Nothing in subsection (b) shall derogate from the duties and functions of the Register of Copyrights or otherwise alter current authorities relating to copyright matters.

(4) In exercising the Director's powers under paragraphs (3) and (4)(A) of subsection (b), the Director shall consult with the Administrator of General Services.

(5) In exercising the Director's powers and duties under this section, the Director shall consult with the Register of Copyrights on all copyright and related matters.

(d) *Construction.* — Nothing in this section shall be construed to nullify, void, cancel, or interrupt any pending request-for-proposal let or contract issued by the General Services Administration for the specific purpose of relocating or leasing space to the United States Patent and Trademark Office.

(July 19, 1952, ch. 950, §1, 66 Stat. 792; Jan. 2, 1975, Pub. L. 93-596, §1, 88 Stat. 1949; Nov. 29, 1999, Pub. L. 106-113, §4712, 113 Stat. 1501A-572; Nov. 2, 2002, Pub. L. 107-273, §13206, 116 Stat. 1904; Dec. 15, 2003, Pub. L. 108-178, §4(g), 117 Stat. 2641; Jan. 4, 2011, Pub. L. 111-350, §5, 124 Stat. 3841; Sept. 16, 2011, Pub. L. 112-29, §21, 125 Stat. 335, 337–38.)

§ 3   Officers and employees

(a) *Under Secretary and Director*—

(1) *In general.*—The powers and duties of the United States Patent and Trademark Office shall be vested in an Under Secretary of Commerce for Intellectual Property and Director of the United States Patent and Trademark Office (in this title referred to as the "Director"), who shall be a citizen of the United States and who shall be appointed by the President, by and with the advice and consent of the Senate. The Director shall be a person who has a professional background and experience in patent or trademark law.

(2) *Duties.*—

(A) *In general.*—The Director shall be responsible for providing policy direction and management supervision for the Office and for the issuance of patents and the registration of trademarks. The Director shall perform these duties in a fair, impartial, and equitable manner.

(B) *Consulting with the Public Advisory Committees.*—The Director shall consult with the Patent Public Advisory Committee established in section 5 on a regular basis on matters relating to the patent operations of the Office, shall consult with the Trademark Public Advisory Committee established in section 5 on a regular basis on matters relating to the trademark operations of the Office, and shall consult with the respective Public Advisory Committee before submitting budgetary proposals to the Office of Management and Budget or changing or proposing to change patent or trademark user fees or patent or trademark regulations which are subject to the requirement to provide notice and opportunity for public comment under section 553 of title 5, as the case may be.

(3) *Oath.*—The Director shall, before taking office, take an oath to discharge faithfully the duties of the Office.

(4) *Removal.*—The Director may be removed from office by the President. The President shall provide notification of any such removal to both Houses of Congress.

(b) *Officers and Employees of the Office*—

(1) *Deputy Under Secretary and Deputy Director.*—The Secretary of Commerce, upon nomination by the Director, shall appoint a Deputy Under Secretary of Commerce for Intellectual Property and Deputy

Director of the United States Patent and Trademark Office who shall be vested with the authority to act in the capacity of the Director in the event of the absence or incapacity of the Director. The Deputy Director shall be a citizen of the United States who has a professional background and experience in patent or trademark law.

(2) *Commissioners.* —

(A) *Appointment and duties.* — The Secretary of Commerce shall appoint a Commissioner for Patents and a Commissioner for Trademarks, without regard to chapter 33, 51, or 53 of title 5. The Commissioner for Patents shall be a citizen of the United States with demonstrated management ability and professional background and experience in patent law and serve for a term of 5 years. The Commissioner for Trademarks shall be a citizen of the United States with demonstrated management ability and professional background and experience in trademark law and serve for a term of 5 years. The Commissioner for Patents and the Commissioner for Trademarks shall serve as the chief operating officers for the operations of the Office relating to patents and trademarks, respectively, and shall be responsible for the management and direction of all aspects of the activities of the Office that affect the administration of patent and trademark operations, respectively. The Secretary may reappoint a Commissioner to subsequent terms of 5 years as long as the performance of the Commissioner as set forth in the performance agreement in subparagraph (B) is satisfactory.

(B) *Salary and performance agreement.* — The Commissioners shall be paid an annual rate of basic pay not to exceed the maximum rate of basic pay for the Senior Executive Service established under section 5382 of title 5, including any applicable locality-based comparability payment that may be authorized under section 5304(h)(2)(C) of title 5. The compensation of the Commissioners shall be considered, for purposes of section 207(c)(2)(A) of title 18, to be the equivalent of that described under clause (ii) of section 207(c)(2)(A) of title 18. In addition, the Commissioners may receive a bonus in an amount of up to, but not in excess of, 50 percent of the Commissioners' annual rate of basic pay, based upon an evaluation by the Secretary of Commerce, acting through the Director, of the Commissioners' performance as defined in an annual performance agreement between the Commissioners and the Secretary. The annual performance agreements shall incorporate measurable organization and individual goals in key operational areas as delineated in an annual performance plan agreed to by the Commissioners and the Secretary. Payment of a bonus under this subparagraph may be made to the Commissioners only to the extent that such payment does not cause the Commissioners' total aggregate compensation in a calendar year to equal or exceed the amount of the salary of the Vice President under section 104 of title 3.

(C) *Removal.*—The Commissioners may be removed from office by the Secretary for misconduct or nonsatisfactory performance under the performance agreement described in subparagraph (B), without regard to the provisions of title 5. The Secretary shall provide notification of any such removal to both Houses of Congress.

(3) *Other officers and employees.*—The Director shall—

(A) appoint such officers, employees (including attorneys), and agents of the Office as the Director considers necessary to carry out the functions of the Office; and

(B) define the title, authority, and duties of such officers and employees and delegate to them such of the powers vested in the Office as the Director may determine.

The Office shall not be subject to any administratively or statutorily imposed limitation on positions or personnel, and no positions or personnel of the Office shall be taken into account for purposes of applying any such limitation.

(4) *Training of examiners.*—The Office shall submit to the Congress a proposal to provide an incentive program to retain as employees patent and trademark examiners of the primary examiner grade or higher who are eligible for retirement, for the sole purpose of training patent and trademark examiners.

(5) *National security positions.*—The Director, in consultation with the Director of the Office of Personnel Management, shall maintain a program for identifying national security positions and providing for appropriate security clearances, in order to maintain the secrecy of certain inventions, as described in section 181, and to prevent disclosure of sensitive and strategic information in the interest of national security.

(6) *Administrative patent judges and administrative trademark judges.*—The Director may fix the rate of basic pay for the administrative patent judges appointed pursuant to section 6 and the administrative trademark judges

appointed pursuant to section 17 of the Trademark Act of 1946 (15 U.S.C. 1067) at not greater than the rate of basic pay payable for level III of the Executive Schedule under section 5314 of title 5. The payment of a rate of basic pay under this paragraph shall not be subject to the pay limitation under section 5306(e) or 5373 of title 5.

(c) *Continued applicability of Title 5.* —Officers and employees of the Office shall be subject to the provisions of title 5 relating to Federal employees.

(d) *Adoption of existing labor agreements.* —The Office shall adopt all labor agreements which are in effect, as of the day before the effective date of the Patent and Trademark Office Efficiency Act, with respect to such Office (as then in effect).

(e) *Carryover of personnel.* —

(1) *From PTO.* —Effective as of the effective date of the Patent and Trademark Office Efficiency Act, all officers and employees of the Patent and Trademark Office on the day before such effective date shall become officers and employees of the Office, without a break in service.

(2) *Other personnel.* —Any individual who, on the day before the effective date of the Patent and Trademark Office Efficiency Act, is an officer or employee of the Department of Commerce (other than an officer or employee under paragraph (1)) shall be transferred to the Office, as necessary to carry out the purposes of that Act, if—

(A) such individual serves in a position for which a major function is the performance of work reimbursed by the Patent and Trademark Office, as determined by the Secretary of Commerce;

(B) such individual serves in a position that performed work in support of the Patent and Trademark Office during at least half of the incumbent's work time, as determined by the Secretary of Commerce; or

(C) such transfer would be in the interest of the Office, as determined by the Secretary of Commerce in consultation with the Director.

Any transfer under this paragraph shall be effective as of the same effective date as referred to in paragraph (1), and shall be made without a break in service.

35 U.S.C. § 3

(f) *Transition provisions.* —

(1) *Interim appointment of Director.* —On or after the effective date of the Patent and Trademark Office Efficiency Act, the President shall appoint an individual to serve as the Director until the date on which a Director qualifies under subsection (a). The President shall not make more than one such appointment under this subsection.

(2) *Continuation in office of certain officers.* —

(A) The individual serving as the Assistant Commissioner for Patents on the day before the effective date of the Patent and Trademark Office Efficiency Act may serve as the Commissioner for Patents until the date on which a Commissioner for Patents is appointed under subsection (b).

(B) The individual serving as the Assistant Commissioner for Trademarks on the day before the effective date of the Patent and Trademark Office Efficiency Act may serve as the Commissioner for Trademarks until the date on which a Commissioner for Trademarks is appointed under subsection (b).

(July 19, 1952, ch. 950, §1, 66 Stat. 792; Sept. 6, 1958, Pub. L. 85-933, §1, 72 Stat. 1793; Sept. 23, 1959, Pub. L. 86-370, §1(a), 73 Stat. 650; Aug. 14, 1964, Pub. L. 88-426, §305(26), 78 Stat. 425; Jan. 2, 1975, Pub. L. 93-596, §1, 88 Stat. 1949; Jan. 2, 1975, Pub. L. 93-601, §1, 88 Stat. 1956; Aug. 27, 1982, Pub. L. 97-247, §4, 96 Stat. 319; Oct. 15, 1982, Pub. L. 97-366, §4, 96 Stat. 1760; Nov. 8, 1984, Pub. L. 98-622, §405, 98 Stat. 3392; Oct. 28, 1998, Pub. L. 105-304, §401(a), 112 Stat. 2887; Aug. 5, 1999, Pub. L. 106-44, §2(c), 113 Stat. 223; Nov. 29, 1999, Pub. L. 106-113, §4713, 113 Stat. 1501A-575; Nov. 2, 2002, Pub. L. 107-273, §13206, 116 Stat. 1904; Sept. 16, 2011, Pub. L. 112-29, §21, 125 Stat. 336.)

§ 4   Restrictions on officers and employees as to interest in patents

Officers and employees of the Patent and Trademark Office shall be incapable, during the period of their appointments and for one year thereafter, of applying for a patent and of acquiring, directly or indirectly, except by inheritance or bequest, any patent or any right or interest in any patent, issued or to be issued by the Office. In patents applied for thereafter they shall not be entitled to any priority date earlier than one year after the termination of their appointment.

(July 19, 1952, ch. 950, §1, 66 Stat. 793; Jan. 2, 1975, Pub. L. 93-596, §1, 88 Stat. 1949.)

§ 5 Patent and Trademark Office Public Advisory Committees

(a) *Establishment of Public Advisory Committees.* —

(1) *Appointment.* — The United States Patent and Trademark Office shall have a Patent Public Advisory Committee and a Trademark Public Advisory Committee, each of which shall have nine voting members who shall be appointed by the Secretary of Commerce and serve at the pleasure of the Secretary of Commerce. In each year, 3 members shall be appointed to each Advisory Committee for 3-year terms that shall begin on December 1 of that year. Any vacancy on an Advisory Committee shall be filled within 90 days after it occurs. A new member who is appointed to fill a vacancy shall be appointed to serve for the remainder of the predecessor's term.

(2) *Chair.* — The Secretary of Commerce, in consultation with the Director, shall designate a Chair and Vice Chair of each Advisory Committee from among the members appointed under paragraph (1). If the Chair resigns before the completion of his or her term, or is otherwise unable to exercise the functions of the Chair, the Vice Chair shall exercise the functions of the Chair.

(b) *Basis for appointments.* — Members of each Advisory Committee —

(1) shall be citizens of the United States who shall be chosen so as to represent the interests of diverse users of the United States Patent and Trademark Office with respect to patents, in the case of the Patent Public Advisory Committee, and with respect to trademarks, in the case of the Trademark Public Advisory Committee;

(2) shall include members who represent small and large entity applicants located in the United States in proportion to the number of applications filed by such applicants, but in no case shall members who represent small entity patent applicants, including small business concerns, independent inventors, and nonprofit organizations, constitute less than 25 percent of the members of the Patent Public Advisory Committee, and such members shall include at least one independent inventor; and

(3) shall include individuals with substantial background and achievement in finance, management, labor relations, science, technology, and office automation.

In addition to the voting members, each Advisory Committee shall include a representative of each labor organization recognized by the United States

Patent and Trademark Office. Such representatives shall be nonvoting members of the Advisory Committee to which they are appointed.

(c) *Meetings.*—Each Advisory Committee shall meet at the call of the chair to consider an agenda set by the chair.

(d) *Duties.*—Each Advisory Committee shall—

(1) review the policies, goals, performance, budget, and user fees of the United States Patent and Trademark Office with respect to patents, in the case of the Patent Public Advisory Committee, and with respect to Trademarks, in the case of the Trademark Public Advisory Committee, and advise the Director on these matters;

(2) within 60 days after the end of each fiscal year—

(A) prepare an annual report on the matters referred to in paragraph (1);

(B) transmit the report to the Secretary of Commerce, the President, and the Committees on the Judiciary of the Senate and the House of Representatives; and

(C) publish the report in the Official Gazette of the United States Patent and Trademark Office.

(e) *Compensation.*—Each member of each Advisory Committee shall be compensated for each day (including travel time) during which such member is attending meetings or conferences of that Advisory Committee or otherwise engaged in the business of that Advisory Committee, at the rate which is the daily equivalent of the annual rate of basic pay in effect for level III of the Executive Schedule under section 5314 of title 5. While away from such member's home or regular place of business such member shall be allowed travel expenses, including per diem in lieu of subsistence, as authorized by section 5703 of title 5.

(f) *Access to information.*—Members of each Advisory Committee shall be provided access to records and information in the United States Patent and Trademark Office, except for personnel or other privileged information and information concerning patent applications required to be kept in confidence by section 122.

(g) *Applicability of certain ethics laws.*—Members of each Advisory Committee shall be special Government employees within the meaning of section 202 of title 18.

35 U.S.C. § 5

(h) *Inapplicability of Federal Advisory Committee Act.*—The Federal Advisory Committee Act (5 U.S.C. App.) shall not apply to each Advisory Committee.

(i) *Open meetings.*—The meetings of each Advisory Committee shall be open to the public, except that each Advisory Committee may by majority vote meet in executive session when considering personnel, privileged, or other confidential information.

(j) *Inapplicability of Patent Prohibition.*—Section 4 shall not apply to voting members of the Advisory Committees.

(Nov. 29, 1999, Pub. L. 106-113, §4714, 113 Stat. 1501A-578; Nov. 2, 2002, Pub. L. 107-273, §§13203, 13206, 116 Stat. 1902, 1904; Jan. 14, 2013, Pub. L. 112-274, §1(l), 126 Stat. 2458.)

§ 6[1]   Patent Trial and Appeal Board

(a) *In general.*—There shall be in the Office a Patent Trial and Appeal Board. The Director, the Deputy Director, the Commissioner for Patents, the Commissioner for Trademarks, and the administrative patent judges shall constitute the Patent Trial and Appeal Board. The administrative patent judges shall be persons of competent legal knowledge and scientific ability who are appointed by the Secretary, in consultation with the Director. Any reference in any Federal law, Executive order, rule, regulation, or delegation of authority, or any document of or pertaining to the Board of Patent Appeals and Interferences is deemed to refer to the Patent Trial and Appeal Board.

(b) *Duties.*—The Patent Trial and Appeal Board shall—

(1) on written appeal of an applicant, review adverse decisions of examiners upon applications for patents pursuant to section 134(a);

(2) review appeals of reexaminations pursuant to section 134(b);

(3) conduct derivation proceedings pursuant to section 135; and

(4) conduct inter partes reviews and post-grant reviews pursuant to chapters 31 and 32.

(c) *3-member panels.*—Each appeal, derivation proceeding, post-grant review, and inter partes review shall be heard by at least 3 members of the Patent

---

[1] *Ed. Note:* The provisions of section 6, as in effect on September 15, 2012, shall apply to interference proceedings that are declared after September 15, 2012, under section 135, as in effect before the effective date under section 3(n) of the Leahy-Smith America Invents Act. The Patent Trial and Appeal Board may be deemed to be the Board of Patent Appeals and Interferences for purposes of such interference proceedings. See Pub. L. 112-274, section (k)(3).

Trial and Appeal Board, who shall be designated by the Director. Only the Patent Trial and Appeal Board may grant rehearings.

(d) *Treatment of prior appointments.* — The Secretary of Commerce may, in the Secretary's discretion, deem the appointment of an administrative patent judge who, before the date of the enactment of this subsection, held office pursuant to an appointment by the Director to take effect on the date on which the Director initially appointed the administrative patent judge. It shall be a defense to a challenge to the appointment of an administrative patent judge on the basis of the judge's having been originally appointed by the Director that the administrative patent judge so appointed was acting as a de facto officer.

(Sept. 16, 2011, Pub. L. 112-29, §7, 125 Stat. 313.)

§ 7   Library

The Director shall maintain a library of scientific and other works and periodicals, both foreign and domestic, in the Patent and Trademark office to aid the officers in the discharge of their duties.

(July 19, 1952, ch. 950, §1, 66 Stat. 793; Jan. 2, 1975, Pub. L. 93-596, §1, 88 Stat. 1949; Nov. 29, 1999, Pub. L. 106-113, §4717, 113 Stat. 1501A-582.)

§ 8   Classification of patents

The Director may revise and maintain the classification by subject matter of United States letters patent, and such other patents and printed publications as may be necessary or practicable, for the purpose of determining with readiness and accuracy the novelty of inventions for which applications for patent are filed.

(July 19, 1952, ch. 950, § 1, 66 Stat. 784; Nov. 29, 1999, Pub. L. 106-113, §4717, 113 Stat. 1501A-582.)

§ 9   Certified copies of records

The Director may furnish certified copies of specifications and drawings of patents issued by the Patent and Trademark Office, and of other records available either to the public or to the person applying therefor.

(July 19, 1952, ch. 950, §1, 66 Stat. 794; Jan. 2, 1975, Pub. L. 93-596, §1, 88 Stat. 1949; Nov. 29, 1999, Pub. L. 106-113, §4717, 113 Stat. 1501A-582.)

§ 10 Publications

(a) The Director may publish in printed, typewritten, or electronic form, the following:

1. Patents and published applications for patents, including specifications and drawings, together with copies of the same. The Patent and Trademark Office may print the headings of the drawings for patents for the purpose of photolithography.

2. Certificates of trademark registrations, including statements and drawings, together with copies of the same.

3. The Official Gazette of the United States Patent and Trademark Office.

4. Annual indexes of patents and patentees, and of trademarks and registrants.

5. Annual volumes of decisions in patent and trademark cases.

6. Pamphlet copies of the patent laws and rules of practice, laws and rules relating to trademarks, and circulars or other publications relating to the business of the Office.

(b) The Director may exchange any of the publications specified in items 3, 4, 5, and 6 of subsection (a) of this section for publications desirable for the use of the Patent and Trademark Office.

(July 19, 1952, ch. 950, §1, 66 Stat. 794; Jan. 2, 1975, Pub. L. 93-596, §1, 88 Stat. 1949; Nov. 29, 1999, Pub. L. 106-113, §§4507, 4717, 4804, 113 Stat. 1501A-565, 580, 589; Nov. 2, 2002, Pub. L. 107-273, §13205, 116 Stat. 1902.)

§ 11 Exchange of copies of patents and applications with foreign countries

The Director may exchange copies of specifications and drawings of United States patents and published applications for patents for those of foreign countries. The Director shall not enter into an agreement to provide such copies of specifications and drawings of United States patents and applications to a foreign country, other than a NAFTA country or a WTO member country, without the express authorization of the Secretary of Commerce. For purposes of this section, the terms "NAFTA country" and "WTO member country" have the meanings given those terms in section 104(b).

(July 19, 1952, ch. 950, §1, 66 Stat. 794; Nov. 29, 1999, Pub. L. 106-113, §§4507, 4717, 4808, 113 Stat. 1501A-565, 580, 589; Nov. 2, 2002, Pub. L. 107-273, §13205, 116 Stat. 1902.)

§ 12   Copies of patents and applications for public libraries

The Director may supply copies of specifications and drawings of patents in printed or electronic form and published applications for patents to public libraries in the United States which shall maintain such copies for the use of the public, at the rate for each year's issue established for this purpose in section 41(d).

(July 19, 1952, ch. 950, §1, 66 Stat. 794; Aug. 27, 1982, Pub. L. 97-247, §15, 96 Stat. 321; Nov. 29, 1999, Pub. L. 106-113, §§4507, 4717, 4804, 113 Stat. 1501A-565, 580, 589; Nov. 2, 2002, Pub. L. 107-273, §13205, 116 Stat. 1902.)

§ 13   Annual report to Congress

The Director shall report to the Congress, not later than 180 days after the end of each fiscal year, the moneys received and expended by the Office, the purposes for which the moneys were spent, the quality and quantity of the work of the Office, the nature of training provided to examiners, the evaluation of the Commissioner of Patents and the Commissioner of Trademarks by the Secretary of Commerce, the compensation of the Commissioners, and other information relating to the Office.

(July 19, 1952, ch. 950, §1, 66 Stat. 794, Pub. L. 106-113, §§4717, 4718, 113 Stat. 1501A-581.)

CHAPTER 2—PROCEEDINGS IN THE PATENT AND TRADEMARK OFFICE

SEC.

§ 21   Filing date and day for taking action

(a) The Director may by rule prescribe that any paper or fee required to be filed in the Patent and Trademark Office will be considered filed in the Office on the date on which it was deposited with the United States Postal Service or would have been deposited with the United States Postal Service but for postal service interruptions or emergencies designated by the Director.

(b) When the day, or the last day, for taking any action or paying any fee in the United States Patent and Trademark Office falls on Saturday, Sunday, or a federal holiday within the District of Columbia, the action may be taken, or the fee paid, on the next succeeding secular or business day.

(July 19, 1952, ch. 950, §1, 66 Stat. 794; Jan. 2, 1975, Pub. L. 93-596, §1, 88 Stat. 1949; Aug. 27, 1982, Pub. L. 97-247, §12, 96 Stat. 321; Nov. 2, 2002, Pub. L. 107-273, §13206, 116 Stat. 1904.)

§ 22 Printing of papers filed

The Director may require papers filed in the Patent and Trademark Office to be printed, typewritten, or on an electronic medium.

(July 19, 1952, ch. 950, §1, 66 Stat. 795; Jan. 2, 1975, Pub. L. 93-596, §1, 88 Stat. 1949; Nov. 29, 1999, Pub. L. 106-113, §4804, 113 Stat. 1501A-589.)

§ 23 Testimony in Patent and Trademark Office cases

The Director may establish rules for taking affidavits and depositions required in cases in the Patent and Trademark Office. Any officer authorized by law to take depositions to be used in the courts of the United States, or of the State where he resides, may take such affidavits and depositions.

(July 19, 1952, ch. 950, §1, 66 Stat. 795; Jan. 2, 1975, Pub. L. 93-596, §1, 88 Stat. 1949.)

§ 24 Subpoenas, witnesses

The clerk of any United States court for the district wherein testimony is to be taken for use in any contested case in the Patent and Trademark Office, shall, upon the application of any party thereto, issue a subpoena for any witness residing or being within such district, commanding him to appear and testify before an officer in such district authorized to take depositions and affidavits, at the time and place stated in the subpoena. The provisions of the Federal Rules of Civil Procedure relating to the attendance of witnesses and to the production of documents and things shall apply to contested cases in the Patent and Trademark Office.

Every witness subpoenaed and in attendance shall be allowed the fees and traveling expenses allowed to witnesses attending the United States district courts.

A judge of a court whose clerk issued a subpoena may enforce obedience to the process or punish disobedience as in other like cases, on proof that a witness, served with such subpoena, neglected or refused to appear or to testify. No witness shall be deemed guilty of contempt for disobeying such subpoena unless his fees and traveling expenses in going to, and returning from, and one day's attendance at the place of examination, are paid or tendered him at the time of the service of the subpoena; nor for refusing to disclose any secret matter except upon appropriate order of the court which issued the subpoena.

(July 19, 1952, ch. 950, §1, 66 Stat. 795; Jan. 2, 1975, Pub. L. 93-596, §1, 88 Stat. 1949.)

§ 25   Declaration in lieu of oath

(a) The Director may by rule prescribe that any document to be filed in the Patent and Trademark Office and which is required by any law, rule, or other regulation to be under oath may be subscribed to by a written declaration in such form as the Director may prescribe, such declaration to be in lieu of the oath otherwise required.

(b) Whenever such written declaration is used, the document must warn the declarant that willful false statements and the like are punishable by fine or imprisonment, or both (18 U.S.C. 1001).

(Mar. 26, 1964, Pub. L. 88-292, §1, 78 Stat. 171; Jan. 2, 1975, Pub. L. 93-596, §1, 88 Stat. 1949.)

Note: 18 U.S.C. §1001 provides: "Whoever in any matter within the jurisdiction of any department or agency of the United States knowingly and willfully falsifies, conceals or covers up by any trick, scheme, or device a material fact, or makes any false, fictitious or fraudulent statements or representations, or makes or uses any false writing or document knowing the same to contain any false, fictitious or fraudulent statement or entry, shall be fined not more than $10,000 or imprisoned not more than five years, or both." (June 25, 1948, 62 Stat. 749)

§ 26   Effect of defective execution

Any document to be filed in the Patent and Trademark Office and which is required by any law, rule, or other regulation to be executed in a specified manner may be provisionally accepted by the Director despite a defective execution, provided a properly executed document is submitted within such time as may be prescribed.

(Mar. 26, 1964, Pub. L. 88-292, §1, 78 Stat. 171; Jan. 2, 1975, Pub. L. 93-596, §1, 88 Stat. 1949.)

§ 27   Revival of applications; reinstatement of reexamination proceedings

The Director may establish procedures, including the requirement for payment of the fee specified in section 41(a)(7), to revive an unintentionally abandoned application for patent, accept an unintentionally delayed payment of the fee for issuing each patent, or accept an unintentionally delayed response by the patent owner in a reexamination proceeding, upon petition by the applicant for patent or patent owner.

(Dec. 18, 2012, Pub. L. 112-211, §201, 126 Stat. 1534.)

CHAPTER 3—PRACTICE BEFORE PATENT AND TRADEMARK OFFICE

SEC.
32.   Suspension or exclusion from practice.
33.   Unauthorized representation as practitioner.

§ 32[2]   **Suspension or exclusion from practice**

The Director may, after notice and opportunity for a hearing, suspend or exclude, either generally or in any particular case, from further practice before the Patent and Trademark Office, any person, agent, or attorney shown to be incompetent or disreputable, or guilty of gross misconduct, or who does not comply with the regulations established under section 2(b)(2)(D), or who shall, by word, circular, letter, or advertising, with intent to defraud in any manner, deceive, mislead, or threaten any applicant or prospective applicant, or other person having immediate or prospective business before the Office. The reasons for any such suspension or exclusion shall be duly recorded. The Director shall have the discretion to designate any attorney who is an officer or employee of the United States Patent and Trademark Office to conduct the hearing required by this section. *A proceeding under this section shall be commenced not later than the earlier of either the date that is 10 years after the date on which the misconduct forming the basis for the proceeding occurred, or 1 year after the date on which the misconduct forming the basis for the proceeding is made known to an officer or employee of the Office as prescribed in the regulations established under section 2(b)(2)(D).* The United States District Court for the Eastern District of Virginia, under such conditions and upon such proceedings as it by its rules determines, may review the action of the Director upon the petition of the person so refused recognition or so suspended or excluded.

---

[2] *Ed. Note:* The italicized language applies in any case in which the time period for instituting a proceeding under section 32 of title 35 had not lapsed before Sept. 16, 2011, the date of enactment of Pub. L. 112-29. See section 3(k) of Pub. L. 112-29.

(July 19, 1952, ch. 950, §1, 66 Stat. 795; Jan. 2, 1975, Pub. L. 93-596, §1, 88 Stat. 1949; Nov. 29, 1999, Pub. L. 106-113, §§4715, 4719, 113 Stat. 1501A-580, 581; Sept. 16, 2011, Pub. L. 112-29, §§3, 9, 125 Stat. 285, 316.)

§ 33 Unauthorized representation as practitioner

Whoever, not being recognized to practice before the Patent and Trademark Office, holds himself out or permits himself to be held out as so recognized, or as being qualified to prepare or prosecute applications for patent, shall be fined not more than $1,000 for each offense.

(July 19, 1952, ch. 950, §1, 66 Stat. 796; Jan. 2, 1975, Pub. L. 93-596, §1, 88 Stat. 1949.)

CHAPTER 4—PATENT FEES; FUNDING; SEARCH SYSTEMS

SEC.
41. Patent fees; patent and trademark search systems.
42. Patent and Trademark Office funding.

§ 41[3] Patent fees; patent and trademark search systems

(a) *General fees.*—The Director shall charge the following fees:

(1) *Filing and basic national fees.*—

(A) On filing each application for an original patent, except for design, plant, or provisional applications, $330 [$280].

(B) On filing each application for an original design patent, $220 [$180].

(C) On filing each application for an original plant patent, $220 [$180].

(D) On filing each provisional application for an original patent, $220 [$260].

(E) On filing each application for the reissue of a patent, $330 [$280].

(F) The basic national fee for each international application filed under the treaty defined in section 351(a) entering the national stage under section 371, $330 [$280].

(G) In addition, excluding any sequence listing or computer program listing filed in an electronic medium as prescribed by the Director, for any application the specification and drawings of which exceed 100 sheets of paper (or equivalent as prescribed by the Director if filed in

---

[3] *Ed. Note:* The amounts in brackets reflect the fee schedule, effective January 1, 2014. The current patent fee schedule may be found by accessing the website of the United States Patent and Trademark Office at www.uspto.gov.

an electronic medium), $270 [$400] for each additional 50 sheets of paper (or equivalent as prescribed by the Director if filed in an electronic medium) or fraction thereof.

(2) *Excess claims fees.—*

(A) *In general.—*In addition to the fee specified in paragraph (1)—

(i) on filing or on presentation at any other time, $220 [$420] for each claim in independent form in excess of 3;

(ii) on filing or on presentation at any other time, $52 [$80] for each claim (whether dependent or independent) in excess of 20; and

(iii) for each application containing a multiple dependent claim, $390 [$780].

(B) *Multiple dependent claims.—*For the purpose of computing fees under subparagraph (A), a multiple dependent claim referred to in section 112 or any claim depending therefrom shall be considered as separate dependent claims in accordance with the number of claims to which reference is made.

(C) *Refunds; errors in payment.—*The Director may by regulation provide for a refund of any part of the fee specified in subparagraph (A) for any claim that is canceled before an examination on the merits, as prescribed by the Director, has been made of the application under section 131. Errors in payment of the additional fees under this paragraph may be rectified in accordance with regulations prescribed by the Director.

(3) *Examination fees.—*

(A) *In general.—*

(i) For examination of each application for an original patent, except for design, plant, provisional, or international applications, $220 [$720].

(ii) For examination of each application for an original design patent, $140 [$460].

(iii) For examination of each application for an original plant patent, $170 [$580].

(iv) For examination of the national stage of each international application, $220 [$720].

(v) For examination of each application for the reissue of a patent, $650 [$2,160].

(B) *Applicability of other fee provisions.*—The provisions of paragraphs (3) and (4) of section 111(a) relating to the payment of the fee for filing the application shall apply to the payment of the fee specified in sub-paragraph (A) with respect to an application filed under section 111(a). The provisions of section 371(d) relating to the payment of the national fee shall apply to the payment of the fee specified in subparagraph (A) with respect to an international application.

(4) *Issue fees.*—

(A) For issuing each original patent, except for design or plant patents, $1,510 [$960].

(B) For issuing each original design patent, $860 [$560].

(C) For issuing each original plant patent, $1,190 [$760].

(D) For issuing each reissue patent, $1,510 [$960].

(5) *Disclaimer fee.*—On filing each disclaimer, $140 [$160].

(6) *Appeal fees.*—

(A) On filing an appeal from the examiner to the Patent Trial and Appeal Board, $540 [$800].

(B) In addition, on filing a brief in support of the appeal, $540 [$0], and on requesting an oral hearing in the appeal before the Patent Trial and Appeal Board, $1,080 [$1,300].

(7) *Revival fees.*—On filing each petition for the revival of an abandoned application for a patent, for the delayed payment of the fee for issuing each patent, for the delayed response by the patent owner in any reexamination proceeding, for the delayed payment of the fee for maintaining a patent in force, for the delayed submission of a priority or benefit claim, or for the extension of the 12-month period for filing a subsequent application, $1,700.00. The Director may refund any part of the fee specified in this paragraph, in exceptional circumstances as determined by the Director.

(8) *Extension fees.*[4]—For petitions for 1-month extensions of time to take actions required by the Director in an application—

(A) on filing a first petition, $130 [$200];

---

[4] *Ed. Note:* See 37 C.F.R. §1.17(a)(1)–(5) for patent extension time fees.

35 U.S.C. § 41

(B) on filing a second petition, $360 [$400]; and

(C) on filing a third or subsequent petition, $620 [$800].

(b) *Maintenance fees.—*

(1) *In general.—*The Director shall charge the following fees for maintaining in force all patents based on applications filed on or after December 12, 1980:

(A) Three years and 6 months after grant, $980 [$1,600].

(B) Seven years and 6 months after grant, $2,480 [$3,600].

(C) Eleven years and 6 months after grant, $4,110 [$7,400].

(2) *Grace period; surcharge.—*Unless payment of the applicable maintenance fee under paragraph (1) is received in the Office on or before the date the fee is due or within a grace period of 6 months thereafter, the patent shall expire as of the end of such grace period. The Director may require the payment of a surcharge as a condition of accepting within such 6-month grace period the payment of an applicable maintenance fee.

(3) *No maintenance fee for design or plant patent.—*No fee may be established for maintaining a design or plant patent in force.

(c) *Delays in payment of maintenance fees.—*

(1) *Acceptance.—*The Director may accept the payment of any maintenance fee required by subsection (b) after the 6-month grace period if the delay is shown to the satisfaction of the Director to have been unintentional. The Director may require the payment of the fee specified in subsection (a)(7) as a condition of accepting payment of any maintenance fee after the 6-month grace period. If the Director accepts payment of a maintenance fee after the 6-month grace period, the patent shall be considered as not having expired at the end of the grace period.

(2) *Effect on rights of others.—*A patent, the term of which has been maintained as a result of the acceptance of a payment of a maintenance fee under this subsection, shall not abridge or affect the right of any person or that person's successors in business who made, purchased, offered to sell, or used anything protected by the patent within the United States, or imported anything protected by the patent into the United States after the 6-month grace period but prior to the acceptance of a maintenance fee under this subsection, to continue the use of, to offer for sale, or to sell to others to be used, offered for sale, or sold, the specific thing so made, pur-

chased, offered for sale, used, or imported. The court before which such matter is in question may provide for the continued manufacture, use, offer for sale, or sale of the thing made, purchased, offered for sale, or used within the United States, or imported into the United States, as specified, or for the manufacture, use, offer for sale, or sale in the United States of which substantial preparation was made after the 6-month grace period but before the acceptance of a maintenance fee under this subsection, and the court may also provide for the continued practice of any process that is practiced, or for the practice of which substantial preparation was made, after the 6-month grace period but before the acceptance of a maintenance fee under this subsection, to the extent and under such terms as the court deems equitable for the protection of investments made or business commenced after the 6-month grace period but before the acceptance of a maintenance fee under this subsection.

(d) *Patent search and other fees.—*

(1) *Patent search fees.—*

(A) *In general.—*The Director shall charge the fees specified under subparagraph (B) for the search of each application for a patent, except for provisional applications. The Director shall adjust the fees charged under this paragraph to ensure that the fees recover an amount not to exceed the estimated average cost to the Office of searching applications for patent by Office personnel.

(B) *Specific fees.—*The fees referred to in subparagraph (A) are—

(i) $540 [$600] for each application for an original patent, except for design, plant, provisional, or international applications;

(ii) $100 [$120] for each application for an original design patent;

(iii) $330 [$380] for each application for an original plant patent;

(iv) $540 [$600] for the national stage of each international application; and

(v) $540 [$600] for each application for the reissue of a patent.

(C) *Applicability of other provisions.—*The provisions of paragraphs (3) and (4) of section 111(a) relating to the payment of the fee for filing the application shall apply to the payment of the fee specified in this paragraph with respect to an application filed under section 111(a). The provisions of section 371(d) relating to the payment of the national fee shall apply to the payment of the fee specified in this paragraph with respect to an international application.

(D) *Refunds.*—The Director may by regulation provide for a refund of any part of the fee specified in this paragraph for any applicant who files a written declaration of express abandonment as prescribed by the Director before an examination has been made of the application under section 131.

(2) *Other fees.*—

(A) *In general.*—The Director shall establish fees for all other processing, services, or materials relating to patents not specified in this section to recover the estimated average cost to the Office of such processing, services, or materials, except that the Director shall charge the following fees for the following services:

(i) For recording a document affecting title, $40 per property.

(ii) For each photocopy, $.25 per page.

(iii) For each black and white copy of a patent, $3.

(B) *Copies for libraries.*—The yearly fee for providing a library specified in section 12 with uncertified printed copies of the specifications and drawings for all patents in that year shall be $50.

(e) *Waiver of fees; copies regarding notice.*—The Director may waive the payment of any fee for any service or material related to patents in connection with an occasional or incidental request made by a department or agency of the Government, or any officer thereof. The Director may provide any applicant issued a notice under section 132 with a copy of the specifications and drawings for all patents referred to in that notice without charge.

(f) *Adjustment of fees.*—The fees established in subsections (a) and (b) of this section may be adjusted by the Director on October 1, 1992, and every year thereafter, to reflect any fluctuations occurring during the previous 12 months in the Consumer Price Index, as determined by the Secretary of Labor. Changes of less than 1 per centum may be ignored.

[5](h) *Fees for small entities.*—

(1) *Reductions in fees.*—Subject to paragraph (3), fees charged under subsections (a), (b), and (d)(1) shall be reduced by 50 percent with respect to their application to any small business concern as defined under section

---

[5] *Ed. Note*: Subsection (g) was repealed pursuant to section 11(e)(2) of Pub. L. 112-29.

3 of the Small Business Act, and to any independent inventor or nonprofit organization as defined in regulations issued by the Director.

(2) *Surcharges and other fees.*—With respect to its application to any entity described in paragraph (1), any surcharge or fee charged under subsection (c) or (d) shall not be higher than the surcharge or fee required of any other entity under the same or substantially similar circumstances.

(3) *Reduction for electronic filing.*—The fee charged under subsection (a)(1)(A) shall be reduced by 75 percent with respect to its application to any entity to which paragraph (1) applies, if the application is filed by electronic means as prescribed by the Director.

(i) *Electronic patent and trademark data.*—

(1) *Maintenance of collections.*—The Director shall maintain, for use by the public, paper, microform, or electronic collections of United States patents, foreign patent documents, and United States trademark registrations arranged to permit search for and retrieval of information. The Director may not impose fees directly for the use of such collections, or for the use of the public patent or trademark search rooms or libraries.

(2) *Availability of automated search systems.*—The Director shall provide for the full deployment of the automated search systems of the Patent and Trademark Office so that such systems are available for use by the public, and shall assure full access by the public to, and dissemination of, patent and trademark information, using a variety of automated methods, including electronic bulletin boards and remote access by users to mass storage and retrieval systems.

(3) *Access fees.*—The Director may establish reasonable fees for access by the public to the automated search systems of the Patent and Trademark Office. If such fees are established, a limited amount of free access shall be made available to users of the systems for purposes of education and training. The Director may waive the payment by an individual of fees authorized by this subsection upon a showing of need or hardship, and if such a waiver is in the public interest.

(4) *Annual report to Congress.*—The Director shall submit to the Congress an annual report on the automated search systems of the Patent and Trademark Office and the access by the public to such systems. The Director shall also publish such report in the Federal Register. The Director shall provide an opportunity for the submission of comments by interested persons on each such report.

(July 19, 1952, ch. 950, §1, 66 Stat. 796; July 24, 1965, Pub. L. 89-83, §§1-2, 79 Stat. 259; Jan. 2, 1975, Pub. L. 93-596, §1, 88 Stat. 1949; Nov. 14, 1975, Pub. L. 94-131, §3, 89 Stat. 690; Dec. 12, 1980, Pub. L. 96-517, §2, 94 Stat. 3017; Aug. 27, 1982, Pub. L. 97-247, §3, 96 Stat. 317; Sept. 8, 1982, Pub. L. 97-256, §101, 96 Stat. 816; Nov. 8, 1984, Pub. L. 98-622, §204, 98 Stat. 3388; Nov. 6, 1986, Pub. L. 99-607, §1, 100 Stat. 3470; Dec. 10, 1991, Pub. L. 102-204, §5, 105 Stat. 1637-39; Oct. 23, 1992, Pub. L. 102-444, §1, 106 Stat. 2245; Dec. 8, 1994, Pub. L. 103-465, §§532, 533, 108 Stat. 4983, 4988; Nov. 10, 1998, Pub. L. 105-358, §3, 112 Stat. 3272; Nov. 29, 1999, Pub. L. 106-113, §§4202, 4605(a), 4732, 4804, 113 Stat. 1501A-554, 570, 581, 589; Dec. 8, 2004, Pub. L. 108-447, Title VIII, division B, 118 Stat. 2924; Sept. 16, 2011, Pub. L. 112-29, §11, 125 Stat. 320; Dec. 18, 2012, Pub. L. 112-211, §202, 126 Stat. 1535.)

§ 42   Patent and Trademark Office funding

(a) All fees for services performed by or materials furnished by the Patent and Trademark Office will be payable to the Director.

(b) All fees paid to the Director and all appropriations for defraying the costs of the activities of the Patent and Trademark Office will be credited to the Patent and Trademark Office Appropriation Account in the Treasury of the United States.

(c) (1) To the extent and in the amounts provided in advance in appropriations Acts, fees authorized in this title or any other Act to be charged or established by the Director shall be collected by and shall, subject to paragraph (3), be available to the Director to carry out the activities of the Patent and Trademark Office.

(2) There is established in the Treasury a Patent and Trademark Fee Reserve Fund. If fee collections by the Patent and Trademark Office for a fiscal year exceed the amount appropriated to the Office for that fiscal year, fees collected in excess of the appropriated amount shall be deposited in the Patent and Trademark Fee Reserve Fund. To the extent and in the amounts provided in appropriations Acts, amounts in the Fund shall be made available until expended only for obligation and expenditure by the Office in accordance with paragraph (3).

(3) (A) Any fees that are collected under this title, and any surcharges on such fees, may only be used for expenses of the Office relating to the processing of patent applications and for other activities, services, and materials relating to patents and to cover a proportionate share of the administrative costs of the Office.

(B) Any fees that are collected under section 31 of the Trademark Act of 1946, and any surcharges on such fees, may only be used for expenses of the Office relating to the processing of trademark registrations and for other activities, services, and materials relating to trademarks and to cover a proportionate share of the administrative costs of the Office.

(d) The Director may refund any fee paid by mistake or any amount paid in excess of that required.

(e) The Secretary of Commerce shall, on the day each year on which the President submits the annual budget to the Congress, provide to the Committees on the Judiciary of the Senate and the House of Representatives—

(1) a list of patent and trademark fee collections by the Patent and Trademark Office during the preceding fiscal year;

(2) a list of activities of the Patent and Trademark Office during the preceding fiscal year which were supported by patent fee expenditures, trademark fee expenditures, and appropriations;

(3) budget plans for significant programs, projects, and activities of the Office, including out-year funding estimates;

(4) any proposed disposition of surplus fees by the Office; and

(5) such other information as the committees consider necessary.

(July 19, 1952, ch. 950, §1, 66 Stat. 796; Nov. 14, 1975, Pub. L. 94-131, §4, 89 Stat. 690; Dec. 12, 1980, Pub. L. 96-517, §3, 94 Stat. 3018; Aug. 27, 1982, Pub. L. 97-247, §3, 96 Stat. 319; Sept. 13, 1982, Pub. L. 97-258, §3, 96 Stat. 1065; Dec. 10, 1991, Pub. L. 102-204, §§4-5, 105 Stat. 1637, 1640; Nov. 10, 1998, Pub. L. 105-358, §4, 112 Stat. 3274; Nov. 29, 1999, Pub. L. 106-113, §4205, 113 Stat. 1501A-555; Aug. 7, 2009, Pub. L. 111-45, §1, 123 Stat. 1968; Sept. 16, 2011, Pub. L. 112-29, §22, 125 Stat. 336; Jan. 14, 2013, Pub. L. 112-274, §1(e)–(j), 126 Stat. 2457.)

PART II—PATENTABILITY OF INVENTIONS AND GRANT OF PATENTS

CHAPTER 10—PATENTABILITY OF INVENTIONS

§ 100 Definitions

(a) The term "invention" means invention or discovery.

(b) The term "process" means process, art or method, and includes a new use of a known process, machine, manufacture, composition of matter, or material.

(c) The terms "United States" and "this country" mean the United States of America, its territories and possessions.

(d) The word "patentee" includes not only the patentee to whom the patent was issued but also the successors in title to the patentee.

(e) The term "third-party requester" means a person requesting ex parte reexamination under section 302 who is not the patent owner.

(f) The term "inventor" means the individual or, if a joint invention, the individuals collectively who invented or discovered the subject matter of the invention.

(g) The terms "joint inventor" and "coinventor" mean any 1 of the individuals who invented or discovered the subject matter of a joint invention.

(h) The term "joint research agreement" means a written contract, grant, or cooperative agreement entered into by 2 or more persons or entities for the performance of experimental, developmental, or research work in the field of the claimed invention.

(i)(1) The term "effective filing date" for a claimed invention in a patent or application for patent means—

(A) if subparagraph (B) does not apply, the actual filing date of the patent or the application for the patent containing a claim to the invention; or

(B) the filing date of the earliest application for which the patent or application is entitled, as to such invention, to a right of priority under section 119, 365(a), 365(b), 386(a), or 386(b) or to the benefit of an earlier filing date under section 120, 121, 365(c), or 386(c).

(2) The effective filing date for a claimed invention in an application for reissue or reissued patent shall be determined by deeming the claim to the invention to have been contained in the patent for which reissue was sought.

(j) The term "claimed invention" means the subject matter defined by a claim in a patent or an application for a patent.

(July 19, 1952, ch. 950, §1, 66 Stat. 797; Nov. 29, 1999, Pub. L. 106-113, §4603, 113 Stat. 1501A-567; Sept. 16, 2011, Pub. L. 112-29, §3, 125 Stat. 285; Dec. 18, 2012, Pub. L. 112-211, §101, 126 Stat. 1531.)

§ 101[6] Inventions patentable

Whoever invents or discovers any new and useful process, machine, manufacture, or composition of matter, or any new and useful improvement thereof, may obtain a patent therefor, subject to the conditions and requirements of this title.

(July 19, 1952, ch. 950, §1, 66 Stat. 797.)

§ 102[7] Conditions for patentability; novelty

(a) *Novelty; Prior Art.*— A person shall be entitled to a patent unless—

(1) the claimed invention was patented, described in a printed publication, or in public use, on sale, or otherwise available to the public before the effective filing date of the claimed invention; or

---

[6] *Ed. Note:* Pursuant to section 33 of Pub. L. 112-29, no patent may issue on a claim directed to or encompassing a human organism. This provision applies to any application for patent that is pending on, or filed on or after Sept. 16, 2011, the date of enactment of Pub. L. 112-29.

[7] *Ed. Note:* Pursuant to Pub. L. 112-29, effective March 16, 2013, this version of §102 replaced the prior version of §102, which appears in the bracketed text immediately below. The new provisions of §102 shall apply to any application for patent and to any patent issuing thereon that contains or contained at any time a claim that has an effective filing date on or after March 16, 2013 or a specific reference under Section 120, 121, or 365(c) to any patent or application that contains or contained at any time such a claim. See text of Pub. L. 112-29 on the CD-ROM that accompanies this edition of the book. A table of effective dates for all changes set forth in Pub. L. 112-29 may also be found on the CD-ROM. See also section 14 of Pub. L. 112-29 relating to tax strategies deemed within the prior art, which appears in "Uncodified Provisions of the America Invents Act," below.

(2) the claimed invention was described in a patent issued under section 151, or in an application for patent published or deemed published under section 122(b), in which the patent or application, as the case may be, names another inventor and was effectively filed before the effective filing date of the claimed invention.

(b) *Exceptions.* —

(1) Disclosures made 1 year or less before the effective filing date of the claimed invention. — A disclosure made 1 year or less before the effective filing date of a claimed invention shall not be prior art to the claimed invention under subsection (a)(1) if—

(A) the disclosure was made by the inventor or joint inventor or by another who obtained the subject matter disclosed directly or indirectly from the inventor or a joint inventor; or

(B) the subject matter disclosed had, before such disclosure, been publicly disclosed by the inventor or a joint inventor or another who obtained the subject matter disclosed directly or indirectly from the inventor or a joint inventor.

(2) *Disclosures appearing in applications and patents.* — A disclosure shall not be prior art to a claimed invention under subsection (a)(2) if—

(A) the subject matter disclosed was obtained directly or indirectly from the inventor or a joint inventor;

(B) the subject matter disclosed had, before such subject matter was effectively filed under subsection (a)(2), been publicly disclosed by the inventor or a joint inventor or another who obtained the subject matter disclosed directly or indirectly from the inventor or a joint inventor; or

(C) the subject matter disclosed and the claimed invention, not later than the effective filing date of the claimed invention, were owned by the same person or subject to an obligation of assignment to the same person.

(c) *Common Ownership Under Joint Research Agreements.* — Subject matter disclosed and a claimed invention shall be deemed to have been owned by the same person or subject to an obligation of assignment to the same person in applying the provisions of subsection (b)(2)(C) if—

(1) the subject matter disclosed was developed and the claimed invention was made by, or on behalf of, 1 or more parties to a joint research agree-

35 U.S.C. § 102

ment that was in effect on or before the effective filing date of the claimed invention;

(2) the claimed invention was made as a result of activities undertaken within the scope of the joint research agreement; and

(3) the application for patent for the claimed invention discloses or is amended to disclose the names of the parties to the joint research agreement.

(d) *Patents and Published Applications Effective as Prior Art.*—For purposes of determining whether a patent or application for patent is prior art to a claimed invention under subsection (a)(2), such patent or application shall be considered to have been effectively filed, with respect to any subject matter described in the patent or application—

(1) if paragraph (2) does not apply, as of the actual filing date of the patent or the application for patent; or

(2) if the patent or application for patent is entitled to claim a right of priority under section 119, 365(a), 365(b), 386(a), or 386(b), or to claim the benefit of an earlier filing date under section 120, 121, 365(c), or 386(c) based upon 1 or more prior filed applications for patent, as of the filing date of the earliest such application that describes the subject matter.

[§ 102[8] Conditions for patentability; novelty and loss of right to patent

A person shall be entitled to a patent unless—

(a) the invention was known or used by others in this country, or patented or described in a printed publication in this or a foreign country, before the invention thereof by the applicant for patent, or

(b) the invention was patented or described in a printed publication in this or a foreign country or in public use or on sale in this country, more than one year prior to the date of the application for patent in the United States, or

---

[8] *Ed. Note:* Pursuant to Pub. L. 112-29, effective March 16, 2013, this version of §102, shown here in brackets, is replaced by new §102, which appears immediately above. The new provisions of §102 shall apply to any application for patent and to any patent issuing thereon that contains or contained at any time a claim that has an effective filing date on or after March 16, 2013 or a specific reference under Section 120, 121, or 365(c) to any patent or application that contains or contained at any time such a claim. See text of Pub. L. 112-29 on the CD-ROM that accompanies this edition of the book. A table of effective dates for all changes set forth in Pub. L. 112-29 may also be found on the CD-ROM. See also section 14 of Pub. L. 112-29 relating to tax strategies deemed within the prior art, which appears in "Uncodified Provisions of the America Invents Act," below.

35 U.S.C. § 102

(c) he has abandoned the invention, or

(d) the invention was first patented or caused to be patented, or was the subject of an inventor's certificate, by the applicant or his legal representatives or assigns in a foreign country prior to the date of the application for patent in this country on an application for patent or inventor's certificate filed more than twelve months before the filing of the application in the United States, or

(e)[9] the invention was described in (1) an application for patent, published under section 122(b), by another filed in the United States before the invention by the applicant for patent or (2) a patent granted on an application for patent by another filed in the United States before the invention by the applicant for patent, except that an international application filed under the treaty defined in section 351(a) shall have the effects for the purposes of this subsection of an application filed in the United States only if the international application designated the United States and was published under Article 21(2) of such treaty in the English language; or

(f) he did not himself invent the subject matter sought to be patented, or

(g)[10](1) during the course of an interference conducted under section 135 or section 291, another inventor involved therein establishes, to the extent permitted in section 104, that before such person's invention thereof the invention was made by such other inventor and not abandoned, suppressed, or concealed, or (2) before such person's invention thereof, the invention was made in this country by another inventor who had not abandoned, suppressed, or concealed it. In determining priority of invention under this subsection, there shall be considered not only the respective dates of conception and reduction to practice of the invention, but also the reasonable diligence of one who was first to conceive and last to reduce to practice, from a time prior to conception by the other.]

(July 19, 1952, ch. 950, §1, 66 Stat. 797; July 28, 1972, Pub. L. 92-358, §2, 86 Stat. 502; Nov. 14, 1975, Pub. L. 94-131, §5, 89 Stat. 691; Nov. 29, 1999, Pub. L. 106-113, §§4505,

---

[9] *Ed. Note:* Pursuant to sec. 13205 of Pub. L. 107-273, this version of 35 U.S.C. §102(e) shall be effective as of November 29, 2000 and shall apply to all patents and all patent applications pending on or filed after November 29, 2000. Patents resulting from an international application filed before November 29, 2000 and applications published pursuant to section 122(b) or Article 21(2) of the treaty defined in section 351(a) resulting from an international application filed before November 29, 2000 shall not be effective as prior art as of the filing date of the international application; however, such patents shall be effective as prior art in accordance with section 102(e) in effect on November 28, 2000.

[10] *Ed. Note:* The provisions of §102(g) in effect on the day prior to March 16, 2013 shall apply to each claim of an application for patent, and any patent issued thereon, that contains or contained at any time a claim to a claimed invention or a specific reference under Section 120, 121, or 365(c) to any patent or application that has an effective filing date prior to March 16, 2013. See Pub. L. 112-29, §3(n)(2), 125 Stat. 293.

35 U.S.C. § 102

4806, 113 Stat. 1501A-565, 590; Nov. 2, 2002, Pub. L. 107-273, §13205, 116 Stat. 1902; Sept. 16, 2011, Pub. L. 112-29, §3, 125 Stat. 285; Dec. 18, 2012, Pub. L. 112-211, §101, 126 Stat. 1531.)

§ 103[11] Conditions for patentability; non-obvious subject matter

A patent for a claimed invention may not be obtained, notwithstanding that the claimed invention is not identically disclosed as set forth in section 102, if the differences between the claimed invention and the prior art are such that the claimed invention as a whole would have been obvious before the effective filing date of the claimed invention to a person having ordinary skill in the art to which the claimed invention pertains. Patentability shall not be negated by the manner in which the invention was made.

[§ 103[12] Conditions for patentability; nonobvious subject matter

(a) A patent may not be obtained though the invention is not identically disclosed or described as set forth in section 102, if the differences between the subject matter sought to be patented and the prior art are such that the subject matter as a whole would have been obvious at the time the invention was made to a person having ordinary skill in the art to which said subject matter pertains. Patentability shall not be negatived by the manner in which the invention was made.

(b) (1) Notwithstanding subsection (a), and upon timely election by the applicant for patent to proceed under this subsection, a biotechnological process using or resulting in a composition of matter that is novel under section 102 and nonobvious under subsection (a) of this section shall be considered nonobvious if—

---

[11] *Ed. Note:* Pursuant to Pub. L. 112-29, effective March 16, 2013, this version of §103 replaced the prior version of §103, which appears in the bracketed text immediately below. The new provisions of §103 shall apply to any application for patent and to any patent issuing thereon that contains or contained at any time a claim that has an effective filing date on or after March 16, 2013 or a specific reference under Section 120, 121, or 365(c) to any patent or application that contains or contained at any time such a claim. See text of Pub. L. 112-29 on the CD-ROM that accompanies this edition of the book. A table of effective dates for all changes set forth in Pub. L. 112-29 may also be found on the CD-ROM. See also section 14 of Pub. L. 112-29 relating to tax strategies deemed within the prior art, which appears in "Uncodified Provisions of the America Invents Act," below.

[12] *Ed. Note:* Pursuant to Pub. L. 112-29, effective March 16, 2013, this version of §103, shown here in brackets, is replaced by new §103, which appears immediately above. The new provisions of §103 shall apply to any application for patent and to any patent issuing thereon that contains or contained at any time a claim that has an effective filing date on or after March 16, 2013 or a specific reference under Section 120, 121, or 365(c) to any patent or application that contains or contained at any time such a claim. See text of Pub. L. 112-29 on the CD-ROM that accompanies this edition of the book. A table of effective dates for all changes set forth in Pub. L. 112-29 may also be found on the CD-ROM. See also section 14 of Pub. L. 112-29 relating to tax strategies deemed within the prior art, which appears in "Uncodified Provisions of the America Invents Act," below.

(A) claims to the process and the composition of matter are contained in either the same application for patent or in separate applications having the same effective filing date; and

(B) the composition of matter, and the process at the time it was invented, were owned by the same person or subject to an obligation of assignment to the same person.

(2) A patent issued on a process under paragraph (1)—

(A) shall also contain the claims to the composition of matter used in or made by that process, or

(B) shall, if such composition of matter is claimed in another patent, be set to expire on the same date as such other patent, notwithstanding section 154.

(3) For purposes of paragraph (1), the term "biotechnological process" means—

(A) a process of genetically altering or otherwise inducing a single—or multi-celled organism to—

(i) express an exogenous nucleotide sequence,

(ii) inhibit, eliminate, augment, or alter expression of an endogenous nucleotide sequence, or

(iii) express a specific physiological characteristic not naturally associated with said organism;

(B) cell fusion procedures yielding a cell line that expresses a specific protein, such as a monoclonal antibody; and

(C) a method of using a product produced by a process defined by subparagraph (A) or (B), or a combination of subparagraphs (A) and (B).

(c) (1) Subject matter developed by another person, which qualifies as prior art only under one or more of subsections (e), (f), and (g) of section 102, shall not preclude patentability under this section where the subject matter and the claimed invention were, at the time the claimed invention was made, owned by the same person or subject to an obligation of assignment to the same person.

(2) For purposes of this subsection, subject matter developed by another person and a claimed invention shall be deemed to have been owned by

the same person or subject to an obligation of assignment to the same person if—

(A) the claimed invention was made by or on behalf of parties to a joint research agreement that was in effect on or before the date the claimed invention was made;

(B) the claimed invention was made as a result of activities undertaken within the scope of the joint research agreement; and

(C) the application for patent for the claimed invention discloses or is amended to disclose the names of the parties to the joint research agreement.

(3) For purposes of paragraph (2), the term "joint research agreement" means a written contract, grant, or cooperative agreement entered into by two or more persons or entities for the performance of experimental, developmental, or research work in the field of the claimed invention.]

(July 19, 1952, ch. 950, §1, 66 Stat. 798; Nov. 8, 1984, Pub. L. 98-622, §103, 98 Stat. 3384; Nov. 1, 1995, Pub. L. 104-41, §1, 109 Stat. 351; Nov. 29, 1999, Pub. L. 106-113, §4807, 113 Stat. 1501A-591, Dec. 10, 2004, Pub. L. 108-453, §2, 118 Stat. 3596; Sept. 16, 2011, Pub. L. 112-29, §3, 125 Stat. 287.)

§ 104 (old)   Invention made abroad [Repealed]

(July 19, 1952, ch. 950, §1, 66 Stat. 798; Jan. 2, 1975, Pub. L. 93-596, §1, 88 Stat. 1949; Nov. 14, 1975, Pub. L. 94-131, §6, 89 Stat. 691; Nov. 8, 1984, Pub. L. 98-622, §403, 98 Stat. 3392; Dec. 8, 1993, Pub. L. 103-182, §331, 107 Stat. 2113; Sept. 16, 2011, Pub. L. 112-29, §3, 125 Stat. 287.)]

§ 104 (new)   Invention made abroad [Repealed]

(July 19, 1952, ch. 950, §1, 66 Stat. 798; Jan. 2, 1975, Pub. L. 93-596, §1, 88 Stat. 1949; Nov. 14, 1975, Pub. L. 94-131, §6, 89 Stat. 691; Nov. 8, 1984, Pub. L. 98-622, §403, 98 Stat. 3392; Dec. 8, 1993, Pub. L. 103-182, §331, 107 Stat. 2113; Dec. 8, 1994, Pub. L. 103-465, §531, 108 Stat. 4982; Sept. 16, 2011, Pub. L. 112-29, §3, 125 Stat. 287.)]

§ 105   Inventions in outer space

(a) Any invention made, used or sold in outer space on a space object or component thereof under the jurisdiction or control of the United States shall be considered to be made, used or sold within the United States for the purposes of this title, except with respect to any space object or component thereof that is specifically identified and otherwise provided for by an international agreement to which the United States is a party, or with respect to any space object or component thereof that is carried on the registry of a foreign state in accordance with the Convention on Registration of Objects Launched into Outer Space.

35 U.S.C. § 104 (old)

(b) Any invention made, used or sold in outer space on a space object or component thereof that is carried on the registry of a foreign state in accordance with the Convention on Registration of Objects Launched into Outer Space, shall be considered to be made, used or sold within the United States for the purposes of this title if specifically so agreed in an international agreement between the United States and the state of registry.

(Nov. 15, 1990, Pub. L. 101-580, §1, 104 Stat. 2863.)

CHAPTER 11 — APPLICATION FOR PATENT

SEC.

§ 111 Application

(a) *In General.* —

(1) *Written application.* — An application for patent shall be made, or authorized to be made, by the inventor, except as otherwise provided in this title, in writing to the Director.

(2) *Contents.* — Such application shall include—

(A) a specification as prescribed by section 112;

(B) a drawing as prescribed by section 113; and

(C) an oath or declaration as prescribed by section 115.

(3) *Fee, oath or declaration, and claims.* — The application shall be accompanied by the fee required by law. The fee, oath or declaration, and 1 or more claims may be submitted after the filing date of the application, within such period and under such conditions, including the payment of a surcharge, as may be prescribed by the Director. Upon failure to submit

35 U.S.C. § 111

the fee, oath or declaration, and 1 or more claims within such prescribed period, the application shall be regarded as abandoned.

(4) *Filing date.*—The filing date of an application shall be the date on which a specification, with or without claims, is received in the United States Patent and Trademark Office.

(b) *Provisional application.*—

(1) *Authorization.*—A provisional application for patent shall be made or authorized to be made by the inventor, except as otherwise provided in this title, in writing to the Director. Such application shall include—

(A) a specification as prescribed by section 112(a); and

(B) a drawing as prescribed by section 113.

(2) *Claim.*—A claim, as required by subsections (b) through (e) of section 112, shall not be required in a provisional application.

(3) *Fee.*—The application shall be accompanied by the fee required by law. The fee may be submitted after the filing date of the application, within such period and under such conditions, including the payment of a surcharge, as may be prescribed by the Director. Upon failure to submit the fee within such prescribed period, the application shall be regarded as abandoned.

(4) *Filing date.*—The filing date of a provisional application shall be the date on which a specification, with or without claims, is received in the United States Patent and Trademark Office.

(5) *Abandonment.*—Notwithstanding the absence of a claim, upon timely request and as prescribed by the Director, a provisional application may be treated as an application filed under subsection (a). Subject to section 119(e)(3), if no such request is made, the provisional application shall be regarded as abandoned 12 months after the filing date of such application and shall not be subject to revival after such 12-month period.

(6) *Other basis for provisional application.*—Subject to all the conditions in this subsection and section 119(e), and as prescribed by the Director, an application for patent filed under subsection (a) may be treated as a provisional application for patent.

(7) *No right of priority or benefit of earliest filing date.*—A provisional application shall not be entitled to the right of priority of any other application under section 119, 365(a), or 386(a) or to the benefit of an earlier filing date in the United States under section 120, 121, 365(c), or 386(c).

35 U.S.C. § 111

(8) *Applicable provisions.* — The provisions of this title relating to applications for patent shall apply to provisional applications for patent, except as otherwise provided, and except that provisional applications for patent shall not be subject to sections 131 and 135.

(c) *Prior Filed Application.* — Notwithstanding the provisions of subsection (a), the Director may prescribe the conditions, including the payment of a surcharge, under which a reference made upon the filing of an application under subsection (a) to a previously filed application, specifying the previously filed application by application number and the intellectual property authority or country in which the application was filed, shall constitute the specification and any drawings of the subsequent application for purposes of a filing date. A copy of the specification and any drawings of the previously filed application shall be submitted within such period and under such conditions as may be prescribed by the Director. A failure to submit the copy of the specification and any drawings of the previously filed application within the prescribed period shall result in the application being regarded as abandoned. Such application shall be treated as having never been filed, unless —

(1) the application is revived under section 27; and

(2) a copy of the specification and any drawings of the previously filed application are submitted to the Director.

(July 19, 1952, ch. 950, §1, 66 Stat. 798; Aug. 27, 1982, Pub. L. 97-247, §5, 96 Stat. 319; Dec. 8, 1994, Pub. L. 103-465, §532, 108 Stat. 4983; Nov. 29, 1999, Pub. L. 106-113, §4801, 113 Stat. 1501A-588; Sept. 16, 2011, Pub. L. 112-29, §3, 125 Stat. 287, 295–96; Dec. 18, 2012, Pub. L. 112-211, §201, 126 Stat. 1533; Dec. 18, 2012, Pub. L. 112-211, §101, 126 Stat. 1531.)

§ 112   Specification

(a) *In general.* — The specification shall contain a written description of the invention, and of the manner and process of making and using it, in such full, clear, concise, and exact terms as to enable any person skilled in the art to which it pertains, or with which it is most nearly connected, to make and use the same, and shall set forth the best mode contemplated by the inventor or joint inventor of carrying out the invention.

(b) *Conclusion.* — The specification shall conclude with one or more claims particularly pointing out and distinctly claiming the subject matter which the inventor or a joint inventor regards as the invention.

(c) *Form.*—A claim may be written in independent or, if the nature of the case admits, in dependent or multiple dependent form.

(d) *Reference in dependent forms.*— Subject to subsection (e), a claim in dependent form shall contain a reference to a claim previously set forth and then specify a further limitation of the subject matter claimed. A claim in dependent form shall be construed to incorporate by reference all the limitations of the claim to which it refers.

(e) *Reference in multiple dependent form.*—A claim in multiple dependent form shall contain a reference, in the alternative only, to more than one claim previously set forth and then specify a further limitation of the subject matter claimed. A multiple dependent claim shall not serve as a basis for any other multiple dependent claim. A multiple dependent claim shall be construed to incorporate by reference all the limitations of the particular claim in relation to which it is being considered.

(f) *Element in claim for a combination.*— An element in a claim for a combination may be expressed as a means or step for performing a specified function without the recital of structure, material, or acts in support thereof, and such claim shall be construed to cover the corresponding structure, material, or acts described in the specification and equivalents thereof.

(July 19, 1952, ch. 950, §1, 66 Stat. 798; July 24, 1965, Pub. L. 89-83, §9, 79 Stat. 261; Nov. 14, 1975, Pub. L. 94-131, §7, 89 Stat. 691; Sept. 16, 2011, Pub. L. 112-29, §118, 125 Stat. 296.)

§ 113   Drawings

The applicant shall furnish a drawing where necessary for the understanding of the subject matter sought to be patented. When the nature of such subject matter admits of illustration by a drawing and the applicant has not furnished such a drawing, the Director may require its submission within a time period of not less than two months from the sending of a notice thereof. Drawings submitted after the filing date of the application may not be used (i) to overcome any insufficiency of the specification due to lack of an enabling disclosure or otherwise inadequate disclosure therein, or (ii) to supplement the original disclosure thereof for the purpose of interpretation of the scope of any claim.

(July 19, 1952, ch. 950, §1, 66 Stat. 799; Nov. 14, 1975, Pub. L. 94-131, §8, 89 Stat. 691.)

§ 114   Models, specimens

The Director may require the applicant to furnish a model of convenient size to exhibit advantageously the several parts of his invention.

35 U.S.C. § 113

When the invention relates to a composition of matter, the Director may require the applicant to furnish specimens or ingredients for the purpose of inspection or experiment.

(July 19, 1952, ch. 950, §1, 66 Stat. 799.)

§ 115   Inventor's oath or declaration

(a) *Naming the inventor; inventor's oath or declaration.*—An application for patent that is filed under section 111(a) or commences the national stage under section 371 shall include, or be amended to include, the name of the inventor for any invention claimed in the application. Except as otherwise provided in this section, each individual who is the inventor or a joint inventor of a claimed invention in an application for patent shall execute an oath or declaration in connection with the application.

(b) *Required statements.*—An oath or declaration under subsection (a) shall contain statements that—

(1) the application was made or was authorized to be made by the affiant or declarant; and

(2) such individual believes himself or herself to be the original inventor or an original joint inventor of a claimed invention in the application.

(c) *Additional requirements.*—The Director may specify additional information relating to the inventor and the invention that is required to be included in an oath or declaration under subsection (a).

(d) *Substitute statement.*—

(1) *In general.*—In lieu of executing an oath or declaration under subsection (a), the applicant for patent may provide a substitute statement under the circumstances described in paragraph (2) and such additional circumstances that the Director may specify by regulation.

(2) *Permitted circumstances.*—A substitute statement under paragraph (1) is permitted with respect to any individual who—

(A) is unable to file the oath or declaration under subsection (a) because the individual—

(i) is deceased;

(ii) is under legal incapacity; or

(iii) cannot be found or reached after diligent effort; or

(B) is under an obligation to assign the invention but has refused to make the oath or declaration required under subsection (a).

(3) *Contents.* — A substitute statement under this subsection shall —

(A) identify the individual with respect to whom the statement applies;

(B) set forth the circumstances representing the permitted basis for the filing of the substitute statement in lieu of the oath or declaration under subsection (a); and

(C) contain any additional information, including any showing, required by the Director. .

(e) *Making required statements in assignment of record.* — An individual who is under an obligation of assignment of an application for patent may include the required statements under subsections (b) and (c) in the assignment executed by the individual, in lieu of filing such statements separately.

(f) *Time for filing.* — The applicant for patent shall provide each required oath or declaration under subsection (a), substitute statement under subsection (d), or recorded assignment meeting the requirements of subsection (e) no later than the date on which the issue fee for the patent is paid.

(g) *Earlier-filed application containing required statements or substitute statement.* —

(1) *Exception.* — The requirements under this section shall not apply to an individual with respect to an application for patent in which the individual is named as the inventor or a joint inventor and that claims the benefit under section 120, 121, 365(c), or 386(c) of the filing of an earlier-filed application, if —

(A) an oath or declaration meeting the requirements of subsection (a) was executed by the individual and was filed in connection with the earlier-filed application;

(B) a substitute statement meeting the requirements of subsection (d) was filed in connection with the earlier filed application with respect to the individual; or

(C) an assignment meeting the requirements of subsection (e) was executed with respect to the earlier-filed application by the individual and was recorded in connection with the earlier-filed application.

(2) *Copies of oaths, declarations, statements, or assignments.* — Notwithstanding paragraph (1), the Director may require that a copy of the executed

oath or declaration, the substitute statement, or the assignment filed in connection with the earlier-filed application be included in the later-filed application.

(h) *Supplemental and corrected statements; filing additional statements.* —

(1) *In general.* — Any person making a statement required under this section may withdraw, replace, or otherwise correct the statement at any time. If a change is made in the naming of the inventor requiring the filing of 1 or more additional statements under this section, the Director shall establish regulations under which such additional statements may be filed.

(2) *Supplemental statements not required.* — If an individual has executed an oath or declaration meeting the requirements of subsection (a) or an assignment meeting the requirements of subsection (e) with respect to an application for patent, the Director may not thereafter require that individual to make any additional oath, declaration, or other statement equivalent to those required by this section in connection with the application for patent or any patent issuing thereon.

(3) *Savings clause.* — A patent shall not be invalid or unenforceable based upon the failure to comply with a requirement under this section if the failure is remedied as provided under paragraph (1).

(i) *Acknowledgment of penalties.* — Any declaration or statement filed pursuant to this section shall contain an acknowledgment that any willful false statement made in such declaration or statement is punishable under section 1001 of title 18 by fine or imprisonment of not more than 5 years, or both.

(July 19, 1952, ch. 950, §1, 66 Stat. 799; Aug. 27, 1982, Pub. L. 97-247, §14, 96 Stat. 321; Oct. 21, 1998, Pub. L. 105-277, §2222, 112 Stat. 2681–818; Sept. 16, 2011, Pub. L. 112-29, §3, 125 Stat. 293; Jan. 14, 2013, Pub. L. 112-274, §1(f), 126 Stat. 2456-57; Dec. 18, 2012, Pub. L. 112-211, §101, 126 Stat. 1531.)

§ 116   Inventors

(a) *Joint inventors.* — When an invention is made by two or more persons jointly, they shall apply for patent jointly and each make the required oath, except as otherwise provided in this title. Inventors may apply for a patent jointly even though (1) they did not physically work together or at the same time, (2) each did not make the same type or amount of contribution, or (3) each did not make a contribution to the subject matter of every claim of the patent.

(b) *Omitted inventor.*—If a joint inventor refuses to join in an application for patent or cannot be found or reached after diligent effort, the application may be made by the other inventor on behalf of himself and the omitted inventor. The Director, on proof of the pertinent facts and after such notice to the omitted inventor as he prescribes, may grant a patent to the inventor making the application, subject to the same rights which the omitted inventor would have had if he had been joined. The omitted inventor may subsequently join in the application.

(c) *Correction of errors in application.*—Whenever through error a person is named in an application for patent as the inventor, or through an error an inventor is not named in an application, the Director may permit the application to be amended accordingly, under such terms as he prescribes.

(July 19, 1952, ch. 950, §1, 66 Stat. 799; Aug. 27, 1982, Pub. L. 97-247, §6, 96 Stat. 320; Nov. 8, 1984, Pub. L. 98-622, §104, 98 Stat. 3384; Sept. 16, 2011, Pub. L. 112-29, §20, 125 Stat. 333–34.)

§ 117   Death or incapacity of inventor

Legal representatives of deceased inventors and of those under legal incapacity may make application for patent upon compliance with the requirements and on the same terms and conditions applicable to the inventor.

(July 19, 1952, ch. 950, §1, 66 Stat. 799.)

§ 118   Filing by other than inventor

A person to whom the inventor has assigned or is under an obligation to assign the invention may make an application for patent. A person who otherwise shows sufficient proprietary interest in the matter may make an application for patent on behalf of and as agent for the inventor on proof of the pertinent facts and a showing that such action is appropriate to preserve the rights of the parties. If the Director grants a patent on an application filed under this section by a person other than the inventor, the patent shall be granted to the real party in interest and upon such notice to the inventor as the Director considers to be sufficient.

(July 19, 1952, ch. 950, §1, 66 Stat. 799; Sept. 16, 2011, Pub. L. 112-29, §3, 125 Stat. 296.)

§ 119   Benefit of earlier filing date; right of priority

(a) An application for patent for an invention filed in this country by any person who has, or whose legal representatives or assigns have, previously regularly filed an application for a patent for the same invention in a foreign country which affords similar privileges in the case of applications filed in the United States or to citizens of the United States, or in a WTO member country, shall have the same effect as the same application would have if filed in this country on the date on which the application for patent for the same invention was first filed in such foreign country, if the application in this country is filed within 12 months from the earliest date on which such foreign application was filed. The Director may prescribe regulations, including the requirement for payment of the fee specified in section 41(a)(7), pursuant to which the 12-month period set forth in this subsection may be extended by an additional 2 months if the delay in filing the application in this country within the 12-month period was unintentional.

(b)(1) No application for patent shall be entitled to this right of priority unless a claim is filed in the Patent and Trademark Office, identifying the foreign application by specifying the application number on that foreign application, the intellectual property authority or country in or for which the application was filed, and the date of filing the application, at such time during the pendency of the application as required by the Director.

(2) The Director may consider the failure of the applicant to file a timely claim for priority as a waiver of any such claim. The Director may establish procedures, including the requirement for payment of the fee specified in section 41(a)(7), to accept an unintentionally delayed claim under this section.

(3) The Director may require a certified copy of the original foreign application, specification, and drawings upon which it is based, a translation if not in the English language, and such other information as the Director considers necessary. Any such certification shall be made by the foreign intellectual property authority in which the foreign application was filed and show the date of the application and of the filing of the specification and other papers.

(c) In like manner and subject to the same conditions and requirements, the right provided in this section may be based upon a subsequent regularly filed application in the same foreign country instead of the first filed foreign application, provided that any foreign application filed prior to such subsequent application has been withdrawn, abandoned, or otherwise disposed of, without having been laid open to public inspection and without leaving any rights outstanding, and has not served, nor thereafter shall serve, as a basis for claiming a right of priority.

(d) Applications for inventors' certificates filed in a foreign country in which applicants have a right to apply, at their discretion, either for a patent or for an inventor's certificate shall be treated in this country in the same manner and have the same effect for purpose of the right of priority under this section as applications for patents, subject to the same conditions and requirements of this section as apply to applications for patents, provided such applicants are entitled to the benefits of the Stockholm Revision of the Paris Convention at the time of such filing.

(e) (1) An application for patent filed under section 111(a) or section 363 for an invention disclosed in the manner provided by section 112(a) (other than the requirement to disclose the best mode) in a provisional application filed under section 111(b), by an inventor or inventors named in the provisional application, shall have the same effect, as to such invention, as though filed on the date of the provisional application filed under section 111(b), if the application for patent filed under section 111(a) or section 363 is filed not later than 12 months after the date on which the provisional application was filed and if it contains or is amended to contain a specific reference to the provisional application. The Director may prescribe regulations, including the requirement for payment of the fee specified in section 41(a)(7), pursuant to which the 12-month period set forth in this subsection may be extended by an additional 2 months if the delay in filing the application under section 111(a) or section 363 within the 12-month period was unintentional. No application shall be entitled to the benefit of an earlier filed provisional application under this subsection unless an amendment containing the specific reference to the earlier filed provisional application is submitted at such time during the pendency of the application as required by the Director. The Director may consider the failure to submit such an amendment within that time period as a waiver of any benefit under this subsection. The Director may establish procedures, including the payment of the fee specified in section 41(a)(7), to accept an unintentionally delayed submission of an amendment under this subsection.

(2) A provisional application filed under section 111(b) may not be relied upon in any proceeding in the Patent and Trademark Office unless the fee set forth in subparagraph (A) or (C) of section 41(a)(1) has been paid.

(3) If the day that is 12 months after the filing date of a provisional application falls on a Saturday, Sunday, or Federal holiday within the District of Columbia, the period of pendency of the provisional application shall be extended to the next succeeding secular or business day. For

an application for patent filed under section 363 in a Receiving Office other than the Patent and Trademark Office, the 12-month and additional 2-month period set forth in this subsection shall be extended as provided under the treaty and Regulations as defined in section 351.

(f) Applications for plant breeder's rights filed in a WTO member country (or in a foreign UPOV Contracting Party) shall have the same effect for the purpose of the right of priority under subsections (a) through (c) of this section as applications for patents, subject to the same conditions and requirements of this section as apply to applications for patents.

(g) As used in this section—

(1) the term "WTO member country" has the same meaning as the term is defined in section 104(b)(2) ; and

(2) the term "UPOV Contracting Party" means a member of the International Convention for the Protection of New Varieties of Plants.

(July 19, 1952, ch. 950, §1, 66 Stat. 800; Oct. 3, 1961, Pub. L. 87-333, §1, 75 Stat. 748; July 28, 1972, Pub. L. 92-358, §1, 86 Stat. 502; Jan. 2, 1975, Pub. L. 93-596, §1, 88 Stat. 1949; Dec. 8, 1994, Pub. L. 103-465, §532, 108 Stat. 4983; Nov. 29, 1999, Pub. L. 106-113, §§4503, 4801, 4802, 113 Stat. 1501A-563, 588, 589; Sept. 16, 2011, Pub. L. 112-29, §15, 125 Stat. 328; Sept. 16, 2011, Pub. L. 112-29, §3, 125 Stat. 288; Dec. 18, 2012, Pub. L. 112-211, §§201, 202, 126 Stat. 1534, 1536.)

§ 120   Benefit of earlier filing date in the United States

An application for patent for an invention disclosed in the manner provided by section 112(a) (other than the requirement to disclose the best mode) in an application previously filed in the United States, or as provided by section 363 or 385, which names an inventor or joint inventor in the previously filed application shall have the same effect, as to such invention, as though filed on the date of the prior application, if filed before the patenting or abandonment of or termination of proceedings on the first application or on an application similarly entitled to the benefit of the filing date of the first application and if it contains or is amended to contain a specific reference to the earlier filed application. No application shall be entitled to the benefit of an earlier filed application under this section unless an amendment containing the specific reference to the earlier filed application is submitted at such time during the pendency of the application as required by the Director. The Director may consider the failure to submit such an amendment within that time period as a waiver of any benefit under this section. The Director may establish procedures, including the requirement for payment of the fee specified in section 41(a)(7), to accept an unintentionally delayed submission of an amendment under this section.

(July 19, 1952, ch. 950, §1, 66 Stat. 800; Nov. 14, 1975, Pub. L. 94-131, §9, 89 Stat. 691; Nov. 8, 1984, Pub. L. 98-622, §104, 98 Stat. 3385; Nov. 29, 1999, Pub. L. 106-113, §4503, 113 Stat. 1501A-563; Sept. 16, 2011, Pub. L. 112-29, §§3,15, 125 Stat. 288, 328; Dec. 18, 2012, Pub. L. 112-211, §202, 126 Stat. 1536; Dec. 18, 2012, Pub. L. 112-211, §101, 126 Stat. 1531.)

§ 121   Divisional applications

If two or more independent and distinct inventions are claimed in one application, the Director may require the application to be restricted to one of the inventions. If the other invention is made the subject of a divisional application which complies with the requirements of section 120 it shall be entitled to the benefit of the filing date of the original application. A patent issuing on an application with respect to which a requirement for restriction under this section has been made, or on an application filed as a result of such a requirement, shall not be used as a reference either in the Patent and Trademark Office or in the courts against a divisional application or against the original application or any patent issued on either of them, if the divisional application is filed before the issuance of the patent on the other application. The validity of a patent shall not be questioned for failure of the Director to require the application to be restricted to one invention.

(July 19, 1952, ch. 950, §1, 66 Stat. 800; Jan. 2, 1975, Pub. L. 93-596, §1, 88 Stat. 1949; Sept. 16, 2011, Pub. L. 112-29, §3, 125 Stat. 295.)

§ 122   Confidential status of applications; publication of patent applications

(a) *Confidentiality.*—Except as provided in subsection (b), applications for patents shall be kept in confidence by the Patent and Trademark Office and no information concerning the same given without authority of the applicant or owner unless necessary to carry out the provisions of an Act of Congress or in such special circumstances as may be determined by the Director.

(b) *Publication.*—

(1) *In general.*—(A) Subject to paragraph (2), each application for a patent shall be published, in accordance with procedures determined by the Director, promptly after the expiration of a period of 18 months from the earliest filing date for which a benefit is sought under this title. At the request of the applicant, an application may be published earlier than the end of such 18-month period.

(B) No information concerning published patent applications shall be made available to the public except as the Director determines.

(C) Notwithstanding any other provision of law, a determination by the Director to release or not to release information concerning a published patent application shall be final and nonreviewable.

(2) *Exceptions.*—(A) An application shall not be published if that application is—

(i) no longer pending;

(ii) subject to a secrecy order under section 181 ;

(iii) a provisional application filed under section 111(b) ; or

(iv) an application for a design patent filed under chapter 16.

(B)(i) If an applicant makes a request upon filing, certifying that the invention disclosed in the application has not and will not be the subject of an application filed in another country, or under a multilateral international agreement, that requires publication of applications 18 months after filing, the application shall not be published as provided in paragraph (1).

(ii) An applicant may rescind a request made under clause (i) at any time.

(iii) An applicant who has made a request under clause (i) but who subsequently files, in a foreign country or under a multilateral international agreement specified in clause (i), an application directed to the invention disclosed in the application filed in the Patent and Trademark Office, shall notify the Director of such filing not later than 45 days after the date of the filing of such foreign or international application. A failure of the applicant to provide such notice within the prescribed period shall result in the application being regarded as abandoned.

(iv) If an applicant rescinds a request made under clause (i) or notifies the Director that an application was filed in a foreign country or under a multilateral international agreement specified in clause (i), the application shall be published in accordance with the provisions of paragraph (1) on or as soon as is practical after the date that is specified in clause (i).

35 U.S.C. § 122

(v) If an applicant has filed applications in one or more foreign countries, directly or through a multilateral international agreement, and such foreign filed applications corresponding to an application filed in the Patent and Trademark Office or the description of the invention in such foreign filed applications is less extensive than the application or description of the invention in the application filed in the Patent and Trademark Office, the applicant may submit a redacted copy of the application filed in the Patent and Trademark Office eliminating any part or description of the invention in such application that is not also contained in any of the corresponding applications filed in a foreign country. The Director may only publish the redacted copy of the application unless the redacted copy of the application is not received within 16 months after the earliest effective filing date for which a benefit is sought under this title. The provisions of section 154(d) shall not apply to a claim if the description of the invention published in the redacted application filed under this clause with respect to the claim does not enable a person skilled in the art to make and use the subject matter of the claim.

(c) *Protest and pre-issuance opposition.*—The Director shall establish appropriate procedures to ensure that no protest or other form of pre-issuance opposition to the grant of a patent on an application may be initiated after publication of the application without the express written consent of the applicant.

(d) *National security.*—No application for patent shall be published under subsection (b)(1) if the publication or disclosure of such invention would be detrimental to the national security. The Director shall establish appropriate procedures to ensure that such applications are promptly identified and the secrecy of such inventions is maintained in accordance with chapter 17.

(e) *Preissuance submissions by third parties.*—

(1) *In general.*—Any third party may submit for consideration and inclusion in the record of a patent application, any patent, published patent application, or other printed publication of potential relevance to the examination of the application, if such submission is made in writing before the earlier of—

(A) the date a notice of allowance under section 151 is given or mailed in the application for patent; or

(B) the later of—

(i) 6 months after the date on which the application for patent is first published under section 122 by the Office, or

(ii) the date of the first rejection under section 132 of any claim by the examiner during the examination of the application for patent.

(2) *Other requirements.*—Any submission under paragraph (1) shall—

(A) set forth a concise description of the asserted relevance of each submitted document;

(B) be accompanied by such fee as the Director may prescribe; and

(C) include a statement by the person making such submission affirming that the submission was made in compliance with this section.

(July 19, 1952, ch. 950, §1, 66 Stat. 801; Jan. 2, 1975, Pub. L. 93-596, §1, 88 Stat. 1949; Nov. 29, 1999, Pub. L. 106-113, §4502, 113 Stat. 1501A-561; Sept. 16, 2011, Pub. L. 112-29, §8, 125 Stat. 315; Dec. 18, 2012, Pub. L. 112-211, §202, 126 Stat. 1536.)

§ 123   Micro entity defined

(a) *In general.*—For purposes of this title, the term "micro entity" means an applicant who makes a certification that the applicant—

(1) qualifies as a small entity, as defined in regulations issued by the Director;

(2) has not been named as an inventor on more than 4 previously filed patent applications, other than applications filed in another country, provisional applications under section 111(b), or international applications filed under the treaty defined in section 351(a) for which the basic national fee under section 41(a) was not paid;

(3) did not, in the calendar year preceding the calendar year in which the applicable fee is being paid, have a gross income, as defined in section 61(a) of the Internal Revenue Code of 1986, exceeding 3 times the median household income for that preceding calendar year, as most recently reported by the Bureau of the Census; and

(4) has not assigned, granted, or conveyed, and is not under an obligation by contract or law to assign, grant, or convey, a license or other ownership interest in the application concerned to an entity that, in the calendar year preceding the calendar year in which the applicable fee is being paid, had a gross income, as defined in section 61(a) of the Internal Revenue Code of 1986, exceeding 3 times the median household income for that preceding calendar year, as most recently reported by the Bureau of the Census.

35 U.S.C. § 123

(b) *Applications resulting from prior employment.*—An applicant is not considered to be named on a previously filed application for purposes of subsection (a)(2) if the applicant has assigned, or is under an obligation by contract or law to assign, all ownership rights in the application as the result of the applicant's previous employment.

(c) *Foreign currency exchange rate.*—If an applicant's or entity's gross income in the preceding calendar year is not in United States dollars, the average currency exchange rate, as reported by the Internal Revenue Service, during that calendar year shall be used to determine whether the applicant's or entity's gross income exceeds the threshold specified in paragraphs (3) or (4) of subsection (a).

(d) *Institutions of higher education.*—For purposes of this section, a micro entity shall include an applicant who certifies that—

(1) the applicant's employer, from which the applicant obtains the majority of the applicant's income, is an institution of higher education as defined in section 101(a) of the Higher Education Act of 1965 (20 U.S.C. 1001(a)); or

(2) the applicant has assigned, granted, conveyed, or is under an obligation by contract or law, to assign, grant, or convey, a license or other ownership interest in the particular applications to such an institution of higher education.

(e) *Director's authority.*—In addition to the limits imposed by this section, the Director may, in the Director's discretion, impose income limits, annual filing limits, or other limits on who may qualify as a micro entity pursuant to this section if the Director determines that such additional limits are reasonably necessary to avoid an undue impact on other patent applicants or owners or are otherwise reasonably necessary and appropriate. At least 3 months before any limits proposed to be imposed pursuant to this subsection take effect, the Director shall inform the Committee on the Judiciary of the House of Representatives and the Committee on the Judiciary of the Senate of any such proposed limits.

(Sept. 16, 2011, Pub. L. 112-29, §10, 125 Stat. 316; Jan. 14, 2013, Pub. L. 112-274, §1(m), 126 Stat. 2459.)

CHAPTER 12—EXAMINATION OF APPLICATION

SEC.
131.   Examination of application.
132.   Notice of rejection; reexamination.

35 U.S.C. § 123

133.   Time for prosecuting application.
134.   Appeal to the Patent Trial and Appeal Board.
135.   Derivation proceedings. [Interferences.]

§ 131   Examination of application

The Director shall cause an examination to be made of the application and the alleged new invention; and if on such examination it appears that the applicant is entitled to a patent under the law, the Director shall issue a patent therefor.

(July 19, 1952, ch. 950, §1, 66 Stat. 801.)

§ 132   Notice of rejection; reexamination

(a) Whenever, on examination, any claim for a patent is rejected, or any objection or requirement made, the Director shall notify the applicant thereof, stating the reasons for such rejection, or objection or requirement, together with such information and references as may be useful in judging of the propriety of continuing the prosecution of his application; and if after receiving such notice, the applicant persists in his claim for a patent, with or without amendment, the application shall be reexamined. No amendment shall introduce new matter into the disclosure of the invention.

(b)[13] The Director shall prescribe regulations to provide for the continued examination of applications for patent at the request of the applicant. The Director may establish appropriate fees for such continued examination and shall provide a 50 percent reduction in such fees for small entities that qualify for reduced fees under section 41(h)(1).

(July 19, 1952, ch. 950, §1, 66 Stat. 801; Nov. 29, 1999, Pub. L. 106-113, §4403, 113 Stat. 1501A-568.)

§ 133   Time for prosecuting application

Upon failure of the applicant to prosecute the application within six months after any action therein, of which notice has been given or mailed to the applicant, or within such shorter time, not less than thirty days, as fixed by the Director in such action, the application shall be regarded as abandoned by the parties thereto.

(July 19, 1952, ch. 950, §1, 66 Stat. 801; Dec. 18, 2012, Pub. L. 112-211, §202, 126 Stat. 1536.)

---

[13] *Ed. Note:* Pursuant to §4405 of Pub. L. 106-113, this provision took effect on May 29, 2000 and applies to all applications filed under §111(a) on or after June 8, 1995, and all applications complying with §371 that resulted from international applications filed on or after June 8, 1995, and does not apply to applications for design patents.

35 U.S.C. § 133

§ 134 Appeal to the Patent Trial and Appeal Board

(a) *Patent applicant.*—An applicant for a patent, any of whose claims has been twice rejected, may appeal from the decision of the primary examiner to the Patent Trial and Appeal Board, having once paid the fee for such appeal.

(b) *Patent owner.*—A patent owner in a reexamination may appeal from the final rejection of any claim by the primary examiner to the Patent Trial and Appeal Board, having once paid the fee for such appeal.

(July 19, 1952, ch. 950, §1, 66 Stat. 801; Nov. 8, 1984, Pub. L. 98-622, §204, 98 Stat. 3388; Nov. 29, 1999, Pub. L. 106-113, §4605(b), 113 Stat. 1501A-570; Nov. 2, 2002, Pub. L. 107-273, §§13106, 13202, 116 Stat. 1901; Sept. 16, 2011, Pub. L. 112-29, §7, 125 Stat. 290–91, 313–14; Sept. 16, 2011, Pub. L. 112-29, §3, 125 Stat. 290.)

§ 135[14] Derivation proceedings

(a) *Institution of Proceeding.*—

(1) *In general.*—An applicant for patent may file a petition with respect to an invention to institute a derivation proceeding in the Office. The petition shall set forth with particularity the basis for finding that an individual named in an earlier application as the inventor or a joint inventor derived such invention from an individual named in the petitioner's application as the inventor or a joint inventor and, without authorization, the earlier application claiming such invention was filed. Whenever the Director determines that a petition filed under this subsection demonstrates that the standards for instituting a derivation proceeding are met, the Director may institute a derivation proceeding.

(2) *Time for filing.*—A petition under this section with respect to an invention that is the same or substantially the same invention as a claim contained in a patent issued on an earlier application, or contained in an earlier application when published or deemed published under section 122(b), may not be filed unless such petition is filed during the 1-year period following the date on which the patent containing such claim was granted or the earlier application containing such claim was published, whichever is earlier.

---

[14] *Ed. Note:* Pursuant to §3(i) of Pub. L. 112-29, effective March 16, 2013, this version of section 135, entitled Derivation Proceedings, replaced the prior version of section 135, which appears in the bracketed text immediately below. See text of Pub. L. 112-29 on the CD-ROM that accompanies this edition of the book. A table of effective dates for all changes set forth in Pub. L. 112-29 may also be found on the CD-ROM. The provisions of §135 in effect on the day prior to March 16, 2013 shall apply to each claim of an application for patent, and any patent issued thereon, that contains or contained at any time a claim to an invention that has an effective filing date prior to March 16, 2013, or a specific reference under Section 120, 121, or 365(c) to any patent or application that contains or contained at any time such a claim. See Pub. L. 112-29, §3(n)(2), 125 Stat. 293.

(3) *Earlier application.*—For purposes of this section, an application shall not be deemed to be an earlier application with respect to an invention, relative to another application, unless a claim to the invention was or could have been made in such application having an effective filing date that is earlier than the effective filing date of any claim to the invention that was or could have been made in such other application.

(4) *No appeal.*—A determination by the Director whether to institute a derivation proceeding under paragraph (1) shall be final and not appealable.

(b) *Determination by Patent Trial and Appeal Board.*—In a derivation proceeding instituted under subsection (a), the Patent Trial and Appeal Board shall determine whether an inventor named in the earlier application derived the claimed invention from an inventor named in the petitioner's application and, without authorization, the earlier application claiming such invention was filed. In appropriate circumstances, the Patent Trial and Appeal Board may correct the naming of the inventor in any application or patent at issue. The Director shall prescribe regulations setting forth standards for the conduct of derivation proceedings, including requiring parties to provide sufficient evidence to prove and rebut a claim of derivation.

(c) *Deferral of Decision.*—The Patent Trial and Appeal Board may defer action on a petition for a derivation proceeding until the expiration of the 3-month period beginning on the date on which the Director issues a patent that includes the claimed invention that is the subject of the petition. The Patent Trial and Appeal Board also may defer action on a petition for a derivation proceeding, or stay the proceeding after it has been instituted, until the termination of a proceeding under chapter 30, 31, or 32 involving the patent of the earlier applicant.

(d) *Effect of Final Decision.*—The final decision of the Patent Trial and Appeal Board, if adverse to claims in an application for patent, shall constitute the final refusal by the Office on those claims. The final decision of the Patent Trial and Appeal Board, if adverse to claims in a patent, shall, if no appeal or other review of the decision has been or can be taken or had, constitute cancellation of those claims, and notice of such cancellation shall be endorsed on copies of the patent distributed after such cancellation.

(e) *Settlement.*—Parties to a proceeding instituted under subsection (a) may terminate the proceeding by filing a written statement reflecting the agreement of the parties as to the correct inventor of the claimed invention in

35 U.S.C. § 135

dispute. Unless the Patent Trial and Appeal Board finds the agreement to be inconsistent with the evidence of record, if any, it shall take action consistent with the agreement. Any written settlement or understanding of the parties shall be filed with the Director. At the request of a party to the proceeding, the agreement or understanding shall be treated as business confidential information, shall be kept separate from the file of the involved patents or applications, and shall be made available only to Government agencies on written request, or to any person on a showing of good cause.

(f) *Arbitration.*—Parties to a proceeding instituted under subsection (a) may, within such time as may be specified by the Director by regulation, determine such contest or any aspect thereof by arbitration. Such arbitration shall be governed by the provisions of title 9, to the extent such title is not inconsistent with this section. The parties shall give notice of any arbitration award to the Director, and such award shall, as between the parties to the arbitration, be dispositive of the issues to which it relates. The arbitration award shall be unenforceable until such notice is given. Nothing in this subsection shall preclude the Director from determining the patentability of the claimed inventions involved in the proceeding.

[§ 135[15] Interferences

(a) Whenever an application is made for a patent which, in the opinion of the Director, would interfere with any pending application, or with any unexpired patent, an interference may be declared and the Director shall give notice of such declaration to the applicants, or applicant and patentee, as the case may be. The Patent Trial and Appeal Board shall determine questions of priority of the inventions and may determine questions of patentability. Any final decision, if adverse to the claim of an applicant, shall constitute the final refusal by the Patent and Trademark Office of the claims involved, and the Director may issue a patent to the applicant who is adjudged the prior inventor. A final judgment adverse to a patentee from which no appeal or other review has been or can be taken or had shall constitute cancellation of

---

[15] *Ed. Note:* Pursuant to §3(i) of Pub. L. 112-29, effective March 16, 2013, this version of section 135, shown here in brackets, was replaced by new section 135, which appears immediately above. The text appears in italics below. See text of Pub. L. 112-29 on the CD-ROM that accompanies this edition of the book. A table of effective dates for all changes set forth in Pub. L. 112-29 may also be found on the CD-ROM. The provisions of §135 in effect on the day prior to March 16, 2013 shall apply to each claim of an application for patent, and any patent issued thereon, that contains or contained at any time a claim to an invention that has an effective filing date prior to March 16, 2013, or a specific reference under Section 120, 121, or 365(c) to any patent or application that contains or contained at any time such a claim. See Pub. L. 112-29, §3(n)(2), 125 Stat. 293.

35 U.S.C. § 135

the claims involved in the patent, and notice of such cancellation shall be endorsed on copies of the patent distributed after such cancellation by the Patent and Trademark Office.

(b) (1) A claim which is the same as, or for the same or substantially the same subject matter as, a claim of an issued patent may not be made in any application unless such a claim is made prior to one year from the date on which the patent was granted.

(2)[16] A claim which is the same as, or for the same or substantially the same subject matter as, a claim of an application published under section 122(b) may be made in an application filed after the application is published only if the claim is made before 1 year after the date on which the application is published.

(c) Any agreement or understanding between parties to an interference, including any collateral agreements referred to therein, made in connection with or in contemplation of the termination of the interference, shall be in writing and a true copy thereof filed in the Patent and Trademark Office before the termination of the interference as between the said parties to the agreement or understanding. If any party filing the same so requests, the copy shall be kept separate from the file of the interference, and made available only to Government agencies on written request, or to any person on a showing of good cause. Failure to file the copy of such agreement or understanding shall render permanently unenforceable such agreement or understanding and any patent of such parties involved in the interference or any patent subsequently issued on any application of such parties so involved. The Director may, however, on a showing of good cause for failure to file within the time prescribed, permit the filing of the agreement or understanding during the six-month period subsequent to the termination of the interference as between the parties to the agreement or understanding.

The Director shall give notice to the parties or their attorneys of record, a reasonable time prior to said termination, of the filing requirement of this section. If the Director gives such notice at a later time, irrespective of the right to file such agreement or understanding within the six-month period on a showing of good cause, the parties may file such agreement or understanding within sixty days of the receipt of such notice.

---

[16] *Ed. Note:* Pursuant to §4508 of Pub. L. 106-113, this provision took effect on Nov. 29, 2000 and applies to all applications filed under §111(a) on or after that date, and all applications complying with §371 that resulted from international applications filed on or after that date.

35 U.S.C. § 135

Any discretionary action of the Director under this subsection shall be reviewable under section 10 of the Administrative Procedure Act.

(d) Parties to a patent interference, within such time as may be specified by the Director by regulation, may determine such contest or any aspect thereof by arbitration. Such arbitration shall be governed by the provisions of title 9 to the extent such title is not inconsistent with this section. The parties shall give notice of any arbitration award to the Director, and such award shall, as between the parties to the arbitration, be dispositive of the issues to which it relates. The arbitration award shall be unenforceable until such notice is given. Nothing in this subsection shall preclude the Director from determining patentability of the invention involved in the interference.]

(July 19, 1952, ch. 950, §1, 66 Stat. 801; Oct. 15, 1962, Pub. L. 87-831, 76 Stat. 958; Jan. 2, 1975, Pub. L. 93-596, §1, 88 Stat. 1949; Nov. 8, 1984, Pub. L. 98-622, §§105 and 202, 98 Stat. 3385–86; Nov. 29, 1999, Pub. L. 106-113, §4507, 113 Stat. 1501A-565; Sept. 16, 2011, Pub. L. 112-29, §3, 125 Stat. 289; Jan. 14, 2013, Pub. L. 112-274, §1(e), (k), 126 Stat. 2456, 2457.)

CHAPTER 13—REVIEW OF PATENT AND TRADEMARK OFFICE DECISION

§ 141   Appeal to Court of Appeals for the Federal Circuit

(a) *Examinations.*—An applicant who is dissatisfied with the final decision in an appeal to the Patent Trial and Appeal Board under section 134(a) may appeal the Board's decision to the United States Court of Appeals for the Federal Circuit. By filing such an appeal, the applicant waives his or her right to proceed under section 145.

(b) *Reexaminations.*—A patent owner who is dissatisfied with the final decision in an appeal of a reexamination to the Patent Trial and Appeal Board under section 134(b) may appeal the Board's decision only to the United States Court of Appeals for the Federal Circuit.

(c) *Post-grant and inter partes reviews.*—A party to an inter partes review or a post-grant review who is dissatisfied with the final written decision of the Patent Trial and Appeal Board under section 318(a) or 328(a) (as the case may be) may appeal the Board's decision only to the United States Court of Appeals for the Federal Circuit.

(d) *Derivation proceedings.* —A party to a derivation proceeding who is dissatisfied with the final decision of the Patent Trial and Appeal Board in the proceeding may appeal the decision to the United States Court of Appeals for the Federal Circuit, but such appeal shall be dismissed if any adverse party to such derivation proceeding, within 20 days after the appellant has filed notice of appeal in accordance with section 142, files notice with the Director that the party elects to have all further proceedings conducted as provided in section 146. If the appellant does not, within 30 days after the filing of such notice by the adverse party, file a civil action under section 146, the Board's decision shall govern the further proceedings in the case.

(Sept. 16, 2011, Pub. L. 112-29, §7, 125 Stat. 314.)

[§ 141[17] Appeal to Court of Appeals for the Federal Circuit

An applicant dissatisfied with the decision in an appeal to the Board of Patent Appeals and Interferences under section 134 may appeal the decision to the United States Court of Appeals for the Federal Circuit. By filing such an appeal the applicant waives his or her right to proceed under section 145. A patent owner, or a third-party requester in an inter partes reexamination proceeding, who is in any reexamination proceeding dissatisfied with the final decision in an appeal to the Board of Patent Appeals and Interferences under section 134 may appeal the decision only to the United States Court of Appeals for the Federal Circuit. A party to an interference dissatisfied with the decision of the Board of Patent Appeals and Interferences on the interference may appeal the decision to the United States Court of Appeals for the Federal Circuit, but such appeal shall be dismissed if any adverse party to such interference, within twenty days after the appellant has filed notice of appeal in accordance with section 142, files notice with the Director that the party elects to have all further proceedings conducted as provided in section 146. If the appellant does not, within thirty days after the filing of such notice by the adverse party, file a civil action under section 146, the decision appealed from shall govern the further proceedings in the case.

---

[17] *Ed. Note:* Pursuant to Pub. L. 112-29, effective Sept. 16, 2012, this version of section 141, shown here in brackets, is replaced by new section 141, which appears immediately above. The provisions of §141 in effect prior to Sept. 16, 2012 continue to apply to inter partes reexaminations requested before Sept. 16, 2012. See text of Pub. L. 112-29 on the CD-ROM that accompanies this edition of the book. A table of effective dates for all changes set forth in Pub. L. 112-29 may also be found on the CD-ROM.

(July 19, 1952, ch. 950, §1, 66 Stat. 802; Apr. 2, 1982, Pub. L. 97-164, §163, 96 Stat. 49-50; Nov. 8, 1984, Pub. L. 98-622, §203, 98 Stat. 3387; Nov. 29, 1999, Pub. L. 106-113, §4605, 113 Stat. 1501A-570; Nov. 2, 2002, Pub. L. 107-273, §13106, 116 Stat. 1900.)]

§ 142   Notice of appeal

When an appeal is taken to the United States Court of Appeals for the Federal Circuit, the appellant shall file in the Patent and Trademark Office a written notice of appeal directed to the Director, within such time after the date of the decision from which the appeal is taken as the Director prescribes, but in no case less than 60 days after that date.

(July 19, 1952, ch. 950, §1, 66 Stat. 802; Jan. 2, 1975, Pub. L. 93-596, §1, 88 Stat. 1949; Apr. 2, 1982, Pub. L. 97-164, §163, 96 Stat. 49; Nov. 8, 1984, Pub. L. 98-620, §414, 98 Stat. 3363.)

§ 143   Proceedings on appeal

With respect to an appeal described in section 142, the Director shall transmit to the United States Court of Appeals for the Federal Circuit a certified list of the documents comprising the record in the Patent and Trademark Office. The court may request that the Director forward the original or certified copies of such documents during pendency of the appeal. In an ex parte case, the Director shall submit to the court in writing the grounds for the decision of the Patent and Trademark Office, addressing all of the issues raised in the appeal. The Director shall have the right to intervene in an appeal from a decision entered by the Patent Trial and Appeal Board in a derivation proceeding under section 135 or in an inter partes or post-grant review under chapter 31 or 32.

(July 19, 1952, ch. 950, §1, 66 Stat. 802; Jan. 2, 1975, Pub. L. 93-596, §1, 88 Stat. 1949; Apr. 2, 1982, Pub. L. 97-164, §163, 96 Stat. 49; Nov. 8, 1984, Pub. L. 98-620, §414, 98 Stat. 3363; Nov. 29, 1999, Pub. L. 106-113, §4605, 113 Stat. 1501A-570; Nov. 2, 2002, Pub. L. 107-273, §13202, 116 Stat. 1901; Sept. 16, 2011, Pub. L. 112-29, §141, 125 Stat. 314–15.)

§ 144   Decision on appeal

The United States Court of Appeals for the Federal Circuit shall review the decision from which an appeal is taken on the record before the Patent and Trademark Office. Upon its determination the court shall issue to the Director its mandate and opinion, which shall be entered of record in the Patent and Trademark Office and shall govern the further proceedings in the case.

(July 19, 1952, ch. 950, §1, 66 Stat. 802; Jan. 2, 1975, Pub. L. 93-596, §1, 88 Stat. 1949; Apr. 2, 1982, Pub. L. 97-164, §163, 96 Stat. 49; Nov. 8, 1984, Pub. L. 98-620, §414, 98 Stat. 3363.)

§ 145 Civil action to obtain patent

An applicant dissatisfied with the decision of the Patent Trial and Appeal Board in an appeal under section 134(a) may, unless appeal has been taken to the United States Court of Appeals for the Federal Circuit, have remedy by civil action against the Director in the United States District Court for the Eastern District of Virginia if commenced within such time after such decision, not less than sixty days, as the Director appoints. The court may adjudge that such applicant is entitled to receive a patent for his invention, as specified in any of his claims involved in the decision of the Patent Trial and Appeal Board, as the facts in the case may appear and such adjudication shall authorize the Director to issue such patent on compliance with the requirements of law. All the expenses of the proceedings shall be paid by the applicant.

(July 19, 1952, ch. 950, §1, 66 Stat. 803; Apr. 2, 1982, Pub. L. 97-164, §163, 96 Stat. 49; Nov. 8, 1984, Pub. L. 98-622, §203, 98 Stat. 3387; Nov. 29, 1999, Pub. L. 106-113, §4605, 113 Stat. 1501A-570; Sept. 16, 2011, Pub. L. 112-29, §9, 125 Stat. 316; Sept. 16, 2011, Pub. L. 112-29, §3, 125 Stat. 290.)

§ 146 Civil action in case of derivation proceeding

Any party to a derivation proceeding dissatisfied with the decision of the Patent Trial and Appeal Board on the derivation proceeding, may have remedy by civil action, if commenced within such time after such decision, not less than sixty days, as the Director appoints or as provided in section 141, unless he has appealed to the United States Court of Appeals for the Federal Circuit, and such appeal is pending or has been decided. In such suits the record in the Patent and Trademark Office shall be admitted on motion of either party upon the terms and conditions as to costs, expenses, and the further cross-examination of the witnesses as the court imposes, without prejudice to the right of the parties to take further testimony. The testimony and exhibits of the record in the Patent and Trademark Office when admitted shall have the same effect as if originally taken and produced in the suit.

Such suit may be instituted against the party in interest as shown by the records of the Patent and Trademark Office at the time of the decision complained of, but any party in interest may become a party to the action. If there be adverse parties residing in a plurality of districts not embraced within the same state, or an adverse party residing in a foreign country, the United States District Court for the Eastern District of Virginia shall have jurisdiction and may issue summons against the adverse parties directed to the marshal of any district in which any adverse party resides. Summons against adverse parties residing in foreign countries may be served by publication or otherwise as the court directs. The Director shall not be a necessary party but he shall be notified of the filing of the suit by the clerk of the court in which it is filed and shall have the right to intervene. Judgment of the court in favor of the right of an applicant to a patent shall authorize the Director to issue such patent on the filing in the Patent and Trademark Office of a certified copy of the judgment and on compliance with the requirements of law.

(July 19, 1952, ch. 950, §1, 66 Stat. 803; Jan. 2, 1975, Pub. L. 93-596, §1, 88 Stat. 1949; Apr. 2, 1982, Pub. L. 97-164, §163, 96 Stat. 49; Nov. 8, 1984, Pub. L. 98-622, §203, 98 Stat. 3387; Sept. 16, 2011, Pub. L. 112-29, §9, 125 Stat. 316; Sept. 16, 2011, Pub. L. 112-29, §3, 125 Stat. 290.)

CHAPTER 14—ISSUE OF PATENT

§ 151   Issue of patent

(a) *In general.*—If it appears that an applicant is entitled to a patent under the law, a written notice of allowance of the application shall be given or mailed to the applicant. The notice shall specify a sum, constituting the issue fee and any required publication fee, which shall be paid within 3 months thereafter.

(b) *Effect of payment.*—Upon payment of this sum the patent may issue, but if payment is not timely made, the application shall be regarded as abandoned.

(July 19, 1952, ch. 950, §1, 66 Stat. 803; July 24, 1965, Pub. L. 89-83, §§4 and 6, 79 Stat. 260-61; Jan. 2, 1975, Pub. L. 93-601, §3, 88 Stat. 1956; Dec. 18, 2012, Pub. L. 112-211, §202, 126 Stat. 1536.)

§ 152 Issue of patent to assignee

Patents may be granted to the assignee of the inventor of record in the Patent and Trademark Office, upon the application made and the specification sworn to by the inventor, except as otherwise provided in this title.

(July 19, 1952, ch. 950, §1, 66 Stat. 804; Jan. 2, 1975, Pub. L. 93-596, §1, 88 Stat. 1949.)

§ 153 How issued

Patents shall be issued in the name of the United States of America, under the seal of the Patent and Trademark Office, and shall be signed by the Director or have his signature placed thereon and shall be recorded in the Patent and Trademark Office.

(July 19, 1952, ch. 950, §1, 66 Stat. 804; Jan. 2, 1975, Pub. L. 93-596, §1, 88 Stat. 1949; Nov. 2, 2002, Pub. L. 107-273, §13203, 116 Stat. 1902.)

§ 154[18] Contents and term of patent; provisional rights

(a) *In general.—*

(1) *Contents.—*Every patent shall contain a short title of the invention and a grant to the patentee, his heirs or assigns, of the right to exclude others from making, using, offering for sale, or selling the invention throughout the United States or importing the invention into the United States, and, if the invention is a process, of the right to exclude others from using, offering for sale or selling throughout the United States, or importing into the United States, products made by that process, referring to the specification for the particulars thereof.

(2) *Term.—*Subject to the payment of fees under this title, such grant shall be for a term beginning on the date on which the patent issues and ending 20 years from the date on which the application for the patent was filed in the United States or, if the application contains a specific reference to an earlier filed application or applications under section 120, 121, 365(c), or 386(c), from the date on which the earliest such application was filed.

(3) *Priority.—*Priority under section 119, 365(a), 365(b), 386(a), or 386(b) shall not be taken into account in determining the term of a patent.

(4) *Specification and drawing.—*A copy of the specification and drawing shall be annexed to the patent and be a part of such patent.

---

[18] *Ed. Note:* Pursuant to section 534 of Pub. L. 103-465, the term of a patent granted on an application filed on or after June 8, 1995, and that contains a specific reference to an earlier application filed under section 120, 121, or 365(c) of title 35, U.S.C., shall be measured from the filing date of the earliest filed application.

(b)[19] *Adjustment of patent term.* —

  (1) *Patent term guarantees.* —

    (A) *Guarantee of prompt Patent and Trademark Office responses.* —Subject to the limitations under paragraph (2), if the issue of an original patent is delayed due to the failure of the Patent and Trademark Office to—

      (i) provide at least one of the notifications under section 132 or a notice of allowance under section 151 not later than 14 months after—

        (I) the date on which an application was filed under section 111(a); or

        (II) the date of commencement of the national stage under section 371 in an international application;

      (ii) respond to a reply under section 132, or to an appeal taken under section 134, within 4 months after the date on which the reply was filed or the appeal was taken;

      (iii) act on an application within 4 months after the date of a decision by the Patent Trial and Appeal Board under section 134 or 135 or a decision by a Federal court under section 141, 145, or 146 in a case in which allowable claims remain in the application; or

      (iv) issue a patent within 4 months after the date on which the issue fee was paid under section 151 and all outstanding requirements were satisfied,

    the term of the patent shall be extended 1 day for each day after the end of the period specified in clause (i), (ii), (iii), or (iv), as the case may be, until the action described in such clause is taken.

    (B) *Guarantee of no more than 3-year application pendency.* —Subject to the limitations under paragraph (2), if the issue of an original patent is delayed due to the failure of the United States Patent and Trademark Office to issue a patent within 3 years after the actual filing date of the application under section 111(a) in the United States or, in the case of an international application, the date of commencement of the national stage under section 371 in the international application, not including—

---

[19] *Ed. Note:* Pursuant to §4405 of Pub. L. 106-113, the provisions of §154(b) took effect on May 29, 2000, and, except for a design patent application, apply to all applications filed on or after that date.

35 U.S.C. § 154

(i) any time consumed by continued examination of the application requested by the applicant under section 132(b);

(ii) any time consumed by a proceeding under section 135(a), any time consumed by the imposition of an order under section 181, or any time consumed by appellate review by the Patent Trial and Appeal Board or by a Federal court; or

(iii) any delay in the processing of the application by the United States Patent and Trademark Office requested by the applicant except as permitted by paragraph (3)(C),

the term of the patent shall be extended 1 day for each day after the end of that 3-year period until the patent is issued.

(C) *Guarantee of adjustments for delays due to derivation proceedings, secrecy orders, and appeals.*—Subject to the limitations under paragraph (2), if the issue of an original patent is delayed due to—

(i) a proceeding under section 135(a);

(ii) the imposition of an order under section 181; or

(iii) appellate review by the Patent Trial and Appeal Board or by a Federal court in a case in which the patent was issued under a decision in the review reversing an adverse determination of patentability,

the term of the patent shall be extended 1 day for each day of the pendency of the proceeding, order, or review, as the case may be.

(2) *Limitations.*—

(A) *In general.*—To the extent that periods of delay attributable to grounds specified in paragraph (1) overlap, the period of any adjustment granted under this subsection shall not exceed the actual number of days the issuance of the patent was delayed.

(B) *Disclaimed term.*—No patent the term of which has been disclaimed beyond a specified date may be adjusted under this section beyond the expiration date specified in the disclaimer.

(C) *Reduction of period of adjustment.*—

(i) The period of adjustment of the term of a patent under paragraph (1) shall be reduced by a period equal to the period of time during which the applicant failed to engage in reasonable efforts to conclude prosecution of the application.

35 U.S.C. § 154

(ii) With respect to adjustments to patent term made under the authority of paragraph (1)(B), an applicant shall be deemed to have failed to engage in reasonable efforts to conclude processing or examination of an application for the cumulative total of any periods of time in excess of 3 months that are taken to respond to a notice from the Office making any rejection, objection, argument, or other request, measuring such 3-month period from the date the notice was given or mailed to the applicant.

(iii) The Director shall prescribe regulations establishing the circumstances that constitute a failure of an applicant to engage in reasonable efforts to conclude processing or examination of an application.

(3) *Procedures for patent term adjustment determination.* —

(A) The Director shall prescribe regulations establishing procedures for the application for and determination of patent term adjustments under this subsection.

(B) Under the procedures established under subparagraph (A), the Director shall—

(i) make a determination of the period of any patent term adjustment under this subsection, and shall transmit a notice of that determination no later than the date of issuance of the patent; and

(ii) provide the applicant one opportunity to request reconsideration of any patent term adjustment determination made by the Director.

(C) The Director shall reinstate all or part of the cumulative period of time of an adjustment under paragraph (2)(C) if the applicant, prior to the issuance of the patent, makes a showing that, in spite of all due care, the applicant was unable to respond within the 3-month period, but in no case shall more than three additional months for each such response beyond the original 3-month period be reinstated.

(D) The Director shall proceed to grant the patent after completion of the Director's determination of a patent term adjustment under the procedures established under this subsection, notwithstanding any appeal taken by the applicant of such determination.

35 U.S.C. § 154

(4) *Appeal of patent term adjustment determination.* —

(A) An applicant dissatisfied with the Director's decision on the applicant's request for reconsideration under paragraph (3)(B)(ii) shall have exclusive remedy by a civil action against the Director filed in the United States District Court for the Eastern District of Virginia within 180 days after the date of the Director's decision on the applicant's request for reconsideration. Chapter 7 of title 5 shall apply to such action. Any final judgment resulting in a change to the period of adjustment of the patent term shall be served on the Director, and the Director shall thereafter alter the term of the patent to reflect such change.

(B) The determination of a patent term adjustment under this subsection shall not be subject to appeal or challenge by a third party prior to the grant of the patent.

(c) *Continuation.* —

(1) *Determination.* —The term of a patent that is in force on or that results from an application filed before the date that is 6 months after the date of the enactment of the Uruguay Round Agreements Act[20] shall be the greater of the 20-year term as provided in subsection (a), or 17 years from grant, subject to any terminal disclaimers.

(2) *Remedies.* —The remedies of sections 283, 284, and 285 shall not apply to acts which—

(A) were commenced or for which substantial investment was made before the date that is 6 months after the date of the enactment of the Uruguay Round Agreements Act; and

(B) became infringing by reason of paragraph (1).

(3) *Remuneration.* —The acts referred to in paragraph (2) may be continued only upon the payment of an equitable remuneration to the patentee that is determined in an action brought under chapter 28 and chapter 29 (other than those provisions excluded by paragraph (2)).

(d)[21] *Provisional rights.* —

(1) *In general.* —In addition to other rights provided by this section, a patent shall include the right to obtain a reasonable royalty from any per-

---

[20] *Ed. Note:* The Uruguay Round Agreements Act was enacted on December 8, 1994.
[21] *Ed. Note:* Pursuant to §4508 of Pub. L. 106-113, §154(d) took effect one year after the Nov. 29, 1999 date of enactment and applies to all applications filed under §111 on or after that date and all applications complying with §371 that resulted from international applications filed on or after that date.

35 U.S.C. § 154

son who, during the period beginning on the date of publication of the application for such patent under section 122(b), or in the case of an international application filed under the treaty defined in section 351(a) designating the United States under Article 21(2)(a) of such treaty or an international design application filed under the treaty defined in section 381(a)(1) designating the United States under Article 5 of such treaty, the date of publication of the application, and ending on the date the patent is issued—

(A)(i) makes, uses, offers for sale, or sells in the United States the invention as claimed in the published patent application or imports such an invention into the United States; or

(ii) if the invention as claimed in the published patent application is a process, uses, offers for sale, or sells in the United States or imports into the United States products made by that process as claimed in the published patent application; and

(B) had actual notice of the published patent application and, in a case in which the right arising under this paragraph is based upon an international application designating the United States that is published in a language other than English, had a translation of the international application into the English language.

(2) *Right based on substantially identical inventions.*—The right under paragraph (1) to obtain a reasonable royalty shall not be available under this subsection unless the invention as claimed in the patent is substantially identical to the invention as claimed in the published patent application.

(3) *Time limitation on obtaining a reasonable royalty.*—The right under paragraph (1) to obtain a reasonable royalty shall be available only in an action brought not later than 6 years after the patent is issued. The right under paragraph (1) to obtain a reasonable royalty shall not be affected by the duration of the period described in paragraph (1).

(4) *Requirements for international applications.* —

(A) *Effective date.*—The right under paragraph (1) to obtain a reasonable royalty based upon the publication under the treaty defined in section 351(a) of an international application designating the United States shall commence on the date of publication under the treaty of the international application, or, if the publication under the treaty of the international application is in a language other than English, on the date on which the Patent and Trademark Office receives a translation of the publication in the English language.

(B) *Copies.*—The Director may require the applicant to provide a copy of the international application and a translation thereof.

(July 19, 1952, ch. 950, §1, 66 Stat. 804; July 24, 1965, Pub. L. 89-83, §5, 79 Stat. 261; Dec. 12, 1980, Pub. L. 96-517, §4, 94 Stat. 3018; Aug. 23, 1988, Pub. L. 100-418, §9002, 102 Stat. 1563; Dec. 8, 1994, Pub. L. 103-465, §532, 108 Stat. 4983; Oct. 11, 1996, Pub. L. 104-295, §20, 110 Stat. 3529; Nov. 29, 1999, Pub. L. 106-113, §§4402, 4504, 113 Stat. 1501A-557, 564; Nov. 2, 2002, Pub. L. 107-273, §§13204, 13206, 116 Stat. 1904; Sept. 16, 2011, Pub. L. 112-29, §3, 125 Stat. 290; Jan. 14, 2013, Pub. L. 112-274, §1(h), 126 Stat. 2457; Dec. 18, 2012, Pub. L. 112-211, §101, 126 Stat. 1531.)

§ 155 Patent term extension [Repealed]

(Jan. 4, 1983, Pub. L. 97-414, §11, 96 Stat. 2065; Nov. 29, 1999, Pub. L. 106-113, §4732, 113 Stat. 1501A-581.)

§ 155A Patent term restoration [Repealed]

(Jan. 4, 1983, Pub. L. 97-414, §11, 96 Stat. 2065; Nov. 29, 1999, Pub. L. 106-113, §4732, 113 Stat. 1501A-581.)

§ 156 Extension of patent term

(a) The term of a patent which claims a product, a method of using a product, or a method of manufacturing a product shall be extended in accordance with this section from the original expiration date of the patent, which shall include any patent term adjustment granted under section 154(b), if—

(1) the term of the patent has not expired before an application is submitted under subsection (d)(1) for its extension;

(2) the term of the patent has never been extended under subsection (e)(1) of this section;

(3) an application for extension is submitted by the owner of record of the patent or its agent and in accordance with the requirements of paragraphs (1) through (4) of subsection (d);

(4) the product has been subject to a regulatory review period before its commercial marketing or use;

(5) (A) except as provided in subparagraph (B) or (C), the permission for the commercial marketing or use of the product after such regulatory review period is the first permitted commercial marketing or use of

the product under the provision of law under which such regulatory review period occurred;

(B) in the case of a patent which claims a method of manufacturing the product which primarily uses recombinant DNA technology in the manufacture of the product, the permission for the commercial marketing or use of the product after such regulatory review period is the first permitted commercial marketing or use of a product manufactured under the process claimed in the patent; or

(C) for purposes of subparagraph (A), in the case of a patent which—

(i) claims a new animal drug or a veterinary biological product which (I) is not covered by the claims in any other patent which has been extended, and (II) has received permission for the commercial marketing or use in non-food-producing animals and in food-producing animals, and

(ii) was not extended on the basis of the regulatory review period for use in non-food-producing animals,

the permission for the commercial marketing or use of the drug or product after the regulatory review period for use in food-producing animals is the first permitted commercial marketing or use of the drug or product for administration to a food-producing animal.

The product referred to in paragraphs (4) and (5) is hereinafter in this section referred to as the "approved product".

(b) Except as provided in subsection (d)(5)(F), the rights derived from any patent the term of which is extended under this section shall during the period during which the term of the patent is extended—

(1) in the case of a patent which claims a product, be limited to any use approved for the product—

(A) before the expiration of the term of the patent—

(i) under the provision of law under which the applicable regulatory review occurred, or

(ii) under the provision of law under which any regulatory review described in paragraph (1), (4), or (5) of subsection (g) occurred, and

(B) on or after the expiration of the regulatory review period upon which the extension of the patent was based;

35 U.S.C. § 156

(2) in the case of a patent which claims a method of using a product, be limited to any use claimed by the patent and approved for the product—

(A) before the expiration of the term of the patent—

(i) under any provision of law under which an applicable regulatory review occurred, and

(ii) under the provision of law under which any regulatory review described in paragraph (1), (4), or (5) of subsection (g) occurred, and

(B) on or after the expiration of the regulatory review period upon which the extension of the patent was based; and

(3) in the case of a patent which claims a method of manufacturing a product, be limited to the method of manufacturing as used to make—

(A) the approved product, or

(B) the product if it has been subject to a regulatory review period described in paragraph (1), (4), or (5) of subsection (g).

As used in this subsection, the term "product" includes an approved product.

(c) The term of a patent eligible for extension under subsection (a) shall be extended by the time equal to the regulatory review period for the approved product which period occurs after the date the patent is issued, except that—

(1) each period of the regulatory review period shall be reduced by any period determined under subsection (d)(2)(B) during which the applicant for the patent extension did not act with due diligence during such period of the regulatory review period;

(2) after any reduction required by paragraph (1), the period of extension shall include only one-half of the time remaining in the periods described in paragraphs (1)(B)(i), (2)(B)(i), (3)(B)(i), (4)(B)(i), and (5)(B)(i) of subsection (g);

(3) if the period remaining in the term of a patent after the date of the approval of the approved product under the provision of law under which such regulatory review occurred when added to the regulatory review period as revised under paragraphs (1) and (2) exceeds fourteen years, the period of extension shall be reduced so that the total of both such periods does not exceed fourteen years; and

35 U.S.C. § 156

(4) in no event shall more than one patent be extended under subsection (e)(1) for the same regulatory review period for any product.

(d) (1) To obtain an extension of the term of a patent under this section, the owner of record of the patent or its agent shall submit an application to the Director. Except as provided in paragraph (5), such an application may only be submitted within the sixty-day period beginning on the date the product received permission under the provision of law under which the applicable regulatory review period occurred for commercial marketing or use. The application shall contain—

(A) the identity of the approved product and the Federal statute under which regulatory review occurred;

(B) the identity of the patent for which an extension is being sought and the identity of each claim of such patent which claims the approved product or a method of using or manufacturing the approved product;

(C) information to enable the Director to determine under subsections (a) and (b) the eligibility of a patent for extension and the rights that will be derived from the extension and information to enable the Director and the Secretary of Health and Human Services or the Secretary of Agriculture to determine the period of the extension under subsection (g);

(D) a brief description of the activities undertaken by the applicant during the applicable regulatory review period with respect to the approved product and the significant dates applicable to such activities; and

(E) such patent or other information as the Director may require.

[22]*For purposes of determining the date on which a product receives permission under the second sentence of this paragraph, if such permission is transmitted after 4:30 P.M., Eastern Time, on a business day, or is transmitted on a day that is not a business day, the product shall be deemed to receive such permission on the next business day. For purposes of the preceding sentence, the term "business day" means any Monday, Tuesday, Wednesday, Thursday, or Friday, excluding any legal holiday under section 6103 of title 5.*

---

[22] *Ed. Note:* The italicized language applies to any application for extension of a patent term under section 156 of title 35 that was pending on, that is filed after, or as to which a decision regarding the application was subject to judicial review on Sept. 16, 2011, the date of enactment of Pub. L. 112-29. See §37 of Pub. L. 112-29.

35 U.S.C. § 156

(2) (A) Within 60 days of the submittal of an application for extension of the term of a patent under paragraph (1), the Director shall notify—

    (i) the Secretary of Agriculture if the patent claims a drug product or a method of using or manufacturing a drug product and the drug product is subject to the Virus-Serum-Toxin Act, and

    (ii) the Secretary of Health and Human Services if the patent claims any other drug product, a medical device, or a food additive or color additive or a method of using or manufacturing such a product, device, or additive and if the product, device, and additive are subject to the Federal Food, Drug, and Cosmetic Act,

of the extension application and shall submit to the Secretary who is so notified a copy of the application. Not later than 30 days after the receipt of an application from the Director, the Secretary receiving the application shall review the dates contained in the application pursuant to paragraph (1)(C) and determine the applicable regulatory review period, shall notify the Director of the determination, and shall publish in the Federal Register a notice of such determination.

(B) (i) If a petition is submitted to the Secretary making the determination under subparagraph (A), not later than 180 days after the publication of the determination under subparagraph (A), upon which it may reasonably be determined that the applicant did not act with due diligence during the applicable regulatory review period, the Secretary making the determination shall, in accordance with regulations promulgated by such Secretary, determine if the applicant acted with due diligence during the applicable regulatory review period. The Secretary making the determination shall make such determination not later than 90 days after the receipt of such a petition. For a drug product, device, or additive subject to the Federal Food, Drug, and Cosmetic Act or the Public Health Service Act, the Secretary may not delegate the authority to make the determination prescribed by this clause to an office below the Office of the Director of Food and Drugs. For a product subject to the Virus-Serum-Toxin Act, the Secretary of Agriculture may not delegate the authority to make the determination prescribed by this clause to an office below the Office of the Assistant Secretary for Marketing and Inspection Services.

35 U.S.C. § 156

(ii) The Secretary making a determination under clause (i) shall notify the Director of the determination and shall publish in the Federal Register a notice of such determination together with the factual and legal basis for such determination. Any interested person may request, within the 60-day period beginning on the publication of a determination, the Secretary making the determination to hold an informal hearing on the determination. If such a request is made within such period, such Secretary shall hold such hearing not later than 30 days after the date of the request, or at the request of the person making the request, not later than 60 days after such date. The Secretary who is holding the hearing shall provide notice of the hearing to the owner of the patent involved and to any interested person and provide the owner and any interested person an opportunity to participate in the hearing. Within 30 days after the completion of the hearing, such Secretary shall affirm or revise the determination which was the subject of the hearing and shall notify the Director of any revision of the determination and shall publish any such revision in the Federal Register.

(3) For the purposes of paragraph (2)(B), the term "due diligence" means that degree of attention, continuous directed effort, and timeliness as may reasonably be expected from, and are ordinarily exercised by, a person during a regulatory review period.

(4) An application for the extension of the term of a patent is subject to the disclosure requirements prescribed by the Director.

(5) (A) If the owner of record of the patent or its agent reasonably expects that the applicable regulatory review period described in paragraph (1)(B)(ii), (2)(B)(ii), (3)(B)(ii), (4)(B)(ii), or (5)(B)(ii) of subsection (g) that began for a product that is the subject of such patent may extend beyond the expiration of the patent term in effect, the owner or its agent may submit an application to the Director for an interim extension during the period beginning 6 months, and ending 15 days, before such term is due to expire. The application shall contain—

(i) the identity of the product subject to regulatory review and the Federal statute under which such review is occurring;

(ii) the identity of the patent for which interim extension is being sought and the identity of each claim of such patent which claims the product under regulatory review or a method of using or manufacturing the product;

(iii) information to enable the Director to determine under subsection (a)(1), (2) and (3) the eligibility of a patent for extension;

(iv) a brief description of the activities undertaken by the applicant during the applicable regulatory review period to date with respect to the product under review and the significant dates applicable to such activities; and

(v) such patent or other information as the Director may require.

(B) If the Director determines that, except for permission to market or use the product commercially, the patent would be eligible for an extension of the patent term under this section, the Director shall publish in the Federal Register a notice of such determination, including the identity of the product under regulatory review, and shall issue to the applicant a certificate of interim extension for a period of not more than 1 year.

(C) The owner of record of a patent, or its agent, for which an interim extension has been granted under subparagraph (B), may apply for not more than 4 subsequent interim extensions under this paragraph, except that, in the case of a patent subject to subsection (g)(6)(C), the owner of record of the patent, or its agent, may apply for only 1 subsequent interim extension under this paragraph. Each such subsequent application shall be made during the period beginning 60 days before, and ending 30 days before, the expiration of the preceding interim extension.

(D) Each certificate of interim extension under this paragraph shall be recorded in the official file of the patent and shall be considered part of the original patent.

(E) Any interim extension granted under this paragraph shall terminate at the end of the 60-day period beginning on the date on which the product involved receives permission for commercial marketing or use, except that, if within that 60-day period the applicant notifies the Director of such permission and submits any additional information under paragraph (1) of this subsection not previously contained in the application for interim extension, the patent shall be further extended, in accordance with the provisions of this section—

35 U.S.C. § 156

(i) for not to exceed 5 years from the date of expiration of the original patent term; or

(ii) if the patent is subject to subsection (g)(6)(C), from the date on which the product involved receives approval for commercial marketing or use.

(F) The rights derived from any patent the term of which is extended under this paragraph shall, during the period of interim extension—

(i) in the case of a patent which claims a product, be limited to any use then under regulatory review;

(ii) in the case of a patent which claims a method of using a product, be limited to any use claimed by the patent then under regulatory review; and

(iii) in the case of a patent which claims a method of manufacturing a product, be limited to the method of manufacturing as used to make the product then under regulatory review.

(e) (1) A determination that a patent is eligible for extension may be made by the Director solely on the basis of the representations contained in the application for the extension. If the Director determines that a patent is eligible for extension under subsection (a) and that the requirements of paragraphs (1) through (4) of subsection (d) have been complied with, the Director shall issue to the applicant for the extension of the term of the patent a certificate of extension, under seal, for the period prescribed by subsection (c). Such certificate shall be recorded in the official file of the patent and shall be considered as part of the original patent.

(2) If the term of a patent for which an application has been submitted under subsection (d)(1) would expire before a certificate of extension is issued or denied under paragraph (1) respecting the application, the Director shall extend, until such determination is made, the term of the patent for periods of up to one year if he determines that the patent is eligible for extension.

(f) For purposes of this section:

(1) The term "product" means:

(A) A drug product.

(B) Any medical device, food additive, or color additive subject to regulation under the Federal Food, Drug, and Cosmetic Act.

(2) The term "drug product" means the active ingredient of—

(A) a new drug, antibiotic drug, or human biological product (as those terms are used in the Federal Food, Drug, and Cosmetic Act and the Public Health Service Act), or

(B) a new animal drug or veterinary biological product (as those terms are used in the Federal Food, Drug, and Cosmetic Act and the Virus-Serum-Toxin Act) which is not primarily manufactured using recombinant DNA, recombinant RNA, hybridoma technology, or other processes involving site specific genetic manipulation techniques,

including any salt or ester of the active ingredient, as a single entity or in combination with another active ingredient.

(3) The term "major health or environmental effects test" means a test which is reasonably related to the evaluation of the health or environmental effects of a product, which requires at least six months to conduct, and the data from which is submitted to receive permission for commercial marketing or use. Periods of analysis or evaluation of test results are not to be included in determining if the conduct of a test required at least six months.

(4) (A) Any reference to section 351 is a reference to section 351 of the Public Health Service Act.

(B) Any reference to section 503, 505, 512, or 515 is a reference to section 503, 505, 512, or 515 of the Federal Food, Drug, and Cosmetic Act.

(C) Any reference to the Virus-Serum-Toxin Act is a reference to the Act of March 4, 1913 (21 U.S.C. 151–158).

(5) The term "informal hearing" has the meaning prescribed for such term by section 201(y) of the Federal Food, Drug, and Cosmetic Act.

(6) The term "patent" means a patent issued by the United States Patent and Trademark Office.

(7) The term "date of enactment" as used in this section means September 24, 1984, for a human drug product, a medical device, food additive, or color additive.

(8) The term "date of enactment" as used in this section means the date of enactment of the Generic Animal Drug and Patent Term Restoration Act for an animal drug or a veterinary biological product.

35 U.S.C. § 156

(g) For purposes of this section, the term "regulatory review period" has the following meanings:

(1) (A) In the case of a product which is a new drug, antibiotic drug, or human biological product, the term means the period described in subparagraph (B) to which the limitation described in paragraph (6) applies.

(B) The regulatory review period for a new drug, antibiotic drug, or human biological product is the sum of—

(i) the period beginning on the date an exemption under subsection (i) of section 505 or subsection (d) of section 507 became effective for the approved product and ending on the date an application was initially submitted for such drug product under section 351, 505, or 507, and

(ii) the period beginning on the date the application was initially submitted for the approved product under section 351, subsection (b) of section 505, or section 507 and ending on the date such application was approved under such section.

(2) (A) In the case of a product which is a food additive or color additive, the term means the period described in subparagraph (B) to which the limitation described in paragraph (6) applies.

(B) The regulatory review period for a food or color additive is the sum of—

(i) the period beginning on the date a major health or environmental effects test on the additive was initiated and ending on the date a petition was initially submitted with respect to the product under the Federal Food, Drug, and Cosmetic Act requesting the issuance of a regulation for use of the product, and

(ii) the period beginning on the date a petition was initially submitted with respect to the product under the Federal Food, Drug, and Cosmetic Act requesting the issuance of a regulation for use of the product, and ending on the date such regulation became effective or, if objections were filed to such regulation, ending on the date such objections were resolved and commercial marketing was permitted or, if commercial marketing was permitted and later revoked pending further proceedings as a result of such objections, ending on the date such proceedings were finally resolved and commercial marketing was permitted.

(3) (A) In the case of a product which is a medical device, the term means the period described in subparagraph (B) to which the limitation described in paragraph (6) applies.

(B) The regulatory review period for a medical device is the sum of—

(i) the period beginning on the date a clinical investigation on humans involving the device was begun and ending on the date an application was initially submitted with respect to the device under section 515, and

(ii) the period beginning on the date an application was initially submitted with respect to the device under section 515 and ending on the date such application was approved under such Act or the period beginning on the date a notice of completion of a product development protocol was initially submitted under section 515(f)(5) and ending on the date the protocol was declared completed under section 515(f)(6).

(4) (A) In the case of a product which is a new animal drug, the term means the period described in subparagraph (B) to which the limitation described in paragraph (6) applies.

(B) The regulatory review period for a new animal drug product is the sum of—

(i) the period beginning on the earlier of the date a major health or environmental effects test on the drug was initiated or the date an exemption under subsection (j) of section 512 became effective for the approved new animal drug product and ending on the date an application was initially submitted for such animal drug product under section 512, and

(ii) the period beginning on the date the application was initially submitted for the approved animal drug product under subsection (b) of section 512 and ending on the date such application was approved under such section.

(5) (A) In the case of a product which is a veterinary biological product, the term means the period described in subparagraph (B) to which the limitation described in paragraph (6) applies.

35 U.S.C. § 156

(B) The regulatory period for a veterinary biological product is the sum of—

(i) the period beginning on the date the authority to prepare an experimental biological product under the Virus-Serum-Toxin Act became effective and ending on the date an application for a license was submitted under the Virus-Serum-Toxin Act, and

(ii) the period beginning on the date an application for a license was initially submitted for approval under the Virus-Serum-Toxin Act and ending on the date such license was issued.

(6) A period determined under any of the preceding paragraphs is subject to the following limitations:

(A) If the patent involved was issued after the date of the enactment of this section, the period of extension determined on the basis of the regulatory review period determined under any such paragraph may not exceed five years.

(B) If the patent involved was issued before the date of the enactment of this section and—

(i) no request for an exemption described in paragraph (1)(B) or (4)(B) was submitted and no request for the authority described in paragraph (5)(B) was submitted,

(ii) no major health or environmental effects test described in paragraph (2)(B) or (4)(B) was initiated and no petition for a regulation or application for registration described in such paragraph was submitted, or

(iii) no clinical investigation described in paragraph (3) was begun or product development protocol described in such paragraph was submitted,

before such date for the approved product the period of extension determined on the basis of the regulatory review period determined under any such paragraph may not exceed five years.

(C) If the patent involved was issued before the date of the enactment of this section and if an action described in subparagraph (B) was taken before the date of enactment of this section with respect to the approved product and the commercial marketing or use of the product has not been approved before such date, the period of extension determined on the basis of the regulatory review period determined under such paragraph may not exceed two years or in the case of an approved product which is a new animal drug or veterinary biological product (as those terms are used in the Federal Food, Drug, and Cosmetic Act or the Virus-Serum-Toxin Act), three years.

(h) The Director may establish such fees as the Director determines appropriate to cover the costs to the Office of receiving and acting upon applications under this section.

(Sept. 24, 1984, Pub. L., 98-417, §201, 98 Stat. 1598-1602; Nov. 16, 1988, Pub. L. 100-670, §201, 102 Stat. 3984-3988; Dec. 3, 1993, Pub. L. 103-179, §§5-6, 107 Stat. 2040; Dec. 8, 1994, Pub. L. 103-465, §532, 108 Stat. 4983; Nov. 21, 1997, Pub. L. 105-115, §125, 111 Stat. 2326; Nov. 29, 1999, Pub. L. 106-113, §4404, 113 Stat. 1501A-560; Nov. 2, 2002, Pub. L. 107-273, §13206, 116 Stat. 1904; Sept. 16, 2011, Pub. L. 112-29, §37, 125 Stat. 341.)

§ 157   Statutory invention registration [Repealed]

(Nov. 8, 1984, Pub. L. 98-622, §102, 98 Stat. 3383; Nov. 29, 1999, Pub. L. 106-113, §4732, 113 Stat. 1501A-581; Sept. 16, 2011, Pub. L. 112-29, §3(e), 125 Stat. 287.)

CHAPTER 15—PLANT PATENTS

SEC.

§ 161   Patents for plants

Whoever invents or discovers and asexually reproduces any distinct and new variety of plant, including cultivated sports, mutants, hybrids, and newly found seedlings, other than a tuber propagated plant or a plant found in an uncultivated state, may obtain a patent therefor, subject to the conditions and requirements of this title.

The provisions of this title relating to patents for inventions shall apply to patents for plants, except as otherwise provided.

(July 19, 1952, ch. 950, §1, 66 Stat. 804; Sept. 3, 1954, ch. 1259, 68 Stat. 1190.)

§ 162   Description, claim

No plant patent shall be declared invalid for noncompliance with section 112 if the description is as complete as is reasonably possible.

The claim in the specification shall be in formal terms to the plant shown and described.

(July 19, 1952, ch. 950, §1, 66 Stat. 804.)

§ 163   Grant

In the case of a plant patent, the grant shall include the right to exclude others from asexually reproducing the plant, and from using, offering for sale, or selling the plant so reproduced, or any of its parts, throughout the United States, or from importing the plant so reproduced, or any parts thereof, into the United States.

(July 19, 1952, ch. 950, §1, 66 Stat. 804; Oct. 27, 1998, §3, 112 Stat. 2781.)

§ 164   Assistance of Department of Agriculture

The President may by Executive order direct the Secretary of Agriculture, in accordance with the requests of the Director, for the purpose of carrying into effect the provisions of this title with respect to plants (1) to furnish available information of the Department of Agriculture, (2) to conduct through the appropriate bureau or division of the Department research upon special problems, or (3) to detail to the Director officers and employees of the Department.

(July 19, 1952, ch. 950, §1, 66 Stat. 804.)

CHAPTER 16—DESIGNS

§ 171   Patents for designs

(a) *In general.*—Whoever invents any new, original and ornamental design for an article of manufacture may obtain a patent therefor, subject to the conditions and requirements of this title.

(b) *Applicability of this title.*—The provisions of this title relating to patents for inventions shall apply to patents for designs, except as otherwise provided.

35 U.S.C. § 163

(c) *Filing Date.* — The filing date of an application for patent for design shall be the date on which the specification as prescribed by section 112 and any required drawings are filed.

(July 19, 1952, ch. 950, §1, 66 Stat. 805; Dec. 18, 2012, Pub. L. 112-211, §202, 126 Stat. 1535.)

§ 172   Right of priority

The right of priority provided for by subsections (a) through (d) of section 119 shall be six months in the case of designs. The right of priority provided for by section 119(e) shall not apply to designs.

(July 19, 1952, ch. 950, §1, 66 Stat. 805; Dec. 8, 1994, Pub. L. 103-465, §532, 108 Stat. 4983; Sept. 16, 2011, Pub. L. 112-29, §3, 125 Stat. 288).

§ 173   Term of design patent

Patents for designs shall be granted for the term of 15 years from the date of grant.

(July 19, 1952, ch. 950, §1, 66 Stat. 805; Aug. 27, 1982, Pub. L. 97-247, §16, 96 Stat. 321; Dec. 8, 1994, Pub. L. 103-465, §532, 108 Stat. 4983; Dec. 18, 2012, Pub. L. 112-211, §101, 126 Stat. 1532.)

CHAPTER 17 — SECRECY OF CERTAIN INVENTIONS AND FILING APPLICATIONS IN FOREIGN COUNTRY

SEC.
181.   Secrecy of certain inventions and withholding of patent.
182.   Abandonment of invention for unauthorized disclosure.
183.   Right to compensation.
184.   Filing of application in foreign country.
185.   Patent barred for filing without license.
186.   Penalty.
187.   Nonapplicability to certain persons.
188.   Rules and regulations, delegation of power.

§ 181   Secrecy of certain inventions and withholding of patent

Whenever publication or disclosure by the publication of an application or by the grant of a patent on an invention in which the Government has a property interest might, in the opinion of the head of the interested Government agency, be detrimental to the national security, the Commissioner of Patents upon being so notified shall order that the invention be kept secret and shall withhold the publication of the application or the grant of a patent therefor under the conditions set forth hereinafter.

Whenever the publication or disclosure of an invention by the publication of an application or by the granting of a patent, in which the Government does not have a property interest, might, in the opinion of the Commissioner of Patents, be detrimental to the national security, he shall make the application for patent in which such invention is disclosed available for inspection to the Atomic Energy Commission, the Secretary of Defense, and the chief officer of any other department or agency of the Government designated by the President as a defense agency of the United States.

Each individual to whom the application is disclosed shall sign a dated acknowledgment thereof, which acknowledgment shall be entered in the file of the application. If, in the opinion of the Atomic Energy Commission, the Secretary of a Defense Department, or the chief officer of another department or agency so designated, the publication or disclosure of the invention by the publication of the application or by the granting of a patent therefor would be detrimental to the national security, the Atomic Energy Commission, the Secretary of a Defense Department, or such other chief officer shall notify the Commissioner of Patents and the Commissioner of Patents shall order that the invention be kept secret and shall withhold the publication of the application or the grant of a patent for such period as the national interest requires, and notify the applicant thereof. Upon proper showing by the head of the department or agency who caused the secrecy order to be issued that the examination of the application might jeopardize the national interest, the Commissioner of Patents shall thereupon maintain the application in a sealed condition and notify the applicant thereof. The owner of an application which has been placed under a secrecy order shall have a right to appeal from the order to the Secretary of Commerce under rules prescribed by him.

An invention shall not be ordered kept secret and the publication of an application or the grant of a patent withheld for a period of more than one year. The Commissioner of Patents shall renew the order at the end thereof, or at the end of any renewal period, for additional periods of one year upon notification by the head of the department or the chief officer of the agency who caused the order to be issued that an affirmative determination has been made that the national interest continues so to require. An order in effect, or issued, during a time when the United States is at war, shall remain in effect for the duration of hostilities and one year following cessation of hostilities. An order in effect, or issued, during a national emergency declared by the President shall remain in effect for the duration of the national emergency and six months thereafter. The Commissioner of Patents may rescind any

35 U.S.C. § 181

order upon notification by the heads of the departments and the chief officers of the agencies who caused the order to be issued that the publication or disclosure of the invention is no longer deemed detrimental to the national security.

(July 19, 1952, ch. 950, §1, 66 Stat. 805; Nov. 29, 1999, Pub. L. 106-113, §4507, 113 Stat. 1501A-565).

§ 182 Abandonment of invention for unauthorized disclosure

The invention disclosed in an application for patent subject to an order made pursuant to section 181 may be held abandoned upon its being established by the Commissioner of Patents that in violation of said order the invention has been published or disclosed or that an application for a patent therefor has been filed in a foreign country by the inventor, his successors, assigns, or legal representatives, or anyone in privity with him or them, without the consent of the Commissioner of Patents. The abandonment shall be held to have occurred as of the time of violation. The consent of the Commissioner of Patents shall not be given without the concurrence of the heads of the departments and the chief officers of the agencies who caused the order to be issued. A holding of abandonment shall constitute forfeiture by the applicant, his successors, assigns, or legal representatives, or anyone in privity with him or them, of all claims against the United States based upon such invention.

(July 19, 1952, ch. 950, §1, 66 Stat. 806.)

§ 183 Right to compensation

An applicant, his successors, assigns, or legal representatives, whose patent is withheld as herein provided, shall have the right, beginning at the date the applicant is notified that, except for such order, his application is otherwise in condition for allowance, or February 1, 1952, whichever is later, and ending six years after a patent is issued thereon, to apply to the head of any department or agency who caused the order to be issued for compensation for the damage caused by the order of secrecy and/or for the use of the invention by the Government, resulting from his disclosure. The right to compensation for use shall begin on the date of the first use of the invention by the Government. The head of the department or agency is authorized, upon the presentation of a claim, to enter into an agreement with the applicant, his successors, assigns, or legal representatives, in full settlement for the damage and/or use. This settlement agreement shall be conclusive for all purposes notwithstanding any other provision of law to the contrary. If full settlement of the claim cannot be effected, the head of the department or agency may award and pay to such applicant, his successors, assigns, or legal representatives, a sum not exceeding 75 per centum of the sum which the head of the department or agency considers just compensation for the damage and/or use. A claimant may bring suit against the United States in the United States Claims Court[23] or in the District Court of the United States for the district in which such claimant is a resident for an amount which when added to the award shall constitute just compensation for the damage and/or use of the invention by the Government. The owner of any patent issued upon an application that was subject to a secrecy order issued pursuant to section 181, who did not apply for compensation as above provided, shall have the right, after the date of issuance of such patent, to bring suit in the United States Claims Court for just compensation for the damage caused by reason of the order of secrecy and/or use by the Government of the invention resulting from his disclosure. The right to compensation for use shall begin on the date of the first use of the invention by the Government. In a suit under the provisions of this section the United States may avail itself of all defenses it may plead in an action under section 1498 of title 28. This section shall not confer a right of action on anyone or his successors, assigns, or legal representatives who, while in the full-time employment or service of the United States, discovered, invented, or developed the invention on which the claim is based.

(July 19, 1952, ch. 950, §1, 66 Stat. 806; Apr. 2, 1982, Pub. L. 97-164, §160, 96 Stat. 48.)

§ 184　Filing of application in foreign country

(a) *Filing in foreign country.*—Except when authorized by a license obtained from the Commissioner of Patents a person shall not file or cause or authorize to be filed in any foreign country prior to six months after filing in the United states an application for patent or for the registration of a utility model, industrial design, or model in respect of an invention made in this country. A license shall not be granted with respect to an invention subject to an order issued by the Commissioner of Patents pursuant to section 181 without the concurrence of the head of the departments and the chief officers of the agencies who caused the order to be issued. The license may be granted retroactively where an application has been filed abroad through

---

[23] *Ed. Note:* Pursuant to the Court of Federal Claims Technical and Procedural Improvements Act of 1992, §902(b)(2), Pub. L. 102-572, 106 Stat. 4516, statutory references to the U.S. Claims Court are deemed to refer to the U.S. Court of Federal Claims.

35 U.S.C. § 184

error and the application does not disclose an invention within the scope of section 181.

(b) *Application.* —The term "application" when used in this chapter includes applications and any modifications, amendments, or supplements thereto, or divisions thereof.

(c) *Subsequent modifications, amendments, and supplements.* —The scope of a license shall permit subsequent modifications, amendments, and supplements containing additional subject matter if the application upon which the request for the license is based is not, or was not, required to be made available for inspection under section 181 and if such modifications, amendments, and supplements do not change the general nature of the invention in a manner which would require such application to be made available for inspection under such section 181. In any case in which a license is not, or was not, required in order to file an application in any foreign country, such subsequent modifications, amendments, and supplements may be made, without a license, to the application filed in the foreign country if the United States application was not required to be made available for inspection under section 181 and if such modifications, amendments, and supplements do not, or did not, change the general nature of the invention in a manner which would require the United States application to have been made available for inspection under such section 181.

(July 19, 1952, ch. 950, §1, 66 Stat. 807; Aug. 23, 1988, Pub. L. 100-418, §9101, 102 Stat. 1567–68; Sept. 16, 2011, Pub. L. 112-29, §20, 125 Stat. 333.)

§ 185   Patent barred for filing without license

Notwithstanding any other provisions of law any person, and his successors, assigns, or legal representatives, shall not receive a United States patent for an invention if that person, or his successors, assigns, or legal representatives shall, without procuring the license prescribed in section 184, have made, or consented to or assisted another's making, application in a foreign country for a patent or for the registration of a utility model, industrial design, or model in respect of the invention. A United States patent issued to such person, his successors, assigns, or legal representatives shall be invalid, unless the failure to procure such license was through error, and the patent does not disclose subject matter within the scope of section 181.

(July 19, 1952, ch. 950, §1, 66 Stat. 807; Aug. 23, 1988, Pub. L. 100-418, §9101, 102 Stat. 1568; Nov. 2, 2002, Pub. L. 107-273, §13206, 116 Stat. 1904; Sept. 16, 2011, Pub. L. 112-29, §20, 125 Stat. 333.)

35 U.S.C. § 185

§ 186   Penalty

Whoever, during the period or periods of time an invention has been ordered to be kept secret and the grant of a patent thereon withheld pursuant to section 181, shall, with knowledge of such order and without due authorization, willfully publish or disclose or authorize or cause to be published or disclosed the invention, or material information with respect thereto, or whoever willfully, in violation of the provisions of section 184, shall file or cause or authorize to be filed in any foreign country an application for patent or for the registration of a utility model, industrial design, or model in respect of any invention made in the United States, shall, upon conviction, be fined not more than $10,000 or imprisoned for not more than two years, or both.

(July 19, 1952, ch. 950, §1, 66 Stat. 807; Aug. 23, 1988, Pub. L. 100-418, §9101, 102 Stat. 1568.)

§ 187   Nonapplicability to certain persons

The prohibitions and penalties of this chapter shall not apply to any officer or agent of the United States acting within the scope of his authority, nor to any person acting upon his written instructions or permission.

(July 19, 1952, ch. 950, §1, 66 Stat. 808.)

§ 188   Rules and regulations, delegation of power

The Atomic Energy Commission, the Secretary of a defense department, the chief officer of any other department or agency of the Government designated by the President as a defense agency of the United States, and the Secretary of Commerce, may separately issue rules and regulations to enable the respective department or agency to carry out the provisions of this chapter, and may delegate any power conferred by this chapter.

(July 19, 1952, ch. 950, §1, 66 Stat. 808.)

CHAPTER 18—PATENT RIGHTS IN INVENTIONS MADE WITH
FEDERAL ASSISTANCE

35 U.S.C. § 186

§ 200 Policy and objective

It is the policy and objective of the Congress to use the patent system to promote the utilization of inventions arising from federally supported research or development; to encourage maximum participation of small business firms in federally supported research and development efforts; to promote collaboration between commercial concerns and nonprofit organizations, including universities; to ensure that inventions made by nonprofit organizations and small business firms are used in a manner to promote free competition and enterprise without unduly encumbering future research and discovery; to promote the commercialization and public availability of inventions made in the United States by United States industry and labor; to ensure that the Government obtains sufficient rights in federally supported inventions to meet the needs of the Government and protect the public against nonuse or unreasonable use of inventions; and to minimize the costs of administering policies in this area.

(Dec. 12, 1980, Pub. L. 96-517, §6, 94 Stat. 3019; Nov. 1, 2000, Pub. L. 106-404, §5, 114 Stat. 1745.)

§ 201 Definitions

As used in this chapter—

(a) The term "Federal agency" means any executive agency as defined in section 105 of title 5, and the military departments as defined by section 102 of title 5.

(b) The term "funding agreement" means any contract, grant, or cooperative agreement entered into between any Federal agency, other than the Tennessee Valley Authority, and any contractor for the performance of experimental, developmental, or research work funded in whole or in part by the Federal Government. Such term includes any assignment, substitution of parties, or subcontract of any type entered into for the performance of experimental, developmental, or research work under a funding agreement as herein defined.

(c) The term "contractor" means any person, small business firm, or nonprofit organization that is a party to a funding agreement.

(d) The term "invention" means any invention or discovery which is or may be patentable or otherwise protectable under this title or any novel variety of plant which is or may be protectable under the Plant Variety Protection Act (7 U.S.C. 2321 et seq.).

(e) The term "subject invention" means any invention of the contractor conceived or first actually reduced to practice in the performance of work under a funding agreement: *Provided,* That in the case of a variety of plant, the date of determination (as defined in section 41(d) of the Plant Variety Protection Act (7 U.S.C. 2401(d)) must also occur during the period of contract performance.

(f) The term "practical application" means to manufacture in the case of a composition or product, to practice in the case of a process or method, or to operate in the case of a machine or system; and, in each case, under such conditions as to establish that the invention is being utilized and that its benefits are to the extent permitted by law or Government regulations available to the public on reasonable terms.

(g) The term "made" when used in relation to any invention means the conception or first actual reduction to practice of such invention.

(h) The term "small business firm" means a small business concern as defined at section 2 of Pub. L. 85-536 (15 U.S.C. 632) and implementing regulations of the Administrator of the Small Business Administration.

(i) The term "nonprofit organization" means universities and other institutions of higher education or an organization of the type described in section 501(c)(3) of the Internal Revenue Code of 1954 (26 U.S.C. 501(c)) and exempt from taxation under section 501(a) of the Internal Revenue Code (26 U.S.C. 501(a)) or any nonprofit scientific or educational organization qualified under a State nonprofit organization statute.

(Dec. 12, 1980, Pub. L. 96-517, §6, 94 Stat. 3019; Nov. 8, 1984, Pub. L. 98-620, §501, 98 Stat. 3364; Nov. 2, 2002, Pub. L. 107-273, §13206, 116 Stat. 1904.)

35 U.S.C. § 201

§ 202 Disposition of rights

(a) Each nonprofit organization or small business firm may, within a reasonable time after disclosure as required by paragraph (c)(1) of this section, elect to retain title to any subject invention: Provided, however, That a funding agreement may provide otherwise (i) when the contractor is not located in the United States or does not have a place of business located in the United States or is subject to the control of a foreign government, (ii) in exceptional circumstances when it is determined by the agency that restriction or elimination of the right to retain title to any subject invention will better promote the policy and objectives of this chapter, (iii) when it is determined by a Government authority which is authorized by statute or Executive order to conduct foreign intelligence or counter-intelligence activities that the restriction or elimination of the right to retain title to any subject invention is necessary to protect the security of such activities or (iv) when the funding agreement includes the operation of a Government-owned, contractor-operated facility of the Department of Energy primarily dedicated to that Department's naval nuclear propulsion or weapons related programs and all funding agreement limitations under this subparagraph on the contractor's right to elect title to a subject invention are limited to inventions occurring under the above two programs of the Department of Energy. The rights of the nonprofit organization or small business firm shall be subject to the provisions of paragraph (c) of this section and the other provisions of this chapter.

(b) (1) The rights of the Government under subsection (a) shall not be exercised by a Federal agency unless it first determines that at least one of the conditions identified in clauses (i) through (iv) of subsection (a) exists. Except in the case of subsection (a)(iii), the agency shall file with the Secretary of Commerce, within thirty days after the award of the applicable funding agreement, a copy of such determination. In the case of a determination under subsection (a)(ii), the statement shall include an analysis justifying the determination. In the case of determinations applicable to funding agreements with small business firms, copies shall also be sent to the Chief Counsel for Advocacy of the Small Business Administration. If the Secretary of Commerce believes that any individual determination or pattern of determinations is contrary to the policies and objectives of this chapter or otherwise not in conformance with this chapter, the Secretary shall so advise the head of the agency concerned and the Administrator of the Office of Federal Procurement Policy, and recommend corrective actions.

(2) Whenever the Administrator of the Office of Federal Procurement Policy has determined that one or more Federal agencies are utilizing the authority of clause (i) or (ii) of subsection (a) of this section in a manner that is contrary to the policies and objectives of this chapter the Administrator is authorized to issue regulations describing classes of situations in which agencies may not exercise the authorities of those clauses.

(3) If the contractor believes that a determination is contrary to the policies and objectives of this chapter or constitutes an abuse of discretion by the agency, the determination shall be subject to section 203(b).

(c) Each funding agreement with a small business firm or nonprofit organization shall contain appropriate provisions to effectuate the following:

(1) That the contractor disclose each subject invention to the Federal agency within a reasonable time after it becomes known to contractor personnel responsible for the administration of patent matters, and that the Federal Government may receive title to any subject invention not disclosed to it within such time.

(2) That the contractor make a written election within two years after disclosure to the Federal agency (or such additional time as may be approved by the Federal agency) whether the contractor will retain title to a subject invention: Provided, That in any case where the 1-year period referred to in section 102(b) would end before the end of that 2-year period, the period for election may be shortened by the Federal agency to a date that is not more than sixty days before the end of that 1-year period: And provided further, That the Federal Government may receive title to any subject invention in which the contractor does not elect to retain rights or fails to elect rights within such times.

(3) That a contractor electing rights in a subject invention agrees to file a patent application prior to the expiration of the 1-year period referred to in section 102(b), and shall thereafter file corresponding patent applications in other countries in which it wishes to retain title within reasonable times, and that the Federal Government may receive title to any subject inventions in the United States or other countries in which the contractor has not filed patent applications on the subject invention within such times.

35 U.S.C. § 202

(4) With respect to any invention in which the contractor elects rights, the Federal agency shall have a nonexclusive, nontransferable, irrevocable, paid-up license to practice or have practiced for or on behalf of the United States any subject invention throughout the world: *Provided,* That the funding agreement may provide for such additional rights, including the right to assign or have assigned foreign patent rights in the subject invention, as are determined by the agency as necessary for meeting the obligations of the United States under any treaty, international agreement, arrangement of cooperation, memorandum of understanding, or similar arrangement, including military agreements relating to weapons development and production.

(5) The right of the Federal agency to require periodic reporting on the utilization or efforts at obtaining utilization that are being made by the contractor or his licensees or assignees: *Provided,* That any such information, as well as any information on utilization or efforts at obtaining utilization obtained as part of a proceeding under section 203 of this chapter shall be treated by the Federal agency as commercial and financial information obtained from a person and privileged and confidential and not subject to disclosure under section 552 of title 5.

(6) An obligation on the part of the contractor, in the event a United States patent application is filed by or on its behalf or by any assignee of the contractor, to include within the specification of such application and any patent issuing thereon, a statement specifying that the invention was made with Government support and that the Government has certain rights in the invention.

(7) In the case of a nonprofit organization, (A) a prohibition upon the assignment of rights to a subject invention in the United States without the approval of the Federal agency, except where such assignment is made to an organization which has as one of its primary functions the management of inventions (provided that such assignee shall be subject to the same provisions as the contractor); (B) a requirement that the contractor share royalties with the inventor; (C) except with respect to a funding agreement for the operation of a Government-owned-contractor-operated facility, a requirement that the balance of any royalties or income earned by the contractor with respect to subject inventions, after payment of expenses (including payments to inventors) incidental to the administration of subject inventions, be utilized for the support of scientific research or education; (D) a requirement that, except where it is determined to be

35 U.S.C. § 202

infeasible following a reasonable inquiry, a preference in the licensing of subject inventions shall be given to small business firms; and (E) with respect to a funding agreement for the operation of a Government-owned-contractor-operated facility, requirements (i) that after payment of patenting costs, licensing costs, payments to inventors, and other expenses incidental to the administration of subject inventions, 100 percent of the balance of any royalties or income earned and retained by the contractor during any fiscal year up to an amount equal to 5 percent of the annual budget of the facility, shall be used by the contractor for scientific research, development, and education consistent with the research and development mission and objectives of the facility, including activities that increase the licensing potential of other inventions of the facility; provided that if said balance exceeds 5 percent of the annual budget of the facility, that 15 percent of such excess shall be paid to the Treasury of the United States and the remaining 85 percent shall be used for the same purposes as described above in this clause and (ii) that, to the extent it provides the most effective technology transfer, the licensing of subject inventions shall be administered by contractor employees on location at the facility.

(8) The requirements of sections 203 and 204 of this chapter.

(d) If a contractor does not elect to retain title to a subject invention in cases subject to this section, the Federal agency may consider and after consultation with the contractor grant requests for retention of rights by the inventor subject to the provisions of this Act and regulations promulgated hereunder.

(e) In any case when a Federal employee is a coinventor of any invention made with a nonprofit organization, a small business firm, or a non-Federal inventor, the Federal agency employing such coinventor may, for the purpose of consolidating rights in the invention and if it finds that it would expedite the development of the invention—

(1) license or assign whatever rights it may acquire in the subject invention to the nonprofit organization, small business firm, or non-Federal inventor in accordance with the provisions of this chapter; or

(2) acquire any rights in the subject invention from the nonprofit organization, small business firm, or non-Federal inventor, but only to the extent the party from whom the rights are acquired voluntarily enters into the transaction and no other transaction under this chapter is conditioned on such acquisition.

35 U.S.C. § 202

(f) (1) No funding agreement with a small business firm or nonprofit organization shall contain a provision allowing a Federal agency to require the licensing to third parties of inventions owned by the contractor that are not subject inventions unless such provision has been approved by the head of the agency and a written justification has been signed by the head of the agency. Any such provision shall clearly state whether the licensing may be required in connection with the practice of a subject invention, a specifically identified work object, or both. The head of the agency may not delegate the authority to approve provisions or sign justifications required by this paragraph.

(2) A Federal agency shall not require the licensing of third parties under any such provision unless the head of the agency determines that the use of the invention by others is necessary for the practice of a subject invention or for the use of a work object of the funding agreement and that such action is necessary to achieve the practical application of the subject invention or work object. Any such determination shall be on the record after an opportunity for an agency hearing. Any action commenced for judicial review of such determination shall be brought within sixty days after notification of such determination.

(Dec. 12, 1980, Pub. L. 96-517, §6, 94 Stat. 3020; Nov. 8, 1984, Pub. L. 98-620, §501, 98 Stat. 3364-66; Dec. 10, 1991, Pub. L. 102-204, §10, 105 Stat. 1641; Nov. 29, 1999, Pub. L. 106-113, §4732, 113 Stat. 1501A-581; Nov. 1, 2000, Pub. L. 106-404, §6(1), 114 Stat. 1745; Nov. 2, 2002, Pub. L. 107-273, §13206, 116 Stat. 1904; Mar. 11, 2009, Pub. L. 111-8, §1301(h), 123 Stat. 829; Sept. 16, 2011, Pub. L. 112-29, §§3, 13, 125 Stat. 288, 327.)

§ 203 March-in rights

(a) With respect to any subject invention in which a small business firm or nonprofit organization has acquired title under this chapter, the Federal agency under whose funding agreement the subject invention was made shall have the right, in accordance with such procedures as are provided in regulations promulgated hereunder to require the contractor, an assignee or exclusive licensee of a subject invention to grant a nonexclusive, partially exclusive, or exclusive license in any field of use to a responsible applicant or applicants, upon terms that are reasonable under the circumstances, and if the contractor, assignee, or exclusive licensee refuses such request, to grant such a license itself, if the Federal agency determines that such—

(1) action is necessary because the contractor or assignee has not taken, or is not expected to take within a reasonable time, effective steps to achieve practical application of the subject invention in such field of use;

(2) action is necessary to alleviate health or safety needs which are not reasonably satisfied by the contractor, assignee, or their licensees;

(3) action is necessary to meet requirements for public use specified by Federal regulations and such requirements are not reasonably satisfied by the contractor, assignee, or licensees; or

(4) action is necessary because the agreement required by section 204 has not been obtained or waived or because a licensee of the exclusive right to use or sell any subject invention in the United States is in breach of its agreement obtained pursuant to section 204.

(b) A determination pursuant to this section or section 202(b)(4) shall not be subject to chapter 71 of title 41. An administrative appeals procedure shall be established by regulations promulgated in accordance with section 206. Additionally, any contractor, inventor, assignee, or exclusive licensee adversely affected by a determination under this section may, at any time within sixty days after the determination is issued, file a petition in the United States Claims Court,[24] which shall have jurisdiction to determine the appeal on the record and to affirm, reverse, remand or modify as appropriate, the determination of the Federal agency. In cases described in paragraphs (1) and (3) of subsection (a), the agency's determination shall be held in abeyance pending the exhaustion of appeals or petitions filed under the preceding sentence.

(Dec. 12, 1980, Pub. L. 96-517, §6, 94 Stat. 3022; Nov. 8, 1984, Pub. L. 98-620, §501, 98 Stat. 3367; Nov. 2, 2002, Pub. L. 107-273, §13206, 116 Stat. 1904; Jan. 4, 2011, Pub. L. 111-350, §5, 124 Stat. 3841.)

§ 204   Preference for United States industry

Notwithstanding any other provision of this chapter, no small business firm or nonprofit organization which receives title to any subject invention and no assignee of any such small business firm or nonprofit organization shall grant to any person the exclusive right to use or sell any subject invention in the United States unless such person agrees that any products embodying the subject invention or produced through the use of the subject invention will be manufactured substantially in the United States. However, in individual cases, the requirement for such an agreement may be waived by the Federal agency under whose funding agreement the invention was made upon a

---

[24] *Ed. Note:* Pursuant to the Court of Federal Claims Technical and Procedural Improvements Act of 1992, §902(b)(2), Pub. L. 102-572, 106 Stat. 4516, statutory references to the U.S. Claims Court are deemed to refer to the U.S. Court of Federal Claims.

showing by the small business firm, nonprofit organization, or assignee that reasonable but unsuccessful efforts have been made to grant licenses on similar terms to potential licensees that would be likely to manufacture substantially in the United States or that under the circumstances domestic manufacture is not commercially feasible.

(Dec. 12, 1980, Pub. L. 96-517, §6, 94 Stat. 3023.)

§ 205   Confidentiality

Federal agencies are authorized to withhold from disclosure to the public information disclosing any invention in which the Federal Government owns or may own a right, title, or interest (including a nonexclusive license) for a reasonable time in order for a patent application to be filed. Furthermore, Federal agencies shall not be required to release copies of any document which is part of an application for patent filed with the United States Patent and Trademark Office or with any foreign patent office.

(Dec. 12, 1980, Pub. L. 96-517, §6, 94 Stat. 3023.)

§ 206   Uniform clauses and regulations

The Secretary of Commerce may issue regulations which may be made applicable to Federal agencies implementing the provisions of sections 202 through 204 of this chapter and shall establish standard funding agreement provisions required under this chapter. The regulations and the standard funding agreement shall be subject to public comment before their issuance.

(Dec. 12, 1980, Pub. L. 96-517, §6, 94 Stat. 3023; Nov. 8, 1984, Pub. L. 98-620, §501, 98 Stat. 3367.)

§ 207   Domestic and foreign protection of federally owned inventions

(a) Each Federal agency is authorized to—

(1) apply for, obtain, and maintain patents or other forms of protection in the United States and in foreign countries on inventions in which the Federal Government owns a right, title, or interest;

(2) grant nonexclusive, exclusive, or partially exclusive licenses under federally owned inventions, royalty-free or for royalties or other consideration, and on such terms and conditions, including the grant to the licensee of the right of enforcement pursuant to the provisions of chapter 29 as determined appropriate in the public interest;

(3) undertake all other suitable and necessary steps to protect and administer rights to federally owned inventions on behalf of the Federal Gov-

ernment either directly or through contract, including acquiring rights for and administering royalties to the Federal Government in any invention, but only to the extent the party from whom the rights are acquired voluntarily enters into the transaction, to facilitate the licensing of a federally owned invention; and

(4) transfer custody and administration, in whole or in part, to another Federal agency, of the right, title, or interest in any federally owned invention.

(b) For the purpose of assuring the effective management of Government-owned inventions, the Secretary of Commerce is authorized to—

(1) assist Federal agency efforts to promote the licensing and utilization of Government-owned inventions;

(2) assist Federal agencies in seeking protection and maintaining inventions in foreign countries, including the payment of fees and costs connected therewith; and

(3) consult with and advise Federal agencies as to areas of science and technology research and development with potential for commercial utilization.

(Dec. 12, 1980, Pub. L. 96-517, §6, 94 Stat. 3023; Nov. 8, 1984, Pub. L. 98-620, §501, 98 Stat. 3367; Nov. 1, 2000, Pub. L. 106-404, §6(2), 114 Stat. 1745.)

§ 208 Regulations governing Federal licensing

The Secretary of Commerce is authorized to promulgate regulations specifying the terms and conditions upon which any federally owned invention, other than inventions owned by the Tennessee Valley Authority, may be licensed on a nonexclusive, partially exclusive, or exclusive basis.

(Dec. 12, 1980, Pub. L. 96-517, §6, 94 Stat. 3024; Nov. 8, 1984, Pub. L. 98-620, §501, 98 Stat. 3367.)

§ 209 Licensing federally owned inventions

(a) *Authority.* — A Federal agency may grant an exclusive or partially exclusive license on a federally owned invention under section 207(a)(2) only if—

(1) granting the license is a reasonable and necessary incentive to—

(A) call forth the investment capital and expenditures needed to bring the invention to practical application; or

(B) otherwise promote the invention's utilization by the public;

(2) the Federal agency finds that the public will be served by the granting of the license, as indicated by the applicant's intentions, plans, and ability to bring the invention to practical application or otherwise promote the invention's utilization by the public, and that the proposed scope of exclusivity is not greater than reasonably necessary to provide the incentive for bringing the invention to practical application, as proposed by the applicant, or otherwise to promote the invention's utilization by the public;

(3) the applicant makes a commitment to achieve practical application of the invention within a reasonable time, which time may be extended by the agency upon the applicant's request and the applicant's demonstration that the refusal of such extension would be unreasonable;

(4) granting the license will not tend to substantially lessen competition or create or maintain a violation of the Federal antitrust laws; and

(5) in the case of an invention covered by a foreign patent application or patent, the interests of the Federal Government or United States industry in foreign commerce will be enhanced.

(b) *Manufacture in United States.* — A Federal agency shall normally grant a license under section 207(a)(2) to use or sell any federally owned invention in the United States only to a licensee who agrees that any products embodying the invention or produced through the use of the invention will be manufactured substantially in the United States.

(c) *Small business.* — First preference for the granting of any exclusive or partially exclusive licenses under section 207(a)(2) shall be given to small business firms having equal or greater likelihood as other applicants to bring the invention to practical application within a reasonable time.

(d) *Terms and conditions.* — Any licenses granted under section 207(a)(2) shall contain such terms and conditions as the granting agency considers appropriate, and shall include provisions —

(1) retaining a non-transferable, irrevocable, paid-up license for any Federal agency to practice the invention or have the invention practiced throughout the world by or on behalf of the Government of the United States;

(2) requiring periodic reporting on utilization of the invention, and utilization efforts, by the licensee, but only to the extent necessary to enable the Federal agency to determine whether the terms of the license are being complied with, except that any such report shall be treated by the

Federal agency as commercial and financial information obtained from a person and privileged and confidential and not subject to disclosure under section 552 of title 5; and

(3) empowering the Federal agency to terminate the license in whole or in part if the agency determines that—

(A) the licensee is not executing its commitment to achieve practical application of the invention, including commitments contained in any plan submitted in support of its request for a license, and the licensee cannot otherwise demonstrate to the satisfaction of the Federal agency that it has taken, or can be expected to take within a reasonable time, effective steps to achieve practical application of the invention;

(B) the licensee is in breach of an agreement described in subsection (b);

(C) termination is necessary to meet requirements for public use specified by Federal regulations issued after the date of the license, and such requirements are not reasonably satisfied by the licensee; or

(D) the licensee has been found by a court of competent jurisdiction to have violated the Federal antitrust laws in connection with its performance under the license agreement.

(e) *Public notice.*—No exclusive or partially exclusive license may be granted under section 207(a)(2) unless public notice of the intention to grant an exclusive or partially exclusive license on a federally owned invention has been provided in an appropriate manner at least 15 days before the license is granted, and the Federal agency has considered all comments received before the end of the comment period in response to that public notice. This subsection shall not apply to the licensing of inventions made under a cooperative research and development agreement entered into under section 12 of the Stevenson-Wydler Technology Innovation Act of 1980 (15 U.S.C. 3710a).

(f) *Plan.*—No Federal agency shall grant any license under a patent or patent application on a federally owned invention unless the person requesting the license has supplied the agency with a plan for development or marketing of the invention, except that any such plan shall be treated by the Federal agency as commercial and financial information obtained from a person and privileged and confidential and not subject to disclosure under section 552 of title 5.

35 U.S.C. § 209

(Dec. 12, 1980, Pub. L. 96-517, §6, 94 Stat. 3024; Nov. 1, 2000, Pub. L. 106-404, §4, 114 Stat. 1743; Nov. 2, 2002, Pub. L. 107-273, §13206, 116 Stat. 1904; Sept. 16, 2011, Pub. L. 112-29, §20, 125 Stat. 335.)

§ 210   Precedence of chapter

(a) This chapter shall take precedence over any other Act which would require a disposition of rights in subject inventions of small business firms or nonprofit organizations contractors in a manner that is inconsistent with this chapter, including but not necessarily limited to the following:

(1) section 10(a) of the Act of June 29, 1935, as added by title I of the Act of August 14, 1946 (7 U.S.C. 427i(a); 60 Stat. 1085);

(2) section 205(a) of the Act of August 14, 1946 (7 U.S.C. 1624(a); 60 Stat. 1090);

(3) section 501(c) of the Federal Mine Safety and Health Act of 1977 (30 U.S.C. 951(c); 83 Stat. 742);

(4) section 106(c) of the National Traffic and Motor Vehicle Safety Act of 1966 (15 U.S.C. 1395(c); 80 Stat. 721);

(5) section 12 of the National Science Foundation Act of 1950 (42 U.S.C. 1871(a); 82 Stat. 360);

(6) section 152 of the Atomic Energy Act of 1954 (42 U.S.C. 2182; 68 Stat. 943);

(7) section 20135 of title 51;

(8) section 6 of the Coal Research and Development Act of 1960 (30 U.S.C. 666; 74 Stat. 337);

(9) section 4 of the Helium Act Amendments of 1960 (50 U.S.C. 167b; 74 Stat. 920);

(10) section 32 of the Arms Control and Disarmament Act of 1961 (22 U.S.C. 2572; 75 Stat. 634);

(11) section 9 of the Federal Nonnuclear Energy Research and Development Act of 1974 (42 U.S.C. 5908; 88 Stat. 1878);

(12) section 5(d) of the Consumer Product Safety Act (15 U.S.C. 2054(d); 86 Stat. 1211);

(13) section 3 of the Act of April 5, 1944 (30 U.S.C. 323; 58 Stat. 191);

(14) section 8001(c)(3) of the Solid Waste Disposal Act (42 U.S.C. 6981(c); 90 Stat. 2829);

(15) section 219 of the Foreign Assistance Act of 1961 (22 U.S.C. 2179; 83 Stat. 806);

(16) section 427(b) of the Federal Mine Health and Safety Act of 1977 (30 U.S.C. 937(b); 86 Stat. 155);

(17) section 306(d) of the Surface Mining and Reclamation Act of 1977 (30 U.S.C. 1226(d); 91 Stat. 455);

(18) section 21(d) of the Federal Fire Prevention and Control Act of 1974 (15 U.S.C. 2218(d); 88 Stat. 1548);

(19) section 6(b) of the Solar Photovoltaic Energy Research Development and Demonstration Act of 1978 (42 U.S.C. 5585(b); 92 Stat. 2516);

(20) section 12 of the Native Latex Commercialization and Economic Development Act of 1978 (7 U.S.C. 178j; 92 Stat. 2533); and

(21) section 408 of the Water Resources and Development Act of 1978 (42 U.S.C. 7879; 92 Stat. 1360).

The Act creating this chapter shall be construed to take precedence over any future Act unless that Act specifically cites this Act and provides that it shall take precedence over this Act.

(b) Nothing in this chapter is intended to alter the effect of the laws cited in paragraph (a) of this section or any other laws with respect to the disposition of rights in inventions made in the performance of funding agreements with persons other than nonprofit organizations or small business firms.

(c) Nothing in this chapter is intended to limit the authority of agencies to agree to the disposition of rights in inventions made in the performance of work under funding agreements with persons other than nonprofit organizations or small business firms in accordance with the Statement of Government Patent Policy issued on February 18, 1983, agency regulations, or other applicable regulations or to otherwise limit the authority of agencies to allow such persons to retain ownership of inventions, except that all funding agreements, including those with other than small business firms and nonprofit organizations, shall include the requirements established in section 202(c)(4) and section 203. Any disposition of rights in inventions made in accordance with the Statement or implementing regulations, including any disposition occurring before enactment of this section, are hereby authorized.

(d) Nothing in this chapter shall be construed to require the disclosure of intelligence sources or methods or to otherwise affect the authority granted to the Director of Central Intelligence by statute or Executive order for the protection of intelligence sources or methods.

(e) The provisions of the Stevenson-Wydler Technology Innovation Act of 1980 shall take precedence over the provisions of this chapter to the extent that they permit or require a disposition of rights in subject inventions which is inconsistent with this chapter.

(Dec. 12, 1980, Pub. L. 96-517, §6, 94 Stat. 3026-3027; Nov. 8, 1984, Pub. L. 98-620, §501, 98 Stat. 3367; Oct. 20, 1986, Pub. L. 99-502, §9, 100 Stat. 1796; Mar. 7, 1996, Pub. L. 104-113, §7, 110 Stat. 779; Nov. 13, 1998, Pub. L. 105-393, §220(c), 112 Stat. 3625; Nov. 2, 2002, Pub. L. 107-273, §13206, 116 Stat. 1904; Aug. 8, 2005, Pub. L. No. 109-58, §1009, 119 Stat. 934; Dec. 18, 2010, Pub. L. 111-314, §4, 124 Stat. 3440.)

§ 211   Relationship to antitrust laws

Nothing in this chapter shall be deemed to convey to any person immunity from civil or criminal liability, or to create any defenses to actions, under any antitrust law.

(Dec. 12, 1980, Pub. L. 96-517, §6, 94 Stat. 3027).

§ 212   Disposition of rights in educational awards

No scholarship, fellowship, training grant, or other funding agreement made by a Federal agency primarily to an awardee for educational purposes will contain any provision giving the Federal agency any rights to inventions made by the awardee.

(Nov. 8, 1984, Pub. L. 98-620, §501, 98 Stat. 3368.)

PART III—PATENTS AND PROTECTION OF PATENT RIGHTS

CHAPTER 25—AMENDMENT AND CORRECTION OF PATENTS

§ 251   Reissue of defective patents

(a) *In general.*—Whenever any patent is, through error, deemed wholly or partly inoperative or invalid, by reason of a defective specification or drawing, or by reason of the patentee claiming more or less than he had a right to claim in the patent, the Director shall, on the surrender of such patent and the payment of the fee required by law, reissue the patent for the invention disclosed in the original patent, and in accordance with a new and amended application, for the unexpired part of the term of the original patent. No new matter shall be introduced into the application for reissue.

(b) *Multiple reissued patents.*—The Director may issue several reissued patents for distinct and separate parts of the thing patented, upon demand of the applicant, and upon payment of the required fee for a reissue for each of such reissued patents.

(c) *Applicability of this title.*—The provisions of this title relating to applications for patent shall be applicable to applications for reissue of a patent, except that application for reissue may be made and sworn to by the assignee of the entire interest if the application does not seek to enlarge the scope of the claims of the original patent or the application for the original patent was filed by the assignee of the entire interest.

(d) *Reissue patent enlarging scope of claims.*—No reissued patent shall be granted enlarging the scope of the claims of the original patent unless applied for within two years from the grant of the original patent.

(July 19, 1952, ch. 950, §1, 66 Stat. 808; Sept. 16, 2011, Pub. L. 112-29, §§118, 20, 125 Stat. 296, 333–34.)

35 U.S.C. § 251

§ 252 Effect of reissue

The surrender of the original patent shall take effect upon the issue of the reissued patent, and every reissued patent shall have the same effect and operation in law, on the trial of actions for causes thereafter arising, as if the same had been originally granted in such amended form, but in so far as the claims of the original and reissued patents are substantially identical, such surrender shall not affect any action then pending nor abate any cause of action then existing, and the reissued patent, to the extent that its claims are substantially identical with the original patent, shall constitute a continuation thereof and have effect continuously from the date of the original patent.

A reissued patent shall not abridge or affect the right of any person or that person's successors in business who, prior to the grant of a reissue, made, purchased, offered to sell, or used within the United States, or imported into the United States, anything patented by the reissued patent, to continue the use of, to offer to sell, or to sell to others to be used, offered for sale, or sold, the specific thing so made, purchased, offered for sale, used, or imported unless the making, using, offering for sale, or selling of such thing infringes a valid claim of the reissued patent which was in the original patent. The court before which such matter is in question may provide for the continued manufacture, use, offer for sale, or sale of the thing made, purchased, offered for sale, used, or imported as specified, or for the manufacture, use, offer for sale, or sale in the United States of which substantial preparation was made before the grant of the reissue, and the court may also provide for the continued practice of any process patented by the reissue that is practiced, or for the practice of which substantial preparation was made, before the grant of the reissue, to the extent and under such terms as the court deems equitable for the protection of investments made or business commenced before the grant of the reissue.

(July 19, 1952, ch. 950, §1, 66 Stat. 808; Dec. 8, 1994, Pub. L. 103-465, §533, 108 Stat. 4988; Nov. 29, 1999, Pub. L. 106-113, §4507, 113 Stat. 1501A-565.)

§ 253 Disclaimer

(a) *In general.* —Whenever a claim of a patent is invalid the remaining claims shall not thereby be rendered invalid. A patentee, whether of the whole or any sectional interest therein, may, on payment of the fee required by law, make disclaimer of any complete claim, stating therein the extent of his interest in such patent. Such disclaimer shall be in writing, and recorded in the Patent and Trademark Office; and it shall thereafter be considered as part of the original patent to the extent of the interest possessed by the disclaimant and by those claiming under him.

(b) *Additional disclaimer or dedication.* — In the manner set forth in subsection (a), any patentee or applicant may disclaim or dedicate to the public the entire term, or any terminal part of the term, of the patent granted or to be granted.

(July 19, 1952, ch. 950, §1, 66 Stat. 809; Jan. 2, 1975, Pub. L. 93-596, §1, 88 Stat. 1949; Sept. 16, 2011, Pub. L. 112-29, §20, 125 Stat. 334.)

§ 254   Certificate of correction of Patent and Trademark Office mistake

Whenever a mistake in a patent, incurred through the fault of the Patent and Trademark Office, is clearly disclosed by the records of the Office, the Director may issue a certificate of correction stating the fact and nature of such mistake, under seal, without charge, to be recorded in the records of patents. A printed copy thereof shall be attached to each printed copy of the patent, and such certificate shall be considered as part of the original patent. Every such patent, together with such certificate, shall have the same effect and operation in law on the trial of actions for causes thereafter arising as if the same had been originally issued in such corrected form. The Director may issue a corrected patent without charge in lieu of and with like effect as a certificate of correction.

(July 19, 1952, ch. 950, §1, 66 Stat. 809; Jan. 2, 1975, Pub. L. 93-596, §1, 88 Stat. 1949.)

§ 255   Certificate of correction of applicant's mistake

Whenever a mistake of a clerical or typographical nature, or of minor character, which was not the fault of the Patent and Trademark Office, appears in a patent and a showing has been made that such mistake occurred in good faith, the Director may, upon payment of the required fee, issue a certificate of correction, if the correction does not involve such changes in the patent as would constitute new matter or would require reexamination. Such patent, together with the certificate, shall have the same effect and operation in law on the trial of actions for causes thereafter arising as if the same had been originally issued in such corrected form.

(July 19, 1952, ch. 950, §1, 66 Stat. 809; Jan. 2, 1975, Pub. L. 93-596, §1, 88 Stat. 1949.)

§ 256   Correction of named inventor

(a) *Correction.* — Whenever through error a person is named in an issued patent as the inventor, or through error an inventor is not named in an issued patent, the Director may, on application of all the parties and assignees, with proof of the facts and such other requirements as may be imposed, issue a certificate correcting such error.

(b) *Patent valid if error corrected.*—The error of omitting inventors or naming persons who are not inventors shall not invalidate the patent in which such error occurred if it can be corrected as provided in this section. The court before which such matter is called in question may order correction of the patent on notice and hearing of all parties concerned and the Director shall issue a certificate accordingly.

(July 19, 1952, ch. 950, §1, 66 Stat. 810; Aug. 27, 1982, Pub. L. 97-247, §6, 96 Stat. 320; Sept. 16, 2011, Pub. L. 112-29, §20, 125 Stat. 334.)

§ 257[25] Supplemental examinations to consider, reconsider, or correct information

(a) *Request for supplemental examination.*—A patent owner may request supplemental examination of a patent in the Office to consider, reconsider, or correct information believed to be relevant to the patent, in accordance with such requirements as the Director may establish. Within 3 months after the date a request for supplemental examination meeting the requirements of this section is received, the Director shall conduct the supplemental examination and shall conclude such examination by issuing a certificate indicating whether the information presented in the request raises a substantial new question of patentability.

(b) *Reexamination ordered.*—If the certificate issued under subsection (a) indicates that a substantial new question of patentability is raised by 1 or more items of information in the request, the Director shall order reexamination of the patent. The reexamination shall be conducted according to procedures established by chapter 30, except that the patent owner shall not have the right to file a statement pursuant to section 304. During the reexamination, the Director shall address each substantial new question of patentability identified during the supplemental examination, notwithstanding the limitations in chapter 30 relating to patents and printed publication or any other provision of such chapter.

---

[25] *Ed. Note:* Pursuant to Pub. L. 112-29, a new section 257 took effect Sept. 16, 2012 and applies to any patent issued before, on, or after that date. See text of Pub. L. 112-29 on the CD-ROM that accompanies this edition of the book. A table of effective dates for all changes set forth in Pub. L. 112-29 may also be found on the CD-ROM.

(c) *Effect.*—

(1) *In general.*—A patent shall not be held unenforceable on the basis of conduct relating to information that had not been considered, was inadequately considered, or was incorrect in a prior examination of the patent if the information was considered, reconsidered, or corrected during a supplemental examination of the patent. The making of a request under subsection (a), or the absence thereof, shall not be relevant to enforceability of the patent under section 282.

(2) *Exceptions.*—

(A) *Prior allegations.*—Paragraph (1) shall not apply to an allegation pled with particularity in a civil action, or set forth with particularity in a notice received by the patent owner under section 505(j)(2)(B)(iv)(II) of the Federal Food, Drug, and Cosmetic Act (21 U.S.C. 355(j)(2)(B)(iv)(II)), before the date of a supplemental examination request under subsection (a) to consider, reconsider, or correct information forming the basis for the allegation.

(B) *Patent enforcement actions.*—In an action brought under section 337(a) of the Tariff Act of 1930 (19 U.S.C. 1337(a)), or section 281, paragraph (1) shall not apply to any defense raised in the action that is based upon information that was considered, reconsidered, or corrected pursuant to a supplemental examination request under subsection (a), unless the supplemental examination, and any reexamination ordered pursuant to the request, are concluded before the date on which the action is brought.

(d) *Fees and regulations.*—

(1) *Fees.*—The Director shall, by regulation, establish fees for the submission of a request for supplemental examination of a patent, and to consider each item of information submitted in the request. If reexamination is ordered under subsection (b), fees established and applicable to ex parte reexamination proceedings under chapter 30 shall be paid, in addition to fees applicable to supplemental examination.

(2) *Regulations.*—The Director shall issue regulations governing the form, content, and other requirements of requests for supplemental examination, and establishing procedures for reviewing information submitted in such requests.

35 U.S.C. § 257

(e) *Fraud.*—If the Director becomes aware, during the course of a supplemental examination or reexamination proceeding ordered under this section, that a material fraud on the Office may have been committed in connection with the patent that is the subject of the supplemental examination, then in addition to any other actions the Director is authorized to take, including the cancellation of any claims found to be invalid under section 307 as a result of a reexamination ordered under this section, the Director shall also refer the matter to the Attorney General for such further action as the Attorney General may deem appropriate. Any such referral shall be treated as confidential, shall not be included in the file of the patent, and shall not be disclosed to the public unless the United States charges a person with a criminal offense in connection with such referral.

(f) *Rule of construction.*—Nothing in this section shall be construed—

(1) to preclude the imposition of sanctions based upon criminal or antitrust laws (including section 1001(a) of title 18, the first section of the Clayton Act, and section 5 of the Federal Trade Commission Act to the extent that section relates to unfair methods of competition);

(2) to limit the authority of the Director to investigate issues of possible misconduct and impose sanctions for misconduct in connection with matters or proceedings before the Office; or

(3) to limit the authority of the Director to issue regulations under chapter 3 relating to sanctions for misconduct by representatives practicing before the Office.

(Sept. 16, 2011, Pub. L. 112-29, §12, 125 Stat. 325.)

CHAPTER 26—OWNERSHIP AND ASSIGNMENT

SEC.
261. Ownership; assignment.
262. Joint owners.

§ 261 Ownership; assignment

Subject to the provisions of this title, patents shall have the attributes of personal property. The Patent and Trademark Office shall maintain a register of interests in patents and applications for patents and shall record any document related thereto upon request, and may require a fee therefor.

Applications for patent, patents, or any interest therein, shall be assignable in law by an instrument in writing. The applicant, patentee, or his assigns or legal representatives may in like manner grant and convey an exclusive right under his application for patent, or patents, to the whole or any specified part of the United States.

A certificate of acknowledgment under the hand and official seal of a person authorized to administer oaths within the United States, or, in a foreign country, of a diplomatic or consular officer of the United States or an officer authorized to administer oaths whose authority is proved by a certificate of a diplomatic or consular officer of the United States, or apostille of an official designated by a foreign country which, by treaty or convention, accords like effect to apostilles of designated officials in the United States, shall be prima facie evidence of the execution of an assignment, grant or conveyance of a patent or application for patent.

An interest that constitutes an assignment, grant or conveyance shall be void as against any subsequent purchaser or mortgagee for a valuable consideration, without notice, unless it is recorded in the Patent and Trademark Office within three months from its date or prior to the date of such subsequent purchase or mortgage.

(July 19, 1952, ch. 950, §1, 66 Stat. 810; Jan. 2, 1975, Pub. L. 93-596, §1, 88 Stat. 1949; Aug. 27, 1982, Pub. L. 97-247, §14, 96 Stat. 321; Dec. 18, 2012, Pub. L. 112-211, §201, 126 Stat. 1535.)

§ 262　Joint owners

In the absence of any agreement to the contrary, each of the joint owners of a patent may make, use, offer to sell, or sell the patented invention within the United States, or import the patented invention into the United States without the consent of and without accounting to the other owners.

(July 19, 1952, ch. 950, §1, 66 Stat. 810; Dec. 8, 1994, Pub. L. 103-465, §533, 108 Stat. 4988.)

CHAPTER 27—GOVERNMENT INTERESTS IN PATENTS

SEC.
266. [Repealed.]
267. Time for taking action in Government applications.

§ 266　[Repealed]

(July 24, 1965, Pub. L. 89-83, §8, 79 Stat. 261.)

35 U.S.C. § 262

§ 267 Time for taking action in Government applications

Notwithstanding the provisions of sections 133 and 151, the Director may extend the time for taking any action to three years, when an application has become the property of the United States and the head of the appropriate department or agency of the Government has certified to the Director that the invention disclosed therein is important to the armament or defense of the United States.

(July 19, 1952, ch. 950, §1, 66 Stat. 811.)

CHAPTER 28 — INFRINGEMENT OF PATENTS

Sec.
271. Infringement of patent.
272. Temporary presence in the United States.
273. Defense to infringement based on prior commercial use [amended].
273. Defense to infringement based on earlier inventor [original].

§ 271 Infringement of patent

(a) Except as otherwise provided in this title, whoever without authority makes, uses, offers to sell, or sells any patented invention, within the United States or imports into the United States any patented invention during the term of the patent therefor, infringes the patent.

(b) Whoever actively induces infringement of a patent shall be liable as an infringer.

(c) Whoever offers to sell or sells within the United States or imports into the United States a component of a patented machine, manufacture, combination or composition, or a material or apparatus for use in practicing a patented process, constituting a material part of the invention, knowing the same to be especially made or especially adapted for use in an infringement of such patent, and not a staple article or commodity of commerce suitable for substantial noninfringing use, shall be liable as a contributory infringer.

(d) No patent owner otherwise entitled to relief for infringement or contributory infringement of a patent shall be denied relief or deemed guilty of misuse or illegal extension of the patent right by reason of his having done one or more of the following: (1) derived revenue from acts which if performed by another without his consent would constitute contributory infringement of the patent; (2) licensed or authorized another to perform acts

35 U.S.C. § 271

which if performed without his consent would constitute contributory infringement of the patent; (3) sought to enforce his patent rights against infringement or contributory infringement; (4) refused to license or use any rights to the patent; or (5) conditioned the license of any rights to the patent or the sale of the patented product on the acquisition of a license to rights in another patent or purchase of a separate product, unless, in view of the circumstances, the patent owner has market power in the relevant market for the patent or patented product on which the license or sale is conditioned.

(e) (1) It shall not be an act of infringement to make, use, offer to sell, or sell within the United States or import into the United States a patented invention (other than a new animal drug or veterinary biological product (as those terms are used in the Federal Food, Drug, and Cosmetic Act and the Act of March 4, 1913) which is primarily manufactured using recombinant DNA, recombinant RNA, hybridoma technology, or other processes involving site specific genetic manipulation techniques) solely for uses reasonably related to the development and submission of information under a Federal law which regulates the manufacture, use, or sale of drugs or veterinary biological products.

(2) It shall be an act of infringement to submit—

(A) an application under section 505(j) of the Federal Food, Drug, and Cosmetic Act or described in section 505(b)(2) of such Act for a drug claimed in a patent or the use of which is claimed in a patent,

(B) an application under section 512 of such Act or under the Act of March 4, 1913 (21 U.S.C. 151-158) for a drug or veterinary biological product which is not primarily manufactured using recombinant DNA, recombinant RNA, hybridoma technology, or other processes involving site specific genetic manipulation techniques and which is claimed in a patent or the use of which is claimed in a patent, or

(C) (i) with respect to a patent that is identified in the list of patents described in section 351(l)(3) of the Public Health Service Act (including as provided under section 351(l)(7) of such Act), an application seeking approval of a biological product, or

(ii) if the applicant for the application fails to provide the application and information required under section 351(l)(2)(A) of such Act, an application seeking approval of a biological product for a patent that could be identified pursuant to section 351(l)(3)(A)(i) of such Act,

if the purpose of such submission is to obtain approval under such Act to engage in the commercial manufacture, use, or sale of a drug, veterinary biological product, or biological product claimed in a patent or the use of which is claimed in a patent before the expiration of such patent.

(3) In any action for patent infringement brought under this section, no injunctive or other relief may be granted which would prohibit the making, using, offering to sell, or selling within the United States or importing into the United States of a patented invention under paragraph (1).

(4) For an act of infringement described in paragraph (2) —

(A) the court shall order the effective date of any approval of the drug or veterinary biological product involved in the infringement to be a date which is not earlier than the date of the expiration of the patent which has been infringed,

(B) injunctive relief may be granted against an infringer to prevent the commercial manufacture, use, offer to sell, or sale within the United States or importation into the United States of an approved drug, veterinary biological product, or biological product

(C) damages or other monetary relief may be awarded against an infringer only if there has been commercial manufacture, use, offer to sell, or sale within the United States or importation into the United States of an approved drug, veterinary biological product, or biological product, and

(D) the court shall order a permanent injunction prohibiting any infringement of the patent by the biological product involved in the infringement until a date which is not earlier than the date of the expiration of the patent that has been infringed under paragraph (2)(C), provided the patent is the subject of a final court decision, as defined in section 351(k)(6) of the Public Health Service Act, in an action for infringement of the patent under section 351(l)(6) of such Act, and the biological product has not yet been approved because of section 351(k)(7) of such Act.

The remedies prescribed by subparagraphs (A), (B), (C), and (D) are the only remedies which may be granted by a court for an act of infringement

35 U.S.C. § 271

described in paragraph (2), except that a court may award attorney fees under section 285.

(5) Where a person has filed an application described in paragraph (2) that includes a certification under subsection (b)(2)(A)(iv) or (j)(2)(A)(vii)(IV) of section 505 of the Federal Food, Drug, and Cosmetic Act (21 U.S.C. 355), and neither the owner of the patent that is the subject of the certification nor the holder of the approved application under subsection (b) of such section for the drug that is claimed by the patent or a use of which is claimed by the patent brought an action for infringement of such patent before the expiration of 45 days after the date on which the notice given under subsection (b)(3) or (j)(2)(B) of such section was received, the courts of the United States shall, to the extent consistent with the Constitution, have subject matter jurisdiction in any action brought by such person under section 2201 of title 28 for a declaratory judgment that such patent is invalid or not infringed.

(6) (A) Subparagraph (B) applies, in lieu of paragraph (4), in the case of a patent—

(i) that is identified, as applicable, in the list of patents described in section 351(l)(4) of the Public Health Service Act or the lists of patents described in section 351(l)(5)(B) of such Act with respect to a biological product; and

(ii) for which an action for infringement of the patent with respect to the biological product—

(I) was brought after the expiration of the 30-day period described in subparagraph (A) or (B), as applicable, of section 351(l)(6) of such Act; or

(II) was brought before the expiration of the 30-day period described in subclause (I), but which was dismissed without prejudice or was not prosecuted to judgment in good faith.

(B) In an action for infringement of a patent described in subparagraph (A), the sole and exclusive remedy that may be granted by a court, upon a finding that the making, using, offering to sell, selling, or importation into the United States of the biological product that is the subject of the action infringed the patent, shall be a reasonable royalty.

(C) The owner of a patent that should have been included in the list described in section 351(l)(3)(A) of the Public Health Service Act, including as provided under section 351(l)(7) of such Act for a biological product, but was not timely included in such list, may not bring an action under this section for infringement of the patent with respect to the biological product.

(f) (1) Whoever without authority supplies or causes to be supplied in or from the United States all or a substantial portion of the components of a patented invention, where such components are uncombined in whole or in part, in such manner as to actively induce the combination of such components outside of the United States in a manner that would infringe the patent if such combination occurred within the United States, shall be liable as an infringer.

(2) Whoever without authority supplies or causes to be supplied in or from the United States any component of a patented invention that is especially made or especially adapted for use in the invention and not a staple article or commodity of commerce suitable for substantial noninfringing use, where such component is uncombined in whole or in part, knowing that such component is so made or adapted and intending that such component will be combined outside of the United States in a manner that would infringe the patent if such combination occurred within the United States, shall be liable as an infringer.

(g) Whoever without authority imports into the United States or offers to sell, sells, or uses within the United States a product which is made by a process patented in the United States shall be liable as an infringer, if the importation, offer to sell, sale, or use of the product occurs during the term of such process patent. In an action for infringement of a process patent, no remedy may be granted for infringement on account of the noncommercial use or retail sale of a product unless there is no adequate remedy under this title for infringement on account of the importation or other use, offer to sell, or sale of that product. A product which is made by a patented process will, for purposes of this title, not be considered to be so made after—

(1) it is materially changed by subsequent processes; or

(2) it becomes a trivial and nonessential component of another product.

(h) As used in this section, the term "whoever" includes any State, any instrumentality of a State, and any officer or employee of a State or instru-

35 U.S.C. § 271

mentality of a State acting in his official capacity. Any State, and any such instrumentality, officer, or employee, shall be subject to the provisions of this title in the same manner and to the same extent as any nongovernmental entity.

(i) As used in this section, an "offer for sale" or an "offer to sell" by a person other than the patentee, or any designee of the patentee, is that in which the sale will occur before the expiration of the term of the patent.

(July 19, 1952, ch. 950, §1, 66 Stat. 811; Sept. 24, 1984, Pub. L. 98-417, §202, 98 Stat. 1603; Nov. 8, 1984, Pub. L. 98-622, §101, 98 Stat. 3383; Aug. 23, 1988, Pub. L. 100-418, §9003, 102 Stat. 1563–64; Nov. 16, 1988, Pub. L. 100-670, §201, 102 Stat. 3988-3989; Nov. 19, 1988, Pub. L. 100-703, §201, 102 Stat. 4676; Oct. 28, 1992, Pub. L. 102-560, §2, 106 Stat. 4230; Dec. 8, 1994, Pub. L. 103-465, §533, 108 Stat. 4988; Dec. 8, 2003, Pub. L. 108-173, §1101(d), 117 Stat. 2457; Mar 23, 2010, Pub. L. 111-148, Title VII, Subtitle A §7002, 124 Stat. 815.)

§ 272 Temporary presence in the United States

The use of any invention in any vessel, aircraft or vehicle of any country which affords similar privileges to vessels, aircraft or vehicles of the United States, entering the United States temporarily or accidentally, shall not constitute infringement of any patent, if the invention is used exclusively for the needs of the vessel, aircraft or vehicle and is not offered for sale or sold in or used for the manufacture of anything to be sold in or exported from the United States.

(July 19, 1952, ch. 950, §1, 66 Stat. 812; Dec. 8, 1994, Pub. L. 103-465, §533, 108 Stat. 4989.)

§ 273 [amended]²⁶ Defense to infringement based on prior commercial use

(a) *In general.*—A person shall be entitled to a defense under section 282(b) with respect to subject matter consisting of a process, or consisting of a machine, manufacture, or composition of matter used in a manufacturing or other commercial process, that would otherwise infringe a claimed invention being asserted against the person if—

(1) such person, acting in good faith, commercially used the subject matter in the United States, either in connection with an internal commercial use or an actual arm's length sale or other arm's length commercial transfer of a useful end result of such commercial use; and

---

²⁶ *Ed. Note:* This section applies to any patent issued on or after the date of enactment of Pub. L. 112-29 (Sept. 16, 2011). See §5(c) of Pub. L. 112-29.

(2) such commercial use occurred at least 1 year before the earlier of either—

(A) the effective filing date of the claimed invention; or

(B) the date on which the claimed invention was disclosed to the public in a manner that qualified for the exception from prior art under section 102(b).

(b) *Burden of proof.*—A person asserting a defense under this section shall have the burden of establishing the defense by clear and convincing evidence.

(c) *Additional commercial uses.* —

(1) *Premarketing regulatory review.*—Subject matter for which commercial marketing or use is subject to a premarketing regulatory review period during which the safety or efficacy of the subject matter is established, including any period specified in section 156(g), shall be deemed to be commercially used for purposes of subsection (a)(1) during such regulatory review period.

(2) *Nonprofit laboratory use.*—A use of subject matter by a nonprofit research laboratory or other nonprofit entity, such as a university or hospital, for which the public is the intended beneficiary, shall be deemed to be a commercial use for purposes of subsection (a)(1), except that a defense under this section may be asserted pursuant to this paragraph only for continued and noncommercial use by and in the laboratory or other nonprofit entity.

(d) *Exhaustion of rights.*—Notwithstanding subsection (e)(1), the sale or other disposition of a useful end result by a person entitled to assert a defense under this section in connection with a patent with respect to that useful end result shall exhaust the patent owner's rights under the patent to the extent that such rights would have been exhausted had such sale or other disposition been made by the patent owner.

(e) *Limitations and exceptions.* —

(1) *Personal defense.*—

(A) *In general.*—A defense under this section may be asserted only by the person who performed or directed the performance of the commercial use described in subsection (a), or by an entity that controls, is controlled by, or is under common control with such person.

35 U.S.C. § 273 [amended]

(B) *Transfer of right.*—Except for any transfer to the patent owner, the right to assert a defense under this section shall not be licensed or assigned or transferred to another person except as an ancillary and subordinate part of a good-faith assignment or transfer for other reasons of the entire enterprise or line of business to which the defense relates.

(C) *Restriction on sites.*—A defense under this section, when acquired by a person as part of an assignment or transfer described in subparagraph (B), may only be asserted for uses at sites where the subject matter that would otherwise infringe a claimed invention is in use before the later of the effective filing date of the claimed invention or the date of the assignment or transfer of such enterprise or line of business.

(2) *Derivation.*—A person may not assert a defense under this section if the subject matter on which the defense is based was derived from the patentee or persons in privity with the patentee.

(3) *Not a general license.*—The defense asserted by a person under his section is not a general license under all claims of the patent at issue, but extends only to the specific subject matter for which it has been established that a commercial use that qualifies under this section occurred, except that the defense shall also extend to variations in the quantity or volume of use of the claimed subject matter, and to improvements in the claimed subject matter that do not infringe additional specifically claimed subject matter of the patent.

(4) *Abandonment of use.*—A person who has abandoned commercial use (that qualifies under this section) of subject matter may not rely on activities performed before the date of such abandonment in establishing a defense under this section with respect to actions taken on or after the date of such abandonment.

(5) *University exception.*—

(A) *In general.*—A person commercially using subject matter to which subsection (a) applies may not assert a defense under this section if the claimed invention with respect to which the defense is asserted was, at the time the invention was made, owned or subject to an obligation of assignment to either an institution of higher education (as defined in section 101(a) of the Higher Education Act of 1965 (20 U.S.C. 1001(a)), or a technology transfer organization whose primary purpose is to facilitate the commercialization of technologies developed by one or more such institutions of higher education.

(B) *Exception.*—Subparagraph (A) shall not apply if any of the activities required to reduce to practice the subject matter of the claimed invention could not have been undertaken using funds provided by the Federal Government.

(f) *Unreasonable assertion of defense.*—If the defense under this section is pleaded by a person who is found to infringe the patent and who subsequently fails to demonstrate a reasonable basis for asserting the defense, the court shall find the case exceptional for the purpose of awarding attorney fees under section 285.

(g) *Invalidity.*—A patent shall not be deemed to be invalid under section 102 or 103 solely because a defense is raised or established under this section.

(Nov. 29, 1999, Pub. L. 106-113, §4302, 113 Stat. 1501A-555; Sept. 16, 2011, Pub. L. 112-29, §5, 125 Stat. 297.)

[§ 273 [original]][27]   Defense to infringement based on earlier inventor

(a) *Definitions.*—For purposes of this section—

(1) the terms "commercially used" and "commercial use" mean use of a method in the United States, so long as such use is in connection with an internal commercial use or an actual arm's-length sale or other arm's-length commercial transfer of a useful end result, whether or not the subject matter at issue is accessible to or otherwise known to the public, except that the subject matter for which commercial marketing or use is subject to a premarketing regulatory review period during which the safety or efficacy of the subject matter is established, including any period specified in section 156(g), shall be deemed "commercially used" and in "commercial use" during such regulatory review period;

(2) in the case of activities performed by a nonprofit research laboratory, or nonprofit entity such as a university, research center, or hospital, a use for which the public is the intended beneficiary shall be considered to be a use described in paragraph (1), except that the use—

(A) may be asserted as a defense under this section only for continued use by and in the laboratory or nonprofit entity; and

---

[27] *Ed. Note:* Amended section 273 above applies to any patent issued on or after the date of enactment of Pub. L. 112-29 (Sept. 16, 2011). See §5(c) of Pub. L. 112-29.

35 U.S.C. § 273 [original]

(B) may not be asserted as a defense with respect to any subsequent commercialization or use outside such laboratory or nonprofit entity;

(3) the term "method" means a method of doing or conducting business; and

(4) the "effective filing date" of a patent is the earlier of the actual filing date of the application for the patent or the filing date of any earlier United States, foreign, or international application to which the subject matter at issue is entitled under section 119, 120, or 365.

(b) *Defense to infringement.—*

(1) *In general.—*It shall be a defense to an action for infringement under section 271 with respect to any subject matter that would otherwise infringe one or more claims for a method in the patent being asserted against a person, if such person had, acting in good faith, actually reduced the subject matter to practice at least 1 year before the effective filing date of such patent, and commercially used the subject matter before the effective filing date of such patent.

(2) *Exhaustion of right.—*The sale or other disposition of a useful end product produced by a patented method, by a person entitled to assert a defense under this section with respect to that useful end result shall exhaust the patent owner's rights under the patent to the extent such rights would have been exhausted had such sale or other disposition been made by the patent owner.

(3) *Limitations and qualifications of defense.—*The defense to infringement under this section is subject to the following:

(A) *Patent.—*A person may not assert the defense under this section unless the invention for which the defense is asserted is for a method.

(B) *Derivation.—*A person may not assert the defense under this section if the subject matter on which the defense is based was derived from the patentee or persons in privity with the patentee.

(C) *Not a general license.—*The defense asserted by a person under this section is not a general license under all claims of the patent at issue, but extends only to the specific subject matter claimed in the patent with respect to which the person can assert a defense under this chapter, except that the defense shall also extend to variations in the quantity or volume of use of the claimed subject matter, and to improvements in the claimed subject matter that do not infringe additional specifically claimed subject matter of the patent.

(4) *Burden of proof.*—A person asserting the defense under this section shall have the burden of establishing the defense by clear and convincing evidence.

(5) *Abandonment of use.*—A person who has abandoned commercial use of subject matter may not rely on activities performed before the date of such abandonment in establishing a defense under this section with respect to actions taken after the date of such abandonment.

(6) *Personal defense.*—The defense under this section may be asserted only by the person who performed the acts necessary to establish the defense and, except for any transfer to the patent owner, the right to assert the defense shall not be licensed or assigned or transferred to another person except as an ancillary and subordinate part of a good faith assignment or transfer for other reasons of the entire enterprise or line of business to which the defense relates.

(7) *Limitation on sites.*—A defense under this section, when acquired as part of a good faith assignment or transfer of an entire enterprise or line of business to which the defense relates, may only be asserted for uses at sites where the subject matter that would otherwise infringe one or more of the claims is in use before the later of the effective filing date of the patent or the date of the assignment or transfer of such enterprise or line of business.

(8) *Unsuccessful assertion of defense.*—If the defense under this section is pleaded by a person who is found to infringe the patent and who subsequently fails to demonstrate a reasonable basis for asserting the defense, the court shall find the case exceptional for the purpose of awarding attorney fees under section 285.

(9) *Invalidity.*—A patent shall not be deemed to be invalid under section 102 or 103 solely because a defense is raised or established under this section.

(Nov. 29, 1999, Pub. L. 106-113, §4302, 113 Stat. 1501A-555).]

CHAPTER 29—REMEDIES FOR INFRINGEMENT OF PATENT, AND OTHER ACTIONS

SEC.
281.   Remedy for infringement of patent.

35 U.S.C. § 273 [original]

§ 281   Remedy for infringement of patent

A patentee shall have remedy by civil action for infringement of his patent.

(July 19, 1952, ch. 950, §1, 66 Stat. 812.)

§ 282   Presumption of validity; defenses

(a) *In general.*—A patent shall be presumed valid. Each claim of a patent (whether in independent, dependent, or multiple dependent form) shall be presumed valid independently of the validity of other claims; dependent or multiple dependent claims shall be presumed valid even though dependent upon an invalid claim. The burden of establishing invalidity of a patent or any claim thereof shall rest on the party asserting such invalidity.

(b) *Defenses.*—The following shall be defenses in any action involving the validity or infringement of a patent and shall be pleaded:

(1) Noninfringement, absence of liability for infringement or unenforceability.

(2) Invalidity of the patent or any claim in suit on any ground specified in part II as a condition for patentability.

(3) Invalidity of the patent or any claim in suit for failure to comply with—

(A) any requirement of section 112, except that the failure to disclose the best mode shall not be a basis on which any claim of a patent may be canceled or held invalid or otherwise unenforceable; or

(B) any requirement of section 251.

(4) Any other fact or act made a defense by this title.

(c) *Notice of actions; actions during extension of patent term.*—In an action involving the validity or infringement of a patent the party asserting invalidity or noninfringement shall give notice in the pleadings or otherwise in writing to the adverse party at least thirty days before the trial, of the country, number, date, and name of the patentee of any patent, the title, date, and page numbers of any publication to be relied upon as anticipation of the patent in suit or, except in actions in the United States Court of Federal Claims, as showing the state of the art, and the name and address of any person who may be relied upon as the prior inventor or as having prior knowledge of or as having previously used or offered for sale the invention of the patent in suit. In the absence of such notice proof of the said matters may not be made at the trial except on such terms as the court requires. Invalidity of the extension of a patent term or any portion thereof under section 154(b) or 156 because of the material failure—

(1) by the applicant for the extension, or

(2) by the Director,

to comply with the requirements of such section shall be a defense in any action involving the infringement of a patent during the period of the extension of its term and shall be pleaded. A due diligence determination under section 156(d)(2) is not subject to review in such an action.

(July 19, 1952, ch. 950, §1, 66 Stat. 812; July 24, 1965, Pub. L. 89-83, §10, 79 Stat. 261; Nov. 14, 1975, Pub. L. 94-131, §10, 89 Stat. 692; Apr. 2, 1982, Pub. L. 97-164, §161, 96 Stat. 49; Sept. 24, 1984, Pub. L. 98-417, §203, 98 Stat. 1603; Nov. 1, 1995, Pub. L. 104-41, §2, 109 Stat. 352; Nov. 29, 1999, Pub. L. 106-113, §4402, 113 Stat. 1501A-557; Sept. 16, 2011, Pub. L. 112-29, §§15, 20, 125 Stat. 328, 334.)

§ 283　Injunction

The several courts having jurisdiction of cases under this title may grant injunctions in accordance with the principles of equity to prevent the violation of any right secured by patent, on such terms as the court deems reasonable.

(July 19, 1952, ch. 950, §1, 66 Stat. 812.)

§ 284   Damages

Upon finding for the claimant the court shall award the claimant damages adequate to compensate for the infringement, but in no event less than a reasonable royalty for the use made of the invention by the infringer, together with interest and costs as fixed by the court.

When the damages are not found by a jury, the court shall assess them. In either event the court may increase the damages up to three times the amount found or assessed. Increased damages under this paragraph shall not apply to provisional rights under section 154(d).

The court may receive expert testimony as an aid to the determination of damages or of what royalty would be reasonable under the circumstances.

(July 19, 1952, ch. 950, §1, 66 Stat. 813; Nov. 29, 1999, Pub. L. 106-113, §4507, 113 Stat. 1501A-565.)

§ 285   Attorney fees

The court in exceptional cases may award reasonable attorney fees to the prevailing party.

(July 19, 1952, ch. 950, §1, 66 Stat. 813.)

§ 286   Time limitation on damages

Except as otherwise provided by law, no recovery shall be had for any infringement committed more than six years prior to the filing of the complaint or counterclaim for infringement in the action.

In the case of claims against the United States Government for use of a patented invention, the period before bringing suit, up to six years, between the date of receipt of a written claim for compensation by the department or agency of the Government having authority to settle such claim, and the date of mailing by the Government of a notice to the claimant that his claim has been denied shall not be counted as part of the period referred to in the preceding paragraph.

(July 19, 1952, ch. 950, §1, 66 Stat. 813.)

§ 287[28] Limitation on damages and other remedies; marking and notice

(a) Patentees, and persons making, offering for sale, or selling within the United States any patented article for or under them or importing any patented article into the United States, may give notice to the public that the same is patented, either by fixing thereon the word "patent" or the abbreviation "pat.", together with the number of the patent, *or by fixing thereon the word "patent" or the abbreviation "pat." together with an address of a posting on the Internet, accessible to the public without charge for accessing the address, that associates the patented article with the number of the patent, or when,* from the character of the article, this can not be done, by fixing to it, or to the package wherein one or more of them is contained, a label containing a like notice. In the event of failure so to mark, no damages shall be recovered by the patentee in any action for infringement, except on proof that the infringer was notified of the infringement and continued to infringe thereafter, in which event damages may be recovered only for infringement occurring after such notice. Filing of an action for infringement shall constitute such notice.

(b) (1) An infringer under section 271(g) shall be subject to all the provisions of this title relating to damages and injunctions except to the extent those remedies are modified by this subsection or section 9006 of the Process Patent Amendments Act of 1988. The modifications of remedies provided in this subsection shall not be available to any person who—

  (A) practiced the patented process;

  (B) owns or controls, or is owned or controlled by, the person who practiced the patented process; or

  (C) had knowledge before the infringement that a patented process was used to make the product the importation, use, offer for sale, or sale of which constitutes the infringement.

(2) No remedies for infringement under section 271(g) shall be available with respect to any product in the possession of, or in transit to, the person subject to liability under such section before that person had notice of infringement with respect to that product. The person subject to liability shall bear the burden of proving any such possession or transit.

---

[28] *Ed. Note:* Pursuant to Pub. L. 112-29, the italicized language in subsection (a) applies to any case that is pending on, or commenced on or after Sept. 16, 2011, the date of enactment of Pub. L. 112-29. See §16(a)(2) of Pub. L. 112-29.

(3) (A) In making a determination with respect to the remedy in an action brought for infringement under section 271(g), the court shall consider—

> (i) the good faith demonstrated by the defendant with respect to a request for disclosure,
>
> (ii) the good faith demonstrated by the plaintiff with respect to a request for disclosure, and
>
> (iii) the need to restore the exclusive rights secured by the patent.

(B) For purposes of subparagraph (A), the following are evidence of good faith:

> (i) a request for disclosure made by the defendant;
>
> (ii) a response within a reasonable time by the person receiving the request for disclosure; and
>
> (iii) the submission of the response by the defendant to the manufacturer, or if the manufacturer is not known, to the supplier, of the product to be purchased by the defendant, together with a request for a written statement that the process claimed in any patent disclosed in the response is not used to produce such product.

The failure to perform any acts described in the preceding sentence is evidence of absence of good faith unless there are mitigating circumstances. Mitigating circumstances include the case in which, due to the nature of the product, the number of sources for the product, or like commercial circumstances, a request for disclosure is not necessary or practicable to avoid infringement.

(4) (A) For purposes of this subsection, a "request for disclosure" means a written request made to a person then engaged in the manufacture of a product to identify all process patents owned by or licensed to that person, as of the time of the request, that the person then reasonably believes could be asserted to be infringed under section 271(g) if that product were imported into, or sold, offered for sale, or used in, the United States by an unauthorized person. A request for disclosure is further limited to a request—

> (i) which is made by a person regularly engaged in the United States in the sale of the same type of products as those manufac-

tured by the person to whom the request is directed, or which includes facts showing that the person making the request plans to engage in the sale of such products in the United States;

(ii) which is made by such person before the person's first importation, use, offer for sale, or sale of units of the product produced by an infringing process and before the person had notice of infringement with respect to the product; and

(iii) which includes a representation by the person making the request that such person will promptly submit the patents identified pursuant to the request to the manufacturer, or if the manufacturer is not known, to the supplier, of the product to be purchased by the person making the request, and will request from that manufacturer or supplier a written statement that none of the processes claimed in those patents is used in the manufacture of the product.

(B) In the case of a request for disclosure received by a person to whom a patent is licensed, that person shall either identify the patent or promptly notify the licensor of the request for disclosure.

(C) A person who has marked, in the manner prescribed by subsection (a), the number of the process patent on all products made by the patented process which have been offered for sale or sold by that person in the United States, or imported by the person into the United States, before a request for disclosure is received is not required to respond to the request for disclosure. For purposes of the preceding sentence, the term "all products" does not include products made before the effective date of the Process Patent Amendments Act of 1988.

(5) (A) For purposes of this subsection, notice of infringement means actual knowledge, or receipt by a person of a written notification, or a combination thereof, of information sufficient to persuade a reasonable person that it is likely that a product was made by a process patented in the United States.

(B) A written notification from the patent holder charging a person with infringement shall specify the patented process alleged to have been used and the reasons for a good faith belief that such process was used. The patent holder shall include in the notification such information as is reasonably necessary to explain fairly the patent holder's belief, except that the patent holder is not required to disclose any trade secret information.

(C) A person who receives a written notification described in subparagraph (B) or a written response to a request for disclosure described in paragraph (4) shall be deemed to have notice of infringement with respect to any patent referred to in such written notification or response unless that person, absent mitigating circumstances—

(i) promptly transmits the written notification or response to the manufacturer or, if the manufacturer is not known, to the supplier, of the product purchased or to be purchased by that person; and

(ii) receives a written statement from the manufacturer or supplier which on its face sets forth a well grounded factual basis for a belief that the identified patents are not infringed.

(D) For purposes of this subsection, a person who obtains a product made by a process patented in the United States in a quantity which is abnormally large in relation to the volume of business of such person or an efficient inventory level shall be rebuttably presumed to have actual knowledge that the product was made by such patented process.

(6) A person who receives a response to a request for disclosure under this subsection shall pay to the person to whom the request was made a reasonable fee to cover actual costs incurred in complying with the request, which may not exceed the cost of a commercially available automated patent search of the matter involved, but in no case more than $500.

(c) (1) With respect to a medical practitioner's performance, of a medical activity that constitutes an infringement under section 271 (a) or (b), the provisions of sections 281, 283, 284, and 285 shall not apply against the medical practitioner or against a related health care entity with respect to such medical activity.

(2) For the purposes of this subsection:

(A) the term "medical activity" means the performance of a medical or surgical procedure on a body, but shall not include (i) the use of a patented machine, manufacture, or composition of matter in violation of such patent, (ii) the practice of a patented use of a composition of matter in violation of such patent, or (iii) the practice of a process in violation of a biotechnology patent.

35 U.S.C. § 287

(B) the term "medical practitioner" means any natural person who is licensed by a State to provide the medical activity described in subsection (c)(1) or who is acting under the direction of such person in the performance of the medical activity.

(C) the term "related health care entity" shall mean an entity with which a medical practitioner has a professional affiliation under which the medical practitioner performs the medical activity, including but not limited to nursing home, hospital, university, medical school, health maintenance organization, group medical practice, or a medical clinic.

(D) the term "professional affiliation" shall mean staff privileges, medical staff membership, employment or contractual relationship, partnership or ownership interest, academic appointment, or other affiliation under which a medical practitioner provides the medical activity on behalf of, or in association with, the health care entity.

(E) the term "body" shall mean a human body, organ or cadaver, or a nonhuman animal used in medical research or instruction directly relating to the treatment of humans.

(F) the term "patented use of a composition of matter" does not include a claim for a method of performing a medical or surgical procedure on a body that recites the use of a composition of matter where the use of that composition of matter does not directly contribute to achievement of the objective of the claimed method.

(G) the term "State" shall mean any State or territory of the United States, the District of Columbia, and the Commonwealth of Puerto Rico.

(3) This subsection does not apply to the activities of any person, or employee or agent of such person (regardless of whether such person is a tax exempt organization under section 501(c) of the Internal Revenue Code), who is engaged in the commercial development, manufacture, sale, importation, or distribution of a machine, manufacture, or composition of matter or the provision of pharmacy or clinical laboratory services (other than clinical laboratory services provided in a physician's office), where such activities are:

(A) directly related to the commercial development, manufacture, sale, importation, or distribution of a machine, manufacture, or composition of matter or the provision of pharmacy or clinical laboratory services (other than clinical laboratory services provided in a physician's office), and

(B) regulated under the Federal Food, Drug, and Cosmetic Act, the Public Health Service Act, or the Clinical Laboratories Improvement Act.

(4) This subsection shall not apply to any patent issued based on an application which has an effective filing date before September 30, 1996.

(July 19, 1952, ch. 950, §1, 66 Stat. 813; Aug. 23, 1988, Pub. L. 100-418, §9004, 102 Stat. 1564-66; Dec. 8, 1994, Pub. L. 103-465, §533, 108 Stat. 4988; Sept. 30, 1996, Pub. L. 104-208, §616, 110 Stat. 3009-67; Nov. 29, 1999, Pub. L. 106-113, §4803, 113 Stat. 1501A-589; Sept. 16, 2011, Pub. L. 112-29, §§ 3, 16(a), 20, 125 Stat. 288, 328, 335.)

§ 288   Action for infringement of a patent containing an invalid claim

Whenever a claim of a patent is invalid, an action may be maintained for the infringement of a claim of the patent which may be valid. The patentee shall recover no costs unless a disclaimer of the invalid claim has been entered at the Patent and Trademark Office before the commencement of the suit.

(July 19, 1952, ch. 950, §1, 66 Stat. 813; Jan. 2, 1975, Pub. L. 93-596, §1, 88 Stat. 1949; Sept. 16, 2011, Pub. L. 112-29, §20, 125 Stat. 334.)

§ 289   Additional remedy for infringement of design patent

Whoever during the term of a patent for a design, without license of the owner, (1) applies the patented design, or any colorable imitation thereof, to any article of manufacture for the purpose of sale, or (2) sells or exposes for sale any article of manufacture to which such design or colorable imitation has been applied shall be liable to the owner to the extent of his total profit, but not less than $250, recoverable in any United States district court having jurisdiction of the parties.

Nothing in this section shall prevent, lessen, or impeach any other remedy which an owner of an infringed patent has under the provisions of this title, but he shall not twice recover the profit made from the infringement.

(July 19, 1952, ch. 950, §1, 66 Stat. 813.)

§ 290   Notice of patent suits

The clerks of the courts of the United States, within one month after the filing of an action under this title shall give notice thereof in writing to the Director, setting forth so far as known the names and addresses of the parties, name of the inventor, and the designated number of the patent upon which the action has been brought. If any other patent is subsequently included in the action he shall give like notice thereof. Within one month after the decision is rendered or a judgment issued the clerk of the court shall give notice thereof to the Director. The Director shall, on receipt of such notices, enter the same in the file of such patent.

(July 19, 1952, ch. 950, §1, 66 Stat. 814.)

§ 291[29] Derived patents

(a) *In general.*—The owner of a patent may have relief by civil action against the owner of another patent that claims the same invention and has an earlier effective filing date, if the invention claimed in such other patent was derived from the inventor of the invention claimed in the patent owned by the person seeking relief under this section.

(b) *Filing limitation.*—An action under this section may be filed only before the end of the 1-year period beginning on the date of the issuance of the first patent containing a claim to the allegedly derived invention and naming an individual alleged to have derived such invention as the inventor or joint inventor.

[§ 291 Interfering patents

The owner of an interfering patent may have relief against the owner of another by civil action, and the court may adjudge the question of the validity of any of the interfering patents, in whole or in part. The provisions of the second paragraph of section 146 shall apply to actions brought under this section.]

(July 19, 1952, ch. 950, §1, 66 Stat. 814; Sept. 16, 2011, Pub. L. 112-29, §3, 125 Stat. 288.)

§ 292 False marking

(a) Whoever, without the consent of the patentee, marks upon, or affixes to, or uses in advertising in connection with anything made, used, offered for sale, or sold by such person within the United States, or imported by the

---

[29] *Ed. Note:* Pursuant to §3(h) of Pub. L. 112-29, effective March 16, 2013, this version of section 291 replaced the prior version of section 291, which appears in the bracketed text immediately below. See text of Pub. L. 112-29 on the CD-ROM that accompanies this edition of the book. A table of effective dates for all changes set forth in Pub. L. 112-29 may also be found on the CD-ROM. The provisions of §291 in effect on the day prior to March 16, 2013 shall apply to each claim of an application for patent, and any patent issued thereon, that contains or contained at any time a claim to an invention that has an effective filing date prior to March 16, 2013, or a specific reference under Section 120, 121, or 365(c) to any patent or application that contains or contained at any time such a claim. *See* Pub. L. 112-29, §3(n)(2), 125 Stat. 293.

person into the United States, the name or any imitation of the name of the patentee, the patent number, or the words "patent," "patentee," or the like, with the intent of counterfeiting or imitating the mark of the patentee, or of deceiving the public and inducing them to believe that the thing was made, offered for sale, sold, or imported into the United States by or with the consent of the patentee; or

Whoever marks upon, or affixes to, or uses in advertising in connection with any unpatented article, the word "patent" or any word or number importing that the same is patented, for the purpose of deceiving the public; or

Whoever marks upon, or affixes to, or uses in advertising in connection with any article, the words "patent applied for," "patent pending," or any word importing that an application for patent has been made, when no application for patent has been made, or if made, is not pending, for the purpose of deceiving the public—

Shall be fined not more than $500 for every such offense. Only the United States may sue for the penalty authorized by this subsection.

(b) A person who has suffered a competitive injury as a result of a violation of this section may file a civil action in a district court of the United States for recovery of damages adequate to compensate for the injury.

(c) The marking of a product, in a manner described in subsection (a), with matter relating to a patent that covered that product but has expired is not a violation of this section.

(July 19, 1952, ch. 950, §1, 66 Stat. 814; Dec. 8, 194, Pub. L. 103-465, §533, 108 Stat. 4988; Sept. 16, 2011, Pub. L. 112-29, §16(b), 125 Stat. 329.)

§ 293   Nonresident patentee; service and notice

Every patentee not residing in the United States may file in the Patent and Trademark Office a written designation stating the name and address of a person residing within the United States on whom may be served process or notice of proceedings affecting the patent or rights thereunder. If the person designated cannot be found at the address given in the last designation, or if no person has been designated, the United States District Court for the Eastern District of Virginia shall have jurisdiction and summons shall be served by publication or otherwise as the court directs. The court shall have the same jurisdiction to take any action respecting the patent or rights thereunder that it would have if the patentee were personally within the jurisdiction of the court.

35 U.S.C. § 293

(July 19, 1952, ch. 950, §1, 66 Stat. 814; Jan. 2, 1975, Pub. L. 93-596, §1, 88 Stat. 1949; Sept. 16, 2011, Pub. L. 112-29, §9, 125 Stat. 316.)

§ 294 Voluntary arbitration

(a) A contract involving a patent or any right under a patent may contain a provision requiring arbitration of any dispute relating to patent validity or infringement arising under the contract. In the absence of such a provision, the parties to an existing patent validity or infringement dispute may agree in writing to settle such dispute by arbitration. Any such provision or agreement shall be valid, irrevocable, and enforceable, except for any grounds that exist at law or in equity for revocation of a contract.

(b) Arbitration of such disputes, awards by arbitrators and confirmation of awards shall be governed by title 9, to the extent such title is not inconsistent with this section. In any such arbitration proceeding, the defenses provided for under section 282 shall be considered by the arbitrator if raised by any party to the proceeding.

(c) An award by an arbitrator shall be final and binding between the parties to the arbitration but shall have no force or effect on any other person. The parties to an arbitration may agree that in the event a patent which is the subject matter of an award is subsequently determined to be invalid or unenforceable in a judgment rendered by a court of competent jurisdiction from which no appeal can or has been taken, such award may be modified by any court of competent jurisdiction upon application by any party to the arbitration. Any such modification shall govern the rights and obligations between such parties from the date of such modification.

(d) When an award is made by an arbitrator, the patentee, his assignee or licensee shall give notice thereof in writing to the Director. There shall be a separate notice prepared for each patent involved in such proceeding. Such notice shall set forth the names and addresses of the parties, the name of the inventor, and the name of the patent owner, shall designate the number of the patent, and shall contain a copy of the award. If an award is modified by a court, the party requesting such modification shall give notice of such modification to the Director. The Director shall, upon receipt of either notice, enter the same in the record of the prosecution of such patent. If the required notice is not filed with the Director, any party to the proceeding may provide such notice to the Director.

(e) The award shall be unenforceable until the notice required by subsection (d) is received by the Director.

(Aug. 27, 1982, Pub. L. 97-247, §17, 96 Stat. 322; (Nov. 2, 2002, Pub. L. 107-273, §13206, 116 Stat. 1904.)

§ 295 Presumption: Product made by patented process

In actions alleging infringement of a process patent based on the importation, sale, offer for sale, or use of a product which is made from a process patented in the United States, if the court finds—

(1) that a substantial likelihood exists that the product was made by the patented process, and

(2) that the plaintiff has made a reasonable effort to determine the process actually used in the production of the product and was unable to so determine,

the product shall be presumed to have been so made, and the burden of establishing that the product was not made by the process shall be on the party asserting that it was not so made.

(Aug. 23, 1988, Pub. L. 100-418, §9005, 102 Stat. 1566; Dec. 8, 1994, Pub. L. 103-465, §533, 108 Stat. 4988.)

§ 296 Liability of States, instrumentalities of States, and State officials for infringement of patents

(a) *In general.*—Any State, any instrumentality of a State, and any officer or employee of a State or instrumentality of a State acting in his official capacity, shall not be immune, under the eleventh amendment of the Constitution of the United States or under any other doctrine of sovereign immunity, from suit in Federal court by any person, including any governmental or nongovernmental entity, for infringement of a patent under section 271, or for any other violation under this title.

(b) *Remedies.*—In a suit described in subsection (a) for a violation described in that subsection, remedies (including remedies both at law and in equity) are available for the violation to the same extent as such remedies are available for such a violation in a suit against any private entity. Such remedies include damages, interest, costs, and treble damages under section 284, attorney fees under section 285, and the additional remedy for infringement of design patents under section 289.

(Oct. 28, 1992, Pub. L. 102-560, §2, 106 Stat. 4230.)

35 U.S.C. § 295

§ 297 Improper and deceptive invention promotion

(a) *In general.*—An invention promoter shall have a duty to disclose the following information to a customer in writing, prior to entering into a contract for invention promotion services:

(1) the total number of inventions evaluated by the invention promoter for commercial potential in the past 5 years, as well as the number of those inventions that received positive evaluations, and the number of those inventions that received negative evaluations;

(2) the total number of customers who have contracted with the invention promoter in the past 5 years, not including customers who have purchased trade show services, research, advertising, or other nonmarketing services from the invention promoter, or who have defaulted in their payment to the invention promoter;

(3) the total number of customers known by the invention promoter to have received a net financial profit as a direct result of the invention promotion services provided by such invention promoter;

(4) the total number of customers known by the invention promoter to have received license agreements for their inventions as a direct result of the invention promotion services provided by such invention promoter; and

(5) the names and addresses of all previous invention promotion companies with which the invention promoter or its officers have collectively or individually been affiliated in the previous 10 years.

(b) *Civil action.*—(1) Any customer who enters into a contract with an invention promoter and who is found by a court to have been injured by any material false or fraudulent statement or representation, or any omission of material fact, by that invention promoter (or any agent, employee, director, officer, partner, or independent contractor of such invention promoter), or by the failure of that invention promoter to disclose such information as required under subsection (a), may recover in a civil action against the invention promoter (or the officers, directors, or partners of such invention promoter), in addition to reasonable costs and attorneys' fees—

(A) the amount of actual damages incurred by the customer; or

(B) at the election of the customer at any time before final judgment is rendered, statutory damages in a sum of not more than $5,000, as the court considers just.

(2) Notwithstanding paragraph (1), in a case where the customer sustains the burden of proof, and the court finds, that the invention promoter intentionally misrepresented or omitted a material fact to such customer, or willfully failed to disclose such information as required under subsection (a), with the purpose of deceiving that customer, the court may increase damages to not more than three times the amount awarded, taking into account past complaints made against the invention promoter that resulted in regulatory sanctions or other corrective actions based on those records compiled by the Commissioner of Patents under subsection (d).

(c) *Definitions.* — For purposes of this section —

(1) a "contract for invention promotion services" means a contract by which an invention promoter undertakes invention promotion services for a customer;

(2) a "customer" is any individual who enters into a contract with an invention promoter for invention promotion services;

(3) the term "invention promoter" means any person, firm, partnership, corporation, or other entity who offers to perform or performs invention promotion services for, or on behalf of, a customer, and who holds itself out through advertising in any mass media as providing such services, but does not include —

(A) any department or agency of the Federal Government or of a State or local government;

(B) any nonprofit, charitable, scientific, or educational organization, qualified under applicable State law or described under section 170(b)(1)(A) of the Internal Revenue Code of 1986;

(C) any person or entity involved in the evaluation to determine commercial potential of, or offering to license or sell, a utility patent or a previously filed nonprovisional utility patent application;

(D) any party participating in a transaction involving the sale of the stock or assets of a business; or

(E) any party who directly engages in the business of retail sales of products or the distribution of products; and

(4) the term "invention promotion services" means the procurement or attempted procurement for a customer of a firm, corporation, or other entity to develop and market products or services that include the invention of the customer.

(d) *Records of complaints.* —

(1) *Release of complaints.* —The Commissioner of Patents shall make all complaints received by the Patent and Trademark Office involving invention promoters publicly available, together with any response of the invention promoters. The Commissioner of Patents shall notify the invention promoter of a complaint and provide a reasonable opportunity to reply prior to making such complaint publicly available.

(2) *Request for complaints.* —The Commissioner of Patents may request complaints relating to invention promotion services from any Federal or State agency and include such complaints in the records maintained under paragraph (1), together with any response of the invention promoters.

(Nov. 29, 1999, Pub. L. 106-113, §4102, 113 Stat. 1501A-552.)

§ 298[30] Advice of counsel

The failure of an infringer to obtain the advice of counsel with respect to any allegedly infringed patent, or the failure of the infringer to present such advice to the court or jury, may not be used to prove that the accused infringer willfully infringed the patent or that the infringer intended to induce infringement of the patent.

(Sept. 16, 2011, Pub. L. 112-29, §17, 125 Stat. 329.)

§ 299[31] Joinder of parties

(a) *Joinder of accused infringers.* —With respect to any civil action arising under any Act of Congress relating to patents, other than an action or trial in which an act of infringement under section 271(e)(2) has been pled, parties that are accused infringers may be joined in one action as defendants or counterclaim defendants, or have their actions consolidated for trial, or counterclaim defendants only if—

---

[30] *Ed. Note:* This section applies to any civil action commenced on or after the date of enactment of Pub. L. 112-274 (Jan. 14, 2013). See section 1(a) of Pub. L. 112-274.

[31] *Ed. Note:* This section applies to any civil action commenced on or after the date of enactment of Pub. L. 112-29 (Sept. 16, 2011). See section 19(e) of Pub. L. 112-29.

(1) any right to relief is asserted against the parties jointly, severally, or in the alternative with respect to or arising out of the same transaction, occurrence, or series of transactions or occurrences relating to the making, using, importing into the United States, offering for sale, or selling of the same accused product or process; and

(2) questions of fact common to all defendants or counterclaim defendants will arise in the action.

(b) *Allegations insufficient for joinder.*—For purposes of this subsection, accused infringers may not be joined in one action as defendants or counterclaim defendants, or have their actions consolidated for trial, based solely on allegations that they each have infringed the patent or patents in suit.

(c) *Waiver.*—A party that is an accused infringer may waive the limitations set forth in this section with respect to that party.

(Sept. 16, 2011, Pub. L. 112-29, §19, 125 Stat. 331.)

CHAPTER 30—PRIOR ART CITATIONS TO OFFICE AND EX PARTE
REEXAMINATION OF PATENTS

SEC.
301. Citation of prior art and written statements.
302. Request for reexamination.
303. Determination of issue by Director.
304. Reexamination order by Director.
305. Conduct of reexamination proceedings.
306. Appeal.
307. Certificate of patentability, unpatentability, and claim cancellation.

§ 301 Citation of prior art and written statements

(a) *In general.*—Any person at any time may cite to the Office in writing—

(1) prior art consisting of patents or printed publications which that person believes to have a bearing on the patentability of any claim of a particular patent; or

(2) statements of the patent owner filed in a proceeding before a Federal court or the Office in which the patent owner took a position on the scope of any claim of a particular patent.

(b) *Official file.*—If the person citing prior art or written statements pursuant to subsection (a) explains in writing the pertinence and manner of applying

35 U.S.C. § 301

the prior art or written statements to at least 1 claim of the patent, the citation of the prior art or written statements and the explanation thereof shall become a part of the official file of the patent.

(c) *Additional information.*—A party that submits a written statement pursuant to subsection (a)(2) shall include any other documents, pleadings, or evidence from the proceeding in which the statement was filed that addresses the written statement.

(d) *Limitations.*—A written statement submitted pursuant to subsection (a)(2), and additional information submitted pursuant to subsection (c), shall not be considered by the Office for any purpose other than to determine the proper meaning of a patent claim in a proceeding that is ordered or instituted pursuant to section 304, 314, or 324. If any such written statement or additional information is subject to an applicable protective order, such statement or information shall be redacted to exclude information that is subject to that order.

(e) *Confidentiality.*—Upon the written request of the person citing prior art or written statements pursuant to subsection (a), that person's identity shall be excluded from the patent file and kept confidential.

(Sept. 16, 2011, Pub. L. 112-29, §6, 125 Stat. 311.)

§ 302   Request for reexamination

Any person at any time may file a request for reexamination by the Office of any claim of a patent on the basis of any prior art cited under the provisions of section 301. The request must be in writing and must be accompanied by payment of a reexamination fee established by the Director pursuant to the provisions of section 41. The request must set forth the pertinency and manner of applying cited prior art to every claim for which reexamination is requested. Unless the requesting person is the owner of the patent, the Director promptly will send a copy of the request to the owner of record of the patent.

(Dec. 12, 1980, Pub. L. 96-517, §1, 94 Stat. 3015; Nov. 29, 1999, Pub. L. 106-113, §4732, 113 Stat. 1501A-581.)

§ 303   Determination of issue by Director

(a) Within three months following the filing of a request for reexamination under the provisions of section 302, the Director will determine whether a substantial new question of patentability affecting any claim of the patent concerned is raised by the request, with or without consideration of other patents or printed publications. On his own initiative, and any time, the Director may determine whether a substantial new question of patentability is raised by patents and publications discovered by him or cited under the provisions of section 301 or 302. The existence of a substantial new question of patentability is not precluded by the fact that a patent or printed publication was previously cited by or to the Office or considered by the Office.

(b) A record of the Director's determination under subsection (a) of this section will be placed in the official file of the patent, and a copy promptly will be given or mailed to the owner of record of the patent and to the person requesting reexamination, if any.

(c) A determination by the Director pursuant to subsection (a) of this section that no substantial new question of patentability has been raised will be final and nonappealable. Upon such a determination, the Director may refund a portion of the reexamination fee required under section 302.

(Dec. 12, 1980, Pub. L. 96-517, §1, 94 Stat. 3015; Nov. 29, 1999, Pub. L. 106-113, §4732, 113 Stat. 1501A-581; Nov. 2, 2002, Pub. L. 107-273, §13105, 116 Stat. 1900; Sept. 16, 2011, Pub. L. 112-29, §6, 125 Stat. 312.)

§ 304   Reexamination order by Director

If, in a determination made under the provisions of subsection 303(a), the Director finds that a substantial new question of patentability affecting any claim of a patent is raised, the determination will include an order for reexamination of the patent for resolution of the question. The patent owner will be given a reasonable period, not less than two months from the date a copy of the determination is given or mailed to him, within which he may file a statement on such question, including any amendment to his patent and new claim or claims he may wish to propose, for consideration in the reexamination. If the patent owner files such a statement, he promptly will serve a copy of it on the person who has requested reexamination under the provisions of section 302. Within a period of two months from the date of service, that person may file and have considered in the reexamination a reply to any statement filed by the patent owner. That person promptly will serve on the patent owner a copy of any reply filed.

(Dec. 12, 1980, Pub. L. 96-517, §1, 94 Stat. 3016.)

§ 305   Conduct of reexamination proceedings

After the times for filing the statement and reply provided for by section 304 have expired, reexamination will be conducted according to the procedures established for initial examination under the provisions of sections 132 and

133. In any reexamination proceeding under this chapter, the patent owner will be permitted to propose any amendment to his patent and a new claim or claims thereto, in order to distinguish the invention as claimed from the prior art cited under the provisions of section 301, or in response to a decision adverse to the patentability of a claim of a patent. No proposed amended or new claim enlarging the scope of a claim of the patent will be permitted in a reexamination proceeding under this chapter. All reexamination proceedings under this section, including any appeal to the Patent Trial and Appeal Board, will be conducted with special dispatch within the Office.

(Dec. 12, 1980, Pub. L. 96-517, §1, 94 Stat. 3016; Nov. 8, 1984, Pub. L. 98-622, §204, 98 Stat. 3388; Sept. 16, 2011, Pub. L. 112-29, §3, 125 Stat. 290.)

§ 306   Appeal

The patent owner involved in a reexamination proceeding under this chapter may appeal under the provisions of section 134, and may seek court review under the provisions of sections 141 to 144, with respect to any decision adverse to the patentability of any original or proposed amended or new claim of the patent.

(Dec. 12, 1980, Pub. L. 96-517, §1, 94 Stat. 3016; Sept. 16, 2011, Pub. L. 112-29, §6, 125 Stat. 299.)

§ 307   Certificate of patentability, unpatentability, and claim cancellation

(a) In a reexamination proceeding under this chapter, when the time for appeal has expired or any appeal proceeding has terminated, the Director will issue and publish a certificate canceling any claim of the patent finally determined to be unpatentable, confirming any claim of the patent determined to be patentable, and incorporating in the patent any proposed amended or new claim determined to be patentable.

(b) Any proposed amended or new claim determined to be patentable and incorporated into a patent following a reexamination proceeding will have the same effect as that specified in section 252 for reissued patents on the right of any person who made, purchased, or used within the United States, or imported into the United States, anything patented by such proposed amended or new claim, or who made substantial preparation for the same, prior to issuance of a certificate under the provisions of subsection (a) of this section.

(Dec. 12, 1980, Pub. L. 96-517, §1, 94 Stat. 3016; Dec. 8, 1994, Pub. L. 103-465, §533, 108 Stat. 4988.)

CHAPTER 31[32] — INTER PARTES REVIEW

SEC.

§ 311   Inter partes review

(a) *In general.* —Subject to the provisions of this chapter, a person who is not the owner of a patent may file with the Office a petition to institute an inter partes review of the patent. The Director shall establish, by regulation, fees to be paid by the person requesting the review, in such amounts as the Director determines to be reasonable, considering the aggregate costs of the review.

(b) *Scope.* —A petitioner in an inter partes review may request to cancel as unpatentable 1 or more claims of a patent only on a ground that could be raised under section 102 or 103 and only on the basis of prior art consisting of patents or printed publications.

(c) *Filing deadline.*[33] —A petition for inter partes review shall be filed after the later of either—

(1) the date that is 9 months after the grant of a patent; or

(2) if a post-grant review is instituted under chapter 32, the date of the termination of such post-grant review.

(Sept. 16, 2011, Pub. L. 112-29, §6, 125 Stat. 299; Jan. 14, 2013, Pub. L. 112-274, §1(d), 126 Stat. 2456.)

---

[32] *Ed. Note:* Pursuant to Pub. L. 112-29, effective Sept. 16, 2012, chapter 31 is amended as set forth in the text below, and applies to any patent issued before, on, or after Sept. 16, 2012. See text of Pub. L. 112-29 on the CD-ROM that accompanies this edition of the book. A table of effective dates for all changes set forth in Pub. L. 112-29 may also be found on the CD-ROM.

[33] *Ed. Note:* Section 311(c) shall not apply to a petition to institute an inter partes review of a patent that is not a patent described in section 3(n)(1) of the Leahy-Smith America Invents Act. See Pub. L. 112-274, section 1(d).

§ 312   Petitions

(a) *Requirements of petition.*—A petition filed under section 311 may be considered only if—

(1) the petition is accompanied by payment of the fee established by the Director under section 311;

(2) the petition identifies all real parties in interest;

(3) the petition identifies, in writing and with particularity, each claim challenged, the grounds on which the challenge to each claim is based, and the evidence that supports the grounds for the challenge to each claim, including—

(A) copies of patents and printed publications that the petitioner relies upon in support of the petition; and

(B) affidavits or declarations of supporting evidence and opinions, if the petitioner relies on expert opinions;

(4) the petition provides such other information as the Director may require by regulation; and

(5) the petitioner provides copies of any of the documents required under paragraphs (2), (3), and (4) to the patent owner or, if applicable, the designated representative of the patent owner.

(b) *Public availability.*—As soon as practicable after the receipt of a petition under section 311, the Director shall make the petition available to the public.

(Sept. 16, 2011, Pub. L. 112-29, §6, 125 Stat. 300.)

§ 313   Preliminary response to petition

If an inter partes review petition is filed under section 311, the patent owner shall have the right to file a preliminary response to the petition, within a time period set by the Director, that sets forth reasons why no inter partes review should be instituted based upon the failure of the petition to meet any requirement of this chapter.

(Sept. 16, 2011, Pub. L. 112-29, §6, 125 Stat. 300.)

§ 314   Institution of inter partes review

(a) *Threshold.*—The Director may not authorize an inter partes review to be instituted unless the Director determines that the information presented in the petition filed under section 311 and any response filed under section 313 shows that there is a reasonable likelihood that the petitioner would prevail with respect to at least 1 of the claims challenged in the petition.

(b) *Timing.*—The Director shall determine whether to institute an inter partes review under this chapter pursuant to a petition filed under section 311 within 3 months after—

(1) receiving a preliminary response to the petition under section 313; or

(2) if no such preliminary response is filed, the last date on which such response may be filed.

(c) *Notice.*—The Director shall notify the petitioner and patent owner, in writing, of the Director's determination under subsection (a), and shall make such notice available to the public as soon as is practicable. Such notice shall include the date on which the review shall commence.

(d) *No appeal.*—The determination by the Director whether to institute an inter partes review under this section shall be final and nonappealable.

(Sept. 16, 2011, Pub. L. 112-29, §6, 125 Stat. 300.)

§ 315 Relation to other proceedings or actions

(a) *Infringer's civil action.*—

(1) *Inter partes review barred by civil action.*—An inter partes review may not be instituted if, before the date on which the petition for such a review is filed, the petitioner or real party in interest filed a civil action challenging the validity of a claim of the patent.

(2) *Stay of civil action.*—If the petitioner or real party in interest files a civil action challenging the validity of a claim of the patent on or after the date on which the petitioner files a petition for inter partes review of the patent, that civil action shall be automatically stayed until either—

(A) the patent owner moves the court to lift the stay;

(B) the patent owner files a civil action or counterclaim alleging that the petitioner or real party in interest has infringed the patent; or

(C) the petitioner or real party in interest moves the court to dismiss the civil action.

(3) *Treatment of counterclaim.*—A counterclaim challenging the validity of a claim of a patent does not constitute a civil action challenging the validity of a claim of a patent for purposes of this subsection.

35 U.S.C. § 315

(b) *Patent owner's action.*—An inter partes review may not be instituted if the petition requesting the proceeding is filed more than 1 year after the date on which the petitioner, real party in interest, or privy of the petitioner is served with a complaint alleging infringement of the patent. The time limitation set forth in the preceding sentence shall not apply to a request for joinder under subsection (c).

(c) *Joinder.*—If the Director institutes an inter partes review, the Director, in his or her discretion, may join as a party to that inter partes review any person who properly files a petition under section 311 that the Director, after receiving a preliminary response under section 313 or the expiration of the time for filing such a response, determines warrants the institution of an inter partes review under section 314.

(d) *Multiple proceedings.*—Notwithstanding sections 135(a), 251, and 252, and chapter 30, during the pendency of an inter partes review, if another proceeding or matter involving the patent is before the Office, the Director may determine the manner in which the inter partes review or other proceeding or matter may proceed, including providing for stay, transfer, consolidation, or termination of any such matter or proceeding.

(e) *Estoppel.*—

(1) *Proceedings before the office.*—The petitioner in an inter partes review of a claim in a patent under this chapter that results in a final written decision under section 318(a), or the real party in interest or privy of the petitioner, may not request or maintain a proceeding before the Office with respect to that claim on any ground that the petitioner raised or reasonably could have raised during that inter partes review.

(2) *Civil actions and other proceedings.*—The petitioner in an inter partes review of a claim in a patent under this chapter that results in a final written decision under section 318(a), or the real party in interest or privy of the petitioner, may not assert either in a civil action arising in whole or in part under section 1338 of title 28 or in a proceeding before the International Trade Commission under section 337 of the Tariff Act of 1930 that the claim is invalid on any ground that the petitioner raised or reasonably could have raised during that inter partes review.

(Sept. 16, 2011, Pub. L. 112-29, §6, 125 Stat. 300–02.)

35 U.S.C. § 315

§ 316   Conduct of inter partes review

(a) *Regulations.*—The Director shall prescribe regulations—

(1) providing that the file of any proceeding under this chapter shall be made available to the public, except that any petition or document filed with the intent that it be sealed shall, if accompanied by a motion to seal, be treated as sealed pending the outcome of the ruling on the motion;

(2) setting forth the standards for the showing of sufficient grounds to institute a review under section 314(a);

(3) establishing procedures for the submission of supplemental information after the petition is filed;

(4) establishing and governing inter partes review under this chapter and the relationship of such review to other proceedings under this title;

(5) setting forth standards and procedures for discovery of relevant evidence, including that such discovery shall be limited to—

   (A) the deposition of witnesses submitting affidavits or declarations; and

   (B) what is otherwise necessary in the interest of justice;

(6) prescribing sanctions for abuse of discovery, abuse of process, or any other improper use of the proceeding, such as to harass or to cause unnecessary delay or an unnecessary increase in the cost of the proceeding;

(7) providing for protective orders governing the exchange and submission of confidential information;

(8) providing for the filing by the patent owner of a response to the petition under section 313 after an inter partes review has been instituted, and requiring that the patent owner file with such response, through affidavits or declarations, any additional factual evidence and expert opinions on which the patent owner relies in support of the response;

(9) setting forth standards and procedures for allowing the patent owner to move to amend the patent under subsection (d) to cancel a challenged claim or propose a reasonable number of substitute claims, and ensuring that any information submitted by the patent owner in support of any amendment entered under subsection (d) is made available to the public as part of the prosecution history of the patent;

(10) providing either party with the right to an oral hearing as part of the proceeding;

(11) requiring that the final determination in an inter partes review be issued not later than 1 year after the date on which the Director notices the institution of a review under this chapter, except that the Director may, for good cause shown, extend the 1-year period by not more than 6 months, and may adjust the time periods in this paragraph in the case of joinder under section 315(c);

(12) setting a time period for requesting joinder under section 315(c); and

(13) providing the petitioner with at least 1 opportunity to file written comments within a time period established by the Director.

(b) *Considerations.*—In prescribing regulations under this section, the Director shall consider the effect of any such regulation on the economy, the integrity of the patent system, the efficient administration of the Office, and the ability of the Office to timely complete proceedings instituted under this chapter.

(c) *Patent Trial and Appeal Board.*—The Patent Trial and Appeal Board shall, in accordance with section 6, conduct each inter partes review instituted under this chapter.

(d) *Amendment of the patent.*—

(1) *In general.*—During an inter partes review instituted under this chapter, the patent owner may file 1 motion to amend the patent in 1 or more of the following ways:

(A) Cancel any challenged patent claim.

(B) For each challenged claim, propose a reasonable number of substitute claims.

(2) *Additional motions.*—Additional motions to amend may be permitted upon the joint request of the petitioner and the patent owner to materially advance the settlement of a proceeding under section 317, or as permitted by regulations prescribed by the Director.

(3) *Scope of claims.*—An amendment under this subsection may not enlarge the scope of the claims of the patent or introduce new matter.

(e) *Evidentiary standards.*—In an inter partes review instituted under this chapter, the petitioner shall have the burden of proving a proposition of unpatentability by a preponderance of the evidence.

(Sept. 16, 2011, Pub. L. 112-29, §6, 125 Stat. 302–03.)

35 U.S.C. § 316

§ 317   Settlement

(a) *In general.* — An inter partes review instituted under this chapter shall be terminated with respect to any petitioner upon the joint request of the petitioner and the patent owner, unless the Office has decided the merits of the proceeding before the request for termination is filed. If the inter partes review is terminated with respect to a petitioner under this section, no estoppel under section 315(e) shall attach to the petitioner, or to the real party in interest or privy of the petitioner, on the basis of that petitioner's institution of that inter partes review. If no petitioner remains in the inter partes review, the Office may terminate the review or proceed to a final written decision under section 318(a).

(b) *Agreements in writing.* — Any agreement or understanding between the patent owner and a petitioner, including any collateral agreements referred to in such agreement or understanding, made in connection with, or in contemplation of, the termination of an inter partes review under this section shall be in writing and a true copy of such agreement or understanding shall be filed in the Office before the termination of the inter partes review as between the parties. At the request of a party to the proceeding, the agreement or understanding shall be treated as business confidential information, shall be kept separate from the file of the involved patents, and shall be made available only to Federal Government agencies on written request, or to any person on a showing of good cause.

(Sept. 16, 2011, Pub. L. 112-29, §6, 125 Stat. 303.)

§ 318   Decision of the Board

(a) *Final written decision.* — If an inter partes review is instituted and not dismissed under this chapter, the Patent Trial and Appeal Board shall issue a final written decision with respect to the patentability of any patent claim challenged by the petitioner and any new claim added under section 316(d).

(b) *Certificate.* — If the Patent Trial and Appeal Board issues a final written decision under subsection (a) and the time for appeal has expired or any appeal has terminated, the Director shall issue and publish a certificate canceling any claim of the patent finally determined to be unpatentable, confirming any claim of the patent determined to be patentable, and incorporating in the patent by operation of the certificate any new or amended claim determined to be patentable.

(c) *Intervening rights.* — Any proposed amended or new claim determined to be patentable and incorporated into a patent following an inter partes review under this chapter shall have the same effect as that specified in section 252 for reissued patents on the right of any person who made, purchased, or used within the United States, or imported into the United States, anything patented by such proposed amended or new claim, or who made substantial preparation therefor, before the issuance of a certificate under subsection (b).

(d) *Data on length of review.* — The Office shall make available to the public data describing the length of time between the institution of, and the issuance of a final written decision under subsection (a) for, each inter partes review.

(Sept. 16, 2011, Pub. L. 112-29, §6, 125 Stat. 303–04.)

§ 319   Appeal

A party dissatisfied with the final written decision of the Patent Trial and Appeal Board under section 318(a) may appeal the decision pursuant to sections 141 through 144. Any party to the inter partes review shall have the right to be a party to the appeal.

(Sept. 16, 2011, Pub. L. 112-29, §6, 125 Stat. 304.)

[CHAPTER 31[34] — OPTIONAL INTER PARTES REEXAMINATION PROCEDURES

SEC.

---

[34] *Ed. Note:* Pursuant to Pub. L. 112-29, effective Sept. 16, 2012, this version of chapter 31 is replaced by new chapter 31, which appears immediately above. The provisions of the replaced chapter 31 continue to apply to requests for inter partes reexamination filed before Sept. 16, 2012. See text of Pub. L. 112-29 on the CD-ROM that accompanies this edition of the book. A table of effective dates for all changes set forth in Pub. L. 112-29 may also be found on the CD-ROM.

[§ 311[35] [36] Request for inter partes reexamination

(a) *In general.*—Any third-party requester at any time may file a request for inter partes reexamination by the Office of a patent on the basis of any prior art cited under the provisions of section 301.

(b) *Requirements.*—The request shall—

(1) be in writing, include the identity of the real party in interest, and be accompanied by payment of an inter partes reexamination fee established by the Director under section 41; and

(2) set forth the pertinency and manner of applying cited prior art to every claim for which reexamination is requested.

(c) *Copy.*—The Director promptly shall send a copy of the request to the owner of record of the patent.

(Nov. 2, 2002, Pub. L. 107-273, §13202, 116 Stat. 1901.)]

[§ 312[37] [38] Determination of issue by Director

(a) *Reexamination.*—Not later than 3 months after the filing of a request for inter partes reexamination under section 311, the Director shall determine whether *the information presented in the request shows that there is a reasonable likelihood that the requester would prevail with respect to at least 1 of the claims challenged in the request,* with or without consideration of other patents or printed publications. *A showing that there is a reasonable likelihood that the requester would prevail with respect to at least 1 of the claims challenged in the request* is not precluded by the fact that a patent or printed publication was previously cited by or to the Office or considered by the Office.

(b) *Record.*—A record of the Director's determination under subsection (a) shall be placed in the official file of the patent, and a copy shall be promptly given or mailed to the owner of record of the patent and to the third-party requester.

---

[35] *Ed. Note:* See Ed. Note to chapter 31.

[36] *Ed. Note:* Pursuant to section 4607 of Pub. L. 106-113 (113 Stat. 1501A-571), "Any party who requests an inter partes reexamination under section 311 of title 35, United States Code, is estopped from challenging at a later time, in any civil action, any fact determined during the process of such reexamination, except with respect to a fact determination later proved to be erroneous based on information unavailable at the time of the inter partes reexamination decision."

[37] *Ed. Note:* See Ed. Note to chapter 31.

[38] *Ed. Note:* The italicized language applies to requests for inter partes reexamination filed on or after the date of enactment of Pub. L. 112-29 (Sept. 16, 2011) but before Sept. 16, 2012. See section 6(c)(3)(B) of Pub. L. 112-29.

35 U.S.C. § 311

(c) *Final decision.*—A determination by the Director under subsection (a) shall be final and non-appealable. Upon a determination that *the showing required by subsection (a) has not been made,* the Director may refund a portion of the inter partes reexamination fee required under section 311.

(Nov. 2, 2002, Pub. L. 107-273, §§13105, 13202, 116 Stat. 1901; Sept. 16, 2011, Pub. L. 112-29, §6, 125 Stat. 299.)]

[§ 313[39][40] Inter partes reexamination order by Director

If, in a determination made under section 312(a), the Director finds that *it has been shown that there is a reasonable likelihood that the requester would prevail with respect to at least 1 of the claims challenged in the request,* the determination shall include an order for inter partes reexamination of the patent for resolution of the question. The order may be accompanied by the initial action of the Patent and Trademark Office on the merits of the inter partes reexamination conducted in accordance with section 314.

(Sept. 16, 2011, Pub. L. 112-29, §6, 125 Stat. 299.)]

[§ 314[41] Conduct of inter partes reexamination proceedings

(a) *In general.*—Except as otherwise provided in this section, reexamination shall be conducted according to the procedures established for initial examination under the provisions of sections 132 and 133. In any inter partes reexamination proceeding under this chapter, the patent owner shall be permitted to propose any amendment to the patent and a new claim or claims, except that no proposed amended or new claim enlarging the scope of the claims of the patent shall be permitted.

(b) *Response.*—(1) With the exception of the inter partes reexamination request, any document filed by either the patent owner or the third-party requester shall be served on the other party. In addition, the Office shall send to the third-party requester a copy of any communication sent by the Office to the patent owner concerning the patent subject to the inter partes reexamination proceeding.

(2) Each time that the patent owner files a response to an action on the merits from the Patent and Trademark Office, the third-party requester shall have one opportunity to file written comments addressing issues

---

[39] *Ed. Note:* See Ed. Note to chapter 31.

[40] *Ed. Note:* The italicized language applies to requests for inter partes reexamination filed on or after the date of enactment of Pub. L. 112-29 (Sept. 16, 2011) but before Sept. 16, 2012. See section 6(c)(3)(B) of Pub. L. 112-29.

[41] *Ed. Note:* See Ed. Note to chapter 31.

raised by the action of the Office or the patent owner's response thereto, if those written comments are received by the Office within 30 days after the date of service of the patent owner's response.

(c) *Special dispatch.*—Unless otherwise provided by the Director for good cause, all inter partes reexamination proceedings under this section, including any appeal to the Board of Patent Appeals and Interferences, shall be conducted with special dispatch within the Office.

(Nov. 2, 2002, Pub. L. 107-273, §13202, 116 Stat. 1901.)]

[§ 315[42] Appeal

(a) *Patent owner.*—The patent owner involved in an inter partes reexamination proceeding under this chapter—

(1) may appeal under the provisions of section 134 and may appeal under the provisions of sections 141 through 144, with respect to any decision adverse to the patentability of any original or proposed amended or new claim of the patent; and

(2) may be a party to any appeal taken by a third-party requester under subsection (b).

(b) *Third-Party Requester.* —A third-party requester—

(1) may appeal under the provisions of section 134, and may appeal under the provisions of sections 141 through 144, with respect to any final decision favorable to the patentability of any original or proposed amended or new claim of the patent; and

(2) may, subject to subsection (c), be a party to any appeal taken by the patent owner under the provisions of section 134 or sections 141 through 144.

(c) *Civil action.*—A third-party requester whose request for an inter partes reexamination results in an order under section 313 is estopped from asserting at a later time, in any civil action arising in whole or in part under section 1338 of title 28, the invalidity of any claim finally determined to be valid and patentable on any ground which the third-party requester raised or could have raised during the inter partes reexamination proceedings. This subsection does not prevent the assertion of invalidity based on newly discovered prior art unavailable to the third-party requester and the Patent and Trademark Office at the time of the inter partes reexamination proceedings.

(Nov. 2, 2002, Pub. L. 107-273, §§13106, 13202, 116 Stat. 1901.)]

---

[42] *Ed. Note:* See Ed. Note to chapter 31.

[§ 316[43] Certificate of patentability, unpatentability, and claim cancellation

(a) *In general.* — In an inter partes reexamination proceeding under this chapter, when the time for appeal has expired or any appeal proceeding has terminated, the Director shall issue and publish a certificate canceling any claim of the patent finally determined to be unpatentable, confirming any claim of the patent determined to be patentable, and incorporating in the patent any proposed amended or new claim determined to be patentable.

(b) *Amended or new claim.* — Any proposed amended or new claim determined to be patentable and incorporated into a patent following an inter partes reexamination proceeding shall have the same effect as that specified in section 252 for reissued patents on the right of any person who made, purchased, or used within the United States, or imported into the United States, anything patented by such proposed amended or new claim, or who made substantial preparation therefor, prior to issuance of a certificate under the provisions of subsection (a) of this section.

(Nov. 29, 1999, Pub. L. 106-113, §1000(a)(9), 113 Stat. 1536, 1501A-569; Nov. 2, 2002, Pub. L. 107-273, §13202(c)(1), 116 Stat. 1902.)]

[§ 317[44] Inter partes reexamination prohibited

(a) *Order for reexamination.* — Notwithstanding any provision of this chapter, once an order for inter partes reexamination of a patent has been issued under section 313, neither the third-party requester nor its privies may file a subsequent request for inter partes reexamination of the patent until an inter partes reexamination certificate is issued and published under section 316, unless authorized by the Director.

(b) *Final decision.* — Once a final decision has been entered against a party in a civil action arising in whole or in part under section 1338 of title 28, that the party has not sustained its burden of proving the invalidity of any patent claim in suit or if a final decision in an inter partes reexamination proceeding instituted by a third-party requester is favorable to the patentability of any original or proposed amended or new claim of the patent, then neither that party nor its privies may thereafter request an inter partes reexamination of any such patent claim on the basis of issues which that party or its privies raised or could have raised in such civil action or inter partes reexamination proceeding, and an inter partes reexamination requested by that party or its privies on the basis of such issues may not thereafter be maintained by the

---

[43] *Ed. Note:* See Ed. Note to chapter 31.
[44] *Ed. Note:* See Ed. Note to chapter 31.

Office, notwithstanding any other provision of this chapter. This subsection does not prevent the assertion of invalidity based on newly discovered prior art unavailable to the third-party requester and the Patent and Trademark Office at the time of the inter partes reexamination proceedings.

(Nov. 2, 2002, Pub. L. 107-273, §13202, 116 Stat. 1901.)]

[§ 318[45] Stay of litigation

Once an order for inter partes reexamination of a patent has been issued under section 313, the patent owner may obtain a stay of any pending litigation which involves an issue of patentability of any claims of the patent which are the subject of the inter partes reexamination order, unless the court before which such litigation is pending determines that a stay would not serve the interests of justice.

(Nov. 29, 1999, Pub. L. 106-113, §4604, 113 Stat. 1501A-567.)]

CHAPTER 32[46] — POST-GRANT REVIEW

SEC.

§ 321   Post-grant review

(a) *In general.* —Subject to the provisions of this chapter, a person who is not the owner of a patent may file with the Office a petition to institute a post-grant review of the patent. The Director shall establish, by regulation, fees to be paid by the person requesting the review, in such amounts as the Director determines to be reasonable, considering the aggregate costs of the post-grant review.

---

[45] *Ed. Note:* See Ed. Note to chapter 31.

[46] *Ed. Note:* Pursuant to Pub. L. 112-29, this chapter took effect on Sept. 16, 2012 and, in general, applies only to patents described in §3(n)(1) of Pub. L. 112-29. See text of Pub. L. 112-29 on the CD-ROM that accompanies this edition of the book. A table of effective dates for all changes set forth in Pub. L. 112-29 may also be found on the CD-ROM.

(b) *Scope.*—A petitioner in a post-grant review may request to cancel as unpatentable 1 or more claims of a patent on any ground that could be raised under paragraph (2) or (3) of section 282(b) (relating to invalidity of the patent or any claim).

(c) *Filing deadline.*—A petition for a post-grant review may only be filed not later than the date that is 9 months after the date of the grant of the patent or of the issuance of a reissue patent (as the case may be).

(Sept. 16, 2011, Pub. L. 112-29, §6, 125 Stat. 306.)

§ 322 Petitions

(a) *Requirements of petition.*—A petition filed under section 321 may be considered only if—

(1) the petition is accompanied by payment of the fee established by the Director under section 321;

(2) the petition identifies all real parties in interest;

(3) the petition identifies, in writing and with particularity, each claim challenged, the grounds on which the challenge to each claim is based, and the evidence that supports the grounds for the challenge to each claim, including—

(A) copies of patents and printed publications that the petitioner relies upon in support of the petition; and

(B) affidavits or declarations of supporting evidence and opinions, if the petitioner relies on other factual evidence or on expert opinions;

(4) the petition provides such other information as the Director may require by regulation; and

(5) the petitioner provides copies of any of the documents required under paragraphs (2), (3), and (4) to the patent owner or, if applicable, the designated representative of the patent owner.

(b) *Public availability.*—As soon as practicable after the receipt of a petition under section 321, the Director shall make the petition available to the public.

(Sept. 16, 2011, Pub. L. 112-29, §6, 125 Stat. 306.)

§ 323 Preliminary response to petition

If a post-grant review petition is filed under section 321, the patent owner shall have the right to file a preliminary response to the petition, within a time period set by the Director, that sets forth reasons why no post-grant review should be instituted based upon the failure of the petition to meet any requirement of this chapter.

(Sept. 16, 2011, Pub. L. 112-29, §6, 125 Stat. 306.)

§ 324   Institution of post-grant review

(a) *Threshold.*—The Director may not authorize a post-grant review to be instituted unless the Director determines that the information presented in the petition filed under section 321, if such information is not rebutted, would demonstrate that it is more likely than not that at least 1 of the claims challenged in the petition is unpatentable.

(b) *Additional grounds.*—The determination required under subsection (a) may also be satisfied by a showing that the petition raises a novel or unsettled legal question that is important to other patents or patent applications.

(c) *Timing.*—The Director shall determine whether to institute a post-grant review under this chapter pursuant to a petition filed under section 321 within 3 months after—

(1) receiving a preliminary response to the petition under section 323; or

(2) if no such preliminary response is filed, the last date on which such response may be filed.

(d) *Notice.*—The Director shall notify the petitioner and patent owner, in writing, of the Director's determination under subsection (a) or (b), and shall make such notice available to the public as soon as is practicable. Such notice shall include the date on which the review shall commence.

(e) *No appeal.*—The determination by the Director whether to institute a post-grant review under this section shall be final and nonappealable.

(Sept. 16, 2011, Pub. L. 112-29, §6, 125 Stat. 306–07.)

§ 325   Relation to other proceedings or actions

(a) *Infringer's civil action.*—

(1) *Post-grant review barred by civil action.*—A post-grant review may not be instituted under this chapter if, before the date on which the petition for such a review is filed, the petitioner or real party in interest filed a civil action challenging the validity of a claim of the patent.

(2) *Stay of civil action.*—If the petitioner or real party in interest files a civil action challenging the validity of a claim of the patent on or after the date

on which the petitioner files a petition for post-grant review of the patent, that civil action shall be automatically stayed until either—

(A) the patent owner moves the court to lift the stay;

(B) the patent owner files a civil action or counterclaim alleging that the petitioner or real party in interest has infringed the patent; or

(C) the petitioner or real party in interest moves the court to dismiss the civil action.

(3) *Treatment of counterclaim.*—A counterclaim challenging the validity of a claim of a patent does not constitute a civil action challenging the validity of a claim of a patent for purposes of this subsection.

(b) *Preliminary injunctions.*—If a civil action alleging infringement of a patent is filed within 3 months after the date on which the patent is granted, the court may not stay its consideration of the patent owner's motion for a preliminary injunction against infringement of the patent on the basis that a petition for post-grant review has been filed under this chapter or that such a post-grant review has been instituted under this chapter.

(c) *Joinder.*—If more than 1 petition for a post-grant review under this chapter is properly filed against the same patent and the Director determines that more than 1 of these petitions warrants the institution of a post-grant review under section 324, the Director may consolidate such reviews into a single post-grant review.

(d) *Multiple proceedings.*—Notwithstanding sections 135(a), 251, and 252, and chapter 30, during the pendency of any post-grant review under this chapter, if another proceeding or matter involving the patent is before the Office, the Director may determine the manner in which the post-grant review or other proceeding or matter may proceed, including providing for the stay, transfer, consolidation, or termination of any such matter or proceeding. In determining whether to institute or order a proceeding under this chapter, chapter 30, or chapter 31, the Director may take into account whether, and reject the petition or request because, the same or substantially the same prior art or arguments previously were presented to the Office.

(e) *Estoppel.*—

(1) *Proceedings before the office.*—The petitioner in a post-grant review of a claim in a patent under this chapter that results in a final written decision under section 328(a), or the real party in interest or privy of the petitioner, may not request or maintain a proceeding before the Office with respect to

35 U.S.C. § 325

that claim on any ground that the petitioner raised or reasonably could have raised during that post-grant review.

(2) *Civil actions and other proceedings.*—The petitioner in a post-grant review of a claim in a patent under this chapter that results in a final written decision under section 328(a), or the real party in interest or privy of the petitioner, may not assert either in a civil action arising in whole or in part under section 1338 of title 28 or in a proceeding before the International Trade Commission under section 337 of the Tariff Act of 1930 that the claim is invalid on any ground that the petitioner raised or reasonably could have raised during that post-grant review.

(f) *Reissue patents.*—A post-grant review may not be instituted under this chapter if the petition requests cancellation of a claim in a reissue patent that is identical to or narrower than a claim in the original patent from which the reissue patent was issued, and the time limitations in section 321(c) would bar filing a petition for a post-grant review for such original patent.

(Sept. 16, 2011, Pub. L. 112-29, §6, 125 Stat. 307–08.)

§ 326   Conduct of post-grant review

(a) *Regulations.*—The Director shall prescribe regulations—

(1) providing that the file of any proceeding under this chapter shall be made available to the public, except that any petition or document filed with the intent that it be sealed shall, if accompanied by a motion to seal, be treated as sealed pending the outcome of the ruling on the motion;

(2) setting forth the standards for the showing of sufficient grounds to institute a review under subsections (a) and (b) of section 324;

(3) establishing procedures for the submission of supplemental information after the petition is filed;

(4) establishing and governing a post-grant review under this chapter and the relationship of such review to other proceedings under this title;

(5) setting forth standards and procedures for discovery of relevant evidence, including that such discovery shall be limited to evidence directly related to factual assertions advanced by either party in the proceeding;

(6) prescribing sanctions for abuse of discovery, abuse of process, or any other improper use of the proceeding, such as to harass or to cause unnecessary delay or an unnecessary increase in the cost of the proceeding;

(7) providing for protective orders governing the exchange and submission of confidential information;

(8) providing for the filing by the patent owner of a response to the petition under section 323 after a post-grant review has been instituted, and requiring that the patent owner file with such response, through affidavits or declarations, any additional factual evidence and expert opinions on which the patent owner relies in support of the response;

(9) setting forth standards and procedures for allowing the patent owner to move to amend the patent under subsection (d) to cancel a challenged claim or propose a reasonable number of substitute claims, and ensuring that any information submitted by the patent owner in support of any amendment entered under subsection (d) is made available to the public as part of the prosecution history of the patent;

(10) providing either party with the right to an oral hearing as part of the proceeding;

(11) requiring that the final determination in any post-grant review be issued not later than 1 year after the date on which the Director notices the institution of a proceeding under this chapter, except that the Director may, for good cause shown, extend the 1-year period by not more than 6 months, and may adjust the time periods in this paragraph in the case of joinder under section 325(c); and

(12) providing the petitioner with at least 1 opportunity to file written comments within a time period established by the Director.

(b) *Considerations.* — In prescribing regulations under this section, the Director shall consider the effect of any such regulation on the economy, the integrity of the patent system, the efficient administration of the Office, and the ability of the Office to timely complete proceedings instituted under this chapter.

(c) *Patent Trial and Appeal Board.* — The Patent Trial and Appeal Board shall, in accordance with section 6, conduct each post-grant review instituted under this chapter.

(d) *Amendment of the patent.* —

(1) *In general.* — During a post-grant review instituted under this chapter, the patent owner may file 1 motion to amend the patent in 1 or more of the following ways:

(A) Cancel any challenged patent claim.

35 U.S.C. § 326

(B) For each challenged claim, propose a reasonable number of substitute claims.

(2) *Additional motions.*—Additional motions to amend may be permitted upon the joint request of the petitioner and the patent owner to materially advance the settlement of a proceeding under section 327, or upon the request of the patent owner for good cause shown.

(3) *Scope of claims.*—An amendment under this subsection may not enlarge the scope of the claims of the patent or introduce new matter.

(e) *Evidentiary standards.*—In a post-grant review instituted under this chapter, the petitioner shall have the burden of proving a proposition of unpatentability by a preponderance of the evidence.

(Sept. 16, 2011, Pub. L. 112-29, §6, 125 Stat. 308–09.)

§ 327 Settlement

(a) *In general.*—A post-grant review instituted under this chapter shall be terminated with respect to any petitioner upon the joint request of the petitioner and the patent owner, unless the Office has decided the merits of the proceeding before the request for termination is filed. If the post-grant review is terminated with respect to a petitioner under this section, no estoppel under section 325(e) shall attach to the petitioner, or to the real party in interest or privy of the petitioner, on the basis of that petitioner's institution of that post-grant review. If no petitioner remains in the post-grant review, the Office may terminate the post-grant review or proceed to a final written decision under section 328(a).

(b) *Agreements in writing.*—Any agreement or understanding between the patent owner and a petitioner, including any collateral agreements referred to in such agreement or understanding, made in connection with, or in contemplation of, the termination of a post-grant review under this section shall be in writing, and a true copy of such agreement or understanding shall be filed in the Office before the termination of the post-grant review as between the parties. At the request of a party to the proceeding, the agreement or understanding shall be treated as business confidential information, shall be kept separate from the file of the involved patents, and shall be made available only to Federal Government agencies on written request, or to any person on a showing of good cause.

(Sept. 16, 2011, Pub. L. 112-29, §6, 125 Stat. 310).

§ 328   Decision of the Board

(a) *Final written decision.*—If a post-grant review is instituted and not dismissed under this chapter, the Patent Trial and Appeal Board shall issue a final written decision with respect to the patentability of any patent claim challenged by the petitioner and any new claim added under section 326(d).

(b) *Certificate.*—If the Patent Trial and Appeal Board issues a final written decision under subsection (a) and the time for appeal has expired or any appeal has terminated, the Director shall issue and publish a certificate canceling any claim of the patent finally determined to be unpatentable, confirming any claim of the patent determined to be patentable, and incorporating in the patent by operation of the certificate any new or amended claim determined to be patentable.

(c) *Intervening rights.*—Any proposed amended or new claim determined to be patentable and incorporated into a patent following a post-grant review under this chapter shall have the same effect as that specified in section 252 for reissued patents on the right of any person who made, purchased, or used within the United States, or imported into the United States, anything patented by such proposed amended or new claim, or who made substantial preparation therefor, before the issuance of a certificate under subsection (b).

(d) *Data on length of review.*—The Office shall make available to the public data describing the length of time between the institution of, and the issuance of a final written decision under subsection (a) for, each post-grant review.

(Sept. 16, 2011, Pub. L. 112-29, §6, 125 Stat. 310.)

§ 329   Appeal

A party dissatisfied with the final written decision of the Patent Trial and Appeal Board under section 328(a) may appeal the decision pursuant to sections 141 through 144. Any party to the post-grant review shall have the right to be a party to the appeal.

(Sept. 16, 2011, Pub. L. 112-29, §6, 125 Stat. 311.)

PART IV—PATENT COOPERATION TREATY

35 U.S.C. § 329

CHAPTER 35—DEFINITIONS

SEC.
351.   Definitions.

§ 351   Definitions

When used in this part unless the context otherwise indicates—

(a) The term "treaty" means the Patent Cooperation Treaty done at Washington, on June 19, 1970.

(b) The term "Regulations", when capitalized, means the Regulations under the treaty done at Washington on the same date as the treaty. The term "regulations", when not capitalized, means the regulations established by the Director under this title.

(c) The term "international application" means an application filed under the treaty.

(d) The term "international application originating in the United States" means an international application filed in the Patent and Trademark Office when it is acting as a Receiving Office under the treaty, irrespective of whether or not the United States has been designated in that international application.

(e) The term "international application designating the United States" means an international application specifying the United States as a country in which a patent is sought, regardless where such international application is filed.

(f) The term "Receiving Office" means a national patent office or intergovernmental organization which receives and processes international applications as prescribed by the treaty and the Regulations.

(g) The terms "International Searching Authority" and "International Preliminary Examining Authority" mean a national patent office or intergovernmental organization as appointed under the treaty which processes international applications as prescribed by the treaty and the Regulations.

(h) The term "International Bureau" means the international intergovernmental organization which is recognized as the coordinating body under the treaty and the Regulations.

(i) Terms and expressions not defined in this part are to be taken in the sense indicated by the treaty and the Regulations.

35 U.S.C. § 351

(Nov. 14, 1975, Pub. L. 94-131, §1, 89 Stat. 685; Nov. 8, 1984, Pub. L. 98-622, §403, 98 Stat. 3392; Nov. 6, 1986, Pub. L. 99-616, §2, 100 Stat. 3485.)

CHAPTER 36—INTERNATIONAL STAGE

§ 361   Receiving Office

(a) The Patent and Trademark Office shall act as a Receiving Office for international applications filed by nationals or residents of the United States. In accordance with any agreement made between the United States and another country, the Patent and Trademark Office may also act as a Receiving Office for international applications filed by residents or nationals of such country who are entitled to file international applications.

(b) The Patent and Trademark Office shall perform all acts connected with the discharge of duties required of a Receiving Office, including the collection of international fees and their transmittal to the International Bureau.

(c) International applications filed in the Patent and Trademark Office shall be filed in the English language, or an English translation shall be filed within such later time as may be fixed by the Director.

(d) The international fee, and the transmittal and search fees prescribed under section 376(a) of this part, shall either be paid on filing of an international application or within such later time as may be fixed by the Director.

(Nov. 14, 1975, Pub. L. 94-131, §1, 89 Stat. 686; Nov. 8, 1984, Pub. L. 98-622, §§401, 403, 98 Stat. 3391-92; Nov. 6, 1986, Pub. L. 99-616, §2, 100 Stat. 3485; Dec. 18, 2012, Pub. L. 112-211, §202, 126 Stat. 1536.)

§ 362   International Searching Authority and International Preliminary Examining Authority

(a) The Patent and Trademark Office may act as an International Searching Authority and International Preliminary Examining Authority with respect

35 U.S.C. § 362

to international applications in accordance with the terms and conditions of an agreement which may be concluded with the International Bureau, and may discharge all duties required of such Authorities, including the collection of handling fees and their transmittal to the International Bureau.

(b) The handling fee, preliminary examination fee, and any additional fees due for international preliminary examination shall be paid within such time as may be fixed by the Director.

(Nov. 14, 1975, Pub. L. 94-131, §1, 89 Stat. 686; Nov. 8, 1984, Pub. L. 98-622, §403, 98 Stat. 3392; Nov. 6, 1986, Pub. L. 99-616, §4, 100 Stat. 3485.)

§ 363   International application designating the United States: Effect

An international application designating the United States shall have the effect, from its international filing date under article 11 of the treaty, of a national application for patent regularly filed in the Patent and Trademark Office.

(Nov. 14, 1975, Pub. L. 94-131, §1, 89 Stat. 686; Nov. 8, 1984, Pub. L. 98-622, §403, 98 Stat. 3392; Sept. 16, 2011, Pub. L. 112-29, §3, 125 Stat. 288.)

§ 364   International stage: Procedure

(a) International applications shall be processed by the Patent and Trademark Office when acting as a Receiving Office, International Searching Authority, or International Preliminary Examining Authority, in accordance with the applicable provisions of the treaty, the Regulations, and this title.

(b) An applicant's failure to act within prescribed time limits in connection with requirements pertaining to an international application may be excused as provided in the treaty and the Regulations.

(Nov. 14, 1975, Pub. L. 94-131, §1, 89 Stat. 686; Nov. 8, 1984, Pub. L. 98-622, §403, 98 Stat. 3392; Nov. 6, 1986, Pub. L. 99-616, §5, 100 Stat. 3484, 3487; Dec. 18, 2012, Pub. L. 112-211, §202, 126 Stat. 1536.)

§ 365   Right of priority; benefit of the filing date of a prior application

(a) In accordance with the conditions and requirements of subsections (a) through (d) of section 119, a national application shall be entitled to the right of priority based on a prior filed international application which designated at least one country other than the United States.

(b) In accordance with the conditions and requirement of section 119(a) and the treaty and the Regulations, an international application designating the United States shall be entitled to the right of priority based on a prior foreign application, or a prior international application designating at least one country other than the United States. The Director may establish procedures, including the requirement for payment of the fee specified in section 41(a)(7), to accept an unintentionally delayed claim for priority under the treaty and the Regulations, and to accept a priority claim that pertains to an application that was not filed within the priority period specified in the treaty and Regulations, but was filed within the additional 2-month period specified under section 119(a) or the treaty and Regulations.

(c) In accordance with the conditions and requirements of section 120, an international application designating the United States shall be entitled to the benefit of the filing date of a prior national application, a prior international application designating the United States, or a prior international design application as defined in section 381(a)(6) designating the United States, and a national application shall be entitled to the benefit of the filing date of a prior international application designating the United States. If any claim for the benefit of an earlier filing date is based on a prior international application which designated but did not originate in the United States or a prior international design application as defined in section 381(a)(6) which designated but did not originate in the United States, the Director may require the filing in the Patent and Trademark Office of a certified copy of such application together with a translation thereof into the English language, if it was filed in another language.

(Nov. 14, 1975, Pub. L. 94-131, §1, 89 Stat. 686; Nov. 8, 1984, Pub. L. 98-622, §403, 98 Stat. 3392; Dec. 8, 1994, Pub. L. 103-465, §532, 108 Stat. 4983; Dec. 18, 2012, Pub. L. 112-211, §201, 126 Stat. 1535; Dec. 18, 2012, Pub. L. 112-211, §101, 126 Stat. 1532.)

§ 366   Withdrawn international application

Subject to section 367 of this part, if an international application designating the United States is withdrawn or considered withdrawn, either generally or as to the United States, under the conditions of the treaty and the Regulations, before the applicant has complied with the applicable requirements prescribed by section 371(c) of this part, the designation of the United States shall have no effect after the date of withdrawal, and shall be considered as not having been made, unless a claim for benefit of a prior filing date under section 365(c) of this section was made in a national application, or an international application designating the United States, or a claim for benefit under section 386(c) was made in an international design application designating the United States, filed before the date of such withdrawal. However, such withdrawn international application may serve as the basis for a claim of priority under section 365(a) and (b), or under section 386(a) or (b), if it designated a country other than the United States.

(Nov. 14, 1975, Pub. L. 94-131, §1, 89 Stat. 687; Nov. 8, 1984, Pub. L. 98-622, §401, 98 Stat. 3391; Dec. 18, 2012, Pub. L. 112-211, §101, 126 Stat. 1532.)

§ 367   Actions of other authorities: Review

(a) Where a Receiving Office other than the Patent and Trademark Office has refused to accord an international filing date to an international application designating the United States or where it has held such application to be withdrawn either generally or as to the United States, the applicant may request review of the matter by the Director, on compliance with the requirements of and within the time limits specified by the treaty and the Regulations. Such review may result in a determination that such application be considered as pending in the national stage.

(b) The review under subsection (a) of this section, subject to the same requirements and conditions, may also be requested in those instances where an international application designating the United States is considered withdrawn due to a finding by the International Bureau under article 12(3) of the treaty.

(Nov. 14, 1975, Pub. L. 94-131, §1, 89 Stat. 687; Nov. 8, 1984, Pub. L. 98-622, §403, 98 Stat. 3392.)

§ 368   Secrecy of certain inventions; filing international applications in foreign countries

(a) International applications filed in the Patent and Trademark Office shall be subject to the provisions of chapter 17.

(b) In accordance with article 27(8) of the treaty, the filing of an international application in a country other than the United States on the invention made in this country shall be considered to constitute the filing of an application in a foreign country within the meaning of chapter 17, whether or not the United states is designated in that international application.

(c) If a license to file in a foreign country is refused or if an international application is ordered to be kept secret and a permit refused, the Patent and Trademark Office when acting as a Receiving Office, International Searching Authority, or International Preliminary Examining Authority, may not disclose the contents of such application to anyone not authorized to receive such disclosure.

(Nov. 14, 1975, Pub. L. 94-131, §1, 89 Stat. 687; Nov. 8, 1984, Pub. L. 98-622, §403, 98 Stat. 3392; Nov. 6, 1986, Pub. L. 99-616, §6, 100 Stat. 3486.)

CHAPTER 37—NATIONAL STAGE

§ 371   National stage: Commencement

(a) Receipt from the International Bureau of copies of international applications with any amendments to the claims, international search reports, and international preliminary examination reports including any annexes thereto may be required in the case of international applications designating or electing the United States.

(b) Subject to subsection (f) of this section, the national stage shall commence with the expiration of the applicable time limit under article 22(1) or (2), or under article 39(1)(a) of the treaty.

(c) The applicant shall file in the Patent and Trademark Office—

(1) the national fee provided in section 41(a);

(2) a copy of the international application, unless not required under subsection (a) of this section or already communicated by the International Bureau, and a translation into the English language of the international application, if it was filed in another language;

(3) amendments, if any, to the claims in the international application, made under article 19 of the treaty, unless such amendments have been communicated to the Patent and Trademark Office by the International Bureau, and a translation into the English language if such amendments were made in another language;

(4) an oath or declaration of the inventor (or other person authorized under chapter 11) complying with the requirements of section 115 and with regulations prescribed for oaths or declarations of applicants;

(5) a translation into the English language of any annexes to the international preliminary examination report, if such annexes were made in another language.

(d) The requirements with respect to the national fee referred to in subsection (c)(1), the translation referred to in subsection (c)(2), and the oath or declaration referred to in subsection (c)(4) of this section shall be complied with by the date of the commencement of the national stage or by such later time as may be fixed by the Director. The copy of the international application referred to in subsection (c)(2) shall be submitted by the date of the commencement of the national stage. Failure to comply with these requirements shall be regarded as abandonment of the application by the parties thereof. The payment of a surcharge may be required as a condition of accepting the national fee referred to in subsection (c)(1) or the oath or declaration referred to in subsection (c)(4) of this section if these requirements are not met by the date of the commencement of the national stage. The requirements of subsection (c)(3) of this section shall be complied with by the date of the commencement of the national stage, and failure to do so shall be regarded as a cancellation of the amendments to the claims in the international application made under article 19 of the treaty. The requirement of subsection (c)(5) shall be complied with at such time as may be fixed by the Director and failure to do so shall be regarded as cancellation of the amendments made under article 34(2)(b) of the treaty.

(e) After an international application has entered the national stage, no patent may be granted or refused thereon before the expiration of the applicable time limit under article 28 or article 41 of the treaty, except with the express consent of the applicant. The applicant may present amendments to the specification, claims, and drawings of the application after the national stage has commenced.

(f) At the express request of the applicant, the national stage of processing may be commenced at any time at which the application is in order for such purpose and the applicable requirements of subsection (c) of this section have been complied with.

(Nov. 14, 1975, Pub. L. 94-131, §1, 89 Stat. 688; Nov. 8, 1984, Pub. L. 98-622, §§402-03, 98 Stat. 3391-92; Nov. 6, 1986, Pub. L. 99-616, §7, 100 Stat. 3486; Dec. 10, 1991, Pub. L. 102-204, §5, 105 Stat. 1641; Nov. 2, 2002, Pub. L. 107-273, §13206, 116 Stat. 1904; Sept. 16, 2011, Pub. L. 112-29, §20, 125 Stat. 335; Dec. 18, 2012, Pub. L. 112-211, §202, 126 Stat. 1536.)

§ 372   National stage: Requirements and procedure

(a) All questions of substance and, within the scope of the requirements of the treaty and Regulations, procedure in an international application designating the United States shall be determined as in the case of national applications regularly filed in the Patent and Trademark Office.

(b) In case of international applications designating but not originating in, the United States—

(1) the Director may cause to be reexamined questions relating to form and contents of the application in accordance with the requirements of the treaty and the Regulations;

(2) the Director may cause the question of unity of invention to be reexamined under section 121, within the scope of the requirements of the treaty and the Regulations; and

(3) the Director may require a verification of the translation of the international application or any other document pertaining to the application if the application or other document was filed in a language other than English.

(c) [Repealed]

(Nov. 14, 1975, Pub. L. 94-131, §1, 89 Stat. 689; Nov. 8, 1984, Pub. L. 98-622, §§402-03, 98 Stat. 3392.)

§ 373   Improper applicant [Repealed]

(Nov. 14, 1975, Pub. L. 94-131, §1, 89 Stat. 689; Nov. 8, 1984, Pub. L. 98-622, §403, 98 Stat. 3392; Dec. 8, 1994, Pub. L. 103-465, §532, 108 Stat. 4983; Jan. 14, 2013, Pub. L. 112-274, §1(i), 126 Stat. 2457.)

§ 374   Publication of international application

The publication under the treaty defined in section 351(a), of an international application designating the United States shall be deemed a publication under section 122(b), except as provided in section 154(d).

(Nov. 14, 1975, Pub. L. 94-131, §1, 89 Stat. 689; Nov. 29, 1999, Pub. L. 106-113, §4507, 113 Stat. 1501A-565; Nov. 2, 2002, Pub. L. 107-273, §13205, 116 Stat. 1902; Sept. 16, 2011, Pub. L. 112-29, §3, 125 Stat. 288.)

§ 375   Patent issued on international application: Effect

(a) A patent may be issued by the Director based on an international application designating the United States, in accordance with the provisions of this title. Such patent shall have the force and effect of a patent issued on a national application filed under the provisions of chapter 11.

(b) Where due to an incorrect translation the scope of a patent granted on an international application designating the United States, which was not originally filed in the English language, exceeds the scope of the international application in its original language, a court of competent jurisdiction may retroactively limit the scope of the patent, by declaring it unenforceable to the extent that it exceeds the scope of the international application in its original language.

(Nov. 14, 1975, Pub. L. 94-131, §1, 89 Stat. 689; Sept. 16, 2011, Pub. L. 112-29, §3, 125 Stat. 288.)

§ 376   Fees

(a) The required payment of the international fee and the handling fee, which amounts are specified in the Regulations, shall be paid in United States currency. The Patent and Trademark Office shall charge a national fee as provided in section 41(a), and may also charge the following fees:

(1) A transmittal fee (see section 361(d)).

(2) A search fee (see section 361(d)).

(3) A supplemental search fee (to be paid when required).

(4) A preliminary examination fee and any additional fees (see section 362(b));

(5) Such other fees as established by the Director.

(b) The amounts of fees specified in subsection (a) of this section, except the international fee and the handling fee, shall be prescribed by the Director. He may refund any sum paid by mistake or in excess of the fees so specified, or if required under the treaty and the Regulations. The Director may also refund any part of the search fee, the national fee, the preliminary examination fee, and any additional fees where he determines such refund to be warranted.

(Nov. 14, 1975, Pub. L. 94-131, §1, 89 Stat. 690; amended Nov. 8, 1984, Pub. L. 98-622, §§402-03, 98 Stat. 3392; Nov. 6, 1986, Pub. L. 99-616, §8, 100 Stat. 3486; Dec. 10, 1991, Pub. L. 102-204, §5, 105 Stat. 1640; Nov. 2, 2002, Pub. L. 107-273, §13206, 116 Stat. 1904.)

CHAPTER 38—INTERNATIONAL DESIGN APPLICATIONS

§ 381 Definitions

(a) *In general.*—When used in this part, unless the context otherwise indicates—

(1) the term "treaty" means the Geneva Act of the Hague Agreement Concerning the International Registration of Industrial Designs adopted at Geneva on July 2, 1999;

(2) the term "regulations"—

(A) when capitalized, means the Common Regulations under the treaty; and

(B) when not capitalized, means the regulations established by the Director under this title;

(3) the terms "designation", "designating", and "designate" refer to a request that an international registration have effect in a Contracting Party to the treaty;

(4) the term "International Bureau" means the international intergovernmental organization that is recognized as the coordinating body under the treaty and the Regulations;

(5) the term "effective registration date" means the date of international registration determined by the International Bureau under the treaty;

(6) the term "international design application" means an application for international registration; and

(7) the term "international registration" means the international registration of an industrial design filed under the treaty.

(b) *Rule of construction.*—Terms and expressions not defined in this part are to be taken in the sense indicated by the treaty and the Regulations.

§ 382 Filing international design applications

(a) *In general.*—Any person who is a national of the United States, or has a domicile, a habitual residence, or a real and effective industrial or commercial establishment in the United States, may file an international design application by submitting to the Patent and Trademark Office an application in such form, together with such fees, as may be prescribed by the Director.

(b) *Required action.*—The Patent and Trademark Office shall perform all acts connected with the discharge of its duties under the treaty, including the collection of international fees and transmittal thereof to the International Bureau. Subject to chapter 17, international design applications shall be forwarded by the Patent and Trademark Office to the International Bureau, upon payment of a transmittal fee.

(c) *Applicability of chapter 16.*—Except as otherwise provided in this chapter, the provisions of chapter 16 shall apply.

(d) *Application filed in another country.*—An international design application on an industrial design made in this country shall be considered to constitute the filing of an application in a foreign country within the meaning of chapter 17 if the international design application is filed—

(1) in a country other than the United States;

(2) at the International Bureau; or

(3) with an intergovernmental organization.

§ 383 International design application

In addition to any requirements pursuant to chapter 16, the international design application shall contain—

(1) a request for international registration under the treaty;

(2) an indication of the designated Contracting Parties;

(3) data concerning the applicant as prescribed in the treaty and the Regulations;

(4) copies of a reproduction or, at the choice of the applicant, of several different reproductions of the industrial design that is the subject of the international design application, presented in the number and manner prescribed in the treaty and the Regulations;

(5) an indication of the product or products that constitute the industrial design or in relation to which the industrial design is to be used, as prescribed in the treaty and the Regulations;

(6) the fees prescribed in the treaty and the Regulations; and

(7) any other particulars prescribed in the Regulations.

§ 384 Filing date

(a) *In general.*—Subject to subsection (b), the filing date of an international design application in the United States shall be the effective registration date. Notwithstanding the provisions of this part, any international design application designating the United States that otherwise meets the requirements of chapter 16 may be treated as a design application under chapter 16.

(b) *Review.*—An applicant may request review by the Director of the filing date of the international design application in the United States. The Director may determine that the filing date of the international design application in the United States is a date other than the effective registration date. The Director may establish procedures, including the payment of a surcharge, to review the filing date under this section. Such review may result in a determination that the application has a filing date in the United States other than the effective registration date.

§ 385 Effect of international design application

An international design application designating the United States shall have the effect, for all purposes, from its filing date determined in accordance with section 384, of an application for patent filed in the Patent and Trademark Office pursuant to chapter 16.

§ 386 Right of priority

(a) *National application.*—In accordance with the conditions and requirements of subsections (a) through (d) of section 119 and section 172, a national application shall be entitled to the right of priority based on a prior international design application that designated at least 1 country other than the United States.

(b) *Prior foreign application.*—In accordance with the conditions and requirements of subsections (a) through (d) of section 119 and section 172 and the treaty and the Regulations, an international design application designating the United States shall be entitled to the right of priority based on a prior foreign application, a prior international application as defined in section 351(c) designating at least 1 country other than the United States, or a prior international design application designating at least 1 country other than the United States.

(c) *Prior national application.*—In accordance with the conditions and requirements of section 120, an international design application designating the

United States shall be entitled to the benefit of the filing date of a prior national application, a prior international application as defined in section 351(c) designating the United States, or a prior international design application designating the United States, and a national application shall be entitled to the benefit of the filing date of a prior international design application designating the United States. If any claim for the benefit of an earlier filing date is based on a prior international application as defined in section 351(c) which designated but did not originate in the United States or a prior international design application which designated but did not originate in the United States, the Director may require the filing in the Patent and Trademark Office of a certified copy of such application together with a translation thereof into the English language, if it was filed in another language.

§ 387   Relief from prescribed time limits

An applicant's failure to act within prescribed time limits in connection with requirements pertaining to an international design application may be excused as to the United States upon a showing satisfactory to the Director of unintentional delay and under such conditions, including a requirement for payment of the fee specified in section 41(a)(7), as may be prescribed by the Director.

§ 388   Withdrawn or abandoned international design application

Subject to sections 384 and 387, if an international design application designating the United States is withdrawn, renounced or canceled or considered withdrawn or abandoned, either generally or as to the United States, under the conditions of the treaty and the Regulations, the designation of the United States shall have no effect after the date of withdrawal, renunciation, cancellation, or abandonment and shall be considered as not having been made, unless a claim for benefit of a prior filing date under section 386(c) was made in a national application, or an international design application designating the United States, or a claim for benefit under section 365(c) was made in an international application designating the United States, filed before the date of such withdrawal, renunciation, cancellation, or abandonment. However, such withdrawn, renounced, canceled, or abandoned international design application may serve as the basis for a claim of priority under subsections (a) and (b) of section 386, or under subsection (a) or (b) of section 365, if it designated a country other than the United States.

§ 389 Examination of international design application

(a) In general.—The Director shall cause an examination to be made pursuant to this title of an international design application designating the United States.

(b) Applicability of chapter 16.—All questions of substance and, unless otherwise required by the treaty and Regulations, procedures regarding an international design application designating the United States shall be determined as in the case of applications filed under chapter 16.

(c) Fees.—The Director may prescribe fees for filing international design applications, for designating the United States, and for any other processing, services, or materials relating to international design applications, and may provide for later payment of such fees, including surcharges for later submission of fees.

(d) Issuance of patent.—The Director may issue a patent based on an international design application designating the United States, in accordance with the provisions of this title. Such patent shall have the force and effect of a patent issued on an application filed under chapter 16.

§ 390 Publication of international design application

The publication under the treaty of an international design application designating the United States shall be deemed a publication under section 122(b).

(Dec. 18, 2012, Pub. L. 112-211, §101, 126 Stat. 1527.)

UNCODIFIED PROVISIONS OF THE AMERICA INVENTS ACT

Sec.
- 10. Fee setting authority.
- 14. Tax strategies deemed within the prior art.
- 18. Transitional program for covered business method patents.

§ 10[47] Fee setting authority

(a) *Fee setting.*—

(1) *In general.*—The Director may set or adjust by rule any fee established, authorized, or charged under title 35, United States Code, or the Trade-

---

[47] *Ed. Note:* The authority of the Director to set or adjust any fee under subsection (a) will terminate seven years after the date of enactment of Pub. L. 112-29. See §10(i)(2) of Pub. L. 112-29.

America Invents Act § 10

mark Act of 1946 (15 U.S.C. 1051 et seq.), for any services performed by or materials furnished by, the Office, subject to paragraph (2).

(2) *Fees to recover costs.*—Fees may be set or adjusted under paragraph (1) only to recover the aggregate estimated costs to the Office for processing, activities, services, and materials relating to patents (in the case of patent fees) and trademarks (in the case of trademark fees), including administrative costs of the Office with respect to such patent or trademark fees (as the case may be).

(b) *Small and micro entities.*—The fees set or adjusted under subsection (a) for filing, searching, examining, issuing, appealing, and maintaining patent applications and patents shall be reduced by 50 percent with respect to the application of such fees to any small entity that qualifies for reduced fees under section 41(h)(1) of title 35, United States Code, and shall be reduced by 75 percent with respect to the application of such fees to any micro entity as defined in section 123 of that title (as added by subsection (g) of this section).

(c) *Reduction of fees in certain fiscal years.*—In each fiscal year, the Director—

(1) shall consult with the Patent Public Advisory Committee and the Trademark Public Advisory Committee on the advisability of reducing any fees described in subsection (a); and

(2) after the consultation required under paragraph (1), may reduce such fees.

(d) *Role of the Public Advisory Committee.*—The Director shall—

(1) not less than 45 days before publishing any proposed fee under subsection (a) in the Federal Register, submit the proposed fee to the Patent Public Advisory Committee or the Trademark Public Advisory Committee, or both, as appropriate;

(2)(A) provide the relevant advisory committee described in paragraph (1) a 30-day period following the submission of any proposed fee, in which to deliberate, consider, and comment on such proposal;

(B) require that, during that 30-day period, the relevant advisory committee hold a public hearing relating to such proposal; and

(C) assist the relevant advisory committee in carrying out that public hearing, including by offering the use of the resources of the Office to notify and promote the hearing to the public and interested stakeholders;

(3) require the relevant advisory committee to make available to the public a written report setting forth in detail the comments, advice, and recommendations of the committee regarding the proposed fee; and

(4) consider and analyze any comments, advice, or recommendations received from the relevant advisory committee before setting or adjusting (as the case may be) the fee.

(e) *Publication in the Federal Register.*—

(1) *Publication and rationale.*—The Director shall—

(A) publish any proposed fee change under this section in the Federal Register;

(B) include, in such publication, the specific rationale and purpose for the proposal, including the possible expectations or benefits resulting from the proposed change; and

(C) notify, through the Chair and Ranking Member of the Committees on the Judiciary of the Senate and the House of Representatives, the Congress of the proposed change not later than the date on which the proposed change is published under subparagraph (A).

(2) *Public comment period.*—The Director shall, in the publication under paragraph (1), provide the public a period of not less than 45 days in which to submit comments on the proposed change in fees.

(3) *Publication of final rule.*—The final rule setting or adjusting a fee under this section shall be published in the Federal Register and in the Official Gazette of the Patent and Trademark Office.

(4) *Congressional comment period.*—A fee set or adjusted under subsection (a) may not become effective—

(A) before the end of the 45-day period beginning on the day after the date on which the Director publishes the final rule adjusting or setting the fee under paragraph (3); or

(B) if a law is enacted disapproving such fee.

(5) *Rule of construction.*—Rules prescribed under this section shall not diminish—

(A) the rights of an applicant for a patent under title 35, United States Code, or for a mark under the Trademark Act of 1946; or

(B) any rights under a ratified treaty.

(f) *Retention of authority.*—The Director retains the authority under subsection (a) to set or adjust fees only during such period as the Patent and Trademark Office remains an agency within the Department of Commerce.

(Sept. 16, 2011, Pub. L. 112-29, §10, 125 Stat. 316.)

§ 14   Tax strategies deemed within the prior art

(a) *In general.*—For purposes of evaluating an invention under section 102 or 103 of title 35, United States Code, any strategy for reducing, avoiding, or deferring tax liability, whether known or unknown at the time of the invention or application for patent, shall be deemed insufficient to differentiate a claimed invention from the prior art.

(b) *Definition.*—For purposes of this section, the term "tax liability" refers to any liability for a tax under any Federal, State, or local law, or the law of any foreign jurisdiction, including any statute, rule, regulation, or ordinance that levies, imposes, or assesses such tax liability.

(c) *Exclusions.*—This section does not apply to that part of an invention that—

(1) is a method, apparatus, technology, computer program product, or system, that is used solely for preparing a tax or information return or other tax filing, including one that records, transmits, transfers, or organizes data related to such filing; or

(2) is a method, apparatus, technology, computer program product, or system used solely for financial management, to the extent that it is severable from any tax strategy or does not limit the use of any tax strategy by any taxpayer or tax advisor.

(d) *Rule of construction.*—Nothing in this section shall be construed to imply that other business methods are patentable or that other business method patents are valid.

(e) *Effective date; applicability.*—This section shall take effect on the date of the enactment of this Act and shall apply to any patent application that is pending on, or filed on or after, that date, and to any patent that is issued on or after that date.

(Sept. 16, 2011, Pub. L. 112-29, §14, 125 Stat. 327.)

§ 18   Transitional program for covered business method patents

(a) *Transitional program.*—

(1) *Establishment.*—Not later than the date that is 1 year after the date of the enactment of this Act, the Director shall issue regulations establishing

and implementing a transitional post-grant review proceeding for review of the validity of covered business method patents. The transitional proceeding implemented pursuant to this subsection shall be regarded as, and shall employ the standards and procedures of, a post-grant review under chapter 32 of title 35, United States Code, subject to the following:

(A) Section 321(c) of title 35, United States Code, and subsections (b), (e)(2), and (f) of section 325 of such title shall not apply to a transitional proceeding.

(B) A person may not file a petition for a transitional proceeding with respect to a covered business method patent unless the person or the person's real party in interest or privy has been sued for infringement of the patent or has been charged with infringement under that patent.

(C) A petitioner in a transitional proceeding who challenges the validity of 1 or more claims in a covered business method patent on a ground raised under section 102 or 103 of title 35, United States Code, as in effect on the day before the effective date set forth in section 3(n)(1),[48] may support such ground only on the basis of—

(i) prior art that is described by section 102(a) of such title (as in effect on the day before such effective date); or

(ii) prior art that—

(I) discloses the invention more than 1 year before the date of the application for patent in the United States; and

(II) would be described by section 102(a) of such title (as in effect on the day before the effective date set forth in section 3(n)(1)) if the disclosure had been made by another before the invention thereof by the applicant for patent.

(D) The petitioner in a transitional proceeding that results in a final written decision under section 328(a) of title 35, United States Code, with respect to a claim in a covered business method patent, or the petitioner's real party in interest, may not assert, either in a civil action arising in whole or in part under section 1338 of title 28, United States Code, or in a proceeding before the International Trade Commission under section 337 of the Tariff Act of 1930 (19 U.S.C. 1337), that the claim is invalid on any ground that the petitioner raised during that transitional proceeding.

---

[48] *Ed. Note*: In general, the effective date set forth in §3(n)(1) is the expiration of 18 months from the date of enactment of Pub. L. 112-29 (Sept. 16, 2011).

America Invents Act § 18

(E) The Director may institute a transitional proceeding only for a patent that is a covered business method patent.

(2) *Effective date.*—The regulations issued under paragraph (1) shall take effect upon the expiration of the 1-year period beginning on the date of the enactment of this Act and shall apply to any covered business method patent issued before, on, or after that effective date, except that the regulations shall not apply to a patent described in section 6(f)(2)(A) of this Act during the period in which a petition for post-grant review of that patent would satisfy the requirements of section 321(c) of title 35, United States Code.

(3) *Sunset.*—

(A) *In general.*—This subsection, and the regulations issued under this subsection, are repealed effective upon the expiration of the 8-year period beginning on the date that the regulations issued under to paragraph (1) take effect.

(B) *Applicability.*—Notwithstanding subparagraph (A), this subsection and the regulations issued under this subsection shall continue to apply, after the date of the repeal under subparagraph (A), to any petition for a transitional proceeding that is filed before the date of such repeal.

(b) *Request for stay.*—

(1) *In general.*—If a party seeks a stay of a civil action alleging infringement of a patent under section 281 of title 35, United States Code, relating to a transitional proceeding for that patent, the court shall decide whether to enter a stay based on—

(A) whether a stay, or the denial thereof, will simplify the issues in question and streamline the trial;

(B) whether discovery is complete and whether a trial date has been set;

(C) whether a stay, or the denial thereof, would unduly prejudice the nonmoving party or present a clear tactical advantage for the moving party; and

(D) whether a stay, or the denial thereof, will reduce the burden of litigation on the parties and on the court.

(2) *Review.*—A party may take an immediate interlocutory appeal from a district court's decision under paragraph (1). The United States Court of

Appeals for the Federal Circuit shall review the district court's decision to ensure consistent application of established precedent, and such review may be de novo.

(c) *ATM exemption for venue purposes.*—In an action for infringement under section 281 of title 35, United States Code, of a covered business method patent, an automated teller machine shall not be deemed to be a regular and established place of business for purposes of section 1400(b) of title 28, United States Code.

(d) *Definition.*—

(1) *In general.*—For purposes of this section, the term "covered business method patent" means a patent that claims a method or corresponding apparatus for performing data processing or other operations used in the practice, administration, or management of a financial product or service, except that the term does not include patents for technological inventions.

(2) *Regulations.*—To assist in implementing the transitional proceeding authorized by this section, the Director shall issue regulations for determining whether a patent is for a technological invention.

(e) *Rule of construction.*—Nothing in this section shall be construed as amending or interpreting categories of patent-eligible subject matter set forth under section 101 of title 35, United States Code.

(Sept. 16, 2011, Pub. L. 112-29, §18, 125 Stat. 329; Jan. 14, 2013, Pub. L. 112-274, §1(b), 126 Stat. 2456.)

Part 2

TRADEMARKS

UNITED STATES CODE

TITLE 15, CHAPTER 22—TRADEMARKS

TITLE 15, CHAPTER 107—PROTECTION OF INTELLECTUAL PROPERTY RIGHTS

UNITED STATES CODE
TITLE 15, CHAPTER 22—TRADEMARKS

CHAPTER 22—TRADEMARKS

SUBCHAPTER I—THE PRINCIPAL REGISTER

§ 1051 Registration; application; payment of fees; designation of resident for service of process and notice [Section 1]

Section 1. (a)(1) The owner of a trademark used in commerce may request registration of its trademark on the principal register hereby established by paying the prescribed fee and filing in the Patent and Trademark Of-

15 U.S.C. § 1051

fice an application and a verified statement, in such form as may be prescribed by the Director[1], and such number of specimens or facsimiles of the mark as used as may be required by the Director.

(2) The application shall include specification of the applicant's domicile and citizenship, the date of the applicant's first use of the mark, the date of the applicant's first use of the mark in commerce, the goods in connection with which the mark is used, and a drawing of the mark.

(3) The statement shall be verified by the applicant and specify that—

(A) the person making the verification believes that he or she, or the juristic person in whose behalf he or she makes the verification, to be the owner of the mark sought to be registered;

(B) to the best of the verifier's knowledge and belief, the facts recited in the application are accurate;

(C) the mark is in use in commerce; and

(D) to the best of the verifier's knowledge and belief, no other person has the right to use such mark in commerce either in the identical form thereof or in such near resemblance thereto as to be likely, when used on or in connection with the goods of such other person, to cause confusion, or to cause mistake, or to deceive, except that, in the case of every application claiming concurrent use, the applicant shall—

(i) state exceptions to the claim of exclusive use; and

(ii) shall specify, to the extent of the verifier's knowledge—

(I) any concurrent use by others;

(II) the goods on or in connection with which and the areas in which each concurrent use exists;

(III) the periods of each use; and

(IV) the goods and area for which the applicant desires registration.

(4) The applicant shall comply with such rules or regulations as may be prescribed by the Director. The Director shall promulgate rules prescribing the requirements for the application and for obtaining a filing date herein.

---

[1] *Ed. Note:* Pursuant to §4732(b)(1) (B) of Pub. L. 106-113, the term "Commissioner" is to be replaced with the term "Director" each place it appears in the Trademark Act of 1946.

15 U.S.C. § 1051

(b)(1) A person who has a bona fide intention, under circumstances showing the good faith of such person, to use a trademark in commerce may request registration of its trademark on the principal register hereby established by paying the prescribed fee and filing in the Patent and Trademark Office an application and a verified statement, in such form as may be prescribed by the Director.

(2) The application shall include specification of the applicant's domicile and citizenship, the goods in connection with which the applicant has a bona fide intention to use the mark, and a drawing of the mark.

(3) The statement shall be verified by the applicant and specify—

(A) that the person making the verification believes that he or she, or the juristic person in whose behalf he or she makes the verification, to be entitled to use the mark in commerce;

(B) the applicant's bona fide intention to use the mark in commerce;

(C) that, to the best of the verifier's knowledge and belief, the facts recited in the application are accurate; and

(D) that, to the best of the verifier's knowledge and belief, no other person has the right to use such mark in commerce either in the identical form thereof or in such near resemblance thereto as to be likely, when used on or in connection with the goods of such other person, to cause confusion, or to cause mistake, or to deceive.

Except for applications filed pursuant to section 44, no mark shall be registered until the applicant has met the requirements of subsections (c) and (d) of this section.

(4) The applicant shall comply with such rules or regulations as may be prescribed by the Director. The Director shall promulgate rules prescribing the requirements for the application and for obtaining a filing date herein.

(c) At any time during examination of an application filed under subsection (b), an applicant who has made use of the mark in commerce may claim the benefits of such use for purposes of this Act, by amending his or her application to bring it into conformity with the requirements of subsection (a).

(d) (1) Within six months after the date on which the notice of allowance with respect to a mark is issued under section 13(b)(2) [§1063(b)(2)] to an applicant under subsection (b) of this section, the applicant shall file in the

Patent and Trademark Office, together with such number of specimens or facsimiles of the mark as used in commerce as may be required by the Director and payment of the prescribed fee, a verified statement that the mark is in use in commerce and specifying the date of the applicant's first use of the mark in commerce and those goods or services specified in the notice of allowance on or in connection with which the mark is used in commerce. Subject to examination and acceptance of the statement of use, the mark shall be registered in the Patent and Trademark Office, a certificate of registration shall be issued for those goods or services recited in the statement of use for which the mark is entitled to registration, and notice of registration shall be published in the Official Gazette of the Patent and Trademark Office. Such examination may include an examination of the factors set forth in subsections (a) through (e) of section 2 [§1052]. The notice of registration shall specify the goods or services for which the mark is registered.

(2) The Director shall extend, for one additional 6-month period, the time for filing the statement of use under paragraph (1), upon written request of the applicant before the expiration of the 6-month period provided in paragraph (1). In addition to an extension under the preceding sentence, the Director may, upon a showing of good cause by the applicant, further extend the time for filing the statement of use under paragraph (1) for periods aggregating not more than 24 months, pursuant to written request of the applicant made before the expiration of the last extension granted under this paragraph. Any request for an extension under this paragraph shall be accompanied by a verified statement that the applicant has a continued bona fide intention to use the mark in commerce and specifying those goods or services identified in the notice of allowance on or in connection with which the applicant has a continued bona fide intention to use the mark in commerce. Any request for an extension under this paragraph shall be accompanied by payment of the prescribed fee. The Director shall issue regulations setting forth guidelines for determining what constitutes good cause for purposes of this paragraph.

(3) The Director shall notify any applicant who files a statement of use of the acceptance or refusal thereof and, if the statement of use is refused, the reasons for the refusal. An applicant may amend the statement of use.

(4) The failure to timely file a verified statement of use under paragraph (1) or an extension request under paragraph (2) shall result in abandon-

ment of the application, unless it can be shown to the satisfaction of the Director that the delay in responding was unintentional, in which case the time for filing may be extended, but for a period not to exceed the period specified in paragraphs (1) and (2) for filing a statement of use.

(e) If the applicant is not domiciled in the United States the applicant may designate, by a document filed in the United States Patent and Trademark Office, the name and address of a person resident in the United States on whom may be served notices or process in proceedings affecting the mark. Such notices or process may be served upon the person so designated by leaving with that person or mailing to that person a copy thereof at the address specified in the last designation so filed. If the person so designated cannot be found at the address given in the last designation, or if the registrant does not designate by a document filed in the United States Patent and Trademark Office the name and address of a person resident in the United States on whom may be served notices or process in proceedings affecting the mark, such notices or process may be served on the Director.

(July 5, 1946, ch. 540, §1, 60 Stat. 427; Oct. 9, 1962, Pub. L. 87-772, §1, 76 Stat. 769; Jan. 2, 1975, Pub. L. 93-596, §1, 88 Stat. 1949; Nov. 16, 1988, Pub. L. 100-667, §103, 102 Stat. 3935–37; Oct. 30, 1998, Pub. L. 105-330, §§103, 201, 112 Stat. 3064, 3069; Nov. 2, 2002, Pub. L. 107-273, §13207, 116 Stat. 1906.)

§ 1052 Trademarks registrable on principal register; concurrent registration [Section 2]

No trademark by which the goods of the applicant may be distinguished from the goods of others shall be refused registration on the principal register on account of its nature unless it—

(a) Consists of or comprises immoral, deceptive, or scandalous matter; or matter which may disparage or falsely suggest a connection with persons, living or dead, institutions, beliefs, or national symbols, or bring them into contempt, or disrepute; or a geographical indication which, when used on or in connection with wines or spirits, identifies a place other than the origin of the goods and is first used on or in connection with wines or spirits by the applicant on or after one year after the date on which the WTO Agreement (as defined in section 2(9) of the Uruguay Round Agreements Act) enters into force with respect to the United States.[2]

---

[2] *Ed. Note:* The WTO Agreement entered into force with respect to the United States on Jan. 1, 1995. Thus, the language after the second semicolon in §1052(a) took effect on Jan. 1, 1996.

15 U.S.C. § 1052

(b) Consists of or comprises the flag or coat of arms or other insignia of the United States, or of any State or municipality, or of any foreign nation, or any simulation thereof.

(c) Consists of or comprises a name, portrait, or signature identifying a particular living individual except by his written consent, or the name, signature, or portrait of a deceased President of the United States during the life of his widow, if any, except by the written consent of the widow.

(d) Consists of or comprises a mark which so resembles a mark registered in the Patent and Trademark Office, or a mark or trade name previously used in the United States by another and not abandoned, as to be likely, when used on or in connection with the goods of the applicant, to cause confusion, or to cause mistake, or to deceive: *Provided,* That if the Director determines that confusion, mistake, or deception is not likely to result from the continued use by more than one person of the same or similar marks under conditions and limitations as to the mode or place of use of the marks or the goods on or in connection with which such marks are used, concurrent registrations may be issued to such persons when they have become entitled to use such marks as a result of their concurrent lawful use in commerce prior to (1) the earliest of the filing dates of the applications pending or of any registration issued under this Act; (2) July 5, 1947, in the case of registrations previously issued under the Act of March 3, 1881, or February 20, 1905, and continuing in full force and effect on that date; or (3) July 5, 1947, in the case of applications filed under the Act of February 20, 1905, and registered after July 5, 1947. Use prior to the filing date of any pending application or a registration shall not be required when the owner of such application or registration consents to the grant of a concurrent registration to the applicant. Concurrent registrations may also be issued by the Director when a court of competent jurisdiction has finally determined that more than one person is entitled to use the same or similar marks in commerce. In issuing concurrent registrations, the Director shall prescribe conditions and limitations as to the mode or place of use of the mark or the goods on or in connection with which such mark is registered to the respective persons.

(e) Consists of a mark which (1) when used on or in connection with the goods of the applicant is merely descriptive or deceptively misdescriptive of them, (2) when used on or in connection with the goods of the applicant is primarily geographically descriptive of them, except as indications of regional origin may be registrable under section 4, (3) when used on or in connection with the goods of the applicant is primarily geographically deceptively misdescriptive of them, (4) is primarily merely a surname, or (5) comprises any matter that, as a whole, is functional.

(f) Except as expressly excluded in subsections (a), (b), (c), (d), (e)(3), and (e)(5) of this section, nothing herein shall prevent the registration of a mark used by the applicant which has become distinctive of the applicant's goods in commerce. The Director may accept as prima facie evidence that the mark has become distinctive, as used on or in connection with the applicant's goods in commerce, proof of substantially exclusive and continuous use thereof as a mark by the applicant in commerce for the five years before the date on which the claim of distinctiveness is made. Nothing in this section shall prevent the registration of a mark which, when used on or in connection with the goods of the applicant, is primarily geographically deceptively misdescriptive of them, and which became distinctive of the applicant's goods in commerce before the date of the enactment of the North American Free Trade Agreement Implementation Act.[3]

A mark which would be likely to cause dilution by blurring or dilution by tarnishment under section 43(c), may be refused registration only pursuant to a proceeding brought under section 13. A registration for a mark which would be likely to cause dilution by blurring or dilution by tarnishment under section 43(c), may be canceled pursuant to a proceeding brought under either section 14 or section 24.

(July 5, 1946, ch. 540, title I, §2, 60 Stat. 428; Oct. 9, 1962, Pub. L. 87-772, §2, 76 Stat. 769; Jan. 2, 1975, Pub. L. 93-596, §1, 88 Stat. 1949; Nov. 16, 1988, Pub. L. 100-667, §104, 102 Stat. 3937-38; Dec. 8, 1993, Pub. L. 103-182, §333, 107 Stat. 2114; Dec. 8, 1994, Pub. L. 103-465, §522, 108 Stat. 4982; Oct. 30, 1998, Pub. L. 105-330, §201, 112 Stat. 3069; Aug. 5, 1999, Pub. L. 106-43, §2, 113 Stat. 218, Oct. 6, 2006, Pub. L. 109-312, §3(a), 120 Stat. 1732.)

§ 1053 Service marks registrable [Section 3]

Subject to the provisions relating to the registration of trademarks, so far as they are applicable, service marks shall be registrable, in the same manner and with the same effect as are trademarks, and when registered they shall be entitled to the protection provided herein in the case of trademarks. Applications and procedure under this section shall conform as nearly as practicable to those prescribed for the registration of trademarks.

---

[3] *Ed. Note:* The North American Free Trade Agreement Implementation Act was enacted on Dec. 8, 1993.

15 U.S.C. § 1053

(July 5, 1946, ch. 540, title I, §3, 60 Stat. 429; Nov. 16, 1988, Pub. L. 100-667, §105, 102 Stat. 3938.)

§ 1054   Collective marks and certification marks registrable [Section 4]

Subject to the provisions relating to the registration of trademarks, so far as they are applicable, collective and certification marks, including indications of regional origin, shall be registrable under this act, in the same manner and with the same effect as are trademarks, by persons, and nations, States, municipalities, and the like, exercising legitimate control over the use of the marks sought to be registered, even though not possessing an industrial or commercial establishment, and when registered they shall be entitled to the protection provided herein in the case of trademarks, except in the case of certification marks when used so as to represent falsely that the owner or a user thereof makes or sells the goods or performs the services on or in connection with which such mark is used. Applications and procedure under this section shall conform as nearly as practicable to those prescribed for the registration of trademarks.

(July 5, 1946, ch. 540, title I, §4, 60 Stat. 429; Nov. 16, 1988, Pub. L. 100-667, §106, 102 Stat. 3938.)

§ 1055   Use by related companies affecting validity and registration
      [Section 5]

Where a registered mark or a mark sought to be registered is or may be used legitimately by related companies, such use shall inure to the benefit of the registrant or applicant for registration, and such use shall not affect the validity of such mark or of its registration, provided such mark is not used in such manner as to deceive the public. If first use of a mark by a person is controlled by the registrant or applicant for registration of the mark with respect to the nature and quality of the goods or services, such first use shall inure to the benefit of the registrant or applicant, as the case may be.

(July 5, 1946, ch. 540, title I, §5, 60 Stat. 429; Nov. 16, 1988, Pub. L. 100-667, §107, 102 Stat. 3938.)

§ 1056   Disclaimer of unregistrable matter [Section 6]

(a) The Director may require the applicant to disclaim an unregistrable component of a mark otherwise registrable. An applicant may voluntarily disclaim a component of a mark sought to be registered.

(b) No disclaimer, including those made under subsection (e) of section 7 [§1057] of this Act shall prejudice or affect the applicant's or registrant's rights then existing or thereafter arising in the disclaimed matter, or his right of registration on another application if the disclaimed matter be or shall have become distinctive of his goods or services.

(July 5, 1946, ch. 540, title I, §6, 60 Stat. 429; Oct. 9, 1962, Pub. L. 87-772, §3, 76 Stat. 769; Nov. 16, 1988, Pub. L. 100-667, §108, 102 Stat. 3938.)

§ 1057   Certificates of registration [Section 7]

(a) *Issuance and form.*—Certificates of registration of marks registered upon the principal register shall be issued in the name of the United States of America, under the seal of the United States Patent and Trademark Office, and shall be signed by the Director or have his signature placed thereon, and a record thereof shall be kept in the United States Patent and Trademark Office. The registration shall reproduce the mark, and state that the mark is registered on the principal register under this Act, the date of the first use of the mark, the date of the first use of the mark in commerce, the particular goods or services for which it is registered, the number and date of the registration, the term thereof, the date on which the application for registration was received in the United States Patent and Trademark Office, and any conditions and limitations that may be imposed in the registration.

(b) *Certificate as prima facie evidence.*—A certificate of registration of a mark upon the principal register provided by this Act shall be prima facie evidence of the validity of the registered mark and of the registration of the mark, of the owner's ownership of the mark, and of the owner's exclusive right to use the registered mark in commerce on or in connection with the goods or services specified in the certificate, subject to any conditions or limitations stated in the certificate.

(c) *Constructive use.*—Contingent on the registration of a mark on the principal register provided by this Act, the filing of the application to register such mark shall constitute constructive use of the mark, conferring a right of priority, nationwide in effect, on or in connection with the goods or services specified in the registration against any other person except for a person whose mark has not been abandoned and who, prior to such filing—

(1) has used the mark;

(2) has filed an application to register the mark which is pending or has resulted in registration of the mark; or

15 U.S.C. § 1057

(3) has filed a foreign application to register the mark on the basis of which he or she has acquired a right of priority, and timely files an application under section 44(d) [§1126(d)] to register the mark which is pending or has resulted in registration of the mark.

(d) *Issuance to assignee.*—A certificate of registration of a mark may be issued to the assignee of the applicant, but the assignment must first be recorded in the United States Patent and Trademark Office. In case of change of ownership the Director shall, at the request of the owner and upon a proper showing and the payment of the prescribed fee, issue to such assignee a new certificate of registration of the said mark in the name of such assignee, and for the unexpired part of the original period.

(e) *Surrender, cancellation, or amendment by registrant.*—Upon application of the owner the Director may permit any registration to be surrendered for cancellation, and upon cancellation appropriate entry shall be made in the records of the United States Patent and Trademark Office. Upon application of the owner and payment of the prescribed fee, the Director for good cause may permit any registration to be amended or to be disclaimed in part: *Provided,* That the amendment or disclaimer does not alter materially the character of the mark. Appropriate entry shall be made in the records of the United States Patent and Trademark Office and upon the certificate of registration.

(f) *Copies of United States Patent and Trademark Office records as evidence.*— Copies of any records, books, papers, or drawings belonging to the United States Patent and Trademark Office relating to marks, and copies of registrations, when authenticated by the seal of the United States Patent and Trademark Office and certified by the Director, or in his name by an employee of the Office duly designated by the Director, shall be evidence in all cases wherein the originals would be evidence; and any person making application therefor and paying the prescribed fee shall have such copies.

(g) *Correction of Patent and Trademark Office mistake.*— Whenever a material mistake in a registration, incurred through the fault of the United States Patent and Trademark Office, is clearly disclosed by the records of the Office a certificate stating the fact and nature of such mistake shall be issued without charge and recorded and a printed copy thereof shall be attached to each printed copy of the registration and such corrected registration shall thereafter have the same effect as if the same had been originally issued in such corrected form, or in the discretion of the Director a new certificate of registration may be issued without charge. All certificates of correction heretofore issued in accordance with the rules of the United States Patent and Trademark Office and the registrations to which they are attached shall have the same force and effect as if such certificates and their issue had been specifically authorized by statute.

(h) *Correction of applicant's mistake.*—Whenever a mistake has been made in a registration and a showing has been made that such mistake occurred in good faith through the fault of the applicant, the Director is authorized to issue a certificate of correction or, in his discretion, a new certificate upon the payment of the prescribed fee: *Provided,* That the correction does not involve such changes in the registration as to require republication of the mark.

(July 5, 1946, ch. 540, title I, §7, 60 Stat. 430; Aug 17, 1950, ch. 733, 64 Stat. 459; Oct. 9, 1962, Pub. L. 87-772, §4, 76 Stat. 769; Jan. 2, 1975, Pub. L. 93-596, §1, 88 Stat. 1949; Nov. 16, 1988, Pub. L. 100-667, §109, 102 Stat. 3938-39; Mar. 17, 2010, Pub. L. 111-146, §3(a), 124 Stat. 66.)

§ 1058 Duration, affidavits and fees [Section 8]

(a) *Time periods for required affidavits.*—Each registration shall remain in force for 10 years, except that the registration of any mark shall be canceled by the Director unless the owner of the registration files in the United States Patent and Trademark Office affidavits that meet the requirements of subsection (b), within the following time periods:

(1) Within the 1-year period immediately preceding the expiration of 6 years following the date of registration under this Act or the date of the publication under section 12(c).

(2) Within the 1-year period immediately preceding the expiration of 10 years following the date of registration, and each successive 10-year period following the date of registration.

(3) The owner may file the affidavit required under this section within the 6-month grace period immediately following the expiration of the periods established in paragraphs (1) and (2), together with the fee described in subsection (b) and the additional grace period surcharge prescribed by the Director.

(b) *Requirements for affidavit.*—The affidavit referred to in subsection (a) shall—

(1) (A) state that the mark is in use in commerce;

(B) set forth the goods and services recited in the registration on or in connection with which the mark is in use in commerce;

(C) be accompanied by such number of specimens or facsimiles showing current use of the mark in commerce as may be required by the Director; and

(D) be accompanied by the fee prescribed by the Director; or

(2) (A) set forth the goods and services recited in the registration on or in connection with which the mark is not in use in commerce;

(B) include a showing that any nonuse is due to special circumstances which excuse such nonuse and is not due to any intention to abandon the mark; and

(C) be accompanied by the fee prescribed by the Director.

(c) *Deficient affidavit.*—If any submission filed within the period set forth in subsection (a) is deficient, including that the affidavit was not filed in the name of the owner of the registration, the deficiency may be corrected after the statutory time period, within the time prescribed after notification of the deficiency. Such submission shall be accompanied by the additional deficiency surcharge prescribed by the Director.

(d) *Notice of requirement.*—Special notice of the requirement for such affidavit shall be attached to each certificate of registration and notice of publication under section 12(c).

(e) *Notification of acceptance or refusal.*—The Director shall notify any owner who files any affidavit required by this section of the Director's acceptance or refusal thereof and, in the case of a refusal, the reasons therefor.

(f) *Designation of resident for service of process and notices.*—If the owner is not domiciled in the United States, the owner may designate, by a document filed in the United States Patent and Trademark Office, the name and address of a person resident in the United States on whom may be served notices or process in proceedings affecting the mark. Such notices or process may be served upon the person so designated by leaving with that person or mailing to that person a copy thereof at the address specified in the last designation so filed. If the person so designated cannot be found at the last designated address, or if the owner does not designate by a document filed in the United States Patent and Trademark Office the name and address of a person resident in the United States on whom may be served notices or process in proceedings affecting the mark, such notices or process may be served on the Director.

(July 5, 1946, ch. 540, §8, 60 Stat. 431; Jan. 2, 1975, Pub. L. 93-596, §1, 88 Stat. 1949; Aug. 27, 1982, Pub. L. 97-247, §8, 96 Stat. 320; Nov. 16, 1988, Pub. L. 100-667, §110, 102 Stat. 3939; Oct. 30, 1998, Pub. L. 105-330, §105, 112 Stat. 3066; Nov. 2, 2002, Pub. L. 107-273, §13207, 116 Stat. 1906; Mar. 17, 2010, Pub. L. 111-146, §3(d)(1), 124 Stat. 67.)

§ 1059   Renewal of registration [Section 9]

(a) Subject to the provisions of section 8, each registration may be renewed for periods of 10 years at the end of each successive 10-year period following the date of registration upon payment of the prescribed fee and the filing of a written application, in such form as may be prescribed by the Director. Such application may be made at any time within 1 year before the end of each successive 10-year period for which the registration was issued or renewed, or it may be made within a grace period of 6 months after the end of each successive 10-year period, upon payment of a fee and surcharge prescribed therefor. If any application filed under this section is deficient, the deficiency may be corrected within the time prescribed after notification of the deficiency, upon payment of a surcharge prescribed therefor.

(b) If the Director refuses to renew the registration, the Director shall notify the registrant of the Director's refusal and the reasons therefor.

(c) If the registrant is not domiciled in the United States the registrant may designate, by a document filed in the United States Patent and Trademark Office, the name and address of a person resident in the United States on whom may be served notices or process in proceedings affecting the mark. Such notices or process may be served upon the person so designated by leaving with that person or mailing to that person a copy thereof at the address specified in the last designation so filed. If the person so designated cannot be found at the address given in the last designation, or if the registrant does not designate by a document filed in the United States Patent and Trademark Office the name and address of a person resident in the United States on whom may be served notices or process in proceedings affecting the mark, such notices or process may be served on the Director.

(July 5, 1946, ch. 540, title I, §9, 60 Stat. 431; Oct. 9, 1962, Pub. L. 87-772, §5, 76 Stat. 770; Nov. 16, 1988, Pub. L. 100-667, §111, 102 Stat. 3939; Oct. 30, 1998, Pub. L. 105-330, §106, 112 Stat. 3067; Nov. 2, 2002, Pub. L. 107-273, §13207, 116 Stat. 1906.)

§ 1060 Assignment of mark; execution; recording; purchaser without notice [Section 10]

(a) (1) A registered mark or a mark for which an application to register has been filed shall be assignable with the good will of the business in which the mark is used, or with that part of the good will of the business connected with the use of and symbolized by the mark. Notwithstanding the preceding sentence, no application to register a mark under section 1(b) shall be assignable prior to the filing of an amendment under section 1(c) to bring the application into conformity with section 1(a) or the filing of the verified statement of use under section 1(d), except for an assignment to a successor to the business of the applicant, or portion thereof, to which the mark pertains, if that business is ongoing and existing.

(2) In any assignment authorized by this section, it shall not be necessary to include the good will of the business connected with the use of and symbolized by any other mark used in the business or by the name or style under which the business is conducted.

(3) Assignments shall be by instruments in writing duly executed. Acknowledgment shall be prima facie evidence of the execution of an assignment, and when the prescribed information reporting the assignment is recorded in the United States Patent and Trademark Office, the record shall be prima facie evidence of execution.

(4) An assignment shall be void against any subsequent purchaser for valuable consideration without notice, unless the prescribed information reporting the assignment is recorded in the United States Patent and Trademark Office within 3 months after the date of the assignment or prior to the subsequent purchase.

(5) The United States Patent and Trademark Office shall maintain a record of information on assignments, in such form as may be prescribed by the Director.

(b) An assignee not domiciled in the United States may designate by a document filed in the United States Patent and Trademark Office the name and address of a person resident in the United States on whom may be served notices or process in proceedings affecting the mark. Such notices or process may be served upon the person so designated by leaving with that person or mailing to that person a copy thereof at the address specified in the last designation so filed. If the person so designated cannot be found at the address given in the last designation, or if the assignee does not designate by a document filed in the United States Patent and Trademark Office the name and address of a person resident in the United States on whom may be served notices or process in proceedings affecting the mark, such notices or process may be served upon the Director.

(July 5, 1946, ch. 540, 310, 60 Stat. 431; Oct. 9, 1962, Pub. L. 87-772, §6, 76 Stat. 770; Jan. 2, 1975, Pub. L. 93-596, §1, 88 Stat. 1949; Nov. 16, 1988, Pub. L. 100-667, §112, 102 Stat. 3939; Oct. 30, 1998, Pub. L. 105-330, §107, 112 Stat. 3068; Aug. 5, 1999, Pub. L. 106-43, §6, 113 Stat. 220; Nov. 2, 2002, Pub. L. 107-273, §13207, 116 Stat. 1906.)

§ 1061 Execution of acknowledgments and verifications [Section 11]

Acknowledgments and verifications required hereunder may be made before any person within the United States authorized by law to administer oaths, or, when made in a foreign country, before any diplomatic or consular officer of the United States or before any official authorized to administer oaths in the foreign country concerned whose authority is proved by a certificate of a diplomatic or consular officer of the United States, or apostille of an official designated by a foreign country which, by treaty or convention, accords like effect to apostilles of designated officials in the United States, and shall be valid if they comply with the laws of the state or country where made.

(July 5, 1946, ch. 540, title I, §11, 60 Stat. 432; Aug. 27, 1982, Pub. L. 97-247, §14, 96 Stat. 321.)

§ 1062 Publication; proceedings on refusal of registration; republication of marks registered under prior acts [Section 12]

(a) Upon the filing of an application for registration and payment of the prescribed fee, the Director shall refer the application to the examiner in charge of the registration of marks, who shall cause an examination to be made and, if on such examination it shall appear that the applicant is entitled to registration, or would be entitled to registration upon the acceptance of the statement of use required by section 1(d) [§1051(d)] of this Act, the Director shall cause the mark to be published in the Official Gazette of the Patent and Trademark Office: *Provided,* That in the case of an applicant claiming concurrent use, or in the case of an application to be placed in an interference as provided for in section 16 [§1066] of this Act, the mark, if otherwise registrable, may be published subject to the determination of the rights of the parties to such proceedings.

15 U.S.C. § 1062

(b) If the applicant is found not entitled to registration, the examiner shall advise the applicant thereof and of the reasons therefor. The applicant shall have a period of six months in which to reply or amend his application, which shall then be reexamined. This procedure may be repeated until (1) the examiner finally refuses registration of the mark or (2) the applicant fails for a period of six months to reply or amend or appeal, whereupon the application shall be deemed to have been abandoned, unless it can be shown to the satisfaction of the Director that the delay in responding was unintentional, whereupon such time may be extended.

(c) A registrant of a mark registered under the provisions of the Act of March 3, 1881, or the Act of February 20, 1905, may, at any time prior to the expiration of the registration thereof, upon the payment of the prescribed fee file with the Director an affidavit setting forth those goods stated in the registration on which said mark is in use in commerce and that the registrant claims the benefits of this Act for said mark. The Director shall publish notice thereof with a reproduction of said mark in the Official Gazette, and notify the registrant of such publication and of the requirement for the affidavit of use or nonuse as provided for in subsection (b) of section 8 [§1058(b)] of this Act. Marks published under this subsection shall not be subject to the provisions of section 13 [§1063] of this Act.

(July 5, 1946, ch. 540, title I, §12, 60 Stat. 432; Oct. 9, 1962, Pub. L. 87-772, §7, 76 Stat. 770; Jan. 2, 1975, Pub. L. 43-596, §1, 88 Stat. 1949; Nov. 16, 1988, Pub. L. 100-667, §113, 102 Stat. 3940; Oct. 30, 1998, Pub. L. 105-330, §104, 112 Stat. 3066.)

§ 1063   Opposition to registration [Section 13]

(a) Any person who believes that he would be damaged by the registration of a mark upon the principal register, including the registration of any mark which would be likely to cause dilution by blurring or dilution by tarnishment under section 43(c), may, upon payment of the prescribed fee, file an opposition in the Patent and Trademark Office, stating the grounds therefor, within thirty days after the publication under subsection (a) of section 12 [§1062] of this Act of the mark sought to be registered. Upon written request prior to the expiration of the thirty-day period, the time for filing opposition shall be extended for an additional thirty days, and further extensions of time for filing opposition may be granted by the Director for good cause when requested prior to the expiration of an extension. The Director shall notify the applicant of each extension of the time for filing opposition. An opposition may be amended under such conditions as may be prescribed by the Director.

(b) Unless registration is successfully opposed—

(1) a mark entitled to registration on the principal register based on an application filed under section 1(a) [§1051(a)] or pursuant to section 44 [§1126] shall be registered in the Patent and Trademark Office, a certificate of registration shall be issued, and notice of the registration shall be published in the Official Gazette of the Patent and Trademark Office; or

(2) a notice of allowance shall be issued to the applicant if the applicant applied for registration under section 1(b) [§1051(b)].

(July 5, 1946, ch. 540, §13, 60 Stat. 433; Oct. 9, 1962, Pub. L. 87-772, §8, 76 Stat. 771; Jan. 2, 1975, Pub. L. 93-596, §1, 88 Stat. 1949; Jan. 2, 1975, Pub. L. 93-600, §1, 88 Stat. 1955; Aug. 27, 1982, Pub. L. 97-247, §9, 96 Stat. 320; Nov. 16, 1988, Pub. L. 100-667, §114, 102 Stat. 3940; Aug. 5, 1999, Pub. L. 106-43, §2, 113 Stat. 218 , Oct. 6, 2006, Pub. L. 109-312, §3(b), 120 Stat. 1732.)

§ 1064   Cancellation of registration [Section 14]

A petition to cancel a registration of a mark, stating the grounds relied upon, may, upon payment of the prescribed fee, be filed as follows by any person who believes that he is or will be damaged, including as a result of a likelihood of dilution by blurring or dilution by tarnishment under section 43(c), by the registration of a mark on the principal register established by this Act, or under the Act of March 3, 1881, or the Act of February 20, 1905:

(1) Within five years from the date of the registration of the mark under this Act.

(2) Within five years from the date of publication under section 12(c) hereof [§1062(c)] of a mark registered under the Act of March 3, 1881, or the Act of February 20, 1905.

(3) At any time if the registered mark becomes the generic name for the goods or services, or a portion thereof, for which it is registered, or is functional, or has been abandoned, or its registration was obtained fraudulently or contrary to the provisions of section 4 [§1054] or of subsection (a), (b), or (c) of section 2 [§1052] for a registration under this Act, or contrary to similar prohibitory provisions of such prior Acts for a registration under such Acts, or if the registered mark is being used by, or with the permission of, the registrant so as to misrepresent the source of the goods or services on or in connection with which the mark is used. If the registered

mark becomes the generic name for less than all of the goods or services for which it is registered, a petition to cancel the registration for only those goods or services may be filed. A registered mark shall not be deemed to be the generic name of goods or services solely because such mark is also used as a name of or to identify a unique product or service. The primary significance of the registered mark to the relevant public rather than purchaser motivation shall be the test for determining whether the registered mark has become the generic name of goods or services on or in connection with which it has been used.

(4) At any time if the mark is registered under the Act of March 3, 1881, or the Act of February 20, 1905, and has not been published under the provisions of subsection (c) of section 12 [§1062] of this Act.

(5) At any time in the case of a certification mark on the ground that the registrant (A) does not control, or is not able legitimately to exercise control over, the use of such mark, or (B) engages in the production or marketing of any goods or services to which the certification mark is applied, or (C) permits the use of the certification mark for purposes other than to certify, or (D) discriminately refuses to certify or to continue to certify the goods or services of any person who maintains the standards or conditions which such mark certifies:

Provided, That the Federal Trade Commission may apply to cancel on the grounds specified in paragraphs (3) and (5) of this section any mark registered on the principal register established by this chapter, and the prescribed fee shall not be required.

Nothing in paragraph (5) shall be deemed to prohibit the registrant from using its certification mark in advertising or promoting recognition of the certification program or of the goods or services meeting the certification standards of the registrant. Such uses of the certification mark shall not be grounds for cancellation under paragraph (5), so long as the registrant does not itself produce, manufacture, or sell any of the certified goods or services to which its identical certification mark is applied.

(July 5, 1946, ch. 540, title I, §14, 60 Stat. 433; Oct. 9, 1962, Pub. L. 87-772, §9, 76 Stat. 771; Aug. 27, 1982, Pub. L. 97-247, §9(b), 96 Stat. 320; Nov. 8, 1984; Pub. L. 98-620; §102, 98 Stat. 3335; Nov. 16, 1988, Pub. L. 100-667, §115, 102 Stat. 3940-41; Oct. 30, 1998, Pub. L. 105-330, §§201, 301, 112 Stat. 3069, 3070; Aug. 5, 1999, Pub. L. 106-43, §2, 113 Stat. 218, Oct. 6, 2006, Pub. L. 109-312, §3(c), 120 Stat. 1732.)

15 U.S.C. § 1064

§ 1065 Incontestability of right to use mark under certain conditions
[Section 15]

Except on a ground for which application to cancel may be filed at any time under paragraphs (3) and (5) of section 14 [§1064] of this Act, and except to the extent, if any, to which the use of a mark registered on the principal register infringes a valid right acquired under the law of any State or Territory by use of a mark or trade name continuing from a date prior to the date of registration under this Act of such registered mark, the right of the owner to use such registered mark in commerce for the goods or services on or in connection with which such registered mark has been in continuous use for five consecutive years subsequent to the date of such registration and is still in use in commerce, shall be incontestable: *Provided,* That—

(1) there has been no final decision adverse to the owner's claim of ownership of such mark for such goods or services, or to the owner's right to register the same or to keep the same on the register; and

(2) there is no proceeding involving said rights pending in the United States Patent and Trademark Office or in a court and not finally disposed of; and

(3) an affidavit is filed with the Director within one year after the expiration of any such five-year period setting forth those goods or services stated in the registration on or in connection with which such mark has been in continuous use for such five consecutive years and is still in use in commerce, and the other matters specified in paragraphs (1) and (2) of this section; and

(4) no incontestable right shall be acquired in a mark which is the generic name for the goods or services or a portion thereof, for which it is registered.

Subject to the conditions above specified in this section, the incontestable right with reference to a mark registered under this Act shall apply to a mark registered under the Act of March 3, 1881, or the Act of February 20, 1905, upon the filing of the required affidavit with the Director within one year after the expiration of any period of five consecutive years after the date of publication of a mark under the provisions of subsection (c) of section 12 [§1062] of this Act.

The Director shall notify any registrant who files the above-prescribed affidavit of the filing thereof.

15 U.S.C. § 1065

(July 5, 1946, ch. 540, §15, 60 Stat. 433; Oct. 9, 1962, Pub. L. 87-772, §10, 76 Stat. 771; Jan. 2, 1975, Pub. L. 93-596, §1, 88 Stat. 1949; Aug. 27, 1982, Pub. L. 97-247, §10, 96 Stat. 320; Nov. 16, 1988, Pub. L. 100-667, §116, 102 Stat. 3941; Mar. 17, 2010, Pub. L. 111-146, §3(b), 124 Stat. 67.)

§ 1066   Interference; declaration by Director [Section 16]

Upon petition showing extraordinary circumstances, the Director may declare that an interference exists when application is made for the registration of a mark which so resembles a mark previously registered by another, or for the registration of which another has previously made application, as to be likely when used on or in connection with the goods or services of the applicant to cause confusion or mistake or to deceive. No interference shall be declared between an application and the registration of a mark the right to the use of which has become incontestable.

(July 5, 1946, ch. 540, title I, §16, 60 Stat. 434; Oct. 9, 1962, Pub. L. 87-772, §11, 76 Stat. 771; Aug. 27, 1982, Pub. L. 97-247, §11, 96 Stat. 321; Nov. 16, 1988, Pub. L. 100-667, §117, 102 Stat. 3941.)

§ 1067   Interference, opposition, and proceedings for concurrent use registration or for cancellation; notice; Trademark Trial and Appeal Board [Section 17]

(a) In every case of interference, opposition to registration, application to register as a lawful concurrent user, or application to cancel the registration of a mark, the Director shall give notice to all parties and shall direct a Trademark Trial and Appeal Board to determine and decide the respective rights of registration.

(b) The Trademark Trial and Appeal Board shall include the Director, the Deputy Director of the United States Patent and Trademark Office, the Commissioner for Patents, the Commissioner for Trademarks, and administrative trademark judges who are appointed by the Secretary of Commerce, in consultation with the Director.

(c) *Authority of the Secretary.* — The Secretary of Commerce may, in his or her discretion, deem the appointment of an administrative trademark judge who, before the date of the enactment of this subsection, held office pursuant to an appointment by the Director to take effect on the date on which the Director initially appointed the administrative trademark judge.

(d) *Defense to Challenge of Appointment.* — It shall be a defense to a challenge to the appointment of an administrative trademark judge on the basis of the judge's having been originally appointed by the Director that the administrative trademark judge so appointed was acting as a de facto officer.

(July 5, 1946, ch. 540, §17, 60 Stat. 434; Aug. 8, 1958, Pub. L. 85-609, §1, 72 Stat. 540; Jan. 2, 1975, Pub. L. 93-596, §1, 88 Stat. 1949; Oct. 15, 1980, Pub. L. 96-455, §1, 94 Stat. 2024; Nov. 29, 1999, Pub. L. 106-113, §4716, 113 Stat. 1501A-580; Nov. 2, 2002, Pub. L. 107-273, §13203, 116 Stat. 1902; Aug. 12, 2008, Pub. L. 110-313, §1, 122 Stat. 3014.)

§ 1068   Same; action of Director [Section 18]

In such proceedings the Director may refuse to register the opposed mark, may cancel the registration, in whole or in part, may modify the application or registration by limiting the goods or services specified therein, may otherwise restrict or rectify with respect to the register the registration of a registered mark, may refuse to register any or all of several interfering marks, or may register the mark or marks for the person or persons entitled thereto, as the rights of the parties under this chapter may be established in the proceedings: *Provided*, That in the case of the registration of any mark based on concurrent use, the Director shall determine and fix the conditions and limitations provided for in subsection (d) of section 2 [§1052] of this Act. However, no final judgment shall be entered in favor of an applicant under section 1(b) [§1051(b)] before the mark is registered, if such applicant cannot prevail without establishing constructive use pursuant to section 7(c) [§1057(c)].

(July 5, 1946, ch. 540, title I, §18, 60 Stat. 434; Nov. 16, 1988, Pub. L. 100-667, §118, 102 Stat. 3941.)

§ 1069   Application of equitable principles in inter partes proceedings [Section 19]

In all inter partes proceedings equitable principles of laches, estoppel, and acquiescence, where applicable may be considered and applied.

(July 5, 1946, ch. 540, §19, 60 Stat. 434; Jan. 2, 1975, Pub. L. 93-596, §1, 88 Stat. 1949; Nov. 16, 1988, Pub. L. 100-667, §119, 102 Stat. 3941.)

§ 1070   Appeals to Trademark Trial and Appeal Board from decisions of examiners [Section 20]

An appeal may be taken to the Trademark Trial and Appeal Board from any final decision of the examiner in charge of the registration of marks upon the payment of the prescribed fee.

(July 5, 1946, ch. 540, title I, §20, 60 Stat. 435; Aug. 8, 1958, Pub. L. 85-609, §1, 72 Stat. 540.)

§ 1071 Appeal to courts [Section 21]

(a) (1) An applicant for registration of a mark, party to an interference proceeding, party to an opposition proceeding, party to an application to register as a lawful concurrent user, party to a cancellation proceeding, a registrant who has filed an affidavit as provided in section 8 [§1058] or section 71 [§1141k] of this Act, or an applicant for renewal, who is dissatisfied with the decision of the Director or Trademark Trial and Appeal Board, may appeal to the United States Court of Appeals for the Federal Circuit thereby waiving his right to proceed under subsection (b) of this section: *Provided,* That such appeal shall be dismissed if any adverse party to the proceeding, other than the Director, shall, within twenty days after the appellant has filed notice of appeal according to paragraph (2) of this subsection, files notice with the Director that he elects to have all further proceedings conducted as provided in subsection (b) of this section. Thereupon the appellant shall have thirty days thereafter within which to file a civil action under said subsection (b) of this section, in default of which the decision appealed from shall govern the further proceedings in the case.

(2) When an appeal is taken to the United States Court of Appeals for the Federal Circuit, the appellant shall file in the United States Patent and Trademark Office a written notice of appeal directed to the Director, within such time after the date of the decision from which the appeal is taken as the Director prescribes, but in no case less than 60 days after that date.

(3) The Director shall transmit to the United States Court of Appeals for the Federal Circuit a certified list of the documents comprising the record in the United States Patent and Trademark Office. The court may request that the Director forward the original or certified copies of such documents during pendency of the appeal. In an ex parte case, the Director shall submit to that court a brief explaining the grounds for the decision of the United States Patent and Trademark Office, addressing all the issues involved in the appeal. The court shall, before hearing an appeal, give notice of the time and place of the hearing to the Director and the parties in the appeal.

(4) The United States Court of Appeals for the Federal Circuit shall review the decision from which the appeal is taken on the record before the United States Patent and Trademark Office. Upon its determination the court shall issue its mandate and opinion to the Director, which shall be entered

of record in the United States Patent and Trademark Office and shall govern the further proceedings in the case. However, no final judgment shall be entered in favor of an applicant under section 1(b) [§1051(b)] before the mark is registered, if such applicant cannot prevail without establishing constructive use pursuant to section 7(c) [§1057(c)].

(b) (1) Whenever a person authorized by subsection (a) of this section to appeal to the United States Court of Appeals for the Federal Circuit is dissatisfied with the decision of the Director or Trademark Trial and Appeal Board, said person may, unless appeal has been taken to said United States Court of Appeals for the Federal Circuit, have remedy by a civil action if commenced within such time after such decision, not less than sixty days, as the Director appoints or as provided in subsection (a) of this section. The court may adjudge that an applicant is entitled to a registration upon the application involved, that a registration involved should be canceled, or such other matter as the issues in the proceeding require, as the facts in the case may appear. Such adjudication shall authorize the Director to take any necessary action, upon compliance with the requirements of law. However, no final judgment shall be entered in favor of an applicant under section 1(b) [§1051(b)] before the mark is registered, if such applicant cannot prevail without establishing constructive use pursuant to section 7(c) [§1057(c)].

(2) The Director shall not be made a party to an inter partes proceeding under this subsection, but he shall be notified of the filing of the complaint by the clerk of the court in which it is filed and shall have the right to intervene in the action.

(3) In any case where there is no adverse party, a copy of the complaint shall be served on the Director, and, unless the court finds the expenses to be unreasonable, all the expenses of the proceeding shall be paid by the party bringing the case, whether the final decision is in favor of such party or not. In suits brought hereunder, the record in the United States Patent and Trademark Office shall be admitted on motion of any party, upon such terms and conditions as to costs, expenses, and the further cross-examination of the witnesses as the court imposes, without prejudice to the right of any party to take further testimony. The testimony and exhibits of the record in the United States Patent and Trademark Office, when admitted, shall have the same effect as if originally taken and produced in the suit.

15 U.S.C. § 1071

(4) Where there is an adverse party, such suit may be instituted against the party in interest as shown by the records of the United States Patent and Trademark Office at the time of the decision complained of, but any party in interest may become a party to the action. If there are adverse parties residing in a plurality of districts not embraced within the same State, or an adverse party residing in a foreign country, the United States District Court for the Eastern District of Virginia shall have jurisdiction and may issue summons against the adverse parties directed to the marshal of any district in which any adverse party resides. Summons against adverse parties residing in foreign countries may be served by publication or otherwise as the court directs.

(July 5, 1946, ch. 540, §21, 60 Stat. 435; July 19, 1952, ch. 950, §2, 66 Stat. 814; Aug. 8, 1958, Pub. L. 85-609, §1, 72 Stat. 540; Oct. 9, 1962, Pub. L. 87-772, §12, 76 Stat. 771; Jan. 2, 1975, Pub. L. 93-596, §1, 88 Stat. 1949; Jan. 2, 1975, Pub. L. 93-600, §2, 88 Stat. 1955; Apr. 2, 1982, Pub. L. 97-164, §162, 96 Stat. 49; Nov. 8, 1984, Pub. L. 98-620, §414, 98 Stat. 3363; Nov. 16, 1988, Pub. L. 100-667, §120, 102 Stat. 3942; Mar. 17, 2010, Pub. L. 111-146, §3(c), 124 Stat. 67; Sept. 16, 2011, Pub. L. 112-29, §9, 125 Stat. 316.)

§ 1072   Registration as constructive notice of claim of ownership
[Section 22]

Registration of a mark on the principal register provided by this Act or under the Act of March 3, 1881, or the Act of February 20, 1905, shall be constructive notice of the registrant's claim of ownership thereof.

(July 5, 1946, ch. 540, title I, §22, 60 Stat. 435.)

SUBCHAPTER II — THE SUPPLEMENTAL REGISTER

§ 1091 Marks registrable on supplemental register; application and proceedings for registration; nature of mark; mark used in foreign commerce [Section 23]

(a) In addition to the principal register, the Director shall keep a continuation of the register provided in paragraph (b) of section 1 of the Act of March 19, 1920, entitled "An Act to give effect to certain provisions of the convention for the protection of trademarks and commercial names, made and signed in the city of Buenos Aires, in the Argentine Republic, August 20, 1910, and for other purposes," to be called the supplemental register. All marks capable of distinguishing applicant's goods or services and not registrable on the principal register herein provided, except those declared to be unregistrable under subsections (a), (b), (c), and (d) and (e)(3) of section 2 [§1052] of this Act, which are in lawful use in commerce by the owner thereof, on or in connection with any goods or services may be registered on the supplemental register upon the payment of the prescribed fee and compliance with the provisions of subsections (a) and (e) of section 1 [§1051] so far as they are applicable. Nothing in this section shall prevent the registration on the supplemental register of a mark, capable of distinguishing the applicant's goods or services and not registrable on the principal register under this Act, that is declared to be unregistrable under section 2(e)(3), if such mark has been in lawful use in commerce by the owner thereof, on or in connection with any goods or services, since before the date of the enactment of the North American Free Trade Agreement Implementation Act.[4]

(b) Upon the filing of an application for registration on the supplemental register and payment of the prescribed fee the Director shall refer the application to the examiner in charge of the registration of marks, who shall cause an examination to be made and if on such examination it shall appear that the applicant is entitled to registration, the registration shall be granted. If the applicant is found not entitled to registration the provisions of subsection (b) of section 12 [§1062] of this Act shall apply.

(c) For the purposes of registration on the supplemental register, a mark may consist of any trademark, symbol, label, package, configuration of goods, name, word, slogan, phrase, surname, geographical name, numeral, device, any matter that as a whole is not functional, or any combination of any of the foregoing, but such mark must be capable of distinguishing the applicant's goods or services.

---

[4] *Ed. Note:* The North American Free Trade Agreement Implementation Act was enacted on Dec. 8, 1993.

15 U.S.C. § 1091

(July 5, 1946, ch. 540, title II, §23, 60 Stat. 435; Oct. 9, 1962, Pub. L. 87-772, §13, 76 Stat. 773; Nov. 16, 1988, Pub. L. 100-667, §121, 102 Stat. 3942-43; Dec. 8, 1993, Pub. L. 103-182, §333, 107 Stat. 2114; Oct. 30, 1998, Pub. L. 105-330, §201, 112 Stat. 3070; Nov. 2, 2002, Pub. L. 107-273, §13207, 116 Stat. 1906.)

§ 1092 Publication; not subject to opposition; cancellation [Section 24]

Marks for the supplemental register shall not be published for or be subject to opposition, but shall be published on registration in the Official Gazette of the Patent and Trademark Office. Whenever any person believes that such person is or will be damaged by the registration of a mark on the supplemental register—

(1) for which the effective filing date is after the date on which such person's mark became famous and which would be likely to cause dilution by blurring or dilution by tarnishment under section 43(c); or

(2) on grounds other than dilution by blurring or dilution by tarnishment, such person may at any time, upon payment of the prescribed fee and the filing of a petition stating the ground therefor, apply to the Director to cancel such registration.

The Director shall refer such application to the Trademark Trial and Appeal Board which shall give notice thereof to the registrant. If it is found after a hearing before the Board that the registrant is not entitled to registration, or that the mark has been abandoned, the registration shall be canceled by the Director. However, no final judgment shall be entered in favor of an applicant under section 1(b) [§1051(b)] before the mark is registered, if such applicant cannot prevail without establishing constructive use pursuant to section 7(c) [§1057(c)].

(July 5, 1946, ch. 540, §24, 60 Stat. 436; Aug. 8, 1958, Pub. L. 85-609. §1, 72 Stat. 540; Oct. 9, 1962, Pub. L. 87-772, §14, 76 Stat. 773; Jan. 2, 1975, Pub. L. 93-596, §1, 88 Stat. 1949; Nov. 16, 1988, Pub. L. 100-667, §122, 102 Stat. 3943; Aug. 5, 1999, Pub. L. 106-43, §2, 113 Stat. 218, Oct. 6, 2006, Pub. L. 109-312, §3(d), 120 Stat. 1732.)

§ 1093 Registration certificates for marks on principal and supplemental registers to be different [Section 25]

The certificates of registration for marks registered on the supplemental register shall be conspicuously different from certificates issued for marks registered on the principal register.

(July 5, 1946, ch. 540, title II, §25, 60 Stat. 436.)

§ 1094 Provisions of chapter applicable to registrations on supplemental register [Section 26]

The provisions of this chapter shall govern so far as applicable applications for registration and registrations on the supplemental register as well as those on the principal register, but applications for and registrations on the supplemental register shall not be subject to or receive the advantages of sections 1(b), 2(e), 2(f), 7(b), 7(c), 12(a), 13 to 18, inclusive, 22, 33, and 42 of this Act [§§1051(b), 1052(e), 1052(f), 1057(b), 1057(c), 1062(a), 1063-1068, 1072, 1115, and 1124].

(July 5, 1946, ch. 540, title II, §26, 60 Stat. 436; Nov. 16, 1988, Pub. L. 100-667, §123, 102 Stat. 3943.)

§ 1095 Registration on principal register not precluded [Section 27]

Registration of a mark on the supplemental register, or under the Act of March 19, 1920, shall not preclude registration by the registrant on the principal register established by this chapter. Registration of a mark on the supplemental register shall not constitute an admission that the mark has not acquired distinctiveness.

(July 5, 1946, ch. 540, title II, §27, 60 Stat. 436; Nov. 16, 1988, Pub. L. 100-667, §124, 102 Stat. 3943.)

§ 1096 Registration on supplemental register not used to stop importations [Section 28]

Registration on the supplemental register or under the Act of March 19, 1920, shall not be filed in the Department of the Treasury or be used to stop importations.

(July 5, 1946, ch. 540, title II, §28, 60 Stat. 436.)

SUBCHAPTER III — GENERAL PROVISIONS

SEC.
1111. Notice of registration; display with mark; recovery of profits and damages in infringement suit.
1112. Classification of goods and services; registration in plurality of classes.
1113. Fees.
1114. Remedies; infringement; innocent infringement by printers and publishers.
1115. Registration on principal register as evidence of exclusive right to use mark; defenses.
1116. Injunctions; enforcement; notice to Director.

15 U.S.C. § 1096

1117.   Recovery for violation of rights; profits, damages and costs; attorney fees.
1118.   Destruction of infringing articles.
1119.   Power of court over registration.
1120.   Civil liability for false or fraudulent registration.
1121.   Jurisdiction of Federal courts.
1122.   Liability of States, Instrumentalities of States, and State Officials.
1123.   Rules and regulations for conduct of proceedings in Patent and Trademark Office.
1124.   Importation of goods bearing infringing marks or names forbidden.
1125.   False designations of origin, false descriptions, and dilution.
1126.   International conventions.
1127.   Construction and definitions; intent of chapter.
1128.   [Repealed].
1129.   Cyberpiracy protections for individuals [Transferred].

§ 1111   Notice of registration; display with mark; recovery of profits and damages in infringement suit [Section 29]

Notwithstanding the provisions of section 22 [§1072] hereof, a registrant of a mark registered in the Patent and Trademark Office may give notice that his mark is registered by displaying with the mark the words "Registered in U.S. Patent and Trademark Office" or "Reg. U.S. Pat. & Tm. Off." or the letter R enclosed within a circle, thus ®; and in any suit for infringement under this Act by such a registrant failing to give such notice of registration, no profits and no damages shall be recovered under the provisions of this Act unless the defendant had actual notice of the registration.

(July 5, 1946, ch. 540, §29, 60 Stat. 436; Oct. 9, 1962, Pub. L. 87-772, §15, 76 Stat. 773; Jan. 2, 1975, Pub. L. 93-596, §§1 and 2, 88 Stat. 1949; Nov. 16, 1988, Pub. L. 100-667, §125, 102 Stat. 3943.)

§ 1112   Classification of goods and services; registration in plurality of classes [Section 30]

The Director may establish a classification of goods and services, for convenience of Patent and Trademark Office administration, but not to limit or extend the applicant's or registrant's rights. The applicant may apply to register a mark for any or all of the goods or services upon or in connection with which he or she is using or has a bona fide intention to use the mark in commerce: *Provided,* That if the Director by regulation permits the filing of an application for the registration of a mark for goods or services which fall within a plurality of classes, a fee equaling the sum of the fees for filing an application in each class shall be paid, and the Director may issue a single certificate of registration for such mark.

(July 5, 1946, ch. 540, §30, 60 Stat. 436; Oct. 9, 1962, Pub. L. 87-772, §16, 76 Stat. 773; Jan. 2, 1975, Pub. L. 93-596, §1, 88 Stat. 1949; Nov. 16, 1988, Pub. L. 100-667, §126, 102 Stat. 3943.)

§ 1113   Fees[5] [Section 31]

(a) The Director shall establish fees for the filing and processing of an application for the registration of a trademark or other mark and for all other services performed by and materials furnished by the Patent and Trademark Office related to trademarks and other marks. Fees established under this subsection may be adjusted by the Director once each year to reflect, in the aggregate, any fluctuations during the preceding 12 months in the Consumer Price Index, as determined by the Secretary of Labor. Changes of less than 1 percent may be ignored. No fee established under this section shall take effect until at least 30 days after notice of the fee has been published in the Federal Register and in the Official Gazette of the Patent and Trademark Office.

(b) The Director may waive the payment of any fee for any service or material related to trademarks or other marks in connection with an occasional request made by a department or agency of the Government, or any officer thereof. The Indian Arts and Crafts Board will not be charged any fee to register Government trademarks of genuineness and quality for Indian products or for products of particular Indian tribes and groups.

(July 5, 1946, ch. 540, §31, 60 Stat. 437; Aug. 8, 1958, Pub. L. 85-609, §1, 72 Stat. 540; July 24, 1965, Pub. L. 89-83, §3, 79 Stat. 260; Jan. 2, 1975, Pub. L. 93-596, §1, 88 Stat. 1949; Dec. 12, 1980, Pub. L. 96-517, §5, 94 Stat. 3018; Aug. 27, 1982, Pub. L. 97-247, §3, 96 Stat. 319; Sept. 8, 1982, Pub. L. 97-256, §103, 96 Stat. 256; Dec. 10, 1991, Pub. L. 102-204, §5, 105 Stat. 1640).

§ 1114   Remedies; infringement; innocent infringement by printers and publishers [Section 32]

(1) Any person who shall, without the consent of the registrant—

   (a) use in commerce any reproduction, counterfeit, copy, or colorable imitation of a registered mark in connection with the sale, offering for sale, distribution, or advertising of any goods or services on or in connection

---

[5] *Ed. Note:* The current trademark fee schedule may be found by accessing the website of the United States Patent and Trademark office at www.uspto.gov.

with which such use is likely to cause confusion, or to cause mistake, or to deceive; or

(b) reproduce, counterfeit, copy, or colorably imitate a registered mark and apply such reproduction, counterfeit, copy, or colorable imitation to labels, signs, prints, packages, wrappers, receptacles or advertisements intended to be used in commerce upon or in connection with the sale, offering for sale, distribution, or advertising of goods or services on or in connection with which such use is likely to cause confusion, or to cause mistake, or to deceive;

shall be liable in a civil action by the registrant for the remedies hereinafter provided. Under subsection (b) hereof, the registrant shall not be entitled to recover profits or damages unless the acts have been committed with knowledge that such imitation is intended to be used to cause confusion, or to cause mistake, or to deceive.

As used in this paragraph, the term "any person" includes the United States, all agencies and instrumentalities thereof, and all individuals, firms, corporations, or other persons acting for the United States and with the authorization and consent of the United States, and any State, any instrumentality of a State, and any officer or employee of a State or instrumentality of a State acting in his or her official capacity. The United States, all agencies and instrumentalities thereof, and all individuals, firms, corporations, other persons acting for the United States and with the authorization and consent of the United States, and any State, and any such instrumentality, officer, or employee, shall be subject to the provisions of this Act in the same manner and to the same extent as any nongovernmental entity.

(2) Notwithstanding any other provision of this Act, the remedies given to the owner of a right infringed under this Act or to a person bringing an action under section 43(a) or (d) [§1125(a) or (d)] shall be limited as follows:

(A) Where an infringer or violator is engaged solely in the business of printing the mark or violating matter for others and establishes that he or she was an innocent infringer or innocent violator, the owner of the right infringed or person bringing the action under section 43(a) [§1125(a)] shall be entitled as against such infringer or violator only to an injunction against future printing.

(B) Where the infringement or violation complained of is contained in or is part of paid advertising matter in a newspaper, magazine, or other similar periodical or in an electronic communication as defined in section

2510(12) of title 18, United States Code, the remedies of the owner of the right infringed or person bringing the action under section 43(a) [§1125(a)] as against the publisher or distributor of such newspaper, magazine, or other similar periodical or electronic communication shall be limited to an injunction against the presentation of such advertising matter in future issues of such newspapers, magazines, or other similar periodicals or in future transmissions of such electronic communications. The limitations of this subparagraph shall apply only to innocent infringers and innocent violators.

(C) Injunctive relief shall not be available to the owner of the right infringed or person bringing the action under section 43(a) [§1125(a)] with respect to an issue of a newspaper, magazine, or other similar periodical or an electronic communication containing infringing matter or violating matter where restraining the dissemination of such infringing matter or violating matter in any particular issue of such periodical or in an electronic communication would delay the delivery of such issue or transmission of such electronic communication after the regular time for such delivery or transmission, and such delay would be due to the method by which publication and distribution of such periodical or transmission of such electronic communication is customarily conducted in accordance with sound business practice, and not due to any method or device adopted to evade this section or to prevent or delay the issuance of an injunction or restraining order with respect to such infringing matter or violating matter.

(D)(i)(I) A domain name registrar, a domain name registry, or other domain name registration authority that takes any action described under clause (ii) affecting a domain name shall not be liable for monetary relief or, except as provided in subclause (II), for injunctive relief, to any person for such action, regardless of whether the domain name is finally determined to infringe or dilute the mark.

(II) A domain name registrar, domain name registry, or other domain name registration authority described in subclause (I) may be subject to injunctive relief only if such registrar, registry, or other registration authority has—

(aa) not expeditiously deposited with a court, in which an action has been filed regarding the disposition of the domain name, documents sufficient for the court to establish the court's control and authority regarding the disposition of the registration and use of the domain name;

(bb) transferred, suspended, or otherwise modified the domain name during the pendency of the action, except upon order of the court; or

(cc) willfully failed to comply with any such court order.

(ii) An action referred to under clause (i)(I) is any action of refusing to register, removing from registration, transferring, temporarily disabling, or permanently canceling a domain name—

(I) in compliance with a court order under section 43(d); or

(II) in the implementation of a reasonable policy by such registrar, registry, or authority prohibiting the registration of a domain name that is identical to, confusingly similar to, or dilutive of another's mark.

(iii) A domain name registrar, a domain name registry, or other domain name registration authority shall not be liable for damages under this section for the registration or maintenance of a domain name for another absent a showing of bad faith intent to profit from such registration or maintenance of the domain name.

(iv) If a registrar, registry, or other registration authority takes an action described under clause (ii) based on a knowing and material misrepresentation by any other person that a domain name is identical to, confusingly similar to, or dilutive of a mark, the person making the knowing and material misrepresentation shall be liable for any damages, including costs and attorney's fees, incurred by the domain name registrant as a result of such action. The court may also grant injunctive relief to the domain name registrant, including the reactivation of the domain name or the transfer of the domain name to the domain name registrant.

(v) A domain name registrant whose domain name has been suspended, disabled, or transferred under a policy described under clause (ii)(II) may, upon notice to the mark owner, file a civil action to establish that the registration or use of the domain name by such registrant is not unlawful under this Act. The court may grant injunctive relief to the domain name registrant, including the reactivation of the domain name or transfer of the domain name to the domain name registrant.

(E) As used in this paragraph—

(i) the term "violator" means a person who violates section 43(a) [§1125(a)]; and

(ii) the term "violating matter" means matter that is the subject of a violation under section 43(a) [§1125(a)].

(3) (A) Any person who engages in the conduct described in paragraph (11) of section 110 of title 17, United States Code, and who complies with the requirements set forth in that paragraph is not liable on account of such conduct for a violation of any right under this Act. This subparagraph does not preclude liability, nor shall it be construed to restrict the defenses or limitations on rights granted under this Act, of a person for conduct not described in paragraph (11) of section 110 of title 17, United States Code, even if that person also engages in conduct described in paragraph (11) of section 110 of such title.

(B) A manufacturer, licensee, or licensor of technology that enables the making of limited portions of audio or video content of a motion picture imperceptible as described in subparagraph (A) is not liable on account of such manufacture or license for a violation of any right under this Act, if such manufacturer, licensee, or licensor ensures that the technology provides a clear and conspicuous notice at the beginning of each performance that the performance of the motion picture is altered from the performance intended by the director or copyright holder of the motion picture. The limitations on liability in subparagraph (A) and this subparagraph shall not apply to a manufacturer, licensee, or licensor of technology that fails to comply with this paragraph.

(C) The requirement under subparagraph (B) to provide notice shall apply only with respect to technology manufactured after the end of the 180-day period beginning on the date of the enactment of the Family Movie Act of 2005.

(D) Any failure by a manufacturer, licensee, or licensor of technology to qualify for the exemption under subparagraphs (A) and (B) shall not be construed to create an inference that any such party that engages in conduct described in paragraph (11) of section 110 of title 17, United States Code, is liable for trademark infringement by reason of such conduct.

15 U.S.C. § 1114

(July 5, 1946, ch. 540, title VI, §32, 60 Stat. 437; Oct. 9, 1962, Pub. L. 87-772, §17, 76 Stat. 773; Nov. 16, 1988, Pub. L. 100-667, §127, 102 Stat. 3943-44; Oct. 27, 1992, Pub. L. 102-542, §3, 106 Stat. 3567; Oct. 30, 1998, Pub. L. 105-330, §201, 112 Stat. 3070; Aug. 5, 1999, Pub. L. 106-43, §4, 113 Stat. 219; Nov. 29, 1999, Pub. L. 106-113, §3004, 113 Stat. 1501A-549; April 27, 2005, Pub. L. 109-9, §202, 119 Stat. 223.)

§ 1115 Registration on principal register as evidence of exclusive right to use mark; defenses [Section 33]

(a) Any registration issued under the Act of March 3, 1881, or the Act of February 20, 1905, or of a mark registered on the principal register provided by this Act and owned by a party to an action shall be admissible in evidence and shall be prima facie evidence of the validity of the registered mark and of the registration of the mark, of the registrant's ownership of the mark, and of the registrant's exclusive right to use the registered mark in commerce on or in connection with the goods or services specified in the registration subject to any conditions or limitations stated therein, but shall not preclude another person from proving any legal or equitable defense or defect, including those set forth in subsection (b), which might have been asserted if such mark had not been registered.

(b) To the extent that the right to use the registered mark has become incontestable under section 15 [§1065], the registration shall be conclusive evidence of the validity of the registered mark and of the registration of the mark, of the registrant's ownership of the mark, and of the registrant's exclusive right to use the registered mark in commerce. Such conclusive evidence shall relate to the exclusive right to use the mark on or in connection with the goods or services specified in the affidavit filed under the provisions of section 15 [§1065], or in the renewal application filed under the provisions of section 9 [§1059] if the goods or services specified in the renewal are fewer in number, subject to any conditions or limitations in the registration or in such affidavit or renewal application. Such conclusive evidence of the right to use the registered mark shall be subject to proof of infringement as defined in section 32 [§1114], and shall be subject to the following defenses or defects:

(1) That the registration or the incontestable right to use the mark was obtained fraudulently; or

(2) That the mark has been abandoned by the registrant; or

(3) That the registered mark is being used, by or with the permission of the registrant or a person in privity with the registrant, so as to misrepre-

sent the source of the goods or services on or in connection with which the mark is used; or

(4) That the use of the name, term, or device charged to be an infringement is a use, otherwise than as a mark, of the party's individual name in his own business, or of the individual name of anyone in privity with such party, or of a term or device which is descriptive of and used fairly and in good faith only to describe the goods or services of such party, or their geographic origin; or

(5) That the mark whose use by a party is charged as an infringement was adopted without knowledge of the registrant's prior use and has been continuously used by such party or those in privity with him from a date prior to (A) the date of constructive use of the mark established pursuant to section 7(c) [§1057(c)], (B) the registration of the mark under this Act if the application for registration is filed before the effective date of the Trademark Law Revision Act of 1988, or (C) publication of the registered mark under subsection (c) of section 12 [§1062] of this Act: *Provided, however*, That this defense or defect shall apply only for the area in which such continuous prior use is proved; or

(6) That the mark whose use is charged as an infringement was registered and used prior to the registration under this Act or publication under subsection (c) of section 12 [§1062] of this Act of the registered mark of the registrant, and not abandoned: *Provided, however*, That this defense or defect shall apply only for the area in which the mark was used prior to such registration or such publication of the registrant's mark; or

(7) That the mark has been or is being used to violate the antitrust laws of the United States; or

(8) That the mark is functional; or

(9) That equitable principles, including laches, estoppel, and acquiescence are applicable.

(July 5, 1946, ch. 540, title VI, §33, 60 Stat. 438; Oct. 9, 1962, Pub. L. 87-772, §18, 76 Stat. 774; Nov. 16, 1988, Pub. L. 100-667, §128, 102 Stat. 3944-45; Oct. 30, 1998, Pub. L. 105-330, §201, 112 Stat. 3070; Nov. 2, 2002, Pub. L. 107-273, §13207, 116 Stat. 1906.)

§ 1116   Injunctions; enforcement; notice to Director [Section 34]

(a) The several courts vested with jurisdiction of civil actions arising under this Act shall have power to grant injunctions, according to the principles of equity and upon such terms as the court may deem reasonable, to prevent the violation of any right of the registrant of a mark registered in the Patent and Trademark Office or to prevent a violation of subsection (a), (c), or (d) of section 43 [§1125(a), (c), or (d)]. Any such injunction may include a provision directing the defendant to file with the court and serve on the plaintiff within thirty days after the service on the defendant of such injunction, or such extended period as the court may direct, a report in writing under oath setting forth in detail the manner and form in which the defendant has complied with the injunction. Any such injunction granted upon hearing, after notice to the defendant, by any district court of the United States, may be served on the parties against whom such injunction is granted anywhere in the United States where they may be found, and shall be operative and may be enforced by proceedings to punish for contempt, or otherwise, by the court by which such injunction was granted, or by any other United States district court in whose jurisdiction the defendant may be found.

(b) The said courts shall have jurisdiction to enforce said injunction, as herein provided, as fully as if the injunction had been granted by the district court in which it is sought to be enforced. The clerk of the court or judge granting the injunction shall, when required to do so by the court before which application to enforce said injunction is made, transfer without delay to said court a certified copy of all papers on file in his office upon which said injunction was granted.

(c) It shall be the duty of the clerks of such courts within one month after the filing of any action, suit, or proceeding involving a mark registered under the provisions of this Act to give notice thereof in writing to the Director setting forth in order so far as known the names and addresses of the litigants and the designating number or numbers of the registration or registrations upon which the action, suit, or proceeding has been brought, and in the event any other registration be subsequently included in the action, suit, or proceeding by amendment, answer, or other pleading, the clerk shall give like notice thereof to the Director, and within one month after the judgment is entered or an appeal is taken the clerk of the court shall give notice thereof to the Director, and it shall be the duty of the Director on receipt of such notice forthwith to endorse the same upon the file wrapper of the said registration or registrations and to incorporate the same as a part of the contents of said file wrapper.

(d) (1) (A) In the case of a civil action arising under section 32(1)(a) of this Act (15 U.S.C. 1114) or section 220506 of title 36, United States Code, with respect to a violation that consists of using a counterfeit mark in connection with the sale, offering for sale, or distribution of goods or services, the court may, upon ex parte application, grant an order under subsection (a) of this section pursuant to this subsection providing for the seizure of goods and counterfeit marks involved in such violation and the means of making such marks, and records documenting the manufacturer, sale, or receipt of things involved in such violation.

(B) As used in this subsection the term "counterfeit mark" means—

(i) a counterfeit of a mark that is registered on the principal register in the United States Patent and Trademark Office for such goods or services sold, offered for sale, or distributed and that is in use, whether or not the person against whom relief is sought knew such mark was so registered; or

(ii) a spurious designation that is identical with, or substantially indistinguishable from, a designation as to which the remedies of this Act are made available by reason of section 220506 of title 36, United States Code;

but such term does not include any mark or designation used on or in connection with goods or services of which the manufacturer or producer was, at the time of the manufacture or production in question, authorized to use the mark or designation for the type of goods or services so manufactured or produced, by the holder of the right to use such mark or designation.

(2) The court shall not receive an application under this subsection unless the applicant has given such notice of the application as is reasonable under the circumstances to the United States attorney for the judicial district in which such order is sought. Such attorney may participate in the proceedings arising under such application if such proceedings may affect evidence of an offense against the United States. The court may deny such application if the court determines that the public interest in a potential prosecution so requires.

(3) The application for an order under this subsection shall—

(A) be based on an affidavit or the verified complaint establishing facts sufficient to support the findings of fact and conclusions of law required for such order; and

15 U.S.C. § 1116

(B) contain the additional information required by paragraph (5) of this subsection to be set forth in such order.

(4) The court shall not grant such an application unless—

(A) the person obtaining an order under this subsection provides the security determined adequate by the court for the payment of such damages as any person may be entitled to recover as a result of a wrongful seizure or wrongful attempted seizure under this subsection; and

(B) the court finds that it clearly appears from specific facts that—

(i) an order other than an ex parte seizure order is not adequate to achieve the purposes of section 32 of this Act (15 U.S.C. 1114);

(ii) the applicant has not publicized the requested seizure;

(iii) the applicant is likely to succeed in showing that the person against whom seizure would be ordered used a counterfeit mark in connection with the sale, offering for sale, or distribution of goods or services;

(iv) an immediate and irreparable injury will occur if such seizure is not ordered;

(v) the matter to be seized will be located at the place identified in the application;

(vi) the harm to the applicant of denying the application outweighs the harm to the legitimate interests of the person against whom seizure would be ordered of granting the application; and

(vii) the person against whom seizure would be ordered, or persons acting in concert with such person, would destroy, move, hide, or otherwise make such matter inaccessible to the court, if the applicant were to proceed on notice to such person.

(5) An order under this subsection shall set forth—

(A) the findings of fact and conclusions of law required for the order;

(B) a particular description of the matter to be seized, and a description of each place at which such matter is to be seized;

(C) the time period, which shall end not later than seven days after the date on which such order is issued, during which the seizure is to be made;

(D) the amount of security required to be provided under this subsection; and

(E) a date for the hearing required under paragraph (10) of this subsection.

(6) The court shall take appropriate action to protect the person against whom an order under this subsection is directed from publicity, by or at the behest of the plaintiff, about such order and any seizure under such order.

(7) Any materials seized under this subsection shall be taken into the custody of the court. For seizures made under this section, the court shall enter an appropriate protective order with respect to discovery and use of any records or information that has been seized. The protective order shall provide for appropriate procedures to ensure that confidential, private, proprietary, or privileged information contained in such records is not improperly disclosed or used.

(8) An order under this subsection, together with the supporting documents, shall be sealed until the person against whom the order is directed has an opportunity to contest such order, except that any person against whom such order is issued shall have access to such order and supporting documents after the seizure has been carried out.

(9) The court shall order that service of a copy of the order under this subsection shall be made by a Federal law enforcement officer (such as a United States marshal or an officer or agent of the United States Customs Service, Secret Service, Federal Bureau of Investigation, or Post Office) or may be made by a State or local law enforcement officer, who, upon making service, shall carry out the seizure under the order. The court shall issue orders, when appropriate, to protect the defendant from undue damage from the disclosure of trade secrets or other confidential information during the course of the seizure, including, when appropriate, orders restricting the access of the applicant (or any agent or employee of the applicant) to such secrets or information.

(10) (A) The court shall hold a hearing, unless waived by all the parties, on the date set by the court in the order of seizure. That date shall be not sooner than ten days after the order is issued and not later than fifteen days after the order is issued, unless the applicant for the order shows good cause for another date or unless the party against whom

15 U.S.C. § 1116

such order is directed consents to another date for such hearing. At such hearing the party obtaining the order shall have the burden to prove that the facts supporting findings of fact and conclusions of law necessary to support such order are still in effect. If that party fails to meet that burden, the seizure order shall be dissolved or modified appropriately.

(B) In connection with a hearing under this paragraph, the court may make such orders modifying the time limits for discovery under the Rules of Civil Procedure as may be necessary to prevent the frustration of the purposes of such hearing.

(11) A person who suffers damage by reason of a wrongful seizure under this subsection has a cause of action against the applicant for the order under which such seizure was made, and shall be entitled to recover such relief as may be appropriate, including damages for lost profits, cost of materials, loss of good will, and punitive damages in instances where the seizure was sought in bad faith, and, unless the court finds extenuating circumstances, to recover a reasonable attorney's fee. The court in its discretion may award prejudgment interest on relief recovered under this paragraph, at an annual interest rate established under section 6621(a)(2) of the Internal Revenue Code of 1986, commencing on the date of service of the claimant's pleading setting forth the claim under this paragraph and ending on the date such recovery is granted, or for such shorter time as the court deems appropriate.

(July 5, 1946, ch. 540, title VI, §34, 60 Stat. 439; Jan. 2, 1975, Pub. L. 93-596, §1, 88 Stat. 1949; Oct. 12, 1984, Pub. L. 98-473, §1503, 98 Stat. 2179; Nov. 16, 1988, Pub. L. 100-667, §128, 102 Stat. 3944-45; July 2, 1996, Pub. L. 104-153, §6, 110 Stat. 1388; Aug. 5, 1999, Pub. L. 106-43, §3, 113 Stat. 218; Nov. 29, 1999, Pub. L. 106-113, §3003, 113 Stat. 1501A-548; Nov. 2, 2002, Pub. L. 107-273, §13207, 116 Stat. 1906; Oct. 13, 2008, Pub. L. 110-403, §102, 122 Stat. 4258.)

§ 1117   Recovery for violation of rights; profits, damages and costs; attorney fees [Section 35]

(a) When a violation of any right of the registrant of a mark registered in the Patent and Trademark Office, a violation under section 43(a) or (d) [§1125(a) or (d)], or a willful violation under section 43(c), shall have been established in any civil action arising under this Act, the plaintiff shall be entitled, subject to the provisions of sections 29 and 32 [§1111, 1114] of this Act, and subject to the principles of equity, to recover (1) defendant's profits, (2) any damages sustained by the plaintiff, and (3) the costs of the action. The court shall assess such profits and damages or cause the same to be assessed under its direction. In assessing profits the plaintiff shall be required to prove defendant's sales only; defendant must prove all elements of cost or deduction claimed. In assessing damages the court may enter judgment, according to the circumstances of the case, for any sum above the amount found as actual damages, not exceeding three times such amount. If the court shall find that the amount of the recovery based on profits is either inadequate or excessive the court may in its discretion enter judgment for such sum as the court shall find to be just, according to the circumstances of the case. Such sum in either of the above circumstances shall constitute compensation and not a penalty. The court in exceptional cases may award reasonable attorney fees to the prevailing party.

(b) In assessing damages under subsection (a) for any violation of section 32(1)(a) of this Act or section 220506 of title 36, United States Code, in a case involving use of a counterfeit mark or designation (as defined in section 34(d) of this Act), the court shall, unless the court finds extenuating circumstances, enter judgment for three times such profits or damages, whichever amount is greater, together with a reasonable attorney's fee, if the violation consists of—

(1) intentionally using a mark or designation, knowing such mark or designation is a counterfeit mark (as defined in section 34(d) of this Act), in connection with the sale, offering for sale, or distribution of goods or services; or

(2) providing goods or services necessary to the commission of a violation specified in paragraph (1), with the intent that the recipient of the goods or services would put the goods or services to use in committing the violation.

In such a case, the court may award prejudgment interest on such amount at an annual interest rate established under section 6621(a)(2) of the Internal Revenue Code of 1986, beginning on the date of the service of the claimant's pleadings setting forth the claim for such entry of judgment and ending on the date such entry is made, or for such shorter time as the court considers appropriate.

(c) In a case involving the use of a counterfeit mark (as defined in section 34(d) (15 U.S.C. 1116(d)) in connection with the sale, offering for sale, or distribution of goods or services, the plaintiff may elect, at any time before final judgment is rendered by the trial court, to recover, instead of actual damages and profits under subsection (a), an award of statutory damages for any such use in connection with the sale, offering for sale, or distribution of goods or services in the amount of—

(1) not less than $1000 or more than $200,000 per counterfeit mark per type of goods or services sold, offered for sale, or distributed, as the court considers just; or

(2) if the court finds that the use of the counterfeit mark was willful, not more than $2,000,000 per counterfeit mark per type of goods or services sold, offered for sale, or distributed, as the court considers just.

(d) In a case involving a violation of section 43(d)(1), the plaintiff may elect, at any time before final judgment is rendered by the trial court, to recover, instead of actual damages and profits, an award of statutory damages in the amount of not less than $1,000 and not more than $100,000 per domain name, as the court considers just.

(e) In the case of a violation referred to in this section, it shall be a rebuttable presumption that the violation is willful for purposes of determining relief if the violator, or a person acting in concert with the violator, knowingly provided or knowingly caused to be provided materially false contact information to a domain name registrar, domain name registry, or other domain name registration authority in registering, maintaining, or renewing a domain name used in connection with the violation. Nothing in this subsection limits what may be considered a willful violation under this section.

(July 5, 1946, ch. 540, title VI, §35, 60 Stat. 439; Oct. 9, 1962, Pub. L. 87-772, §19, 76 Stat. 774; Jan. 2, 1975, Pub. L. 93-596, §1, 88 Stat. 1949, Jan. 2, 1975, Pub. L. 93-600, §3, 88 Stat. 1955; Oct. 12, 1984, Pub. L. 98-473, §1503, 98 Stat. 2182; Nov. 16, 1988, Pub. L. 100-667, §129, 102 Stat. 3945; July 2, 1996, Pub. L. 104-153, §7, 110 Stat. 1388; Aug. 5, 1999, Pub. L. 106-43, §3, 113 Stat. 219 Nov. 29, 1999, Pub. L. 106-113, §3003, 113 Stat. 1501A-548; Nov. 2, 2002, Pub. L. 107-273, §13207, 116 Stat. 1906; Dec. 23, 2004, Pub. L. 108-482, §202, 118 Stat. 3916; Oct. 13, 2008, Pub. L. 110-403, §§103, 104, 122 Stat 4259.)

§ 1118 Destruction of infringing articles [Section 36]

In any action arising under this Act, in which a violation of any right of the registrant of a mark registered in the Patent and Trademark Office, a violation under section 43(a) [§1125(a)], or a willful violation under section 43(c), shall have been established, the court may order that all labels, signs, prints, packages, wrappers, receptacles, and advertisements in the possession of the defendant, bearing the registered mark or, in the case of a violation of section

43(a) [§1125(a)] or a willful violation under section 43(c), the word, term, name, symbol, device, combination thereof, designation, description, or representation that is the subject of the violation, or any reproduction, counterfeit, copy, or colorable imitation thereof, and all plates, molds, matrices, and other means of making the same, shall be delivered up and destroyed. The party seeking an order under this section for destruction of articles seized under section 34(d) (15 U.S.C. 1116(d)) shall give ten days' notice to the United States attorney for the judicial district in which such order is sought (unless good cause is shown for lesser notice) and such United States attorney may, if such destruction may affect evidence of an offense against the United States, seek a hearing on such destruction or participate in any hearing otherwise to be held with respect to such destruction.

(July 5, 1946, ch. 540, title VI, §36, 60 Stat 440; Jan. 2, 1975, Pub. L. 93-596, §1, 88 Stat. 1949; Oct. 12, 1984, Pub. L. 98-473, §1503, 98 Stat. 2182; Nov. 16, 1988, Pub. L. 100-667, §130, 102 Stat. 3945; Aug. 5, 1999, Pub. L. 106-43, §3, 113 Stat. 219.)

§ 1119   Power of court over registration [Section 37]

In any action involving a registered mark the court may determine the right to registration, order the cancelation of registrations, in whole or in part, restore canceled registrations, and otherwise rectify the register with respect to the registrations of any party to the action. Decrees and orders shall be certified by the court to the Director, who shall make appropriate entry upon the records of the Patent and Trademark Office, and shall be controlled thereby.

(July 5, 1946, ch. 540, title VI, §37, 60 Stat. 440; Jan. 2, 1975, Pub. L. 93-596, §1, 88 Stat. 1949.)

§ 1120   Civil liability for false or fraudulent registration [Section 38]

Any person who shall procure registration in the Patent and Trademark Office of a mark by a false or fraudulent declaration or representation, oral or in writing, or by any false means, shall be liable in a civil action by any person injured thereby for any damages sustained in consequence thereof.

(July 5, 1946, ch. 540, title VI, §38, 60 Stat. 440; Jan. 2, 1975, Pub. L. 93-596, §1, 88 Stat. 1949.)

§ 1121   Jurisdiction of Federal courts [Section 39]

(a) The district and territorial courts of the United States shall have original jurisdiction, [and] the courts of appeal of the United States (other than the United States Court of Appeals for the Federal Circuit) [and the United States Court of Appeals for the District of Columbia][6] shall have appellate jurisdiction, of all actions arising under this Act, without regard to the amount in controversy or to diversity or lack of diversity of the citizenship of the parties.

(b) No State or other jurisdiction of the United States or any political subdivision or any agency thereof may require alteration of a registered mark, or require that additional trademarks, service marks, trade names, or corporate names that may be associated with or incorporated into the registered mark be displayed in the mark in a manner differing from the display of such additional trademarks, service marks, trade names, or corporate names contemplated by the registered mark as exhibited in the certificate of registration issued by the United States Patent and Trademark Office.

(July 5, 1946, ch. 540, title VI, §39, 60 Stat. 440; June 25, 1948, ch. 646, §§1 and 32(a), 62 Stat. 870, 991; May 24, 1949, ch. 139, §127, 63 Stat. 107; Apr. 2, 1982, title I, Pub. L. 97-164, §148, 96 Stat. 46; Oct. 12, 1982, Pub. L. 97-296, 96 Stat. 1316; Nov. 16, 1988, Pub. L. 100-667, §131, 102 Stat. 3946.)

§ 1122   Liability of States, Instrumentalities of States, and State Officials [Section 40]

(a) *Waiver of Sovereign Immunity by the United States.* — The United States, all agencies and instrumentalities thereof, and all individuals, firms, corporations, other persons acting for the United States and with the authorization and consent of the United States, shall not be immune from suit in Federal or State court by any person, including any governmental or nongovernmental entity, for any violation under this Act.

(b) *Waiver of Sovereign Immunity by States.* — Any State, instrumentality of a State or any officer or employee of a State or instrumentality of a State acting in his or her official capacity, shall not be immune, under the eleventh amendment of the Constitution of the United States or under any other doctrine of sovereign immunity, from suit in Federal court by any person, including any governmental or nongovernmental entity for any violation under this Act.

---

[6] *Ed. Note:* This bracketed language is technically part of the statute, but is superfluous.

15 U.S.C. § 1121

(c) In a suit described in subsection (a) or (b) for a violation described therein, remedies (including remedies both at law and in equity) are available for the violation to the same extent as such remedies are available for such a violation in a suit against any person other than the United States or any agency or instrumentality thereof, or any individual, firm, corporation, or other person acting for the United States and with authorization and consent of the United States, or a State, instrumentality of a State, or officer or employee of a State or instrumentality of a State acting in his or her official capacity. Such remedies include injunctive relief under section 34 [§1116], actual damages, profits, costs and attorney's fees under section 35 [§1117], destruction of infringing articles under section 36 [§1118], the remedies provided for under sections 32, 37, 38, 42, and 43 [§§1114, 1119, 1120, 1124, and 1125] and for any other remedies provided under this Act.

(Added Oct. 27, 1992, Pub. L. 102-542, §3, 106 Stat. 3567-3568; Aug. 5, 1999, Pub. L. 106-43, §4, 113 Stat. 219.)

§ 1123 Rules and regulations for conduct of proceedings in Patent and Trademark Office [Section 41]

The Director shall make rules and regulations, not inconsistent with law, for the conduct of proceedings in the Patent and Trademark Office under this Act.

(July 5, 1946, ch. 540, title VI, §41, 60 Stat. 440; Jan. 2, 1975, Pub. L. 93-596, §1, 88 Stat. 1949.)

§ 1124 Importation of goods bearing infringing marks or names forbidden [Section 42]

Except as provided in subsection (d) of section 526 of the Tariff Act of 1930 19 U.S.C.S. 1526(d), no article of imported merchandise which shall copy or simulate the name of any domestic manufacture, or manufacturer, or trader, or of any manufacturer or trader located in any foreign country which, by treaty, convention, or law affords similar privileges to citizens of the United States, or which shall copy or simulate a trademark registered in accordance with the provisions of this Act or shall bear a name or mark calculated to induce the public to believe that the article is manufactured in the United States, or that it is manufactured in any foreign country or locality other than the country or locality in which it is in fact manufactured, shall be admitted to entry at any customhouse of the United States; and, in order to aid the officers of the customs in enforcing this prohibition, any domestic manufacturer or trader, and any foreign manufacturer or trader, who is entitled under the provisions of a treaty, conviction, declaration, or agreement between the United States and any foreign country to the advantages afforded by law to citizens of the United States in respect to trademarks and commercial names, may require his name and residence, and the name of the locality in which his goods are manufactured, and a copy of the certificate of registration of his trademark, issued in accordance with the provisions of this Act, to be recorded in books which shall be kept for this purpose in the Department of the Treasury, under such regulations as the Secretary of the Treasury shall prescribe, and may furnish to the Department facsimiles of his name, the name of the locality in which his goods are manufactured, or of his registered trademark, and thereupon the Secretary of the Treasury shall cause one or more copies of the same to be transmitted to each collector or other proper officer of customs.

(July 5, 1946, ch. 540, §42, 60 Stat. 440; Oct. 3, 1978, Pub. L. 95-410, title II, §211, 92 Stat. 903; Oct. 30, 1998, Pub. L. 105-330, §201, 112 Stat. 3070.)

§ 1125 False designations of origin, false descriptions, and dilution
[Section 43]

(a) (1) Any person who, on or in connection with any goods or services, or any container for goods, uses in commerce any word, term, name, symbol, or device, or any combination thereof, or any false designation of origin, false or misleading description of fact, or false or misleading representation of fact, which—

(A) is likely to cause confusion, or to cause mistake, or to deceive as to the affiliation, connection, or association of such person with another person, or as to the origin, sponsorship, or approval of his or her goods, services, or commercial activities by another person, or

(B) in commercial advertising or promotion, misrepresents the nature, characteristics, qualities, or geographic origin of his or her or another person's goods, services, or commercial activities,

shall be liable in a civil action by any person who believes that he or she is or is likely to be damaged by such act.

(2) As used in this subsection, the term "any person" includes any State, instrumentality of a State or employee of a State or instrumentality of a State acting in his or her official capacity. Any State, and any such instrumentality, officer, or employee, shall be subject to the provisions of this

Act in the same manner and to the same extent as any nongovernmental entity.

(3) In a civil action for trade dress infringement under this Act for trade dress not registered on the principal register, the person who asserts trade dress protection has the burden of proving that the matter sought to be protected is not functional.

(b) Any goods marked or labeled in contravention of the provisions of this section shall not be imported into the United States or admitted to entry at any customhouse of the United States. The owner, importer, or consignee of goods refused entry at any customhouse under this section may have any recourse by protest or appeal that is given under the customs revenue laws or may have the remedy given by this Act in cases involving goods refused entry or seized.

(c) *Dilution by Blurring; Dilution by Tarnishment.—*

(1) *Injunctive relief.—*Subject to the principles of equity, the owner of a famous mark that is distinctive, inherently or through acquired distinctiveness, shall be entitled to an injunction against another person who, at any time after the owner's mark has become famous, commences use of a mark or trade name in commerce that is likely to cause dilution by blurring or dilution by tarnishment of the famous mark, regardless of the presence or absence of actual or likely confusion, of competition, or of actual economic injury.

(2) *Definitions.—*

(A) For purposes of paragraph (1), a mark is famous if it is widely recognized by the general consuming public of the United States as a designation of source of the goods or services of the mark's owner. In determining whether a mark possesses the requisite degree of recognition, the court may consider all relevant factors, including the following:

(i) The duration, extent, and geographic reach of advertising and publicity of the mark, whether advertised or publicized by the owner or third parties.

(ii) The amount, volume, and geographic extent of sales of goods or services offered under the mark.

(iii) The extent of actual recognition of the mark.

15 U.S.C. § 1125

(iv) Whether the mark was registered under the Act of March 3, 1881, or the Act of February 20, 1905, or on the principal register.

(B) For purposes of paragraph (1), "dilution by blurring" is association arising from the similarity between a mark or trade name and a famous mark that impairs the distinctiveness of the famous mark. In determining whether a mark or trade name is likely to cause dilution by blurring, the court may consider all relevant factors, including the following:

(i) The degree of similarity between the mark or trade name and the famous mark.

(ii) The degree of inherent or acquired distinctiveness of the famous mark.

(iii) The extent to which the owner of the famous mark is engaging in substantially exclusive use of the mark.

(iv) The degree of recognition of the famous mark.

(v) Whether the user of the mark or trade name intended to create an association with the famous mark.

(vi) Any actual association between the mark or trade name and the famous mark.

(C) For purposes of paragraph (1), "dilution by tarnishment" is association arising from the similarity between a mark or trade name and a famous mark that harms the reputation of the famous mark.

(3) *Exclusions.*—The following shall not be actionable as dilution by blurring or dilution by tarnishment under this subsection:

(A) Any fair use, including a nominative or descriptive fair use, or facilitation of such fair use, of a famous mark by another person other than as a designation of source for the person's own goods or services, including use in connection with—

(i) advertising or promotion that permits consumers to compare goods or services; or

(ii) identifying and parodying, criticizing, or commenting upon the famous mark owner or the goods or services of the famous mark owner.

(B) All forms of news reporting and news commentary.

15 U.S.C. § 1125

(C) Any noncommercial use of a mark.

(4) *Burden of proof.*—In a civil action for trade dress dilution under this Act for trade dress not registered on the principal register, the person who asserts trade dress protection has the burden of proving that—

(A) the claimed trade dress, taken as a whole, is not functional and is famous; and

(B) if the claimed trade dress includes any mark or marks registered on the principal register, the unregistered matter, taken as a whole, is famous separate and apart from any fame of such registered marks.

(5) *Additional remedies.*—In an action brought under this subsection, the owner of the famous mark shall be entitled to injunctive relief as set forth in section 34. The owner of the famous mark shall also be entitled to the remedies set forth in sections 35(a) and 36, subject to the discretion of the court and the principles of equity if—

(A) the mark or trade name that is likely to cause dilution by blurring or dilution by tarnishment was first used in commerce by the person against whom the injunction is sought after the date of enactment of the Trademark Dilution Revision Act of 2006; and

(B) in a claim arising under this subsection—

(i) by reason of dilution by blurring, the person against whom the injunction is sought willfully intended to trade on the recognition of the famous mark; or

(ii) by reason of dilution by tarnishment, the person against whom the injunction is sought willfully intended to harm the reputation of the famous mark.

(6) *Ownership of valid registration a complete bar to action.*—The ownership by a person of a valid registration under the Act of March 3, 1881, or the Act of February 20, 1905, or on the principal register under this Act shall be a complete bar to an action against that person, with respect to that mark, that—

(A) is brought by another person under the common law or a statute of a State; and

(B)(i) seeks to prevent dilution by blurring or dilution by tarnishment; or

(ii) asserts any claim of actual or likely damage or harm to the distinctiveness or reputation of a mark, label, or form of advertisement.

(7) *Savings clause.*—Nothing in this subsection shall be construed to impair, modify, or supersede the applicability of the patent laws of the United States.

(d)(1)(A) A person shall be liable in a civil action by the owner of a mark, including a personal name which is protected as a mark under this section, if, without regard to the goods or services of the parties, that person—

(i) has a bad faith intent to profit from that mark, including a personal name which is protected as a mark under this section; and

(ii) registers, traffics in, or uses a domain name that—

(I) in the case of a mark that is distinctive at the time of registration of the domain name, is identical or confusingly similar to that mark;

(II) in the case of a famous mark that is famous at the time of registration of the domain name, is identical or confusingly similar to or dilutive of that mark; or

(III) is a trademark, word, or name protected by reason of section 706 of title 18, United States Code, or section 220506 of title 36, United States Code.

(B)(i) In determining whether a person has a bad faith intent described under subparagraph (A), a court may consider factors such as, but not limited to—

(I) the trademark or other intellectual property rights of the person, if any, in the domain name;

(II) the extent to which the domain name consists of the legal name of the person or a name that is otherwise commonly used to identify that person;

(III) the person's prior use, if any, of the domain name in connection with the bona fide offering of any goods or services;

(IV) the person's bona fide noncommercial or fair use of the mark in a site accessible under the domain name;

(V) the person's intent to divert consumers from the mark owner's online location to a site accessible under the domain name that could harm the goodwill represented by the mark, either for commercial gain or with the intent to tarnish or disparage the mark, by creating a likelihood of confusion as to the source, sponsorship, affiliation, or endorsement of the site;

(VI) the person's offer to transfer, sell, or otherwise assign the domain name to the mark owner or any third party for financial gain without having used, or having an intent to use, the domain name in the bona fide offering of any goods or services, or the person's prior conduct indicating a pattern of such conduct;

(VII) the person's provision of material and misleading false contact information when applying for the registration of the domain name, the person's intentional failure to maintain accurate contact information, or the person's prior conduct indicating a pattern of such conduct;

(VIII) the person's registration or acquisition of multiple domain names which the person knows are identical or confusingly similar to marks of others that are distinctive at the time of registration of such domain names, or dilutive of famous marks of others that are famous at the time of registration of such domain names, without regard to the goods or services of the parties; and

(IX) the extent to which the mark incorporated in the person's domain name registration is or is not distinctive and famous within the meaning of subsection (c).

(ii) Bad faith intent described under subparagraph (A) shall not be found in any case in which the court determines that the person believed and had reasonable grounds to believe that the use of the domain name was a fair use or otherwise lawful.

(C) In any civil action involving the registration, trafficking, or use of a domain name under this paragraph, a court may order the forfeiture or cancellation of the domain name or the transfer of the domain name to the owner of the mark.

15 U.S.C. § 1125

(D) A person shall be liable for using a domain name under subparagraph (A) only if that person is the domain name registrant or that registrant's authorized licensee.

(E) As used in this paragraph, the term "traffics in" refers to transactions that include, but are not limited to, sales, purchases, loans, pledges, licenses, exchanges of currency, and any other transfer for consideration or receipt in exchange for consideration.

(2)(A) The owner of a mark may file an in rem civil action against a domain name in the judicial district in which the domain name registrar, domain name registry, or other domain name authority that registered or assigned the domain name is located if—

(i) the domain name violates any right of the owner of a mark registered in the Patent and Trademark Office, or protected under subsection (a) or (c); and

(ii) the court finds that the owner—

(I) is not able to obtain in personam jurisdiction over a person who would have been a defendant in a civil action under paragraph (1); or

(II) through due diligence was not able to find a person who would have been a defendant in a civil action under paragraph (1) by—

(aa) sending a notice of the alleged violation and intent to proceed under this paragraph to the registrant of the domain name at the postal and e-mail address provided by the registrant to the registrar; and

(bb) publishing notice of the action as the court may direct promptly after filing the action.

(B) The actions under subparagraph (A)(ii) shall constitute service of process.

(C) In an in rem action under this paragraph, a domain name shall be deemed to have its situs in the judicial district in which—

(i) the domain name registrar, registry, or other domain name authority that registered or assigned the domain name is located; or

(ii) documents sufficient to establish control and authority regarding the disposition of the registration and use of the domain name are deposited with the court.

(D)(i) The remedies in an in rem action under this paragraph shall be limited to a court order for the forfeiture or cancellation of the domain name or the transfer of the domain name to the owner of the mark. Upon receipt of written notification of a filed, stamped copy of a complaint filed by the owner of a mark in a United States district court under this paragraph, the domain name registrar, domain name registry, or other domain name authority shall—

(I) expeditiously deposit with the court documents sufficient to establish the court's control and authority regarding the disposition of the registration and use of the domain name to the court; and

(II) not transfer, suspend, or otherwise modify the domain name during the pendency of the action, except upon order of the court.

(ii) The domain name registrar or registry or other domain name authority shall not be liable for injunctive or monetary relief under this paragraph except in the case of bad faith or reckless disregard, which includes a willful failure to comply with any such court order.

(3) The civil action established under paragraph (1) and the in rem action established under paragraph (2), and any remedy available under either such action, shall be in addition to any other civil action or remedy otherwise applicable.

(4) The in rem jurisdiction established under paragraph (2) shall be in addition to any other jurisdiction that otherwise exists, whether in rem or in personam.

(July 5, 1946, ch. 540, title VIII, §43, 60 Stat. 441; Nov. 16, 1988, Pub. L. 100-667, §132, 102 Stat. 3946; Oct. 27, 1992, Pub. L. 102-542, §3, 106 Stat. 3568; Jan. 16, 1996, Pub. L. 104-98, 109 Stat. 985; Aug. 5, 1999, Pub. L. 106-43, §3, 113 Stat. 219; Aug. 5, 1999, Pub. L. 106-43, §5, 113 Stat. 219; Nov. 29, 1999, Pub. L. 106-113, §3002, 113 Stat. 1501A-545, Oct. 6, 2006, Pub. L. 109-312, §2, 120 Stat. 1730, 1732; Oct. 5, 2012, Pub. L. 112-90, §1, 126 Stat. 1436.)

15 U.S.C. § 1125

§ 1126   International conventions [Section 44]

(a) *Register of marks communicated by international bureaus.* — The Director shall keep a register of all marks communicated to him by the international bureaus provided for by the conventions for the protection of industrial property, trademarks, trade and commercial names, and the repression of unfair competition to which the United States is or may become a party, and upon the payment of the fees required by such conventions and the fees required in this Act may place the marks so communicated upon such register. This register shall show a facsimile of the mark or trade or commercial name; the name, citizenship, and address of the registrant; the number, date, and place of the first registration of the mark, including the dates on which application for such registration was filed and granted and the term of such registration; a list of goods or services to which the mark is applied as shown by the registration in the country of origin, and such other data as may be useful concerning the mark. This register shall be a continuation of the register provided in section 1(a) of the Act of March 19, 1920.

(b) *Benefits of section to persons whose country of origin is party to convention or treaty.* — Any person whose country of origin is a party to any convention or treaty relating to trademarks, trade or commercial names, or the repression of unfair competition, to which the United States is also a party, or extends reciprocal rights to nationals of the United States by law, shall be entitled to the benefits of this section under the conditions expressed herein to the extent necessary to give effect to any provision of such convention, treaty or reciprocal law, in addition to the rights to which any owner of a mark is otherwise entitled by this Act.

(c) *Prior registration in country of origin; country of origin defined.* — No registration of a mark in the United States by a person described in subsection (b) of this section shall be granted until such mark has been registered in the country of origin of the applicant, unless the applicant alleges use in commerce. For the purposes of this section, the country of origin of the applicant is the country in which he has a bona fide and effective industrial or commercial establishment, or if he has not such an establishment the country in which he is domiciled, or if he has not a domicile in any of the countries described in subsection (b) of this section, the country of which he is a national.

(d) *Right of priority.* — An application for registration of a mark under sections 1, 3, 4, or 23 of this Act or under subsection (e) of this section filed by a person described in subsection (b) of this section who has previously duly filed an application for registration of the same mark in one of the countries described in subsection (b) shall be accorded the same force and effect as would be accorded to the same application if filed in the United States on the same date on which the application was first filed in such foreign country: *Provided,* that—

(1) the application in the United States is filed within six months from the date on which the application was first filed in the foreign country;

(2) the application conforms as nearly as practicable to the requirements of this Act, including a statement that the applicant has a bona fide intention to use the mark in commerce;

(3) the rights acquired by third parties before the date of the filing of the first application in the foreign country shall in no way be affected by a registration obtained on an application filed under this subsection;

(4) nothing in this subsection shall entitle the owner of a registration granted under this section to sue for acts committed prior to the date on which his mark was registered in this country unless the registration is based on use in commerce.

In like manner and subject to the same conditions and requirements, the right provided in this section may be based upon a subsequent regularly filed application in the same foreign country, instead of the first filed foreign application: *Provided,* That any foreign application filed prior to such subsequent application has been withdrawn, abandoned, or otherwise disposed of, without having been laid open to public inspection and without leaving any rights outstanding, and has not served, nor thereafter shall serve, as a basis for claiming a right of priority.

(e) *Registration on principal or supplemental register; copy of foreign registration.—* A mark duly registered in the country of origin of the foreign applicant may be registered on the principal register if eligible, otherwise on the supplemental register herein provided. Such applicant shall submit, within such time period as may be prescribed by the Director, a true copy, a photocopy, a certification, or a certified copy of the registration in the country of origin of the applicant. The application must state the applicant's bona fide intention to use the mark in commerce, but use in commerce shall not be required prior to registration.

15 U.S.C. § 1126

(f) *Domestic registration independent of foreign registration.*—The registration of a mark under the provisions of subsections (c), (d), and (e) of this section by a person described in subsection (b) shall be independent of the registration in the country of origin and the duration, validity, or transfer in the United States of such registration shall be governed by the provisions of this Act.

(g) *Trade or commercial names of foreign nationals protected without registration.*— Trade names or commercial names of persons described in subsection (b) of this section shall be protected without the obligation of filing or registration whether or not they form parts of marks.

(h) *Protection of foreign nationals against unfair competition.*—Any person designated in subsection (b) of this section as entitled to the benefits and subject to the provisions of this Act shall be entitled to effective protection against unfair competition, and the remedies provided herein for infringement of marks shall be available so far as they may be appropriate in repressing acts of unfair competition.

(i) *Citizens or residents of United States entitled to benefits of section.*—Citizens or residents of the United States shall have the same benefits as are granted by this section to persons described in subsection (b) of this section.

(July 5, 1946, ch. 540, title IX, §44, 60 Stat. 441; Oct. 3, 1961, Pub. L. 87-333, §2, 75 Stat. 748; Oct. 9, 1962, Pub. L. 87-772, §20, 76 Stat. 774; Nov. 16, 1988, Pub. L. 100-667, §133, 102 Stat. 3946; Oct. 30, 1998, Pub. L. 105-330, §108, 112 Stat. 3068; Nov. 2, 2002, Pub. L. 107-273, §13207, 116 Stat. 1906.)

§ 1127 Construction and definitions; intent of chapter [Section 45]

In the construction of this Act, unless the contrary is plainly apparent from the context—

The United States includes and embraces all territory which is under its jurisdiction and control.

The word "commerce" means all commerce which may lawfully be regulated by Congress.

The term "principal register" refers to the register provided for by sections 1 through 22 hereof [§§1051-1072], and the term "supplemental register" refers to the register provided for by sections 23 through 28 thereof [§§1091-1096].

The term "person" and any other word or term used to designate the applicant or other entitled to a benefit or privilege or rendered liable under the provisions of this Act includes a juristic person as well as a natural person. The term "juristic person" includes a firm, corporation, union, association, or other organization capable of suing and being sued in a court of law.

The term "person" also includes the United States, any agency or instrumentality thereof; or any individual, firm, or corporation acting for the United States and with the authorization and consent of the United States. The United States, any agency or instrumentality thereof, and any individual, firm, or corporation acting for the United States and with the authorization and consent of the United States, shall be subject to the provisions of this Act in the same manner and to the same extent as any nongovernmental entity.

The term "person" also includes any State, any instrumentality of a State, and any officer or employee of a State or instrumentality of a State acting in his or her official capacity. Any State, and any such instrumentality, officer, or employee, shall be subject to the provisions of this Act in the same manner and to the same extent as any nongovernmental entity.

The terms "applicant" and "registrant" embrace the legal representatives, predecessors, successors and assigns of such applicant or registrant.

The term "Director" means the Under Secretary of Commerce for Intellectual Property and Director of the United States Patent and Trademark Office.

The term "related company" means any person whose use of a mark is controlled by the owner of the mark with respect to the nature and quality of the goods or services on or in connection with which the mark is used.

The terms "trade name" and "commercial name" mean any name used by a person to identify his or her business or vocation.

The term "trademark" includes any word, name, symbol, or device, or any combination thereof—

(1) used by a person, or

(2) which a person has a bona fide intention to use in commerce and applies to register on the principal register established by this Act,

to identify and distinguish his or her goods, including a unique product, from those manufactured or sold by others and to indicate the source of the goods, even if that source is unknown.

The term "service mark" means any word, name, symbol, or device, or any combination thereof—

(1) used by a person, or

(2) which a person has a bona fide intention to use in commerce and applies to register on the principal register established by this Act,

to identify and distinguish the services of one person, including a unique service, from the services of others and to indicate the source of the services, even if that source is unknown. Titles, character names, and other distinctive features of radio or television programs may be registered as service marks notwithstanding that they, or the programs, may advertise the goods of the sponsor.

The term "certification mark" means any word, name, symbol, or device, or any combination thereof—

(1) used by a person other than its owner, or

(2) which its owner has a bona fide intention to permit a person other than the owner to use in commerce and files an application to register on the principal register established by this Act,

to certify regional or other origin, material, mode of manufacture, quality, accuracy, or other characteristics of such person's goods or services or that the work or labor on the goods or services was performed by members of a union or other organization.

The term "collective mark" means a trademark or service mark—

(1) used by the members of a cooperative, an association, or other collective group or organization, or

(2) which such cooperative, association, or other collective group or organization has a bona fide intention to use in commerce and applies to register on the principal register established by this Act,

and includes marks indicating membership in a union, an association, or other organization.

The term "mark" includes any trademark, service mark, collective mark, or certification mark.

The term "use in commerce" means the bona fide use of a mark in the ordinary course of trade, and not made merely to reserve a right in a mark. For purposes of this Act, a mark shall be deemed to be in use in commerce—

(1) on goods when—

(A) it is placed in any manner on the goods or their containers or the displays associated therewith or on the tags or labels affixed thereto, or if the nature of the goods makes such placement impracticable, then on documents associated with the goods or their sale, and

(B) the goods are sold or transported in commerce, and

(2) on services when it is used or displayed in the sale or advertising of services and the services are rendered in commerce, or the services are rendered in more than one State or in the United States and a foreign country and the person rendering the services is engaged in commerce in connection with the services.

A mark shall be deemed to be "abandoned" when either of the following occurs:

(1) When its use has been discontinued with intent not to resume such use. Intent not to resume may be inferred from circumstances. Nonuse for 3 consecutive years shall be prima facie evidence of abandonment. "Use" of a mark means the bona fide use of that mark made in the ordinary course of trade, and not made merely to reserve a right in a mark.

(2) When any course of conduct of the owner, including acts of omission as well as commission, causes the mark to become the generic name for the goods or services on or in connection with which it is used or otherwise to lose its significance as a mark. Purchaser motivation shall not be a test for determining abandonment under this paragraph.

The term "colorable imitation" includes any mark which so resembles a registered mark as to be likely to cause confusion or mistake or to deceive.

The term "registered mark" means a mark registered in the United States Patent and Trademark Office under this Act or under the Act of March 3, 1881, or the Act of February 20, 1905, or the Act of March 19, 1920. The phrase "marks registered in the Patent and Trademark Office" means registered marks.

The term "Act of March 3, 1881," "Act of February 20, 1905," or "Act of March 19, 1920," means the respective Act as amended.

A "counterfeit" is a spurious mark which is identical with, or substantially indistinguishable from, a registered mark.

The term "domain name" means any alphanumeric designation which is registered with or assigned by any domain name registrar, domain name registry, or other domain name registration authority as part of an electronic address on the Internet.

15 U.S.C. § 1127

The term "Internet" has the meaning given that term in section 230(f)(1) of the Communications Act of 1934 (47 U.S.C. 230(f)(1)).

Words used in the singular include the plural and vice versa.

The intent of this Act is to regulate commerce within the control of Congress by making actionable the deceptive and misleading use of marks in such commerce; to protect registered marks used in such commerce from interference by State, or territorial legislation; to protect persons engaged in such commerce against unfair competition; to prevent fraud and deception in such commerce by the use of reproductions, copies, counterfeits, or colorable imitations of registered marks; and to provide rights and remedies stipulated by treaties and conventions respecting trademarks, trade names, and unfair competition entered into between the United States and foreign nations.

(July 5, 1946, ch. 540, title X, §45, 60 Stat. 443; Oct. 9, 1962, Pub. L. 87-772, §21, 76 Stat. 774; Jan. 2, 1975, Pub. L. 93-596, §1, 88 Stat. 1949; Nov. 8, 1984, Pub. L. 98-620, §103, 98 Stat. 3336; Nov. 16, 1988, Pub. L. 100-667, §134, 102 Stat. 3946-48; Oct. 27, 1992, Pub. L. 102-542, §3, 106 Stat. 3568; Dec. 8, 1994, Pub. L. 103-465, §521, 108 Stat. 4981; Jan. 16, 1996, Pub. L. 104-98, 109 Stat. 986; Aug. 5, 1999, Pub. L. 106-43, §4, 113 Stat. 219; Nov. 29, 1999, Pub. L. 106-113, §§3005, 4732, 113 Stat. 1501A-550, 581, Oct. 6, 2006, Pub. L. 109-312, §3(e), 120 Stat. 1733.)

§ 1128 [Repealed]

(Sept. 29, 1999, Pub. L. 106-58, §653, 113 Stat. 480; Dec. 8, 2004, Pub. L. 108-447, §210, 118 Stat. 2884; Oct. 13, 2008, Pub. L. 110-403, §305, 122 Stat. 4270.)

§ 1129[7] Cyberpiracy protections for individuals [Transferred]

---

[7] *Ed. Note*: In 2008 this section was recodified at 15 U.S.C. §8131.

SUBCHAPTER IV — THE MADRID PROTOCOL

§ 1141   Definitions [Section 60]

In this title:

(1) *Basic application.* — The term "basic application" means the application for the registration of a mark that has been filed with an Office of a Contracting Party and that constitutes the basis for an application for the international registration of that mark.

(2) *Basic registration.* — The term "basic registration" means the registration of a mark that has been granted by an Office of a Contracting Party and that constitutes the basis for an application for the international registration of that mark.

(3) *Contracting Party.* — The term "Contracting Party" means any country or inter-governmental organization that is a party to the Madrid Protocol.

(4) *Date of recordal.* — The term "date of recordal" means the date on which a request for extension of protection, filed after an international registration is granted, is recorded on the International Register.

(5) *Declaration of bona fide intention to use the mark in commerce.* — The term "declaration of bona fide intention to use the mark in commerce" means a declaration that is signed by the applicant for, or holder of, an international registration who is seeking extension of protection of a mark to the United States and that contains a statement that —

> (A) the applicant or holder has a bona fide intention to use the mark in commerce;

> (B) the person making the declaration believes himself or herself, or the firm, corporation, or association in whose behalf he or she makes the declaration, to be entitled to use the mark in commerce; and

> (C) no other person, firm, corporation, or association, to the best of his or her knowledge and belief, has the right to use such mark in commerce either in the identical form of the mark or in such near resemblance to the mark as to be likely, when used on or in connection with the goods of such other person, firm, corporation, or association, to cause confusion, mistake, or deception.

(6) *Extension of protection.* — The term "extension of protection" means the protection resulting from an international registration that extends to the

15 U.S.C. § 1141

United States at the request of the holder of the international registration, in accordance with the Madrid Protocol.

(7) *Holder of an international registration.*—A "holder" of an international registration is the natural or juristic person in whose name the international registration is recorded on the International Register.

(8) *International application.*—The term "international application" means an application for international registration that is filed under the Madrid Protocol.

(9) *International Bureau.*—The term "International Bureau" means the International Bureau of the World Intellectual Property Organization.

(10) *International Register.*—The term "International Register" means the official collection of data concerning international registrations maintained by the International Bureau that the Madrid Protocol or its implementing regulations require or permit to be recorded.

(11) *International registration.*—The term "international registration" means the registration of a mark granted under the Madrid Protocol.

(12) *International registration date.*—The term "international registration date" means the date assigned to the international registration by the International Bureau.

(13) *Madrid Protocol.*—The term "Madrid Protocol" means the Protocol Relating to the Madrid Agreement Concerning the International Registration of Marks, adopted at Madrid, Spain, on June 27, 1989.

(14) *Notification of refusal.*—The term "notification of refusal" means the notice sent by the United States Patent and Trademark Office to the International Bureau declaring that an extension of protection cannot be granted.

(15) *Office of a Contracting Party.*—The term "Office of a Contracting Party" means—

> (A) the office, or governmental entity, of a Contracting Party that is responsible for the registration of marks; or

> (B) the common office, or governmental entity, of more than 1 Contracting Party that is responsible for the registration of marks and is so recognized by the International Bureau.

15 U.S.C. § 1141

(16) *Office of origin.*—The term "office of origin" means the Office of a Contracting Party with which a basic application was filed or by which a basic registration was granted.

(17) *Opposition period.*—The term "opposition period" means the time allowed for filing an opposition in the United States Patent and Trademark Office, including any extension of time granted under section 13.

§ 1141a   International applications based on United States applications or registrations [Section 61]

(a) *In general.*—The owner of a basic application pending before the United States Patent and Trademark Office, or the owner of a basic registration granted by the United States Patent and Trademark Office may file an international application by submitting to the United States Patent and Trademark Office a written application in such form, together with such fees, as may be prescribed by the Director.

(b) *Qualified owners.*—A qualified owner, under subsection (a), shall—

(1) be a national of the United States;

(2) be domiciled in the United States; or

(3) have a real and effective industrial or commercial establishment in the United States.

§ 1141b   Certification of the international application [Section 62]

(a) *Certification procedure.*—Upon the filing of an application for international registration and payment of the prescribed fees, the Director shall examine the international application for the purpose of certifying that the information contained in the international application corresponds to the information contained in the basic application or basic registration at the time of the certification.

(b) *Transmittal.*—Upon examination and certification of the international application, the Director shall transmit the international application to the International Bureau.

15 U.S.C. § 1141b

§ 1141c Restriction, abandonment, cancellation, or expiration of a basic application or basic registration [Section 63]

With respect to an international application transmitted to the International Bureau under section 62, the Director shall notify the International Bureau whenever the basic application or basic registration which is the basis for the international application has been restricted, abandoned, or canceled, or has expired, with respect to some or all of the goods and services listed in the international registration—

(1) within 5 years after the international registration date; or

(2) more than 5 years after the international registration date if the restriction, abandonment, or cancellation of the basic application or basic registration resulted from an action that began before the end of that 5-year period.

§ 1141d Request for extension of protection subsequent to international registration [Section 64]

The holder of an international registration that is based upon a basic application filed with the United States Patent and Trademark Office or a basic registration granted by the Patent and Trademark Office may request an extension of protection of its international registration by filing such a request—

(1) directly with the International Bureau; or

(2) with the United States Patent and Trademark Office for transmittal to the International Bureau, if the request is in such form, and contains such transmittal fee, as may be prescribed by the Director.

§ 1141e Extension of protection of an international registration to the United States under the Madrid Protocol [Section 65]

(a) *In general.*—Subject to the provisions of section 68, the holder of an international registration shall be entitled to the benefits of extension of protection of that international registration to the United States to the extent necessary to give effect to any provision of the Madrid Protocol.

(b) *If the United States is office of origin.*—Where the United States Patent and Trademark Office is the office of origin for a trademark application or registration, any international registration based on such application or registration cannot be used to obtain the benefits of the Madrid Protocol in the United States.

§ 1141f   Effect of filing a request for extension of protection of an international registration to the United States [Section 66]

(a) *Requirement for request for extension of protection.*—A request for extension of protection of an international registration to the United States that the International Bureau transmits to the United States Patent and Trademark Office shall be deemed to be properly filed in the United States if such request, when received by the International Bureau, has attached to it a declaration of bona fide intention to use the mark in commerce that is verified by the applicant for, or holder of, the international registration.

(b) *Effect of proper filing.*—Unless extension of protection is refused under section 68, the proper filing of the request for extension of protection under subsection (a) shall constitute constructive use of the mark, conferring the same rights as those specified in section 7(c), as of the earliest of the following:

(1) The international registration date, if the request for extension of protection was filed in the international application.

(2) The date of recordal of the request for extension of protection, if the request for extension of protection was made after the international registration date.

(3) The date of priority claimed pursuant to section 67.

§ 1141g   Right of priority for request for extension of protection to the United States [Section 67]

The holder of an international registration with a request for an extension of protection to the United States shall be entitled to claim a date of priority based on a right of priority within the meaning of Article 4 of the Paris Convention for the Protection of Industrial Property if—

(1) the request for extension of protection contains a claim of priority; and

(2) the date of international registration or the date of the recordal of the request for extension of protection to the United States is not later than 6 months after the date of the first regular national filing (within the meaning of Article 4(A)(3) of the Paris Convention for the Protection of Indus-

trial Property) or a subsequent application (within the meaning of Article 4(C)(4) of the Paris Convention for the Protection of Industrial Property).

§ 1141h Examination of and opposition to request for extension of protection; notification of refusal [Section 68]

(a) *Examination and opposition.*—(1) A request for extension of protection described in section 66(a) shall be examined as an application for registration on the Principal Register under this Act, and if on such examination it appears that the applicant is entitled to extension of protection under this title, the Director shall cause the mark to be published in the Official Gazette of the United States Patent and Trademark Office.

(2) Subject to the provisions of subsection (c), a request for extension of protection under this title shall be subject to opposition under section 13.

(3) Extension of protection shall not be refused on the ground that the mark has not been used in commerce.

(4) Extension of protection shall be refused to any mark not registrable on the Principal Register.

(b) *Notification of refusal.*—If, a request for extension of protection is refused under subsection (a), the Director shall declare in a notification of refusal (as provided in subsection (c)) that the extension of protection cannot be granted, together with a statement of all grounds on which the refusal was based.

(c) *Notice to International Bureau.*—(1) Within 18 months after the date on which the International Bureau transmits to the Patent and Trademark Office a notification of a request for extension of protection, the Director shall transmit to the International Bureau any of the following that applies to such request:

(A) A notification of refusal based on an examination of the request for extension of protection.

(B) A notification of refusal based on the filing of an opposition to the request.

(C) A notification of the possibility that an opposition to the request may be filed after the end of that 18-month period.

(2) If the Director has sent a notification of the possibility of opposition under paragraph (1)(C), the Director shall, if applicable, transmit to the International Bureau a notification of refusal on the basis of the opposi-

tion, together with a statement of all the grounds for the opposition, within 7 months after the beginning of the opposition period or within 1 month after the end of the opposition period, whichever is earlier.

(3) If a notification of refusal of a request for extension of protection is transmitted under paragraph (1) or (2), no grounds for refusal of such request other than those set forth in such notification may be transmitted to the International Bureau by the Director after the expiration of the time periods set forth in paragraph (1) or (2), as the case may be.

(4) If a notification specified in paragraph (1) or (2) is not sent to the International Bureau within the time period set forth in such paragraph, with respect to a request for extension of protection, the request for extension of protection shall not be refused and the Director shall issue a certificate of extension of protection pursuant to the request.

(d) *Designation of agent for service of process.*—In responding to a notification of refusal with respect to a mark, the holder of the international registration of the mark may designate, by a document filed in the United States Patent and Trademark Office, the name and address of a person residing in the United States on whom notices or process in proceedings affecting the mark may be served. Such notices or process may be served upon the person designated by leaving with that person, or mailing to that person, a copy thereof at the address specified in the last designation filed. If the person designated cannot be found at the address given in the last designation, or if the holder does not designate by a document filed in the United States Patent and Trademark Office the name and address of a person residing in the United States for service of notices or process in proceedings affecting the mark, the notice or process may be served on the Director.

§ 1141i Effect of extension of protection [Section 69]

(a) *Issuance of extension of protection.*—Unless a request for extension of protection is refused under section 68, the Director shall issue a certificate of extension of protection pursuant to the request and shall cause notice of such certificate of extension of protection to be published in the Official Gazette of the United States Patent and Trademark Office.

(b) *Effect of extension of protection.*—From the date on which a certificate of extension of protection is issued under subsection (a)—

(1) such extension of protection shall have the same effect and validity as a registration on the Principal Register; and

(2) the holder of the international registration shall have the same rights and remedies as the owner of a registration on the Principal Register.

§ 1141j   Dependence of extension of protection to the United States on the underlying international registration [Section 70]

(a) *Effect of cancellation of international registration.*—If the International Bureau notifies the United States Patent and Trademark Office of the cancellation of an international registration with respect to some or all of the goods and services listed in the international registration, the Director shall cancel any extension of protection to the United States with respect to such goods and services as of the date on which the international registration was canceled.

(b) *Effect of failure to renew international registration.*—If the International Bureau does not renew an international registration, the corresponding extension of protection to the United States shall cease to be valid as of the date of the expiration of the international registration.

(c) *Transformation of an extension of protection into a United States Application.*— The holder of an international registration canceled in whole or in part by the International Bureau at the request of the office of origin, under article 6(4) of the Madrid Protocol, may file an application, under section 1 or 44 of this Act, for the registration of the same mark for any of the goods and services to which the cancellation applies that were covered by an extension of protection to the United States based on that international registration. Such an application shall be treated as if it had been filed on the international registration date or the date of recordal of the request for extension of protection with the International Bureau, whichever date applies, and, if the extension of protection enjoyed priority under section 67 of this title, shall enjoy the same priority. Such an application shall be entitled to the benefits conferred by this subsection only if the application is filed not later than 3 months after the date on which the international registration was canceled, in whole or in part, and only if the application complies with all the requirements of this Act which apply to any application filed pursuant to section 1 or 44.

§ 1141k   Duration, affidavits and fees [Section 71]

(a) *Time periods for required affidavits.*—Each extension of protection for which a certificate has been issued under section 69 shall remain in force for the term of the international registration upon which it is based, except that the extension of protection of any mark shall be canceled by the Director unless the holder of the international registration files in the United States Patent and Trademark Office affidavits that meet the requirements of subsection (b), within the following time periods:

(1) Within the 1-year period immediately preceding the expiration of 6 years following the date of issuance of the certificate of extension of protection.

(2) Within the 1-year period immediately preceding the expiration of 10 years following the date of issuance of the certificate of extension of protection, and each successive 10-year period following the date of issuance of the certificate of extension of protection.

(3) The holder may file the affidavit required under this section within a grace period of 6 months after the end of the applicable time period established in paragraph (1) or (2), together with the fee described in subsection (b) and the additional grace period surcharge prescribed by the Director.

(b) *Requirements for affidavit.*—The affidavit referred to in subsection (a) shall—

(1) (A) state that the mark is in use in commerce;

(B) set forth the goods and services recited in the extension of protection on or in connection with which the mark is in use in commerce;

(C) be accompanied by such number of specimens or facsimiles showing current use of the mark in commerce as may be required by the Director; and

(D) be accompanied by the fee prescribed by the Director; or

(2) (A) set forth the goods and services recited in the extension of protection on or in connection with which the mark is not in use in commerce;

(B) include a showing that any nonuse is due to special circumstances which excuse such nonuse and is not due to any intention to abandon the mark; and

15 U.S.C. § 1141k

(C) be accompanied by the fee prescribed by the Director.

(c) *Deficient affidavit.*—If any submission filed within the period set forth in subsection (a) is deficient, including that the affidavit was not filed in the name of the holder of the international registration, the deficiency may be corrected after the statutory time period, within the time prescribed after notification of the deficiency. Such submission shall be accompanied by the additional deficiency surcharge prescribed by the Director.

(d) *Notice of requirement.*—Special notice of the requirement for such affidavit shall be attached to each certificate of extension of protection.

(e) *Notification of acceptance or refusal.*—The Director shall notify the holder of the international registration who files any affidavit required by this section of the Director's acceptance or refusal thereof and, in the case of a refusal, the reasons therefor.

(f) *Designation of resident for service of process and notices.*—If the holder of the international registration of the mark is not domiciled in the United States, the holder may designate, by a document filed in the United States Patent and Trademark Office, the name and address of a person resident in the United States on whom may be served notices or process in proceedings affecting the mark. Such notices or process may be served upon the person so designated by leaving with that person or mailing to that person a copy thereof at the address specified in the last designation so filed. If the person so designated cannot be found at the last designated address, or if the holder does not designate by a document filed in the United States Patent and Trademark Office the name and address of a person resident in the United States on whom may be served notices or process in proceedings affecting the mark, such notices or process may be served on the Director.

§ 1141l   Assignment of an extension of protection [Section 72]

An extension of protection may be assigned, together with the goodwill associated with the mark, only to a person who is a national of, is domiciled in, or has a bona fide and effective industrial or commercial establishment either in a country that is a Contracting Party or in a country that is a member of an intergovernmental organization that is a Contracting Party.

15 U.S.C. § 1141l

§ 1141m   Incontestability [Section 73]

The period of continuous use prescribed under section 15 for a mark covered by an extension of protection issued under this title may begin no earlier than the date on which the Director issues the certificate of the extension of protection under section 69, except as provided in section 74.

§ 1141n   Rights of extension of protection [Section 74]

When a United States registration and a subsequently issued certificate of extension of protection to the United States are owned by the same person, identify the same mark, and list the same goods or services, the extension of protection shall have the same rights that accrued to the registration prior to issuance of the certificate of extension of protection.

(Nov. 2, 2002, Pub. L. 107-273, §13402, 116 Stat. 1913; Mar. 17, 2010, Pub. L. 111-146, §3(d)(2), 124 Stat. 68.)

§ 46(a)   Time of taking effect—Repeal of prior acts

This Act shall be in force and take effect one year from its enactment, but except as otherwise herein specifically provided shall not affect any suit, proceeding, or appeal then pending. All Acts and parts of Acts inconsistent herewith are hereby repealed effective one year from the enactment hereof, including the following Acts insofar as they are inconsistent herewith: The Act of Congress approved March 3, 1881, entitled "An Act to authorize the registration of trademarks and protect the same"; the Act approved August 5, 1882, entitled "An Act relating to the registration of trademarks"; the Act of February 20, 1905 (U.S.C., title 15, secs. 81 to 109, inclusive), entitled "An Act to authorize the registration of trademarks used in commerce with foreign nations or among the several States or with Indian tribes, and to protect the same", and the amendments thereto by the Acts of May 4, 1906 (U.S.C., title 15, secs. 131 and 132; 34 Stat. 169), March 2, 1907 (34 Stat. 1251, 1252), February 18, 1909 (35 Stat. 627, 628), February 18, 1911 (36 Stat. 918), January 8, 1913 (37 Stat. 649), June 7, 1924 (43 Stat. 647), March 4, 1925 (43 Stat. 1268, 1269), April 11, 1930 (46 Stat. 155), June 10, 1938 (Public, Numbered 586, Seventy-fifth Congress, ch. 332, third session); the Act of March 19, 1920 (U.S.C., title 15, secs. 121 to 128, inclusive), entitled "an Act to give effect to certain provisions of the convention for the protection of trademarks and commercial names made and signed in the city of Buenos Aires, in the Argentine Republic, August 20, 1910, and for other purposes", and the amendments thereto, including the Act of June 10, 1938 (Public, Numbered 586, Seventy-fifth Congress, ch. 332, third session): *Provided,* That this repeal shall not affect the validity of registrations granted or applied for under any of said Acts prior to the effective date of this Act, or rights or remedies thereunder except as provided in sections 8, 12, 14, 15, and 47 [§§1058, 1062, 1064, 1065, and 47 (§47 is uncodified; see below)] of this Act; but nothing contained in this Act shall be construed as limiting, restricting, modifying, or repealing any statute in force on the effective date of this Act which does not relate to trademarks, or as restricting or increasing the authority of any Federal departments or regulatory agency except as may be specifically provided in this Act.

(July 5, 1946, ch. 540, §§46–50, 60 Stat. 444–46.)

§ 46(b) Existing registrations under prior acts

Acts of 1881 and 1905. Registrations now existing under the Act of March 3, 1881, or the Act of February 20, 1905, shall continue in full force and effect for the unexpired terms thereof and may be renewed under the provisions of section 9 [§1059] of this Act. Such registrations and the renewals thereof shall be subject to and shall be entitled to the benefits of the provisions of this Act to the same extent and with the same force and effect as though registered on the principal register established by this Act except as limited in sections 8, 12, 14, and 15 [§§1058, 1062, 1064, and 1065] of this Act. Marks registered under the "ten-year proviso" of section 5 [§1055] of the Act of February 20, 1905, as amended, shall be deemed to have become distinctive of the registrant's goods in commerce under paragraph (f) of section 2 of this Act and may be renewed under section 9 [§1059] hereof as marks coming within said paragraph.

Act of 1920. Registrations now existing under the Act of March 19, 1920, shall expire 5 months after the effective date of this Act, or twenty years from the dates of their registrations, whichever date is later. Such registrations shall be subject to and entitled to the benefits of the provisions of this Act relating to marks registered on the supplemental register established by this Act, and may not be renewed unless renewal is required to support foreign registrations. In that event renewal may be effected on the supplemental register under the provisions of section 9 [§1059] of this Act.

Subject to registration under this Act. Marks registered under previous Acts may, if eligible, also be registered under this Act.

(July 5, 1946, ch. 540, §§46–50, 60 Stat. 444–46.)

§ 47(a) Applications pending on effective date of Act

All applications for registration pending in the Patent and Trademark Office at the effective date of this Act may be amended, if practicable, to bring them under the provisions of this Act. The prosecution of such applications so amended and the grant of registrations thereon shall be proceeded with in accordance with the provisions of this Act. If such amendments are not made, the prosecution of said applications shall be proceeded with and registrations thereon granted in accordance with the Acts under which said applications were filed, and said Acts are hereby continued in force to this extent and for this purpose only, notwithstanding the foregoing general repeal thereof.

(July 5, 1946, ch. 540, §§46–50, 60 Stat. 444–46.)

§ 47(b)   Appeals pending on effective date of Act

In any case in which an appeal is pending before the United States Court of Customs and Patent Appeals or any United States Circuit Court of Appeals or the United States Court of Appeals for the District of Columbia or the United States Supreme Court at the effective date of this Act, the court, if it be of the opinion that the provisions of this Act are applicable to the subject matter of the appeal, may apply such provision or may remand the case to the Director or to the district court for the taking of additional evidence or a new trial or for reconsideration of the decision on the record as made, as the appellate court may deem proper.

(July 5, 1946, ch. 540, §§46–50, 60 Stat. 444–46.)

§ 48   Prior acts not repealed

Section 4 of the Act of January 5, 1905 (U.S.C., title 36, §4), as amended, entitled "An Act to incorporate the National Red Cross", and section 7 of the Act of June 15, 1916 (U.S.C., title 36, §27), entitled "An Act to incorporate the Boy Scouts of America, and for other purposes", and the Act of June 20, 1936 (U.S.C., title 22, §248), entitled "An Act to prohibit the commercial use of the coat of arms of the Swiss Confederation", are not repealed or affected by this Act.[8]

(July 5, 1946, ch. 540, §§46–50, 60 Stat. 444–46.)

§ 49   Preservation of existing rights

Nothing herein shall adversely affect the rights or the enforcement of rights in marks acquired in good faith prior to the effective date of this Act.

(July 5, 1946, ch. 540, §§46–50, 60 Stat. 444–46.)

§ 50   Severability

If any provision of this Act or the application of such provision to any person or circumstance is held invalid, the remainder of the Act shall not be affected thereby.

(July 5, 1946, ch. 540, §§46–50, 60 Stat. 444–46.)

---

[8] *Ed. Note:* The first and third of the laws referred to in this section have been repealed and replaced by sections 706 and 708, respectively, of U.S.C., Title 18, Crimes and Criminal Procedure, enacted June 25, 1948, effective September 1, 1948.

§ 51   Pending Applications

All certificates of registration based upon applications for registration pending in the Patent and Trademark Office on the effective date of the Trademark Law Revision Act of 1988 shall remain in force for a period of 10 years.

(Nov. 16, 1988, Pub. L. 100-667, §135, 102 Stat. 3948.)

UNITED STATES CODE
TITLE 15, CHAPTER 107—PROTECTION OF
INTELLECTUAL PROPERTY RIGHTS

SUBCHAPTER 2—CYBERSQUATTING PROTECTION

SEC.
8131.   Cyberpiracy protections for individuals.

§ 8131   Cyberpiracy protections for individuals

(1) *In general.*—

(A) *Civil liability.*—Any person who registers a domain name that consists of the name of another living person, or a name substantially and confusingly similar thereto, without that person's consent, with the specific intent to profit from such name by selling the domain name for financial gain to that person or any third party, shall be liable in a civil action by such person.

(B) *Exception.*—A person who in good faith registers a domain name consisting of the name of another living person, or a name substantially and confusingly similar thereto, shall not be liable under this paragraph if such name is used in, affiliated with, or related to a work of authorship protected under title 17, including a work made for hire as defined in section 101 of title 17, and if the person registering the domain name is the copyright owner or licensee of the work, the person intends to sell the domain name in conjunction with the lawful exploitation of the work, and such registration is not prohibited by a contract between the registrant and the named person. The exception under this subparagraph shall apply only to a civil action brought under paragraph (1) and shall in no manner limit the protections afforded under the Trademark Act of 1946 (15 U.S.C. 1051 et seq.) or other provision of Federal or State law.

(2) *Remedies.*—In any civil action brought under paragraph (1), a court may award injunctive relief, including the forfeiture or cancellation of the domain name or the transfer of the domain name to the plaintiff. The court may also, in its discretion, award costs and attorneys fees to the prevailing party.

15 U.S.C. § 8131

(3) *Definition.*—In this section, the term "domain name" has the meaning given that term in section 45 of the Trademark Act of 1946 (15 U.S.C. 1127).

(4) *Effective date.*—This section shall apply to domain names registered on or after November 29, 1999.

(Nov. 29, 1999, Pub. L. 106-113, §3002(b), 113 Stat. 1536.)

Part 3

TECHNOLOGY INNOVATION

UNITED STATES CODE

TITLE 15, CHAPTER 63—TECHNOLOGY INNOVATION

§ 3701 Findings

The Congress finds and declares that:

(1) Technology and industrial innovation are central to the economic, environmental, and social well-being of citizens of the United States.

(2) Technology and industrial innovation offer an improved standard of living, increased public and private sector productivity, creation of new

industries and employment opportunities, improved public services and enhanced competitiveness of United States products in world markets.

(3) Many new discoveries and advances in science occur in universities and Federal laboratories, while the application of this new knowledge to commercial and useful public purposes depends largely upon actions by business and labor. Cooperation among academia, Federal laboratories, labor, and industry, in such forms as technology transfer, personnel exchange, joint research projects, and others, should be renewed, expanded, and strengthened.

(4) Small businesses have performed an important role in advancing industrial and technological innovation.

(5) Industrial and technological innovation in the United States may be lagging when compared to historical patterns and other industrialized nations.

(6) Increased industrial and technological innovation would reduce trade deficits, stabilize the dollar, increase productivity gains, increase employment, and stabilize prices.

(7) Government antitrust, economic, trade, patent, procurement, regulatory, research and development, and tax policies have significant impacts upon industrial innovation and development of technology, but there is insufficient knowledge of their effects in particular sectors of the economy.

(8) No comprehensive national policy exists to enhance technological innovation for commercial and public purposes. There is a need for such a policy, including a strong national policy supporting domestic technology transfer and utilization of the science and technology resources of the Federal Government.

(9) It is in the national interest to promote the adaptation of technological innovations to State and local government uses. Technological innovations can improve services, reduce their costs, and increase productivity in State and local governments.

(10) The Federal laboratories and other performers of federally funded research and development frequently provide scientific and technological developments of potential use to State and local governments and private industry. These developments, which include inventions, computer software, and training technologies, should be made accessible to those gov-

ernments and industry. There is a need to provide means of access and to give adequate personnel and funding support to these means.

(11) The Nation should give fuller recognition to individuals and companies which have made outstanding contributions to the promotion of technology or technological manpower for the improvement of the economic, environmental, or social well-being of the United States.

(Oct. 21, 1980, Pub. L. 96-480, §2, 94 Stat. 2311; Oct. 20, 1986, Pub. L. 99-502, §9, 100 Stat. 1797.)

§ 3702   Purpose

It is the purpose of this Act to improve the economic, environmental, and social well-being of the United States by —

(1) establishing organizations in the executive branch to study and stimulate technology;

(2) promoting technology development through the establishment of cooperative research centers;

(3) stimulating improved utilization of federally funded technology developments, including inventions, software, and training technologies, by State and local governments and the private sector;

(4) providing encouragement for the development of technology through the recognition of individuals and companies which have made outstanding contributions in technology; and

(5) encouraging the exchange of scientific and technical personnel among academia, industry, and Federal laboratories.

(Oct. 21, 1980, Pub. L. 96-480, §3, 94 Stat. 2312; Oct. 20, 1986, Pub. L. 99-502, §9, 100 Stat. 1795, 1797.)

§ 3703   Definitions

As used in this Act, unless the context otherwise requires, the term —

(1) "Secretary" means the Secretary of Commerce.

(2) "Centers" means the Cooperative Research Centers established under section 7 or section 9 [§§3706 or 3708] of this Act.

(3) "Nonprofit institution" means an organization owned and operated exclusively for scientific or educational purposes, no part of the net earn-

15 U.S.C. § 3703

ings of which inures to the benefit of any private shareholder or individual.

(4) "Federal laboratory" means any laboratory, any federally funded research and development center, or any center established under section 7 or section 9 [§§3706 or 3708] of this Act that is owned, leased, or otherwise used by a Federal agency and funded by the Federal Government, whether operated by the Government or by a contractor.

(5) "Supporting agency" means either the Department of Commerce or the National Science Foundation, as appropriate.

(6) "Federal agency" means any executive agency as defined in section 105 of title 5, United States Code, and the military departments as defined in section 102 of such title, as well as any agency of the legislative branch of the Federal Government.

(7) "Invention" means any invention or discovery which is or may be patentable or otherwise protected under title 35, United States Code, or any novel variety of plant which is or may be protectable under the Plant Variety Protection Act (7 U.S.C. 2321 et seq.).

(8) "Made" when used in conjunction with any invention means the conception or first actual reduction to practice of such invention.

(9) "Small business firm" means a small business concern as defined in section 2 of Public Law 85-536 (15 U.S.C. 632) and implementing regulations of the Administrator of the Small Business Administration.

(10) "Training technology" means computer software and related materials which are developed by a Federal agency to train employees of such agency, including but not limited to software for computer-based instructional systems and for interactive video disc systems.

(11) "Clearinghouse" means the Clearinghouse for State and Local Initiatives on Productivity, Technology, and Innovation established by section 6 [§3704a].

(Oct. 21, 1980, Pub. L. 96-480, §4, 94 Stat. 2312; Oct. 20, 1986, Pub. L. 99-502, §9, 100 Stat. 1795, 1796; Aug. 23, 1988, Pub. L. 100-418, §5122, 102 Stat. 1439; Oct. 24, 1988, Pub. L. 100-519, §201, 102 Stat. 2594; Feb. 14, 1992, Pub. L. 102-245, §304, 106 Stat. 20; Nov. 1, 2000, Pub. L. 106-404, §7, 114 Stat. 1745; Aug. 9, 2007, Pub. L. 110-69, §3002, 121 Stat. 586.)

15 U.S.C. § 3703

§ 3704 Experimental Program to Stimulate Competitive Technology

(a) *Program Establishment.—*

(1) *In general.—*Beginning in fiscal year 1999, the Secretary shall establish a program to be known as the Experimental Program to Stimulate Competitive Technology (referred to in this subsection as the "program"). The purpose of the program shall be to strengthen the technological competitiveness of those States that have historically received less Federal research and development funds than those received by a majority of the States.

(2) *Arrangement.—*In carrying out the program, the Secretary shall—

(A) enter into such arrangements as may be necessary to provide for the coordination of the program through the State committees established under the Experimental Program to Stimulate Competitive Research of the National Science Foundation; and

(B) cooperate with—

(i) any State science and technology council established under the program under subparagraph (A); and

(ii) representatives of small business firms and other appropriate technology-based businesses.

(3) *Grants and cooperative agreements.—*In carrying out the program, the Secretary may make grants or enter into cooperative agreements to provide for—

(A) technology research and development;

(B) technology transfer from university research;

(C) technology deployment and diffusion; and

(D) the strengthening of technological capabilities through consortia comprised of—

(i) technology-based small business firms;

(ii) industries and emerging companies;

(iii) universities; and

(iv) State and local development agencies and entities.

15 U.S.C. § 3704

(4) *Requirements for making awards.—*

(A) *In general.—*In making awards under this subsection, the Secretary shall ensure that the awards are awarded on a competitive basis that includes a review of the merits of the activities that are the subject of the award.

(B) *Matching requirement.—*The non-Federal share of the activities (other than planning activities) carried out under an award under this subsection shall be not less than 25 percent of the cost of those activities.

(5) *Criteria for states.—*The Secretary shall establish criteria for achievement by each State that participates in the program. Upon the achievement of all such criteria, a State shall cease to be eligible to participate in the program.

(b) *Coordination.—*To the extent practicable, in carrying out subsection (a), the Secretary shall coordinate the program with other programs of the Department of Commerce.

(c) *Minority Serving Institution Digital and Wireless Technology Opportunity Program.—*

(1) *In general.—*The Secretary shall establish a Minority Serving Institution Digital and Wireless Technology Opportunity Program that awards grants, cooperative agreements, and contracts to eligible institutions to enable the eligible institutions in acquiring, and augmenting the institutions' use of, digital and wireless networking technologies to improve the quality and delivery of educational services at eligible institutions.

(2) *Application and review procedures.—*

(A) *In general.—*To be eligible to receive a grant, cooperative agreement, or contract under this subsection, an eligible institution shall submit an application to the Secretary at such time, in such manner, and containing such information as the Secretary may require. Such application, at a minimum, shall include a description of how the funds will be used, including a description of any digital and wireless networking technology to be acquired, and a description of how the institution will ensure that digital and wireless networking technology will be made accessible to, and employed by, students, faculty, and administrators. The Secretary, consistent with subparagraph (C) and in consultation with the advisory council established under subparagraph (B), shall establish procedures to review such applications. The Secretary shall publish the application requirements and review criteria in the Federal Register, along with a statement describing the availability of funds.

(B) *Advisory council.* — The Secretary shall establish an advisory council to advise the Secretary on the best approaches to encourage maximum participation by eligible institutions in the program established under paragraph (1), and on the procedures to review applications submitted to the program. In selecting the members of the advisory council, the Secretary shall consult with representatives of appropriate organizations, including representatives of eligible institutions, to ensure that the membership of the advisory council includes representatives of minority businesses and eligible institution communities. The Secretary shall also consult with experts in digital and wireless networking technology to ensure that such expertise is represented on the advisory council.

(C) *Review panels.* — Each application submitted under this subsection by an eligible institution shall be reviewed by a panel of individuals selected by the Secretary to judge the quality and merit of the proposal, including the extent to which the eligible institution can effectively and successfully utilize the proposed grant, cooperative agreement, or contract to carry out the program described in paragraph (1). The Secretary shall ensure that the review panels include representatives of minority serving institutions and others who are knowledgeable about eligible institutions and technology issues. The Secretary shall ensure that no individual assigned under this subsection to review any application has a conflict of interest with regard to that application. The Secretary shall take into consideration the recommendations of the review panel in determining whether to award a grant, cooperative agreement, or contract to an eligible institution.

(3) *Awards.* —

(A) *Limitation.* — An eligible institution that receives a grant, cooperative agreement, or contract under this subsection that exceeds $2,500,000 shall not be eligible to receive another grant, cooperative agreement, or contract under this subsection.

(B) *Consortia.* — Grants, cooperative agreements, and contracts may only be awarded to eligible institutions. Eligible institutions may seek

15 U.S.C. § 3704

funding under this subsection for consortia, which may include other eligible institutions, a State or a State educational agency, local educational agencies, institutions of higher education, community-based organizations, national nonprofit organizations, or businesses, including minority businesses.

(C) *Planning grants.*—The Secretary may provide funds to develop strategic plans to implement grants, cooperative agreements, or contracts awarded under this subsection.

(D) *Institutional diversity.*—In awarding grants, cooperative agreements, and contracts to eligible institutions, the Secretary shall ensure, to the extent practicable, that awards are made to all types of institutions eligible for assistance under this subsection.

(E) *Need.*—In awarding funds under this subsection, the Secretary shall give priority to the eligible institution with the greatest demonstrated need for assistance.

(4) *Authorized activities.*—An eligible institution may use a grant, cooperative agreement, or contract awarded under this subsection—

(A) to acquire equipment, instrumentation, networking capability, hardware and software, digital network technology, wireless technology, and infrastructure to further the objective of the program described in paragraph (1);

(B) to develop and provide training, education, and professional development programs, including faculty development, to increase the use of, and usefulness of, digital and wireless networking technology;

(C) to provide teacher education, including the provision of preservice teacher training and in-service professional development at eligible institutions, library and media specialist training, and preschool and teacher aid certification to individuals who seek to acquire or enhance technology skills in order to use digital and wireless networking technology in the classroom or instructional process, including instruction in science, mathematics, engineering, and technology subjects;

(D) to obtain capacity-building technical assistance, including through remote technical support, technical assistance workshops, and distance learning services; or

(E) to foster the use of digital and wireless networking technology to improve research and education, including scientific, mathematics, engineering, and technology instruction.

(5) *Information dissemination.*—The Secretary shall convene an annual meeting of eligible institutions receiving grants, cooperative agreements, or contracts under this subsection to foster collaboration and capacity-building activities among eligible institutions.

(6) *Matching requirement.*—The Secretary may not award a grant, cooperative agreement, or contract to an eligible institution under this subsection unless such institution agrees that, with respect to the costs incurred by the institution in carrying out the program for which the grant, cooperative agreement, or contract was awarded, such institution shall make available, directly, or through donations from public or private entities, non-Federal contributions in an amount equal to 25 percent of the grant, cooperative agreement, or contract awarded by the Secretary, or $500,000, whichever is the lesser amount. The Secretary shall waive the matching requirement for any institution or consortium with no endowment, or an endowment that has a current dollar value lower than $50,000,000.

(7) *Annual report and assessments.*—

(A) *Annual report required from recipients.*—Each eligible institution that receives a grant, cooperative agreement, or contract awarded under this subsection shall provide an annual report to the Secretary on its use of the grant, cooperative agreement, or contract.

(B) *Independent assessments.*—

(i) *Contract to conduct assessments.*—Not later than 6 months after the date of enactment of this subsection, the Secretary shall enter into a contract with the National Academy of Public Administration to conduct periodic assessments of the program established under paragraph (1). The assessments shall be conducted once every 3 years during the 10-year period following the date of enactment of this subsection.

(ii) *Evaluations and recommendations.*—The assessments described in clause (i) shall include—

(I) an evaluation of the effectiveness of the program established under paragraph (1) in improving the education and training of students, faculty, and staff at eligible institutions

15 U.S.C. § 3704

that have been awarded grants, cooperative agreements, or contracts under the program;

(II) an evaluation of the effectiveness of the program in improving access to, and familiarity with, digital and wireless networking technology for students, faculty, and staff at all eligible institutions;

(III) an evaluation of the procedures established under paragraph (2)(A); and

(IV) recommendations for improving the program, including recommendations concerning the continuing need for Federal support.

(iii) *Review of reports.*—In carrying out the assessments under this subparagraph, the National Academy of Public Administration shall review the reports submitted to the Secretary under subparagraph (A).

(iv) *Report to congress.*—Upon completion of each assessment under this subparagraph, the Secretary shall transmit the assessment to Congress along with a summary of the Secretary's plans, if any, to implement the recommendations of the National Academy of Public Administration.

(8) *Definitions.*—In this subsection:

(A) *Digital and wireless networking technology.*—The term "digital and wireless networking technology" means computer and communications equipment and software that facilitates the transmission of information in a digital format.

(B) *Eligible institution.*—The term "eligible institution" means an institution that is—

(i) a part B institution, as defined in section 322(2) of the Higher Education Act of 1965 (20 U.S.C. 1061(2)), an institution identified in subparagraph (A), (B), or (C) of section 326(e)(1) of such Act (20 U.S.C. 1063b(e)(1)(A), (B), or (C)), or a consortium of institutions described in this clause;

(ii) a Hispanic-serving institution, as defined in section 502(a)(5) of the Higher Education Act of 1965 (20 U.S.C. 1101a(a)(5));

(iii) a Tribal College or University, as defined in section 316(b)(3) of the Higher Education Act of 1965 (20 U.S.C. 1059c(b)(3));

(iv) an Alaska Native-serving institution, as defined in section 317(b) of the Higher Education Act of 1965 (20 U.S.C. 1059d(b));

(v) a Native Hawaiian-serving institution, as defined in section 317(b) of the Higher Education Act of 1965 (20 U.S.C. 1059d(b));

(vi) a Predominately Black Institution, as defined in section 318 of the Higher Education Act of 1965 (20 U.S.C. 1059e);

(vii) a Native American-serving, nontribal institution, as defined in section 319 of the Higher Education Act of 1965 (20 U.S.C. 1059f);

(viii) an Asian American and Native American Pacific Islander-serving institution, as defined in section 320 of the Higher Education Act of 1965 (20 U.S.C. 1059g); or

(ix) a minority institution, as defined in section 365 of the Higher Education Act of 1965 (20 U.S.C. 1067k), with an enrollment of needy students, as defined in section 312(d) of the Higher Education Act of 1965 (20 U.S.C. 1058(d)).

(C) *Institution of higher education.* — The term "institution of higher education" has the meaning given the term in section 101 of the Higher Education Act of 1965 (20 U.S.C. 1001).

(D) *Local educational agency.* — The term "local educational agency" has the meaning given the term in section 9101 of the Elementary and Secondary Education Act of 1965 (20 U.S.C. 7801).

(E) *Minority business.* — The term "minority business" includes HUB-Zone small business concerns (as defined in section 3(p) of the Small Business Act (15 U.S.C. 632(p))).

(F) *Minority individual.* — The term "minority individual" means an American Indian, Alaskan Native, Black (not of Hispanic origin), Hispanic (including persons of Mexican, Puerto Rican, Cuban, and Central or South American origin), or Pacific Islander individual.

(G) *State.* — The term "State" has the meaning given the term in section 9101 of the Elementary and Secondary Education Act of 1965 (20 U.S.C. 7801).

15 U.S.C. § 3704

(H) *State educational agency.*—The term "State educational agency" has the meaning given the term in section 9101 of the Elementary and Secondary Education Act of 1965 (20 U.S.C. 7801).

(Oct. 21, 1980, Pub. L. 96-480, §5, 94 Stat. 2312; Aug. 14, 1986, Pub. L. 99-382, §2, 100 Stat. 811; Oct. 20, 1986, Pub. L. 99-502, §9, 100 Stat. 1795-97; Oct. 24, 1988, Pub. L. 100-519, §201, 102 Stat. 2593, 2594; Feb. 14, 1992, Pub. L. 102-245, §306, 106 Stat. 20; Oct. 30, 1998, Pub. L 105-309, §9, 112 Stat. 2938; Nov. 1, 2000, Pub. L. 106-404, §7, 114 Stat. 1745; Aug. 9, 2007, Pub. L. 110-69, §3002, 121 Stat. 586; Aug. 14, 2008, Pub. L. 110-315, §971, 122 Stat. 3473.)

§ 3704a   Clearinghouse for State and Local Initiatives on Productivity, Technology, and Innovation

(a) *Establishment.*—There is established within the Office of Productivity, Technology, and Innovation a Clearinghouse for State and Local Initiatives on Productivity, Technology, and Innovation. The Clearinghouse shall serve as a central repository of information on initiatives by State and local governments to enhance the competitiveness of American business through the stimulation of productivity, technology, and innovation and Federal efforts to assist State and local governments to enhance competitiveness.

(b) *Responsibilities.*—The Clearinghouse may—

(1) establish relationships with State and local governments, and regional and multistate organizations of such governments, which carry out such initiatives;

(2) collect information on the nature, extent, and effects of such initiatives, particularly information useful to the Congress, Federal agencies, State and local governments, regional and multistate organizations of such governments, businesses, and the public throughout the United States;

(3) disseminate information collected under paragraph (2) through reports, directories, handbooks, conferences, and seminars;

(4) provide technical assistance and advice to such governments with respect to such initiatives, including assistance in determining sources of assistance from Federal agencies which may be available to support such initiatives;

(5) study ways in which Federal agencies, including Federal laboratories, are able to use their existing policies and programs to assist State and local governments, and regional and multistate organizations of such governments, to enhance the competitiveness of American business;

(6) make periodic recommendations to the Secretary, and to other Federal agencies upon their request, concerning modifications in Federal policies and programs which would improve Federal assistance to State and local technology and business assistance programs;

(7) develop methodologies to evaluate State and local programs, and, when requested, advise State and local governments, and regional and multistate organizations of such governments, as to which programs are most effective in enhancing the competitiveness of American business through the stimulation of productivity, technology, and innovation; and

(8) make use of, and disseminate, the nationwide study of State industrial extension programs conducted by the Secretary.

(c) *Contracts.* — In carrying out subsection (b), the Secretary may enter into contracts for the purpose of collecting information on the nature, extent, and effects of initiatives.

(d) *Triennial report.* — The Secretary shall prepare and transmit to the Congress once each 3 years a report on initiatives by State and local governments to enhance the competitiveness of American businesses through the stimulation of productivity, technology, and innovation. The report shall include recommendations to the President, the Congress, and to Federal agencies on the appropriate Federal role in stimulating State and local efforts in this area. The first of these reports shall be transmitted to the Congress before January 1, 1989.

(Oct. 21, 1980, Pub. L. 96-480, §6, as added Aug. 23, 1988, Pub. L. 100-418, §5122, 102 Stat. 1438.)

§ 3704b National Technical Information Service

(a) *Powers.* —

(1) The Secretary of Commerce, acting through the Director of the National Technical Information Service (hereafter in this subtitle referred to as the "Director") is authorized to do the following:

(A) Enter into such contracts, cooperative agreements, joint ventures, and other transactions, in accordance with all relevant provisions of Federal law applicable to such contracts and agreements, and under reasonable terms and conditions, as may be necessary in the conduct of the business of the National Technical Information Service (hereafter in this subtitle referred to as the "Service").

15 U.S.C. § 3704b

(B) In addition to the authority regarding fees contained in section 2 of the Act entitled "An Act to provide for the dissemination of technological, scientific, and engineering information to American business and industry, and for other purposes" enacted September 9, 1950 (15 U.S.C. 1152), retain and, subject to appropriations Acts, utilize its net revenues to the extent necessary to implement the plan submitted under subsection (f)(3)(D).

(C) Enter into contracts for the performance of part or all of the functions performed by the Promotion Division of the Service prior to the date of the enactment of this Act. The details of any such contract, and a statement of its effect on the operations and personnel of the Service, shall be provided to the appropriate committees of the Congress 30 days in advance of the execution of such contract.

(D) Employ such personnel as may be necessary to conduct the business of the Service.

(E) For the period of October 1, 1991 through September 30, 1992, only, retain and use all earned and unearned monies heretofore or hereafter received, including receipts, revenues, and advanced payments and deposits, to fund all obligations and expenses, including inventories and capital equipment.

An increase or decrease in the personnel of the Service shall not affect or be affected by any ceilings on the number or grade of personnel.

(2) The functions and activities of the Service specified in subsection (e)(1) through (6) are permanent Federal functions to be carried out by the Secretary through the Service and its employees, and shall not be transferred from the Service, by contract or otherwise, to the private sector on a permanent or temporary basis without express approval of the Congress. Functions or activities—

(A) for the procurement of supplies, materials, and equipment by the Service;

(B) referred to in paragraph (1)(C); or

(C) to be performed through joint ventures or cooperative agreements which do not result in a reduction in the Federal workforce of the affected programs of the service,

shall not be considered functions or activities for purposes of this paragraph.

15 U.S.C. § 3704b

(3) For the purposes of this subsection, the term "net revenues" means the excess of revenues and receipts from any source, other than royalties and other income described in section 13(a)(4) of the Stevenson-Wydler Technology Innovation Act of 1980 (15 U.S.C. 3710(c)(a)(4)), over operating expenses.

(b) *Director of the Service.*—The management of the Service shall be vested in a Director who shall report to the Director of the National Institute of Standards and Technology and the Secretary of Commerce.

(c) *Advisory Board.*—

(1) There is established the Advisory Board of the National Technical Information Service, which shall be composed of a chairman and four other members appointed by the Secretary.

(2) In appointing members of the Advisory Board the Secretary shall solicit recommendations from the major users and beneficiaries of the Service's activities and shall select individuals experienced in providing or utilizing technical information.

(3) The Advisory Board shall review the general policies and operations of the Service, including policies in connection with fees and charges for its services, and shall advise the Secretary and the Director with respect thereto.

(4) The Advisory Board shall meet at the call of the Secretary, but not less often than once each six months.

(d) *Audits.*—The Secretary of Commerce shall provide for annual independent audits of the Service's financial statements beginning with fiscal year 1988, to be conducted in accordance with generally accepted accounting principles.

(e) *Functions.*—The Secretary of Commerce, acting through the Service, shall—

(1) establish and maintain a permanent repository of nonclassified scientific, technical, and engineering information;

(2) cooperate and coordinate its operations with other Government scientific, technical, and engineering information programs;

(3) make selected bibliographic information products available in a timely manner to depository libraries as part of the Depository Library Program of the Government Printing Office;

15 U.S.C. § 3704b

(4) in conjunction with the private sector as appropriate, collect, translate into English, and disseminate unclassified foreign scientific, technical, and engineering information;

(5) implement new methods or media for the dissemination of scientific, technical, and engineering information, including producing and disseminating information products in electronic format; and

(6) carry out the functions and activities of the Secretary under the act entitled "An Act to provide for the dissemination of technological, scientific, and engineering information to American business and industry, and for other purposes" enacted September 9, 1950, and the functions and activities of the Secretary performed through the National Technical Information Service as of the date of enactment of this Act under the Stevenson-Wydler Technology Innovation Act of 1980, under chapter 63 of this title.

(f) *Notification of Congress.—*

(1) The Secretary of Commerce and the Director shall keep the appropriate committees of Congress fully and currently informed about all activities related to the carrying out of the functions of the Service, including changes in fee policies.

(2) Within 90 days after the date of enactment of this Act, the Secretary of Commerce shall submit to the Congress a report on the current fee structure of the Service, including an explanation of the basis for the fees, taking into consideration all applicable costs, and the adequacy of the fees, along with reasons for the declining sales at the Service of scientific, technical, and engineering publications. Such report shall explain any actions planned or taken to increase such sales at reasonable fees.

(3) The Secretary shall submit an annual report to the Congress which shall—

    (A) summarize the operations of the Service during the preceding year, including financial details and staff levels broken down by major activities;

    (B) detail the operating plan of the Service, including specific expense and staff needs, for the upcoming year;

    (C) set forth details of modernization progress made in the preceding year;

(D) describe the long-term modernization of the Service; and

(E) include the results of the most recent annual audit carried out under subsection (d).

(4) The Secretary shall also give the Congress detailed advance notice of not less than 30 calendar days of—

(A) any proposed reduction-in-force;

(B) any joint venture or cooperative agreement which involves a financial incentive to the joint venturer or contractor; and

(C) any change in the operating plan submitted under paragraph (3)(B) which would result in a variation from such plan with respect to expense levels of more than 10 percent.

(Oct. 24, 1988, Pub. L. 100-519, §212, 102 Stat. 2594; Oct. 28, 1991, Pub. L. 102-140, §200, 105 Stat. 804; Feb.14, 1992, Pub. L. 102-245, §506, 106 Stat. 27; Dec. 26, 2007, Pub. L. 110-161, §109, 121 Stat. 1893.)

§ 3704b-1   Operating costs

Operating costs for the National Technical Information Service associated with the acquisition, processing, storage, bibliographic control, and archiving of information and documents shall be recovered primarily through the collection of fees.

(Feb. 14, 1992, Pub. L. 102-245, §103(c), 106 Stat. 8.)

§ 3704b-2   Transfer of Federal scientific and technical information

(a) *Transfer.*—The head of each Federal executive department or agency shall transfer in a timely manner to the National Technical Information Service unclassified scientific, technical, and engineering information which results from federally funded research and development activities for dissemination to the private sector, academia, State and local governments, and Federal agencies. Only information which would otherwise be available for public dissemination shall be transferred under this subsection. Such information shall include technical reports and information, computer software, application assessments generated pursuant to section 11(c) of the Stevenson-Wydler Technology Innovation Act of 1980 (15 U.S.C. 3710(c)), and information regarding training technology and other federally owned or originated technologies. The Secretary shall issue regulations within one year after February 14, 1992 outlining procedures for the ongoing transfer of such information to the National Technical Information Service.

15 U.S.C. § 3704b-2

(b) *Annual report to Congress.*—As part of the annual report required under section 3704b(f)(3) of this title, the Secretary shall report to Congress on the status of efforts under this section to ensure access to Federal scientific and technical information by the public. Such report shall include—

(1) an evaluation of the comprehensiveness of transfers of information by each Federal executive department or agency under subsection (a) of this section;

(2) a description of the use of Federal scientific and technical information;

(3) plans for improving public access to Federal scientific and technical information; and

(4) recommendations for legislation necessary to improve public access to Federal scientific and technical information.

(Feb. 14, 1992, Pub. L. 102-245, title I, §108, 106 Stat. 13.)

§ 3705 Cooperative Research Centers

(a) *Establishment.*—The Secretary shall provide assistance for the establishment of Cooperative Research Centers. Such Centers shall be affiliated with any university, or other nonprofit institution, or group thereof, that applies for and is awarded a grant or enters into a cooperative agreement under this section. The objective of the Centers is to enhance technological innovation through—

(1) the participation of individuals from industry and universities in cooperative technological innovation activities;

(2) the development of the generic research base, important for technological advance and innovative activity, in which individual firms have little incentive to invest, but which may have significant economic or strategic importance, such as manufacturing technology;

(3) the education and training of individuals in the technological innovation process;

(4) the improvement of mechanisms for the dissemination of scientific, engineering, and technical information among universities and industry;

(5) the utilization of the capability and expertise, where appropriate, that exists in Federal laboratories; and

(6) the development of continuing financial support from other mission agencies, from State and local government, and from industry and universities through, among other means, fees, licenses, and royalties.

(b) *Activities.*—The activities of the Centers shall include, but need not be limited to—

(1) research supportive of technological and industrial innovation including cooperative industry-university research;

(2) assistance to individuals and small businesses in the generation, evaluation and development of technological ideas supportive of industrial innovation and new business ventures;

(3) technical assistance and advisory services to industry, particularly small businesses; and

(4) curriculum development, training, and instruction in invention, entrepreneurship, and industrial innovation.

Each Center need not undertake all of the activities under this subsection.

(c) *Requirements.*—Prior to establishing a Center, the Secretary shall find that—

(1) consideration has been given to the potential contribution of the activities proposed under the Center to productivity, employment, and economic competitiveness of the United States;

(2) a high likelihood exists of continuing participation, advice, financial support, and other contributions from the private sector;

(3) the host university or other nonprofit institution has a plan for the management and evaluation of the activities proposed within the particular Center, including:

(A) the agreement between the parties as to the allocation of patent rights on a nonexclusive, partially exclusive, or exclusive license basis to and inventions conceived or made under the auspices of the Center; and

(B) the consideration of means to place the Center, to the maximum extent feasible, on a self-sustaining basis;

(4) suitable consideration has been given to the university's or other nonprofit institution's capabilities and geographical location; and

(5) consideration has been given to any effects upon competition of the activities proposed under the Center.

15 U.S.C. § 3705

(d) *Planning grants.*—The Secretary is authorized to make available nonrenewable planning grants to universities or nonprofit institutions for the purpose of developing a plan required under subsection (c)(3).

(e) *Research and development utilization.*—In the promotion of technology from research and development efforts by Centers under this section, chapter 18 of title 35, United States Code, shall apply to the extent not inconsistent with this section.

(Oct. 21, 1980, Pub. L. 96-480, §7, formerly §6, 94 Stat. 2313; Oct. 20, 1986, Pub. L. 99-502, §9, 100 Stat. 1796; Aug. 23, 1988, Pub. L. 100-418, §5122, 102 Stat. 1438.)

§ 3706   Grants and cooperative agreements

(a) *In general.*—The Secretary may make grants and enter into cooperative agreements according to the provisions of this section in order to assist any activity consistent with this Act, including activities performed by individuals. The total amount of any such grant or cooperative agreement may not exceed 75 percent of the total cost of the program.

(b) *Eligibility and procedure.*—Any person or institution may apply to the Secretary for a grant or cooperative agreement available under this section. Application shall be made in such form and manner, and with such content and other submissions, as the Assistant Secretary shall prescribe. The Secretary shall act upon each such application within 90 days after the date on which all required information is received.

(c) *Terms and conditions.*—

(1) Any grant made, or cooperative agreement entered into, under this section shall be subject to the limitations and provisions set forth in paragraph (2) of this subsection, and to such other terms, conditions, and requirements as the Secretary deems necessary or appropriate.

(2) Any person who receives or utilizes any proceeds of any grant made or cooperative agreement entered into under this section shall keep such records as the Secretary shall by regulation prescribe as being necessary and appropriate to facilitate effective audit and evaluation, including records which fully disclose the amount and disposition by such recipient of such proceeds, the total cost of the program or project in connection with which such proceeds were used, and the amount, if any, of such costs which was provided through other sources.

(Oct. 21, 1980, Pub. L. 96-480, §8, formerly §7, 94 Stat. 2315; Aug. 23, 1988, Pub. L. 100-418, §§5115, 5122, 102 Stat. 1433, 1438.)

15 U.S.C. § 3706

§3707   National Science Foundation Cooperative Research Centers

(a) *Establishment and provisions.*—The National Science Foundation shall provide assistance for the establishment of Cooperative Research Centers. Such Centers shall be affiliated with a university, or other nonprofit institution, or a group thereof. The objective of the Centers is to enhance technological innovation as provided in section 7(a) through the conduct of activities as provided in section 7(b).

(b) *Planning grants.*—The National Science Foundation is authorized to make available nonrenewable planning grants to universities or nonprofit institutions for the purpose of developing the plan, as described under section 7(c)(3) [§3706(c)(3)].

(c) *Terms and conditions.*—Grants, contracts, and cooperative agreements entered into by the National Science Foundation in execution of the powers and duties of the National Science Foundation under this Act shall be governed by the National Science Foundation Act of 1950 and other pertinent Acts.

(Oct. 21, 1980, Pub. L. 96-480, §9, formerly §8, 94 Stat. 2316; Oct. 20, 1986, Pub. L. 99-502, §9, 100 Stat. 1796, 1797; Aug. 23, 1988, Pub. L. 100-418, §5122, 102 Stat. 1438; Nov. 1, 2000, Pub. L. 106-404, §7, 114 Stat. 1745.)

§ 3708   Administrative arrangements

(a) *Coordination.*—The Secretary and the National Science Foundation shall, on a continuing basis, obtain the advice and cooperation of departments and agencies whose missions contribute to or are affected by the programs established under this Act, including the development of an agenda for research and policy experimentation. These departments and agencies shall include but not be limited to the Departments of Defense, Energy, Education, Health and Human Services, Housing and Urban Development, the Environmental Protection Agency, National Aeronautics and Space Administration, Small Business Administration, Council of Economic Advisers, Council on Environmental Quality, and Office of Science and Technology Policy.

(b) *Cooperation.*—It is the sense of the Congress that departments and agencies, including the Federal laboratories, whose missions are affected by, or could contribute to, the programs established under this Act, should, within the limits of budgetary authorizations and appropriations, support or participate in activities or projects authorized by this Act.

15 U.S.C. § 3708

(c) *Administrative authorization.* —

(1) Departments and agencies described in subsection (b) are authorized to participate in, contribute to, and serve as resources for the Centers and for any other activities authorized under this Act.

(2) The Secretary and the National Science Foundation are authorized to receive moneys and to receive other forms of assistance from other departments or agencies to support activities of the Centers and any other activities authorized under this Act.

(d) *Cooperative efforts.* —The Secretary and the National Science Foundation shall, on a continuing basis, provide each other the opportunity to comment on any proposed program of activity under section 7, 9, 11, 15, 17, or 20 of this Act [§§3705, 3707, 3710, 3710d, 3711a, or 3712] before funds are committed to such program in order to mount complementary efforts and avoid duplication.

(Oct. 21, 1980, Pub. L. 96-480, §10, formerly §9, 94 Stat. 2316; Oct. 20, 1986, Pub. L. 99-502, §9, 100 Stat. 1797; Aug. 20, 1987, Pub. L. 100-107, §3, 101 Stat. 727; Aug. 23, 1988, Pub. L. 100-418, §5122, 102 Stat. 1438, 1439; Dec. 18, 1991, Pub. L. 102-240, §6019, 105 Stat. 2183.)

§ 3709   [Repealed] (Oct. 20, 1986, Pub. L. 99-502, §9, 100 Stat. 1795).

§ 3710   Utilization of Federal technology

(a) *Policy.* —

(1) It is the continuing responsibility of the Federal Government to ensure the full use of the results of the Nation's Federal investment in research and development. To this end the Federal Government shall strive where appropriate to transfer federally owned or originated technology to State and local governments and to the private sector.

(2) Technology transfer, consistent with mission responsibilities, is a responsibility of each laboratory science and engineering professional.

(3) Each laboratory director shall ensure that efforts to transfer technology are considered positively in laboratory job descriptions, employee promotion policies, and evaluation of the job performance of scientists and engineers in the laboratory.

(b) *Establishment of Research and Technology Applications Offices.* —Each Federal laboratory shall establish an Office of Research and Technology Applications.

Laboratories having existing organizational structures which perform the functions of this section may elect to combine the Office of Research and Technology Applications within the existing organization. The staffing and funding levels for these offices shall be determined between each Federal laboratory and the Federal agency operating or directing the laboratory, except that (1) each laboratory having 200 or more full-time equivalent scientific, engineering, and related technical positions shall provide one or more full-time equivalent positions as staff for its Office of Research and Technology Applications, and (2) each Federal agency which operates or directs one or more Federal laboratories shall make available sufficient funding, either as a separate line item or from the agency's research and development budget, to support the technology transfer function at the agency and at its laboratories, including support of the Offices of Research and Technology Applications. Furthermore, individuals filling positions in an Office of Research and Technology Applications shall be included in the overall laboratory/agency management development program so as to ensure that highly competent technical managers are full participants in the technology transfer process.

(c) *Functions of Research and Technology Applications Offices.* — It shall be the function of each Office of Research and Technology Applications—

(1) to prepare application assessments for selected research and development projects in which that laboratory is engaged and which in the opinion of the laboratory may have potential commercial applications;

(2) to provide and disseminate information on federally owned or originated products, processes, and services having potential application to State and local governments and to private industry;

(3) to cooperate with and assist the National Technical Information Service, the Federal Laboratory Consortium for Technology Transfer, and other organizations which link the research and development resources of that laboratory and the Federal Government as a whole to potential users in State and local government and private industry;

(4) to provide technical assistance to State and local government officials; and

(5) to participate, where feasible, in regional, State, and local programs designed to facilitate or stimulate the transfer of technology for the benefit

15 U.S.C. § 3710

of the region, State, or local jurisdiction in which the Federal laboratory is located.

Agencies which have established organizational structures outside their Federal laboratories which have as their principal purpose the transfer of federally owned or originated technology to State and local government and to the private sector may elect to perform the functions of this subsection in such organizational structures. No Office of Research and Technology Applications or other organizational structures performing the functions of this subsection shall substantially compete with similar services available in the private sector.

(d) *Dissemination of technical information.* — The National Technical Information Service shall —

(1) serve as a central clearinghouse for the collection, dissemination and transfer of information on federally owned or originated technologies having potential application to State and local governments and to private industry;

(2) utilize the expertise and services of the National Science Foundation and the Federal Laboratory Consortium for Technology Transfer; particularly in dealing with State and local governments;

(3) receive requests for technical assistance from State and local governments, respond to such requests with published information available to the Service, and refer such requests to the Federal Laboratory Consortium for Technology Transfer to the extent that such requests require a response involving more than the published information available to the Service;

(4) provide funding at the discretion of the Secretary, for Federal laboratories to provide the assistance specified in subsection (c)(3);

(5) use appropriate technology transfer mechanisms such as personnel exchanges and computer-based systems; and

(6) maintain a permanent archival repository and clearinghouse for the collection and dissemination of nonclassified scientific, technical, and engineering information.

(e) *Establishment of Federal Laboratory Consortium for Technology Transfer.*—

(1) There is hereby established the Federal Laboratory Consortium for Technology Transfer (hereinafter referred to as the "Consortium") which, in cooperation with Federal laboratories and the private sector, shall—

(A) develop and (with the consent of the Federal laboratory concerned) administer techniques, training courses, and materials concerning technology transfer to increase the awareness of Federal laboratory employees regarding the commercial potential of laboratory technology and innovations;

(B) furnish advice and assistance requested by Federal agencies and laboratories for use in their technology transfer programs (including the planning of seminars for small business and other industry);

(C) provide a clearinghouse for requests, received at the laboratory level, for technical assistance from States and units of local governments, businesses, industrial development organizations, not-for-profit organizations including universities, Federal agencies and laboratories, and other persons, and—

(i) to the extent that such requests can be responded to with published information available to the National Technical Information Service, refer such requests to that Service, and

(ii) otherwise refer these requests to the appropriate Federal laboratories and agencies;

(D) facilitate communication and coordination between Offices of Research and Technology Applications of Federal laboratories;

(E) utilize (with the consent of the agency involved) the expertise and services of the National Science Foundation, the Department of Commerce, the National Aeronautics and Space Administration, and other Federal agencies, as necessary;

(F) with the consent of any Federal laboratory, facilitate the use by such laboratory of appropriate technology transfer mechanisms such as personnel exchanges and computer-based systems;

(G) with the consent of any Federal laboratory, assist such laboratory to establish programs using technical volunteers to provide technical assistance to communities related to such laboratory;

15 U.S.C. § 3710

(H) facilitate communication and cooperation between Offices of Research and Technology Applications of Federal laboratories and regional, State, and local technology transfer organizations;

(I) when requested, assist colleges or universities, businesses, nonprofit organizations, State or local governments, or regional organizations to establish programs to stimulate research and to encourage technology transfer in such areas as technology program development, curriculum design, long-term research planning, personnel needs projections, and productivity assessments;

(J) seek advice in each Federal laboratory consortium region from representatives of State and local governments, large and small business, universities, and other appropriate persons on the effectiveness of the program (and any such advice shall be provided at no expense to the Government); and

(K) work with the Director of the National Institute on Disability and Rehabilitation Research to compile a compendium of current and projected Federal Laboratory technologies and projects that have or will have an intended or recognized impact on the available range of assistive technology for individuals with disabilities (as defined in section 3 of the Assistive Technology Act of 1998), including technologies and projects that incorporate the principles of universal design (as defined in section 3 of such Act), as appropriate.

(2) The membership of the Consortium shall consist of the Federal laboratories described in clause (1) of subsection (b) and such other laboratories as may choose to join the Consortium. The representatives to the Consortium shall include a senior staff member of each Federal laboratory which is a member of the Consortium and a senior representative appointed from each Federal agency with one or more member laboratories.

(3) The representatives to the Consortium shall elect a Chairman of the Consortium.

(4) The Director of the National Institute of Standards and Technology shall provide the Consortium, on a reimbursable basis, with administrative services, such as office space, personnel, and support services of the Institute, as requested by the Consortium and approved by such Director.

(5) Each Federal laboratory or agency shall transfer technology directly to users or representatives of users, and shall not transfer technology directly

to the Consortium. Each Federal laboratory shall conduct and transfer technology only in accordance with the practices and policies of the Federal agency which owns, leases, or otherwise uses such Federal laboratory.

(6) Not later than one year after the date of enactment of this subsection, and every year thereafter, the Chairman of the Consortium shall submit a report to the President, to the appropriate authorization and appropriation committees of both Houses of the Congress, and to each agency with respect to which a transfer of funding is made (for the fiscal year or years involved) under paragraph (7), concerning the activities of the Consortium and the expenditures made by it under this subsection during the year for which the report is made. Such report shall include an annual independent audit of the financial statements of the Consortium, conducted in accordance with generally accepted accounting principles.

(7) (A) Subject to subparagraph (B), an amount equal to 0.008 percent of the budget of each Federal agency from any Federal source, including related overhead, that is to be utilized by or on behalf of the laboratories of such agency for a fiscal year referred to in subparagraph (B)(ii) shall be transferred by such agency to the National Institute of Standards and Technology at the beginning of the fiscal year involved. Amounts so transferred shall be provided by the Institute to the Consortium for the purpose of carrying out activities of the Consortium under this subsection.

(B) A transfer shall be made by any Federal agency under subparagraph (A), for any fiscal year, only if the amount so transferred by that agency (as determined under such subparagraph) would exceed $10,000.

(C) The heads of Federal agencies and their designees, and the directors of Federal laboratories, may provide such additional support for operations of the Consortium as they deem appropriate.

(8) [repealed].

(f) *Agency reports on utilization.—*

(1) *In general.—* Each Federal agency which operates or directs one or more Federal laboratories or which conducts activities under sections 207 and 209 of title 35, United States Code, shall report annually to the Office of Management and Budget, as part of the agency's annual budget submis-

15 U.S.C. § 3710

sion, on the activities performed by that agency and its Federal laboratories under the provisions of this section and of sections 207 and 209 of title 35, United States Code.

(2) *Contents.*—The report shall include—

(A) an explanation of the agency's technology transfer program for the preceding fiscal year and the agency's plans for conducting its technology transfer function, including its plans for securing intellectual property rights in laboratory innovations with commercial promise and plans for managing its intellectual property so as to advance the agency's mission and benefit the competitiveness of United States industry; and

(B) information on technology transfer activities for the preceding fiscal year, including—

(i) the number of patent applications filed;

(ii) the number of patents received;

(iii) the number of fully-executed licenses which received royalty income in the preceding fiscal year, categorized by whether they are exclusive, partially-exclusive, or non-exclusive, and the time elapsed from the date on which the license was requested by the licensee in writing to the date the license was executed;

(iv) the total earned royalty income including such statistical information as the total earned royalty income, of the top 1 percent, 5 percent, and 20 percent of the licenses, the range of royalty income, and the median, except where disclosure of such information would reveal the amount of royalty income associated with an individual license or licensee;

(v) what disposition was made of the income described in clause (iv);

(vi) the number of licenses terminated for cause; and

(vii) any other parameters or discussion that the agency deems relevant or unique to its practice of technology transfer.

(3) *Copy to Secretary; Attorney General; Congress.*—The agency shall transmit a copy of the report to the Secretary of Commerce and the Attorney General for inclusion in the annual report to Congress and the President required by subsection (g)(2).

15 U.S.C. § 3710

(4) *Public availability.*—Each Federal agency reporting under this subsection is also strongly encouraged to make the information contained in such report available to the public through Internet sites or other electronic means.

(g) *Functions of the Secretary.* —

(1) The Secretary, in consultation with other Federal agencies, may—

(A) make available to interested agencies the expertise of the Department of Commerce regarding the commercial potential of inventions and methods and options for commercialization which are available to the Federal laboratories, including research and development limited partnerships;

(B) develop and disseminate to appropriate agency and laboratory personnel model provisions for use on a voluntary basis in cooperative research and development arrangements; and

(C) furnish advice and assistance, upon request, to Federal agencies concerning their cooperative research and development programs and projects.

(2) *Reports.*—

(A) *Annual report required.*—The Secretary, in consultation with the Attorney General and the Commissioner of Patents and Trademarks, shall submit each fiscal year, beginning 1 year after the enactment of the Technology Transfer Commercialization Act of 2000, a summary report to the President, the United States Trade Representative, and the Congress on the use by Federal agencies and the Secretary of the technology transfer authorities specified in this Act and in sections 207 and 209 of title 35, United States Code.

(B) *Content.*—The report shall—

(i) draw upon the reports prepared by the agencies under subsection (f);

(ii) discuss technology transfer best practices and effective approaches in the licensing and transfer of technology in the context of the agencies' missions; and

(iii) discuss the progress made toward development of additional useful measures of the outcomes of technology transfer programs of Federal agencies.

15 U.S.C. § 3710

(C) *Public availability.*—The Secretary shall make the report available to the public through Internet sites or other electronic means.

(3) Not later than one year after the date of enactment of the Federal Technology Transfer Act of 1986, the Secretary shall submit to the President and the Congress a report regarding—

(A) any copyright provisions or other types of barriers which tend to restrict or limit the transfer of federally funded computer software to the private sector and to State and local governments, and agencies of such State and local governments; and

(B) the feasibility and cost of compiling and maintaining a current and comprehensive inventory of all federally funded training software.

(h) *Duplication of reporting.*—The reporting obligations imposed by this section—

(1) are not intended to impose requirements that duplicate requirements imposed by the Government Performance and Results Act of 1993 (31 U.S.C. 1101 note);

(2) are to be implemented in coordination with the implementation of that Act; and

(3) are satisfied if an agency provided the information concerning technology transfer activities described in this section in its annual submission under the Government Performance and Results Act of 1993 (31 U.S.C. 1101 note).

(i) *Research equipment.*—The Director of a laboratory, or the head of any Federal agency or department, may loan, lease, or give research equipment that is excess to the needs of the laboratory, agency, or department to an educational institution or nonprofit organization for the conduct of technical and scientific education and research activities. Title of ownership shall transfer with a gift under this section.

(Oct. 21, 1980, Pub. L. 96-480, §11, 94 Stat. 2318; Oct. 20, 1986, Pub. L. 99-502, §§3-5, 9, 100 Stat. 1787, 1789, 1791, 1797; Aug. 23, 1988, Pub. L. 100-418, §§5115, 5122, 5162, 5163, 102 Stat. 1433, 1438, 1450-51; Oct. 24, 1988, Pub. L. 100-519, §§201, 212, 102 Stat. 2594-95; Nov. 29, 1989, Pub. L. 101-189, §3133, 103 Stat. 1679; Feb. 14, 1992, Pub. L. 102-245, §§301, 303, 106 Stat. 20; Mar. 7, 1996, Pub. L. 104-113, §9, 110 Stat. 775; Nov. 13, 1998, Pub. L. 105-394, §212(d), 112 Stat. 3655; Nov. 1, 2000, Pub. L. 106-404, §§7, 10, 114 Stat. 1745, 1747; Aug. 9, 2007, Pub. L. 110-69, §3002, 121 Stat. 586.)

15 U.S.C. § 3710

§ 3710a Cooperative research and development agreements

(a) *General authority.*—Each Federal agency may permit the director of any of its Government-operated Federal laboratories, and, to the extent provided in an agency-approved joint work statement or, if permitted by the agency, in an agency-approved annual strategic plan, the director of any of its Government-owned, contractor-operated laboratories—

(1) to enter into cooperative research and development agreements on behalf of such agency (subject to subsection (c) of this section) with other Federal agencies; units of State or local government; industrial organizations (including corporations, partnerships, and limited partnerships, and industrial development organizations); public and private foundations; nonprofit organizations (including universities); or other persons (including licensees of inventions owned by the Federal agency); and

(2) to negotiate licensing agreements under section 207 of title 35, United States Code, or under other authorities (in the case of a Government-owned, contractor-operated laboratory, subject to subsection (c) of this section) for inventions made or other intellectual property developed at the laboratory and other inventions or other intellectual property that may be voluntarily assigned to the Government.

(b) *Enumerated authority.*—

(1) Under an agreement entered into pursuant to subsection (a)(1), the laboratory may grant, or agree to grant in advance, to a collaborating party patent licenses or assignments, or options thereto, in any invention made in whole or in part by a laboratory employee under the agreement, for reasonable compensation when appropriate. The laboratory shall ensure, through such agreement, that the collaborating party has the option to choose an exclusive license for a pre-negotiated field of use for any such invention under the agreement or, subject to section 209 of title 35, United States Code, may grant a license to an invention which is federally owned, for which a patent application was filed before the signing of the agreement, and directly within the scope of the work under the agreement, or, if there is more than one collaborating party, that the collaborating parties are offered the option to hold licensing rights that collectively encompass the rights that would be held under such an exclusive license by one party. In consideration for the Government's contribution under the agreement, grants under this paragraph shall be subject to the following explicit conditions:

15 U.S.C. § 3710a

(A) A nonexclusive, nontransferable, irrevocable, paid-up license from the collaborating party to the laboratory to practice the invention or have the invention practiced throughout the world by or on behalf of the Government. In the exercise of such license, the Government shall not publicly disclose trade secrets or commercial or financial information that is privileged or confidential within the meaning of section 552(b)(4) of title 5, United States Code, or which would be considered as such if it had been obtained from a non-Federal party.

(B) If a laboratory assigns title or grants an exclusive license to such an invention, the Government shall retain the right—

(i) to require the collaborating party to grant to a responsible applicant a nonexclusive, partially exclusive, or exclusive license to use the invention in the applicant's licensed field of use, on terms that are reasonable under the circumstances; or

(ii) if the collaborating party fails to grant such a license, to grant the license itself.

(C) The Government may exercise its right retained under subparagraph (B) only in exceptional circumstances and only if the Government determines that—

(i) the action is necessary to meet health or safety needs that are not reasonably satisfied by the collaborating party;

(ii) the action is necessary to meet requirements for public use specified by Federal regulations, and such requirements are not reasonably satisfied by the collaborating party; or

(iii) the collaborating party has failed to comply with an agreement containing provisions described in subsection (c)(4)(B).

This determination is subject to administrative appeal and judicial review under section 203(2) of title 35, United States Code.

(2) Under agreements entered into pursuant to subsection (a)(1), the laboratory shall ensure that a collaborating party may retain title to any invention made solely by its employee in exchange for normally granting the Government a nonexclusive, nontransferable, irrevocable, paid-up license to practice the invention or have the invention practiced throughout the world by or on behalf of the Government for research or other Government purposes.

15 U.S.C. § 3710a

(3) Under an agreement entered into pursuant to subsection (a)(1), a laboratory may—

(A) accept, retain, and use funds, personnel, services, and property from a collaborating party and provide personnel, services, and property to a collaborating party;

(B) use funds received from a collaborating party in accordance with subparagraph (A) to hire personnel to carry out the agreement who will not be subject to full-time-equivalent restrictions of the agency;

(C) to the extent consistent with any applicable agency requirements or standards of conduct, permit an employee or former employee of the laboratory to participate in an effort to commercialize an invention made by the employee or former employee while in the employment or service of the Government; and

(D) waive, subject to reservation by the Government of a nonexclusive, irrevocable, paid-up license to practice the invention or have the invention practiced throughout the world by or on behalf of the Government, in advance, in whole or in part, any right of ownership which the Federal Government may have to any subject invention made under the agreement by a collaborating party or employee of a collaborating party.

(4) A collaborating party in an exclusive license in any invention made under an agreement entered into pursuant to subsection (a)(1) shall have the right of enforcement under chapter 29 of title 35, United States Code.

(5) A Government-owned, contractor-operated laboratory that enters into a cooperative research and development agreement pursuant to subsection (a)(1) may use or obligate royalties or other income accruing to the laboratory under such agreement with respect to any invention only—

(A) for payments to inventors;

(B) for purposes described in clauses (i), (ii), (iii), and (iv) of section 14(a)(1)(B); and

(C) for scientific research and development consistent with the research and development missions and objectives of the laboratory.

[1](6) (A) In the case of a laboratory that is part of the National Nuclear Security Administration, a designated official of that Administration

---

[1] *Ed. Note:* This provision expired on October 30, 2005.

may waive any license retained by the Government under paragraph (1)(A), (2), or (3)(D), in whole or in part and according to negotiated terms and conditions, if the designated official finds that the retention of the license by the Government would substantially inhibit the commercialization of an invention that would otherwise serve an important national security mission.

(B) The authority to grant a waiver under subparagraph (A) shall expire on the date that is five years after the date of the enactment of the Floyd D. Spence National Defense Authorization Act for Fiscal Year 2001. The expiration under the preceding sentence of authority to grant a waiver under subparagraph (A) shall not affect any waiver granted under that subparagraph before the expiration of such authority.

(C) Not later than February 15 of each year, the Administrator for Nuclear Security shall submit to Congress a report on any waivers granted under this paragraph during the preceding year.

(c) *Contract considerations.* —

(1) A Federal agency may issue regulations on suitable procedures for implementing the provisions of this section; however, implementation of this section shall not be delayed until issuance of such regulations.

(2) The agency in permitting a Federal laboratory to enter into agreements under this section shall be guided by the purposes of this Act.

(3) (A) Any agency using the authority given it under subsection (a) shall review standards of conduct for its employees for resolving potential conflicts of interest to make sure they adequately establish guidelines for situations likely to arise through the use of this authority, including but not limited to cases where present or former employees or their partners negotiate licenses or assignments of titles to inventions or negotiate cooperative research and development agreements with Federal agencies (including the agency with which the employee involved is or was formerly employed).

(B) If, in implementing subparagraph (A), an agency is unable to resolve potential conflicts of interest within its current statutory framework, it shall propose necessary statutory changes to be forwarded to its authorizing committees in Congress.

15 U.S.C. § 3710a

(4) The laboratory director in deciding what cooperative research and development agreements to enter into shall—

(A) give special consideration to small business firms, and consortia involving small business firms; and

(B) give preference to business units located in the United States which agree that products embodying inventions made under the cooperative research and development agreement or produced through the use of such inventions will be manufactured substantially in the United States and, in the case of any industrial organization or other person subject to the control of a foreign company or government, as appropriate, take into consideration whether or not such foreign government permits United States agencies, organizations, or other persons to enter into cooperative research and development agreements and licensing agreements.

(5) (A) If the head of the agency or his designee desires an opportunity to disapprove or require the modification of any such agreement presented by the director of a Government-operated laboratory, the agreement shall provide a 30-day period within which such action must be taken beginning on the date the agreement is presented to him or her by the head of the laboratory concerned.

(B) In any case in which the head of an agency or his designee disapproves or requires the modification of an agreement presented by the director of a Government-operated laboratory under this section, the head of the agency or such designee shall transmit a written explanation of such disapproval or modification to the head of the laboratory concerned.

(C) (i) Any non-Federal entity that operates a laboratory pursuant to a contract with a Federal agency shall submit to the agency any cooperative research and development agreement that the entity proposes to enter into and the joint work statement if required with respect to that agreement.

(ii) A Federal agency that receives a proposed agreement and joint work statement under clause (i) shall review and approve, request specific modifications to, or disapprove the proposed agreement and joint work statement within 30 days after such submission. No agreement may be entered into by a Government-owned, contractor-operated laboratory under this section before both approval of the agreement and approval of a joint work statement under this clause.

(iii) In any case in which an agency which has contracted with an entity referred to in clause (i) disapproves or requests the modification of a cooperative research and development agreement or joint work statement submitted under that clause, the agency shall transmit a written explanation of such disapproval or modification to the head of the laboratory concerned.

(iv) Any agency that has contracted with a non-Federal entity to operate a laboratory may develop and provide to such laboratory one or more model cooperative research and development agreements for purposes of standardizing practices and procedures, resolving common legal issues, and enabling review of cooperative research and development agreements to be carried out in a routine and prompt manner.

(v) A Federal agency may waive the requirements of clause (i) or (ii) under such circumstances as the agency considers appropriate.

(6) Each agency shall maintain a record of all agreements entered into under this section.

(7) (A) No trade secrets or commercial or financial information that is privileged or confidential, under the meaning of section 552(b)(4) of title 5, United States Code, which is obtained in the conduct of research or as a result of activities under this Act from a non-Federal party participating in a cooperative research and development agreement shall be disclosed.

(B) The director, or in the case of a contractor-operated laboratory, the agency, for a period of up to 5 years after development of information that results from research and development activities conducted under this Act and that would be a trade secret or commercial or financial information that is privileged or confidential if the information had been obtained from a non-Federal party participating in a cooperative research and development agreement, may provide appropriate protections against the dissemination of such information, including exemption from subchapter II of chapter 5 of title 5, United States Code.

15 U.S.C. § 3710a

(d) *Definitions.* — As used in this section —

(1) the term "cooperative research and development agreement" means any agreement between one or more Federal laboratories and one or more non-Federal parties under which the Government, through its laboratories, provides personnel, services, facilities, equipment, intellectual property, or other resources with or without reimbursement (but not funds to non-Federal parties) and the non-Federal parties provide funds, personnel, services, facilities, equipment, intellectual property, or other resources toward the conduct of specified research or development efforts which are consistent with the missions of the laboratory; except that such term does not include a procurement contract or cooperative agreement as those terms are used in sections 6303, 6304, and 6305 of title 31, United States Code;

(2) the term "laboratory" means —

(A) a facility or group of facilities owned, leased, or otherwise used by a Federal agency, a substantial purpose of which is the performance of research, development, or engineering by employees of the Federal Government;

(B) a group of Government-owned, contractor-operated facilities under a common contract, when a substantial purpose of the contract is the performance of research and development for the Federal Government; and

(C) a Government-owned, contractor-operated facility that is not under a common contract described in subparagraph (B), and the primary purpose of which is the performance of research and development for the Federal Government,

but such term does not include any facility covered by Executive Order No. 12344, dated February 1, 1982, pertaining to the naval nuclear propulsion program; and

(3) the term "joint work statement" means a proposal prepared for a Federal agency by the director of a Government-owned, contractor-operated laboratory describing the purpose and scope of a proposed cooperative research and development agreement, and assigning rights and responsibilities among the agency, the laboratory, and any other party or parties to the proposed agreement.

15 U.S.C. § 3710a

(e) *Determination of laboratory missions.* —

For purposes of this section, an agency shall make separate determinations of the mission or missions of each of its laboratories.

(f) *Relationship to other laws.* —

Nothing in this section is intended to limit or diminish existing authorities of any agency.

(g) *Principles.* — In implementing this section, each agency which has contracted with a non-Federal entity to operate a laboratory shall be guided by the following principles:

(1) The implementation shall advance program missions at the laboratory, including any national security mission.

(2) Classified information and unclassified sensitive information protected by law, regulation, or Executive order shall be appropriately safeguarded.

(Oct. 21, 1980, Pub. L. 96-480, §12, as added Oct. 20, 1986, Pub. L. 99-502, §§2, 9, 100 Stat. 1785, 1797; Aug. 23, 1988, Pub. L. 100-418, §5122, 102 Stat. 1438; Oct. 24, 1980, Pub. L. 100-519, §301, 102 Stat. 2597; Nov. 29, 1989, Pub. L. 101-189, §3133, 103 Stat. 1675; April 6, 1991, Pub. L. 102-25, §705, 105 Stat. 121; Feb. 14, 1992, Pub. L. 102-245, §302, 106 Stat. 20; Oct. 23, 1992, Pub. L. 102-484, §3135, 106 Stat. 2640-41; Mar. 7, 1996, Pub. L. 104-113, §4, 110 Stat. 775; Oct. 30, 2000, Pub. L. 106-398, §3196, 114 Stat. 1654A-481-2; Nov. 1, 2000, Pub. L. 106-404, §3, 114 Stat. 1742.)

§ 3710b Rewards for scientific, engineering, and technical personnel of Federal agencies

The head of each Federal agency that is making expenditures at a rate of more than $50,000,000 per fiscal year for research and development in its Government-operated laboratories shall use the appropriate statutory authority to develop and implement a cash awards program to reward its scientific, engineering, and technical personnel for—

(1) inventions, innovations, computer software, or other outstanding scientific or technological contributions of value to the United States due to commercial application or due to contributions to missions of the Federal agency or the Federal government or

(2) exemplary activities that promote the domestic transfer of science and technology development within the Federal Government and result in utilization of such science and technology by American industry or business, universities, State or local governments, or other non-Federal parties.

(Oct. 21, 1980, Pub. L. 96-480, §13, as added Oct. 20, 1986, Pub. L. 99-502, §§6, 9, 100 Stat. 1792, 1797; Aug. 23, 1988, Pub. L. 100-418, §5122, 102 Stat. 1438; Oct. 24, 1988, Pub. L. 100-519, §302, 102 Stat. 2597.)

§ 3710c Distribution of royalties received by Federal agencies

(a) *In general.—*

(1) Except as provided in paragraphs (2) and (4), any royalties or other payments received by a Federal agency from the licensing and assignment of inventions under agreements entered into by Federal laboratories under section 12, and from the licensing of inventions of Federal laboratories under section 207 of title 35, United States Code, or under any other provision of law, shall be retained by the laboratory which produced the invention and shall be disposed of as follows:

(A) (i) The head of the agency or laboratory, or such individual's designee, shall pay each year the first $2,000, and thereafter at least 15 percent, of the royalties or other payments, other than payments of patent costs as delineated by a license or assignment agreement, to the inventor or coinventors, if the inventor's or coinventor's rights are assigned to the United States.

(ii) An agency or laboratory may provide appropriate incentives, from royalties, or other payments, to laboratory employees who are not an inventor of such inventions but who substantially increased the technical value of such inventions.

(iii) The agency or laboratory shall retain the royalties and other payments received from an invention until the agency or laboratory makes payments to employees of a laboratory under clause (i) or (ii).

(B) The balance of the royalties or other payments shall be transferred by the agency to its laboratories, with the majority share of the royalties or other payments from any invention going to the laboratory where the invention occurred. The royalties or other payments so transferred to any laboratory may be used or obligated by that laboratory during the fiscal year in which they are received or during the 2 succeeding fiscal years—

(i) to reward scientific, engineering, and technical employees of the laboratory, including developers of sensitive or classified technology, regardless of whether the technology has commercial applications;

(ii) to further scientific exchange among the laboratories of the agency;

(iii) for education and training of employees consistent with the research and development missions and objectives of the agency or laboratory, and for other activities that increase the potential for transfer of the technology of the laboratories of the agency;

(iv) for payment of expenses incidental to the administration and licensing of intellectual property by the agency or laboratory with respect to inventions made at that laboratory, including the fees or other costs for the services of other agencies, persons, or organizations for intellectual property management and licensing services; or

(v) for scientific research and development consistent with the research and development missions and objectives of the laboratory.

(C) All royalties or other payments retained by the agency or laboratory after payments have been made pursuant to subparagraphs (A) and (B) that is unobligated and unexpended at the end of the second fiscal year succeeding the fiscal year in which the royalties and other payments were received shall be paid into the Treasury.

(2) If, after payments to inventors under paragraph (1), the royalties or other payments received by an agency in any fiscal year exceed 5 percent of the budget of the agency for that year, 75 percent of such excess shall be paid to the Treasury of the United States and the remaining 25 percent may be used or obligated under paragraph (1)(B). Any funds not so used or obligated shall be paid into the Treasury of the United States.

(3) Any payment made to an employee under this section shall be in addition to the regular pay of the employee and to any other awards made to the employee, and shall not affect the entitlement of the employee to any regular pay, annuity, or award to which he is otherwise entitled or for which he is otherwise eligible or limit the amount thereof. Any payment made to an inventor as such shall continue after the inventor leaves the laboratory or agency. Payments made under this section shall not exceed $150,000 per year to any one person, unless the President ap-

proves a larger award (with the excess over $150,000 being treated as a Presidential award under section 4504 of title 5, United States Code).

(4) A Federal agency receiving royalties or other payments as a result of invention management services performed for another Federal agency or laboratory under section 207 of title 35, United States Code, may retain such royalties or payments to the extent required to offset payments to inventors under clause (i) of paragraph (1)(A), costs and expenses incurred under clause (iv) of paragraph (1)(B), and the cost of foreign patenting and maintenance for any invention of the other agency. All royalties and other payments remaining after offsetting the payments to inventors, costs, and expenses described in the preceding sentence shall be transferred to the agency for which the services were performed, for distribution in accordance with paragraph (1)(B).

(b) *Certain assignments.*—If the invention involved was one assigned to the Federal agency—

(1) by a contractor, grantee, or participant, or an employee of a contractor, grantee, or participant, in an agreement or other arrangement with the agency, or

(2) by an employee of the agency who was not working in the laboratory at the time the invention was made,

the agency unit that was involved in such assignment shall be considered to be a laboratory for purposes of this section.

(c) *Reports.*— The Comptroller General shall transmit a report to the appropriate committees of the Senate and House of Representatives on the effectiveness of Federal technology transfer programs, including findings, conclusions, and recommendations for improvements in such programs. The report shall be integrated with, and submitted at the same time as, the report required by section 202(b)(3) of title 35, United States Code.

(Oct. 21, 1980, Pub. L. 96-480, §14, as added Oct. 20, 1986, Pub. L. 99-502, §§7, 9, 100 Stat. 1792, 1797; Aug. 23, 1988, Pub. L. 100-418, §§5122, 5162, 102 Stat. 1438, 1450; Oct. 24, 1988, Pub. L. 100-519, §303, 102 Stat. 2597; Nov. 29, 1989, Pub. L. 101-189, §3133, 103 Stat. 1677; Mar. 7, 1996, Pub. L. 104-113, §5, 110 Stat. 777; Nov. 1, 2000, Pub. L. 106-404, §§7, 10, 114 Stat. 1745, 1747.)

§ 3710d Employee activities

(a) *In general.*—If a Federal agency which has ownership of or the right of ownership to an invention made by a Federal employee does not intend to file for a patent application or otherwise to promote commercialization of such invention, the agency shall allow the inventor, if the inventor is a Government employee or former employee who made the invention during the course of employment with the Government, to obtain or retain title to the invention (subject to reservation by the Government of a nonexclusive, nontransferrable, irrevocable, paid-up license to practice the invention or have the invention practiced throughout the world by or on behalf of the Government). In addition, the agency may condition the inventor's right to title on the timely filing of a patent application in cases when the Government determines that it has or may have a need to practice the invention.

(b) *"Special Government employees" defined.*—For purposes of this section, Federal employees include "special Government employees" as defined in section 202 of title 18, United States Code.

(c) *Relationship to other laws.*—Nothing in this section is intended to limit or diminish existing authorities of any agency.

(Oct. 21, 1980, Pub. L. 96-480, §15, as added Oct. 20, 1986, Pub. L. 99-502, §§8, 9, 100 Stat. 1794, 1797; Aug. 23, 1988, Pub. L. 100-418, §5122, 102 Stat. 1438; Mar. 7, 1996, Pub. L. 104-113, §6, 110 Stat. 779.)

§ 3711 National Technology and Innovation Medal

(a) *Establishment.*—There is hereby established a National Technology and Innovation Medal, which shall be of such design and materials and bear such inscriptions as the President, on the basis of recommendations submitted by the Office of Science and Technology Policy, may prescribe.

(b) *Award.*—The President shall periodically award the medal, on the basis of recommendations received from the Secretary or on the basis of such other information and evidence as he deems appropriate, to individuals or companies, which in his judgment are deserving of special recognition by reason of their outstanding contributions to the promotion of technology or technological manpower for the improvement of the economic, environmental, or social well-being of the United States.

(c) *Presentation.*—The presentation of the award shall be made by the President with such ceremonies as he may deem proper.

(Oct. 21, 1980, Pub. L. 96-480, §16, 94 Stat. 2319; Oct. 20, 1986, Pub. L. 99-502, §§2, 9, 100 Stat. 1785, 1797; Aug. 23, 1988, Pub. L. 100-418, §5122, 102 Stat. 1438; Aug. 9, 2007, Pub. L. 110-69, §1003, 121 Stat. 576-577.)

§ 3711a Malcolm Baldrige National Quality Award

(a) *Establishment.*—There is hereby established the Malcolm Baldrige National Quality Award, which shall be evidenced by a medal bearing the inscriptions "Malcolm Baldrige National Quality Award" and "The Quest for Excellence". The medal shall be of such design and materials and bear such additional inscriptions as the Secretary may prescribe.

(b) *Making and presentation of award.*—

(1) The President (on the basis of recommendations received from the Secretary), or the Secretary, shall periodically make the award to companies and other organizations which in the judgment of the President or the Secretary have substantially benefited the economic or social well-being of the United States through improvements in the quality of their goods or services resulting from the effective practice of quality management, and which as a consequence are deserving of special recognition.

(2) The presentation of the award shall be made by the President or the Secretary with such ceremonies as the President or the Secretary may deem proper.

(3) An organization to which an award is made under this section, and which agrees to help other American organizations improve their quality management, may publicize its receipt of such award and use the award in its advertising, but it shall be ineligible to receive another such award in the same category for a period of 5 years.

(c) *Categories in which award may be given.*—

(1) Subject to paragraph (2), separate awards shall be made to qualifying organizations in each of the following categories—

(A) Small businesses.

(B) Companies or their subsidiaries.

(C) Companies which primarily provide services.

(D) Health care providers.

(E) Education providers.

(F) Nonprofit organizations.

(2) The Secretary may at any time expand, subdivide, or otherwise modify the list of categories within which awards may be made as initially in effect under paragraph (1), and may establish separate awards for other

15 U.S.C. § 3711a

organizations including units of government, upon a determination that the objectives of this section would be better served thereby; except that any such expansion, subdivision, modification, or establishment shall not be effective unless and until the Secretary has submitted a detailed description thereof to the Congress and a period of 30 days has elapsed since that submission.

(3) In any year, not more than 18 awards may be made under this section to recipients who have not previously received an award under this section, and no award shall be made within any category described in paragraph (1) if there are no qualifying enterprises in that category.

(d) *Criteria for qualification.*—

(1) An organization may qualify for an award under this section only if it—

(A) applies to the Director of the National Institute of Standards and Technology in writing, for the award,

(B) permits a rigorous evaluation of the way in which its business and other operations have contributed to improvements in the quality of goods and services, and

(C) meets such requirements and specifications as the Secretary, after receiving recommendations from the Board of Overseers established under paragraph (2)(B) and the Director of the National Institute of Standards and Technology determines to be appropriate to achieve the objectives of this section.

In applying the provisions of subparagraph (C) with respect to any organization, the Director of the National Institute of Standards and Technology shall rely upon an intensive evaluation by a competent board of examiners which shall review the evidence submitted by the organization and, through a site visit, verify the accuracy of the quality improvements claimed. The examination should encompass all aspects of the organization's current practice of quality management, as well as the organization's provision for quality management in its future goals. The award shall be given only to organizations which have made outstanding improvements in the quality of their goods or services (or both) and which demonstrate effective quality management through the training and involvement of all levels of personnel in quality improvement.

15 U.S.C. § 3711a

(2) (A) The Director of the National Institute of Standards and Technology shall, under appropriate contractual arrangements, carry out the Director's responsibilities under subparagraphs (A) and (B) of paragraph (1) through one or more broad-based nonprofit entities which are leaders in the field of quality management and which have a history of service to society.

(B) The Secretary shall appoint a board of overseers for the award, consisting of at least five persons selected for their preeminence in the field of quality management. This board shall meet annually to review the work of the contractor or contractors and make such suggestions for the improvement of the award process as they deem necessary. The board shall report the results of the award activities to the Director of the National Institute of Standards and Technology each year, along with its recommendations for improvement of the process.

(e) *Information and technology transfer program.*—The Director of the National Institute of Standards and Technology shall ensure that all program participants receive the complete results of their audits as well as detailed explanations of all suggestions for improvements. The Director shall also provide information about the awards and the successful quality improvement strategies and programs of the award-winning participants to all participants and other appropriate groups.

(f) *Funding.*—The Secretary is authorized to seek and accept gifts from public and private sources to carry out the program under this section. If additional sums are needed to cover the full cost of the program, the Secretary shall impose fees upon the organizations applying for the award in amounts sufficient to provide such additional sums. The Director is authorized to use appropriated funds to carry out responsibilities under this Act.

(g) *Report.*—The Secretary shall prepare and submit to the President and the Congress, within 3 years after the date of the enactment of this section, a report on the progress, findings, and conclusions of activities conducted pursuant to this section along with recommendations for possible modifications thereof.

(Oct. 21, 1980, Pub. L. 96-480, §17, as added Aug. 20, 1987, Pub. L. 100-107, §3, 101 Stat. 725; Aug. 23, 1988, Pub. L. 100-418, §§5115, 5122, 102 Stat. 1433, 1438; Feb. 14, 1992, Pub. L. 102-245, §305, 106 Stat. 20; Oct. 30, 1998, Pub. L. 105-309, §3, 112 Stat. 2935; Oct. 5, 2004, Pub. L. 108-320, §1, 118 Stat. 1213; Aug. 9, 2007, Pub. L. 110-69, §3010, 121 Stat. 592.)

15 U.S.C. § 3711a

§ 3711b Conference on advanced automotive technologies

Not later than 180 days after the date of the enactment of this section, the Secretary of Commerce, through the Under Secretary of Commerce for Technology, in consultation with other appropriate officials, shall convene a conference of domestic motor vehicle manufacturers, parts suppliers, Federal laboratories, and motor vehicle users to explore ways in which cooperatively they can improve the competitiveness of the United States motor vehicle industry by developing new technologies which will enhance the safety and energy savings, and lessen the environmental impact of domestic motor vehicles, and the results of such conference shall be published and then submitted to the President and to the Committees on Science, Space, and Technology and Public Works and Transportation of the House of Representatives and the Committee on Commerce, Science, and Transportation of the Senate.

(Oct. 21, 1980, Pub. L. 96-480, §18, as added Dec. 18, 1991, Pub. L. 102-240, §6019, 105 Stat. 2183.)

§ 3711c Advanced motor vehicle research award

(a) *Establishment.*—There is established a National Award for the Advancement of Motor Vehicle Research and Development. The award shall consist of a medal, and a cash prize if funding is available for the prize under subsection (c). The medal shall be of such design and materials and bear inscriptions as is determined by the Secretary of Transportation.

(b) *Making and presenting award.*—The Secretary of Transportation shall periodically make and present the award to domestic motor vehicle manufacturers, suppliers, or Federal laboratory personnel who, in the opinion of the Secretary of Transportation, have substantially improved domestic motor vehicle research and development in safety, energy savings, or environmental impact. No person may receive the award more than once every 5 years.

(c) *Funding for award.*—The Secretary of Transportation may seek and accept gifts of money from private sources for the purpose of making cash prize awards under this section. Such money may be used only for that purpose, and only such money may be used for that purpose.

(Added Dec. 18, 1991, Pub. L. 102-240, §6019, 105 Stat. 2183–84.)

(Oct. 21, 1980, Pub. L. 96-480, §19, as added Dec. 18, 1991, Pub. L. 102-240, §6019, 105 Stat. 2183.)

§ 3712   Personnel exchanges

The Secretary, the Secretary of Energy, and the Director of the National Science Foundation, jointly, shall establish a program to foster the exchange of scientific and technical personnel among academia, industry, and Federal laboratories. Such program shall include both (1) federally supported exchanges and (2) efforts to stimulate exchanges without Federal funding.

(Oct. 21, 1980, Pub. L. 96-480, §20, 94 Stat. 2319; Oct. 20, 1986, Pub. L. 99-502, §§2, 9, 100 Stat. 1785, 1797; Aug. 20, 1987, Pub. L. 100-107, §3, 101 Stat. 725; Aug. 23, 1988, Pub. L. 100-418, §5122, 102 Stat. 1438; Dec. 18, 1991, Pub. L. 102-240, §6019, 105 Stat. 2183; Aug. 8, 2005, Pub. L. No. 109-58, §1009, 119 Stat. 936.)

§ 3713   Authorization of appropriations

(a) (1) There is authorized to be appropriated to the Secretary for the purposes of carrying out sections 11(g) and 16 of this Act [§§3710(g) and 3711] not to exceed $3,400,000 for the fiscal year ending September 30, 1988.

(2) Of the amount authorized under paragraph (1) of this subsection, $2,400,000 is authorized only for the Office of Productivity, Technology, and Innovation; and $500,000 is authorized only for the patent licensing activities of the National Technical Information Service.

(b) In addition to the authorization of appropriations provided under subsection (a) of this section, there is authorized to be appropriated to the Secretary for the purposes of carrying out section 6 of this Act [§3704a] not to exceed $500,000 for the fiscal year ending September 30, 1988, $1,000,000 for the fiscal year ending September 30, 1989, and $1,500,000 for the fiscal year ending September 30, 1990.

(c) Such sums as may be appropriated under subsections (a) and (b) shall remain available until expended.

(d) To enable the National Science Foundation to carry out its powers and duties under this Act only such sums may be appropriated as the Congress may authorize by law.

(Oct. 21, 1980, Pub. L. 96-480, §21, 94 Stat. 2319; Oct. 20, 1986, Pub. L. 99-502, §§2, 9, 100 Stat. 1785, 1797; Aug. 20, 1987, Pub. L. 100-107, §3, 101 Stat. 725; Aug. 23, 1988, Pub. L. 100-418, §§5122, 5152, 102 Stat. 1438, 1449; Dec. 18, 1991, Pub. L. 102-240, §6019, 105 Stat. 2183; Aug. 9, 2007, Pub. L. 110-69, §3002, 121 Stat. 586.)

§ 3714 Spending authority

No payments shall be made or contracts shall be entered into pursuant to the provisions of this Act (other than sections 12, 13, and 14) except to such extent or in such amounts as are provided in advance in appropriation Acts.

(Oct. 21, 1980, Pub. L. 96-480, §22, 94 Stat. 2319; Oct. 20, 1986, Pub. L. 99-502, §§2, 9, 100 Stat. 1785, 1796-97; Aug. 20, 1987, Pub. L. 100-107, §3, 101 Stat. 725; Aug. 23, 1988, Pub. L. 100-418, §5122, 102 Stat. 1438; Dec. 18, 1991, Pub. L. 102-240, §6019, 105 Stat. 2183; Nov. 1, 2000, Pub. L. 106-404, §7, 114 Stat. 1745.)

§ 3715 Use of partnership intermediaries

(a) *Authority.*—Subject to the approval of the Secretary or head of the affected department or agency, the Director of a Federal laboratory, or in the case of a federally funded research and development center that is not a laboratory (as defined in section 12(d)(2) [§3710a(d)(2)]), the Federal employee who is the contract officer, may—

(1) enter into a contract or memorandum of understanding with a partnership intermediary that provides for the partnership intermediary to perform services for the Federal laboratory that increase the likelihood of success in the conduct of cooperative or joint activities of such Federal laboratory with small business firms, institutions of higher education as defined in section 1201(a) of the Higher Education Act of 1965 (20 U.S.C. 1141(a)), or educational institutions within the meaning of section 2194 of title 10, United States Code; and

(2) pay the Federal costs of such contract or memorandum of understanding out of funds available for the support of the technology transfer function pursuant to section 11(b) of this Act [§3710(b)].

(b) *Partnership progress reports.*—The Secretary shall include in each triennial report required under section 6(d) [§3704a(d)] of this Act a discussion and evaluation of the activities carried out pursuant to this section during the period covered by the report.

(c) *Definition.*—For purposes of this section, the term "partnership intermediary" means an agency of a State or local government, or a nonprofit entity owned in whole or in part by, chartered by, funded in whole or in part by, or operated in whole or in part by or on behalf of a State or local government, that assists, counsels, advises, evaluates, or otherwise cooperates with small business firms, institutions of higher education as defined in section 1201(a) of the Higher Education Act of 1965 (20 U.S.C. 1141(a)), or educational institutions within the meaning of section 2194 of title 10, United States Code, that need or can make demonstrably productive use of technology-related assistance from a Federal laboratory, including State programs receiving funds under cooperative agreements entered into under section 5121(b) of the Omnibus Trade and Competitiveness Act of 1988 (15 U.S.C. 2781 note).

(Oct. 21, 1980, Pub. L. 96-480, §23, as added Nov. 5, 1990, Pub. L. 101-510, §827, 104 Stat. 1606; Dec. 5, 1991, Pub. L. 102-190, §836, 105 Stat. 1448; Dec. 18, 1991, Pub. L. 102-240, §6019, 105 Stat. 2183; Nov. 1, 2000, Pub. L. 106-404, §9, 114 Stat. 1747.)

§ 3716 Critical industries

(a) *Identification of industries and development of plan.* —The Secretary shall—

(1) identify those civilian industries in the United States that are necessary to support a robust manufacturing infrastructure and critical to the economic security of the United States; and

(2) list the major research and development initiatives being undertaken, and the substantial investments being made, by the Federal Government, including its research laboratories, in each of the critical industries identified under paragraph (1).

(b) *Initial report.* —The Secretary shall submit a report to the Congress within 1 year after February 14, 1992, on the actions taken under subsection (a) of this section.

(c) *Annual updates.* —The Secretary shall annually submit to the Congress an update of the report submitted under subsection (b) of this section. Each such update shall—

(1) describe the status of each identified critical industry, including the advances and declines occurring since the most recent report; and

(2) identify any industries that should be added to the list of critical industries.

(Feb. 14, 1992, Pub. L. 102-245, §504, 106 Stat. 24.)

§ 3717 National Quality Council

(a) *Establishment and functions.* —There is established a National Quality Council (hereafter in this section referred to as the "Council"). The functions of the Council shall be—

(1) to establish national goals and priorities for Quality performance in business, education, government, and all other sectors of the Nation;

(2) to encourage and support the voluntary adoption of these goals and priorities by companies, unions, professional and business associations, coalition groups, and units of government, as well as private and nonprofit organizations;

(3) to arouse and maintain the interest of the people of the United States in Quality performance, and to encourage the adoption and institution of Quality performance methods by all corporations, government agencies, and other organizations; and

(4) to conduct a White House Conference on Quality Performance in the American Workplace that would bring together in a single forum national leaders in business, labor, education, professional societies, the media, government, and politics to address Quality performance as a means of improving United States competitiveness.

(b) *Membership.*—The Council shall consist of not less than 17 or more than 20 members, appointed by the Secretary. Members shall include—

(1) at least 2 but not more than 3 representatives from manufacturing industry;

(2) at least 2 but not more than 3 representatives from service industry;

(3) at least 2 but not more than 3 representatives from national Quality not-for-profit organizations;

(4) two representatives from education, one with expertise in elementary and secondary education, and one with expertise in post-secondary education;

(5) one representative from labor;

(6) one representative from professional societies;

(7) one representative from local and State government;

(8) one representative from the Federal Quality Institute;

(9) one representative from the National Institute of Standards and Technology;

(10) one representative from the Department of Defense;

(11) one representative from a civilian Federal agency not otherwise represented on the Council, to be rotated among such agencies every 2 years; and

(12) one representative from the Foundation for the Malcolm Baldrige National Quality Award.

(c) *Terms.*—The term of office of each member of the Council appointed under paragraphs (1) through (7) of subsection (b) of this section shall be 2 years, except that when making the initial appointments under such paragraphs; the Secretary shall appoint not more than 50 percent of the members to 1 year terms. No member appointed under such paragraphs shall serve on the Council for more than 2 consecutive terms.

(d) *Chairman and Vice Chairman.*—The Secretary shall designate one of the members initially appointed to the Council as Chairman. Thereafter, the members of the Council shall annually elect one of their number as Chairman. The members of the Council shall also annually elect one of their members as Vice Chairman. No individual shall serve as Chairman or Vice Chairman for more than 2 consecutive years.

(e) *Executive Director and employees.*—The Council shall appoint and fix the compensation of an Executive Director, who shall hire and fix the compensation of such additional employees as may be necessary to assist the Council in carrying out its functions. In hiring such additional employees, the Executive Director shall ensure than no individual hired has a conflict of interest with the responsibilities of the Council.

(f) *Funding.*—There is established in the Treasury of the United States a National Quality Performance Trust Fund, into which all funds received by the Council, through private donations or otherwise, shall be deposited. Amounts in such Trust Fund shall be available to the Council, to the extent provided in advance in appropriations Acts, for the purpose of carrying out the functions of the Council under this Act.

(g) *Contributions.*—The Council may not accept private donations from a single source in excess of $25,000 per year. Private donations from a single source in excess of $10,000 per year may be accepted by the Council only on approval of two-thirds of the Council.

(h) *Annual report.*—The Council shall annually submit to the President and the Congress a comprehensive and detailed report on—

(1) the progress in meeting the goals and priorities established by the Council;

(2) the Council's operations, activities, and financial condition;

(3) contributions to the Council from non-Federal sources;

15 U.S.C. § 3717

(4) plans for the Council's operations and activities for the future; and

(5) any other information or recommendations the Council considers appropriate.

(Feb. 14, 1992, Pub. L. 102-245, §507, 106 Stat. 27.)

15 U.S.C. § 3717

Part 4

COPYRIGHTS

UNITED STATES CODE
TITLE 17—COPYRIGHTS

UNITED STATES CODE

TITLE 17—COPYRIGHTS

Chapter 1—Subject Matter and Scope of Copyright

§ 101   Definitions

As used in this title, the following terms and their variant forms mean the following:

An "anonymous work" is a work on the copies or phonorecords of which no natural person is identified as author.

An "architectural work" is the design of a building as embodied in any tangible medium of expression, including a building, architectural plans, or drawings. The work includes the overall form as well as the arrangement and composition of spaces and elements in the design, but does not include individual standard features.

"Audiovisual works" are works that consist of a series of related images which are intrinsically intended to be shown by the use of machines or devices such as projectors, viewers, or electronic equipment, together with accompanying sounds, if any, regardless of the nature of the material objects, such as films or tapes, in which the works are embodied.

The "Berne Convention" is the Convention for the Protection of Literary and Artistic Works, signed at Berne, Switzerland, on September 9, 1886, and all acts, protocols, and revisions thereto.

The "best edition" of a work is the edition, published in the United States at any time before the date of deposit, that the Library of Congress determines to be most suitable for its purposes.

A person's "children" are that person's immediate offspring, whether legitimate or not, and any children legally adopted by that person.

A "collective work" is a work, such as a periodical issue, anthology, or encyclopedia, in which a number of contributions, constituting separate and independent works in themselves, are assembled into a collective whole.

A "compilation" is a work formed by the collection and assembling of preexisting materials or of data that are selected, coordinated, or arranged in such a way that the resulting work as a whole constitutes an original work of authorship. The term "compilation" includes collective works.

A "computer program" is a set of statements or instructions to be used directly or indirectly in a computer in order to bring about a certain result.

"Copies" are material objects, other than phonorecords, in which a work is fixed by any method now known or later developed, and from which the work can be perceived, reproduced, or otherwise communicated, either directly or with the aid of a machine or device. The term "copies" includes the material object, other than a phonorecord, in which the work is first fixed.

"Copyright owner", with respect to any one of the exclusive rights comprised in a copyright, refers to the owner of that particular right.

A "Copyright Royalty Judge" is a Copyright Royalty Judge appointed under section 802 of this title, and includes any individual serving as an interim Copyright Royalty Judge under such section.

A work is "created" when it is fixed in a copy or phonorecord for the first time; where a work is prepared over a period of time, the portion of it that has been fixed at any particular time constitutes the work as of that time, and where the work has been prepared in different versions, each version constitutes a separate work.

A "derivative work" is a work based upon one or more preexisting works, such as a translation, musical arrangement, dramatization, fictionalization, motion picture version, sound recording, art reproduction, abridgment, condensation, or any other form in which a work may be recast, transformed, or adapted. A work consisting of editorial revisions, annotations, elaborations, or other modifications which, as a whole, represent an original work of authorship, is a "derivative work".

A "device", "machine", or "process" is one now known or later developed.

A "digital transmission" is a transmission in whole or in part in a digital or other non-analog format.

To "display" a work means to show a copy of it, either directly or by means of a film, slide, television image, or any other device or process or, in the case of a motion picture or other audiovisual work, to show individual images nonsequentially.

An "establishment" is a store, shop, or any similar place of business open to the general public for the primary purpose of selling goods or services in which the majority of the gross square feet of space that is nonresidential is used for that purpose, and in which nondramatic musical works are performed publicly.

The term "financial gain" includes receipt, or expectation of receipt, of anything of value, including the receipt of other copyrighted works.

A work is "fixed" in a tangible medium of expression when its embodiment in a copy or phonorecord, by or under the authority of the author, is sufficiently permanent or stable to permit it to be perceived, reproduced, or otherwise communicated for a period of more than transitory duration. A work consisting of sounds, images, or both, that are being transmitted, is "fixed" for purposes of this title if a fixation of the work is being made simultaneously with its transmission.

A "food service or drinking establishment" is a restaurant, inn, bar, tavern, or any other similar place of business in which the public or patrons assemble for the primary purpose of being served food or drink, in which the majority of the gross square feet of space that is nonresidential is used for that purpose, and in which nondramatic musical works are performed publicly.

The "Geneva Phonograms Convention" is the Convention for the Protection of Producers of Phonograms Against Unauthorized Duplication of Their Phonograms, concluded at Geneva, Switzerland, on October 29, 1971.

The "gross square feet of space" of an establishment means the entire interior space of that establishment, and any adjoining outdoor space used to serve patrons, whether on a seasonal basis or otherwise.

The terms "including" and "such as" are illustrative and not limitative.

An "international agreement" is—

(1) the Universal Copyright Convention;

(2) the Geneva Phonograms Convention;

(3) the Berne Convention;

(4) the WTO Agreement;

(5) the WIPO Copyright Treaty;

(6) the WIPO Performances and Phonograms Treaty; and

(7) any other copyright treaty to which the United States is a party.

A "joint work" is a work prepared by two or more authors with the intention that their contributions be merged into inseparable or interdependent parts of a unitary whole.

"Literary works" are works, other than audiovisual works, expressed in words, numbers, or other verbal or numerical symbols or indicia, regardless of the nature of the material objects, such as books, periodicals, manuscripts, phonorecords, film, tapes, disks, or cards, in which they are embodied.

The term "motion picture exhibition facility" means a movie theater, screening room, or other venue that is being used primarily for the exhibition of a copyrighted motion picture, if such exhibition is open to the public or is made to an assembled group of viewers outside of a normal circle of a family and its social acquaintances.

"Motion pictures" are audiovisual works consisting of a series of related images which, when shown in succession, impart an impression of motion, together with accompanying sounds, if any.

To "perform" a work means to recite, render, play, dance, or act it, either directly or by means of any device or process or, in the case of a motion picture or other audiovisual work, to show its images in any sequence or to make the sounds accompanying it audible.

A "performing rights society" is an association, corporation, or other entity that licenses the public performance of nondramatic musical works on behalf of copyright owners of such works, such as the American Society of Composers, Authors and Publishers (ASCAP), Broadcast Music, Inc. (BMI), and SESAC, Inc.

"Phonorecords" are material objects in which sounds, other than those accompanying a motion picture or other audiovisual work, are fixed by any method now known or later developed, and from which the sounds can be perceived, reproduced, or otherwise communicated, either directly or with the aid of a machine or device. The term "phonorecords" includes the material object in which the sounds are first fixed.

"Pictorial, graphic, and sculptural works" include two-dimensional and three-dimensional works of fine, graphic, and applied art, photographs, prints and art reproductions, maps, globes, charts, diagrams, models, and technical drawings, including architectural plans. Such works shall include works of artistic craftsmanship insofar as their form but not their mechanical or utilitarian aspects are concerned; the design of a useful article, as defined in this section, shall be considered a pictorial, graphic, or sculptural work only if, and only to the extent that, such design incorporates pictorial, graphic, or sculptural features that can be identified separately from, and are capable of existing independently of, the utilitarian aspects of the article.

For purposes of section 513, a "proprietor" is an individual, corporation, partnership, or other entity, as the case may be, that owns an establishment or a food service or drinking establishment, except that no owner or operator of a radio or television station licensed by the Federal Communications Commission, cable system or satellite carrier, cable or satellite carrier service or programmer, provider of online services or network access or the operator of facilities therefor, telecommunications company, or any other such audio or audiovisual service or programmer now known or as may be developed in the future, commercial subscription music service, or owner or operator of any other transmission service, shall under any circumstances be deemed to be a proprietor.

A "pseudonymous work" is a work on the copies or phonorecords of which the author is identified under a fictitious name.

"Publication" is the distribution of copies or phonorecords of a work to the public by sale or other transfer of ownership, or by rental, lease, or lending. The offering to distribute copies or phonorecords to a group of persons for purposes of further distribution, public performance, or public display, constitutes publication. A public performance or display of a work does not of itself constitute publication.

To perform or display a work "publicly" means—

(1) to perform or display it at a place open to the public or at any place where a substantial number of persons outside of a normal circle of a family and its social acquaintances is gathered; or

(2) to transmit or otherwise communicate a performance or display of the work to a place specified by clause (1) or to the public, by means of any device or process, whether the members of the public capable of receiving the performance or display receive it in the same place or in separate places and at the same time or at different times.

"Registration", for purposes of sections 205(c)(2), 405, 406, 410(d), 411, 412, and 506(e), means a registration of a claim in the original or renewed and extended term of copyright.

"Sound recordings" are works that result from the fixation of a series of musical, spoken, or other sounds, but not including the sounds accompanying a motion picture or other audiovisual work, regardless of the nature of the material objects, such as disks, tapes, or other phonorecords, in which they are embodied.

"State" includes the District of Columbia and the Commonwealth of Puerto Rico, and any territories to which this title is made applicable by an Act of Congress.

17 U.S.C. § 101

A "transfer of copyright ownership" is an assignment, mortgage, exclusive license, or any other conveyance, alienation, or hypothecation of a copyright or of any of the exclusive rights comprised in a copyright, whether or not it is limited in time or place of effect, but not including a nonexclusive license.

A "transmission program" is a body of material that, as an aggregate, has been produced for the sole purpose of transmission to the public in sequence and as a unit.

To "transmit" a performance or display is to communicate it by any device or process whereby images or sounds are received beyond the place from which they are sent.

A "treaty party" is a country or intergovernmental organization other than the United States that is a party to an international agreement.

The "United States", when used in a geographical sense, comprises the several States, the District of Columbia and the Commonwealth of Puerto Rico, and the organized territories under the jurisdiction of the United States Government.

For purposes of section 411, a work is a "United States work" only if—

(1) in the case of a published work, the work is first published—

(A) in the United States;

(B) simultaneously in the United States and another treaty party or parties, whose law grants a term of copyright protection that is the same as or longer than the term provided in the United States;

(C) simultaneously in the United States and a foreign nation that is not a treaty party; or

(D) in a foreign nation that is not a treaty party, and all of the authors of the work are nationals, domiciliaries, or habitual residents of, or in the case of an audiovisual work legal entities with headquarters in, the United States;

(2) in the case of an unpublished work, all the authors of the work are nationals, domiciliaries, or habitual residents of the United States, or, in the case of an unpublished audiovisual work, all the authors are legal entities with headquarters in the United States; or

(3) in the case of a pictorial, graphic, or sculptural work incorporated in a building or structure, the building or structure is located in the United States.

17 U.S.C. § 101

A "useful article" is an article having an intrinsic utilitarian function that is not merely to portray the appearance of the article or to convey information. An article that is normally a part of a useful article is considered a "useful article".

The author's "widow" or "widower" is the author's surviving spouse under the law of the author's domicile at the time of his or her death, whether or not the spouse has later remarried.

The "WIPO Copyright Treaty" is the WIPO Copyright Treaty concluded at Geneva, Switzerland, on December 20, 1996.

The "WIPO Performances and Phonograms Treaty" is the WIPO Performances and Phonograms Treaty concluded at Geneva, Switzerland, on December 20, 1996.

A "work of visual art" is—

(1) a painting, drawing, print, or sculpture, existing in a single copy, in a limited edition of 200 copies or fewer that are signed and consecutively numbered by the author, or, in the case of a sculpture, in multiple cast, carved, or fabricated sculptures of 200 or fewer that are consecutively numbered by the author and bear the signature or other identifying mark of the author; or

(2) a still photographic image produced for exhibition purposes only, existing in a single copy that is signed by the author, or in a limited edition of 200 copies or fewer that are signed and consecutively numbered by the author.

A work of visual art does not include—

(A) (i) any poster, map, globe, chart, technical drawing, diagram, model, applied art, motion picture or other audiovisual work, book, magazine, newspaper, periodical, data base, electronic information service, electronic publication, or similar publication;

(ii) any merchandising item or advertising, promotional, descriptive, covering, or packaging material or container;

(iii) any portion or part of any item described in clause (i) or (ii);

(B) any work made for hire; or

(C) any work not subject to copyright protection under this title.

17 U.S.C. § 101

A "work of the United States Government" is a work prepared by an officer or employee of the United States Government as part of that person's official duties.

A "work made for hire" is—

(1) a work prepared by an employee within the scope of his or her employment; or

(2) a work specially ordered or commissioned for use as a contribution to a collective work, as a part of a motion picture or other audiovisual work, as a translation, as a supplementary work, as a compilation, as an instructional text, as a test, as answer material for a test, or as an atlas, if the parties expressly agree in a written instrument signed by them that the work shall be considered a work made for hire. For the purpose of the foregoing sentence, a "supplementary work" is a work prepared for publication as a secondary adjunct to a work by another author for the purpose of introducing, concluding, illustrating, explaining, revising, commenting upon, or assisting in the use of the other work, such as forewords, afterwords, pictorial illustrations, maps, charts, tables, editorial notes, musical arrangements, answer material for tests, bibliographies, appendixes, and indexes, and an "instructional text" is a literary, pictorial, or graphic work prepared for publication and with the purpose of use in systematic instructional activities.

In determining whether any work is eligible to be considered a work made for hire under paragraph (2), neither the amendment contained in section 1011(d) of the Intellectual Property and Communications Omnibus Reform Act of 1999, as enacted by section 1000(a)(9) of Public Law 106-113, nor the deletion of the words added by that amendment—

(A) shall be considered or otherwise given any legal significance, or

(B) shall be interpreted to indicate congressional approval or disapproval of, or acquiescence in, any judicial determination,

by the courts or the Copyright Office. Paragraph (2) shall be interpreted as if both section 2(a)(1) of the Work Made For Hire and Copyright Corrections Act of 2000 and section 1011(d) of the Intellectual Property and Communications Omnibus Reform Act of 1999, as enacted by section 1000(a)(9) of Public Law 106-113, were never enacted, and without regard to any inaction or awareness by the Congress at any time of any judicial determinations.

17 U.S.C. § 101

The terms "WTO Agreement" and "WTO member country" have the meanings given those terms in paragraphs (9) and (10), respectively, of section 2 of the Uruguay Round Agreements Act.

(Oct. 19, 1976, Pub. L. 94-553, §101, 90 Stat. 2541; Dec. 12, 1980, Pub. L. 96-517, §10, 94 Stat. 3028; Oct. 31, 1988, Pub. L. 100-568, §4, 102 Stat. 2854; Dec. 1, 1990, Pub. L. 101-650, §602 and 702, 104 Stat. 5128, 5133; June 26, 1992, Pub. L. 102-307, §102(b), 106 Stat. 266; Nov. 1. 1995, Pub. L. 104-39, §5(a), 109 Stat. 348; Nov. 13, 1997, Pub. L. 105-80, §12, 111 Stat. 1534; Dec. 16, 1997, Pub. L. 105-147, §2(a), 111 Stat. 2678; Oct. 28, 1998; Pub. L. 105-304; §102(a), 112 Stat. 2861; Aug. 5, 1999, Pub. L. 106-44, §1(g), 113 Stat. 222; Nov. 29, 1999, Pub. L. 106-113, §1011, 113 Stat. 1501A-543; Oct. 27, 2000, Pub. L. 106-379, §2, 114 Stat. 1444; Nov. 2, 2002, Pub. L. 107-273, §13210, 116 Stat. 1909; Nov. 30, 2004, Pub. L. 108-419, §4, 118 Stat. 2361; April 27, 2005, Pub. L. 109-9, §102, 119 Stat. 220; Dec. 9, 2010, Pub. L. 111-295, §6, 124 Stat. 3181.)

§ 102   Subject matter of copyright: In general

(a) Copyright protection subsists, in accordance with this title, in original works of authorship fixed in any tangible medium of expression, now known or later developed, from which they can be perceived, reproduced, or otherwise communicated, either directly or with the aid of a machine or device. Works of authorship include the following categories:

(1) literary works;

(2) musical works, including any accompanying words;

(3) dramatic works, including any accompanying music;

(4) pantomimes and choreographic works;

(5) pictorial, graphic, and sculptural works;

(6) motion pictures and other audiovisual works;

(7) sound recordings; and

(8) architectural works.

(b) In no case does copyright protection for an original work of authorship extend to any idea, procedure, process, system, method of operation, concept, principle, or discovery, regardless of the form in which it is described, explained, illustrated, or embodied in such work.

(Oct. 19, 1976, Pub. L. 94-553, §101, 90 Stat. 2544; Dec. 1, 1990, Pub. L. 101-650, §703, 104 Stat. 5133.)

§ 103   Subject matter of copyright: Compilations and derivative works

(a) The subject matter of copyright as specified by section 102 includes compilations and derivative works, but protection for a work employing preexisting material in which copyright subsists does not extend to any part of the work in which such material has been used unlawfully.

(b) The copyright in a compilation or derivative work extends only to the material contributed by the author of such work, as distinguished from the preexisting material employed in the work, and does not imply any exclusive right in the preexisting material. The copyright in such work is independent of, and does not affect or enlarge the scope, duration, ownership, or subsistence of, any copyright protection in the preexisting material.

(Oct. 19, 1976, Pub. L. 94-553, §101, 90 Stat. 2545.)

§ 104 Subject matter of copyright: National origin

(a) *Unpublished Works*

The works specified by sections 102 and 103, while unpublished, are subject to protection under this title without regard to the nationality or domicile of the author.

(b) *Published Works*

The works specified by sections 102 and 103, when published, are subject to protection under this title if—

(1) on the date of first publication, one or more of the authors is a national or domiciliary of the United States, or is a national, domiciliary, or sovereign authority of a treaty party, or is a stateless person, wherever that person may be domiciled; or

(2) the work is first published in the United States or in a foreign nation that, on the date of first publication, is a treaty party; or

(3) the work is a sound recording that was first fixed in a treaty party; or

(4) the work is a pictorial, graphic, or sculptural work that is incorporated in a building or other structure, or an architectural work that is embodied in a building and the building or structure is located in the United States or a treaty party; or

(5) the work is first published by the United Nations or any of its specialized agencies, or by the Organization of American States; or

(6) the work comes within the scope of a Presidential proclamation. Whenever the President finds that a particular foreign nation extends, to works by authors who are nationals or domiciliaries of the United States or to works that are first published in the United States, copyright protection on substantially the same basis as that on which the foreign nation

17 U.S.C. § 104

extends protection to works of its own nationals and domiciliaries and works first published in that nation, the President may by proclamation extend protection under this title to works of which one or more of the authors is, on the date of first publication, a national, domiciliary, or sovereign authority of that nation, or which was first published in that nation. The President may revise, suspend, or revoke any such proclamation or impose any conditions or limitations on protection under a proclamation.

For purposes of paragraph (2), a work that is published in the United States or a treaty party within 30 days after publication in a foreign nation that is not a treaty party shall be considered to be first published in the United States or such treaty party, as the case may be.

(c) *Effect of Berne Convention.*—No right or interest in a work eligible for protection under this title may be claimed by virtue of, or in reliance upon, the provisions of the Berne Convention, or the adherence of the United States thereto. Any rights in a work eligible for protection under this title that derive from this title, other Federal or State statutes, or the common law, shall not be expanded or reduced by virtue of, or in reliance upon, the provisions of the Berne Convention, or the adherence of the United States thereto.

(d) *Effect of phonograms treaties.*—Notwithstanding the provisions of subsection (b), no works other than sound recordings shall be eligible for protection under this title solely by virtue of the adherence of the United States to the Geneva Phonograms Convention or the WIPO Performances and Phonograms Treaty.

(Oct. 19, 1976, Pub. L. 94-553, §101, 90 Stat. 2545; Oct. 31, 1988, Pub. L. 100-568, §4, 102 Stat. 2855; Oct. 28, 1998, Pub. L. 105-304, §102(b), 112 Stat. 2862.)

§ 104A Copyright in restored works

(a) *Automatic protection and term.* —

    (1) *Term.* —

        (A) Copyright subsists, in accordance with this section, in restored works, and vests automatically on the date of restoration.

        (B) Any work in which copyright is restored under this section shall subsist for the remainder of the term of copyright that the work would have otherwise been granted in the United States if the work never entered the public domain in the United States.

(2) *Exception.*—Any work in which the copyright was ever owned or administered by the Alien Property Custodian and in which the restored copyright would be owned by a government or instrumentality thereof, is not a restored work.

(b) *Ownership of restored copyright.*—A restored work vests initially in the author or initial rightholder of the work as determined by the law of the source country of the work.

(c) *Filing of notice of intent to enforce restored copyright against reliance parties.*— On or after the date of restoration, any person who owns a copyright in a restored work or an exclusive right therein may file with the Copyright Office a notice of intent to enforce that person's copyright or exclusive right or may serve such a notice directly on a reliance party. Acceptance of a notice by the Copyright Office is effective as to any reliance parties but shall not create a presumption of the validity of any of the facts stated therein. Service on a reliance party is effective as to that reliance party and any other reliance parties with actual knowledge of such service and of the contents of that notice.

(d) *Remedies for infringement of restored copyrights.*—

(1) *Enforcement of copyright in restored works in the absence of a reliance party.*—As against any party who is not a reliance party, the remedies provided in chapter 5 of this title shall be available on or after the date of restoration of a restored copyright with respect to an act of infringement of the restored copyright that is commenced on or after the date of restoration.

(2) *Enforcement of copyright in restored works as against reliance parties.*—As against a reliance party, except to the extent provided in paragraphs (3) and (4), the remedies provided in chapter 5 of this title shall be available, with respect to an act of infringement of a restored copyright, on or after the date of restoration of the restored copyright if the requirements of either of the following subparagraphs are met:

(A) (i) The owner of the restored copyright (or such owner's agent) or the owner of an exclusive right therein (or such owner's agent) files with the Copyright Office, during the 24-month period beginning on the date of restoration, a notice of intent to enforce the restored copyright; and

(ii) (I) the act of infringement commenced after the end of the 12-month period beginning on the date of publication of the notice in the Federal Register;

(II) the act of infringement commenced before the end of the 12-month period described in subclause (I) and continued after the end of that 12-month period, in which case remedies shall be available only for infringement occurring after the end of that 12-month period; or

(III) copies or phonorecords of a work in which copyright has been restored under this section are made after publication of the notice of intent in the Federal Register.

(B) (i) The owner of the restored copyright (or such owner's agent) or the owner of an exclusive right therein (or such owner's agent) serves upon a reliance party a notice of intent to enforce a restored copyright; and

(ii) (I) the act of infringement commenced after the end of the 12-month period beginning on the date the notice of intent is received;

(II) the act of infringement commenced before the end of the 12-month period described in subclause (I) and continued after the end of that 12-month period, in which case remedies shall be available only for the infringement occurring after the end of that 12-month period; or

(III) copies or phonorecords of a work in which copyright has been restored under this section are made after receipt of the notice of intent.

In the event that notice is provided under both subparagraphs (A) and (B), the 12-month period referred to in such subparagraphs shall run from the earlier of publication or service of notice.

(3) *Existing derivative works.* —

(A) In the case of a derivative work that is based upon a restored work and is created —

(i) before the date of the enactment of the Uruguay Round Agreements Act, if the source country of the restored work is an eligible country on such date, or

(ii) before the date on which the source country of the restored work becomes an eligible country, if that country is not an eligible country on such date of enactment,

a reliance party may continue to exploit that derivative work for the duration of the restored copyright if the reliance party pays to the owner of the restored copyright reasonable compensation for conduct which would be subject to a remedy for infringement but for the provisions of this paragraph.

(B) In the absence of an agreement between the parties, the amount of such compensation shall be determined by an action in United States district court, and shall reflect any harm to the actual or potential market for or value of the restored work from the reliance party's continued exploitation of the work, as well as compensation for the relative contributions of expression of the author of the restored work and the reliance party to the derivative work.

(4) *Commencement of infringement for reliance parties.*—For purposes of section 412, in the case of reliance parties, infringement shall be deemed to have commenced before registration when acts which would have constituted infringement had the restored work been subject to copyright were commenced before the date of restoration.

(e) *Notices of intent to enforce a restored copyright.*—

(1) *Notices of intent filed with the Copyright Office.*—

(A) (i) A notice of intent filed with the Copyright Office to enforce a restored copyright shall be signed by the owner of the restored copyright or the owner of an exclusive right therein, who files the notice under subsection (d)(2)(A)(i) (hereafter in this paragraph referred to as the "owner"), or by the owner's agent, shall identify the title of the restored work, and shall include an English translation of the title and any other alternative titles known to the owner by which the restored work may be identified, and an address and telephone number at which the owner may be contacted. If the notice is signed by an agent, the agency relationship must have been constituted in a writing signed by the owner before the filing of the notice. The Copyright Office may specifically require in regulations other information to be included in the notice, but failure to provide such other information shall not invalidate the notice or be a basis for refusal to list the restored work in the Federal Register.

(ii) If a work in which copyright is restored has no formal title, it shall be described in the notice of intent in detail sufficient to identify it.

(iii) Minor errors or omissions may be corrected by further notice at any time after the notice of intent is filed. Notices of corrections for such minor errors or omissions shall be accepted after the period established in subsection (d)(2)(A)(i). Notices shall be published in the Federal Register pursuant to subparagraph (B).

(B) (i) The Register of Copyrights shall publish in the Federal Register, commencing not later than 4 months after the date of restoration for a particular nation and every 4 months thereafter for a period of 2 years, lists identifying restored works and the ownership thereof if a notice of intent to enforce a restored copyright has been filed.

(ii) Not less than 1 list containing all notices of intent to enforce shall be maintained in the Public Information Office of the Copyright Office and shall be available for public inspection and copying during regular business hours pursuant to sections 705 and 708.

(C) The Register of Copyrights is authorized to fix reasonable fees based on the costs of receipt, processing, recording, and publication of notices of intent to enforce a restored copyright and corrections thereto.

(D) (i) Not later than 90 days before the date the Agreement on Trade-Related Aspects of Intellectual Property referred to in section 101(d)(15) of the Uruguay Round Agreements Act enters into force with respect to the United States,[1] the Copyright Office shall issue and publish in the Federal Register regulations governing the filing under this subsection of notices of intent to enforce a restored copyright.

(ii) Such regulations shall permit owners of restored copyrights to file simultaneously for registration of the restored copyright.

---

[1] *Ed. Note:* The TRIPs Agreement entered into force with respect to the U.S. on Jan. 1, 1996.

17 U.S.C. § 104A

(2) *Notices of intent served on a reliance party.* —

(A) Notices of intent to enforce a restored copyright may be served on a reliance party at any time after the date of restoration of the restored copyright.

(B) Notices of intent to enforce a restored copyright served on a reliance party shall be signed by the owner or the owner's agent, shall identify the restored work and the work in which the restored work is used, if any, in detail sufficient to identify them, and shall include an English translation of the title, any other alternative titles known to the owner by which the work may be identified, the use or uses to which the owner objects, and an address and telephone number at which the reliance party may contact the owner. If the notice is signed by an agent, the agency relationship must have been constituted in writing and signed by the owner before service of the notice.

(3) *Effect of material false statements.* —Any material false statement knowingly made with respect to any restored copyright identified in any notice of intent shall make void all claims and assertions made with respect to such restored copyright.

(f) *Immunity from warranty and related liability.* —

(1) *In general.* —Any person who warrants, promises, or guarantees that a work does not violate an exclusive right granted in section 106 shall not be liable for legal, equitable, arbitral, or administrative relief if the warranty, promise, or guarantee is breached by virtue of the restoration of copyright under this section, if such warranty, promise, or guarantee is made before January 1, 1995.

(2) *Performances.* —No person shall be required to perform any act if such performance is made infringing by virtue of the restoration of copyright under the provisions of this section, if the obligation to perform was undertaken before January 1, 1995.

(g) *Proclamation of copyright restoration.* —Whenever the President finds that a particular foreign nation extends, to works by authors who are nationals or domiciliaries of the United States, restored copyright protection on substantially the same basis as provided under this section, the President may by proclamation extend restored protection provided under this section to any work—

17 U.S.C. § 104A

(1) of which one or more of the authors is, on the date of first publication, a national, domiciliary, or sovereign authority of that nation; or

(2) which was first published in that nation. The President may revise, suspend, or revoke any such proclamation or impose any conditions or limitations on protection under such a proclamation.

(h) *Definitions.*—For purposes of this section and section 109(a):

(1) The term "date of adherence or proclamation" means the earlier of the date on which a foreign nation which, as of the date the WTO Agreement enters into force with respect to the United States, is not a nation adhering to the Berne Convention or a WTO member country, becomes—

(A) a nation adhering to the Berne Convention;

(B) a WTO member country;

(C) a nation adhering to the WIPO Copyright Treaty;

(D) a nation adhering to the WIPO Performances and Phonograms Treaty; or

(E) subject to a Presidential proclamation under subsection (g).

(2) The "date of restoration" of a restored copyright is the later of—

(A) January 1, 1996, if the source country of the restored work is a nation adhering to the Berne Convention or a WTO member country on such date; or

(B) the date of adherence or proclamation, in the case of any other source country of the restored work.

(3) The term "eligible country" means a nation, other than the United States, that —

(A) becomes a WTO member country after the date of the enactment of the Uruguay Round Agreements Act;

(B) on such date of enactment is, or after such date of enactment becomes, a nation adhering to the Berne Convention;

(C) a nation adhering to the WIPO Copyright Treaty;

(D) a nation adhering to the WIPO Performances and Phonograms Treaty; or

17 U.S.C. § 104A

(E) after such date of enactment becomes subject to a proclamation under subsection (g).

For purposes of this section, a nation that is a member of the Berne Convention on the date of the enactment of the Uruguay Round Agreements Act shall be construed to become an eligible country on such date of enactment.

(4) The term "reliance party" means any person who—

(A) with respect to a particular work, engages in acts, before the source country of that work becomes an eligible country, which would have violated section 106 if the restored work had been subject to copyright protection, and who, after the source country becomes an eligible country, continues to engage in such acts;

(B) before the source country of a particular work becomes an eligible country, makes or acquires 1 or more copies or phonorecords of that work; or

(C) as the result of the sale or other disposition of a derivative work covered under subsection (d)(3), or significant assets of a person described in subparagraph (A) or (B), is a successor, assignee, or licensee of that person.

(5) The term "restored copyright" means copyright in a restored work under this section.

(6) The term "restored work" means an original work of authorship that—

(A) is protected under subsection (a);

(B) is not in the public domain in its source country through expiration of term of protection;

(C) is in the public domain in the United States due to—

(i) noncompliance with formalities imposed at any time by United States copyright law, including failure of renewal, lack of proper notice, or failure to comply with any manufacturing requirements;

(ii) lack of subject matter protection in the case of sound recordings fixed before February 15, 1972; or

(iii) lack of national eligibility;

(D) has at least one author or rightholder who was, at the time the work was created, a national or domiciliary of an eligible country, and

17 U.S.C. § 104A

if published, was first published in an eligible country and not published in the United States during the 30-day period following publication in such eligible country; and

(E) if the source country for the work is an eligible country solely by virtue of its adherence to the WIPO Performances and Phonograms Treaty, is a sound recording.

(7) The term "rightholder" means the person—

(A) who, with respect to a sound recording, first fixes a sound recording with authorization, or

(B) who has acquired rights from the person described in subparagraph (A) by means of any conveyance or by operation of law.

(8) The "source country" of a restored work is—

(A) a nation other than the United States;

(B) in the case of an unpublished work—

(i) the eligible country in which the author or rightholder is a national or domiciliary, or, if a restored work has more than 1 author or rightholder, of which the majority of foreign authors or rightholders are nationals or domiciliaries; or

(ii) if the majority of authors or rightholders are not foreign, the nation other than the United States which has the most significant contacts with the work; and

(C) in the case of a published work—

(i) the eligible country in which the work is first published, or

(ii) if the restored work is published on the same day in 2 or more eligible countries, the eligible country which has the most significant contacts with the work.

(Dec. 8, 1994; Pub. L. 103-465, §514, 108 Stat. 4976; Oct. 11, 1996, Pub. L. 104-295, Title V(2), 110 Stat. 3529; Nov. 13, 1997, Pub. L. 105-80, §2, 111 Stat. 1530-31; Oct. 28, 1998; Pub. L. 105-304; §102(c), 112 Stat. 2862.)

§ 105 Subject matter of copyright: United States Government works

Copyright protection under this title is not available for any work of the United States Government, but the United States Government is not precluded from receiving and holding copyrights transferred to it by assignment, bequest, or otherwise.

(Oct. 19, 1976, Pub. L. 94-553, §101, 90 Stat. 2546.)

§ 106 Exclusive rights in copyrighted works

Subject to sections 107 through 122, the owner of copyright under this title has the exclusive rights to do and to authorize any of the following:

(1) to reproduce the copyrighted work in copies or phonorecords;

(2) to prepare derivative works based upon the copyrighted work;

(3) to distribute copies or phonorecords of the copyrighted work to the public by sale or other transfer of ownership, or by rental, lease, or lending;

(4) in the case of literary, musical, dramatic, and choreographic works, pantomimes, and motion pictures and other audiovisual works, to perform the copyrighted work publicly;

(5) in the case of literary, musical, dramatic, and choreographic works, pantomimes, and pictorial, graphic, or sculptural works, including the individual images of a motion picture or other audiovisual work, to display the copyrighted work publicly; and

(6) in the case of sound recordings, to perform the copyrighted work publicly by means of a digital audio transmission.

(Oct. 19, 1976, Pub. L. 94-553, §101, 90 Stat. 2546; July 3, 1990, Pub. L. 101-318, §3, 104 Stat. 288; Dec. 1, 1990, Pub. L. 101-650, §704, 104 Stat. 5134; Nov. 1, 1995, Pub. L. 104-39, §2, 109 Stat. 336; Aug. 5, 1999, Pub. L. 106-44, §1(g), 113 Stat. 222; Nov. 2, 2002, Pub. L. 107-273, §13210, 116 Stat. 1909.)

§ 106A Rights of certain authors to attribution and integrity

(a) *Rights of attribution and integrity.*—Subject to section 107 and independent of the exclusive rights provided in section 106, the author of a work of visual art—

(1) shall have the right—

(A) to claim authorship of that work, and

(B) to prevent the use of his or her name as the author of any work of visual art which he or she did not create;

(2) shall have the right to prevent the use of his or her name as the author of the work of visual art in the event of a distortion, mutilation, or other modification of the work which would be prejudicial to his or her honor or reputation; and

(3) subject to the limitations set forth in section 113(d), shall have the right—

(A) to prevent any intentional distortion, mutilation, or other modification of that work which would be prejudicial to his or her honor or reputation, and any intentional distortion, mutilation, or modification of that work is a violation of that right, and

(B) to prevent any destruction of a work of recognized stature, and any intentional or grossly negligent destruction of that work is a violation of that right.

(b) *Scope and exercise of rights.*—Only the author of a work of visual art has the rights conferred by subsection (a) in that work, whether or not the author is the copyright owner. The authors of a joint work of visual art are coowners of the rights conferred by subsection (a) in that work.

(c) *Exceptions.*—

(1) The modification of a work of visual art which is a result of the passage of time or the inherent nature of the materials is not a distortion, mutilation, or other modification described in subsection (a)(3)(A).

(2) The modification of a work of visual art which is the result of conservation, or of the public presentation, including lighting and placement, of the work is not a destruction, distortion, mutilation, or other modification described in subsection (a)(3) unless the modification is caused by gross negligence.

(3) The rights described in paragraphs (1) and (2) of subsection (a) shall not apply to any reproduction, depiction, portrayal, or other use of a work in, upon, or in any connection with any item described in subparagraph (A) or (B) of the definition of "work of visual art" in section 101, and any such reproduction, depiction, portrayal, or other use of a work is not a destruction, distortion, mutilation, or other modification described in paragraph (3) of subsection (a).

(d) *Duration of rights.*—

(1) With respect to works of visual art created on or after the effective date set forth in section 610(a) of the Visual Artists Rights Act of 1990, the rights conferred by subsection (a) shall endure for a term consisting of the life of the author.

17 U.S.C. § 106A

(2) With respect to works of visual art created before the effective date set forth in section 610(a) of the Visual Artists Rights Act of 1990, but title to which has not, as of such effective date, been transferred from the author, the rights conferred by subsection (a) shall be coextensive with, and shall expire at the same time as, the rights conferred by section 106.

(3) In the case of a joint work prepared by two or more authors, the rights conferred by subsection (a) shall endure for a term consisting of the life of the last surviving author.

(4) All terms of the rights conferred by subsection (a) run to the end of the calendar year in which they would otherwise expire.

(e) *Transfer and waiver.*—

(1) The rights conferred by subsection (a) may not be transferred, but those rights may be waived if the author expressly agrees to such waiver in a written instrument signed by the author. Such instrument shall specifically identify the work, and uses of that work, to which the waiver applies, and the waiver shall apply only to the work and uses so identified. In the case of a joint work prepared by two or more authors, a waiver of rights under this paragraph made by one such author waives such rights for all such authors.

(2) Ownership of the rights conferred by subsection (a) with respect to a work of visual art is distinct from ownership of any copy of that work, or of a copyright or any exclusive right under a copyright in that work. Transfer of ownership of any copy of a work of visual art, or of a copyright or any exclusive right under a copyright, shall not constitute a waiver of the rights conferred by subsection (a). Except as may otherwise be agreed by the author in a written instrument signed by the author, a waiver of the rights conferred by subsection (a) with respect to a work of visual art shall not constitute a transfer of ownership of any copy of that work, or of ownership of a copyright or of any exclusive right under a copyright in that work.

(Dec. 1, 1990, Pub. L. 101-650, §603, 104 Stat. 5128.)

§ 107   Limitations on exclusive rights: Fair use

Notwithstanding the provisions of sections 106 and 106A, the fair use of a copyrighted work, including such use by reproduction in copies or phonorecords or by any other means specified by that section, for purposes such as criticism, comment, news reporting, teaching (including multiple copies for classroom use), scholarship, or research, is not an infringement of copyright. In determining whether the use made of a work in any particular case is a fair use the factors to be considered shall include—

(1) the purpose and character of the use, including whether such use is of a commercial nature or is for nonprofit educational purposes;

(2) the nature of the copyrighted work;

(3) the amount and substantiality of the portion used in relation to the copyrighted work as a whole; and

(4) the effect of the use upon the potential market for or value of the copyrighted work.

The fact that a work is unpublished shall not itself bar a finding of fair use if such finding is made upon consideration of all the above factors.

(Oct. 19, 1976, Pub. L. 94-533, §101, 90 Stat. 2546; Dec. 1, 1990, Pub. L. 101-650, §607, 104 Stat. 5132; Oct. 24, 1992, Pub. L. 102-492, 106 Stat. 3145.)

§ 108   Limitations on exclusive rights: Reproduction by libraries and archives

(a) Except as otherwise provided in this title and notwithstanding the provisions of section 106, it is not an infringement of copyright for a library or archives, or any of its employees acting within the scope of their employment, to reproduce no more than one copy or phonorecord of a work, except as provided in subsections (b) and (c), or to distribute such copy or phonorecord, under the conditions specified by this section, if—

(1) the reproduction or distribution is made without any purpose of direct or indirect commercial advantage;

(2) the collections of the library or archives are (i) open to the public, or (ii) available not only to researchers affiliated with the library or archives or with the institution of which it is a part, but also to other persons doing research in a specialized field; and

(3) the reproduction or distribution of the work includes a notice of copyright that appears on the copy or phonorecord that is reproduced under the provisions of this section, or includes a legend stating that the work may be protected by copyright if no such notice can be found on the copy or phonorecord that is reproduced under the provisions of this section.

(b) The rights of reproduction and distribution under this section apply to three copies or phonorecords of an unpublished work duplicated solely for purposes of preservation and security or for deposit for research use in another library or archives of the type described by clause (2) of subsection (a), if—

(1) the copy or phonorecord reproduced is currently in the collections of the library or archives; and

(2) any such copy or phonorecord that is reproduced in digital format is not otherwise distributed in that format and is not made available to the public in that format outside the premises of the library or archives.

(c) The right of reproduction under this section applies to three copies or phonorecords of a published work duplicated solely for the purpose of replacement of a copy or phonorecord that is damaged, deteriorating, lost, or stolen, or if the existing format in which the work is stored has become obsolete, if —

(1) the library or archives has, after a reasonable effort, determined that an unused replacement cannot be obtained at a fair price; and

(2) any such copy or phonorecord that is reproduced in digital format is not made available to the public in that format outside the premises of the library or archives in lawful possession of such copy.

For purposes of this subsection, a format shall be considered obsolete if the machine or device necessary to render perceptible a work stored in that format is no longer manufactured or is no longer reasonably available in the commercial marketplace.

(d) The rights of reproduction and distribution under this section apply to a copy, made from the collection of a library or archives where the user makes his or her request or from that of another library or archives, of no more than one article or other contribution to a copyrighted collection or periodical issue, or to a copy or phonorecord of a small part of any other copyrighted work, if—

(1) the copy or phonorecord becomes the property of the user, and the library or archives has had no notice that the copy or phonorecord would be used for any purpose other than private study, scholarship, or research; and

(2) the library or archives displays prominently, at the place where orders are accepted, and includes on its order form, a warning of copyright in accordance with requirements that the Register of Copyrights shall pre-scribe by regulation.

17 U.S.C. § 108

(e) The rights of reproduction and distribution under this section apply to the entire work, or to a substantial part of it, made from the collection of a library or archives where the user makes his or her request or from that of another library or archives, if the library or archives has first determined, on the basis of a reasonable investigation, that a copy or phonorecord of the copyrighted work cannot be obtained at a fair price, if—

(1) the copy or phonorecord becomes the property of the user, and the library or archives has had no notice that the copy or phonorecord would be used for any purpose other than private study, scholarship, or research; and

(2) the library or archives displays prominently, at the place where orders are accepted, and includes on its order form, a warning of copyright in accordance with requirements that the Register of Copyrights shall prescribe by regulation.

(f) Nothing in this section—

(1) shall be construed to impose liability for copyright infringement upon a library or archives or its employees for the unsupervised use of reproducing equipment located on its premises: *Provided,* That such equipment displays a notice that the making of a copy may be subject to the copyright law;

(2) excuses a person who uses such reproducing equipment or who requests a copy or phonorecord under subsection (d) from liability for copyright infringement for any such act, or for any later use of such copy or phonorecord, if it exceeds fair use as provided by section 107;

(3) shall be construed to limit the reproduction and distribution by lending of a limited number of copies and excerpts by a library or archives of an audiovisual news program, subject to clauses (1), (2), and (3) of subsection (a); or

(4) in any way affects the right of fair use as provided by section 107, or any contractual obligations assumed at any time by the library or archives when it obtained a copy or phonorecord of a work in its collections.

(g) The rights of reproduction and distribution under this section extend to the isolated and unrelated reproduction or distribution of a single copy or phonorecord of the same material on separate occasions, but do not extend to cases where the library or archives, or its employee—

(1) is aware or has substantial reason to believe that it is engaging in the related or concerted reproduction or distribution of multiple copies or phonorecords of the same material, whether made on one occasion or over a period of time, and whether intended for aggregate use by one or more individuals or for separate use by the individual members of a group; or

(2) engages in the systematic reproduction or distribution of single or multiple copies or phonorecords of material described in subsection (d): *Provided,* That nothing in this clause prevents a library or archives from participating in interlibrary arrangements that do not have, as their purpose or effect, that the library or archives receiving such copies or phonorecords for distribution does so in such aggregate quantities as to substitute for a subscription to or purchase of such work.

(h)(1) For purposes of this section, during the last 20 years of any term of copyright of a published work, a library or archives, including a nonprofit educational institution that functions as such, may reproduce, distribute, display, or perform in facsimile or digital form a copy or phonorecord of such work, or portions thereof, for purposes of preservation, scholarship, or research, if such library or archives has first determined, on the basis of a reasonable investigation, that none of the conditions set forth in subparagraphs (A), (B), and (C) of paragraph (2) apply.

(2) No reproduction, distribution, display, or performance is authorized under this subsection if—

(A) the work is subject to normal commercial exploitation;

(B) a copy or phonorecord of the work can be obtained at a reasonable price; or

(C) the copyright owner or its agent provides notice pursuant to regulations promulgated by the Register of Copyrights that either of the conditions set forth in subparagraphs (A) and (B) applies.

(3) The exemption provided in this subsection does not apply to any subsequent uses by users other than such library or archives.

(i) The rights of reproduction and distribution under this section do not apply to a musical work, a pictorial, graphic or sculptural work, or a motion picture or other audiovisual work other than an audiovisual work dealing with news, except that no such limitation shall apply with respect to rights granted by subsections (b), (c), and (h) or with respect to pictorial or graphic works published as illustrations, diagrams, or similar adjuncts to works of which copies are reproduced or distributed in accordance with subsections (d) and (e).

(Oct. 19, 1976, Pub. L. 94-553, §101, 90 Stat. 2546; June 26, 1992, Pub. L. 102-307, §301, 106 Stat. 272; Nov. 13, 1997, Pub. L. 105-80, §12, 111 Stat. 1534; Oct. 27, 1998, Pub, L, 105-298, §104, 112 Stat. 2829; Oct. 28, 1998, Pub. L. 105-304, §404, 112 Stat. 2889; April 27, 2005, Pub. L. 109-9, §402, 119 Stat. 227.)

§ 109 Limitations on exclusive rights: Effect of transfer of particular copy or phonorecord

(a) Notwithstanding the provisions of section 106(3), the owner of a particular copy or phonorecord lawfully made under this title, or any person authorized by such owner, is entitled, without the authority of the copyright owner, to sell or otherwise dispose of the possession of that copy or phonorecord. Notwithstanding the preceding sentence, copies or phonorecords of works subject to restored copyright under section 104A that are manufactured before the date of restoration of copyright or, with respect to reliance parties, before publication or service of notice under section 104A(e), may be sold or otherwise disposed of without the authorization of the owner of the restored copyright for purposes of direct or indirect commercial advantage only during the 12-month period beginning on—

(1) the date of the publication in the Federal Register of the notice of intent filed with the Copyright Office under section 104A(d)(2)(A), or

(2) the date of the receipt of actual notice served under section 104A(d)(2)(B),

whichever occurs first.

(b) (1) (A) Notwithstanding the provisions of subsection (a), unless authorized by the owners of copyright in the sound recording or the owner of copyright in a computer program (including any tape, disk, or other medium embodying such program), and in the case of a sound recording in the musical works embodied therein, neither the owner of a particular phonorecord nor any person in possession of a particular copy of a computer program (including any tape, disk, or other medium embodying such program), may, for the purposes of direct or indirect commercial advantage, dispose of, or authorize the disposal of, the possession of that phonorecord or computer program (including any tape, disk, or other medium embodying such program) by rental, lease, or lending, or by any other act or practice in the nature of rental, lease, or lending. Nothing in the preceding sentence shall apply to the rental, lease, or lending of a phonorecord for nonprofit purposes by a nonprofit library or nonprofit educational institution. The transfer of possession of a lawfully made copy of a computer program by a non-profit educational institution to another nonprofit educational institution or to faculty, staff, and students does not constitute rental, lease, or lending for direct or indirect commercial purposes under this sub-section.

(B) This subsection does not apply to—

(i) a computer program which is embodied in a machine or product and which cannot be copied during the ordinary operation or use of the machine or product; or

(ii) a computer program embodied in or used in conjunction with a limited purpose computer that is designed for playing video games and may be designed for other purposes.

(C) Nothing in this subsection affects any provision of chapter 9 of this title.

(2) (A) Nothing in this subsection shall apply to the lending of a computer program for nonprofit purposes by a nonprofit library, if each copy of a computer program which is lent by such library has affixed to the packaging containing the program a warning of copyright in accord-ance with requirements that the Register of Copyrights shall prescribe by regulation.

(B) Not later than three years after the date of the enactment of the Computer Software Rental Amendments Act of 1990, and at such times thereafter as the Register of Copyrights considers appropriate, the Register of Copyrights, after consultation with representatives of copyright owners and librarians, shall submit to the Congress a report stating whether this paragraph has achieved its intended purpose of maintaining the integrity of the copyright system while providing nonprofit libraries the capability to fulfill their function. Such report shall advise the Congress as to any information or recommendations that the Register of Copyrights considers necessary to carry out the purposes of this subsection.

(3) Nothing in this subsection shall affect any provision of the antitrust laws. For purposes of the preceding sentence, "antitrust laws" has the

meaning given that term in the first section of the Clayton Act and includes section 5 of the Federal Trade Commission Act to the extent that section relates to unfair methods of competition.

(4) Any person who distributes a phonorecord or a copy of a computer program (including any tape, disk, or other medium embodying such program) in violation of paragraph (1) is an infringer of copyright under section 501 of this title and is subject to the remedies set forth in sections 502, 503, 504, and 505. Such violation shall not be a criminal offense under section 506 or cause such person to be subject to the criminal penalties set forth in section 2319 of title 18.

(c) Notwithstanding the provisions of section 106(5), the owner of a particular copy lawfully made under this title, or any person authorized by such owner, is entitled, without the authority of the copyright owner, to display that copy publicly, either directly or by the projection of no more than one image at a time, to viewers present at the place where the copy is located.

(d) The privileges prescribed by subsections (a) and (c) do not, unless authorized by the copyright owner, extend to any person who has acquired possession of the copy or phonorecord from the copyright owner, by rental, lease, loan, or otherwise, without acquiring ownership of it.

(e) Notwithstanding the provisions of sections 106(4) and 106(5), in the case of an electronic audiovisual game intended for use in coin-operated equipment, the owner of a particular copy of such a game lawfully made under this title, is entitled, without the authority of the copyright owner of the game, to publicly perform or display that game in coin-operated equipment, except that this subsection shall not apply to any work of authorship embodied in the audiovisual game if the copyright owner of the electronic audiovisual game is not also the copyright owner of the work of authorship.[2]

(Oct. 19, 1976, Pub. L. 94-553, §101, 90 Stat. 2548; Oct. 4, 1984, Pub. L. 98-450, §2, 98 Stat. 1727; Nov. 5, 1988, Pub. L. 100-617, §2, 102 Stat. 3194; Dec. 1, 1990, Pub. L. 101-650, §802-03, 104 Stat. 5134-35; Dec. 8, 1994, Pub. L. 103-465, §514, 108 Stat. 4976; Nov. 13, 1997, Pub. L. 105-80, §12, 111 Stat. 1534; Oct. 13, 2008, Pub. L. 110-403, §209, 122 Stat. 4264.)

---

[2] *Ed. Note:* Pursuant to section 804 of Public Law 101-650, the amendment made by section 803 took effect one year from date of enactment, which was December 1, 1990. The amendments made by section 803 (enacting §(e)) do not apply to public performances or displays that occur on or after October 1, 1995.

17 U.S.C. § 109

§ 110   Limitations on exclusive rights: Exemption of certain performances and displays

Notwithstanding the provisions of section 106, the following are not infringements of copyright:

(1) performance or display of a work by instructors or pupils in the course of face-to-face teaching activities of a nonprofit educational institution, in a classroom or similar place devoted to instruction, unless, in the case of a motion picture or other audiovisual work, the performance, or the display of individual images, is given by means of a copy that was not lawfully made under this title, and that the person responsible for the performance knew or had reason to believe was not lawfully made;

(2) except with respect to a work produced or marketed primarily for performance or display as part of mediated instructional activities transmitted via digital networks, or a performance or display that is given by means of a copy or phonorecord that is not lawfully made and acquired under this title, and the transmitting government body or accredited nonprofit educational institution knew or had reason to believe was not lawfully made and acquired, the performance of a nondramatic literary or musical work or reasonable and limited portions of any other work, or display of a work in an amount comparable to that which is typically displayed in the course of a live classroom session, by or in the course of a transmission, if—

(A) the performance or display is made by, at the direction of, or under the actual supervision of an instructor as an integral part of a class session offered as a regular part of the systematic mediated instructional activities of a governmental body or an accredited nonprofit educational institution;

(B) the performance or display is directly related and of material assistance to the teaching content of the transmission;

(C) the transmission is made solely for, and, to the extent technologically feasible, the reception of such transmission is limited to—

(i) students officially enrolled in the course for which the transmission is made; or

(ii) officers or employees of governmental bodies as a part of their official duties or employment; and

(D) the transmitting body or institution—

17 U.S.C. § 110

(i) institutes policies regarding copyright, provides informational materials to faculty, students, and relevant staff members that accurately describe, and promote compliance with, the laws of the United States relating to copyright, and provides notice to students that materials used in connection with the course may be subject to copyright protection; and

(ii) in the case of digital transmissions—

(I) applies technological measures that reasonably prevent—

(aa) retention of the work in accessible form by recipients of the transmission from the transmitting body or institution for longer than the class session; and

(bb) unauthorized further dissemination of the work in accessible form by such recipients to others; and

(II) does not engage in conduct that could reasonably be expected to interfere with technological measures used by copyright owners to prevent such retention or unauthorized further dissemination;

(3) performance of a nondramatic literary or musical work or of a dramatico-musical work of a religious nature, or display of a work, in the course of services at a place of worship or other religious assembly;

(4) performance of a nondramatic literary or musical work otherwise than in a transmission to the public, without any purpose of direct or indirect commercial advantage and without payment of any fee or other compensation for the performance to any of its performers, promoters, or organizers, if—

(A) there is no direct or indirect admission charge; or

(B) the proceeds, after deducting the reasonable costs of producing the performance, are used exclusively for educational, religious, or charitable purposes and not for private financial gain, except where the copyright owner has served notice of objection to the performance under the following conditions:

(i) the notice shall be in writing and signed by the copyright owner or such owner's duly authorized agent; and

(ii) the notice shall be served on the person responsible for the performance at least seven days before the date of the performance, and shall state the reasons for the objection; and

(iii) the notice shall comply, in form, content, and manner of service, with requirements that the Register of Copyrights shall prescribe by regulation;

(5)(A) except as provided in subparagraph (B), communication of a transmission embodying a performance or display of a work by the public reception of the transmission on a single receiving apparatus of a kind commonly used in private homes, unless—

(i) a direct charge is made to see or hear the transmission; or

(ii) the transmission thus received is further transmitted to the public;

(B) communication by an establishment of a transmission or retransmission embodying a performance or display of a nondramatic musical work intended to be received by the general public, originated by a radio or television broadcast station licensed as such by the Federal Communications Commission, or, if an audiovisual transmission, by a cable system or satellite carrier, if—

(i) in the case of an establishment other than a food service or drinking establishment, either the establishment in which the communication occurs has less than 2,000 gross square feet of space (excluding space used for customer parking and for no other purpose), or the establishment in which the communication occurs has 2,000 or more gross square feet of space (excluding space used for customer parking and for no other purpose) and—

(I) if the performance is by audio means only, the performance is communicated by means of a total of not more than 6 loudspeakers, of which not more than 4 loudspeakers are located in any 1 room or adjoining outdoor space; or

(II) if the performance or display is by audiovisual means, any visual portion of the performance or display is communicated by means of a total of not more than 4 audiovisual devices, of which not more than 1 audiovisual device is located in any 1 room, and no such audiovisual device has a diagonal screen size greater than 55 inches, and any audio portion of the per-

17 U.S.C. § 110

formance or display is communicated by means of a total of not more than 6 loudspeakers, of which not more than 4 loudspeakers are located in any 1 room or adjoining outdoor space;

(ii) in the case of a food service or drinking establishment, either the establishment in which the communication occurs has less than 3,750 gross square feet of space (excluding space used for customer parking and for no other purpose), or the establishment in which the communication occurs has 3,750 gross square feet of space or more (excluding space used for customer parking and for no other purpose) and—

(I) if the performance is by audio means only, the performance is communicated by means of a total of not more than 6 loudspeakers, of which not more than 4 loudspeakers are located in any 1 room or adjoining outdoor space; or

(II) if the performance or display is by audiovisual means, any visual portion of the performance or display is communicated by means of a total of not more than 4 audiovisual devices, of which not more than one audiovisual device is located in any 1 room, and no such audiovisual device has a diagonal screen size greater than 55 inches, and any audio portion of the performance or display is communicated by means of a total of not more than 6 loudspeakers, of which not more than 4 loudspeakers are located in any 1 room or adjoining outdoor space;

(iii) no direct charge is made to see or hear the transmission or retransmission;

(iv) the transmission or retransmission is not further transmitted beyond the establishment where it is received; and

(v) the transmission or retransmission is licensed by the copyright owner of the work so publicly performed or displayed;

(6) performance of a nondramatic musical work by a governmental body or a nonprofit agricultural or horticultural organization, in the course of an annual agricultural or horticultural fair or exhibition conducted by such body or organization; the exemption provided by this clause shall extend to any liability for copyright infringement that would otherwise be

imposed on such body or organization, under doctrines of vicarious liability or related infringement, for a performance by a concessionnaire, business establishment, or other person at such fair or exhibition, but shall not excuse any such person from liability for the performance;

(7) performance of a nondramatic musical work by a vending establishment open to the public at large without any direct or indirect admission charge, where the sole purpose of the performance is to promote the retail sale of copies or phonorecords of the work, or of the audiovisual or other devices utilized in such performance, and the performance is not transmitted beyond the place where the establishment is located and is within the immediate area where the sale is occurring;

(8) performance of a nondramatic literary work, by or in the course of a transmission specifically designed for and primarily directed to blind or other handicapped persons who are unable to read normal printed material as a result of their handicap, or deaf or other handicapped persons who are unable to hear the aural signals accompanying a transmission of visual signals, if the performance is made without any purpose of direct or indirect commercial advantage and its transmission is made through the facilities of: (i) a governmental body; or (ii) a noncommercial educational broadcast station (as defined in section 397 of title 47); or (iii) a radio subcarrier authorization (as defined in 47 CFR 73.293–73.295 and 73.593–73.595); or (iv) a cable system (as defined in section 111(f)).

(9) performance on a single occasion of a dramatic literary work published at least ten years before the date of the performance, by or in the course of a transmission specifically designed for and primarily directed to blind or other handicapped persons who are unable to read normal printed material as a result of their handicap, if the performance is made without any purpose of direct or indirect commercial advantage and its transmission is made through the facilities of a radio subcarrier authorization referred to in clause (8)(iii), *Provided,* That the provisions of this clause shall not be applicable to more than one performance of the same work by the same performers or under the auspices of the same organization;

(10) notwithstanding paragraph (4), the following is not an infringement of copyright: performance of a nondramatic literary or musical work in the course of a social function which is organized and promoted by a nonprofit veterans' organization or a nonprofit fraternal organization to which the general public is not invited, but not including the invitees of

17 U.S.C. § 110

the organizations, if the proceeds from the performance, after deducting the reasonable costs of producing the performance, are used exclusively for charitable purposes and not for financial gain. For purposes of this section the social functions of any college or university fraternity or sorority shall not be included unless the social function is held solely to raise funds for a specific charitable purpose; and

(11) the making imperceptible, by or at the direction of a member of a private household, of limited portions of audio or video content of a motion picture, during a performance in or transmitted to that household for private home viewing, from an authorized copy of the motion picture, or the creation or provision of a computer program or other technology that enables such making imperceptible and that is designed and marketed to be used, at the direction of a member of a private household, for such making imperceptible, if no fixed copy of the altered version of the motion picture is created by such computer program or other technology.

The exemptions provided under paragraph (5) shall not be taken into account in any administrative, judicial, or other governmental proceeding to set or adjust the royalties payable to copyright owners for the public performance or display of their works. Royalties payable to copyright owners for any public performance or display of their works other than such performances or displays as are exempted under paragraph (5) shall not be diminished in any respect as a result of such exemption.

In paragraph (2), the term "mediated instructional activities" with respect to the performance or display of a work by digital transmission under this section refers to activities that use such work as an integral part of the class experience, controlled by or under the actual supervision of the instructor and analogous to the type of performance or display that would take place in a live classroom setting. The term does not refer to activities that use, in 1 or more class sessions of a single course, such works as textbooks, course packs, or other material in any media, copies or phonorecords of which are typically purchased or acquired by the students in higher education for their independent use and retention or are typically purchased or acquired for elementary and secondary students for their possession and independent use.

For purposes of paragraph (2), accreditation—

(A) with respect to an institution providing post-secondary education, shall be as determined by a regional or national accrediting agency recognized by the Council on Higher Education Accreditation or the United States Department of Education; and

(B) with respect to an institution providing elementary or secondary education, shall be as recognized by the applicable state certification or licensing procedures.

For purposes of paragraph (2), no governmental body or accredited nonprofit educational institution shall be liable for infringement by reason of the transient or temporary storage of material carried out through the automatic technical process of a digital transmission of the performance or display of that material as authorized under paragraph (2). No such material stored on the system or network controlled or operated by the transmitting body or institution under this paragraph shall be maintained on such system or network in a manner ordinarily accessible to anyone other than anticipated recipients. No such copy shall be maintained on the system or network in a manner ordinarily accessible to such anticipated recipients for a longer period than is reasonably necessary to facilitate the transmissions for which it was made.

For purposes of paragraph (11), the term "making imperceptible" does not include the addition of audio or video content that is performed or displayed over or in place of existing content in a motion picture.

Nothing in paragraph (11) shall be construed to imply further rights under section 106 of this title, or to have any effect on defenses or limitations on rights granted under any other section of this title or under any other paragraph of this section.

(Oct. 19, 1976, Pub. L. 94-553, §101, 90 Stat. 2549; Oct. 15, 1982, Pub. L. 97-366, §3, 96 Stat. 1759; Nov. 13, 1997, Pub. L. 105-80, §12, 111 Stat. 1534; Oct. 27, 1998, Pub. L. 105-298, §202(a), (b) , 112 Stat. 2830, 2831; Aug. 5, 1999, Pub. L. 106-44, §1(a), 113 Stat. 221; Nov. 2, 2002, Pub. L. 107-273, §§13210, 13301, 116 Stat. 1910; April 27, 2005, Pub. L. 109-9, §202, 119 Stat. 223.)

§ 111 Limitations on exclusive rights: Secondary transmissions of broadcast programming by cable

(a) *Certain secondary transmissions exempted.*—The secondary transmission of a performance or display of a work embodied in a primary transmission is not an infringement of copyright if—

(1) the secondary transmission is not made by a cable system, and consists entirely of the relaying, by the management of a hotel, apartment house, or similar establishment, of signals transmitted by a broadcast station

licensed by the Federal Communications Commission, within the local service area of such station, to the private lodgings of guests or residents of such establishment, and no direct charge is made to see or hear the secondary transmission; or

(2) the secondary transmission is made solely for the purpose and under the conditions specified by paragraph (2) of section 110; or

(3) the secondary transmission is made by any carrier who has no direct or indirect control over the content or selection of the primary transmission or over the particular recipients of the secondary transmission, and whose activities with respect to the secondary transmission consist solely of providing wires, cables, or other communications channels for the use of others: *Provided,* That the provisions of this paragraph extend only to the activities of said carrier with respect to secondary transmissions and do not exempt from liability the activities of others with respect to their own primary or secondary transmissions;

(4) the secondary transmission is made by a satellite carrier pursuant to a statutory license under section 119 or section 122;

(5) the secondary transmission is not made by a cable system but is made by a governmental body, or other nonprofit organization, without any purpose of direct or indirect commercial advantage, and without charge to the recipients of the secondary transmission other than assessments necessary to defray the actual and reasonable costs of maintaining and operating the secondary transmission service.

(b) *Secondary transmission of primary transmission to controlled group.—* Notwithstanding the provisions of subsections (a) and (c), the secondary transmission to the public of a performance or display of a work embodied in a primary transmission is actionable as an act of infringement under section 501, and is fully subject to the remedies provided by sections 502 through 506, if the primary transmission is not made for reception by the public at large but is controlled and limited to reception by particular members of the public: *Provided,* however, That such secondary transmission is not actionable as an act of infringement if—

(1) the primary transmission is made by a broadcast station licensed by the Federal Communications Commission; and

(2) the carriage of the signals comprising the secondary transmission is required under the rules, regulations, or authorizations of the Federal Communications Commission; and

(3) the signal of the primary transmitter is not altered or changed in any way by the secondary transmitter.

(c) *Secondary transmissions by cable systems.* —

(1) Subject to the provisions of paragraphs (2), (3), and (4) of this subsection and section 114(d), secondary transmissions to the public by a cable system of a performance or display of a work embodied in a primary transmission made by a broadcast station licensed by the Federal Communications Commission or by an appropriate governmental authority of Canada or Mexico shall be subject to statutory licensing upon compliance with the requirements of subsection (d) where the carriage of the signals comprising the secondary transmission is permissible under the rules, regulations, or authorizations of the Federal Communications Commission.

(2) Notwithstanding the provisions of paragraph (1) of this subsection, the willful or repeated secondary transmission to the public by a cable system of a primary transmission made by a broadcast station licensed by the Federal Communications Commission or by an appropriate governmental authority of Canada or Mexico and embodying a performance or display of a work is actionable as an act of infringement under section 501, and is fully subject to the remedies provided by sections 502 through 506, in the following cases:

(A) where the carriage of the signals comprising the secondary transmission is not permissible under the rules, regulations, or authorizations of the Federal Communications Commission; or

(B) where the cable system has not deposited the statement of account and royalty fee required by subsection (d).

(3) Notwithstanding the provisions of paragraph (1) of this subsection and subject to the provisions of subsection (e) of this section, the secondary transmission to the public by a cable system of a performance or display of a work embodied in a primary transmission made by a broadcast station licensed by the Federal Communications Commission or by an appropriate governmental authority of Canada or Mexico is actionable as an act of infringement under section 501, and is fully subject to the remedies

provided by sections 502 through 506 and section 510, if the content of the particular program in which the performance or display is embodied, or any commercial advertising or station announcements transmitted by the primary transmitter during, or immediately before or after, the transmission of such program, is in any way willfully altered by the cable system through changes, deletions, or additions, except for the alteration, deletion, or substitution of commercial advertisements performed by those engaged in television commercial advertising market research: *Provided,* That the research company has obtained the prior consent of the advertiser who has purchased the original commercial advertisement, the television station broadcasting that commercial advertisement, and the cable system performing the secondary transmission: *And provided further,* That such commercial alteration, deletion, or substitution is not performed for the purpose of deriving income from the sale of that commercial time.

(4) Notwithstanding the provisions of paragraph (1) of this subsection, the secondary transmission to the public by a cable system of a primary transmission made by a broadcast station licensed by an appropriate governmental authority of Canada or Mexico and embodying a performance or display of a work is actionable as an act of infringement under section 501, and is fully subject to the remedies provided by sections 502 through 506, if (A) with respect to Canadian signals, the community of the cable system is located more than 150 miles from the United States-Canadian border and is also located south of the forty-second parallel of latitude, or (B) with respect to Mexican signals, the secondary transmission is made by a cable system which received the primary transmission by means other than direct interception of a free space radio wave emitted by such broadcast television station, unless prior to April 15, 1976, such cable system was actually carrying, or was specifically authorized to carry, the signal of such foreign station on the system pursuant to the rules, regulations, or authorizations of the Federal Communications Commission.

(d) *Statutory license for secondary transmissions by cable systems.* —

(1) *Statement of account and royalty fees.* —Subject to paragraph (5), a cable system whose secondary transmissions have been subject to statutory licensing under subsection (c) shall, on a semiannual basis, deposit with the Register of Copyrights, in accordance with requirements that the Register shall prescribe by regulation the following:

(A) A statement of account, covering the six months next preceding, specifying the number of channels on which the cable system made secondary transmissions to its subscribers, the names and locations of all primary transmitters whose transmissions were further transmitted by the cable system, the total number of subscribers, the gross amounts paid to the cable system for the basic service of providing secondary transmissions of primary broadcast transmitters, and such other data as the Register of Copyrights may from time to time prescribe by regulation. In determining the total number of subscribers and the gross amounts paid to the cable system for the basic service of providing secondary transmissions of primary broadcast transmitters, the system shall not include subscribers and amounts collected from subscribers receiving secondary transmissions pursuant to section 119. Such statement shall also include a special statement of account covering any non-network television programming that was carried by the cable system in whole or in part beyond the local service area of the primary transmitter, under rules, regulations, or authorizations of the Federal Communications Commission permitting the substitution or addition of signals under certain circumstances, together with logs showing the times, dates, stations, and programs involved in such substituted or added carriage.

(B) Except in the case of a cable system whose royalty fee is specified in subparagraph (E) or (F), a total royalty fee payable to copyright owners pursuant to paragraph (3) for the period covered by the statement, computed on the basis of specified percentages of the gross receipts from subscribers to the cable service during such period for the basic service of providing secondary transmissions of primary broadcast transmitters, as follows:

(i) 1.064 percent of such gross receipts for the privilege of further transmitting, beyond the local service area of such primary transmitter, any non-network programming of a primary transmitter in whole or in part, such amount to be applied against the fee, if any, payable pursuant to clauses (ii) through (iv);

(ii) 1.064 percent of such gross receipts for the first distant signal equivalent;

(iii) 0.701 percent of such gross receipts for each of the second, third, and fourth distant signal equivalents; and

(iv) 0.330 percent of such gross receipts for the fifth distant signal equivalent and each distant signal equivalent thereafter.

(C) In computing amounts under clauses (ii) through (iv) of subparagraph (B)—

(i) any fraction of a distant signal equivalent shall be computed at its fractional value;

(ii) in the case of any cable system located partly within and partly outside of the local service area of a primary transmitter, gross receipts shall be limited to those gross receipts derived from subscribers located outside of the local service area of such primary transmitter; and

(iii) if a cable system provides a secondary transmission of a primary transmitter to some but not all communities served by that cable system—

(I) the gross receipts and the distant signal equivalent values for such secondary transmission shall be derived solely on the basis of the subscribers in those communities where the cable system provides such secondary transmission; and

(II) the total royalty fee for the period paid by such system shall not be less than the royalty fee calculated under subparagraph (B)(i) multiplied by the gross receipts from all subscribers to the system.

(D) A cable system that, on a statement submitted before the date of the enactment of the Satellite Television Extension and Localism Act of 2010, computed its royalty fee consistent with the methodology under subparagraph (C)(iii), or that amends a statement filed before such date of enactment to compute the royalty fee due using such methodology, shall not be subject to an action for infringement, or eligible for any royalty refund or offset, arising out of its use of such methodology on such statement.

(E) If the actual gross receipts paid by subscribers to a cable system for the period covered by the statement for the basic service of providing secondary transmissions of primary broadcast transmitters are $263,800 or less—

(i) gross receipts of the cable system for the purpose of this paragraph shall be computed by subtracting from such actual gross receipts the amount by which $263,800 exceeds such actual gross receipts, except that in no case shall a cable system's gross receipts be reduced to less than $10,400; and

(ii) the royalty fee payable under this paragraph to copyright owners pursuant to paragraph (3) shall be 0.5 percent, regardless of the number of distant signal equivalents, if any.

(F) If the actual gross receipts paid by subscribers to a cable system for the period covered by the statement for the basic service of providing secondary transmissions of primary broadcast transmitters are more than $263,800 but less than $527,600, the royalty fee payable under this paragraph to copyright owners pursuant to paragraph (3) shall be—

(i) 0.5 percent of any gross receipts up to $263,800, regardless of the number of distant signal equivalents, if any; and

(ii) 1 percent of any gross receipts in excess of $263,800, but less than $527,600, regardless of the number of distant signal equivalents, if any.

(G) A filing fee, as determined by the Register of Copyrights pursuant to section 708(a).

(2) *Handling of fees.*—The Register of Copyrights shall receive all fees (including the filing fee specified in paragraph (1)(G)) deposited under this section and, after deducting the reasonable costs incurred by the Copyright Office under this section, shall deposit the balance in the Treasury of the United States, in such manner as the Secretary of the Treasury directs. All funds held by the Secretary of the Treasury shall be invested in interest-bearing United States securities for later distribution with interest by the Librarian of Congress upon authorization by the Copyright Royalty Judges.

(3) *Distribution of royalty fees to copyright owners.*—The royalty fees thus deposited shall, in accordance with the procedures provided by paragraph (4), be distributed to those among the following copyright owners who claim that their works were the subject of secondary transmissions by cable systems during the relevant semiannual period:

(A) Any such owner whose work was included in a secondary transmission made by a cable system of a non-network television program in whole or in part beyond the local service area of the primary transmitter.

(B) Any such owner whose work was included in a secondary transmission identified in a special statement of account deposited under paragraph (1)(A).

(C) Any such owner whose work was included in non-network programming consisting exclusively of aural signals carried by a cable system in whole or in part beyond the local service area of the primary transmitter of such programs.

(4) *Procedures for royalty fee distribution.*—The royalty fees thus deposited shall be distributed in accordance with the following procedures:

(A) During the month of July in each year, every person claiming to be entitled to statutory license fees for secondary transmissions shall file a claim with the Copyright Royalty Judges, in accordance with requirements that the Copyright Royalty Judges shall prescribe by regulation. Notwithstanding any provisions of the antitrust laws, for purposes of this clause any claimants may agree among themselves as to the proportionate division of statutory licensing fees among them, may lump their claims together and file them jointly or as a single claim, or may designate a common agent to receive payment on their behalf.

(B) After the first day of August of each year, the Copyright Royalty Judges shall determine whether there exists a controversy concerning the distribution of royalty fees. If the Copyright Royalty Judges determine that no such controversy exists, the Copyright Royalty Judges shall authorize the Librarian of Congress to proceed to distribute such fees to the copyright owners entitled to receive them, or to their designated agents, subject to the deduction of reasonable administrative costs under this section. If the Copyright Royalty Judges find the existence of a controversy, the Copyright Royalty Judges shall, pursuant to chapter 8 of this title, conduct a proceeding to determine the distribution of royalty fees.

(C) During the pendency of any proceeding under this subsection, the Copyright Royalty Judges shall have the discretion to authorize the Librarian of Congress to proceed to distribute any amounts that are not in controversy.

(5) *3.75 percent rate and syndicated exclusivity surcharge not applicable to multicast streams.*—The royalty rates specified in sections 256.2(c) and 256.2(d) of title 37, Code of Federal Regulations (commonly referred to as the "3.75 percent rate" and the "syndicated exclusivity surcharge", respec-

tively), as in effect on the date of the enactment of the Satellite Television Extension and Localism Act of 2010,[3] as such rates may be adjusted, or such sections redesignated, thereafter by the Copyright Royalty Judges, shall not apply to the secondary transmission of a multicast stream.

(6) *Verification of accounts and fee payments.*—The Register of Copyrights shall issue regulations to provide for the confidential verification by copyright owners whose works were embodied in the secondary transmissions of primary transmissions pursuant to this section of the information reported on the semiannual statements of account filed under this subsection for accounting periods beginning on or after January 1, 2010, in order that the auditor designated under subparagraph (A) is able to confirm the correctness of the calculations and royalty payments reported therein. The regulations shall—

(A) establish procedures for the designation of a qualified independent auditor—

(i) with exclusive authority to request verification of such a statement of account on behalf of all copyright owners whose works were the subject of secondary transmissions of primary transmissions by the cable system (that deposited the statement) during the accounting period covered by the statement; and

(ii) who is not an officer, employee, or agent of any such copyright owner for any purpose other than such audit;

(B) establish procedures for safeguarding all non-public financial and business information provided under this paragraph;

(C)(i) require a consultation period for the independent auditor to review its conclusions with a designee of the cable system;

(ii) establish a mechanism for the cable system to remedy any errors identified in the auditor's report and to cure any underpayment identified; and

(iii) provide an opportunity to remedy any disputed facts or conclusions;

(D) limit the frequency of requests for verification for a particular cable system and the number of audits that a multiple system operator can be required to undergo in a single year; and

---

[3] The date of enactment was Feb. 27, 2010.

(E) permit requests for verification of a statement of account to be made only within 3 years after the last day of the year in which the statement of account is filed.

(7) *Acceptance of additional deposits.* — Any royalty fee payments received by the Copyright Office from cable systems for the secondary transmission of primary transmissions that are in addition to the payments calculated and deposited in accordance with this subsection shall be deemed to have been deposited for the particular accounting period for which they are received and shall be distributed as specified under this subsection.

(e) *Nonsimultaneous secondary transmissions by cable systems.* —

(1) Notwithstanding those provisions of the subsection (f)(2) relating to nonsimultaneous secondary transmissions by a cable system, any such transmissions are actionable as an act of infringement under section 501, and are fully subject to the remedies provided by sections 502 through 506 and section 510, unless —

(A) the program on the videotape is transmitted no more than one time to the cable system's subscribers;

(B) the copyrighted program, episode, or motion picture videotape, including the commercials contained within such program, episode, or picture, is transmitted without deletion or editing;

(C) an owner or officer of the cable system (i) prevents the duplication of the videotape while in the possession of the system, (ii) prevents unauthorized duplication while in the possession of the facility making the videotape for the system if the system owns or controls the facility, or takes reasonable precautions to prevent such duplication if it does not own or control the facility, (iii) takes adequate precautions to prevent duplication while the tape is being transported, and (iv) subject to paragraph (2), erases or destroys, or causes the erasure or destruction of, the videotape;

(D) within forty-five days after the end of each calendar quarter, an owner or officer of the cable system executes an affidavit attesting (i) to the steps and precautions taken to prevent duplication of the videotape, and (ii) subject to paragraph (2), to the erasure or destruction of all videotapes made or used during such quarter;

(E) such owner or officer places or causes each such affidavit, and affidavits received pursuant to paragraph (2)(C), to be placed in a file, open to public inspection, at such system's main office in the community where the transmission is made or in the nearest community where such system maintains an office; and

(F) the nonsimultaneous transmission is one that the cable system would be authorized to transmit under the rules, regulations, and authorizations of the Federal Communications Commission in effect at the time of the nonsimultaneous transmission if the transmission had been made simultaneously, except that this subparagraph shall not apply to inadvertent or accidental transmissions.

(2) If a cable system transfers to any person a videotape of a program nonsimultaneously transmitted by it, such transfer is actionable as an act of infringement under section 501, and is fully subject to the remedies provided by sections 502 through 506, except that, pursuant to a written, nonprofit contract providing for the equitable sharing of the costs of such videotape and its transfer, a videotape nonsimultaneously transmitted by it, in accordance with paragraph (1), may be transferred by one cable system in Alaska to another system in Alaska, by one cable system in Hawaii permitted to make such nonsimultaneous transmissions to another such cable system in Hawaii, or by one cable system in Guam, the Northern Mariana Islands, the Federated States of Micronesia, the Republic of Palau, or the Republic of the Marshall Islands, to another cable system in any of those five entities, if—

(A) each such contract is available for public inspection in the offices of the cable systems involved, and a copy of such contract is filed, within thirty days after such contract is entered into, with the Copyright Office (which Office shall make each such contract available for public inspection);

(B) the cable system to which the videotape is transferred complies with paragraph (1)(A), (B), (C)(i), (iii), and (iv), and (D) through (F); and

(C) such system provides a copy of the affidavit required to be made in accordance with paragraph (1)(D) to each cable system making a previous nonsimultaneous transmission of the same videotape.

(3) This subsection shall not be construed to supersede the exclusivity protection provisions of any existing agreement, or any such agreement hereafter entered into, between a cable system and a television broadcast station in the area in which the cable system is located, or a network with which such station is affiliated.

(4) As used in this subsection, the term "videotape" means the reproduction of the images and sounds of a program or programs broadcast by a television broadcast station licensed by the Federal Communications Commission, regardless of the nature of the material objects, such as tapes or films, in which the reproduction is embodied.

(f) *Definitions.*—As used in this section, the following terms mean the following:

(1) *Primary transmission.*—A "primary transmission" is a transmission made to the public by a transmitting facility whose signals are being received and further transmitted by a secondary transmission service, regardless of where or when the performance or display was first transmitted. In the case of a television broadcast station, the primary stream and any multicast streams transmitted by the station constitute primary transmissions.

(2) *Secondary transmission.*—A "secondary transmission" is the further transmitting of a primary transmission simultaneously with the primary transmission, or nonsimultaneously with the primary transmission if by a cable system not located in whole or in part within the boundary of the forty-eight contiguous States, Hawaii, or Puerto Rico: *Provided, however,* That a nonsimultaneous further transmission by a cable system located in Hawaii of a primary transmission shall be deemed to be a secondary transmission if the carriage of the television broadcast signal comprising such further transmission is permissible under the rules, regulations, or authorizations of the Federal Communications Commission.

(3) *Cable system.*—A "cable system" is a facility, located in any State, territory, trust territory, or possession of the United States, that in whole or in part receives signals transmitted or programs broadcast by one or more television broadcast stations licensed by the Federal Communications Commission, and makes secondary transmissions of such signals or programs by wires, cables, microwave, or other communications channels to subscribing members of the public who pay for such service. For purposes of determining the royalty fee under subsection (d)(1), two or more cable systems in contiguous communities under common ownership or control or operating from one headend shall be considered as one system.

(4) *Local service area of a primary transmitter.*—The "local service area of a primary transmitter", in the case of both the primary stream and any multicast streams transmitted by a primary transmitter that is a television

broadcast station, comprises the area where such primary transmitter could have insisted upon its signal being retransmitted by a cable system pursuant to the rules, regulations, and authorizations of the Federal Communications Commission in effect on April 15, 1976, or such station's television market as defined in section 76.55(e) of title 47, Code of Federal Regulations (as in effect on September 18, 1993), or any modifications to such television market made, on or after September 18, 1993, pursuant to section 76.55(e) or 76.59 of title 47, Code of Federal Regulations, or within the noise-limited contour as defined in 73.622(e)(1) of title 47, Code of Federal Regulations, or in the case of a television broadcast station licensed by an appropriate governmental authority of Canada or Mexico, the area in which it would be entitled to insist upon its signal being retransmitted if it were a television broadcast station subject to such rules, regulations, and authorizations. In the case of a low power television station, as defined by the rules and regulations of the Federal Communications Commission, the "local service area of a primary transmitter" comprises the designated market area, as defined in section 122(j)(2)(C), that encompasses the community of license of such station and any community that is located outside such designated market area that is either wholly or partially within 35 miles of the transmitter site or, in the case of such a station located in a standard metropolitan statistical area which has one of the 50 largest populations of all standard metropolitan statistical areas (based on the 1980 decennial census of population taken by the Secretary of Commerce), wholly or partially within 20 miles of such transmitter site. The "local service area of a primary transmitter", in the case of a radio broadcast station, comprises the primary service area of such station, pursuant to the rules and regulations of the Federal Communications Commission.

(5) *Distant signal equivalent.—*

(A) *In general.*—Except as provided under subparagraph (B), a "distant signal equivalent"—

(i) is the value assigned to the secondary transmission of any non-network television programming carried by a cable system in whole or in part beyond the local service area of the primary transmitter of such programming; and

(ii) is computed by assigning a value of one to each primary stream and to each multicast stream (other than a simulcast) that is an independent station, and by assigning a value of one-quarter to each primary stream and to each multicast stream (other than a simulcast) that is a network station or a noncommercial educational station.

(B) *Exceptions.*—The values for independent, network, and noncommercial educational stations specified in subparagraph (A) are subject to the following:

(i) Where the rules and regulations of the Federal Communications Commission require a cable system to omit the further transmission of a particular program and such rules and regulations also permit the substitution of another program embodying a performance or display of a work in place of the omitted transmission, or where such rules and regulations in effect on the date of the enactment of the Copyright Act of 1976 permit a cable system, at its election, to effect such omission and substitution of a nonlive program or to carry additional programs not transmitted by primary transmitters within whose local service area the cable system is located, no value shall be assigned for the substituted or additional program.

(ii) Where the rules, regulations, or authorizations of the Federal Communications Commission in effect on the date of the enactment of the Copyright Act of 1976 permit a cable system, at its election, to omit the further transmission of a particular program and such rules, regulations, or authorizations also permit the substitution of another program embodying a performance or display of a work in place of the omitted transmission, the value assigned for the substituted or additional program shall be, in the case of a live program, the value of one full distant signal equivalent multiplied by a fraction that has as its numerator the number of days in the year in which such substitution occurs and as its denominator the number of days in the year.

(iii) In the case of the secondary transmission of a primary transmitter that is a television broadcast station pursuant to the late-night or specialty programming rules of the Federal Communications Commission, or the secondary transmission of a primary transmitter that is a television broadcast station on a part-time basis where full-time carriage is not possible because the cable system lacks the activated channel capacity to retransmit on a full-time basis all signals that it is authorized to carry, the values for independent, network, and noncommercial educational stations set forth in subparagraph (A), as the case may be, shall be multiplied by a fraction that is equal to the ratio of the broadcast hours of such primary transmitter retransmitted by the cable system to the total broadcast hours of the primary transmitter.

(iv) No value shall be assigned for the secondary transmission of the primary stream or any multicast streams of a primary transmitter that is a television broadcast station in any community that is within the local service area of the primary transmitter.

(6) *Network station.* —

(A) *Treatment of primary stream.* —The term "network station" shall be applied to a primary stream of a television broadcast station that is owned or operated by, or affiliated with, one or more of the television networks in the United States providing nationwide transmissions, and that transmits a substantial part of the programming supplied by such networks for a substantial part of the primary stream's typical broadcast day.

(B) *Treatment of multicast streams.* —The term "network station" shall be applied to a multicast stream on which a television broadcast station transmits all or substantially all of the programming of an interconnected program service that—

(i) is owned or operated by, or affiliated with, one or more of the television networks described in subparagraph (A); and

(ii) offers programming on a regular basis for 15 or more hours per week to at least 25 of the affiliated television licensees of the interconnected program service in 10 or more States.

(7) *Independent station.* —The term "independent station" shall be applied to the primary stream or a multicast stream of a television broadcast station that is not a network station or a noncommercial educational station.

(8) *Noncommercial educational station.* —The term "noncommercial educational station" shall be applied to the primary stream or a multicast stream of a television broadcast station that is a noncommercial educational broadcast station as defined in section 397 of the Communications Act of 1934, as in effect on the date of the enactment of the Satellite Television Extension and Localism Act of 2010.

17 U.S.C. § 111

(9) *Primary stream.*—A "primary stream" is—

(A) the single digital stream of programming that, before June 12, 2009, was substantially duplicating the programming transmitted by the television broadcast station as an analog signal; or

(B) if there is no stream described in subparagraph (A), then the single digital stream of programming transmitted by the television broadcast station for the longest period of time.

(10) *Primary transmitter.*—A "primary transmitter" is a television or radio broadcast station licensed by the Federal Communications Commission, or by an appropriate governmental authority of Canada or Mexico, that makes primary transmissions to the public.

(11) *Multicast stream.*—A "multicast stream" is a digital stream of programming that is transmitted by a television broadcast station and is not the station's primary stream.

(12) *Simulcast.*—A "simulcast" is a multicast stream of a television broadcast station that duplicates the programming transmitted by the primary stream or another multicast stream of such station.

(13) *Subscriber; subscribe.*—

(A) *Subscriber.*—The term "subscriber" means a person or entity that receives a secondary transmission service from a cable system and pays a fee for the service, directly or indirectly, to the cable system.

(B) *Subscribe.*—The term "subscribe" means to elect to become a subscriber.

(Oct. 19, 1976, Pub. L. 94-553, §101, 90 Stat. 2550; Aug. 27, 1986, Pub. L. 99-397, §1 and 2, 100 Stat. 848; Nov. 16, 1988, Pub. L. 100-667, §202, 102 Stat. 3949; July 3, 1990, Pub. L. 101-318, §3, 104 Stat. 288; Dec. 17, 1993, Pub. L. 103-198, §6(a), 107 Stat. 2311; Oct. 18, 1994, Pub. L. 103-369, §2, 108 Stat. 3481; Nov. 1, 1995, Pub. L. 104-39, §5(b), 109 Stat. 348; Nov. 29, 1999, Pub. L. 106-113, §1011, 113 Stat. 1501A-543; Nov. 30, 2004, Pub. L. 108-419, §5, 118 Stat. 2361; Dec. 8, 2004, Pub. L. 108-447, §107(b), 118 Stat. 3406, Oct. 6, 2006, Pub. L. 109-303, §4(a), 120 Stat. 1481; May 8, 2008, Pub. L. 110-229, §807, 122 Stat. 874; Oct. 13, 2008, Pub. L. 110-403, §209, 122 Stat. 4264; May 27, 2010,[4] Pub. L. 111-175, §§103, 104, 124 Stat. 1227, 1231; Dec. 4, 2014, Pub. L. 113-200, §§201, 203, 128 Stat. 2066, 2067.)

§ 112   Limitations on exclusive rights: Ephemeral recordings

(a)(1) Notwithstanding the provisions of section 106, and except in the case of a motion picture or other audiovisual work, it is not an infringement of copyright for a transmitting organization entitled to transmit to the public

---

[4] *Ed. Note:* In general, the amendments made by this Public Law took effect on Feb. 27, 2010.

a performance or display of a work, under a license, including a statutory license under section 114(f), or transfer of the copyright or under the limitations on exclusive rights in sound recordings specified by section 114(a), or for a transmitting organization that is a broadcast radio or television station licensed as such by the Federal Communications Commission and that makes a broadcast transmission of a performance of a sound recording in a digital format on a nonsubscription basis, to make no more than one copy or phonorecord of a particular transmission program embodying the performance or display, if—

(A) the copy or phonorecord is retained and used solely by the transmitting organization that made it, and no further copies or phonorecords are reproduced from it; and

(B) the copy or phonorecord is used solely for the transmitting organization's own transmissions within its local service area, or for purposes of archival preservation or security; and

(C) unless preserved exclusively for archival purposes, the copy or phonorecord is destroyed within six months from the date the transmission program was first transmitted to the public.

(2) In a case in which a transmitting organization entitled to make a copy or phonorecord under paragraph (1) in connection with the transmission to the public of a performance or display of a work is prevented from making such copy or phonorecord by reason of the application by the copyright owner of technical measures that prevent the reproduction of the work, the copyright owner shall make available to the transmitting organization the necessary means for permitting the making of such copy or phonorecord as permitted under that paragraph, if it is technologically feasible and economically reasonable for the copyright owner to do so. If the copyright owner fails to do so in a timely manner in light of the transmitting organization's reasonable business requirements, the transmitting organization shall not be liable for a violation of section 1201(a)(1) of this title for engaging in such activities as are necessary to make such copies or phonorecords as permitted under paragraph (1) of this subsection.

(b) Notwithstanding the provisions of section 106, it is not an infringement of copyright for a governmental body or other nonprofit organization entitled to transmit a performance or display of a work, under section 110(2) or under the limitations on exclusive rights in sound recordings specified by section

17 U.S.C. § 112

114(a), to make no more than thirty copies or phonorecords of a particular transmission program embodying the performance or display, if —

(1) no further copies or phonorecords are reproduced from the copies or phonorecords made under this clause; and

(2) except for one copy or phonorecord that may be preserved exclusively for archival purposes, the copies or phonorecords are destroyed within seven years from the date the transmission program was first transmitted to the public.

(c) Notwithstanding the provisions of section 106, it is not an infringement of copyright for a governmental body or other nonprofit organization to make for distribution no more than one copy or phonorecord, for each transmitting organization specified in clause (2) of this subsection, of a particular transmission program embodying a performance of a nondramatic musical work of a religious nature, or of a sound recording of such a musical work, if —

(1) there is no direct or indirect charge for making or distributing any such copies or phonorecords; and

(2) none of such copies or phonorecords is used for any performance other than a single transmission to the public by a transmitting organization entitled to transmit to the public a performance of the work under a license or transfer of the copyright; and

(3) except for one copy or phonorecord that may be preserved exclusively for archival purposes, the copies or phonorecords are all destroyed within one year from the date the transmission program was first transmitted to the public.

(d) Notwithstanding the provisions of section 106, it is not an infringement of copyright for a governmental body or other nonprofit organization entitled to transmit a performance of a work under section 110(8) to make no more than ten copies or phonorecords embodying the performance, or to permit the use of any such copy or phonorecord by any governmental body or nonprofit organization entitled to transmit a performance of a work under section 110(8), if —

(1) any such copy or phonorecord is retained and used solely by the organization that made it, or by a governmental body or nonprofit organization entitled to transmit a performance of a work under section 110(8), and no further copies or phonorecords are reproduced from it; and

17 U.S.C. § 112

(2) any such copy or phonorecord is used solely for transmissions authorized under section 110(8), or for purposes of archival preservation or security; and

(3) the governmental body or nonprofit organization permitting any use of any such copy or phonorecord by any governmental body or nonprofit organization under this subsection does not make any charge for such use.

(e) *Statutory license*—(1) A transmitting organization entitled to transmit to the public a performance of a sound recording under the limitation on exclusive rights specified by section 114(d)(1)(C)(iv) or under a statutory license in accordance with section 114(f) is entitled to a statutory license, under the conditions specified by this subsection, to make no more than 1 phonorecord of the sound recording (unless the terms and conditions of the statutory license allow for more), if the following conditions are satisfied:

(A) The phonorecord is retained and used solely by the transmitting organization that made it, and no further phonorecords are reproduced from it.

(B) The phonorecord is used solely for the transmitting organization's own transmissions originating in the United States under a statutory license in accordance with section 114(f) or the limitation on exclusive rights specified by section 114(d)(1)(C)(iv).

(C) Unless preserved exclusively for purposes of archival preservation, the phonorecord is destroyed within 6 months from the date the sound recording was first transmitted to the public using the phonorecord.

(D) Phonorecords of the sound recording have been distributed to the public under the authority of the copyright owner or the copyright owner authorizes the transmitting entity to transmit the sound recording, and the transmitting entity makes the phonorecord under this subsection from a phonorecord lawfully made and acquired under the authority of the copyright owner.

(2) Notwithstanding any provision of the antitrust laws, any copyright owners of sound recordings and any transmitting organizations entitled to a statutory license under this subsection may negotiate and agree upon royalty rates and license terms and conditions for making phonorecords of such sound recordings under this section and the proportionate divi-

sion of fees paid among copyright owners, and may designate common agents to negotiate, agree to, pay, or receive such royalty payments.

(3) Proceedings under chapter 8 shall determine reasonable rates and terms of royalty payments for the activities specified by paragraph (1) during the 5-year period beginning on January 1 of the second year following the year in which the proceedings are to be commenced, or such other period as the parties may agree. Such rates shall include a minimum fee for each type of service offered by transmitting organizations. Any copyright owners of sound recordings or any transmitting organizations entitled to a statutory license under this subsection may submit to the Copyright Royalty Judges licenses covering such activities with respect to such sound recordings. The parties to each proceeding shall bear their own costs.

(4) The schedule of reasonable rates and terms determined by the Copyright Royalty Judges shall, subject to paragraph (5), be binding on all copyright owners of sound recordings and transmitting organizations entitled to a statutory license under this subsection during the 5-year period specified in paragraph (3), or such other period as the parties may agree. Such rates shall include a minimum fee for each type of service offered by transmitting organizations. The Copyright Royalty Judges shall establish rates that most clearly represent the fees that would have been negotiated in the marketplace between a willing buyer and a willing seller. In determining such rates and terms, the Copyright Royalty Judges shall base their decision on economic, competitive, and programming information presented by the parties, including—

(A) whether use of the service may substitute for or may promote the sales of phonorecords or otherwise interferes with or enhances the copyright owner's traditional streams of revenue; and

(B) the relative roles of the copyright owner and the transmitting organization in the copyrighted work and the service made available to the public with respect to relative creative contribution, technological contribution, capital investment, cost, and risk.

In establishing such rates and terms, the Copyright Royalty Judges may consider the rates and terms under voluntary license agreements described in paragraphs (2) and (3). The Copyright Royalty Judges shall also establish requirements by which copyright owners may receive reasonable notice of the use of their sound recordings under this section, and under which records of such use shall be kept and made available by transmitting organizations entitled to obtain a statutory license under this subsection.

(5) License agreements voluntarily negotiated at any time between 1 or more copyright owners of sound recordings and 1 or more transmitting organizations entitled to obtain a statutory license under this subsection shall be given effect in lieu of any decision by the Librarian of Congress or determination by the Copyright Royalty Judges.

(6) (A) Any person who wishes to make a phonorecord of a sound recording under a statutory license in accordance with this subsection may do so without infringing the exclusive right of the copyright owner of the sound recording under section 106(1) —

(i) by complying with such notice requirements as the Copyright Royalty Judges shall prescribe by regulation and by paying royalty fees in accordance with this subsection; or

(ii) if such royalty fees have not been set, by agreeing to pay such royalty fees as shall be determined in accordance with this subsection.

(B) Any royalty payments in arrears shall be made on or before the 20th day of the month next succeeding the month in which the royalty fees are set.

(7) If a transmitting organization entitled to make a phonorecord under this subsection is prevented from making such phonorecord by reason of the application by the copyright owner of technical measures that prevent the reproduction of the sound recording, the copyright owner shall make available to the transmitting organization the necessary means for permitting the making of such phonorecord as permitted under this subsection, if it is technologically feasible and economically reasonable for the copyright owner to do so. If the copyright owner fails to do so in a timely manner in light of the transmitting organization's reasonable business requirements, the transmitting organization shall not be liable for a violation of section 1201(a)(1) of this title for engaging in such activities as are necessary to make such phonorecords as permitted under this subsection.

(8) Nothing in this subsection annuls, limits, impairs, or otherwise affects in any way the existence or value of any of the exclusive rights of the copyright owners in a sound recording, except as otherwise provided in this subsection, or in a musical work, including the exclusive rights to reproduce and distribute a sound recording or musical work, including by

17 U.S.C. § 112

means of a digital phonorecord delivery, under sections 106(1), 106(3), and 115, and the right to perform publicly a sound recording or musical work, including by means of a digital audio transmission, under sections 106(4) and 106(6).

(f) (1) Notwithstanding the provisions of section 106, and without limiting the application of subsection (b), it is not an infringement of copyright for a governmental body or other nonprofit educational institution entitled under section 110(2) to transmit a performance or display to make copies or phonorecords of a work that is in digital form and, solely to the extent permitted in paragraph (2), of a work that is in analog form, embodying the performance or display to be used for making transmissions authorized under section 110(2), if—

(A) such copies or phonorecords are retained and used solely by the body or institution that made them, and no further copies or phonorecords are reproduced from them, except as authorized under section 110(2); and

(B) such copies or phonorecords are used solely for transmissions authorized under section 110(2).

(2) This subsection does not authorize the conversion of print or other analog versions of works into digital formats, except that such conversion is permitted hereunder, only with respect to the amount of such works authorized to be performed or displayed under section 110(2), if—

(A) no digital version of the work is available to the institution; or

(B) the digital version of the work that is available to the institution is subject to technological protection measures that prevent its use for section 110(2).

(g) The transmission program embodied in a copy or phonorecord made under this section is not subject to protection as a derivative work under this title except with the express consent of the owners of copyright in the preexisting works employed in the program.

(Oct. 19, 1976, Pub. L. 94-553, §101, 90 Stat. 2558; Oct. 28, 1998, Pub. L. 105-304, §§402, 405(b), 112 Stat. 2888, 2899; Aug. 5, 1999, Pub. L. 106-44, §1(b), 113 Stat. 221; Nov. 2, 2002, Pub. L. 107-273, §13301, 116 Stat. 1910; Nov. 30, 2004, Pub. L. 108-419, §5, 118 Stat. 2361.)

17 U.S.C. § 112

§ 113   Scope of exclusive rights in pictorial, graphic, and sculptural works

(a) Subject to the provisions of subsections (b) and (c) of this section, the exclusive right to reproduce a copyrighted pictorial, graphic, or sculptural work in copies under section 106 includes the right to reproduce the work in or on any kind of article, whether useful or otherwise.

(b) This title does not afford, to the owner of copyright in a work that portrays a useful article as such, any greater or lesser rights with respect to the making, distribution, or display of the useful article so portrayed than those afforded to such works under the law, whether title 17 or the common law or statutes of a State, in effect on December 31, 1977, as held applicable and construed by a court in an action brought under this title.

(c) In the case of a work lawfully reproduced in useful articles that have been offered for sale or other distribution to the public, copyright does not include any right to prevent the making, distribution, or display of pictures or photographs of such articles in connection with advertisements or commentaries related to the distribution or display of such articles, or in connection with news reports.

(d) (1) In a case in which—

> (A) a work of visual art has been incorporated in or made part of a building in such a way that removing the work from the building will cause the destruction, distortion, mutilation, or other modification of the work as described in section 106A(a)(3), and

> (B) the author consented to the installation of the work in the building either before the effective date set forth in section 610(a) of the Visual Artists Rights Act of 1990, or in a written instrument executed on or after such effective date that is signed by the owner of the building and the author and that specifies that installation of the work may subject the work to destruction, distortion, mutilation, or other modification, by reason of its removal,

then the rights conferred by paragraphs (2) and (3) of section 106(A(a) shall not apply.

(2) If the owner of a building wishes to remove a work of visual art which is a part of such building and which can be removed from the building without the destruction, distortion, mutilation, or other modification of the work as described in section 106A(a)(3), the author's rights under paragraphs (2) and (3) of section 106A(a) shall apply unless—

(A) the owner has made a diligent, good faith attempt without success to notify the author of the owner's intended action affecting the work of visual art, or

(B) the owner did provide such notice in writing and the person so notified failed, within 90 days after receiving such notice, either to remove the work or to pay its removal.

For purposes of subparagraph (A), an owner shall be presumed to have made a diligent, good faith attempt to send notice if the owner sent such notice by registered mail to the author at the most recent address of the author that was recorded with the Register of Copyrights pursuant to paragraph (3). If the work is removed at the expense of the author, title to that copy of the work shall be deemed to be in the author.

(3) The Register of Copyrights shall establish a system of records whereby any author of a work of visual art that has been incorporated in or made part of a building, may record his or her identity and address with the Copyright Office. The Register shall also establish procedures under which any such author may update the information so recorded, and procedures under which owners of buildings may record with the Copyright Office evidence of their efforts to comply with this subsection.

(Oct. 19, 1976, Pub. L. 94-553, §101, 90 Stat. 2560; Dec. 1, 1990, Pub. L. 101-650, §604, 104 Stat. 5130.)

§ 114   Scope of exclusive rights in sound recordings

(a) The exclusive rights of the owner of copyright in a sound recording are limited to the rights specified by clauses (1), (2), (3) and (6) of section 106, and do not include any right of performance under section 106(4).

(b) The exclusive right of the owner of copyright in a sound recording under clause (1) of section 106 is limited to the right to duplicate the sound recording in the form of phonorecords or copies that directly or indirectly recapture the actual sounds fixed in the recording. The exclusive right of the owner of copyright in a sound recording under clause (2) of section 106 is limited to the right to prepare a derivative work in which the actual sounds fixed in the sound recording are rearranged, remixed, or otherwise altered in sequence or quality. The exclusive rights of the owner of copyright in a sound recording under clauses (1) and (2) of section 106 do not extend to the making or duplication of another sound recording that consists entirely of an independent fixation of other sounds, even though such sounds imitate or simulate those in the copyrighted sound recording. The exclusive rights of the owner of copyright in a sound recording under clauses (1), (2), and (3) of section 106 do not apply to sound recordings included in educational television and radio programs (as defined in section 397 of title 47) distributed or transmitted by or through public broadcasting entities (as defined by section 118(f)): *Provided*, That copies or phonorecords of said programs are not commercially distributed by or through public broadcasting entities to the general public.

(c) This section does not limit or impair the exclusive right to perform publicly, by means of a phonorecord, any of the works specified by section 106(4).

(d) *Limitations on exclusive right.*—Notwithstanding the provisions of section 106(6)—

(1) *Exempt transmissions and retransmissions.*—The performance of a sound recording publicly by means of a digital audio transmission, other than as a part of an interactive service, is not an infringement of section 106(6) if the performance is part of—

(A) a nonsubscription broadcast transmission;

(B) a retransmission of a nonsubscription broadcast transmission: *Provided*, That, in the case of a retransmission of a radio station's broadcast transmission—

(i) the radio station's broadcast transmission is not willfully or repeatedly retransmitted more than a radius of 150 miles from the site of the radio broadcast transmitter, however—

(I) the 150 mile limitation under this clause shall not apply when a nonsubscription broadcast transmission by a radio station licensed by the Federal Communications Commission is retransmitted on a nonsubscription basis by a terrestrial broadcast station, terrestrial translator, or terrestrial repeater licensed by the Federal Communications Commission; and

(II) in the case of a subscription retransmission of a nonsubscription broadcast retransmission covered by subclause (I), the 150 mile radius shall be measured from the transmitter site of such broadcast retransmitter;

(ii) the retransmission is of radio station broadcast transmissions that are—

17 U.S.C. § 114

(I) obtained by the retransmitter over the air;

(II) not electronically processed by the retransmitter to deliver separate and discrete signals; and

(III) retransmitted only within the local communities served by the retransmitter;

(iii) the radio station's broadcast transmission was being retransmitted to cable systems (as defined in section 111(f)) by a satellite carrier on January 1, 1995, and that retransmission was being retransmitted by cable systems as a separate and discrete signal, and the satellite carrier obtains the radio station's broadcast transmission in an analog format: *Provided*, That the broadcast transmission being retransmitted may embody the programming of no more than one radio station; or

(iv) the radio station's broadcast transmission is made by a noncommercial educational broadcast station funded on or after January 1, 1995, under section 396(k) of the Communications Act of 1934 (47 U.S.C. 396(k)), consists solely of noncommercial educational and cultural radio programs, and the retransmission, whether or not simultaneous, is a nonsubscription terrestrial broadcast retransmission; or

(C) a transmission that comes within any of the following categories—

(i) a prior or simultaneous transmission incidental to an exempt transmission, such as a feed received by and then retransmitted by an exempt transmitter: *Provided*, That such incidental transmissions do not include any subscription transmission directly for reception by members of the public;

(ii) a transmission within a business establishment, confined to its premises or the immediately surrounding vicinity;

(iii) a retransmission by any retransmitter, including a multichannel video programming distributor as defined in section 602(12) of the Communications Act of 1934 (47 U.S.C. 522(12)), of a transmission by a transmitter licensed to publicly perform the sound recording as a part of that transmission, if the retransmission is simultaneous with the licensed transmission and authorized by the transmitter; or

(iv) a transmission to a business establishment for use in the ordinary course of its business: *Provided,* That the business recipient does not retransmit the transmission outside of its premises or the immediately surrounding vicinity, and that the transmission does not exceed the sound recording performance complement. Nothing in this clause shall limit the scope of the exemption in clause (ii).

(2) *Statutory licensing of certain transmissions*—The performance of a sound recording publicly by means of a subscription digital audio transmission not exempt under paragraph (1), an eligible nonsubscription transmission, or a transmission not exempt under paragraph (1) that is made by a preexisting satellite digital audio radio service shall be subject to statutory licensing, in accordance with subsection (f) if—

(A)(i) the transmission is not part of an interactive service;

(ii) except in the case of a transmission to a business establishment, the transmitting entity does not automatically and intentionally cause any device receiving the transmission to switch from one program channel to another; and

(iii) except as provided in section 1002(e), the transmission of the sound recording is accompanied, if technically feasible, by the information encoded in that sound recording, if any, by or under the authority of the copyright owner of that sound recording, that identifies the title of the sound recording, the featured recording artist who performs on the sound recording, and related information, including information concerning the underlying musical work and its writer;

(B) in the case of a subscription transmission not exempt under paragraph (1) that is made by a preexisting subscription service in the same transmission medium used by such service on July 31, 1998, or in the case of a transmission not exempt under paragraph (1) that is made by a preexisting satellite digital audio radio service—

(i) the transmission does not exceed the sound recording performance complement; and

(ii) the transmitting entity does not cause to be published by means of an advance program schedule or prior announcement the titles of the specific sound recordings or phonorecords embodying such sound recordings to be transmitted; and

(C) in the case of an eligible nonsubscription transmission or a subscription transmission not exempt under paragraph (1) that is made by a new subscription service or by a preexisting subscription service other than in the same transmission medium used by such service on July 31, 1998—

(i) the transmission does not exceed the sound recording performance complement, except that this requirement shall not apply in the case of a retransmission of a broadcast transmission if the retransmission is made by a transmitting entity that does not have the right or ability to control the programming of the broadcast station making the broadcast transmission, unless—

(I) the broadcast station makes broadcast transmissions—

(aa) in digital format that regularly exceed the sound recording performance complement; or

(bb) in analog format, a substantial portion of which, on a weekly basis, exceed the sound recording performance complement; and

(II) the sound recording copyright owner or its representative has notified the transmitting entity in writing that broadcast transmissions of the copyright owner's sound recordings exceed the sound recording performance complement as provided in this clause;

(ii) the transmitting entity does not cause to be published, or induce or facilitate the publication, by means of an advance program schedule or prior announcement, the titles of the specific sound recordings to be transmitted, the phonorecords embodying such sound recordings, or, other than for illustrative purposes, the names of the featured recording artists, except that this clause does not disqualify a transmitting entity that makes a prior announcement that a particular artist will be featured within an unspecified future time period, and in the case of a retransmission of a broadcast transmission by a transmitting entity that does not have the right or ability to control the programming of the broadcast transmission, the requirement of this clause shall not apply to a prior oral announcement by the broadcast station, or to an advance program schedule published, induced, or facilitated by the broadcast station, if the transmitting entity does not have actual knowledge and has not received written notice from the copyright owner or its representative that the broadcast station publishes or induces or facilitates the publication of such advance program schedule, or if such advance program schedule is a schedule of classical music programming published by the broadcast station in the same manner as published by that broadcast station on or before September 30, 1998;

(iii) the transmission—

(I) is not part of an archived program of less than 5 hours duration

(II) is not part of an archived program of 5 hours or greater in duration that is made available for a period exceeding 2 weeks;

(III) is not part of a continuous program which is of less than 3 hours duration; or

(IV) is not part of an identifiable program in which performances of sound recordings are rendered in a predetermined order, other than an archived or continuous program, that is transmitted at—

(aa) more than 3 times in any 2-week period that have been publicly announced in advance, in the case of a program of less than 1 hour in duration, or

(bb) more than 4 times in any 2-week period that have been publicly announced in advance, in the case of a program of 1 hour or more in duration,

except that the requirement of this subclause shall not apply in the case of a retransmission of a broadcast transmission by a transmitting entity that does not have the right or ability to control the programming of the broadcast transmission, unless the transmitting entity is given notice in writing by the copyright owner of the sound recording that the broadcast station makes broadcast transmissions that regularly violate such requirement;

17 U.S.C. § 114

(iv) the transmitting entity does not knowingly perform the sound recording, as part of a service that offers transmissions of visual images contemporaneously with transmissions of sound recordings, in a manner that is likely to cause confusion, to cause mistake, or to deceive, as to the affiliation, connection, or association of the copyright owner or featured recording artist with the transmitting entity or a particular product or service advertised by the transmitting entity, or as to the origin, sponsorship, or approval by the copyright owner or featured recording artist of the activities of the transmitting entity other than the performance of the sound recording itself;

(v) the transmitting entity cooperates to prevent, to the extent feasible without imposing substantial costs or burdens, a transmission recipient or any other person or entity from automatically scanning the transmitting entity's transmissions alone or together with transmissions by other transmitting entities in order to select a particular sound recording to be transmitted to the transmission recipient, except that the requirement of this clause shall not apply to a satellite digital audio service that is in operation, or that is licensed by the Federal Communications Commission, on or before July 31, 1998;

(vi) the transmitting entity takes no affirmative steps to cause or induce the making of a phonorecord by the transmission recipient, and if the technology used by the transmitting entity enables the transmitting entity to limit the making by the transmission recipient of phonorecords of the transmission directly in a digital format, the transmitting entity sets such technology to limit such making of phonorecords to the extent permitted by such technology;

(vii) phonorecords of the sound recording have been distributed to the public under the authority of the copyright owner or the copyright owner authorizes the transmitting entity to transmit the sound recording, and the transmitting entity makes the transmission from a phonorecord lawfully made under the authority of the copyright owner, except that the requirement of this clause shall not apply to a retransmission of a broadcast transmission by a transmitting entity that does not have the right or ability to control the programming of the broadcast transmission, unless the transmitting entity is given notice in writing by the copyright owner of the sound recording that the broadcast station makes broadcast transmissions that regularly violate such requirement;

(viii) the transmitting entity accommodates and does not interfere with the transmission of technical measures that are widely used by sound recording copyright owners to identify or protect copyrighted works, and that are technically feasible of being transmitted by the transmitting entity without imposing substantial costs on the transmitting entity or resulting in perceptible aural or visual degradation of the digital signal, except that the requirement of this clause shall not apply to a satellite digital audio service that is in operation, or that is licensed under the authority of the Federal Communications Commission, on or before July 31, 1998, to the extent that such service has designed, developed, or made commitments to procure equipment or technology that is not compatible with such technical measures before such technical measures are widely adopted by sound recording copyright owners; and

(ix) the transmitting entity identifies in textual data the sound recording during, but not before, the time it is performed, including the title of the sound recording, the title of the phonorecord embodying such sound recording, if any, and the featured recording artist, in a manner to permit it to be displayed to the transmission recipient by the device or technology intended for receiving the service provided by the transmitting entity, except that the obligation in this clause shall not take effect until 1 year after the date of the enactment of the Digital Millennium Copyright Act and shall not apply in the case of a retransmission of a broadcast transmission by a transmitting entity that does not have the right or ability to control the programming of the broadcast transmission, or in the case in which devices or technology intended for receiving the service provided by the transmitting entity that have the capability to display such textual data are not common in the marketplace.

(3) *Licenses for transmissions by interactive services.* —

(A) No interactive service shall be granted an exclusive license under section 106(6) for the performance of a sound recording publicly by means of digital audio transmission for a period in excess of 12 months, except that with respect to an exclusive license granted to an interactive service by a licensor that holds the copyright to 1,000 or fewer sound recordings, the period of such license shall not exceed 24 months: *Provided, however,* That the grantee of such exclusive license shall be ineligible to receive another exclusive license for the performance of that sound recording for a period of 13 months from the expiration of the prior exclusive license.

(B) The limitation set forth in subparagraph (A) of this paragraph shall not apply if—

(i) the licensor has granted and there remain in effect licenses under section 106(6) for the public performance of sound recordings by means of digital audio transmission by at least 5 different interactive services: *Provided, however,* That each such license must be for a minimum of 10 percent of the copyrighted sound recordings owned by the licensor that have been licensed to interactive services, but in no event less than 50 sound recordings; or

(ii) the exclusive license is granted to perform publicly up to 45 seconds of a sound recording and the sole purpose of the performance is to promote the distribution or performance of that sound recording.

(C) Notwithstanding the grant of an exclusive or nonexclusive license of the right of public performance under section 106(6), an interactive service may not publicly perform a sound recording unless a license has been granted for the public performance of any copyrighted musical work contained in the sound recording: *Provided,* That such license to publicly perform the copyrighted musical work may be granted either by a performing rights society representing the copyright owner or by the copyright owner.

(D) The performance of a sound recording by means of a retransmission of a digital audio transmission is not an infringement of section 106(6) if—

(i) the retransmission is of a transmission by an interactive service licensed to publicly perform the sound recording to a particular member of the public as part of that transmission; and

(ii) the retransmission is simultaneous with the licensed transmission, authorized by the transmitter, and limited to that particular member of the public intended by the interactive service to be the recipient of the transmission.

(E) For the purposes of this paragraph—

(i) a "licensor" shall include the licensing entity and any other entity under any material degree of common ownership, management, or control that owns copyrights in sound recordings; and

(ii) a "performing rights society" is an association or corporation that licenses the public performance of nondramatic musical works on behalf of the copyright owner, such as the American Society of Composers, Authors and Publishers, Broadcast Music, Inc., and SESAC, Inc.

(4) *Rights not otherwise limited.* —

(A) Except as expressly provided in this section, this section does not limit or impair the exclusive right to perform a sound recording publicly by means of a digital audio transmission under section 106(6).

(B) Nothing in this section annuls or limits in any way—

(i) the exclusive right to publicly perform a musical work, including by means of a digital audio transmission, under section 106(4);

(ii) the exclusive rights in a sound recording or the musical work embodied therein under sections 106(1), 106(2) and 106(3); or

(iii) any other rights under any other clause of section 106, or remedies available under this title, as such rights or remedies exist either before or after the date of enactment of the Digital Performance Right in Sound Recordings Act of 1995.

(C) Any limitations in this section on the exclusive right under section 106(6) apply only to the exclusive right under section 106(6) and not to any other exclusive rights under section 106. Nothing in this section shall be construed to annul, limit, impair or otherwise affect in any way the ability of the owner of a copyright in a sound recording to exercise the rights under sections 106(1), 106(2) and 106(3), or to obtain the remedies available under this title pursuant to such rights, as such rights and remedies exist either before or after the date of enactment of the Digital Performance Right in Sound Recordings Act of 1995.

17 U.S.C. § 114

(e) *Authority for negotiations.—*

(1) Notwithstanding any provision of the antitrust laws, in negotiating statutory licenses in accordance with subsection (f), any copyright owners of sound recordings and any entities performing sound recordings affected by this section may negotiate and agree upon the royalty rates and license terms and conditions for the performance of such sound recordings and the proportionate division of fees paid among copyright owners, and may designate common agents on a nonexclusive basis to negotiate, agree to, pay, or receive payments.

(2) For licenses granted under section 106(6), other than statutory licenses, such as for performances by interactive services or performances that exceed the sound recording performance complement—

(A) copyright owners of sound recordings affected by this section may designate common agents to act on their behalf to grant licenses and receive and remit royalty payments: *Provided,* That each copyright owner shall establish the royalty rates and material license terms and conditions unilaterally, that is, not in agreement, combination, or concert with other copyright owners of sound recordings; and

(B) entities performing sound recordings affected by this section may designate common agents to act on their behalf to obtain licenses and collect and pay royalty fees: *Provided,* That each entity performing sound recordings shall determine the royalty rates and material license terms and conditions unilaterally, that is, not in agreement, combination, or concert with other entities performing sound recordings.

(f) *Licenses for certain nonexempt transmissions.—*

(1)(A) Proceedings under chapter 8 shall determine reasonable rates and terms of royalty payments for subscription transmissions by preexisting subscription services and transmissions by pre-existing satellite digital audio radio services specified by subsection (d)(2) during the 5-year period beginning on January 1 of the second year following the year in which the proceedings are to be commenced, except in the case of a different transitional period provided under section 6(b)(3) of the Copyright Royalty and Distribution Reform Act of 2004, or such other period as the parties may agree.

(B) The schedule of reasonable rates and terms determined by the Copyright Royalty Judges shall, subject to paragraph (3), be binding on all copyright owners of sound recordings and entities performing sound recordings affected by this paragraph during the 5-year period specified in subparagraph (A), a transitional period provided under section 6(b)(3) of the Copyright Royalty and Distribution Reform Act of 2004, or such other period as the parties may agree. In establishing rates and terms for preexisting subscription services and preexisting satellite digital audio radio services, in addition to the objectives set forth in section 801(b)(1), the Copyright Royalty Judges may consider the rates and terms for comparable types of subscription digital audio transmission services and comparable circumstances under voluntary license agreements described in subparagraph (A).

(C) The procedures under subparagraphs (A) and (B) also shall be initiated pursuant to a petition filed by any copyright owners of sound recordings, any preexisting subscription services, or any preexisting satellite digital audio radio services indicating that a new type of subscription digital audio transmission service on which sound recordings are performed is or is about to become operational, for the purpose of determining reasonable terms and rates of royalty payments with respect to such new type of transmission service for the period beginning with the inception of such new type of service and ending on the date on which the royalty rates and terms for subscription digital audio transmission services most recently determined under subparagraph (A) or (B) and chapter 8 expire, or such other period as the parties may agree.

(2)(A) Proceedings under chapter 8 shall determine reasonable rates and terms of royalty payments for public performances of sound recordings by means of eligible nonsubscription transmission services and new subscription services specified by subsection (d)(2) during the 5-year period beginning on January 1 of the second year following the year in which the proceedings are to be commenced, except in the case of a different transitional period provided under section 6(b)(3) of the Copyright Royalty and Distribution Reform Act of 2004, or such other period as the parties may agree. Such rates and terms shall distinguish among the different types of eligible nonsubscription transmission services and new subscription services then in operation and shall include a minimum fee for each such type of service. Any copyright

17 U.S.C. § 114

owners of sound recordings or any entities performing sound recordings affected by this paragraph may submit to the Copyright Royalty Judges licenses covering such eligible nonsubscription transmissions and new subscription services with respect to such sound recordings. The parties to each proceeding shall bear their own costs.

(B) The schedule of reasonable rates and terms determined by the Copyright Royalty Judges shall, subject to paragraph (3), be binding on all copyright owners of sound recordings and entities performing sound recordings affected by this paragraph during the 5-year period specified in subparagraph (A), a transitional period provided under section 6(b)(3) of the Copyright Royalty and Distribution Act of 2004, or such other period as the parties may agree. Such rates and terms shall distinguish among the different types of eligible nonsubscription transmission services then in operation and shall include a minimum fee for each such type of service, such differences to be based on criteria including, but not limited to, the quantity and nature of the use of sound recordings and the degree to which use of the service may substitute for or may promote the purchase of phonorecords by consumers. In establishing rates and terms for transmissions by eligible nonsubscription services and new subscription services, the Copyright Royalty Judges shall establish rates and terms that most clearly represent the rates and terms that would have been negotiated in the marketplace between a willing buyer and a willing seller. In determining such rates and terms, the Copyright Royalty Judges shall base their decision on economic, competitive and programming information presented by the parties, including—

> (i) whether use of the service may substitute for or may promote the sales of phonorecords or otherwise may interfere with or may enhance the sound recording copyright owner's other streams of revenue from its sound recordings; and

> (ii) the relative roles of the copyright owner and the transmitting entity in the copyrighted work and the service made available to the public with respect to relative creative contribution, technological contribution, capital investment, cost, and risk.

In establishing such rates and terms, the Copyright Royalty Judges may consider the rates and terms for comparable types of digital audio transmission services and comparable circumstances under voluntary license agreements described in subparagraph (A).

(C) The procedures under subparagraphs (A) and (B) shall also be initiated pursuant to a petition filed by any copyright owners of sound recordings or any eligible nonsubscription service or new subscription service indicating that a new type of eligible nonsubscription service or new subscription service on which sound recordings are performed is or is about to become operational, for the purpose of determining reasonable terms and rates of royalty payments with respect to such new type of service for the period beginning with the inception of such new type of service and ending on the date on which the royalty rates and terms for eligible nonsubscription services and new subscription services, as the case may be, most recently determined under subparagraph (A) or (B) and chapter 8 expire, or such other period as the parties may agree.

(3) License agreements voluntarily negotiated at any time between 1 or more copyright owners of sound recordings and 1 or more entities performing sound recordings shall be given effect in lieu of any decision by the Librarian of Congress or determination by the Copyright Royalty Judges.

(4)(A) The Copyright Royalty Judges shall also establish requirements by which copyright owners may receive reasonable notice of the use of their sound recordings under this section, and under which records of such use shall be kept and made available by entities performing sound recordings. The notice and recordkeeping rules in effect on the day before the effective date of the Copyright Royalty and Distribution Reform Act of 2004 shall remain in effect unless and until new regulations are promulgated by the Copyright Royalty Judges. If new regulations are promulgated under this subparagraph, the Copyright Royalty Judges shall take into account the substance and effect of the rules in effect on the day before the effective date of the Copyright Royalty and Distribution Reform Act of 2004 and shall, to the extent practicable, avoid significant disruption of the functions of any designated agent authorized to collect and distribute royalty fees.

(B) Any person who wishes to perform a sound recording publicly by means of a transmission eligible for statutory licensing under this subsection may do so without infringing the exclusive right of the copyright owner of the sound recording —

(i) by complying with such notice requirements as the Copyright Royalty Judges shall prescribe by regulation and by paying royalty fees in accordance with this subsection; or

(ii) if such royalty fees have not been set, by agreeing to pay such royalty fees as shall be determined in accordance with this subsection.

(C) Any royalty payments in arrears shall be made on or before the twentieth day of the month next succeeding the month in which the royalty fees are set.

(5) (A) Notwithstanding section 112(e) and the other provisions of this subsection, the receiving agent may enter into agreements for the reproduction and performance of sound recordings under section 112(e) and this section by any 1 or more commercial webcasters or noncommercial webcasters for a period of not more than 11 years beginning on January 1, 2005, that, once published in the Federal Register pursuant to subparagraph (B), shall be binding on all copyright owners of sound recordings and other persons entitled to payment under this section, in lieu of any determination by the Copyright Royalty Judges. Any such agreement for commercial webcasters may include provisions for payment of royalties on the basis of a percentage of revenue or expenses, or both, and include a minimum fee. Any such agreement may include other terms and conditions, including requirements by which copyright owners may receive notice of the use of their sound recordings and under which records of such use shall be kept and made available by commercial webcasters or noncommercial webcasters. The receiving agent shall be under no obligation to negotiate any such agreement. The receiving agent shall have no obligation to any copyright owner of sound recordings or any other person entitled to payment under this section in negotiating any such agreement, and no liability to any copyright owner of sound recordings or any other person entitled to payment under this section for having entered into such agreement.

(B) The Copyright Office shall cause to be published in the Federal Register any agreement entered into pursuant to subparagraph (A). Such publication shall include a statement containing the substance of subparagraph (C). Such agreements shall not be included in the Code of Federal Regulations. Thereafter, the terms of such agreement shall be available, as an option, to any commercial webcaster or noncommercial webcaster meeting the eligibility conditions of such agreement.

(C) Neither subparagraph (A) nor any provisions of any agreement entered into pursuant to subparagraph (A), including any rate structure, fees, terms, conditions, or notice and recordkeeping requirements set forth therein, shall be admissible as evidence or otherwise taken into account in any administrative, judicial, or other government proceeding involving the setting or adjustment of the royalties payable for the public performance or reproduction in ephemeral phonorecords or copies of sound recordings, the determination of terms or conditions related thereto, or the establishment of notice or recordkeeping requirements by the Copyright Royalty Judges under paragraph (4) or section 112(e)(4). It is the intent of Congress that any royalty rates, rate structure, definitions, terms, conditions, or notice and recordkeeping requirements, included in such agreements shall be considered as a compromise motivated by the unique business, economic and political circumstances of webcasters, copyright owners, and performers rather than as matters that would have been negotiated in the marketplace between a willing buyer and a willing seller, or otherwise meet the objectives set forth in section 801(b). This subparagraph shall not apply to the extent that the receiving agent and a webcaster that is party to an agreement entered into pursuant to subparagraph (A) expressly authorize the submission of the agreement in a proceeding under this subsection.

(D) Nothing in the Webcaster Settlement Act of 2008, the Webcaster Settlement Act of 2009, or any agreement entered into pursuant to subparagraph (A) shall be taken into account by the United States Court of Appeals for the District of Columbia Circuit in its review of the determination by the Copyright Royalty Judges of May 1, 2007, of rates and terms for the digital performance of sound recordings and ephemeral recordings, pursuant to sections 112 and 114.

(E) As used in this paragraph—

(i) the term "noncommercial webcaster" means a webcaster that—

(I) is exempt from taxation under section 501 of the Internal Revenue Code of 1986 (26 U.S.C. 501);

(II) has applied in good faith to the Internal Revenue Service for exemption from taxation under section 501 of the Internal Revenue Code and has a commercially reasonable expectation that such exemption shall be granted; or

(III) is operated by a State or possession or any governmental entity or subordinate thereof, or by the United States or District of Columbia, for exclusively public purposes;

(ii) the term "receiving agent" shall have the meaning given that term in section 261.2 of title 37, Code of Federal Regulations, as published in the Federal Register on July 8, 2002; and

(iii) the term "webcaster" means a person or entity that has obtained a compulsory license under section 112 or 114 and the implementing regulations therefor.

(F) The authority to make settlements pursuant to subparagraph (A) shall expire at 11:59 p.m. Eastern time on the 30th day after the date of the enactment of the Webcaster Settlement Act of 2009.[6]

(g) *Proceeds from licensing of transmissions.* —

(1) Except in the case of a transmission licensed under a statutory license in accordance with subsection (f) of this section—

(A) a featured recording artist who performs on a sound recording that has been licensed for a transmission shall be entitled to receive payments from the copyright owner of the sound recording in accordance with the terms of the artist's contract; and

(B) a nonfeatured recording artist who performs on a sound recording that has been licensed for a transmission shall be entitled to receive payments from the copyright owner of the sound recording in accordance with the terms of the nonfeatured recording artist's applicable contract or other applicable agreement.

(2) An agent designated to distribute receipts from the licensing of transmissions in accordance with subsection (f) shall distribute such receipts as follows:

---

[6] *Ed. Note:* The date of enactment of the Webcaster Settlement Act of 2009 was June 30, 2009.

17 U.S.C. § 114

(A) 50 percent of the receipts shall be paid to the copyright owner of the exclusive right under section 106(6) of this title to publicly perform a sound recording by means of a digital audio transmission.

(B) 2½ percent of the receipts shall be deposited in an escrow account managed by an independent administrator jointly appointed by copyright owners of sound recordings and the American Federation of Musicians (or any successor entity) to be distributed to nonfeatured musicians (whether or not members of the American Federation of Musicians) who have performed on sound recordings.

(C) 2½ percent of the receipts shall be deposited in an escrow account managed by an independent administrator jointly appointed by copyright owners of sound recordings and the American Federation of Television and Radio Artists (or any successor entity) to be distributed to nonfeatured vocalists (whether or not members of the American Federation of Television and Radio Artists) who have performed on sound recordings.

(D) 45 percent of the receipts shall be paid, on a per sound recording basis, to the recording artist or artists featured on such sound recording (or the persons conveying rights in the artists' performance in the sound recordings).

(3) A nonprofit agent designated to distribute receipts from the licensing of transmissions in accordance with subsection (f) may deduct from any of its receipts, prior to the distribution of such receipts to any person or entity entitled thereto other than copyright owners and performers who have elected to receive royalties from another designated agent and have notified such nonprofit agent in writing of such election, the reasonable costs of such agent incurred after November 1, 1995, in—

(A) the administration of the collection, distribution, and calculation of the royalties;

(B) the settlement of disputes relating to the collection and calculation of the royalties; and

(C) the licensing and enforcement of rights with respect to the making of ephemeral recordings and performances subject to licensing under section 112 and this section, including those incurred in participating in negotiations or arbitration proceedings under section 112 and this section, except that all costs incurred relating to the section 112 ephemeral recordings right may only be deducted from the royalties received pursuant to section 112.

(4) Notwithstanding paragraph (3), any designated agent designated to distribute receipts from the licensing of transmissions in accordance with subsection (f) may deduct from any of its receipts, prior to the distribution of such receipts, the reasonable costs identified in paragraph (3) of such agent incurred after November 1, 1995, with respect to such copyright owners and performers who have entered with such agent a contractual relationship that specifies that such costs may be deducted from such royalty receipts.

(h) *Licensing to affiliates.* —

(1) If the copyright owner of a sound recording licenses an affiliated entity the right to publicly perform a sound recording by means of a digital audio transmission under section 106(6), the copyright owner shall make the licensed sound recording available under section 106(6) on no less favorable terms and conditions to all bona fide entities that offer similar services, except that, if there are material differences in the scope of the requested license with respect to the type of service, the particular sound recordings licensed, the frequency of use, the number of subscribers served, or the duration, then the copyright owner may establish different terms and conditions for such other services.

(2) The limitation set forth in paragraph (1) of this subsection shall not apply in the case where the copyright owner of a sound recording licenses—

(A) an interactive service; or

(B) an entity to perform publicly up to 45 seconds of the sound recording and the sole purpose of the performance is to promote the distribution or performance of that sound recording.

(i) *No effect on royalties for underlying works.*—License fees payable for the public performance of sound recordings under section 106(6) shall not be taken into account in any administrative, judicial, or other governmental proceeding to set or adjust the royalties payable to copyright owners of musical works for the public performance of their works. It is the intent of Congress that royalties payable to copyright owners of musical works for the public performance of their works shall not be diminished in any respect as a result of the rights granted by section 106(6).

17 U.S.C. § 114

(j) *Definitions.*—As used in this section, the following terms have the following meanings:

(1) An "affiliated entity" is an entity engaging in digital audio transmissions covered by section 106(6), other than an interactive service, in which the licensor has any direct or indirect partnership or any ownership interest amounting to 5 percent or more of the outstanding voting or nonvoting stock.

(2) An "archived program" is a predetermined program that is available repeatedly on the demand of the transmission recipient and that is performed in the same order from the beginning, except that an archived program shall not include a recorded event or broadcast transmission that makes no more than an incidental use of sound recordings, as long as such recorded event or broadcast transmission does not contain an entire sound recording or feature a particular sound recording.

(3) A "broadcast" transmission is a transmission made by a terrestrial broadcast station licensed as such by the Federal Communications Commission.

(4) A "continuous program" is a predetermined program that is continuously performed in the same order and that is accessed at a point in the program that is beyond the control of the transmission recipient.

(5) A "digital audio transmission" is a digital transmission as defined in section 101, that embodies the transmission of a sound recording. This term does not include the transmission of any audiovisual work.

(6) An "eligible nonsubscription transmission" is a noninteractive nonsubscription digital audio transmission not exempt under subsection (d)(1) that is made as part of a service that provides audio programming consisting, in whole or in part, of performances of sound recordings, including retransmissions of broadcast transmissions, if the primary purpose of the service is to provide to the public such audio or other entertainment programming, and the primary purpose of the service is not to sell, advertise, or promote particular products or services other than sound recordings, live concerts, or other music-related events.

(7) An "interactive service" is one that enables a member of the public to receive a transmission of a program specially created for the recipient, or on request, a transmission of a particular sound recording, whether or not as part of a program, which is selected by or on behalf of the recipient.

17 U.S.C. § 114

The ability of individuals to request that particular sound recordings be performed for reception by the public at large, or in the case of a subscription service, by all subscribers of the service, does not make a service interactive, if the programming on each channel of the service does not substantially consist of sound recordings that are performed within 1 hour of the request or at a time designated by either the transmitting entity or the individual making such request. If an entity offers both interactive and noninteractive services (either concurrently or at different times), the noninteractive component shall not be treated as part of an interactive service.

(8) A "new subscription service" is a service that performs sound recordings by means of noninteractive subscription digital audio transmissions and that is not a preexisting subscription service or a preexisting satellite digital audio radio service.

(9) A "nonsubscription" transmission is any transmission that is not a subscription transmission.

(10) A "preexisting satellite digital audio radio service" is a subscription satellite digital audio radio service provided pursuant to a satellite digital audio radio service license issued by the Federal Communications Commission on or before July 31, 1998, and any renewal of such license to the extent of the scope of the original license, and may include a limited number of sample channels representative of the subscription service that are made available on a nonsubscription basis in order to promote the subscription service.

(11) A "preexisting subscription service" is a service that performs sound recordings by means of noninteractive audio-only subscription digital audio transmissions, which was in existence and was making such transmissions to the public for a fee on or before July 31, 1998, and may include a limited number of sample channels representative of the subscription service that are made available on a nonsubscription basis in order to promote the subscription service.

(12) A "retransmission" is a further transmission of an initial transmission, and includes any further retransmission of the same transmission. Except as provided in this section, a transmission qualifies as a "retransmission" only if it is simultaneous with the initial transmission. Nothing in this definition shall be construed to exempt a transmission that fails to satisfy a separate element required to qualify for an exemption under section 114(d)(1).

17 U.S.C. § 114

(13) The "sound recording performance complement" is the transmission during any 3-hour period, on a particular channel used by a transmitting entity, of no more than—

(A) 3 different selections of sound recordings from any one phonorecord lawfully distributed for public performance or sale in the United States, if no more than 2 such selections are transmitted consecutively; or

(B) 4 different selections of sound recordings—

(i) by the same featured recording artist; or

(ii) from any set or compilation of phonorecords lawfully distributed together as a unit for public performance or sale in the United States,

if no more than three such selections are transmitted consecutively:

Provided, That the transmission of selections in excess of the numerical limits provided for in clauses (A) and (B) from multiple phonorecords shall nonetheless qualify as a sound recording performance complement if the programming of the multiple phonorecords was not willfully intended to avoid the numerical limitations prescribed in such clauses.

(14) A "subscription" transmission is a transmission that is controlled and limited to particular recipients, and for which consideration is required to be paid or otherwise given by or on behalf of the recipient to receive the transmission or a package of transmissions including the transmission.

(15) A "transmission" is either an initial transmission or a retransmission.

(Oct. 19, 1976, Pub. L. 94-553, §101, 90 Stat. 2560; Nov. 1, 1995, Pub. L. 104-39, §3, 109 Stat. 336; Nov. 13, 1997, Pub. L. 105-80, §3, 111 Stat. 1531; Oct. 28, 1998, Pub. L. 105-304, §405(a), 112 Stat. 2890; Dec. 4, 2002, Pub. L. 107-321, §§4, 5, 116 Stat. 2780; Nov. 30, 2004, Pub. L. 108-419, §5, 118 Stat. 2362; Oct. 6, 2006, Pub. L. 109-303, §4(b), 120 Stat. 1481; Oct. 16, 2008, Pub. L. 110-435, §2, 122 Stat. 4974; June 30, 2009, Pub. L. 111-36, §2, 123 Stat. 1926; Dec. 9, 2010, Pub. L. 111-295, §§5, 6, 124 Stat. 3181.)

§ 115 Scope of exclusive rights in nondramatic musical works: Compulsory license for making and distributing phonorecords

In the case of nondramatic musical works, the exclusive rights provided by clauses (1) and (3) of section 106, to make and to distribute phonorecords of such works, are subject to compulsory licensing under the conditions specified by this section.

(a) *Availability and scope of compulsory license.* —

(1) When phonorecords of a nondramatic musical work have been distributed to the public in the United States under the authority of the copyright owner, any other person, including those who make phonorecords or digital phonorecord deliveries, may, by complying with the provisions of this section, obtain a compulsory license to make and distribute phonorecords of the work. A person may obtain a compulsory license only if his or her primary purpose in making phonorecords is to distribute them to the public for private use, including by means of a digital phonorecord delivery. A person may not obtain a compulsory license for use of the work in the making of phonorecords duplicating a sound recording fixed by another, unless: (i) such sound recording was fixed lawfully; and (ii) the making of the phonorecords was authorized by the owner of copyright in the sound recording or, if the sound recording was fixed before February 15, 1972, by any person who fixed the sound recording pursuant to an express license from the owner of the copyright in the musical work or pursuant to a valid compulsory license for use of such work in a sound recording.

(2) A compulsory license includes the privilege of making a musical arrangement of the work to the extent necessary to conform it to the style or manner of interpretation of the performance involved, but the arrangement shall not change the basic melody or fundamental character of the work, and shall not be subject to protection as a derivative work under this title, except with the express consent of the copyright owner.

(b) *Notice of intention to obtain compulsory license.* —

(1) Any person who wishes to obtain a compulsory license under this section shall, before or within thirty days after making, and before distributing any phonorecords of the work, serve notice of intention to do so on the copyright owner. If the registration or other public records of the Copyright Office do not identify the copyright owner and include an address at which notice can be served, it shall be sufficient to file the notice of intention in the Copyright Office. The notice shall comply, in form, content, and manner of service, with requirements that the Register of Copyrights shall prescribe by regulation.

(2) Failure to serve or file the notice required by clause (1) forecloses the possibility of a compulsory license and, in the absence of a negotiated license, renders the making and distribution of phonorecords actionable

as acts of infringement under section 501 and fully subject to the remedies provided by sections 502 through 506 and 509.

(c) *Royalty payable under compulsory license.*[7]

(1) To be entitled to receive royalties under a compulsory license, the copyright owner must be identified in the registration or other public records of the Copyright Office. The owner is entitled to royalties for phonorecords made and distributed after being so identified, but is not entitled to recover for any phonorecords previously made and distributed.

(2) Except as provided by clause (1), the royalty under a compulsory license shall be payable for every phonorecord made and distributed in accordance with the license. For this purpose, and other than as provided in paragraph (3), a phonorecord is considered "distributed" if the person exercising the compulsory license has voluntarily and permanently parted with its possession. With respect to each work embodied in the phonorecord, the royalty shall be either two and three-fourths cents,[8] or one-half of one cent[9] per minute of playing time or fraction thereof, whichever amount is larger.

(3) (A) A compulsory license under this section includes the right of the compulsory licensee to distribute or authorize the distribution of a phonorecord of a nondramatic musical work by means of a digital transmission which constitutes a digital phonorecord delivery, regardless of whether the digital transmission is also a public performance of the sound recording under section 106(6) of this title or of any nondramatic musical work embodied therein under section 106(4) of this title. For every digital phonorecord delivery by or under the authority of the compulsory licensee—

(i) on or before December 31, 1997, the royalty payable by the compulsory licensee shall be the royalty prescribed under paragraph (2) and chapter 8 of this title; and

(ii) on or after January 1, 1998, the royalty payable by the compulsory licensee shall be the royalty prescribed under subparagraphs (B) through (E) and chapter 8 of this title.

---

[7] *Ed. Note:* Rates are readjusted pursuant to statute. *See* 17 U.S.C. §§801–03.
[8] *Ed. Note:* Rates are readjusted pursuant to statute. *See* 17 U.S.C. §§801–03.
[9] *Ed. Note:* Rates are readjusted pursuant to statute. *See* 17 U.S.C. §§801–03.

(B) Notwithstanding any provision of the antitrust laws, any copyright owners of nondramatic musical works and any persons entitled to obtain a compulsory license under subsection (a)(1) may negotiate and agree upon the terms and rates of royalty payments under this section and the proportionate division of fees paid among copyright owners, and may designate common agents on a nonexclusive basis to negotiate, agree to, pay or receive such royalty payments. Such authority to negotiate the terms and rates of royalty payments includes, but is not limited to, the authority to negotiate the year during which the royalty rates prescribed under this subparagraph and subparagraphs (C) through (E) and chapter 8 of this title shall next be determined.

(C) Proceedings under chapter 8 shall determine reasonable rates and terms of royalty payments for the activities specified by this section during the period beginning with the effective date of such rates and terms, but not earlier than January 1 of the second year following the year in which the petition requesting the proceeding is filed, and ending on the effective date of successor rates and terms, or such other period as the parties may agree. Such terms and rates shall distinguish between (i) digital phonorecord deliveries where the reproduction or distribution of a phonorecord is incidental to the transmission which constitutes the digital phonorecord delivery, and (ii) digital phonorecord deliveries in general. Any copyright owners of nondramatic musical works and any persons entitled to obtain a compulsory license under subsection (a)(1) may submit to the Copyright Royalty Judges licenses covering such activities. The parties to each proceeding shall bear their own costs.

(D) The schedule of reasonable rates and terms determined by the Copyright Royalty Judges shall, subject to subparagraph (E), be binding on all copyright owners of nondramatic musical works and persons entitled to obtain a compulsory license under subsection (a)(1) during the period specified in subparagraph (C), such other period as may be determined pursuant to subparagraphs (B) and (C), or such other period as the parties may agree. Such terms and rates shall distinguish between (i) digital phonorecord deliveries where the reproduction or distribution of a phonorecord is incidental to the transmission which constitutes the digital phonorecord delivery, and (ii) digital phonorecord deliveries in general. In addition to the objectives set forth in section 801(b)(1), in establishing such rates and terms, the Copyright Royalty Judges may consider rates and terms under voluntary license agreements described in subparagraphs (B) and (C). The royalty rates payable for a compulsory license for a digital phonorecord delivery under this section shall be established de novo and no precedential effect shall be given to the amount of the royalty payable by a compulsory licensee for digital phonorecord deliveries on or before December 31, 1997. The Copyright Royalty Judges shall also establish requirements by which copyright owners may receive reasonable notice of the use of their works under this section, and under which records of such use shall be kept and made available by persons making digital phonorecord deliveries.

(E) (i) License agreements voluntarily negotiated at any time between one or more copyright owners of nondramatic musical works and one or more persons entitled to obtain a compulsory license under subsection (a)(1) shall be given effect in lieu of any determination by the Librarian of Congress and Copyright Royalty Judges. Subject to clause (ii), the royalty rates determined pursuant to subparagraph (C) and (D) shall be given effect as to digital phonorecord deliveries in lieu of any contrary royalty rates specified in a contract pursuant to which a recording artist who is the author of a nondramatic musical work grants a license under that person's exclusive rights in the musical work under paragraphs (1) and (3) of section 106 or commits another person to grant a license in that musical work under paragraphs (1) and (3) of section 106, to a person desiring to fix in a tangible medium of expression a sound recording embodying the musical work.

(ii) The second sentence of clause (i) shall not apply to—

(I) a contract entered into on or before June 22, 1995, and not modified thereafter for the purpose of reducing the royalty rates determined pursuant to subparagraph (C) and (D) or of increasing the number of musical works within the scope of the contract covered by the reduced rates, except if a contract entered into on or before June 22, 1995, is modified thereafter for the purpose of increasing the number of musical works within the scope of the contract, any contrary royalty rates specified in the contract shall be given effect in lieu of royalty rates determined pursuant to subparagraph (C) and (D) for the number of musical works within the scope of the contract as of June 22, 1995; and

(II) a contract entered into after the date that the sound recording is fixed in a tangible medium of expression substantially in a form intended for commercial release, if at the time the contract is entered into, the recording artist retains the right to grant licenses as to the musical work under paragraphs (1) and (3) of section 106.

(F) Except as provided in section 1002(e) of this title, a digital phonorecord delivery licensed under this paragraph shall be accompanied by the information encoded in the sound recording, if any, by or under the authority of the copyright owner of that sound recording, that identifies the title of the sound recording, the featured recording artist who performs on the sound recording, and related information, including information concerning the underlying musical work and its writer.

(G) (i) A digital phonorecord delivery of a sound recording is actionable as an act of infringement under section 501, and is fully subject to the remedies provided by sections 502 through 506, unless—

(I) the digital phonorecord delivery has been authorized by the copyright owner of the sound recording; and

(II) the owner of the copyright in the sound recording or the entity making the digital phonorecord delivery has obtained a compulsory license under this section or has otherwise been authorized by the copyright owner of the musical work to distribute or authorize the distribution, by means of a digital phonorecord delivery, of each musical work embodied in the sound recording.

(ii) Any cause of action under this subparagraph shall be in addition to those available to the owner of the copyright in the nondramatic musical work under subsection (c)(6) and section 106(4) and the owner of the copyright in the sound recording under section 106(6).

(H) The liability of the copyright owner of a sound recording for infringement of the copyright in a nondramatic musical work embodied in the sound recording shall be determined in accordance with applicable law, except that the owner of a copyright in a sound recording shall not be liable for a digital phonorecord delivery by a third party if the owner of the copyright in the sound recording does not license the distribution of a phonorecord of the nondramatic musical work.

(I) Nothing in section 1008 shall be construed to prevent the exercise of the rights and remedies allowed by this paragraph, paragraph (6), and chapter 5 in the event of a digital phonorecord delivery, except that no action alleging infringement of copyright may be brought under this title against a manufacturer, importer or distributor of a digital audio recording device, a digital audio recording medium, an analog recording device, or an analog recording medium, or against a consumer, based on the actions described in such section.

(J) Nothing in this section annuls or limits (i) the exclusive right to publicly perform a sound recording or the musical work embodied therein, including by means of a digital transmission, under sections 106(4) and 106(6), (ii) except for compulsory licensing under the conditions specified by this section, the exclusive rights to reproduce and distribute the sound recording and the musical work embodied therein under sections 106(1) and 106(3), including by means of a digital phonorecord delivery, or (iii) any other rights under any other provision of section 106, or remedies available under this title, as such rights or remedies exist either before or after the date of enactment of the Digital Performance Right in Sound Recordings Act of 1995.

(K) The provisions of this section concerning digital phonorecord deliveries shall not apply to any exempt transmissions or retransmissions under section 114(d)(1). The exemptions created in section 114(d)(1) do not expand or reduce the rights of copyright owners under section 106 (1) through (5) with respect to such transmissions and retransmissions.

(4) A compulsory license under this section includes the right of the maker of a phonorecord of a nondramatic musical work under subsection (a)(1) to distribute or authorize distribution of such phonorecord by rental, lease, or lending (or by acts or practices in the nature of rental, lease, or lending). In addition to any royalty payable under clause (2) and chapter 8 of this title, a royalty shall be payable by the compulsory licensee for every act of distribution of a phonorecord by or in the nature of rental, lease, or lending, by or under the authority of the compulsory licensee. With

17 U.S.C. § 115

respect to each nondramatic musical work embodied in the phonorecord, the royalty shall be a proportion of the revenue received by the compulsory licensee from every such act of distribution of the phonorecord under this clause equal to the proportion of the revenue received by the compulsory licensee from distribution of the phonorecord under clause (2) that is payable by a compulsory licensee under that clause and under chapter 8. The Register of Copyrights shall issue regulations to carry out the purpose of this clause.

(5) Royalty payments shall be made on or before the twentieth day of each month and shall include all royalties for the month next preceding. Each monthly payment shall be made under oath and shall comply with requirements that the Register of Copyrights shall prescribe by regulation. The Register shall also prescribe regulations under which detailed cumulative annual statements of account, certified by a certified public accountant, shall be filed for every compulsory license under this section. The regulations covering both the monthly and the annual statements of account shall prescribe the form, content, and manner of certification with respect to the number of records made and the number of records distributed.

(6) If the copyright owner does not receive the monthly payment and the monthly and annual statements of account when due, the owner may give written notice to the licensee that, unless the default is remedied within thirty days from the date of the notice, the compulsory license will be automatically terminated. Such termination renders either the making or the distribution, or both, of all phonorecords for which the royalty has not been paid, actionable as acts of infringement under section 501 and fully subject to the remedies provided by sections 502 through 506.

(d) *Definition.*—As used in this section, the following term has the following meaning: A "digital phonorecord delivery" is each individual delivery of a phonorecord by digital transmission of a sound recording which results in a specifically identifiable reproduction by or for any transmission recipient of a phonorecord of that sound recording, regardless of whether the digital transmission is also a public performance of the sound recording or any nondramatic musical work embodied therein. A digital phonorecord delivery does not result from a real-time, non-interactive subscription transmission of a sound recording where no reproduction of the sound recording or the musical work embodied therein is made from the inception of the transmission

17 U.S.C. § 115

through to its receipt by the transmission recipient in order to make the sound recording audible.

(Oct. 19, 1976, Pub. L. 94-553, §101, 90 Stat. 2561; Oct. 4, 1984, Pub. L. 98-450, §3, 98 Stat. 1727; Nov. 1. 1995, Pub. L. 104-39, §4, 109 Stat. 344; Nov. 13, 1997, Pub. L. 105-80, §§4, 12, 111 Stat. 1531, 1534-5; Nov. 30, 2004, Pub. L. 108-419, §5, 118 Stat. 2364, Oct. 6, 2006, Pub. L. 109-303, §4(c), 120 Stat. 1482; Oct. 13, 2008, Pub. L. 110-403, §209, 122 Stat. 4264.)

§ 116 Negotiated licenses for public performances by means of coin-operated phonorecord players

(a) *Applicability of section.*—This section applies to any nondramatic musical work embodied in a phonorecord.

(b) *Negotiated licenses.*—

(1) *Authority for negotiations.*—Any owners of copyright in works to which this section applies and any operators of coin-operated phonorecord players may negotiate and agree upon the terms and rates of royalty payments for the performance of such works and the proportionate division of fees paid among copyright owners, and may designate common agents to negotiate, agree to, pay, or receive such royalty payments.

(2) *Chapter 8 proceeding.*—Parties not subject to such a negotiation may have the terms and rates and the division of fees described in paragraph (1) determined in a proceeding in accordance with the provisions of chapter 8.

(c) *License agreements superior to determinations by Copyright Royalty Judges.*— License agreements between one or more copyright owners and one or more operators of coin-operated phonorecord players, which are negotiated in accordance with subsection (b), shall be given effect in lieu of any otherwise applicable determination by the Copyright Royalty Judges.

(d) *Definitions.*—As used in this section, the following terms mean the following:

(1) A "coin-operated phonorecord player" is a machine or device that—

(A) is employed solely for the performance of nondramatic musical works by means of phonorecords upon being activated by the insertion of coins, currency, tokens, or other monetary units or their equivalent;

(B) is located in an establishment making no direct or indirect charge for admission;

17 U.S.C. § 116

(C) is accompanied by a list which is comprised of the titles of all the musical works available for performance on it, and is affixed to the phonorecord player or posted in the establishment in a prominent position where it can readily be examined by the public; and

(D) affords a choice of works available for performance and permits the choice to be made by the patrons of the establishment in which it is located.

(2) An "operator" is any person who, alone or jointly with others—

(A) owns a coin-operated phonorecord player;

(B) has the power to make a coin-operated phonorecord player available for placement in an establishment for purposes of public performance; or

(C) has the power to exercise primary control over the selection of the musical works made available for public performance on a coin-operated phonorecord player.

(Oct. 31, 1988, Pub. L. 100-568, §4, 102 Stat. 2855; Dec. 17, 1993, Pub. L. 103-198, §3(b), 107 Stat. 2309; Nov. 13, 1997, Pub. L. 105-80, §5, 111 Stat. 1531; Nov. 30, 2004, Pub. L. 108-419, §5, 118 Stat. 2365.)

§ 117 Limitations on exclusive rights: Computer programs

(a) *Making of additional copy or adaptation by owner of copy.*—Notwithstanding the provisions of section 106, it is not an infringement for the owner of a copy of a computer program to make or authorize the making of another copy or adaptation of that computer program provided:

(1) that such a new copy or adaptation is created as an essential step in the utilization of the computer program in conjunction with a machine and that it is used in no other manner, or

(2) that such new copy or adaptation is for archival purposes only and that all archival copies are destroyed in the event that continued possession of the computer program should cease to be rightful.

(b) *Lease, sale, or other transfer of additional copy or adaptation.*—Any exact copies prepared in accordance with the provisions of this section may be leased, sold, or otherwise transferred, along with the copy from which such copies were prepared, only as part of the lease, sale, or other transfer of all rights in the program. Adaptations so prepared may be transferred only with the authorization of the copyright owner.

(c) *Machine maintenance or repair.*—Notwithstanding the provisions of section 106, it is not an infringement for the owner or lessee of a machine to make or authorize the making of a copy of a computer program if such copy is made solely by virtue of the activation of a machine that lawfully contains an authorized copy of the computer program, for purposes only of maintenance or repair of that machine, if—

(1) such new copy is used in no other manner and is destroyed immediately after the maintenance or repair is completed; and

(2) with respect to any computer program or part thereof that is not necessary for that machine to be activated, such program or part thereof is not accessed or used other than to make such new copy by virtue of the activation of the machine.

(d) *Definitions.*—For purposes of this section—

(1) the "maintenance" of a machine is the servicing of the machine in order to make it work in accordance with its original specifications and any changes to those specifications authorized for that machine; and

(2) the "repair" of a machine is the restoring of the machine to the state of working in accordance with its original specifications and any changes to those specifications authorized for that machine.

(Oct. 19, 1976, Pub. L. 94-553, §101, 90 Stat. 2565; Dec. 12, 1980, Pub. L. 96-517, §10, 94 Stat. 3028; Oct. 28, 1998, Pub. L. 105-304, §302, 112 Stat. 2887.)

§ 118   Scope of exclusive rights: Use of certain works in connection with noncommercial broadcasting

(a) The exclusive rights provided by section 106 shall, with respect to the works specified by subsection (b) and the activities specified by subsection (d), be subject to the conditions and limitations prescribed by this section.

(b) Notwithstanding any provision of the antitrust laws, any owners of copyright in published nondramatic musical works and published pictorial, graphic, and sculptural works and any public broadcasting entities, respectively, may negotiate and agree upon the terms and rates of royalty payments and the proportionate division of fees paid among various copyright owners, and may designate common agents to negotiate, agree to, pay, or receive payments.

(1) Any owner of copyright in a work specified in this subsection or any public broadcasting entity may submit to the Copyright Royalty Judges proposed licenses covering such activities with respect to such works.

(2) License agreements, voluntarily negotiated at any time between one or more copyright owners and one or more public broadcasting entities shall be given effect in lieu of any determination by the Librarian of Congress or the Copyright Royalty Judges, if copies of such agreements are filed with the Copyright Royalty Judges within 30 days of execution in accordance with regulations that the Copyright Royalty Judges shall issue.

(3) Voluntary negotiation proceedings initiated pursuant to a petition filed under section 804(a) for the purpose of determining a schedule of terms and rates of royalty payments by public broadcasting entities to owners of copyright in works specified by this subsection and the proportionate division of fees paid among various copyright owners shall cover the 5-year period beginning on January 1 of the second year following the year in which the petition is filed. The parties to each negotiation proceeding shall bear their own costs.

(4) In the absence of license agreements negotiated under paragraph (2) or (3), the Copyright Royalty Judges shall, pursuant to chapter 8, conduct a proceeding to determine and publish in the Federal Register a schedule of rates and terms which, subject to paragraph (2), shall be binding on all owners of copyright in works specified by this subsection and public broadcasting entities, regardless of whether such copyright owners have submitted proposals to the Copyright Royalty Judges. In establishing such rates and terms the Copyright Royalty Judges may consider the rates for comparable circumstances under voluntary license agreements negotiated as provided in paragraph (2) or (3). The Copyright Royalty Judges shall also establish requirements by which copyright owners may receive reasonable notice of the use of their works under this section, and under which records of such use shall be kept by public broadcasting entities.

(c) Subject to the terms of any voluntary license agreements that have been negotiated as provided by subsection (b)(2) or (3), a public broadcasting entity may, upon compliance with the provisions of this section, including the rates and terms established by the Copyright Royalty Judges under subsection (b)(4), engage in the following activities with respect to published nondramatic musical works and published pictorial, graphic, and sculptural works:

17 U.S.C. § 118

(1) performance or display of a work by or in the course of a transmission made by a noncommercial educational broadcast station referred to in subsection (f); and

(2) production of a transmission program, reproduction of copies or phonorecords of such a transmission program, and distribution of such copies or phonorecords, where such production, reproduction, or distribution is made by a nonprofit institution or organization solely for the purpose of transmissions specified in paragraph (1); and

(3) the making of reproductions by a governmental body or a nonprofit institution of a transmission program simultaneously with its transmission as specified in paragraph (1), and the performance or display of the contents of such program under the conditions specified by paragraph (1) of section 110, but only if the reproductions are used for performances or displays for a period of no more than seven days from the date of the transmission specified in paragraph (1), and are destroyed before or at the end of such period. No person supplying, in accordance with paragraph (2), a reproduction of a transmission program to governmental bodies or nonprofit institutions under this clause shall have any liability as a result of failure of such body or institution to destroy such reproduction: *Provided,* That it shall have notified such body or institution of the requirement for such destruction pursuant to this clause: *And provided further,* That if such body or institution itself fails to destroy such reproduction it shall be deemed to have infringed.

(d) Except as expressly provided in this subsection, this section shall have no applicability to works other than those specified in subsection (b). Owners of copyright in nondramatic literary works and public broadcasting entities may, during the course of voluntary negotiations, agree among themselves, respectively, as to the terms and rates of royalty payments without liability under the antitrust laws. Any such terms and rates of royalty payments shall be effective upon filing with the Copyright Royalty Judges, in accordance with regulations that the Copyright Royalty Judges shall prescribe as provided in section 803(b)(6).

(e) Nothing in this section shall be construed to permit, beyond the limits of fair use as provided by section 107, the unauthorized dramatization of a nondramatic musical work, the production of a transmission program drawn to any substantial extent from a published compilation of pictorial, graphic,

17 U.S.C. § 118

or sculptural works, or the unauthorized use of any portion of an audiovisual work.

(f) As used in this section, the term "public broadcasting entity" means a noncommercial educational broadcast station as defined in section 397 of title 47 and any nonprofit institution or organization engaged in the activities described in paragraph (2) of subsection (c).

(Oct. 19, 1976, Pub. L. 94-553, §101, 90 Stat. 2565; Dec. 17, 1993, Pub. L. 103-198, §4, 107 Stat. 2309; Aug. 5, 1999, Pub. L. 106-44, §1(g), 113 Stat. 222; Nov. 2, 2002, Pub. L. 107-273, §13210, 116 Stat. 1909; Nov. 30, 2004, Pub. L. 108-419, §5, 118 Stat. 2365, Oct. 6, 2006, Pub. L. 109-303, §4(d), 120 Stat. 1482.)

§ 119 Limitations on exclusive rights: Secondary transmissions of distant television programming by satellite[10]

(a) *Secondary transmissions by satellite carriers.* —

(1) *Non-network stations.*—Subject to the provisions of paragraphs (4), (5), and (7) of this subsection and section 114(d), secondary transmissions of a performance or display of a work embodied in a primary transmission made by a non-network station shall be subject to statutory licensing under this section if the secondary transmission is made by a satellite carrier to the public for private home viewing or for viewing in a commercial establishment, with regard to secondary transmissions the satellite carrier is in compliance with the rules, regulations, or authorizations of the Federal Communications Commission governing the carriage of television broadcast station signals, and the carrier makes a direct or indirect charge for each retransmission service to each subscriber receiving the secondary transmission or to a distributor that has contracted with the carrier for direct or indirect delivery of the secondary transmission to the public for private home viewing or for viewing in a commercial establishment.

(2) *Network stations.* —

(A) *In general.*—Subject to the provisions of subparagraph (B) of this paragraph and paragraphs (4), (5), (6), and (7) of this subsection and section 114(d), secondary transmissions of a performance or display of a work embodied in a primary transmission made by a network station shall be subject to statutory licensing under this section if the secondary transmission is made by a satellite carrier to the public for

---

[10] *Ed. Note:* Section 119 expires on Dec. 31, 2014.

17 U.S.C. § 119

private home viewing, with regard to secondary transmissions the satellite carrier is in compliance with the rules, regulations, or authorizations of the Federal Communications Commission governing the carriage of television broadcast station signals, and the carrier makes a direct or indirect charge for such retransmission service to each subscriber receiving the secondary transmission.

(B) *Secondary transmissions to unserved households.* —

(i) *In general.* — The statutory license provided for in subparagraph (A) shall be limited to secondary transmissions of the signals of no more than two network stations in a single day for each television network to persons who reside in unserved households.

(ii) *Accurate determinations of eligibility.* —

(I) *Accurate predictive model.* — In determining presumptively whether a person resides in an unserved household under subsection (d)(10)(A), a court shall rely on the Individual Location Longley-Rice model set forth by the Federal Communications Commission in Docket No. 98-201, as that model may be amended by the Commission over time under section 339(c)(3) of the Communications Act of 1934 to increase the accuracy of that model.

(II) *Accurate measurements.* — For purposes of site measurements to determine whether a person resides in an unserved household under subsection (d)(10)(A), a court shall rely on section 339(c)(4) of the Communications Act of 1934.

(III) *Accurate predictive model with respect to digital signals.* — Notwithstanding subclause (I), in determining presumptively whether a person resides in an unserved household under subsection (d)(10)(A) with respect to digital signals, a court shall rely on a predictive model set forth by the Federal Communications Commission pursuant to a rulemaking as provided in section 339(c)(3) of the Communications Act of 1934 (47 U.S.C. 339(c)(3)), as that model may be amended by the Commission over time under such section to increase the accuracy of that model. Until such time as the Commission sets forth such model, a court shall rely on the predictive model as recommended by the Commission with respect to digital signals in its Report to Congress in ET Docket No. 05-182, FCC 05-199 (released December 9, 2005).

(iii) *C-band exemption to unserved households.* —

(I) *In general.* —The limitations of clause (i) shall not apply to any secondary transmissions by C-band services of network stations that a subscriber to C-band service received before any termination of such secondary transmissions before October 31, 1999.

(II) *Definition.* —In this clause, the term "C-band service" means a service that is licensed by the Federal Communications Commission and operates in the Fixed Satellite Service under part 25 of title 47, Code of Federal Regulations.

(C) *Submission of subscriber lists to networks.* —

(i) *Initial lists.* —A satellite carrier that makes secondary transmissions of a primary transmission made by a network station pursuant to subparagraph (A) shall, not later than 90 days after commencing such secondary transmissions, submit to the network that owns or is affiliated with the network station a list identifying (by name and address, including street or rural route number, city, State, and 9-digit zip code) all subscribers to which the satellite carrier makes secondary transmissions of that primary transmission to subscribers in unserved households.

(ii) *Monthly lists.* —After the submission of the initial lists under clause (i), the satellite carrier shall, not later than the 15th of each month, submit to the network a list, aggregated by designated market area, identifying (by name and address, including street or rural route number, city, State, and 9-digit zip code) any persons who have been added or dropped as subscribers under clause (i) since the last submission under this subparagraph.

(iii) *Use of subscriber information.* —Subscriber information submitted by a satellite carrier under this subparagraph may be used only for purposes of monitoring compliance by the satellite carrier with this subsection.

(iv) *Applicability.* —The submission requirements of this subparagraph shall apply to a satellite carrier only if the network to which the submissions are to be made places on file with the Register of

Copyrights a document identifying the name and address of the person to whom such submissions are to be made. The Register shall maintain for public inspection a file of all such documents.

(3) *Statutory license where retransmissions into local market available.* —

    (A) *Rules for subscribers to signals under subsection (e).* —

        (i) *For those receiving distant signals.* —In the case of a subscriber of a satellite carrier who is eligible to receive the secondary transmission of the primary transmission of a network station solely by reason of subsection (e) (in this subparagraph referred to as a "distant signal"), and who, as of October 1, 2004, is receiving the distant signal of that network station, the following shall apply:

            (I) In a case in which the satellite carrier makes available to the subscriber the secondary transmission of the primary transmission of a local network station affiliated with the same television network pursuant to the statutory license under section 122, the statutory license under paragraph (2) shall apply only to secondary transmissions by that satellite carrier to that subscriber of the distant signal of a station affiliated with the same television network—

                (aa) if, within 60 days after receiving the notice of the satellite carrier under section 338(h)(1) of the Communications Act of 1934, the subscriber elects to retain the distant signal; but

                (bb) only until such time as the subscriber elects to receive such local signal.

            (II) Notwithstanding subclause (I), the statutory license under paragraph (2) shall not apply with respect to any subscriber who is eligible to receive the distant signal of a television network station solely by reason of subsection (e), unless the satellite carrier, within 60 days after the date of the enactment of the Satellite Home Viewer Extension and Reauthorization Act of 2004, submits to that television network a list, aggregated by designated market area (as defined in section 122(j)(2)(C)), that—

(aa) identifies that subscriber by name and address (street or rural route number, city, State, and zip code) and specifies the distant signals received by the subscriber; and

(bb) states, to the best of the satellite carrier's knowledge and belief, after having made diligent and good faith inquiries, that the subscriber is eligible under subsection (e) to receive the distant signals.

(ii) *For those not receiving distant signals.*—In the case of any subscriber of a satellite carrier who is eligible to receive the distant signal of a network station solely by reason of subsection (e) and who did not receive a distant signal of a station affiliated with the same network on October 1, 2004, the statutory license under paragraph (2) shall not apply to secondary transmissions by that satellite carrier to that subscriber of the distant signal of a station affiliated with the same network.

(B) *Rules for lawful subscribers as of date of enactment of 2010 Act.*—In the case of a subscriber of a satellite carrier who, on the day before the date of the enactment of the Satellite Television Extension and Localism Act of 2010, was lawfully receiving the secondary transmission of the primary transmission of a network station under the statutory license under paragraph (2) (in this subparagraph referred to as the "distant signal"), other than subscribers to whom subparagraph (A) applies, the statutory license under paragraph (2) shall apply to secondary transmissions by that satellite carrier to that subscriber of the distant signal of a station affiliated with the same television network, and the subscriber's household shall continue to be considered to be an unserved household with respect to such network, until such time as the subscriber elects to terminate such secondary transmissions, whether or not the subscriber elects to subscribe to receive the secondary transmission of the primary transmission of a local network station affiliated with the same network pursuant to the statutory license under section 122.

(C) *Future applicability.*—

(i) *When local signal available at time of subscription.*—The statutory license under paragraph (2) shall not apply to the secondary transmission by a satellite carrier of the primary transmission of a network station to a person who is not a subscriber lawfully receiving such secondary transmission as of the date of the enactment of the Satellite Television Extension and Localism Act of 2010 and, at the time such person seeks to subscribe to receive such secondary transmission, resides in a local market where the satellite carrier makes available to that person the secondary transmission of the primary transmission of a local network station affiliated with the same network pursuant to the statutory license under section 122.

(ii) *When local signal available after subscription.*—In the case of a subscriber who lawfully subscribes to and receives the secondary transmission by a satellite carrier of the primary transmission of a network station under the statutory license under paragraph (2) (in this clause referred to as the "distant signal") on or after the date of the enactment of the Satellite Television Extension and Localism Act of 2010, the statutory license under paragraph (2) shall apply to secondary transmissions by that satellite carrier to that subscriber of the distant signal of a station affiliated with the same television network, and the subscriber's household shall continue to be considered to be an unserved household with respect to such network, until such time as the subscriber elects to terminate such secondary transmissions, but only if such subscriber subscribes to the secondary transmission of the primary transmission of a local network station affiliated with the same network within 60 days after the satellite carrier makes available to the subscriber such secondary transmission of the primary transmission of such local network station.

(D) *Other provisions not affected.*—This paragraph shall not affect the applicability of the statutory license to secondary transmissions to unserved households included under paragraph (11).

(E) *Waiver.*—A subscriber who is denied the secondary transmission of a network station under subparagraph (B) or (C) may request a waiver from such denial by submitting a request, through the subscriber's satellite carrier, to the network station in the local market affiliated with the same network where the subscriber is located. The network station shall accept or reject the subscriber's request for a waiver within 30 days after receipt of the request. If the network station fails to accept or reject the subscriber's request for a waiver within that 30-day period, that network station shall be deemed to agree to the waiver request. Unless specifically stated by the network station, a waiver that was granted before the date of the enactment of the Satellite Home Viewer Extension and Reauthorization Act of 2004 under section 339(c)(2) of the Communications Act of 1934 shall not constitute a waiver for purposes of this subparagraph.

(F) *Available defined.*—For purposes of this paragraph, a satellite carrier makes available a secondary transmission of the primary transmission of a local station to a subscriber or person if the satellite carrier offers that secondary transmission to other subscribers who reside in the same 9-digit zip code as that subscriber or person.

(4) *Noncompliance with reporting and payment requirements.*— Notwithstanding the provisions of paragraphs (1) and (2), the willful or repeated secondary transmission to the public by a satellite carrier of a primary transmission made by a non-network station or a network station and embodying a performance or display of a work is actionable as an act of infringement under section 501, and is fully subject to the remedies provided by sections 502 through 506, where the satellite carrier has not deposited the statement of account and royalty fee required by subsection (b), or has failed to make the submissions to networks required by paragraph (2)(C).

(5) *Willful alterations.*—Notwithstanding the provisions of paragraphs (1) and (2), the secondary transmission to the public by a satellite carrier of a performance or display of a work embodied in a primary transmission made by a non-network station or a network station is actionable as an act of infringement under section 501, and is fully subject to the remedies provided by sections 502 through 506 and section 510, if the content of the particular program in which the performance or display is embodied, or any commercial advertising or station announcement transmitted by the primary transmitter during, or immediately before or after, the transmission of such program, is in any way willfully altered by the satellite carrier through changes, deletions, or additions, or is combined with programming from any other broadcast signal.

(6) *Violation of territorial restrictions on statutory license for network stations.* —

(A) *Individual violations.*—The willful or repeated secondary transmission by a satellite carrier of a primary transmission made by a network station and embodying a performance or display of a work to a subscriber who is not eligible to receive the transmission under this section is actionable as an act of infringement under section 501 and is fully subject to the remedies provided by sections 502 through 506, except that—

(i) no damages shall be awarded for such act of infringement if the satellite carrier took corrective action by promptly withdrawing service from the ineligible subscriber, and

(ii) any statutory damages shall not exceed $250 for such subscriber for each month during which the violation occurred.

(B) *Pattern of violations.*—If a satellite carrier engages in a willful or repeated pattern or practice of delivering a primary transmission made by a network station and embodying a performance or display of a work to subscribers who are not eligible to receive the transmission under this section, then in addition to the remedies set forth in subparagraph (A)—

(i) if the pattern or practice has been carried out on a substantially nationwide basis, the court shall order a permanent injunction barring the secondary transmission by the satellite carrier, for private home viewing, of the primary transmissions of any primary network station affiliated with the same network, and the court may order statutory damages of not to exceed $2,500,000 for each 3-month period during which the pattern or practice was carried out; and

(ii) if the pattern or practice has been carried out on a local or regional basis, the court shall order a permanent injunction barring the secondary transmission, for private home viewing in that locality or region, by the satellite carrier of the primary transmissions of any primary network station affiliated with the same network, and the court may order statutory damages of not to exceed $2,500,000 for each 6-month period during which the pattern or practice was carried out.

The court shall direct one half of any statutory damages ordered under clause (i) to be deposited with the Register of Copyrights for distribution to copyright owners pursuant to subsection (b). The Copyright Royalty Judges shall issue regulations establishing procedures for distributing such funds, on a proportional basis, to copyright owners whose works were included in the secondary transmissions that were the subject of the statutory damages.[11]

(C) *Previous subscribers excluded.*—Subparagraphs (A) and (B) do not apply to secondary transmissions by a satellite carrier to persons who subscribed to receive such secondary transmissions from the satellite carrier or a distributor before November 16, 1988.

(D) *Burden of proof.*—In any action brought under this paragraph, the satellite carrier shall have the burden of proving that its secondary transmission of a primary transmission by a network station is to a subscriber who is eligible to receive the secondary transmission under this section.[12]

(E) *Exception*— The secondary transmission by a satellite carrier of a performance or display of a work embodied in a primary transmission made by a network station to subscribers who do not reside in un-served households shall not be an act of infringement if—

(i) the station on May 1, 1991, was retransmitted by a satellite carrier and was not on that date owned or operated by or affiliated with a television network that offered interconnected program service on a regular basis for 15 or more hours per week to at least 25 affiliated television licensees in 10 or more States;

(ii) as of July 1, 1998, such station was retransmitted by a satellite carrier under the statutory license of this section; and

(iii) the station is not owned or operated by or affiliated with a television network that, as of January 1, 1995, offered interconnected program service on a regular basis for 15 or more hours per week to at least 25 affiliated television licensees in 10 or more States.

(7) *Discrimination by a satellite carrier.*—Notwithstanding the provisions of paragraph (1), the willful or repeated secondary transmission to the public by a satellite carrier of a performance or display of a work embodied in a primary transmission made by a non-network station or a network station is actionable as an act of infringement under section 501, and is fully sub-

---

[11] *Ed. Note:* The preceding two sentences probably should be inserted here even though Pub. L. 111-175 would place them at the end of section 119(a)(6).

[12] *Ed. Note:* Pursuant to Section 6(b) of Pub. L. 103-369, the provisions of §119(a)(5)(D) took effect on Jan. 1, 1997, with respect to civil matters relating to the eligibility of subscribers who subscribed to service as an unserved household before Oct. 18, 1994.

17 U.S.C. § 119

ject to the remedies provided by sections 502 through 506, if the satellite carrier unlawfully discriminates against a distributor.

(8) *Geographic limitation on secondary transmissions.* —The statutory license created by this section shall apply only to secondary transmissions to households located in the United States.

(9) *Loser pays for signal intensity measurement; recovery of measurement costs in a civil action.* —In any civil action filed relating to the eligibility of subscribing households as unserved households—

    (A) a network station challenging such eligibility shall, within 60 days after receipt of the measurement results and a statement of such costs, reimburse the satellite carrier for any signal intensity measurement that is conducted by that carrier in response to a challenge by the network station and that establishes the household is an unserved household; and

    (B) a satellite carrier shall, within 60 days after receipt of the measurement results and a statement of such costs, reimburse the network station challenging such eligibility for any signal intensity measurement that is conducted by that station and that establishes the household is not an unserved household.

(10) *Inability to conduct measurement.* —If a network station makes a reasonable attempt to conduct a site measurement of its signal at a subscriber's household and is denied access for the purpose of conducting the measurement, and is otherwise unable to conduct a measurement, the satellite carrier shall within 60 days notice thereof, terminate service of the station's network to that household.

(11) *Service to recreational vehicles and commercial trucks.* —

    (A) *Exemption.* —

        (i) *In general.* —For purposes of this subsection, and subject to clauses (ii) and (iii), the term "unserved household" shall include—

            (I) recreational vehicles as defined in regulations of the Secretary of Housing and Urban Development under section 3282.8 of title 24, Code of Federal Regulations; and

(II) commercial trucks that qualify as commercial motor vehicles under regulations of the Secretary of Transportation under section 383.5 of title 49, Code of Federal Regulations.

(ii) *Limitation.* —Clause (i) shall apply only to a recreational vehicle or commercial truck if any satellite carrier that proposes to make a secondary transmission of a network station to the operator of such a recreational vehicle or commercial truck complies with the documentation requirements under subparagraphs (B) and (C).

(iii) *Exclusion.* —For purposes of this subparagraph, the terms "recreational vehicle" and "commercial truck" shall not include any fixed dwelling, whether a mobile home or otherwise.

(B) *Documentation requirements.* —A recreational vehicle or commercial truck shall be deemed to be an unserved household beginning 10 days after the relevant satellite carrier provides to the network that owns or is affiliated with the network station that will be secondarily transmitted to the recreational vehicle or commercial truck the following documents:

(i) *Declaration.* —A signed declaration by the operator of the recreational vehicle or commercial truck that the satellite dish is permanently attached to the recreational vehicle or commercial truck, and will not be used to receive satellite programming at any fixed dwelling.

(ii) *Registration.* —In the case of a recreational vehicle, a copy of the current State vehicle registration for the recreational vehicle.

(iii) *Registration and license.* —In the case of a commercial truck, a copy of—

(I) the current State vehicle registration for the truck; and

(II) a copy of a valid, current commercial driver's license, as defined in regulations of the Secretary of Transportation under section 383 of title 49, Code of Federal Regulations, issued to the operator.

(C) *Updated documentation requirements.* —If a satellite carrier wishes to continue to make secondary transmissions to a recreational vehicle or commercial truck for more than a 2-year period, that carrier shall provide each network, upon request, with updated documentation in the form described under subparagraph (B) during the 90 days before expiration of that 2-year period.

(12) *Statutory license contingent on compliance with FCC rules and remedial steps.*—Notwithstanding any other provision of this section, the willful or repeated secondary transmission to the public by a satellite carrier of a primary transmission embodying a performance or display of a work made by a broadcast station licensed by the Federal Communications Commission is actionable as an act of infringement under section 501, and is fully subject to the remedies provided by sections 502 through 506, if, at the time of such transmission, the satellite carrier is not in compliance with the rules, regulations, and authorizations of the Federal Communications Commission concerning the carriage of television broadcast station signals.

(13) *Waivers.*—A subscriber who is denied the secondary transmission of a signal of a network station under subsection (a)(2)(B) may request a waiver from such denial by submitting a request, through the subscriber's satellite carrier, to the network station asserting that the secondary transmission is prohibited. The network station shall accept or reject a subscriber's request for a waiver within 30 days after receipt of the request. If a television network station fails to accept or reject a subscriber's request for a waiver within the 30-day period after receipt of the request, that station shall be deemed to agree to the waiver request and have filed such written waiver. Unless specifically stated by the network station, a waiver that was granted before the date of the enactment of the Satellite Home Viewer Extension and Reauthorization Act of 2004 under section 339(c)(2) of the Communications Act of 1934, and that was in effect on such date of enactment, shall constitute a waiver for purposes of this paragraph.

(14) *Restricted transmission of out-of-state distant network signals into certain markets.*—

   (A) *Out-of-state network affiliates.*—Notwithstanding any other provision of this title, the statutory license in this subsection and subsection (b) shall not apply to any secondary transmission of the primary transmission of a network station located outside of the State of Alaska to any subscriber in that State to whom the secondary transmission of the primary transmission of a television station located in that State is made available by the satellite carrier pursuant to section 122.

17 U.S.C. § 119

(B) *Exception.* — The limitation in subparagraph (A) shall not apply to the secondary transmission of the primary transmission of a digital signal of a network station located outside of the State of Alaska if at the time that the secondary transmission is made, no television station licensed to a community in the State and affiliated with the same network makes primary transmissions of a digital signal.

(b) *Deposit of statements and fees; verification procedures.* —

(1) *Deposits with the Register of Copyrights.* — A satellite carrier whose secondary transmissions are subject to statutory licensing under subsection (a) shall, on a semiannual basis, deposit with the Register of Copyrights, in accordance with requirements that the Register shall prescribe by regulation —

(A) a statement of account, covering the preceding 6-month period, specifying the names and locations of all non-network stations and network stations whose signals were retransmitted, at any time during that period, to subscribers as described in subsections (a)(1) and (a)(2), the total number of subscribers that received such retransmissions, and such other data as the Register of Copyrights may from time to time prescribe by regulation;

(B) a royalty fee payable to copyright owners pursuant to paragraph (4) for that 6-month period, computed by multiplying the total number of subscribers receiving each secondary transmission of a primary stream or multicast stream of each non-network station or network station during each calendar year month by the appropriate rate in effect under this subsection; and

(C) a filing fee, as determined by the Register of Copyrights pursuant to section 708(a).

(2) *Verification of accounts and fee payments.* — The Register of Copyrights shall issue regulations to permit interested parties to verify and audit the statements of account and royalty fees submitted by satellite carriers under this subsection.

(3) *Investment of fees.* — The Register of Copyrights shall receive all fees (including the filing fee specified in paragraph (1)(C)) deposited under this section and, after deducting the reasonable costs incurred by the Copyright Office under this section (other than the costs deducted under paragraph (5)), shall deposit the balance in the Treasury of the United

States, in such manner as the Secretary of the Treasury directs. All funds held by the Secretary of the Treasury shall be invested in interest-bearing securities of the United States for later distribution with interest by the Librarian of Congress as provided by this title.

(4) *Persons to whom fees are distributed.*—The royalty fees deposited under paragraph (3) shall, in accordance with the procedures provided by paragraph (5), be distributed to those copyright owners whose works were included in a secondary transmission for private home viewing made by a satellite carrier during the applicable 6-month accounting period and who file a claim with the Copyright Royalty Judges under paragraph (5).

(5) *Procedures for distribution.*—The royalty fees deposited under paragraph (3) shall be distributed in accordance with the following procedures:

(A) *Filing of claims for fees.*—During the month of July in each year, each person claiming to be entitled to statutory license fees for secondary transmissions shall file a claim with the Copyright Royalty Judges, in accordance with requirements that the Copyright Royalty Judges shall prescribe by regulation. For purposes of this paragraph, any claimants may agree among themselves as to the proportionate division of statutory license fees among them, may lump their claims together and file them jointly or as a single claim, or may designate a common agent to receive payment on their behalf.

(B) *Determination of controversy; distributions.*—After the first day of August of each year, the Copyright Royalty Judges shall determine whether there exists a controversy concerning the distribution of royalty fees. If the Copyright Royalty Judges determine that no such controversy exists, the Copyright Royalty Judges shall authorize the Librarian of Congress to proceed to distribute such fees to the copyright owners entitled to receive them, or to their designated agents, subject to the deduction of reasonable administrative costs under this section. If the Copyright Royalty Judges find the existence of a controversy, the Copyright Royalty Judges shall, pursuant to chapter 8 of this title, conduct a proceeding to determine the distribution of royalty fees.

(C) *Withholding of fees during controversy.*—During the pendency of any proceeding under this subsection, the Copyright Royalty Judges shall have the discretion to authorize the Librarian of Congress to proceed to distribute any amounts that are not in controversy.

(c) *Adjustment of Royalty Fees.* —

(1) *Applicability and determination of royalty fees for signals.* —

(A) *Initial fee.* — The appropriate fee for purposes of determining the royalty fee under subsection (b)(1)(B) for the secondary transmission of the primary transmissions of network stations and non-network stations shall be the appropriate fee set forth in part 258 of title 37, Code of Federal Regulations, as in effect on July 1, 2009, as modified under this paragraph.

(B) *Fee set by voluntary negotiation.* — On or before June 1, 2010, the Copyright Royalty Judges shall cause to be published in the Federal Register of the initiation of voluntary negotiation proceedings for the purpose of determining the royalty fee to be paid by satellite carriers for the secondary transmission of the primary transmissions of network stations and non-network stations under subsection (b)(1)(B).

(C) *Negotiations.* — Satellite carriers, distributors, and copyright owners entitled to royalty fees under this section shall negotiate in good faith in an effort to reach a voluntary agreement or agreements for the payment of royalty fees. Any such satellite carriers, distributors and copyright owners may at any time negotiate and agree to the royalty fee, and may designate common agents to negotiate, agree to, or pay such fees. If the parties fail to identify common agents, the Copyright Royalty Judges shall do so, after requesting recommendations from the parties to the negotiation proceeding. The parties to each negotiation proceeding shall bear the cost thereof.

(D) *Agreements binding on parties, filing of agreements; public notice.* —

(i) *Voluntary agreements; filing.* — Voluntary agreements negotiated at any time in accordance with this paragraph shall be binding upon all satellite carriers, distributors, and copyright owners that are parties thereto. Copies of such agreements shall be filed with the Copyright Office within 30 days after execution in accordance with regulations that the Register of Copyright shall prescribe.

(ii) *Procedure for adoption of fees.* —

(I) *Publication of notice.* — Within 10 days after publication in the Federal Register of a notice of the initiation of voluntary negotiation proceedings, parties who have reached a voluntary agreement may request that the royalty fees in that agreement be applied to all satellite carriers, distributors, and copyright owners without convening a proceeding under subparagraph (F).

(II) *Public notice of fees.*—Upon receiving a request under subclause (I), the Copyright Royalty Judges shall immediately provide public notice of the royalty fees from the voluntary agreement and afford parties an opportunity to state that they object to those fees.

(III) *Adoption of fees.*—The Copyright Royalty Judges shall adopt the royalty fees from the voluntary agreement for all satellite carriers, distributors, and copyright owners without convening the proceeding under subparagraph (F) unless a party with an intent to participate in that proceeding and a significant interest in the outcome of that proceeding objects under subclause (II).

(E) *Period agreement is in effect.*—The obligation to pay the royalty fees established under a voluntary agreement which has been filed with the Copyright Royalty Judges in accordance with this paragraph shall become effective on the date specified in the agreement, and shall remain in effect until December 31, 2019, or in accordance with the terms of the agreement, whichever is later.

(F) *Fee set by Copyright Royalty Judges proceeding.*—

(i) *Notice of initiation of the proceeding.*—On or before September 1, 2010, the Copyright Royalty Judges shall cause notice to be published in the Federal Register of the initiation of a proceeding for the purpose of determining the royalty fees to be paid for the secondary transmission of the primary transmissions of network stations and non-network stations under subsection (b)(1)(B) by satellite carriers and distributors—

(I) in the absence of a voluntary agreement filed in accordance with subparagraph (D) that establishes royalty fees to be paid by all satellite carriers and distributors; or

(II) if an objection to the fees from a voluntary agreement submitted for adoption by the Copyright Royalty Judges to apply to all satellite carriers, distributors, and copyright owners is received under subparagraph (D) from a party with an intent to participate in the proceeding and a significant interest in the outcome of that proceeding.

Such proceeding shall be conducted under chapter 8.

(ii) *Establishment of royalty fees.*— In determining royalty fees under this subparagraph, the Copyright Royalty Judges shall establish fees for the secondary transmissions of the primary transmissions of network stations and non-network stations that most clearly represent the fair market value of secondary transmissions, except that the Copyright Royalty Judges shall adjust royalty fees to account for the obligations of the parties under any applicable voluntary agreement filed with the Copyright Royalty Judges in accordance with subparagraph (D). In determining the fair market value, the Judges shall base their decision on economic, competitive, and programming information presented by the parties, including—

(I) the competitive environment in which such programming is distributed, the cost of similar signals in similar private and compulsory license marketplaces, and any special features and conditions of the retransmission marketplace;

(II) the economic impact of such fees on copyright owners and satellite carriers; and

(III) the impact on the continued availability of secondary transmissions to the public.

(iii) *Effective date for decision of Copyright Royalty Judges.*—The obligation to pay the royalty fees established under a determination that is made by the Copyright Royalty Judges in a proceeding under this paragraph shall be effective as of January 1, 2010.

(iv) *Persons subject to royalty fees.*—The royalty fees referred to in clause (iii) shall be binding on all satellite carriers, distributors and copyright owners, who are not party to a voluntary agreement filed with the Copyright Office under subparagraph (D).

(2) *Annual royalty fee adjustment.*—Effective January 1 of each year, the royalty fee payable under subsection (b)(1)(B) for the secondary transmission of the primary transmissions of network stations and non-network stations shall be adjusted by the Copyright Royalty Judges to reflect any changes occurring in the cost of living as determined by the most recent Consumer Price Index (for all consumers and for all items) published by

the Secretary of Labor before December 1 of the preceding year. Notification of the adjusted fees shall be published in the Federal Register at least 25 days before January 1.

(d) *Definitions.*—As used in this section—

(1) *Distributor.*—The term "distributor" means an entity that contracts to distribute secondary transmissions from a satellite carrier and, either as a single channel or in a package with other programming, provides the secondary transmission either directly to individual subscribers or indirectly through other program distribution entities in accordance with the provisions of this section.

(2) *Network station.*—The term "network station" means—

(A) a television station licensed by the Federal Communications Commission, including any translator station or terrestrial satellite station that rebroadcasts all or substantially all of the programming broadcast by a network station, that is owned or operated by, or affiliated with, one or more of the television networks in the United States that offer an interconnected program service on a regular basis for 15 or more hours per week to at least 25 of its affiliated television licensees in 10 or more States; or

(B) a noncommercial educational broadcast station (as defined in section 397 of the Communications Act of 1934);

except that the term does not include the signal of the Alaska Rural Communications Service, or any successor entity to that service.

(3) *Primary network station.*—The term "primary network station" means a network station that broadcasts or rebroadcasts the basic programming service of a particular national network.

(4) *Primary transmission.*—The term "primary transmission" has the meaning given that term in section 111(f) of this title.

(5) *Private home viewing.*—The term "private home viewing" means the viewing, for private use in a household by means of satellite reception equipment that is operated by an individual in that household and that serves only such household, of a secondary transmission delivered by a satellite carrier of a primary transmission of a television station licensed by the Federal Communications Commission.

(6) *Satellite carrier.*—The term "satellite carrier" means an entity that uses the facilities of a satellite or satellite service licensed by the Federal Communications Commission and operates in the Fixed-Satellite Service under part 25 of title 47, Code of Federal Regulations, or the Direct Broadcast Satellite Service under part 100 of title 47, Code of Federal Regulations, to establish and operate a channel of communications for point-to-multipoint distribution of television station signals, and that owns or leases a capacity or service on a satellite in order to provide such point-to-multipoint distribution, except to the extent that such entity provides such distribution pursuant to tariff under the Communications Act of 1934, other than for private home viewing pursuant to this section.

(7) *Secondary transmission.*—The term "secondary transmission" has the meaning given that term in section 111(f) of this title.

(8) *Subscriber; subscribe.*—

(A) *Subscriber.*—The term "subscriber" means a person or entity that receives a secondary transmission service from a satellite carrier and pays a fee for the service, directly or indirectly, to the satellite carrier or to a distributor.

(B) *Subscribe.*—The term "subscribe" means to elect to become a subscriber.

(9) *Non-network station.*—The term "non-network station" means a television station, other than a network station, licensed by the Federal Communications Commission, that is secondarily transmitted by a satellite carrier.

(10) *Unserved household.*—The term "unserved household", with respect to a particular television network, means a household that—

(A) cannot receive, through the use of an antenna, an over-the-air signal containing the primary stream, or, on or after the qualifying date, the multicast stream, originating in that household's local market and affiliated with that network of—

(i) if the signal originates as an analog signal, Grade B intensity as defined by the Federal Communications Commission in section 73.683(a) of title 47, Code of Federal Regulations, as in effect on January 1, 1999; or

(ii) if the signal originates as a digital signal, intensity defined in the values for the digital television noise-limited service contour, as defined in regulations issued by the Federal Communications Commission (section 73.622(e) of title 47, Code of Federal Regulations), as such regulations may be amended from time to time;

(B) is subject to a waiver that meets the standards of subsection (a)(13) whether or not the waiver was granted before the date of the enactment of the Satellite Television Extension and Localism Act of 2010.[13]

(C) is a subscriber to whom subsection (e) applies;

(D) is a subscriber to whom subsection (a)(11) applies; or

(E) is a subscriber to whom the exemption under subsection (a)(2)(B)(iii) applies.

(11) *Local market.*—The term "local market" has the meaning given such term under section 122(j).

(12) *Commercial establishment.*—The term "commercial establishment"—

(A) means an establishment used for commercial purposes, such as a bar, restaurant, private office, fitness club, oil rig, retail store, bank or other financial institution, supermarket, automobile or boat dealership, or any other establishment with a common business area; and

(B) does not include a multi-unit permanent or temporary dwelling where private home viewing occurs, such as a hotel, dormitory, hospital, apartment, condominium, or prison.

(13) *Qualifying date.*—The term "qualifying date", for purposes of paragraph (10)(A), means—

(A) October 1, 2010, for multicast streams that exist on March 31, 2010; and

(B) January 1, 2011, for all other multicast streams.

(14) *Multicast stream.*—The term "multicast stream" means a digital stream containing programming and program-related material affiliated with a television network, other than the primary stream.

(15) *Primary stream.*—The term "primary stream" means—

(A) the single digital stream of programming as to which a television broadcast station has the right to mandatory carriage with a satellite carrier under the rules of the Federal Communications Commission in effect on July 1, 2009; or

---

[13] The date of enactment of the Satellite Television Extension and Localism Act of 2010 was Feb. 27, 2010.

17 U.S.C. § 119

(B) if there is no stream described in subparagraph (A), then either—

(i) the single digital stream of programming associated with the network last transmitted by the station as an analog signal; or

(ii) if there is no stream described in clause (i), then the single digital stream of programming affiliated with the network that, as of July 1, 2009, had been offered by the television broadcast station for the longest period of time.

(e) *Moratorium on copyright liability.*—Until December 31, 2019, a subscriber who does not receive a signal of Grade A intensity (as defined in the regulations of the Federal Communications Commission under section 73.683(a) of title 47, Code of Federal Regulations, as in effect on January 1, 1999, or predicted by the Federal Communications Commission using the Individual Location Longley-Rice methodology described by the Federal Communications Commission in Docket No. 98-201) of a local network television broadcast station shall remain eligible to receive signals of network stations affiliated with the same network, if that subscriber had satellite service of such network signal terminated after July 11, 1998, and before October 31, 1999, as required by this section, or received such service on October 31, 1999.

(f) *Expedited consideration by Justice Department of voluntary agreements to provide satellite secondary transmissions to local markets.* —

(1) *In general.*—In a case in which no satellite carrier makes available, to subscribers located in a local market, as defined in section 122(j)(2), the secondary transmission into that market of a primary transmission of one or more television broadcast stations licensed by the Federal Communications Commission, and two or more satellite carriers request a business review letter in accordance with section 50.6 of title 28, Code of Federal Regulations (as in effect on July 7, 2004), in order to assess the legality under the antitrust laws of proposed business conduct to make or carry out an agreement to provide such secondary transmission into such local market, the appropriate official of the Department of Justice shall respond to the request no later than 90 days after the date on which the request is received.

(2) *Definition.*—For purposes of this subsection the term "antitrust laws"—

(A) has the meaning given that term in subsection (a) of the first section of the Clayton Act (15 U.S.C. 12(a)), except that such term includes section 5 of the Federal Trade Commission Act (15 U.S.C. 45) to the extent such section 5 applies to unfair methods of competition; and

(B) includes any State law similar to the laws referred to in paragraph (1).

(g) *Certain waivers granted to providers of local-into-local service to all DMAs.* —

(1) *Injunction waiver.*—A court that issued an injunction pursuant to subsection (a)(7)(B) before the date of the enactment of this subsection shall waive such injunction if the court recognizes the entity against which the injunction was issued as a qualified carrier.

(2) *Limited temporary waiver.* —

(A) *In general.* —Upon a request made by a satellite carrier, a court that issued an injunction against such carrier under subsection (a)(7)(B) before the date of the enactment of this subsection shall waive such injunction with respect to the statutory license provided under subsection (a)(2) to the extent necessary to allow such carrier to make secondary transmissions of primary transmissions made by a network station to unserved households located in short markets in which such carrier was not providing local service pursuant to the license under section 122 as of December 31, 2009.

(B) *Expiration of temporary waiver.*—A temporary waiver of an injunction under subparagraph (A) shall expire after the end of the 120-day period beginning on the date such temporary waiver is issued unless extended for good cause by the court making the temporary waiver.

(C) *Failure to provide local-into-local service to all DMAs.* —

(i) *Failure to act reasonably and in good faith.* —If the court issuing a temporary waiver under subparagraph (A) determines that the satellite carrier that made the request for such waiver has failed to act reasonably or has failed to make a good faith effort to provide local-into-local service to all DMAs, such failure—

(I) is actionable as an act of infringement under section 501 and the court may in its discretion impose the remedies provided for in sections 502 through 506 and subsection (a)(6)(B) of this section; and

(II) shall result in the termination of the waiver issued under subparagraph (A).

(ii) *Failure to provide local-into-local service.* —If the court issuing a temporary waiver under subparagraph (A) determines that the satellite carrier that made the request for such waiver has failed to provide local-into-local service to all DMAs, but determines that the carrier acted reasonably and in good faith, the court may in its discretion impose financial penalties that reflect—

(I) the degree of control the carrier had over the circumstances that resulted in the failure;

(II) the quality of the carrier's efforts to remedy the failure; and

(III) the severity and duration of any service interruption.

(D) *Single temporary waiver available.*—An entity may only receive one temporary waiver under this paragraph.

(E) *Short market defined.*—For purposes of this paragraph, the term "short market" means a local market in which programming of one or more of the four most widely viewed television networks nationwide as measured on the date of the enactment of this subsection is not offered on the primary stream transmitted by any local television broadcast station.

(3) *Establishment of qualified carrier recognition.*—

(A) *Statement of eligibility.*—An entity seeking to be recognized as a qualified carrier under this subsection shall file a statement of eligibility with the court that imposed the injunction. A statement of eligibility must include—

(i) an affidavit that the entity is providing local-into-local service to all DMAs;

(ii) a motion for a waiver of the injunction;

(iii) a motion that the court appoint a special master under Rule 53 of the Federal Rules of Civil Procedure;

(iv) an agreement by the carrier to pay all expenses incurred by the special master under paragraph (4)(B)(ii); and

(v) a certification issued pursuant to section 342(a) of Communications Act of 1934.

(B) *Grant of recognition as a qualified carrier.*—Upon receipt of a statement of eligibility, the court shall recognize the entity as a qualified carrier and issue the waiver under paragraph (1). Upon motion pursuant to subparagraph (A)(iii), the court shall appoint a special master to conduct the examination and provide a report to the court as provided in paragraph (4)(B).

(C) *Voluntary termination.* —At any time, an entity recognized as a qualified carrier may file a statement of voluntary termination with the court certifying that it no longer wishes to be recognized as a qualified carrier. Upon receipt of such statement, the court shall reinstate the injunction waived under paragraph (1).

(D) *Loss of recognition prevents future recognition.* —No entity may be recognized as a qualified carrier if such entity had previously been recognized as a qualified carrier and subsequently lost such recognition or voluntarily terminated such recognition under subparagraph (C).

(4) *Qualified carrier obligations and compliance.* —

(A) *Continuing obligations.* —

(i) *In general.* —An entity recognized as a qualified carrier shall continue to provide local-into-local service to all DMAs.

(ii) *Cooperation with compliance examination.* —An entity recognized as a qualified carrier shall fully cooperate with the special master appointed by the court under paragraph (3)(B) in an examination set forth in subparagraph (B).

(B) *Qualified carrier compliance examination.* —

(i) *Examination and report.* —A special master appointed by the court under paragraph (3)(B) shall conduct an examination of, and file a report on, the qualified carrier's compliance with the royalty payment and household eligibility requirements of the license under this section. The report shall address the qualified carrier's conduct during the period beginning on the date on which the qualified carrier is recognized as such under paragraph (3)(B) and ending on April 30, 2012.

(ii) *Records of qualified carrier.* —Beginning on the date that is one year after the date on which the qualified carrier is recognized as such under paragraph (3)(B), but not later than December 1, 2011, the qualified carrier shall provide the special master with all records that the special master considers to be directly pertinent to the following requirements under this section:

(I) Proper calculation and payment of royalties under the statutory license under this section.

(II) Provision of service under this license to eligible subscribers only.

(iii) *Submission of report.*—The special master shall file the report required by clause (i) not later than July 24, 2012, with the court referred to in paragraph (1) that issued the injunction, and the court shall transmit a copy of the report to the Register of Copyrights, the Committees on the Judiciary and on Energy and Commerce of the House of Representatives, and the Committees on the Judiciary and on Commerce, Science, and Transportation of the Senate.

(iv) *Evidence of infringement.*—The special master shall include in the report a statement of whether the examination by the special master indicated that there is substantial evidence that a copyright holder could bring a successful action under this section against the qualified carrier for infringement.

(v) *Subsequent examination.*—If the special master's report includes a statement that its examination indicated the existence of substantial evidence that a copyright holder could bring a successful action under this section against the qualified carrier for infringement, the special master shall, not later than 6 months after the report under clause (i) is filed, initiate another examination of the qualified carrier's compliance with the royalty payment and household eligibility requirements of the license under this section since the last report was filed under clause (iii). The special master shall file a report on the results of the examination conducted under this clause with the court referred to in paragraph (1) that issued the injunction, and the court shall transmit a copy to the Register of Copyrights, the Committees on the Judiciary and on Energy and Commerce of the House of Representatives, and the Committees on the Judiciary and on Commerce, Science, and Transportation of the Senate. The report shall include a statement described in clause (iv).

(vi) *Compliance.*—Upon motion filed by an aggrieved copyright owner, the court recognizing an entity as a qualified carrier shall terminate such designation upon finding that the entity has failed to cooperate with an examination required by this subparagraph.

(vii) *Oversight.*—During the period of time that the special master is conducting an examination under this subparagraph, the Comptroller General shall monitor the degree to which the entity seeking to be recognized or recognized as a qualified carrier under paragraph (3) is complying with the special master's examination. The qualified carrier shall make available to the Comptroller General all records and individuals that the Comptroller General considers necessary to meet the Comptroller General's obligations under this clause. The Comptroller General shall report the results of the monitoring required by this clause to the Committees on the Judiciary and on Energy and Commerce of the House of Representatives and the Committees on the Judiciary and on Commerce, Science, and Transportation of the Senate at intervals of not less than six months during such period.

(C) *Affirmation.*—A qualified carrier shall file an affidavit with the district court and the Register of Copyrights 30 months after such status was granted stating that, to the best of the affiant's knowledge, it is in compliance with the requirements for a qualified carrier. The qualified carrier shall attach to its affidavit copies of all reports or orders issued by the court, the special master, and the Comptroller General.

(D) *Compliance determination.*—Upon the motion of an aggrieved television broadcast station, the court recognizing an entity as a qualified carrier may make a determination of whether the entity is providing local-into-local service to all DMAs.

(E) *Pleading requirement.*—In any motion brought under subparagraph (D), the party making such motion shall specify one or more designated market areas (as such term is defined in section 122(j)(2)(C)) for which the failure to provide service is being alleged, and, for each such designated market area, shall plead with particularity the circumstances of the alleged failure.

(F) *Burden of proof.*—In any proceeding to make a determination under subparagraph (D), and with respect to a designated market area for which failure to provide service is alleged, the entity recognized as a qualified carrier shall have the burden of proving that the entity provided local-into-local service with a good quality satellite signal to at least 90 percent of the households in such designated market area (based on the most recent census data released by the United States Census Bureau) at the time and place alleged.

(5) *Failure to provide service.* —

(A) *Penalties.* — If the court recognizing an entity as a qualified carrier finds that such entity has willfully failed to provide local-into-local service to all DMAs, such finding shall result in the loss of recognition of the entity as a qualified carrier and the termination of the waiver provided under paragraph (1), and the court may, in its discretion —

(i) treat such failure as an act of infringement under section 501, and subject such infringement to the remedies provided for in sections 502 through 506 and subsection (a)(6)(B) of this section; and

(ii) impose a fine of not less than $250,000 and not more than $5,000,000.

(B) *Exception for nonwillful violation.* — If the court determines that the failure to provide local-into-local service to all DMAs is nonwillful, the court may in its discretion impose financial penalties for noncompliance that reflect —

(i) the degree of control the entity had over the circumstances that resulted in the failure;

(ii) the quality of the entity's efforts to remedy the failure and restore service; and

(iii) the severity and duration of any service interruption.

(6) *Penalties for violations of license.* — A court that finds, under subsection (a)(6)(A), that an entity recognized as a qualified carrier has willfully made a secondary transmission of a primary transmission made by a network station and embodying a performance or display of a work to a subscriber who is not eligible to receive the transmission under this section shall reinstate the injunction waived under paragraph (1), and the court may order statutory damages of not more than $2,500,000.

(7) *Local-into-local service to all DMAs defined.* — For purposes of this subsection:

(A) *In general.* — An entity provides "local-into-local service to all DMAs" if the entity provides local service in all designated market areas (as such term is defined in section 122(j)(2)(C)) pursuant to the license under section 122.

(B) *Household coverage.*—For purposes of subparagraph (A), an entity that makes available local-into-local service with a good quality satellite signal to at least 90 percent of the households in a designated market area based on the most recent census data released by the United States Census Bureau shall be considered to be providing local service to such designated market area.

(C) *Good quality satellite signal defined.*—The term "good quality satellite signal" has the meaning given such term under section 342(e)(2) of Communications Act of 1934.

(h) *Termination of license.*—This section shall cease to be effective on December 31, 2019.

(Nov. 16, 1988, Pub. L. 100-667, §202, 102 Stat. 3949; Dec. 17, 1993, Pub. L. 103-198, §5, 107 Stat. 2310; Oct. 18, 1994, Pub. L. 103-369, §2, 108 Stat. 3477 Nov. 1. 1995, Pub. L. 104-39, §5(c), 109 Stat. 348; Nov. 13, 1997, Pub. L. 105-80, §§2, 12, 111 Stat. 1529-30, 1535; Aug. 5, 1999, Pub. L. 106-44, §1(g), 113 Stat. 222; Nov. 29, 1999, Pub. L. 106-113, §§1004, 1005-1008, 1011, 113 Stat. 1501A-527, 527-31, 543; Nov. 2, 2002, Pub. L. 107-273, §§13209, 13210, 116 Stat. 1909; Nov. 30, 2004, Pub. L. 108-419, §5, 118 Stat. 2367; Dec. 8, 2004, Pub. L. 108-447, §§101-108, 119, 118 Stat. 3394 et seq., Oct. 6, 2006, Pub. L. 109-303, §4(e), 120 Stat. 1482; Oct. 13, 2008, Pub. L. 110-403, §209, 122 Stat. 4264; Dec. 19, 2009, Pub. L. 111-118, §1003, 123 Stat. 3469; Mar. 2, 2010, Pub. L. 111-144, §10, 124 Stat. 47; Mar. 26, 2010, Pub. L. 111-151, §2, 124 Stat. 1027; Apr. 15, 2010, Pub. L. 111-157, §9, 124 Stat. 1118; May 27, 2010,[14] Pub. L. 111-175, §§102, 105, 124 Stat. 1219, 1239; Dec. 9, 2010, Pub. L. 111-295, §6, 124 Stat. 3181; Dec. 4, 2014, Pub. L. 113-200, §§201, 202, 128 Stat. 2066.)

§ 120   Scope of exclusive rights in architectural works

(a) *Pictorial representations permitted.*—The copyright in an architectural work that has been constructed does not include the right to prevent the making, distributing, or public display of pictures, paintings, photographs, or other pictorial representations of the work, if the building in which the work is embodied is located in or ordinarily visible from a public place.

(b) *Alterations to and destruction of buildings.*—Notwithstanding the provisions of section 106(2), the owners of a building embodying an architectural work may, without the consent of the author or copyright owner of the architectural work, make or authorize the making of alterations to such building, and destroy or authorize the destruction of such building.

(Dec. 1, 1990, Pub. L. 101-650, §704, 104 Stat. 5133.)

---

[14] *Ed. Note:* In general, the amendments made by this Public Law took effect on Feb. 27, 2010.

§ 121   Limitations on exclusive rights: Reproduction for blind or other people with disabilities

(a) Notwithstanding the provisions of section 106, it is not an infringement of copyright for an authorized entity to reproduce or to distribute copies or phonorecords of a previously published, nondramatic literary work if such copies or phonorecords are reproduced or distributed in specialized formats exclusively for use by blind or other persons with disabilities.

(b) (1) Copies or phonorecords to which this section applies shall—

> (A) not be reproduced or distributed in a format other than a specialized format exclusively for use by blind or other persons with disabilities;

> (B) bear a notice that any further reproduction or distribution in a format other than a specialized format is an infringement; and

> (C) include a copyright notice identifying the copyright owner and the date of the original publication.

(2) The provisions of this subsection shall not apply to standardized, secure, or norm-referenced tests and related testing material, or to computer programs, except the portions thereof that are in conventional human language (including descriptions of pictorial works) and displayed to users in the ordinary course of using the computer programs.

(c) Notwithstanding the provisions of section 106, it is not an infringement of copyright for a publisher of print instructional materials for use in elementary or secondary schools to create and distribute to the National Instructional Materials Access Center copies of the electronic files described in sections 612(a)(23)(C), 613(a)(6), and section 674(e) of the Individuals with Disabilities Education Act that contain the contents of print instructional materials using the National Instructional Material Accessibility Standard (as defined in section 674(e)(3) of that Act), if—

> (1) the inclusion of the contents of such print instructional materials is required by any State educational agency or local educational agency;

> (2) the publisher had the right to publish such print instructional materials in print formats; and

> (3) such copies are used solely for reproduction or distribution of the contents of such print instructional materials in specialized formats.

(d) For purposes of this section, the term—

(1) "authorized entity" means a nonprofit organization or a governmental agency that has a primary mission to provide specialized services relating to training, education, or adaptive reading or information access needs of blind or other persons with disabilities;

(2) "blind or other persons with disabilities" means individuals who are eligible or who may qualify in accordance with the Act entitled "An Act to provide books for the adult blind", approved March 3, 1931 (2 U.S.C. 135a; 46 Stat. 1487) to receive books and other publications produced in specialized formats;

(3) "print instructional materials" has the meaning given under section 674(e)(3)(C) of the Individuals with Disabilities Education Act; and

(4) "specialized formats" means—

(A) braille, audio, or digital text which is exclusively for use by blind or other persons with disabilities; and

(B) with respect to print instructional materials, includes large print formats when such materials are distributed exclusively for use by blind or other persons with disabilities.

(Sept. 16, 1996, Pub. L. 104-197, §316, 110 Stat. 2416; Oct. 27, 2000, Pub. L. 106-379, §3(b), 114 Stat. 1445; Nov. 2, 2002, Pub. L. 107-273, §13210, 116 Stat. 1909; Dec. 3, 2004, Pub. L. 108-446, §306, 118 Stat. 2807.)

§ 122 Limitations on exclusive rights: Secondary transmissions of local television programming by satellite

(a) *Secondary transmissions into local markets.* —

(1) *Secondary transmissions of television broadcast stations within a local market.* —A secondary transmission of a performance or display of a work embodied in a primary transmission of a television broadcast station into the station's local market shall be subject to statutory licensing under this section if—

(A) the secondary transmission is made by a satellite carrier to the public;

(B) with regard to secondary transmissions, the satellite carrier is in compliance with the rules, regulations, or authorizations of the Federal Communications Commission governing the carriage of television broadcast station signals; and

(C) the satellite carrier makes a direct or indirect charge for the secondary transmission to—

(i) each subscriber receiving the secondary transmission; or

(ii) a distributor that has contracted with the satellite carrier for direct or indirect delivery of the secondary transmission to the public.

(2) *Significantly viewed stations.* —

(A) *In general.* — A secondary transmission of a performance or display of a work embodied in a primary transmission of a television broadcast station to subscribers who receive secondary transmissions of primary transmissions under paragraph (1) shall be subject to statutory licensing under this paragraph if the secondary transmission is of the primary transmission of a network station or a non-network station to a subscriber who resides outside the station's local market but within a community in which the signal has been determined by the Federal Communications Commission to be significantly viewed in such community, pursuant to the rules, regulations, and authorizations of the Federal Communications Commission in effect on April 15, 1976, applicable to determining with respect to a cable system whether signals are significantly viewed in a community.

(B) *Waiver.* — A subscriber who is denied the secondary transmission of the primary transmission of a network station or a non-network station under subparagraph (A) may request a waiver from such denial by submitting a request, through the subscriber's satellite carrier, to the network station or non-network station in the local market affiliated with the same network or non-network where the subscriber is located. The network station or non-network station shall accept or reject the subscriber's request for a waiver within 30 days after receipt of the request. If the network station or non-network station fails to accept or reject the subscriber's request for a waiver within that 30-day period, that network station or non-network station shall be deemed to agree to the waiver request.

(3) *Secondary transmission of low power programming.* —

(A) *In general.* — Subject to subparagraphs (B) and (C), a secondary transmission of a performance or display of a work embodied in a primary transmission of a television broadcast station to subscribers who receive secondary transmissions of primary transmissions under paragraph (1) shall be subject to statutory licensing under this paragraph if the secondary transmission is of the primary transmission of a television broadcast station that is licensed as a low power television station, to a subscriber who resides within the same designated market area as the station that originates the transmission.

(B) *No applicability to repeaters and translators.* —Secondary transmissions provided for in subparagraph (A) shall not apply to any low power television station that retransmits the programs and signals of another television station for more than 2 hours each day.

(C) *No impact on other secondary transmissions obligations.* —A satellite carrier that makes secondary transmissions of a primary transmission of a low power television station under a statutory license provided under this section is not required, by reason of such secondary transmissions, to make any other secondary transmissions.

(4) *Special exceptions.* —A secondary transmission of a performance or display of a work embodied in a primary transmission of a television broadcast station to subscribers who receive secondary transmissions of primary transmissions under paragraph (1) shall, if the secondary transmission is made by a satellite carrier that complies with the requirements of paragraph (1), be subject to statutory licensing under this paragraph as follows:

(A) *States with single full-power network station.* —In a State in which there is licensed by the Federal Communications Commission a single full-power station that was a network station on January 1, 1995, the statutory license provided for in this paragraph shall apply to the secondary transmission by a satellite carrier of the primary transmission of that station to any subscriber in a community that is located within that State and that is not within the first 50 television markets as listed in the regulations of the Commission as in effect on such date (47 C.F.R. 76.51).

(B) *States with all network stations and non-network stations in same local market.* —In a State in which all network stations and non-network stations licensed by the Federal Communications Commission within that State as of January 1, 1995, are assigned to the same local market and that local market does not encompass all counties of that State, the statutory license provided under this paragraph shall apply to the secondary transmission by a satellite carrier of the primary transmissions of such station to all subscribers in the State who reside in a local market that is within the first 50 major television markets as listed in the regulations of the Commission as in effect on such date (section 76.51 of title 47, Code of Federal Regulations).

(C) *Additional stations.* —In the case of that State in which are located 4 counties that—

(i) on January 1, 2004, were in local markets principally comprised of counties in another State, and

(ii) had a combined total of 41,340 television households, according to the U.S. Television Household Estimates by Nielsen Media Research for 2004,

the statutory license provided under this paragraph shall apply to secondary transmissions by a satellite carrier to subscribers in any such county of the primary transmissions of any network station located in that State, if the satellite carrier was making such secondary transmissions to any subscribers in that county on January 1, 2004.

(D) *Certain additional stations.* —If 2 adjacent counties in a single State are in a local market comprised principally of counties located in another State, the statutory license provided for in this paragraph shall apply to the secondary transmission by a satellite carrier to subscribers in those 2 counties of the primary transmissions of any network station located in the capital of the State in which such 2 counties are located, if—

(i) the 2 counties are located in a local market that is in the top 100 markets for the year 2003 according to Nielsen Media Research; and

(ii) the total number of television households in the 2 counties combined did not exceed 10,000 for the year 2003 according to Nielsen Media Research.

(E) *Networks of noncommercial educational broadcast stations.* —In the case of a system of three or more noncommercial educational broadcast stations licensed to a single State, public agency, or political, educational, or special purpose subdivision of a State, the statutory license provided for in this paragraph shall apply to the secondary transmission of the primary transmission of such system to any subscriber in any county or county equivalent within such State, if such subscriber is located in a designated market area that is not otherwise eligible to receive the secondary transmission of the primary transmission of a noncommercial educational broadcast station located within the State pursuant to paragraph (1).

(5) *Applicability of royalty rates and procedures.*—The royalty rates and procedures under section 119(b) shall apply to the secondary transmissions to which the statutory license under paragraph (4) applies.

(b) *Reporting requirements.*—

(1) *Initial lists.*—A satellite carrier that makes secondary transmissions of a primary transmission made by a network station under subsection (a) shall, within 90 days after commencing such secondary transmissions, submit to the network that owns or is affiliated with the network station—

(A) a list identifying (by name in alphabetical order and street address, including county and 9-digit zip code) all subscribers to which the satellite carrier makes secondary transmissions of that primary transmission under subsection (a); and

(B) a separate list, aggregated by designated market area (by name and address, including street or rural route number, city, State, and 9-digit zip code), which shall indicate those subscribers being served pursuant to paragraph (2) of subsection (a).

(2) *Subsequent lists.*—After the list is submitted under paragraph (1), the satellite carrier shall, on the 15th of each month, submit to the network—

(A) a list identifying (by name in alphabetical order and street address, including county and 9-digit zip code) any subscribers who have been added or dropped as subscribers since the last submission under this subsection; and

(B) a separate list, aggregated by designated market area (by name and street address, including street or rural route number, city, State, and 9-digit zip code), identifying those subscribers whose service pursuant to paragraph (2) of subsection (a) has been added or dropped since the last submission under this subsection.

(3) *Use of subscriber information.*—Subscriber information submitted by a satellite carrier under this subsection may be used only for the purposes of monitoring compliance by the satellite carrier with this section.

(4) *Requirements of networks.*—The submission requirements of this subsection shall apply to a satellite carrier only if the network to which the submissions are to be made places on file with the Register of Copyrights a document identifying the name and address of the person to whom

such submissions are to be made. The Register of Copyrights shall maintain for public inspection a file of all such documents.

(c) *No royalty fee required for certain secondary transmissions.*—A satellite carrier whose secondary transmissions are subject to statutory licensing under paragraphs (1), (2), and (3) of subsection (a) shall have no royalty obligation for such secondary transmissions.

(d) *Noncompliance with reporting and regulatory requirements.*—Notwithstanding subsection (a), the willful or repeated secondary transmission to the public by a satellite carrier into the local market of a television broadcast station of a primary transmission embodying a performance or display of a work made by that television broadcast station is actionable as an act of infringement under section 501, and is fully subject to the remedies provided under sections 502 through 506, if the satellite carrier has not complied with the reporting requirements of subsection (b) or with the rules, regulations, and authorizations of the Federal Communications Commission concerning the carriage of television broadcast signals.

(e) *Willful alterations.*—Notwithstanding subsection (a), the secondary transmission to the public by a satellite carrier into the local market of a television broadcast station of a performance or display of a work embodied in a primary transmission made by that television broadcast station is actionable as an act of infringement under section 501, and is fully subject to the remedies provided by sections 502 through 506 and section 510, if the content of the particular program in which the performance or display is embodied, or any commercial advertising or station announcement transmitted by the primary transmitter during, or immediately before or after, the transmission of such program, is in any way willfully altered by the satellite carrier through changes, deletions, or additions, or is combined with programming from any other broadcast signal.

(f) *Violation of territorial restrictions on statutory license for television broadcast stations.*—

(1) *Individual violations.*—The willful or repeated secondary transmission to the public by a satellite carrier of a primary transmission embodying a performance or display of a work made by a television broadcast station to a subscriber who does not reside in that station's local market, and is not subject to statutory licensing under section 119, subject to statutory licensing by reason of paragraph (2)(A), (3), or (4) of subsection (a), or subject to a private licensing agreement, is actionable as an act of in-

fringement under section 501 and is fully subject to the remedies provided by sections 502 through 506, except that—

(A) no damages shall be awarded for such act of infringement if the satellite carrier took corrective action by promptly withdrawing service from the ineligible subscriber; and

(B) any statutory damages shall not exceed $250 for such subscriber for each month during which the violation occurred.

(2) *Pattern of violations.*—If a satellite carrier engages in a willful or repeated pattern or practice of secondarily transmitting to the public a primary transmission embodying a performance or display of a work made by a television broadcast station to subscribers who do not reside in that station's local market, and are not subject to statutory licensing under section 119, subject to statutory licensing by reason of paragraph (2)(A), (3), or (4) of subsection (a), or subject to a private licensing agreement, then in addition to the remedies under paragraph (1)—

(A) if the pattern or practice has been carried out on a substantially nationwide basis, the court—

(i) shall order a permanent injunction barring the secondary transmission by the satellite carrier of the primary transmissions of that television broadcast station (and if such television broadcast station is a network station, all other television broadcast stations affiliated with such network); and

(ii) may order statutory damages not exceeding $2,500,000 for each 6-month period during which the pattern or practice was carried out; and

(B) if the pattern or practice has been carried out on a local or regional basis with respect to more than one television broadcast station, the court—

(i) shall order a permanent injunction barring the secondary transmission in that locality or region by the satellite carrier of the primary transmissions of any television broadcast station; and

(ii) may order statutory damages not exceeding $2,500,000 for each 6-month period during which the pattern or practice was carried out.

(g) *Burden of proof.*—In any action brought under subsection (f), the satellite carrier shall have the burden of proving that its secondary transmission of a primary transmission by a television broadcast station is made only to

17 U.S.C. § 122

subscribers located within that station's local market or subscribers being served in compliance with section 119, paragraph (2)(A), (3), or (4) of subsection (a), or a private licensing agreement.

(h) *Geographic limitations on secondary transmissions.*—The statutory license created by this section shall apply to secondary transmissions to locations in the United States.

(i) *Exclusivity with respect to secondary transmissions of broadcast stations by satellite to members of the public.*—No provision of section 111 or any other law (other than this section and section 119) shall be construed to contain any authorization, exemption, or license through which secondary transmissions by satellite carriers of programming contained in a primary transmission made by a television broadcast station may be made without obtaining the consent of the copyright owner.

(j) *Definitions.*—In this section—

(1) *Distributor.*—The term "distributor" means an entity that contracts to distribute secondary transmissions from a satellite carrier and, either as a single channel or in a package with other programming, provides the secondary transmission either directly to individual subscribers or indirectly through other program distribution entities.

(2) *Local market.*—

(A) *In general.*—The term "local market", in the case of both commercial and noncommercial television broadcast stations, means the designated market area in which a station is located, and—

(i) in the case of a commercial television broadcast station, all commercial television broadcast stations licensed to a community within the same designated market area are within the same local market; and

(ii) in the case of a noncommercial educational television broadcast station, the market includes any station that is licensed to a community within the same designated market area as the noncommercial educational television broadcast station.

(B) *County of license.*—In addition to the area described in subparagraph (A), a station's local market includes the county in which the station's community of license is located.

(C) *Designated market area.*—For purposes of subparagraph (A), the term "designated market area" means a designated market area, as determined by Nielsen Media Research and published in the 1999-

Copyrights • 451

2000 Nielsen Station Index Directory and Nielsen Station Index United States Television Household Estimates or any successor publication.

(D) *Certain areas outside of any designated market area.* — Any census area, borough, or other area in the State of Alaska that is outside of a designated market area, as determined by Nielsen Media Research, shall be deemed to be part of one of the local markets in the State of Alaska. A satellite carrier may determine which local market in the State of Alaska will be deemed to be the relevant local market in connection with each subscriber in such census area, borough, or other area.

(E) *Market determinations.* — The local market area of a commercial television broadcast station may be modified by the Federal Communications Commission in accordance with section 338(l) of the Communications Act of 1934 (47 U.S.C. 338).

(3) *Low power television station.* — The term "low power television station" means a low power TV station as defined in section 74.701(f) of title 47, Code of Federal Regulations, as in effect on June 1, 2004. For purposes of this paragraph, the term "low power television station" includes a low power television station that has been accorded primary status as a Class A television licensee under section 73.6001(a) of title 47, Code of Federal Regulations.

(4) *Network station; non-network station; satellite carrier; secondary transmission.* — The terms "network station", "non-network station", "satellite carrier", and "secondary transmission" have the meanings given such terms under section 119(d).

(5) *Noncommercial educational broadcast station.* — The term "noncommercial educational broadcast station" means a television broadcast station that is a noncommercial educational broadcast station as defined in section 397 of the Communications Act of 1934, as in effect on the date of the enactment of the Satellite Television Extension and Localism Act of 2010.

(6) *Subscriber.* — The term "subscriber" means a person or entity that receives a secondary transmission service from a satellite carrier and pays a fee for the service, directly or indirectly, to the satellite carrier or to a distributor.

(7) *Television broadcast station.* — The term "television broadcast station" —

(A) means an over-the-air, commercial or noncommercial television broadcast station licensed by the Federal Communications Commission under subpart E of part 73 of title 47, Code of Federal Regulations, except that such term does not include a low-power or translator television station; and

(B) includes a television broadcast station licensed by an appropriate governmental authority of Canada or Mexico if the station broadcasts primarily in the English language and is a network station as defined in section 119(d)(2)(A).

(Nov. 29, 1999, Pub. L. 106-113, §1002, 113 Stat. 1501A-523; Nov. 2, 2002, Pub. L. 107-273, §13210, 116 Stat. 1909; Dec.. 8, 2004, Pub. L. 108-447, §111(b), 118 Stat. 3409; Oct. 13, 2008, Pub. L. 110-403, §209, 122 Stat. 4264; May 27, 2010,[14] Pub. L. 111-175, §103, 124 Stat. 1227; Dec. 4, 2014, Pub. L. 113-200, §204, 128 Stat. 2067.)

CHAPTER 2—COPYRIGHT OWNERSHIP AND TRANSFER

§ 201   Ownership of copyright

(a) *Initial ownership.*—Copyright in a work protected under this title vests initially in the author or authors of the work. The authors of a joint work are coowners of copyright in the work.

(b) *Works made for hire.*—In the case of a work made for hire, the employer or other person for whom the work was prepared is considered the author for purposes of this title, and, unless the parties have expressly agreed otherwise in a written instrument signed by them, owns all of the rights comprised in the copyright.

(c) *Contributions to collective works.*—Copyright in each separate contribution to a collective work is distinct from copyright in the collective work as a whole, and vests initially in the author of the contribution. In the absence of an express transfer of the copyright or of any rights under it, the owner of copyright in the collective work is presumed to have acquired only the privilege of reproducing and distributing the contribution as part of that particular collective work, any revision of that collective work, and any later collective work in the same series.

---

[14] *Ed. Note:* In general, the amendments made by this Public Law took effect on Feb. 27, 2010.

(d) *Transfer of ownership.—*

(1) The ownership of a copyright may be transferred in whole or in part by any means of conveyance or by operation of law, and may be bequeathed by will or pass as personal property by the applicable laws of intestate succession.

(2) Any of the exclusive rights comprised in a copyright, including any subdivision of any of the rights specified by section 106, may be transferred as provided by clause (1) and owned separately. The owner of any particular exclusive right is entitled, to the extent of that right, to all of the protection and remedies accorded to the copyright owner by this title.

(e) *Involuntary transfer.—*When an individual author's ownership of a copyright, or of any of the exclusive rights under a copyright, has not previously been transferred voluntarily by that individual author, no action by any governmental body or other official or organization purporting to seize, expropriate, transfer, or exercise rights of ownership with respect to the copyright, or any of the exclusive rights under a copyright, shall be given effect under this title, except as provided under title 11.

(Oct. 16, 1976, Pub. L. 94-553, §101, 90 Stat. 2568; Nov. 6, 1978, Pub. L. 95-598, §313, 92 Stat. 2676.)

§ 202 Ownership of copyright as distinct from ownership of material object

Ownership of a copyright, or of any of the exclusive rights under a copyright, is distinct from ownership of any material object in which the work is embodied. Transfer of ownership of any material object, including the copy or phonorecord in which the work is first fixed, does not of itself convey any rights in the copyrighted work embodied in the object; nor, in the absence of an agreement, does transfer of ownership of a copyright or of any exclusive rights under a copyright convey property rights in any material object.

(Oct. 19, 1976, Pub. L. 94-553, §101, 90 Stat. 2568.)

§ 203 Termination of transfers and licenses granted by the author

(a) *Conditions for termination.—*In the case of any work other than a work made for hire, the exclusive or nonexclusive grant of a transfer or license of copyright or of any right under a copyright, executed by the author on or after January 1, 1978, otherwise than by will, is subject to termination under the following conditions:

(1) In the case of a grant executed by one author, termination of the grant may be effected by that author or, if the author is dead, by the person or persons who, under clause (2) of this subsection, own and are entitled to exercise a total of more than one-half of that author's termination interest. In the case of a grant executed by two or more authors of a joint work, termination of the grant may be effected by a majority of the authors who executed it; if any of such authors is dead, the termination interest of any such author may be exercised as a unit by the person or persons who, under clause (2) of this subsection, own and are entitled to exercise a total of more than one-half of that author's interest.

(2) Where an author is dead, his or her termination interest is owned, and may be exercised, as follows:

(A) The widow or widower owns the author's entire termination interest unless there are any surviving children or grandchildren of the author, in which case the widow or widower owns one-half of the author's interest.

(B) The author's surviving children, and the surviving children of any dead child of the author, own the author's entire termination interest unless there is a widow or widower, in which case the ownership of one-half of the author's interest is divided among them.

(C) The rights of the author's children and grandchildren are in all cases divided among them and exercised on a per stirpes basis according to the number of such author's children represented; the share of the children of a dead child in a termination interest can be exercised only by the action of a majority of them.

(D) in the event that the author's widow or widower, children, and grandchildren are not living, the author's executor, administrator, personal representative, or trustee shall own the author's entire termination interest.

(3) Termination of the grant may be effected at any time during a period of five years beginning at the end of thirty-five years from the date of execution of the grant; or, if the grant covers the right of publication of the work, the period begins at the end of thirty-five years from the date of publication of the work under the grant or at the end of forty years from the date of execution of the grant, whichever term ends earlier.

17 U.S.C. § 203

(4) The termination shall be effected by serving an advance notice in writing, signed by the number and proportion of owners of termination interests required under clauses (1) and (2) of this subsection, or by their duly authorized agents, upon the grantee or the grantee's successor in title.

(A) The notice shall state the effective date of the termination, which shall fall within the five-year period specified by clause (3) of this subsection, and the notice shall be served not less than two or more than ten years before that date. A copy of the notice shall be recorded in the Copyright Office before the effective date of termination, as a condition to its taking effect.

(B) The notice shall comply, in form, content, and manner of service, with requirements that the Register of Copyrights shall prescribe by regulation.

(5) Termination of the grant may be effected notwithstanding any agreement to the contrary, including an agreement to make a will or to make any future grant.

(b) *Effect of termination.*—Upon the effective date of termination, all rights under this title that were covered by the terminated grants revert to the author, authors, and other persons owning termination interests under clauses (1) and (2) of subsection (a), including those owners who did not join in signing the notice of termination under clause (4) of subsection (a), but with the following limitations:

(1) A derivative work prepared under authority of the grant before its termination may continue to be utilized under the terms of the grant after its termination, but this privilege does not extend to the preparation after the termination of other derivative works based upon the copyrighted work covered by the terminated grant.

(2) The future rights that will revert upon termination of the grant become vested on the date the notice of termination has been served as provided by clause (4) of subsection (a). The rights vest in the author, authors, and other persons named in, and in the proportionate shares provided by, clauses (1) and (2) of subsection (a).

(3) Subject to the provisions of clause (4) of this subsection, a further grant, or agreement to make a further grant, of any right covered by a terminated grant is valid only if it is signed by the same number and proportion of the owners, in whom the right has vested under clause (2) of this subsec-

17 U.S.C. § 203

tion, as are required to terminate the grant under clauses (1) and (2) of subsection (a). Such further grant or agreement is effective with respect to all of the persons in whom the right it covers has vested under clause (2) of this subsection, including those who did not join in signing it. If any person dies after rights under a terminated grant have vested in him or her, that person's legal representatives, legatees, or heirs at law represent him or her for purposes of this clause.

(4) A further grant, or agreement to make a further grant, of any right covered by a terminated grant is valid only if it is made after the effective date of the termination. As an exception, however, an agreement for such a further grant may be made between the persons provided by clause (3) of this subsection and the original grantee or such grantee's successor in title, after the notice of termination has been served as provided by clause (4) of subsection (a).

(5) Termination of a grant under this section affects only those rights covered by the grants that arise under this title, and in no way affects rights arising under any other Federal, State, or foreign laws.

(6) Unless and until termination is effected under this section, the grant, if it does not provide otherwise, continues in effect for the term of copyright provided by this title.

(Oct. 19, 1976, Pub. L. 94-553, §101, 90 Stat. 2569; Oct. 27 1998, Pub. L. 105-298, §103, 112 Stat. 2829; Nov. 2, 2002, Pub. L. 107-273, §13210, 116 Stat. 1909.)

§ 204   Execution of transfers of copyright ownership

(a) A transfer of copyright ownership, other than by operation of law, is not valid unless an instrument of conveyance, or a note or memorandum of the transfer, is in writing and signed by the owner of the rights conveyed or such owner's duly authorized agent.

(b) A certificate of acknowledgement is not required for the validity of a transfer, but is prima facie evidence of the execution of the transfer if—

(1) in the case of a transfer executed in the United States, the certificate is issued by a person authorized to administer oaths within the United States; or

(2) in the case of a transfer executed in a foreign country, the certificate is issued by a diplomatic or consular officer of the United States, or by a person authorized to administer oaths whose authority is proved by a certificate of such an officer.

(Oct. 19, 1976, Pub. L. 94-553, §101, 90 Stat. 2570.)

§ 205   Recordation of transfers and other documents

(a) *Conditions for recordation.* — Any transfer of copyright ownership or other document pertaining to a copyright may be recorded in the Copyright Office if the document filed for recordation bears the actual signature of the person who executed it, or if it is accompanied by a sworn or official certification that it is a true copy of the original, signed document. A sworn or official certification may be submitted to the Copyright Office electronically, pursuant to regulations established by the Register of Copyrights.

(b) *Certificate of recordation.* — The Register of Copyrights shall, upon receipt of a document as provided by subsection (a) and of the fee provided by section 708, record the document and return it with a certificate of recordation.

(c) *Recordation as constructive notice.* — Recordation of a document in the Copyright Office gives all persons constructive notice of the facts stated in the recorded document, but only if —

(1) the document, or material attached to it, specifically identifies the work to which it pertains so that, after the document is indexed by the Register of Copyrights, it would be revealed by a reasonable search under the title or registration number of the work; and

(2) registration has been made for the work.

(d) *Priority between conflicting transfers.* — As between two conflicting transfers, the one executed first prevails if it is recorded, in the manner required to give constructive notice under subsection (c), within one month after its execution in the United States or within two months after its execution outside the United States, or at any time before recordation in such manner of the later transfer. Otherwise the later transfer prevails if recorded first in such manner, and if taken in good faith, for valuable consideration or on the basis of a binding promise to pay royalties, and without notice of the earlier transfer.

(e) *Priority between conflicting transfer of ownership and nonexclusive license.* — A nonexclusive license, whether recorded or not, prevails over a conflicting transfer of copyright ownership if the license is evidenced by a written instrument signed by the owner of the rights licensed or such owner's duly authorized agent, and if —

(1) the license was taken before execution of the transfer; or

(2) the license was taken in good faith before recordation of the transfer and without notice of it.

17 U.S.C. § 205

(Oct. 19, 1976, Pub. L. 94-553, §101, 90 Stat. 2571; Oct. 31, 1988, Pub. L. 100-568, §5, 102 Stat. 2857; Dec. 9, 2010, Pub. L. 111-295, §3, 124 Stat. 3180.)

CHAPTER 3—DURATION OF COPYRIGHT

§ 301 Preemption with respect to other laws

(a) On and after January 1, 1978, all legal or equitable rights that are equivalent to any of the exclusive rights within the general scope of copyright as specified by section 106 in works of authorship that are fixed in a tangible medium of expression and come within the subject matter of copyright as specified by sections 102 and 103, whether created before or after that date and whether published or unpublished, are governed exclusively by this title. Thereafter, no person is entitled to any such right or equivalent right in any such work under the common law or statutes of any State.

(b) Nothing in this title annuls or limits any rights or remedies under the common law or statutes of any State with respect to—

(1) subject matter that does not come within the subject matter of copyright as specified by sections 102 and 103, including works of authorship not fixed in any tangible medium of expression; or

(2) any cause of action arising from undertakings commenced before January 1, 1978;

(3) activities violating legal or equitable rights that are not equivalent to any of the exclusive rights within the general scope of copyright as specified by section 106; or

(4) State and local landmarks, historic preservation, zoning, or building codes, relating to architectural works protected under section 102(a)(8).

(c) With respect to sound recordings fixed before February 15, 1972, any rights or remedies under the common law or statutes of any State shall not be annulled or limited by this title until February 15, 2067. The preemptive provisions of subsection (a) shall apply to any such rights and remedies pertaining to any cause of action arising from undertakings commenced on and after February 15, 2067. Notwithstanding the provisions of section 303, no sound recording fixed before February 15, 1972, shall be subject to copyright under this title before, on, or after February 15, 2067.

(d) Nothing in this title annuls or limits any rights or remedies under any other Federal statute.

(e) The scope of Federal preemption under this section is not affected by the adherence of the United States to the Berne Convention or the satisfaction of obligations of the United States thereunder.

(f) (1) On or after the effective date set forth in section 610(a) of the Visual Artists Rights Act of 1990, all legal or equitable rights that are equivalent to any of the rights conferred by section 106A with respect to works of visual art to which the rights conferred by section 106A apply are governed exclusively by section 106A and section 113(d) and the provisions of this title relating to such sections. Thereafter, no person is entitled to any such right or equivalent right in any work of visual art under the common law or statutes of any State.

(2) Nothing in paragraph (1) annuls or limits any rights or remedies under the common law or statutes of any State with respect to—

(A) any cause of action from undertakings commenced before the effective date set forth in section 610(a) of the Visual Artists Rights Act of 1990;

(B) activities violating legal or equitable rights that are not equivalent to any of the rights conferred by section 106A with respect to works of visual art; or

(C) activities violating legal or equitable rights which extend beyond the life of the author.

(Oct. 19, 1976, Pub. L. 94-553, §101, 90 Stat. 2572; Oct. 31, 1988, Pub. L. 100-568, §6, 102 Stat. 2857; Dec. 1, 1990, Pub. L. 101-650, §605, §705, 104 Stat. 5131, 5134; Oct. 27, 1998, Pub. L. 105-298, §102(a), 112 Stat. 2827.)

§ 302 Duration of copyright: Works created on or after January 1, 1978

(a) *In general.*—Copyright in a work created on or after January 1, 1978, subsists from its creation and, except as provided by the following subsections, endures for a term consisting of the life of the author and 70 years after the author's death.

(b) *Joint works.* —In the case of a joint work prepared by two or more authors who did not work for hire, the copyright endures for a term consisting of the life of the last surviving author and 70 years after such last surviving author's death.

(c) *Anonymous works, pseudonymous works, and works made for hire.* —In the case of an anonymous work, a pseudonymous work, or a work made for hire, the copyright endures for a term of 95 years from the year of its first publication, or a term of 120 years from the year of its creation, whichever expires first. If, before the end of such term, the identity of one or more of the authors of an anonymous or pseudonymous work is revealed in the records of a registration made for that work under subsections (a) or (d) of section 408, or in the records provided by this subsection, the copyright in the work endures for the term specified by subsection (a) or (b), based on the life of the author or authors whose identity has been revealed. Any person having an interest in the copyright in an anonymous or pseudonymous work may at any time record, in records to be maintained by the Copyright Office for that purpose, a statement identifying one or more authors of the work; the statement shall also identify the person filing it, the nature of that person's interest, the source of the information recorded, and the particular work affected, and shall comply in form and content with requirements that the Register of Copyrights shall prescribe by regulation.

(d) *Records relating to death of authors.* —Any person having an interest in a copyright may at any time record in the Copyright Office a statement of the date of death of the author of the copyrighted work, or a statement that the author is still living on a particular date. The statement shall identify the person filing it, the nature of that person's interest, and the source of the information recorded, and shall comply in form and content with requirements that the Register of Copyrights shall prescribe by regulation. The Register shall maintain current records of information relating to the death of authors of copyrighted works, based on such recorded statements and, to the extent the Register considers practicable, on data contained in any of the records of the Copyright Office or in other reference sources.

(e) *Presumption as to author's death.* —After a period of 95 years from the year of first publication of a work, or a period of 120 years from the year of its creation, whichever expires first, any person who obtains from the Copyright Office a certified report that the records provided by subsection (d) disclose nothing to indicate that the author of the work is living, or died less than 70 years before, is entitled to the benefits of a presumption that the author has been dead for at least 70 years. Reliance in good faith upon this presumption shall be a complete defense to any action for infringement under this title.

(Oct. 19, 1976, Pub. L. 94-553, §101, 90 Stat. 2572; Oct. 27, 1998, Pub. L. 105-298, §102(b), 112 Stat. 2827.)

§ 303   Duration of copyright: Works created but not published or copyrighted before January 1, 1978

(a) Copyright in a work created before January 1, 1978, but not theretofore in the public domain or copyrighted, subsists from January 1, 1978, and endures for the term provided by section 302. In no case, however, shall the term of copyright in such a work expire before December 31, 2002; and, if the work is published on or before December 31, 2002, the term of copyright shall not expire before December 31, 2047.

(b) The distribution before January 1, 1978, of a phonorecord shall not for any purpose constitute a publication of any musical work, dramatic work, or literary work embodied therein.

(Oct. 19, 1976, Pub. L. 94-553, §101, 90 Stat. 2573; Nov. 13, 1997, Pub. L. 105-80, §11, 111 Stat. 1534; Oct. 27, 1998, Pub. L. 105-298, §102(c), 112 Stat. 2827; Dec. 9, 2010, Pub. L. 111- 295, §5, 124 Stat. 3181.)

§ 304   Duration of copyright: Subsisting copyrights

(a) *Copyrights in their first term on January 1, 1978.* —

  (1) (A) Any copyright, the first term of which is subsisting on January 1, 1978, shall endure for 28 years from the date it was originally secured.

   (B) In the case of—

     (i) any posthumous work or of any periodical, cyclopedic, or other composite work upon which the copyright was originally secured by the proprietor thereof, or

     (ii) any work copyrighted by a corporate body (otherwise than as assignee or licensee of the individual author) or by an employer for whom such work is made for hire,

   the proprietor of such copyright shall be entitled to a renewal and ex-tension of the copyright in such work for the further term of 67 years.

   (C) In the case of any other copyrighted work, including a contribu-tion by an individual author to a periodical or to a cyclopedic or other composite work—

(i) the author of such work, if the author is still living,

(ii) the widow, widower, or children of the author, if the author is not living,

(iii) the author's executors, if such author, widow, widower, or children are not living, or

(iv) the author's next of kin, in the absence of a will of the author,

shall be entitled to a renewal and extension of the copyright in such work for a further term of 67 years.

(2) (A) At the expiration of the original term of copyright in a work specified in paragraph (1)(B) of this subsection, the copyright shall endure for a renewed and extended further term of 67 years, which—

(i) if an application to register a claim to such further term has been made to the Copyright Office within 1 year before the expiration of the original term of copyright, and the claim is registered, shall vest, upon the beginning of such further term, in the proprietor of the copyright who is entitled to claim the renewal of copyright at the time the application is made; or

(ii) if no such application is made or the claim pursuant to such application is not registered, shall vest, upon the beginning of such further term, in the person or entity that was the proprietor of the copyright as of the last day of the original term of copyright.

(B) At the expiration of the original term of copyright in a work specified in paragraph (1)(C) of this subsection, the copyright shall endure for a renewed and extended further term of 67 years, which—

(i) if an application to register a claim to such further term has been made to the Copyright Office within 1 year before the expiration of the original term of copyright, and the claim is registered, shall vest, upon the beginning of such further term, in any person who is entitled under paragraph (1)(C) to the renewal and extension of the copyright at the time the application is made; or

(ii) if no such application is made or the claim pursuant to such application is not registered, shall vest, upon the beginning of such further term, in any person entitled under paragraph (1)(C), as of the last day of the original term of copyright, to the renewal and extension of the copyright.

(3) (A) An application to register a claim to the renewed and extended term of copyright in a work may be made to the Copyright Office—

(i) within 1 year before the expiration of the original term of copyright by any person entitled under paragraph (1) (B) or (C) to such further term of 67 years; and

(ii) at any time during the renewed and extended term by any person in whom such further term vested, under paragraph (2) (A) or (B), or by any successor or assign of such person, if the application is made in the name of such person.

(B) Such an application is not a condition of the renewal and extension of the copyright in a work for a further term of 67 years.

(4) (A) If an application to register a claim to the renewed and extended term of copyright in a work is not made within 1 year before the expiration of the original term of copyright in a work, or if the claim pursuant to such application is not registered, then a derivative work prepared under authority of a grant of a transfer or license of the copyright that is made before the expiration of the original term of copyright may continue to be used under the terms of the grant during the renewed and extended term of copyright without infringing the copyright, except that such use does not extend to the preparation during such renewed and extended term of other derivative works based upon the copyrighted work covered by such grant.

(B) If an application to register a claim to the renewed and extended term of copyright in a work is made within 1 year before its expiration, and the claim is registered, the certificate of such registration shall constitute prima facie evidence as to the validity of the copyright during its renewed and extended term and of the facts stated in the certificate. The evidentiary weight to be accorded the certificates of a registration of a renewed and extended term of copyright made after the end of that 1-year period shall be within the discretion of the court.

(b) *Copyrights in their renewal term at the time of the effective date of the Sonny Bono Copyright Term Extension Act.*—Any copyright still in its renewal term at the time that the Sonny Bono Copyright Term Extension Act becomes effective shall have a copyright term of 95 years from the date copyright was originally secured.

(c) *Termination of transfers and licenses covering extended renewal term.*—In the case of any copyright subsisting in either its first or renewal term on January

17 U.S.C. § 304

1, 1978, other than a copyright in a work made for hire, the exclusive or nonexclusive grant of a transfer or license of the renewal copyright or any right under it, executed before January 1, 1978, by any of the persons designated by subsection (a)(1)(C) of this section, otherwise than by will, is subject to termination under the following conditions:

(1) In the case of a grant executed by a person or persons other than the author, termination of the grant may be effected by the surviving person or persons who executed it. In the case of a grant executed by one or more of the authors of the work, termination of the grant may be effected, to the extent of a particular author's share in the ownership of the renewal copyright, by the author who executed it or, if such author is dead, by the person or persons who, under clause (2) of this subsection, own and are entitled to exercise a total of more than one-half of that author's termination interest.

(2) Where an author is dead, his or her termination interest is owned, and may be exercised, as follows:

(A) The widow or widower owns the author's entire termination interest unless there are any surviving children or grandchildren of the author, in which case the widow or widower owns one-half of the author's interest.

(B) The author's surviving children, and the surviving children of any dead child of the author, own the author's entire termination interest unless there is a widow or widower, in which case the ownership of one-half of the author's interest is divided among them.

(C) The rights of the author's children and grandchildren are in all cases divided among them and exercised on a per stirpes basis according to the number of such author's children represented; the share of the children of a dead child in a termination interest can be exercised only by the action of a majority of them.

(D) in the event that the author's widow or widower, children, and grandchildren are not living, the author's executor, administrator, personal representative, or trustee shall own the author's entire termination interest.

(3) Termination of the grant may be effected at any time during a period of five years beginning at the end of fifty-six years from the date copyright was originally secured, or beginning on January 1, 1978, whichever is later.

17 U.S.C. § 304

(4) The termination shall be effected by serving an advance notice in writing upon the grantee or the grantee's successor in title. In the case of a grant executed by a person or persons other than the author, the notice shall be signed by all of those entitled to terminate the grant under clause (1) of this subsection, or by their duly authorized agents. In the case of a grant executed by one or more of the authors of the work, the notice as to any one author's share shall be signed by that author or his or her duly authorized agent or, if that author is dead, by the number and proportion of the owners of his or her termination interest required under clauses (1) and (2) of this subsection, or by their duly authorized agents.

(A) The notice shall state the effective date of the termination, which shall fall within the five-year period specified by clause (3) of this subsection, or, in the case of a termination under subsection (d), within the five-year period specified by subsection (d)(2), and the notice shall be served not less than two or more than ten years before that date. A copy of the notice shall be recorded in the Copyright Office before the effective date of termination, as a condition to its taking effect.

(B) The notice shall comply, in form, content, and manner of service, with requirements that the Register of Copyrights shall prescribe by regulation.

(5) Termination of the grant may be effected notwithstanding any agreement to the contrary, including an agreement to make a will or to make any future grant.

(6) In the case of a grant executed by a person or persons other than the author, all rights under this title that were covered by the terminated grant revert, upon the effective date of termination, to all of those entitled to terminate the grant under clause (1) of this subsection. In the case of a grant executed by one or more of the authors of the work, all of a particular author's rights under this title that were covered by the terminated grant revert, upon the effective date of termination, to that author or, if that author is dead, to the persons owning his or her termination interest under clause (2) of this subsection, including those owners who did not join in signing the notice of termination under clause (4) of this subsection. In all cases the reversion of rights is subject to the following limitations:

(A) A derivative work prepared under authority of the grant before its termination may continue to be utilized under the terms of the grant after its termination, but this privilege does not extend to the prepara-

17 U.S.C. § 304

tion after the termination of other derivative works based upon the copyrighted work covered by the terminated grant.

(B) The future rights that will revert upon termination of the grant become vested on the date the notice of termination has been served as provided by clause (4) of this subsection.

(C) Where the author's rights revert to two or more persons under clause (2) of this subsection, they shall vest in those persons in the proportionate shares provided by that clause. In such a case, and subject to the provisions of subclause (D) of this clause, a further grant, or agreement to make a further grant, of a particular author's share with respect to any right covered by a terminated grant is valid only if it is signed by the same number and proportion of the owners, in whom the right has vested under this clause, as are required to terminate the grant under clause (2) of this subsection. Such further grant or agreement is effective with respect to all of the persons in whom the right it covers has vested under this subclause, including those who did not join in signing it. If any person dies after rights under a terminated grant have vested in him or her, that person's legal representatives, legatees, or heirs at law represent him or her for purposes of this subclause.

(D) A further grant, or agreement to make a further grant, of any right covered by a terminated grant is valid only if it is made after the effective date of the termination. As an exception, however, an agreement for such a further grant may be made between the author or any of the persons provided by the first sentence of clause (6) of this subsection, or between the persons provided by subclause (C) of this clause, and the original grantee or such grantee's successor in title, after the notice of termination has been served as provided by clause (4) of this subsection.

(E) Termination of a grant under this subsection affects only those rights covered by the grant that arise under this title, and in no way affects rights arising under any other Federal, State, or foreign laws.

(F) Unless and until termination is effected under this subsection, the grant, if it does not provide otherwise, continues in effect for the remainder of the extended renewal term.

(d) *Termination rights provided in subsection (c) which have expired on or before the effective date of the Sonny Bono Copyright Term Extension Act.*—In the case of any copyright other than a work made for hire, subsisting in its renewal term on the effective date of the Sonny Bono Copyright Term Extension Act for which the termination right provided in subsection (c) has expired by such date, where the author or owner of the termination right has not previously exercised such termination right, the exclusive or nonexclusive grant of a transfer or license of the renewal copyright or any right under it, executed before January 1, 1978, by any of the persons designated in subsection (a)(1)(C) of this section, other than by will, is subject to termination under the following conditions:

(1) The conditions specified in subsections (c) (1), (2), (4), (5), and (6) of this section apply to terminations of the last 20 years of copyright term as provided by the amendments made by the Sonny Bono Copyright Term Extension Act.

(2) Termination of the grant may be effected at any time during a period of 5 years beginning at the end of 75 years from the date copyright was originally secured.

(Oct. 19, 1976, Pub. L. 94-553, §101, 90 Stat. 2573; June 26, 1992, Pub. L. 102-307, §102(a) and (d), 106 Stat. 264-66; Nov. 13, 1997, Pub. L. 105-80, §12, 111 Stat. 1535; Oct. 27, 1998, Pub. L. 105-298, §§102(d), 103, 112 Stat. 2827, 2829; Nov. 2, 2002, Pub. L. 107-273, §13210, 116 Stat. 1909.)

§ 305   Duration of copyright: Terminal date

All terms of copyright provided by sections 302 through 304 run to the end of the calendar year in which they would otherwise expire.

(Oct. 19, 1976, Pub. L. 94-553, §101, 90 Stat. 2576.)

CHAPTER 4 — COPYRIGHT NOTICE, DEPOSIT, AND REGISTRATION

411.   Registration and civil infringement actions.
412.   Registration as prerequisite to certain remedies for infringement.

§ 401   Notice of copyright: Visually perceptible copies

(a) *General provisions.*—Whenever a work protected under this title is published in the United States or elsewhere by authority of the copyright owner, a notice of copyright as provided by this section may be placed on publicly distributed copies from which the work can be visually perceived, either directly or with the aid of a machine or device.

(b) *Form of notice.*—If a notice appears on the copies, it shall consist of the following three elements:

(1) the symbol © (the letter C in a circle), or the word "Copyright", or the abbreviation "Copr."; and

(2) the year of first publication of the work; in the case of compilations, or derivative works incorporating previously published material, the year date of first publication of the compilation or derivative work is sufficient. The year date may be omitted where a pictorial, graphic, or sculptural work, with accompanying text matter, if any, is reproduced in or on greeting cards, postcards, stationery, jewelry, dolls, toys, or any useful articles; and

(3) the name of the owner of copyright in the work, or an abbreviation by which the name can be recognized, or a generally known alternative designation of the owner.

(c) *Position of notice.*—The notice shall be affixed to the copies in such manner and location as to give reasonable notice of the claim of copyright. The Register of Copyrights shall prescribe by regulation, as examples, specific methods of affixation and positions of the notice on various types of works that will satisfy this requirement, but these specifications shall not be considered exhaustive.

(d) *Evidentiary weight of notice.*—If a notice of copyright in the form and position specified by this section appears on the published copy or copies to which a defendant in a copyright infringement suit had access, then no weight shall be given to such a defendant's interposition of a defense based on innocent infringement in mitigation of actual or statutory damages, except as provided in the last sentence of section 504(c)(2).

(Oct. 19, 1976, Pub. L. 94-553, §101, 90 Stat. 2576; Oct. 31, 1988, Pub. L. 100-568, §7, 102 Stat. 2857.)

17 U.S.C. § 401

§ 402 Notice of copyright: Phonorecords of sound recordings

(a) *General provisions.* —Whenever a sound recording protected under this title is published in the United States or elsewhere by authority of the copyright owner, a notice of copyright as provided by this section may be placed on publicly distributed phonorecords of the sound recording.

(b) *Form of notice.* —If a notice appears on the phonorecords, it shall consist of the following three elements:

(1) the symbol ℗ (the letter P in a circle); and

(2) the year of first publication of the sound recording; and

(3) the name of the owner of copyright in the sound recording, or an abbreviation by which the name can be recognized, or a generally known alternative designation of the owner; if the producer of the sound recording is named on the phonorecord labels or containers, and if no other name appears in conjunction with the notice, the producer's name shall be considered a part of the notice.

(c) *Position of notice.* —The notice shall be placed on the surface of the phonorecord, or on the phonorecord label or container, in such manner and location as to give reasonable notice of the claim of copyright.

(d) *Evidentiary weight of notice.* —If a notice of copyright in the form and position specified by this section appears on the published phonorecord or phonorecords to which a defendant in a copyright infringement suit had access, then no weight shall be given to such a defendant's interpretation of a defense based on innocent infringement in mitigation of actual or statutory damages, except as provided in the last sentence of section 504(c)(2).

(Oct. 19, 1976, Pub. L. 94-553, §101, 90 Stat. 2577; Oct. 31, 1988, Pub. L. 100-568, §7, 102 Stat. 2857.)

§ 403 Notice of copyright: Publications incorporating United States Government works

Section 401(d) and 402(d) shall not apply to a work published in copies or phonorecords consisting predominantly of one or more works of the United States Government unless the notice of copyright appearing on the published copies or phonorecords to which a defendant in the copyright infringement suit had access includes a statement identifying, either affirmatively or negatively, those portions of the copies or phonorecords embodying any work or works protected under this title.

(Oct. 19, 1976, Pub. L. 94-553, §101, 90 Stat. 2577; Oct. 31, 1988, Pub. L. 100-568, §7, 102 Stat. 2858.)

§ 404 Notice of copyright: Contributions to collective works

(a) A separate contribution to a collective work may bear its own notice of copyright, as provided by section 401 through 403. However, a single notice applicable to the collective work as a whole is sufficient to invoke the provisions of section 401(d) or 402(d), as applicable with respect to the separate contributions it contains (not including advertisements inserted on behalf of persons other than the owner of copyright in the collective work), regardless of the ownership of copyright in the contributions and whether or not they have been previously published.

(b) With respect to copies and phonorecords publicly distributed by authority of the copyright owner before the effective date of the Berne Convention Implementation Act of 1988, where the person named in a single notice applicable to a collective work as a whole is not the owner of copyright in a separate contribution that does not bear its own notice, the case is governed by the provisions of section 406(a).

(Oct. 19, 1976, Pub. L. 94-553, §101, 90 Stat. 2577; Oct. 31, 1988, Pub. L. 100-568, §7, 102 Stat. 2858.)

§ 405 Notice of copyright: Omission of notice

(a) *Effect of omission on copyright.* — With respect to copies and phonorecords publicly distributed by authority of the copyright owner before the effective date of the Berne Convention Implementation Act of 1988, the omission of the copyright notice described in sections 401 through 403 from copies or phonorecords publicly distributed by authority of the copyright owner does not invalidate the copyright in a work if —

(1) the notice has been omitted from no more than a relatively small number of copies or phonorecords distributed to the public; or

(2) registration for the work has been made before or is made within five years after the publication without notice, and a reasonable effort is made to add notice to all copies of phonorecords that are distributed to the public in the United States after the omission has been discovered; or

(3) the notice has been omitted in violation of an express requirement in writing that, as a condition of the copyright owner's authorization of the public distribution of copies or phonorecords, they bear the prescribed notice.

(b) *Effect of omission on innocent infringers.*—Any person who innocently infringes a copyright, in reliance upon an authorized copy or phonorecord from which the copyright notice has been omitted and which was publicly distributed by authority of the copyright owner before the effective date of the Berne Convention Implementation Act of 1988, incurs no liability for actual or statutory damages under section 504 for any infringing act committed before receiving actual notice that registration for the work has been made under section 408, if such person proves that he or she was misled by the omission of notice. In a suit for infringement in such a case the court may allow or disallow recovery of any of the infringer's profits attributable to the infringement, and may enjoin the continuation of the infringing undertaking or may require, as a condition for permitting the continuation of the infringing undertaking, that the infringer pay the copyright owner a reasonable license fee in an amount and on terms fixed by the court.

(c) *Removal of notice.*—Protection under this title is not affected by the removal, destruction, or obliteration of the notice, without the authorization of the copyright owner, from any publicly distributed copies or phonorecords.

(Oct. 19, 1976, Pub. L. 94-553, §101, 90 Stat. 2578; Oct. 31, 1988, Pub. L. 100-568, §7, 102 Stat. 2858; Nov. 13, 1997, Pub. L. 105-80, §12, 111 Stat. 1535.)

§ 406   Notice of copyright: Error in name or date

(a) *Error in name.*—With respect to copies and phonorecords publicly distributed by authority of the copyright owner before the effective date of the Berne Convention Implementation Act of 1988, where the person named in the copyright notice on copies or phonorecords publicly distributed by authority of the copyright owner is not the owner of copyright, the validity and ownership of the copyright are not affected. In such a case, however, any person who innocently begins an undertaking that infringes the copyright has a complete defense to any action for such infringement if such person proves that he or she was misled by the notice and began the undertaking in good faith under a purported transfer or license from the person named therein, unless before the undertaking was begun—

(1) registration for the work had been made in the name of the owner of copyright; or

(2) a document executed by the person named in the notice and showing the ownership of the copyright had been recorded.

17 U.S.C. § 406

(b) *Error in date.*—When the year date in the notice on copies or phonorecords distributed before the effective date of the Berne Convention Implementation Act of 1988 by authority of the copyright owner is earlier than the year in which publication first occurred, any period computed from the year of first publication under section 302 is to be computed from the year in the notice. Where the year date is more than one year later than the year in which publication first occurred, the work is considered to have been published without any notice and is governed by the provisions of section 405.

(c) *Omission of name or date.*—Where copies or phonorecords publicly distributed before the effective date of the Berne Convention Implementation Act of 1988 by authority of the copyright owner contain no name or no date that could reasonably be considered a part of the notice, the work is considered to have been published without any notice and is governed by the provision of section 405 as in effect on the day before the effective date of the Berne Convention Implementation Act of 1988.

(Oct. 19, 1976, Pub. L. 94-553, §101, 90 Stat. 2578; Oct. 31, 1988, Pub. L. 100-568, §7, 102 Stat. 2858.)

§ 407 Deposit of copies or phonorecords for Library of Congress

(a) Except as provided by subsection (c), and subject to the provisions of subsection (e), the owner of copyright or of the exclusive right of publication in a work published in the United States shall deposit, within three months after the date of such publication—

> (1) two complete copies of the best edition; or

> (2) if the work is a sound recording, two complete phonorecords of the best edition, together with any printed or other visually perceptible material published with such phonorecords.

Neither the deposit requirements of this subsection nor the acquisition provisions of subsection (e) are conditions of copyright protection.

(b) The required copies or phonorecords shall be deposited in the Copyright Office for the use or disposition of the Library of Congress. The Register of Copyrights shall, when requested by the depositor and upon payment of the fee prescribed by section 708, issue a receipt for the deposit.

(c) The Register of Copyrights may by regulation exempt any categories of material from the deposit requirements of this section, or require deposit of only one copy or phonorecord with respect to any categories. Such regulations shall provide either for complete exemption from the deposit requirements of this section, or for alternative forms of deposit aimed at providing a satisfactory archival record of a work without imposing practical or financial hardships on the depositor, where the individual author is the owner of copyright in a pictorial, graphic, or sculptural work and (i) less than five copies of the work have been published, or (ii) the work has been published in a limited edition consisting of numbered copies, the monetary value of which would make the mandatory deposit of two copies of the best edition of the work burdensome, unfair, or unreasonable.

(d) At any time after publication of a work as provided by subsection (a), the Register of Copyrights may make written demand for the required deposit on any of the persons obligated to make the deposit under subsection (a). Unless deposit is made within three months after the demand is received, the person or persons on whom the demand was made are liable—

(1) to a fine of not more than $250 for each work; and

(2) to pay into a specially designated fund in the Library of Congress the total retail price of the copies or phonorecords demanded, or, if no retail price has been fixed, the reasonable cost to the Library of Congress of acquiring them; and

(3) to pay a fine of $2,500, in addition to any fine or liability imposed under clauses (1) and (2), if such person willfully or repeatedly fails or refuses to comply with such a demand.

(e) With respect to transmission programs that have been fixed and transmitted to the public in the United States but have not been published, the Register of Copyrights shall, after consulting with the Librarian of Congress and other interested organizations and officials, establish regulations governing the acquisition, through deposit or otherwise, of copies or phonorecords of such programs for the collections of the Library of Congress.

(1) The Librarian of Congress shall be permitted, under the standards and conditions set forth in such regulations, to make a fixation of a transmission program directly from a transmission to the public, and to reproduce one copy or phonorecord from such fixation for archival purposes.

(2) Such regulations shall also provide standards and procedures by which the Register of Copyrights may make written demand, upon the owner of the right of transmission in the United States, for the deposit of a copy or phonorecord of a specific transmission program. Such deposit may, at the option of the owner of the right of transmission in the United

States, be accomplished by gift, by loan for purposes of reproduction, or by sale at a price not to exceed the cost of reproducing and supplying the copy or phonorecord. The regulations established under this clause shall provide reasonable periods of not less than three months for compliance with a demand, and shall allow for extensions of such periods and adjustments in the scope of the demand or the methods for fulfilling it, as reasonably warranted by the circumstances. Willful failure or refusal to comply with the conditions prescribed by such regulations shall subject the owner of the right of transmission in the United States to liability for an amount, not to exceed the cost of reproducing and supplying the copy or phonorecord in question, to be paid into a specially designated fund in the Library of Congress.

(3) Nothing in this subsection shall be construed to require the making or retention, for purposes of deposit, of any copy or phonorecord of an unpublished transmission program, the transmission of which occurs before the receipt of a specific written demand as provided by clause (2).

(4) No activity undertaken in compliance with regulations prescribed under clauses (1) or (2) of this subsection shall result in liability if intended solely to assist in the acquisition of copies or phonorecords under this subsection.

(Oct. 19, 1976, Pub. L. 94-553, §101, 90 Stat. 2579; Oct. 31, 1988, Pub. L. 100-568, §8, 102 Stat. 2859. Nov. 13, 1977, Pub. L. 105-80, §12, 111 Stat. 1535.)

§ 408 Copyright registration in general

(a) *Registration permissive.*—At any time during the subsistence of the first term of copyright in any published or unpublished work in which the copyright was secured before January 1, 1978, and during the subsistence of any copyright secured on or after that date, the owner of copyright or of any exclusive right in the work may obtain registration of the copyright claim by delivering to the Copyright Office the deposit specified by this section, together with the application and fee specified by sections 409 and 708. Such registration is not a condition of copyright protection.

(b) *Deposit for copyright registration.*—Except as provided by subsection (c), the material deposited for registration shall include—

(1) in the case of an unpublished work, one complete copy or phonorecord;

(2) in the case of a published work, two complete copies or phonorecords of the best edition;

(3) in the case of a work first published outside the United States, one complete copy or phonorecord as so published;

(4) in the case of a contribution to a collective work, one complete copy or phonorecord of the best edition of the collective work.

Copies or phonorecords deposited for the Library of Congress under section 407 may be used to satisfy the deposit provisions of this section, if they are accompanied by the prescribed application and fee, and by any additional identifying material that the Register may, by regulation, require. The Register shall also prescribe regulations establishing requirements under which copies or phonorecords acquired for the Library of Congress under subsection (e) of section 407, otherwise than by deposit, may be used to satisfy the deposit provisions of this section.

(c) *Administrative classification and optional deposit.* —

(1) The Register of Copyrights is authorized to specify by regulation the administrative classes into which works are to be placed for purposes of deposit and registration, and the nature of the copies or phonorecords to be deposited in the various classes specified. The regulations may require or permit, for particular classes, the deposit of identifying material instead of copies or phonorecords, the deposit of only one copy or phonorecord where two would normally be required, or a single registration for a group of related works. This administrative classification of works has no significance with respect to the subject matter of copyright or the exclusive rights provided by this title.

(2) Without prejudice to the general authority provided under clause (1), the Register of Copyrights shall establish regulations specifically permitting a single registration for a group of works by the same individual author, all first published as contributions to periodicals, including newspapers, within a twelve-month period, on the basis of a single deposit, application, and registration fee, under the following conditions:

(A) if the deposit consists of one copy of the entire issue of the periodical, or of the entire section in the case of a newspaper, in which each contribution was first published; and

(B) if the application identifies each work separately, including the periodical containing it and its date of first publication.

17 U.S.C. § 408

(3) As an alternative to separate renewal registrations under subsection (a) of section 304, a single renewal registration may be made for a group of works by the same individual author, all first published as contributions to periodicals, including newspapers, upon the filing of a single application and fee, under all of the following conditions:

(A) the renewal claimant or claimants, and the basis of claim or claims under section 304(a), is the same for each of the works; and

(B) the works were all copyrighted upon their first publication, either through separate copyright notice and registration or by virtue of a general copyright notice in the periodical issue as a whole; and

(C) the renewal application and fee are received not more than twenty-eight or less than twenty-seven years after the thirty-first day of December of the calendar year in which all of the works were first published; and

(D) the renewal application identifies each work separately, including the periodical containing it and its date of first publication.

(d) *Corrections and amplifications.* — The Register may also establish, by regulation, formal procedures for the filing of an application for supplementary registration, to correct an error in a copyright registration or to amplify the information given in a registration. Such application shall be accompanied by the fee provided by section 708, and shall clearly identify the registration to be corrected or amplified. The information contained in a supplementary registration augments but does not supersede that contained in the earlier registration.

(e) *Published edition of previously registered work.* — Registration for the first published edition of a work previously registered in unpublished form may be made even though the work as published is substantially the same as the unpublished version.

(f) *Preregistration of works being prepared for commercial distribution* —

(1) *Rulemaking.* — Not later than 180 days after the date of enactment of this subsection, the Register of Copyrights shall issue regulations to establish procedures for preregistration of a work that is being prepared for commercial distribution and has not been published.

(2) *Class of works.* — The regulations established under paragraph (1) shall permit preregistration for any work that is in a class of works that the

Register determines has had a history of infringement prior to authorized commercial distribution.

(3) *Application for registration.*—Not later than 3 months after the first publication of a work preregistered under this subsection, the applicant shall submit to the Copyright Office—

(A) an application for registration of the work;

(B) a deposit; and

(C) the applicable fee.

(4) *Effect of untimely application.*—An action under this chapter for infringement of a work preregistered under this subsection, in a case in which the infringement commenced no later than 2 months after the first publication of the work, shall be dismissed if the items described in Paragraph (3) are not submitted to the Copyright Office in proper form within the earlier of—

(A) 3 months after the first publication of the work; or

(B) 1 month after the copyright owner has learned of the infringement.

(Oct. 19, 1976, Pub. L. 94-553, §101, 90 Stat. 2580; Oct. 31, 1988, Pub. L. 100-568, §9, 102 Stat. 2859; June 26, 1992, Pub. L. 102-307, §102, 106 Stat. 266; April 27, 2005, Pub. L. 109-9, §104, 119 Stat. 221.)

§ 409   Application for copyright registration

The application for copyright registration shall be made on a form prescribed by the Register of Copyrights and shall include—

(1) the name and address of the copyright claimant;

(2) in the case of a work other than an anonymous or pseudonymous work, the name and nationality or domicile of the author or authors, and, if one or more of the authors is dead, the dates of their deaths;

(3) if the work is anonymous or pseudonymous, the nationality or domicile of the author or authors;

(4) in the case of a work made for hire, a statement to this effect;

(5) if the copyright claimant is not the author, a brief statement of how the claimant obtained ownership of the copyright;

(6) the title of the work, together with any previous or alternative titles under which the work can be identified;

(7) the year in which creation of the work was completed;

(8) if the work has been published, the date and nation of its first publication;

(9) in the case of a compilation or derivative work, an identification of any preexisting work or works that it is based on or incorporates, and a brief, general statement of the additional material covered by the copyright claim being registered; and

(10) any other information regarded by the Register of Copyrights as bearing upon the preparation or identification of the work or the existence, ownership, or duration of the copyright.

If an application is submitted for the renewed and extended term provided for in section 304(a)(3)(A) and an original term registration has not been made, the Register may request information with respect to the existence, ownership, or duration of the copyright for the original term.

(Oct. 19, 1976, Pub. L. 94-553, §101, 90 Stat. 2582; June 26, 1992, Pub. L. 102-307, §102(b), 106 Stat. 266; Dec. 9, 2010, Pub. L. 111-295, §4, 124 Stat. 3180.)

§ 410 Registration of claim and issuance of certificate

(a) When, after examination, the Register of Copyrights determines that, in accordance with the provisions of this title, the material deposited constitutes copyrightable subject matter and that the other legal and formal requirements of this title have been met, the Register shall register the claim and issue to the applicant a certificate of registration under the seal of the Copyright Office. The certificate shall contain the information given in the application, together with the number and effective date of the registration.

(b) In any case in which the Register of Copyrights determines that, in accordance with the provisions of this title, the material deposited does not constitute copyrightable subject matter or that the claim is invalid for any other reason, the Register shall refuse registration and shall notify the applicant in writing of the reasons for such refusal.

(c) In any judicial proceedings the certificate of a registration made before or within five years after first publication of the work shall constitute prima facie evidence of the validity of the copyright and of the facts stated in the certificate. The evidentiary weight to be accorded the certificate of a registration made thereafter shall be within the discretion of the court.

(d) The effective date of a copyright registration is the day on which an application, deposit, and fee, which are later determined by the Register of Copyrights or by a court of competent jurisdiction to be acceptable for registration, have all been received in the Copyright Office.

(Oct. 19, 1976, Pub. L. 94-553, §101, 90 Stat. 2582.)

§ 411   Registration and civil infringement actions

(a) Except for an action brought for a violation of the rights of the author under section 106A(a), and subject to the provisions of subsection (b), no civil action for infringement of the copyright in any United States work shall be instituted until preregistration or registration of the copyright claim has been made in accordance with this title. In any case, however, where the deposit, application, and fee required for registration have been delivered to the Copyright Office in proper form and registration has been refused, the applicant is entitled to institute a civil action for infringement if notice thereof, with a copy of the complaint, is served on the Register of Copyrights. The Register may, at his or her option, become a party to the action with respect to the issue of registrability of the copyright claim by entering an appearance within sixty days after such service, but the Register's failure to become a party shall not deprive the court of jurisdiction to determine that issue.

(b)(1) A certificate of registration satisfies the requirements of this section and section 412, regardless of whether the certificate contains any inaccurate information, unless—

(A) the inaccurate information was included on the application for copyright registration with knowledge that it was inaccurate; and

(B) the inaccuracy of the information, if known, would have caused the Register of Copyrights to refuse registration.

(2) In any case in which inaccurate information described under paragraph (1) is alleged, the court shall request the Register of Copyrights to advise the court whether the inaccurate information, if known, would have caused the Register of Copyrights to refuse registration.

(3) Nothing in this subsection shall affect any rights, obligations, or requirements of a person related to information contained in a registration certificate, except for the institution of and remedies in infringement actions under this section and section 412.

17 U.S.C. § 411

(c) In the case of a work consisting of sounds, images, or both, the first fixation of which is made simultaneously with its transmission, the copyright owner may, either before or after such fixation takes place, institute an action for infringement under section 501, fully subject to the remedies provided by sections 502 through 505 and section 510, if, in accordance with requirements that the Register of Copyrights shall prescribe by regulation, the copyright owner—

(1) serves notice upon the infringer, not less than 48 hours before such fixation, identifying the work and the specific time and source of its first transmission, and declaring an intention to secure copyright in the work; and

(2) makes registration for the work, if required by subsection (a), within three months after its first transmission.

(Oct. 19, 1976, Pub. L. 94-553, §101, 90 Stat. 2583; Oct. 31, 1988, Pub. L. 100-568, §9, 102 Stat. 2859; Dec. 1, 1990, Pub. L. 101-650, §606, 104 Stat. 5131; Nov. 13, 1997, Pub. L. 105-80, §6, 111 Stat. 1532; Oct. 28, 1998, Pub. L. 105-304, §102(d), 112 Stat. 2863; April 27, 2005, Pub. L. 109-9, §104, 119 Stat. 222; Oct. 13, 2008, Pub. L. 110-403, §101, §209, 122 Stat. 4257, 4258, 4264.)

§ 412   Registration as prerequisite to certain remedies for infringement

In any action under this title, other than an action brought for a violation of the rights of the author under section 106A(a), an action for infringement of the copyright of a work that has been preregistered under section 408(f) before the commencement of the infringement and that has an effective date of registration not later than the earlier of 3 months after the first publication of the work or 1 month after the copyright owner has learned of the infringement, or an action instituted under section 411(c), no award of statutory damages or of attorney's fees, as provided by sections 504 and 505, shall be made for—

(1) any infringement of copyright in an unpublished work commenced before the effective date of its registration; or

(2) any infringement of copyright commenced after first publication of the work and before the effective date of its registration, unless such registration is made within three months after the first publication of the work.

(Oct. 19, 1976, Pub. L. 94-553, §101, 90 Stat. 2583; Dec. 1, 1990, Pub. L. 101-650, §606, 104 Stat. 5131; April 27, 2005, Pub. L. 109-9, §104, 119 Stat. 222; Oct. 13, 2008, Pub. L. 110-403, §101, 122 Stat. 4258.)

CHAPTER 5—COPYRIGHT INFRINGEMENT AND REMEDIES

§ 501   Infringement of copyright

(a) Anyone who violates any of the exclusive rights of the copyright owner as provided by sections 106 through 122, or of the author as provided in section 106A(a), or who imports copies or phonorecords into the United States in violation of section 602, is an infringer of the copyright or right of the author, as the case may be. For purposes of this chapter (other than Section 506), any reference to copyright shall be deemed to include the rights conferred by Section 106A(a). As used in this subsection, the term "anyone" includes any State, any instrumentality of a State, and any officer or employee of a State or instrumentality of a State acting in his or her official capacity. Any State, and any such instrumentality, officer, or employee, shall be subject to the provisions of this title in the same manner and to the same extent as any nongovernmental entity.

(b) The legal or beneficial owner of an exclusive right under a copyright is entitled, subject to the requirements of section 411, to institute an action for any infringement of that particular right committed while he or she is the owner of it. The court may require such owner to serve written notice of the action with a copy of the complaint upon any person shown, by the records of the Copyright Office or otherwise, to have or claim an interest in the copyright, and shall require that such notice be served upon any person whose interest is likely to be affected by a decision in the case. The court may require the joinder, and shall permit the intervention, of any person having or claiming an interest in the copyright.

(c) For any secondary transmission by a cable system that embodies a performance or a display of a work which is actionable as an act of infringement under subsection (c) of section 111, a television broadcast station holding a copyright or other license to transmit or perform the same version of that work shall, for purposes of subsection (b) of this section, be treated as a legal or beneficial owner if such secondary transmission occurs within the local service area of that television station.

(d) For any secondary transmission by a cable system that is actionable as an act of infringement pursuant to section 111(c)(3), the following shall also have standing to sue: (i) the primary transmitter whose transmission has been altered by the cable system; and (ii) any broadcast station within whose local service area the secondary transmission occurs.

(e) With respect to any secondary transmission that is made by a satellite carrier of a performance or display of a work embodied in a primary transmission and is actionable as an act of infringement under section 119(a)(5), a network station holding a copyright or other license to transmit or perform the same version of that work shall, for purposes of subsection (b) of this section, be treated as a legal or beneficial owner if such secondary transmission occurs within the local service area of that station.

(f)(1) With respect to any secondary transmission that is made by a satellite carrier of a performance or display of a work embodied in a primary transmission and is actionable as an act of infringement under section 122, a television broadcast station holding a copyright or other license to transmit or perform the same version of that work shall, for purposes of subsection (b) of this section, be treated as a legal or beneficial owner if such secondary transmission occurs within the local market of that station.

(2) A television broadcast station may file a civil action against any satellite carrier that has refused to carry television broadcast signals, as required under section 122(a)(2), to enforce that television broadcast station's rights under section 338(a) of the Communications Act of 1934.

(Oct. 19, 1976, Pub. L. 94-553, §101, 90 Stat. 2584; Oct. 31, 1988, Pub. L. 100-568, §10, 102 Stat. 2860; Nov. 16, 1988, Pub. L. 100-667, §202, 102 Stat. 3957; Nov. 15, 1990, Pub. L. 101-553, §2, 104 Stat. 2749; Dec. 1, 1990, Pub. L. 101-650, §606, 104 Stat. 5131; Aug. 5, 1999, Pub. L. 106-44, §1(g), 113 Stat. 222; Nov. 29, 1999, Pub. L. 106-113, §§1002, 1011, 113 Stat. 1501A-523, 543; Nov. 2, 2002, Pub. L. 107-273, §13210, 116 Stat. 1909.)

17 U.S.C. § 501

§ 502   Remedies for infringement: Injunctions

(a) Any court having jurisdiction of a civil action arising under this title may, subject to the provisions of section 1498 of title 28, grant temporary and final injunctions on such terms as it may deem reasonable to prevent or restrain infringement of a copyright.

(b) Any such injunction may be served anywhere in the United States on the person enjoined; it shall be operative throughout the United States and shall be enforceable, by proceedings in contempt or otherwise, by any United States court having jurisdiction of that person. The clerk of the court granting the injunction shall, when requested by any other court in which enforcement of the injunction is sought, transmit promptly to the other court a certified copy of all the papers in the case on file in such clerk's office.

(Oct. 19, 1976, Pub. L. 94-553, §101, 90 Stat. 2584.)

§ 503   Remedies for infringement: Impounding and disposition of infringing articles

(a)(1) At any time while an action under this title is pending, the court may order the impounding, on such terms as it may deem reasonable —

> (A) of all copies or phonorecords claimed to have been made or used in violation of the exclusive right of the copyright owner;

> (B) of all plates, molds, matrices, masters, tapes, film negatives, or other articles by means of which such copies or phonorecords may be reproduced; and

> (C) of records documenting the manufacture, sale, or receipt of things involved in any such violation, provided that any records seized under this subparagraph shall be taken into the custody of the court.

(2) For impoundments of records ordered under paragraph (1)(C), the court shall enter an appropriate protective order with respect to discovery and use of any records or information that has been impounded. The protective order shall provide for appropriate procedures to ensure that confidential, private, proprietary, or privileged information contained in such records is not improperly disclosed or used.

(3) The relevant provisions of paragraphs (2) through (11) of section 34(d) of the Trademark Act (15 U.S.C. 1116(d)(2) through (11)) shall extend to any impoundment of records ordered under paragraph (1)(C) that is based upon an ex parte application, notwithstanding the provisions of

rule 65 of the Federal Rules of Civil Procedure. Any references in paragraphs (2) through (11) of section 34(d) of the Trademark Act to section 32 of such Act shall be read as references to section 501 of this title, and references to use of a counterfeit mark in connection with the sale, offering for sale, or distribution of goods or services shall be read as references to infringement of a copyright.

(b) As part of a final judgment or decree, the court may order the destruction or other reasonable disposition of all copies or phonorecords found to have been made or used in violation of the copyright owner's exclusive rights, and of all plates, molds, matrices, masters, tapes, film negatives, or other articles by means of which such copies or phonorecords may be reproduced.

(Oct. 19, 1976, Pub. L. 94-553, §101, 90 Stat. 2585; Oct. 13, 2008, Pub. L. 110-403, §102, 122 Stat. 4258; Dec. 9, 2010, Pub. L. 111-295, §6, 124 Stat. 3181.)

§ 504   Remedies for infringement: Damages and profits

(a) *In general.*—Except as otherwise provided by this title, an infringer of copyright is liable for either—

(1) the copyright owner's actual damages and any additional profits of the infringer, as provided by subsection (b); or

(2) statutory damages, as provided by subsection (c).

(b) *Actual damages and profits.*—The copyright owner is entitled to recover the actual damages suffered by him or her as a result of the infringement, and any profits of the infringer that are attributable to the infringement and are not taken into account in computing the actual damages. In establishing the infringer's profits, the copyright owner is required to present proof only of the infringer's gross revenue, and the infringer is required to prove his or her deductible expenses and the elements of profit attributable to factors other than the copyrighted work.

(c) *Statutory damages.*—

(1) Except as provided by clause (2) of this subsection, the copyright owner may elect, at any time before final judgment is rendered, to recover, instead of actual damages and profits, an award of statutory damages for all infringements involved in the action, with respect to any one work, for which any one infringer is liable individually, or for which any two or more infringers are liable jointly and severally, in a sum of not less than $750 or more than $30,000 as the court considers just. For the purposes of

this subsection, all the parts of a compilation or derivative work constitute one work.

(2) In a case where the copyright owner sustains the burden of proving, and the court finds, that infringement was committed willfully, the court in its discretion may increase the award of statutory damages to a sum of not more than $150,000. In a case where the infringer sustains the burden of proving, and the court finds, that such infringer was not aware and had no reason to believe that his or her acts constituted an infringement of copyright, the court in its discretion may reduce the award of statutory damages to a sum of not less than $200. The court shall remit statutory damages in any case where an infringer believed and had reasonable grounds for believing that his or her use of the copyrighted work was a fair use under section 107, if the infringer was: (i) an employee or agent of a nonprofit educational institution, library, or archives acting within the scope of his or her employment who, or such institution, library, or archives itself, which infringed by reproducing the work in copies or phonorecords; or (ii) a public broadcasting entity which or a person who, as a regular part of the nonprofit activities of a public broadcasting entity (as defined in section 118(f)) infringed by performing a published non-dramatic literary work or by reproducing a transmission program embodying a performance of such a work.

(3) (A) In a case of infringement, it shall be a rebuttable presumption that the infringement was committed willfully for purposes of determining relief if the violator, or a person acting in concert with the violator, knowingly provided or knowingly caused to be provided materially false contact information to a domain name registrar, domain name registry, or other domain name registration authority in registering, maintaining, or renewing a domain name used in connection with the infringement.

(B) Nothing in this paragraph limits what may be considered willful infringement under this subsection.

(C) For purposes of this paragraph, the term "domain name" has the meaning given that term in section 45 of the Act entitled "An Act to provide for the registration and protection of trademarks used in commerce, to carry out the provisions of certain international conventions, and for other purposes" approved July 5, 1946 (commonly referred to as the "Trademark Act of 1946"; 15 U.S.C. 1127).

17 U.S.C. § 504

(d) *Additional damages in certain cases.*—In any case in which the court finds that a defendant proprietor of an establishment who claims as a defense that its activities were exempt under section 110(5) did not have reasonable grounds to believe that its use of a copyrighted work was exempt under such section, the plaintiff shall be entitled to, in addition to any award of damages under this section, an additional award of two times the amount of the license fee that the proprietor of the establishment concerned should have paid the plaintiff for such use during the preceding period of up to 3 years.

(Oct. 19, 1976, Pub. L. 94-553, §101, 90 Stat. 2585; Oct. 31, 1988, Pub. L. 100-568, §10, 102 Stat. 2860; Nov. 13, 1997, Pub. L. 105-80, §12, 111 Stat. 1535; Oct. 27, 1998, Pub. L. 105-298, §204, 112 Stat. 2833; Dec. 9. 1999, Pub. L. 106-160, §2, 113 Stat. 1774; Nov. 2, 2002, Pub. L. 107-273, §13207, 116 Stat. 1906; Dec. 23, 2004, Pub. L. 108-482, §202, 118 Stat. 3916; Dec. 9, 2010, Pub. L. 111-295, §6, 124 Stat. 3181.)

§ 505 Remedies for infringement: Costs and attorney's fees

In any civil action under this title, the court in its discretion may allow the recovery of full costs by or against any party other than the United States or an officer thereof. Except as otherwise provided by this title, the court may also award a reasonable attorney's fee to the prevailing party as part of the costs.

(Oct. 19, 1976, Pub. L. 94-553, §101, 90 Stat. 2586.)

§ 506 Criminal offenses

(a) *Criminal infringement.* —

(1) *In general.*—Any person who willfully infringes a copyright shall be punished as provided under section 2319 of title 18, if the infringement was committed—

(A) for purposes of commercial advantage or private financial gain;

(B) by the reproduction or distribution, including by electronic means, during any 180-day period, of 1 or more copies or phonorecords of 1 or more copyrighted works, which have a total retail value of more than $1,000; or

(C) by the distribution of a work being prepared for commercial distribution, by making it available on a computer network accessible to members of the public, if such person knew or should have known that the work was intended for commercial distribution.

(2) *Evidence.*—For purposes of this subsection, evidence of reproduction or distribution of a copyrighted work, by itself, shall not be sufficient to establish willful infringement of a copyright.

(3) *Definition.*—In this subsection, the term "work being prepared for commercial distribution" means—

(A) a computer program, a musical work, a motion picture or other audiovisual work, or a sound recording, if, at the time of unauthorized distribution—

(i) the copyright owner has a reasonable expectation of commercial distribution; and

(ii) the copies or phonorecords of the work have not been commercially distributed; or

(B) a motion picture, if, at the time of unauthorized distribution, the motion picture—

(i) has been made available for viewing in a motion picture exhibition facility; and

(ii) has not been made available in copies for sale to the general public in the United States in a format intended to permit viewing outside a motion picture exhibition facility.

(b) *Forfeiture, destruction, and restitution.*—Forfeiture, destruction, and restitution relating to this section shall be subject to section 2323 of title 18, to the extent provided in that section, in addition to any other similar remedies provided by law.

(c) *Fraudulent copyright notice.*—Any person who, with fraudulent intent, places on any article a notice of copyright or words of the same purport that such person knows to be false, or who, with fraudulent intent, publicly distributes or imports for public distribution any article bearing such notice or words that such person knows to be false, shall be fined not more than $2,500.

(d) *Fraudulent removal of copyright notice.*—Any person who, with fraudulent intent, removes or alters any notice of copyright appearing on a copy of a copyrighted work shall be fined not more than $2,500.

(e) *False representation.*—Any person who knowingly makes a false representation of a material fact in the application for copyright registration provided for by section 409, or in any written statement filed in connection with the application, shall be fined not more than $2,500.

(f) *Rights of attribution and integrity.*—Nothing in this section applies to infringement of the rights conferred by Section 106A(a).

(Oct. 19, 1976, Pub. L. 94-553, §101, 90 Stat. 2586; May 24, 1982, Pub. L. 97-180, §5, 96 Stat. 93; Dec. 1, 1990, Pub. L. 101-650, §606, 104 Stat. 5131; Dec. 16, 1997, Pub. L. 105-147, §2(b), 111 Stat. 2678; April 27, 2005, Pub. L. 109-9, §103, 119 Stat. 220; Oct. 13, 2008, Pub. L. 110-403, §201, 122 Stat. 4260.)

§ 507 Limitations on actions

(a) *Criminal proceedings.*—Except as expressly provided otherwise in this title, no criminal proceeding shall be maintained under the provisions of this title unless it is commenced within 5 years after the cause of action arose.

(b) *Civil actions.*—No civil action shall be maintained under the provisions of this title unless it is commenced within three years after the claim accrued.

(Oct. 19, 1976, Pub. L. 94-553, §101, 90 Stat. 2586; Dec. 16, 1997, Pub. L. 105-147, §2(c), 111 Stat. 2678; Oct. 28, 1998, Pub. L. 105-304, §102(e), 112 Stat. 2863.)

§ 508 Notification of filing and determination of actions

(a) Within one month after the filing of any action under this title, the clerks of the courts of the United States shall send written notification to the Register of Copyrights setting forth, as far as is shown by the papers filed in the court, the names and addresses of the parties and the title, author, and registration number of each work involved in the action. If any other copyrighted work is later included in the action by amendment, answer, or other pleading, the clerk shall also send a notification concerning it to the Register within one month after the pleading is filed.

(b) Within one month after any final order or judgment is issued in the case, the clerk of the court shall notify the Register of it, sending with the notification a copy of the order or judgment together with the written opinion, if any, of the court.

(c) Upon receiving the notifications specified in this section, the Register shall make them a part of the public records of the Copyright Office.

(Oct. 19, 1976, Pub. L. 94-553, §101, 90 Stat. 2586.)

§ 509 [Repealed]

(Oct. 19, 1976, Pub. L. 94-553, §101, 90 Stat. 2587; Nov. 13, 1997, Pub. L. 105-80, §12, 111 Stat. 1535; Oct. 13, 2008, Pub. L. 110-403, §201, 122 Stat. 4260.)

§ 510 Remedies for alteration of programming by cable systems

(a) In any action filed pursuant to section 111(c)(3), the following remedies shall be available:

(1) Where an action is brought by a party identified in subsections (b) or (c) of section 501, the remedies provided by sections 502 through 505, and the remedy provided by subsection (b) of this section; and

(2) When an action is brought by a party identified in subsection (d) of section 501, the remedies provided by sections 502 and 505, together with any actual damages suffered by such party as a result of the infringement, and the remedy provided by subsection (b) of this section.

(b) In any action filed pursuant to section 111(c)(3), the court may decree that, for a period not to exceed thirty days, the cable system shall be deprived of the benefit of a statutory license for one or more distant signals carried by such cable system.

(Oct. 19, 1976, Pub. L. 94-553, §101, 90 Stat. 2587; Nov. 29, 1999, Pub. L. 106-113, §1011, 113 Stat. 1501A-543.)

§ 511 Liability of States, instrumentalities of States, and State officials for infringement of copyright

(a) *In general.*—Any State, any instrumentality of a State, and any officer or employee of a State or instrumentality of a State acting in his or her official capacity, shall not be immune, under the Eleventh Amendment of the Constitution of the United States or under any other doctrine of sovereign immunity, from suit in Federal court by any person, including any governmental or nongovernmental entity, for a violation of any of the exclusive rights of a copyright owner provided by sections 106 through 122, for importing copies of phonorecords in violation of section 602, or for any other violation under this title.

(b) *Remedies.*—In a suit described in subsection (a) for a violation described in that subsection, remedies (including remedies both at law and in equity) are available for the violation to the same extent as such remedies are available for such a violation in a suit against any public or private entity other than a State, instrumentality of a State, or officer or employee of a State acting in his or her official capacity. Such remedies include impounding and disposition of infringing articles under section 503, actual damages and profits and statutory damages under section 504, costs and attorney's fees under section 505, and the remedies provided in section 510.

(Added Nov. 15, 1990, Pub. L. 101-553, §2, 104 Stat. 2749-50; Aug. 5, 1999, Pub. L. 106-44, §1(g), 113 Stat. 222; Nov. 2, 2002, Pub. L. 107-273, §13210, 116 Stat. 1909.)

§ 512 Limitations on liability relating to material online

(a) *Transitory digital network communications.* — A service provider shall not be liable for monetary relief, or, except as provided in subsection (j), for injunctive or other equitable relief, for infringement of copyright by reason of the provider's transmitting, routing, or providing connections for, material through a system or network controlled or operated by or for the service provider, or by reason of the intermediate and transient storage of that material in the course of such transmitting, routing, or providing connections, if—

(1) the transmission of the material was initiated by or at the direction of a person other than the service provider;

(2) the transmission, routing, provision of connections, or storage is carried out through an automatic technical process without selection of the material by the service provider;

(3) the service provider does not select the recipients of the material except as an automatic response to the request of another person;

(4) no copy of the material made by the service provider in the course of such intermediate or transient storage is maintained on the system or network in a manner ordinarily accessible to anyone other than anticipated recipients, and no such copy is maintained on the system or network in a manner ordinarily accessible to such anticipated recipients for a longer period than is reasonably necessary for the transmission, routing, or provision of connections; and

(5) the material is transmitted through the system or network without modification of its content.

(b) *System caching.* —

(1) *Limitation on liability.*—A service provider shall not be liable for monetary relief, or, except as provided in subsection (j), for injunctive or other equitable relief, for infringement of copyright by reason of the intermediate and temporary storage of material on a system or network controlled or operated by or for the service provider in a case in which—

(A) the material is made available online by a person other than the service provider;

(B) the material is transmitted from the person described in subparagraph (A) through the system or network to a person other than the person described in subparagraph (A) at the direction of that other person; and

(C) the storage is carried out through an automatic technical process for the purpose of making the material available to users of the system or network who, after the material is transmitted as described in subparagraph (B), request access to the material from the person described in subparagraph (A),

if the conditions set forth in paragraph (2) are met.

(2) *Conditions.* — The conditions referred to in paragraph (1) are that —

(A) the material described in paragraph (1) is transmitted to the subsequent users described in paragraph (1)(C) without modification to its content from the manner in which the material was transmitted from the person described in paragraph (1)(A);

(B) the service provider described in paragraph (1) complies with rules concerning the refreshing, reloading, or other updating of the material when specified by the person making the material available online in accordance with a generally accepted industry standard data communications protocol for the system or network through which that person makes the material available, except that this subparagraph applies only if those rules are not used by the person described in paragraph (1)(A) to prevent or unreasonably impair the intermediate storage to which this subsection applies;

(C) the service provider does not interfere with the ability of technology associated with the material to return to the person described in paragraph (1)(A) the information that would have been available to that person if the material had been obtained by the subsequent users described in paragraph (1)(C) directly from that person, except that this subparagraph applies only if that technology —

(i) does not significantly interfere with the performance of the provider's system or network or with the intermediate storage of the material;

(ii) is consistent with generally accepted industry standard communications protocols; and

17 U.S.C. § 512

(iii) does not extract information from the provider's system or network other than the information that would have been available to the person described in paragraph (1)(A) if the subsequent users had gained access to the material directly from that person;

(D) if the person described in paragraph (1)(A) has in effect a condition that a person must meet prior to having access to the material, such as a condition based on payment of a fee or provision of a password or other information, the service provider permits access to the stored material in significant part only to users of its system or network that have met those conditions and only in accordance with those conditions; and

(E) if the person described in paragraph (1)(A) makes that material available online without the authorization of the copyright owner of the material, the service provider responds expeditiously to remove, or disable access to, the material that is claimed to be infringing upon notification of claimed infringement as described in subsection (c)(3), except that this subparagraph applies only if—

(i) the material has previously been removed from the originating site or access to it has been disabled, or a court has ordered that the material be removed from the originating site or that access to the material on the originating site be disabled; and

(ii) the party giving the notification includes in the notification a statement confirming that the material has been removed from the originating site or access to it has been disabled or that a court has ordered that the material be removed from the originating site or that access to the material on the originating site be disabled.

(c) *Information residing on systems or networks at director of users.* —

(1) *In general.*—A service provider shall not be liable for monetary relief, or, except as provided in subsection (j), for injunctive or other equitable relief, for infringement of copyright by reason of the storage at the direction of a user of material that resides on a system or network controlled or operated by or for the service provider, if the service provider—

(A)(i) does not have actual knowledge that the material or an activity using the material on the system or network is infringing;

(ii) in the absence of such actual knowledge, is not aware of facts or circumstances from which infringing activity is apparent; or

(iii) upon obtaining such knowledge or awareness, acts expeditiously to remove, or disable access to, the material;

(B) does not receive a financial benefit directly attributable to the infringing activity, in a case in which the service provider has the right and ability to control such activity; and

(C) upon notification of claimed infringement as described in paragraph (3), responds expeditiously to remove, or disable access to, the material that is claimed to be infringing or to be the subject of infringing activity.

(2) *Designated agent.*—The limitations on liability established in this subsection apply to a service provider only if the service provider has designated an agent to receive notifications of claimed infringement described in paragraph (3), by making available through its service, including on its website in a location accessible to the public, and by providing to the Copyright Office, substantially the following information:

(A) the name, address, phone number, and electronic mail address of the agent.

(B) other contact information which the Register of Copyrights may deem appropriate.

The Register of Copyrights shall maintain a current directory of agents available to the public for inspection, including through the Internet, and may require payment of a fee by service providers to cover the costs of maintaining the directory.

(3) *Elements of notification.*—

(A) To be effective under this subsection, a notification of claimed infringement must be a written communication provided to the designated agent of a service provider that includes substantially the following:

(i) A physical or electronic signature of a person authorized to act on behalf of the owner of an exclusive right that is allegedly infringed.

(ii) Identification of the copyrighted work claimed to have been infringed, or, if multiple copyrighted works at a single online site are covered by a single notification, a representative list of such works at that site.

17 U.S.C. § 512

(iii) Identification of the material that is claimed to be infringing or to be the subject of infringing activity and that is to be removed or access to which is to be disabled, and information reasonably sufficient to permit the service provider to locate the material.

(iv) Information reasonably sufficient to permit the service provider to contact the complaining party, such as an address, telephone number, and, if available, an electronic mail address at which the complaining party may be contacted.

(v) A statement that the complaining party has a good faith belief that use of the material in the manner complained of is not authorized by the copyright owner, its agent, or the law.

(vi) A statement that the information in the notification is accurate, and under penalty of perjury, that the complaining party is authorized to act on behalf of the owner of an exclusive right that is allegedly infringed.

(B)(i) Subject to clause (ii), a notification from a copyright owner or from a person authorized to act on behalf of the copyright owner that fails to comply substantially with the provisions of subparagraph (A) shall not be considered under paragraph (1)(A) in determining whether a service provider has actual knowledge or is aware of facts or circumstances from which infringing activity is apparent.

(ii) In a case in which the notification that is provided to the service provider's designated agent fails to comply substantially with all the provisions of subparagraph (A) but substantially complies with clauses (ii), (iii), and (iv) of subparagraph (A), clause (i) of this subparagraph applies only if the service provider promptly attempts to contact the person making the notification or takes other reasonable steps to assist in the receipt of notification that substantially complies with all the provisions of subparagraph (A).

(d) *Information location tools.*—A service provider shall not be liable for monetary relief, or, except as provided in subsection (j), for injunctive or other equitable relief, for infringement of copyright by reason of the provider referring or linking users to an online location containing infringing material or infringing activity, by using information location tools, including a directory, index, reference, pointer, or hypertext link, if the service provider—

(1)(A) does not have actual knowledge that the material or activity is infringing;

(B) in the absence of such actual knowledge, is not aware of facts or circumstances from which infringing activity is apparent; or

(C) upon obtaining such knowledge or awareness, acts expeditiously to remove, or disable access to, the material;

(2) does not receive a financial benefit directly attributable to the infringing activity, in a case in which the service provider has the right and ability to control such activity; and

(3) upon notification of claimed infringement as described in subsection (c)(3), responds expeditiously to remove, or disable access to, the material that is claimed to be infringing or to be the subject of infringing activity, except that, for purposes of this paragraph, the information described in subsection (c)(3)(A)(iii) shall be identification of the reference or link, to material or activity claimed to be infringing, that is to be removed or access to which is to be disabled, and information reasonably sufficient to permit the service provider to locate that reference or link.

(e) *Limitation on liability of nonprofit educational institutions.*—

(1) When a public or other nonprofit institution of higher education is a service provider, and when a faculty member or graduate student who is an employee of such institution is performing a teaching or research function, for the purposes of subsections (a) and (b) such faculty member or graduate student shall be considered to be a person other than the institution, and for the purposes of subsections (c) and (d) such faculty member's or graduate student's knowledge or awareness of his or her infringing activities shall not be attributed to the institution, if—

(A) such faculty member's or graduate student's infringing activities do not involve the provision of online access to instructional materials that are or were required or recommended, within the preceding 3-year period, for a course taught at the institution by such faculty member or graduate student;

(B) the institution has not, within the preceding 3-year period, received more than two notifications described in subsection (c)(3) of claimed infringement by such faculty member or graduate student, and such notifications of claimed infringement were not actionable under subsection (f); and

(C) the institution provides to all users of its system or network informational materials that accurately describe, and promote compliance with, the laws of the United States relating to copyright.

(2) For the purposes of this subsection, the limitations on injunctive relief contained in subsections (j)(2) and (j)(3), but not those in (j)(1), shall apply.

(f) *Misrepresentations.*—Any person who knowingly materially misrepresents under this section—

(1) that material or activity is infringing, or

(2) that material or activity was removed or disabled by mistake or misidentification,

shall be liable for any damages, including costs and attorneys' fees, incurred by the alleged infringer, by any copyright owner or copyright owner's authorized licensee, or by a service provider, who is injured by such misrepresentation, as the result of the service provider relying upon such misrepresentation in removing or disabling access to the material or activity claimed to be infringing, or in replacing the removed material or ceasing to disable access to it.

(g) *Replacement of removed or disabled material and limitation on other liability.*—

(1) *No liability for taking down generally.*—Subject to paragraph (2), a service provider shall not be liable to any person for any claim based on the service provider's good faith disabling of access to, or removal of, material or activity claimed to be infringing or based on facts or circumstances from which infringing activity is apparent, regardless of whether the material or activity is ultimately determined to be infringing.

(2) *Exception.*—Paragraph (1) shall not apply with respect to material residing at the direction of a subscriber of the service provider on a system or network controlled or operated by or for the service provider that is removed, or to which access is disabled by the service provider, pursuant to a notice provided under subsection (c)(1)(C), unless the service provider—

(A) takes reasonable steps promptly to notify the subscriber that it has removed or disabled access to the material;

(B) upon receipt of a counter notification described in paragraph (3), promptly provides the person who provided the notification under subsection (c)(1)(C) with a copy of the counter notification, and informs that person that it will replace the removed material or cease disabling access to it in 10 business days; and

(C) replaces the removed material and ceases disabling access to it not less than 10, nor more than 14, business days following receipt of the counter notice, unless its designated agent first receives notice from the person who submitted the notification under subsection (c)(1)(C) that such person has filed an action seeking a court order to restrain the subscriber from engaging in infringing activity relating to the material on the service provider's system or network.

(3) *Contents of counter notification.* — To be effective under this subsection, a counter notification must be a written communication provided to the service provider's designated agent that includes substantially the following:

(A) A physical or electronic signature of the subscriber.

(B) Identification of the material that has been removed or to which access has been disabled and the location at which the material appeared before it was removed or access to it was disabled.

(C) A statement under penalty of perjury that the subscriber has a good faith belief that the material was removed or disabled as a result of mistake or misidentification of the material to be removed or disabled.

(D) The subscriber's name, address, and telephone number, and a statement that the subscriber consents to the jurisdiction of Federal District Court for the judicial district in which the address is located, or if the subscriber's address is outside of the United States, for any judicial district in which the service provider may be found, and that the subscriber will accept service of process from the person who provided notification under subsection (c)(1)(C) or an agent of such person.

(4) *Limitation on other liability.* — A service provider's compliance with paragraph (2) shall not subject the service provider to liability for copyright infringement with respect to the material identified in the notice provided under subsection (c)(1)(C).

17 U.S.C. § 512

(h) *Subpoena to identify infringer.* —

(1) *Request.* — A copyright owner or a person authorized to act on the owner's behalf may request the clerk of any United States district court to issue a subpoena to a service provider for identification of an alleged infringer in accordance with this subsection.

(2) *Contents of request.* — The request may be made by filing with the clerk—

(A) a copy of a notification described in subsection (c)(3)(A);

(B) a proposed subpoena; and

(C) a sworn declaration to the effect that the purpose for which the subpoena is sought is to obtain the identity of an alleged infringer and that such information will only be used for the purpose of protecting rights under this title.

(3) *Contents of subpoena.* — The subpoena shall authorize and order the service provider receiving the notification and the subpoena to expeditiously disclose to the copyright owner or person authorized by the copyright owner information sufficient to identify the alleged infringer of the material described in the notification to the extent such information is available to the service provider.

(4) *Basis for granting subpoena.* — If the notification filed satisfies the provisions of subsection (c)(3)(A), the proposed subpoena is in proper form, and the accompanying declaration is properly executed, the clerk shall expeditiously issue and sign the proposed subpoena and return it to the requester for delivery to the service provider.

(5) *Actions of service provider receiving subpoena.* — Upon receipt of the issued subpoena, either accompanying or subsequent to the receipt of a notification described in subsection (c)(3)(A), the service provider shall expeditiously disclose to the copyright owner or person authorized by the copyright owner the information required by the subpoena, notwithstanding any other provision of law and regardless of whether the service provider responds to the notification.

(6) *Rules applicable to subpoena.* — Unless otherwise provided by this section or by applicable rules of the court, the procedure for issuance and delivery of the subpoena, and the remedies for noncompliance with the subpoena, shall be governed to the greatest extent practicable by those provisions of

the Federal Rules of Civil Procedure governing the issuance, service, and enforcement of a subpoena duces tecum.

(i) *Conditions for eligibility.* —

(1) *Accommodation of technology.* — The limitations on liability established by this section shall apply to a service provider only if the service provider—

(A) has adopted and reasonably implemented, and informs subscribers and account holders of the service provider's system or network of, a policy that provides for the termination in appropriate circumstances of subscribers and account holders of the service provider's system or network who are repeat infringers; and

(B) accommodates and does not interfere with standard technical measures.

(2) *Definition.* — As used in this subsection, the term "standard technical measures" means technical measures that are used by copyright owners to identify or protect copyrighted works and—

(A) have been developed pursuant to a broad consensus of copyright owners and service providers in an open, fair, voluntary, multi-industry standards process;

(B) are available to any person on reasonable and nondiscriminatory terms; and

(C) do not impose substantial costs on service providers or substantial burdens on their systems or networks.

(j) *Injunctions.* — The following rules shall apply in the case of any application for an injunction under section 502 against a service provider that is not subject to monetary remedies under this section:

(1) *Scope of relief.* —

(A) With respect to conduct other than that which qualifies for the limitation on remedies set forth in subsection (a), the court may grant injunctive relief with respect to a service provider only in one or more of the following forms:

(i) An order restraining the service provider from providing access to infringing material or activity residing at a particular online site on the provider's system or network.

17 U.S.C. § 512

(ii) An order restraining the service provider from providing access to a subscriber or account holder of the service provider's system or network who is engaging in infringing activity and is identified in the order, by terminating the accounts of the subscriber or account holder that are specified in the order.

(iii) Such other injunctive relief as the court may consider necessary to prevent or restrain infringement of copyrighted material specified in the order of the court at a particular online location, if such relief is the least burdensome to the service provider among the forms of relief comparably effective for that purpose.

(B) If the service provider qualifies for the limitation on remedies described in subsection (a), the court may only grant injunctive relief in one or both of the following forms:

(i) An order restraining the service provider from providing access to a subscriber or account holder of the service provider's system or network who is using the provider's service to engage in infringing activity and is identified in the order, by terminating the accounts of the subscriber or account holder that are specified in the order.

(ii) An order restraining the service provider from providing access, by taking reasonable steps specified in the order to block access, to a specific, identified, online location outside the United States.

(2) *Considerations.*—The court, in considering the relevant criteria for injunctive relief under applicable law, shall consider—

(A) whether such an injunction, either alone or in combination with other such injunctions issued against the same service provider under this subsection, would significantly burden either the provider or the operation of the provider's system or network;

(B) the magnitude of the harm likely to be suffered by the copyright owner in the digital network environment if steps are not taken to prevent or restrain the infringement;

(C) whether implementation of such an injunction would be technically feasible and effective, and would not interfere with access to noninfringing material at other online locations; and

(D) whether other less burdensome and comparably effective means of preventing or restraining access to the infringing material are available.

(3) *Notice and ex parte orders.*—Injunctive relief under this subsection shall be available only after notice to the service provider and an opportunity for the service provider to appear are provided, except for orders ensuring the preservation of evidence or other orders having no material adverse effect on the operation of the service provider's communications network.

(k) *Definitions.*—

(1) *Service provider.*—

(A) As used in subsection (a), the term "service provider" means an entity offering the transmission, routing, or providing of connections for digital online communications, between or among points specified by a user, of material of the user's choosing, without modification to the content of the material as sent or received.

(B) As used in this section, other than subsection (a), the term "service provider" means a provider of online services or network access, or the operator of facilities therefor, and includes an entity described in subparagraph (A).

(2) *Monetary relief.*—As used in this section, the term "monetary relief" means damages, costs, attorneys' fees, and any other form of monetary payment.

(l) *Other defenses not affected.*—The failure of a service provider's conduct to qualify for limitation of liability under this section shall not bear adversely upon the consideration of a defense by the service provider that the service provider's conduct is not infringing under this title or any other defense.

(m) *Protection of privacy.*—Nothing in this section shall be construed to condition the applicability of subsections (a) through (d) on—

(1) a service provider monitoring its service or affirmatively seeking facts indicating infringing activity, except to the extent consistent with a standard technical measure complying with the provisions of subsection (i); or

(2) a service provider gaining access to, removing, or disabling access to material in cases in which such conduct is prohibited by law.

(n) *Construction.*—Subsections (a), (b), (c), and (d) describe separate and distinct functions for purposes of applying this section. Whether a service

17 U.S.C. § 512

provider qualifies for the limitation on liability in any one of those subsections shall be based solely on the criteria in that subsection, and shall not affect a determination of whether that service provider qualifies for the limitations on liability under any other such subsection.

(Oct. 28, 1998, Pub. L. 105-304, §202, 112 Stat. 2877; Aug. 5, 1999, Pub. L. 106-44, §1(d), 113 Stat. 222; Dec. 9, 2010, Pub. L. 111-295, §3, 124 Stat. 3180.)

§ 513 Determination of reasonable license fees for individual proprietors

In the case of any performing rights society subject to a consent decree which provides for the determination of reasonable license rates or fees to be charged by the performing rights society, notwithstanding the provisions of that consent decree, an individual proprietor who owns or operates fewer than 7 non-publicly traded establishments in which nondramatic musical works are performed publicly and who claims that any license agreement offered by that performing rights society is unreasonable in its license rate or fee as to that individual proprietor, shall be entitled to determination of a reasonable license rate or fee as follows:

(1) The individual proprietor may commence such proceeding for determination of a reasonable license rate or fee by filing an application in the applicable district court under paragraph (2) that a rate disagreement exists and by serving a copy of the application on the performing rights society. Such proceeding shall commence in the applicable district court within 90 days after the service of such copy, except that such 90-day requirement shall be subject to the administrative requirements of the court.

(2) The proceeding under paragraph (1) shall be held, at the individual proprietor's election, in the judicial district of the district court with jurisdiction over the applicable consent decree or in that place of holding court of a district court that is the seat of the Federal circuit (other than the Court of Appeals for the Federal Circuit) in which the proprietor's establishment is located.

(3) Such proceeding shall be held before the judge of the court with jurisdiction over the consent decree governing the performing rights society. At the discretion of the court, the proceeding shall be held before a special master or magistrate judge appointed by such judge. Should that consent decree provide for the appointment of an advisor or advisors to the court for any purpose, any such advisor shall be the special master so named by the court.

17 U.S.C. § 513

(4) In any such proceeding, the industry rate shall be presumed to have been reasonable at the time it was agreed to or determined by the court. Such presumption shall in no way affect a determination of whether the rate is being correctly applied to the individual proprietor.

(5) Pending the completion of such proceeding, the individual proprietor shall have the right to perform publicly the copyrighted musical compositions in the repertoire of the performing rights society by paying an interim license rate or fee into an interest bearing escrow account with the clerk of the court, subject to retroactive adjustment when a final rate or fee has been determined, in an amount equal to the industry rate, or, in the absence of an industry rate, the amount of the most recent license rate or fee agreed to by the parties.

(6) Any decision rendered in such proceeding by a special master or magistrate judge named under paragraph (3) shall be reviewed by the judge of the court with jurisdiction over the consent decree governing the performing rights society. Such proceeding, including such review, shall be concluded within 6 months after its commencement.

(7) Any such final determination shall be binding only as to the individual proprietor commencing the proceeding, and shall not be applicable to any other proprietor or any other performing rights society, and the performing rights society shall be relieved of any obligation of nondiscrimination among similarly situated music users that may be imposed by the consent decree governing its operations.

(8) An individual proprietor may not bring more than one proceeding provided for in this section for the determination of a reasonable license rate or fee under any license agreement with respect to any one performing rights society.

(9) For purposes of this section, the term "industry rate" means the license fee a performing rights society has agreed to with, or which has been determined by the court for, a significant segment of the music user industry to which the individual proprietor belongs.

(Added Oct. 27, 1998, Pub. L. 105-298, §203, 112 Stat. 2831; Aug. 5, 1999, Pub. L. 106-44, §1(c), 113 Stat. 221.)

CHAPTER 6 — IMPORTATION AND EXPORTATION

SEC.
  601.   [Repealed].

602.   Infringing importation or exportation of copies or phonorecords.

603.   Importation prohibitions: Enforcement and disposition of excluded articles.

§ 601   [Repealed]

(Oct. 19, 1976, Pub. L. 94-553, §101, 90 Stat. 2588; July 13, 1982, Pub. L. 97-215, 96 Stat. 178; Nov. 13, 1997, Pub. L. 105-80, §12, 111 Stat. 1535; Oct. 13, 2008, Pub. L. 110-403, §105, 122 Stat. 4260; Dec. 9, 2010, Pub. L. 111-295, §4, 124 Stat. 3180.)

§ 602   Infringing importation or exportation of copies or phonorecords

(a) *Infringing importation or exportation.* —

(1) *Importation.* —Importation into the United States, without the authority of the owner of copyright under this title, of copies or phonorecords of a work that have been acquired outside the United States is an infringement of the exclusive right to distribute copies or phonorecords under section 106, actionable under section 501.

(2) *Importation or exportation of infringing items.* —Importation into the United States or exportation from the United States, without the authority of the owner of copyright under this title, of copies or phonorecords, the making of which either constituted an infringement of copyright, or which would have constituted an infringement of copyright if this title had been applicable, is an infringement of the exclusive right to distribute copies or phonorecords under section 106, actionable under sections 501 and 506.

(3) *Exceptions.* —This subsection does not apply to—

(A) importation or exportation of copies or phonorecords under the authority or for the use of the Government of the United States or of any State or political subdivision of a State, but not including copies or phonorecords for use in schools, or copies of any audiovisual work imported for purposes other than archival use;

(B) importation or exportation, for the private use of the importer or exporter and not for distribution, by any person with respect to no more than one copy or phonorecord of any one work at any one time, or by any person arriving from outside the United States or departing from the United States with respect to copies or phonorecords forming part of such person's personal baggage; or

(C) importation by or for an organization operated for scholarly, educational, or religious purposes and not for private gain, with respect to no more than one copy of an audiovisual work solely for its archival purposes, and no more than five copies or phonorecords of any other work for its library lending or archival purposes, unless the importation of such copies or phonorecords is part of an activity consisting of systematic reproduction or distribution, engaged in by such organization in violation of the provisions of section 108(g)(2).

(b) *Import prohibition.*—In a case where the making of the copies or phonorecords would have constituted an infringement of copyright if this title had been applicable, their importation is prohibited. In a case where the copies or phonorecords were lawfully made, the United States Customs and Border Protection has no authority to prevent their importation. In either case, the Secretary of the Treasury is authorized to prescribe, by regulation, a procedure under which any person claiming an interest in the copyright in a particular work may, upon payment of a specified fee, be entitled to notification by the United States Customs and Border Protection of the importation of articles that appear to be copies or phonorecords of the work.

(Oct. 19, 1976, Pub. L. 94-553, §101, 90 Stat. 2589; Oct. 13, 2008, Pub. L. 110-403, §105, 122 Stat. 4259, 4260; Dec. 9, 2010, Pub. L. 111-295, §4, 124 Stat. 3180.)

§ 603   Importation prohibitions: Enforcement and disposition of excluded articles

(a) The Secretary of the Treasury and the United States Postal Service shall separately or jointly make regulations for the enforcement of the provisions of this title prohibiting importation.

(b) These regulations may require, as a condition for the exclusion of articles under section 602—

(1) that the person seeking exclusion obtain a court order enjoining importation of the articles; or

(2) that the person seeking exclusion furnish proof, of a specified nature and in accordance with prescribed procedures, that the copyright in which such person claims an interest is valid and that the importation would violate the prohibition in section 602; the person seeking exclusion may also be required to post a surety bond for any injury that may result if the detention or exclusion of the articles proves to be unjustified.

(c) Articles imported in violation of the importation prohibitions of this title are subject to seizure and forfeiture in the same manner as property imported in violation of the customs revenue laws. Forfeited articles shall be destroyed as directed by the Secretary of the Treasury or the court, as the case may be.

(Oct. 19, 1976, Pub. L. 94-553, §101, 90 Stat. 2590; July 2, 1996, Pub. L. 104-153, §8, 110 Stat. 1388.)

CHAPTER 7—COPYRIGHT OFFICE

§ 701   The Copyright Office: General responsibilities and organization

(a) All administrative functions and duties under this title, except as otherwise specified, are the responsibility of the Register of Copyrights as director of the Copyright Office of the Library of Congress. The Register of Copyrights, together with the subordinate officers and employees of the Copyright Office, shall be appointed by the Librarian of Congress, and shall act under the Librarian's general direction and supervision.

(b) In addition to the functions and duties set out elsewhere in this chapter, the Register of Copyrights shall perform the following functions:

(1) Advise Congress on national and international issues relating to copyright, other matters arising under this title, and related matters.

(2) Provide information and assistance to Federal departments and agencies and the Judiciary on national and international issues relating to copyright, other matters arising under this title, and related matters.

(3) Participate in meetings of international intergovernmental organizations and meetings with foreign government officials relating to copyright, other matters arising under this title, and related matters, including as a member of United States delegations as authorized by the appropriate Executive branch authority.

(4) Conduct studies and programs regarding copyright, other matters arising under this title, and related matters, the administration of the Copyright Office, or any function vested in the Copyright Office by law, including educational programs conducted cooperatively with foreign intellectual property offices and international intergovernmental organizations.

(5) Perform such other functions as Congress may direct, or as may be appropriate in furtherance of the functions and duties specifically set forth in this title.

(c) The Register of Copyrights shall adopt a seal to be used on and after January 1, 1978, to authenticate all certified documents issued by the Copyright Office.

(d) The Register of Copyrights shall make an annual report to the Librarian of Congress of the work and accomplishments of the Copyright Office during the previous fiscal year. The annual report of the Register of Copyrights shall be published separately and as a part of the annual report of the Librarian of Congress.

(e) Except as provided by section 706(b) and the regulations issued thereunder, all actions taken by the Register of Copyrights under this title are subject to the provisions of the Administrative Procedure Act of June 11, 1946, as amended (c. 324, 60 Stat. 237, title 5, United States Code, Chapter 5, Subchapter II and Chapter 7).

(f) The Register of Copyrights shall be compensated at the rate of pay in effect for level III of the Executive Schedule under section 5314 of title 5. The Librarian of Congress shall establish not more than four positions for Associate Registers of Copyrights, in accordance with the recommendations of the Register of Copyrights. The Librarian shall make appointments to such positions after consultation with the Register of Copyrights. Each Associate Register of Copyrights shall be paid at a rate not to exceed the maximum annual rate of basic pay payable for GS-18 of the General Schedule under section 5332 of title 5.

(Oct. 19, 1976, Pub. L. 94-553, §101, 90 Stat. 2591; July 3, 1990, Pub. L. 101-319, §2, 104 Stat. 290; Oct. 28, 1998, Pub. L. 105-304, §401, 112 Stat. 2887.)

§ 702 Copyright Office regulations

The Register of Copyrights is authorized to establish regulations not inconsistent with law for the administration of the functions and duties made the responsibility of the Register under this title. All regulations established by the Register under this title are subject to the approval of the Librarian of Congress.

(Oct. 19, 1976, Pub. L. 94-553, §101, 90 Stat. 2591.)

§ 703   Effective date of actions in Copyright Office

In any case in which time limits are prescribed under this title for the performance of an action in the Copyright Office, and in which the last day of the prescribed period falls on a Saturday, Sunday, holiday, or other nonbusiness day within the District of Columbia or the Federal Government, the action may be taken on the next succeeding business day, and is effective as of the date when the period expired.

(Oct. 19, 1976, Pub. L. 94-553, §101, 90 Stat. 2591.)

§ 704   Retention and disposition of articles deposited in Copyright Office

(a) Upon their deposit in the Copyright Office under sections 407 and 408, all copies, phonorecords, and identifying material, including those deposited in connection with claims that have been refused registration, are the property of the United States Government.

(b) In the case of published works, all copies, phonorecords, and identifying material deposited are available to the Library of Congress for its collections, or for exchange or transfer to any other library. In the case of unpublished works, the Library is entitled, under regulations that the Register of Copyrights shall prescribe, to select any deposits for its collections or for transfer to the National Archives of the United States or to a Federal records center, as defined in section 2901 of title 44.

(c) The Register of Copyrights is authorized, for specific or general categories of works, to make a facsimile reproduction of all or any part of the material deposited under section 408, and to make such reproduction a part of the Copyright Office records of the registration, before transferring such material to the Library of Congress as provided by subsection (b), or before destroying or otherwise disposing of such material as provided by subsection (d).

(d) Deposits not selected by the Library under subsection (b), or identifying portions or reproductions of them, shall be retained under the control of the Copyright Office, including retention in Government storage facilities, for the longest period considered practicable and desirable by the Register of Copyrights and the Librarian of Congress. After that period it is within the joint discretion of the Register and the Librarian to order their destruction or other disposition; but, in the case of unpublished works, no deposit shall be knowingly or intentionally destroyed or otherwise disposed of during its term of copyright unless a facsimile reproduction of the entire deposit has been made a part of the Copyright Office records as provided by subsection (c).

(e) The depositor of copies, phonorecords, or identifying material under section 408, or the copyright owner of record, may request retention, under the control of the Copyright Office, of one or more of such articles for the full term of copyright in the work. The Register of Copyrights shall prescribe, by regulation, the conditions under which such requests are to be made and granted, and shall fix the fee to be charged under section 708(a) if the request is granted.

(Oct. 19, 1976, Pub. L. 94-553, §101, 90 Stat. 2591; July 3, 1990, Pub. L. 101-318, §2, 104 Stat. 288; Dec. 9, 2010, Pub. L. 111-295, §6, 124 Stat. 3181.)

§ 705 Copyright Office records: Preparation, maintenance, public inspection, and searching

(a) The Register of Copyrights shall ensure that records of deposits, registrations, recordations, and other actions taken under this title are maintained, and that indexes of such records are prepared.

(b) Such records and indexes, as well as the articles deposited in connection with completed copyright registrations and retained under the control of the Copyright Office, shall be open to public inspection.

(c) Upon request and payment of the fee specified by section 708, the Copyright Office shall make a search of its public records, indexes, and deposits, and shall furnish a report of the information they disclose with respect to any particular deposits, registrations, or recorded documents.

(Oct. 19, 1976, Pub. L. 94-553, §101, 90 Stat. 2592; Oct. 27, 2000, Pub. L. 106-379, §3(a), 114 Stat. 1445.)

§ 706 Copies of Copyright Office records

(a) Copies may be made of any public records or indexes of the Copyright Office; additional certificates of copyright registration and copies of any public records or indexes may be furnished upon request and payment of the fees specified by section 708.

(b) Copies or reproductions of deposited articles retained under the control of the Copyright Office shall be authorized or furnished only under the conditions specified by the Copyright Office regulations.

(Oct. 19, 1976, Pub. L. 94-553, §101, 90 Stat. 2592.)

§ 707 Copyright Office forms and publications

(a) *Catalog of copyright entries.* — The Register of Copyrights shall compile and publish at periodic intervals catalogs of all copyright registrations. These catalogs shall be divided into parts in accordance with the various classes of works, and the Register has discretion to determine, on the basis of practicability and usefulness, the form and frequency of publication of each particular part.

(b) *Other publications.* — The Register shall furnish, free of charge upon request, application forms for copyright registration and general informational material in connection with the functions of the Copyright Office. The Register also has the authority to publish compilations of information, bibliographies, and other material he or she considers to be of value to the public.

(c) *Distribution of publications.* — All publications of the Copyright Office shall be furnished to depository libraries as specified under section 1905 of title 44, and, aside from those furnished free of charge, shall be offered for sale to the public at prices based on the cost of reproduction and distribution.

(Oct. 19, 1976, Pub. L. 94-553, §101, 90 Stat. 2592.)

§ 708 Copyright Office fees[16]

(a) *Fees.* — Fees shall be paid to the Register of Copyrights—

(1) on filing each application under section 408 for registration of a copyright claim or for a supplementary registration, including the issuance of a certificate of registration if registration is made;

(2) on filing each application for registration of a claim for renewal of a subsisting copyright under section 304(a), including the issuance of a certificate of registration if registration is made;

(3) for the issuance of a receipt for a deposit under section 407;

(4) for the recordation, as provided by section 205, of a transfer of copyright ownership or other document;

---

[16] *Ed. Note:* The Copyright Office fees may be found at www.copyright.gov/docs/fees.html.

(5) for the filing, under section 115(b), of a notice of intention to obtain a compulsory license;

(6) for the recordation, under section 302(c), of a statement revealing the identity of an author of an anonymous or pseudonymous work, or for the recordation, under section 302(d), of a statement relating to the death of an author;

(7) for the issuance, under section 706, of an additional certificate of registration;

(8) for the issuance of any other certification;

(9) for the making and reporting of a search as provided by section 705, and for any related services;

(10) on filing a statement of account based on secondary transmissions of primary transmissions pursuant to section 119 or 122; and

(11) on filing a statement of account based on secondary transmissions of primary transmissions pursuant to section 111.

The Register is authorized to fix fees for other services, including the cost of preparing copies of Copyright Office records, whether or not such copies are certified, based on the cost of providing the service. Fees established under paragraphs (10) and (11) shall be reasonable and may not exceed one-half of the cost necessary to cover reasonable expenses incurred by the Copyright Office for the collection and administration of the statements of account and any royalty fees deposited with such statements.

(b) *Adjustment of Fees.*—The Register of Copyrights may, by regulation, adjust the fees for the services specified in paragraphs (1) through (9) of subsection (a) in the following manner:

(1) The Register shall conduct a study of the costs incurred by the Copyright Office for the registration of claims, the recordation of documents, and the provision of services. The study shall also consider the timing of any adjustment in fees and the authority to use such fees consistent with the budget.

(2) The Register may, on the basis of the study under paragraph (1), and subject to paragraph (5), adjust fees to not more than that necessary to cover the reasonable costs incurred by the Copyright Office for the services described in paragraph (1), plus a reasonable inflation adjustment to account for any estimated increase in costs.

17 U.S.C. § 708

(3) Any fee established under paragraph (2) shall be rounded off to the nearest dollar, or for a fee less than $12, rounded off to the nearest 50 cents.

(4) Fees established under this subsection shall be fair and equitable and give due consideration to the objectives of the copyright system.

(5) If the Register determines under paragraph (2) that fees should be adjusted, the Register shall prepare a proposed fee schedule and submit the schedule with the accompanying economic analysis to the Congress. The fees proposed by the Register may be instituted after the end of 120 days after the schedule is submitted to the Congress unless, within that 120-day period, a law is enacted stating in substance that the Congress does not approve the schedule.

(c) The fees prescribed by or under this section are applicable to the United States Government and any of its agencies, employees, or officers, but the Register of Copyrights has discretion to waive the requirement of this subsection in occasional or isolated cases involving relatively small amounts.

(d) (1) Except as provided in paragraph (2), all fees received under this section shall be deposited by the Register of Copyrights in the Treasury of the United States and shall be credited to the appropriations for necessary expenses of the Copyright Office. Such fees that are collected shall remain available until expended. The Register may, in accordance with regulations that he or she shall prescribe, refund any sum paid by mistake or in excess of the fee required by this section.

(2) In the case of fees deposited against future services, the Register of Copyrights shall request the Secretary of the Treasury to invest in interest-bearing securities in the United States Treasury any portion of the fees that, as determined by the Register, is not required to meet current deposit account demands. Funds from such portion of fees shall be invested in securities that permit funds to be available to the Copyright Office at all times if they are determined to be necessary to meet current deposit account demands. Such investments shall be in public debt securities with maturities suitable to the needs of the Copyright Office, as determined by the Register of Copyrights, and bearing interest at rates determined by the Secretary of the Treasury, taking into consideration current market yields on outstanding marketable obligations of the United States of comparable maturities.

17 U.S.C. § 708

(3) The income on such investments shall be deposited in the Treasury of the United States and shall be credited to the appropriations for necessary expenses of the Copyright Office.

(Oct. 19, 1976, Pub. L. 94-553, §101, 90 Stat. 2593; Aug. 5, 1977, Pub. L. 95-94, §406, 91 Stat. 682; Oct. 15, 1982, Pub. L. 97-366, §1, 96 Stat. 1759; July 3, 1990, Pub. L. 101-318, §2, 104 Stat. 287-88; June 26, 1992, Pub. L. 102-307, §102(f), 106 Stat. 266; Nov. 13, 1997, Pub. L. 105-80 §7, 111 Stat. 1532-33; Oct. 27, 2000, Pub. L. 106-379, §3(a), 114 Stat. 1445; May 27, 2010, Pub. L. 111-175, §106, 124 Stat. 1244.)

§ 709 Delay in delivery caused by disruption of postal or other services

In any case in which the Register of Copyrights determines, on the basis of such evidence as the Register may by regulation require, that a deposit, application, fee, or any other material to be delivered to the Copyright Office by a particular date, would have been received in the Copyright Office in due time except for a general disruption or suspension of postal or other transportation or communications services, the actual receipt of such material in the Copyright Office within one month after the date on which the Register determines that the disruption or suspension of such services has terminated, shall be considered timely.

(Oct. 19, 1976, Pub. L. 94-553, §101, 90 Stat. 2594.)

§ 710 [Repealed]

(Oct. 19, 1976, Pub. L. 94-553, §101, 90 Stat. 2594; Oct. 27, 2000, Pub. L. 106-379, §3(a), 114 Stat. 1445.)

CHAPTER 8—COPYRIGHT ARBITRATION ROYALTY PANELS

§ 801 Copyright Royalty Judges; appointment and functions

(a) *Appointment.*—The Librarian of Congress shall appoint 3 full-time Copyright Royalty Judges, and shall appoint 1 of the 3 as the Chief Copyright Royalty Judge. The Librarian shall make appointments to such positions after consultation with the Register of Copyrights.

(b) *Functions.*—Subject to the provisions of this chapter, the functions of the Copyright Royalty Judges shall be as follows:

(1) To make determinations and adjustments of reasonable terms and rates of royalty payments as provided in sections 112(e), 114, 115, 116, 118, 119, and 1004. The rates applicable under sections 114(f)(1)(B), 115, and 116 shall be calculated to achieve the following objectives:

(A) To maximize the availability of creative works to the public.

(B) To afford the copyright owner a fair return for his or her creative work and the copyright user a fair income under existing economic conditions.

(C) To reflect the relative roles of the copyright owner and the copyright user in the product made available to the public with respect to relative creative contribution, technological contribution, capital investment, cost, risk, and contribution to the opening of new markets for creative expression and media for their communication.

(D) To minimize any disruptive impact on the structure of the industries involved and on generally prevailing industry practices.

(2) To make determinations concerning the adjustment of the copyright royalty rates under section 111 solely in accordance with the following provisions:

(A) The rates established by section 111(d)(1)(B) may be adjusted to reflect—

(i) national monetary inflation or deflation; or

(ii) changes in the average rates charged cable subscribers for the basic service of providing secondary transmissions to maintain the real constant dollar level of the royalty fee per subscriber which existed as of the date of October 19, 1976,

except that—

(I) if the average rates charged cable system subscribers for the basic service of providing secondary transmissions are changed so that the average rates exceed national monetary inflation, no change in the rates established by section 111(d)(1)(B) shall be permitted; and

(II) no increase in the royalty fee shall be permitted based on any reduction in the average number of distant signal equivalents per subscriber.

The Copyright Royalty Judges may consider all factors relating to the maintenance of such level of payments, including, as an extenuating factor, whether the industry has been restrained by subscriber rate regulating authorities from increasing the rates for the basic service of providing secondary transmissions.

(B) In the event that the rules and regulations of the Federal Communications Commission are amended at any time after April 15, 1976, to permit the carriage by cable systems of additional television broadcast signals beyond the local service area of the primary transmitters of such signals, the royalty rates established by section 111(d)(1)(B) may be adjusted to ensure that the rates for the additional distant signal equivalents resulting from such carriage are reasonable in the light of the changes effected by the amendment to such rules and regulations. In determining the reasonableness of rates proposed following an amendment of Federal Communications Commission rules and regulations, the Copyright Royalty Judges shall consider, among other factors, the economic impact on copyright owners and users; except that no adjustment in royalty rates shall be made under this subparagraph with respect to any distant signal equivalent or fraction thereof represented by—

(i) carriage of any signal permitted under the rules and regulations of the Federal Communications Commission in effect on April 15, 1976, or the carriage of a signal of the same type (that is, independent, network, or noncommercial educational) substituted for such permitted signal; or

(ii) a television broadcast signal first carried after April 15, 1976, pursuant to an individual waiver of the rules and regulations of the Federal Communications Commission, as such rules and regulations were in effect on April 15, 1976.

(C) In the event of any change in the rules and regulations of the Federal Communications Commission with respect to syndicated and sports program exclusivity after April 15, 1976, the rates established by section 111(d)(1)(B) may be adjusted to assure that such rates are reasonable in light of the changes to such rules and regulations, but any such adjustment shall apply only to the affected television broadcast signals carried on those systems affected by the change.

(D) The gross receipts limitations established by section 111(d)(1) (C) and (D) shall be adjusted to reflect national monetary inflation or deflation or changes in the average rates charged cable system subscribers for the basic service of providing secondary transmissions to maintain the real constant dollar value of the exemption provided by such section, and the royalty rate specified therein shall not be subject to adjustment.

(3) (A) To authorize the distribution, under sections 111, 119, and 1007, of those royalty fees collected under sections 111, 119, and 1005, as the case may be, to the extent that the Copyright Royalty Judges have found that the distribution of such fees is not subject to controversy.

(B) In cases where the Copyright Royalty Judges determine that controversy exists, the Copyright Royalty Judges shall determine the distribution of such fees, including partial distributions, in accordance with section 111, 119, or 1007, as the case may be.

(C) Notwithstanding section 804(b)(8), the Copyright Royalty Judges, at any time after the filing of claims under section 111, 119, or 1007, may, upon motion of one or more of the claimants and after publication in the Federal Register of a request for responses to the motion from interested claimants, make a partial distribution of such fees, if, based upon all responses received during the 30-day period beginning on the date of such publication, the Copyright Royalty Judges conclude that no claimant entitled to receive such fees has stated a reasonable objection to the partial distribution, and all such claimants—

(i) agree to the partial distribution;

(ii) sign an agreement obligating them to return any excess amounts to the extent necessary to comply with the final determination on the distribution of the fees made under subparagraph (B);

(iii) file the agreement with the Copyright Royalty Judges; and

(iv) agree that such funds are available for distribution.

(D) The Copyright Royalty Judges and any other officer or employee acting in good faith in distributing funds under subparagraph (C) shall not be held liable for the payment of any excess fees under subparagraph (C). The Copyright Royalty Judges shall, at the time the final determination is made, calculate any such excess amounts.

(4) To accept or reject royalty claims filed under sections 111, 119, and 1007, on the basis of timeliness or the failure to establish the basis for a claim.

(5) To accept or reject rate adjustment petitions as provided in section 804 and petitions to participate as provided in section 803(b) (1) and (2).

(6) To determine the status of a digital audio recording device or a digital audio interface device under sections 1002 and 1003, as provided in section 1010.

(7) (A) To adopt as a basis for statutory terms and rates or as a basis for the distribution of statutory royalty payments, an agreement concerning such matters reached among some or all of the participants in a proceeding at any time during the proceeding, except that—

(i) the Copyright Royalty Judges shall provide to those that would be bound by the terms, rates, or other determination set by any agreement in a proceeding to determine royalty rates an opportunity to comment on the agreement and shall provide to participants in the proceeding under section 803(b)(2) that would be bound by the terms, rates, or other determination set by the agreement an opportunity to comment on the agreement and object to its adoption as a basis for statutory terms and rates; and

(ii) the Copyright Royalty Judges may decline to adopt the agreement as a basis for statutory terms and rates for participants that are not parties to the agreement, if any participant described in clause (i) objects to the agreement and the Copyright Royalty Judges conclude, based on the record before them if one exists, that the agreement does not provide a reasonable basis for setting statutory terms or rates.

(B) License agreements voluntarily negotiated pursuant to section 112(e)(5), 114(f)(3), 115(c)(3)(E)(i), 116(c), or 118(b)(2) that do not result in statutory terms and rates shall not be subject to clauses (i) and (ii) of subparagraph (A).

(C) Interested parties may negotiate and agree to, and the Copyright Royalty Judges may adopt, an agreement that specifies as terms notice and recordkeeping requirements that apply in lieu of those that would otherwise apply under regulations.

(8) To perform other duties, as assigned by the Register of Copyrights within the Library of Congress, except as provided in section 802(g), at times when Copyright Royalty Judges are not engaged in performing the other duties set forth in this section.

(c) *Rulings.*—The Copyright Royalty Judges may make any necessary procedural or evidentiary rulings in any proceeding under this chapter and may, before commencing a proceeding under this chapter, make any such rulings that would apply to the proceedings conducted by the Copyright Royalty Judges.

(d) *Administrative Support.*—The Librarian of Congress shall provide the Copyright Royalty Judges with the necessary administrative services related to proceedings under this chapter.

(e) *Location in Library of Congress.*—The offices of the Copyright Royalty Judges and staff shall be in the Library of Congress.

(f) *Effective Date of Actions.*—On and after the date of the enactment of the Copyright Royalty and Distribution Reform Act of 2004, in any case in which time limits are prescribed under this title for performance of an action with or by the Copyright Royalty Judges, and in which the last day of the prescribed period falls on a Saturday, Sunday, holiday, or other nonbusiness day within the District of Columbia or the Federal Government, the action may be taken on the next succeeding business day, and is effective as of the date when the period expired.

(Nov. 30, 2004, Pub. L. 108-419, §3, 118 Stat. 2341; Dec. 8, 2004, Pub. L. 108-447, §112, 118 Stat. 3409, Oct. 9, 2006, Pub. L. 109-303, §§3, 5, 120 Stat. 1478, 1483.)

§ 802   Copyright Royalty Judgeships; staff

(a) *Qualifications of Copyright Royalty Judges.* —

(1) *In general.*—Each Copyright Royalty Judge shall be an attorney who has at least 7 years of legal experience. The Chief Copyright Royalty Judge shall have at least 5 years of experience in adjudications, arbitrations, or court trials. Of the other 2 Copyright Royalty Judges, 1 shall have significant knowledge of copyright law, and the other shall have significant knowledge of economics. An individual may serve as a Copyright Royalty Judge only if the individual is free of any financial conflict of interest under subsection (h).

(2) *Definition.* —In this subsection, the term "adjudication" has the meaning given that term in section 551 of title 5, but does not include mediation.

(b) *Staff.* —The Chief Copyright Royalty Judge shall hire 3 full-time staff members to assist the Copyright Royalty Judges in performing their functions.

(c) *Terms.* —The individual first appointed as the Chief Copyright Royalty Judge shall be appointed to a term of 6 years, and of the remaining individuals first appointed as Copyright Royalty Judges, 1 shall be appointed to a term of 4 years, and the other shall be appointed to a term of 2 years. Thereafter, the terms of succeeding Copyright Royalty Judges shall each be 6 years. An individual serving as a Copyright Royalty Judge may be reappointed to subsequent terms. The term of a Copyright Royalty Judge shall begin when the term of the predecessor of that Copyright Royalty Judge ends. When the term of office of a Copyright Royalty Judge ends, the individual serving that term may continue to serve until a successor is selected.

(d) *Vacancies or Incapacity.* —

(1) *Vacancies.* —If a vacancy should occur in the position of Copyright Royalty Judge, the Librarian of Congress shall act expeditiously to fill the vacancy, and may appoint an interim Copyright Royalty Judge to serve until another Copyright Royalty Judge is appointed under this section. An individual appointed to fill the vacancy occurring before the expiration of the term for which the predecessor of that individual was appointed shall be appointed for the remainder of that term.

(2) *Incapacity.* —In the case in which a Copyright Royalty Judge is temporarily unable to perform his or her duties, the Librarian of Congress may appoint an interim Copyright Royalty Judge to perform such duties during the period of such incapacity.

(e) *Compensation.* —

(1) *Judges.* —The Chief Copyright Royalty Judge shall receive compensation at the rate of basic pay payable for level AL-1 for administrative law judges pursuant to section 5372(b) of title 5, and each of the other two Copyright Royalty Judges shall receive compensation at the rate of basic pay payable for level AL-2 for administrative law judges pursuant to such section. The compensation of the Copyright Royalty Judges shall not be subject to any regulations adopted by the Office of Personnel Management pursuant to its authority under section 5376(b)(1) of title 5.

17 U.S.C. § 802

(2) *Staff members.*—Of the staff members appointed under subsection (b)—

(A) the rate of pay of 1 staff member shall be not more than the basic rate of pay payable for level 10 of GS-15 of the General Schedule;

(B) the rate of pay of 1 staff member shall be not less than the basic rate of pay payable for GS-13 of the General Schedule and not more than the basic rate of pay payable for level 10 of GS-14 of such Schedule; and

(C) the rate of pay for the third staff member shall be not less than the basic rate of pay payable for GS-8 of the General Schedule and not more than the basic rate of pay payable for level 10 of GS-11 of such Schedule.

(3) *Locality pay.*—All rates of pay referred to under this subsection shall include locality pay.

(f) *Independence of Copyright Royalty Judge.*—

(1) *In making determinations.*—

(A) *In general.*—

(i) Subject to subparagraph (B) and clause (ii) of this subparagraph, the Copyright Royalty Judges shall have full independence in making determinations concerning adjustments and determinations of copyright royalty rates and terms, the distribution of copyright royalties, the acceptance or rejection of royalty claims, rate adjustment petitions, and petitions to participate, and in issuing other rulings under this title, except that the Copyright Royalty Judges may consult with the Register of Copyrights on any matter other than a question of fact

(ii) One or more Copyright Royalty Judges may, or by motion to the Copyright Royalty Judges, any participant in a proceeding may, request from the Register of Copyrights an interpretation of any material questions of substantive law that relate to the construction of provisions of this title and arise in the course of the proceeding. Any request for a written interpretation shall be in writing and on the record, and reasonable provision shall be made to permit participants in the proceeding to comment on the material questions of substantive law in a manner that minimizes duplication and delay. Except as provided in subparagraph (B), the Register of Copyrights shall deliver to the Copyright Royalty

Judges a written response within 14 days after the receipt of all briefs and comments from the participants. The Copyright Royalty Judges shall apply the legal interpretation embodied in the response of the Register of Copyrights if it is timely delivered, and the response shall be included in the record that accompanies the final determination. The authority under this clause shall not be construed to authorize the Register of Copyrights to provide an interpretation of questions of procedure before the Copyright Royalty Judges, the ultimate adjustments and determinations of copyright royalty rates and terms, the ultimate distribution of copyright royalties, or the acceptance or rejection of royalty claims, rate adjustment petitions, or petitions to participate in a proceeding.

(B) *Novel questions.* —

(i) In any case in which a novel material question of substantive law concerning an interpretation of those provisions of this title that are the subject of the proceeding is presented, the Copyright Royalty Judges shall request a decision of the Register of Copyrights, in writing, to resolve such novel question. Reasonable provision shall be made for comment on such request by the participants in the proceeding, in such a way as to minimize duplication and delay. The Register of Copyrights shall transmit his or her decision to the Copyright Royalty Judges within 30 days after the Register of Copyrights receives all of the briefs or comments of the participants. Such decision shall be in writing and included by the Copyright Royalty Judges in the record that accompanies their final determination. If such a decision is timely delivered to the Copyright Royalty Judges, the Copyright Royalty Judges shall apply the legal determinations embodied in the decision of the Register of Copyrights in resolving material questions of substantive law.

(ii) In clause (i), a "novel question of law" is a question of law that has not been determined in prior decisions, determinations, and rulings described in section 803(a).

(C) *Consultation.* —Notwithstanding the provisions of subparagraph (A), the Copyright Royalty Judges shall consult with the Register of Copyrights with respect to any determination or ruling that would require that any act be performed by the Copyright Office, and any such determination or ruling shall not be binding upon the Register of Copyrights.

(D) *Review of legal conclusions by the Register of Copyrights.* — The Register of Copyrights may review for legal error the resolution by the Copyright Royalty Judges of a material question of substantive law under this title that underlies or is contained in a final determination of the Copyright Royalty Judges. If the Register of Copyrights concludes, after taking into consideration the views of the participants in the proceeding, that any resolution reached by the Copyright Royalty Judges was in material error, the Register of Copyrights shall issue a written decision correcting such legal error, which shall be made part of the record of the proceeding. The Register of Copyrights shall issue such written decision not later than 60 days after the date on which the final determination by the Copyright Royalty Judges is issued. Additionally, the Register of Copyrights shall cause to be published in the Federal Register such written decision, together with a specific identification of the legal conclusion of the Copyright Royalty Judges that is determined to be erroneous. As to conclusions of substantive law involving an interpretation of the statutory provisions of this title, the decision of the Register of Copyrights shall be binding as precedent upon the Copyright Royalty Judges in subsequent proceedings under this chapter. When a decision has been rendered pursuant to this subparagraph, the Register of Copyrights may, on the basis of and in accordance with such decision, intervene as of right in any appeal of a final determination of the Copyright Royalty Judges pursuant to section 803(d) in the United States Court of Appeals for the District of Columbia Circuit. If, prior to intervening in such an appeal, the Register of Copyrights gives notification to, and undertakes to consult with, the Attorney General with respect to such intervention, and the Attorney General fails, within a reasonable period after receiving such notification, to intervene in such appeal, the Register of Copyrights may intervene in such appeal in his or her own name by any attorney designated by the Register of Copyrights for such purpose. Intervention by the Register of Copyrights in his or her own name shall not preclude the Attorney General from intervening on behalf of the United States in such an appeal as may be otherwise provided or required by law.

17 U.S.C. § 802

(E) *Effect on judicial review.*—Nothing in this section shall be interpreted to alter the standard applied by a court in reviewing legal determinations involving an interpretation or construction of the provisions of this title or to affect the extent to which any construction or interpretation of the provisions of this title shall be accorded deference by a reviewing court.

(2) *Performance appraisals.*—

(A) *In general.*—Notwithstanding any other provision of law or any regulation of the Library of Congress, and subject to subparagraph (B), the Copyright Royalty Judges shall not receive performance appraisals.

(B) *Relating to sanction or removal.*—To the extent that the Librarian of Congress adopts regulations under subsection (h) relating to the sanction or removal of a Copyright Royalty Judge and such regulations require documentation to establish the cause of such sanction or removal, the Copyright Royalty Judge may receive an appraisal related specifically to the cause of the sanction or removal.

(g) *Inconsistent Duties Barred.*—No Copyright Royalty Judge may undertake duties that conflict with his or her duties and responsibilities as a Copyright Royalty Judge.

(h) *Standards of Conduct.*—The Librarian of Congress shall adopt regulations regarding the standards of conduct, including financial conflict of interest and restrictions against ex parte communications, which shall govern the Copyright Royalty Judges and the proceedings under this chapter.

(i)[17] *Removal or Sanction.*—The Librarian of Congress may sanction or remove a Copyright Royalty Judge *for violation of the standards of conduct adopted under subsection (h), misconduct, neglect of duty, or any disqualifying physical or mental disability. Any such sanction or removal may be made only after notice and opportunity for a hearing, but the Librarian of Congress may suspend the Copyright Royalty Judge during the pendency of such hearing. The Librarian shall appoint an interim Copyright Royalty Judge during the period of any such suspension.*

(Nov. 30, 2004, Pub. L. 108-419, §3, 118 Stat. 2341; Dec. 8, 2004, Pub. L. 108-447, §112, 118 Stat. 3409, Oct. 9, 2006, Pub. L. 109-303, §3, 120 Stat. 1478.)

---

[17] *Ed. Note:* Intercollegiate Broadcasting System v. Copyright Royalty Board, 684 F.3d 1332, 103 U.S.P.Q. 2d 1337 (CADC 2012), held that the italicized language was unconstitutional and such language was invalidated and severed from the remainder of the statute.

17 U.S.C. § 802

524 • Patent, Trademark, & Copyright Laws, June 2015 Edition

§ 803   Proceedings of Copyright Royalty Judges

(a) *Proceedings.* —

(1) *In general.* — The Copyright Royalty Judges shall act in accordance with this title, and to the extent not inconsistent with this title, in accordance with subchapter II of chapter 5 of title 5, in carrying out the purposes set forth in section 801. The Copyright Royalty Judges shall act in accordance with regulations issued by the Copyright Royalty Judges and the Librarian of Congress, and on the basis of a written record, prior determinations and interpretations of the Copyright Royalty Tribunal, Librarian of Congress, the Register of Copyrights, copyright arbitration royalty panels (to the extent those determinations are not inconsistent with a decision of the Librarian of Congress or the Register of Copyrights), and the Copyright Royalty Judges (to the extent those determinations are not inconsistent with a decision of the Register of Copyrights that was timely delivered to the Copyright Royalty Judges pursuant to section 802(f)(1) (A) or (B), or with a decision of the Register of Copyrights pursuant to section 802(f)(1)(D)), under this chapter, and decisions of the court of appeals under this chapter before, on, or after the effective date of the Copyright Royalty and Distribution Reform Act of 2004.

(2) *Judges acting as panel and individually.* — The Copyright Royalty Judges shall preside over hearings in proceedings under this chapter en banc. The Chief Copyright Royalty Judge may designate a Copyright Royalty Judge to preside individually over such collateral and administrative proceedings, and over such proceedings under paragraphs (1) through (5) of subsection (b), as the Chief Judge considers appropriate.

(3) *Determinations.* — Final determinations of the Copyright Royalty Judges in proceedings under this chapter shall be made by majority vote. A Copyright Royalty Judge dissenting from the majority on any determination under this chapter may issue his or her dissenting opinion, which shall be included with the determination.

(b) *Procedures.* —

(1) *Initiation.* —

(A) *Call for petitions to participate.* —

(i) The Copyright Royalty Judges shall cause to be published in the Federal Register notice of commencement of proceedings under this chapter, calling for the filing of petitions to participate in a proceeding under this chapter for the purpose of making the relevant determination under section 111, 112, 114, 115, 116, 118, 119, 1004, or 1007, as the case may be —

(I) promptly upon a determination made under section 804(a);

(II) by no later than January 5 of a year specified in paragraph (2) of section 804(b) for the commencement of proceedings;

(III) by no later than January 5 of a year specified in subparagraph (A) or (B) of paragraph (3) of section 804(b) for the commencement of proceedings, or as otherwise provided in subparagraph (A) or (C) of such paragraph for the commencement of proceedings;

(IV) as provided under section 804(b)(8); or

(V) by no later than January 5 of a year specified in any other provision of section 804(b) for the filing of petitions for the commencement of proceedings, if a petition has not been filed by that date, except that the publication of notice requirement shall not apply in the case of proceedings under section 111 that are scheduled to commence in 2005.

(ii) Petitions to participate shall be filed by no later than 30 days after publication of notice of commencement of a proceeding under clause (i), except that the Copyright Royalty Judges may, for substantial good cause shown and if there is no prejudice to the participants that have already filed petitions, accept late petitions to participate at any time up to the date that is 90 days before the date on which participants in the proceeding are to file their written direct statements. Notwithstanding the preceding sentence, petitioners whose petitions are filed more than 30 days after publication of notice of commencement of a proceeding are not eligible to object to a settlement reached during the voluntary negotiation period under paragraph (3), and any objection filed by such a petitioner shall not be taken into account by the Copyright Royalty Judges.

(B) *Petitions to participate.* —Each petition to participate in a proceeding shall describe the petitioner's interest in the subject matter of the proceeding. Parties with similar interests may file a single petition to participate.

17 U.S.C. § 803

(2) *Participation in general.*—Subject to paragraph (4), a person may participate in a proceeding under this chapter, including through the submission of briefs or other information, only if—

(A) that person has filed a petition to participate in accordance with paragraph (1) (either individually or as a group under paragraph (1)(B));

(B) the Copyright Royalty Judges have not determined that the petition to participate is facially invalid;

(C) the Copyright Royalty Judges have not determined, sua sponte or on the motion of another participant in the proceeding, that the person lacks a significant interest in the proceeding; and

(D) the petition to participate is accompanied by either—

(i) in a proceeding to determine royalty rates, a filing fee of $150; or

(ii) in a proceeding to determine distribution of royalty fees—

(I) a filing fee of $150; or

(II) a statement that the petitioner (individually or as a group) will not seek a distribution of more than $1000, in which case the amount distributed to the petitioner shall not exceed $1000.

(3) *Voluntary negotiation period.*—

(A) *Commencement of proceedings.*—

(i) *Rate adjustment proceeding.*—Promptly after the date for filing of petitions to participate in a proceeding, the Copyright Royalty Judges shall make available to all participants in the proceeding a list of such participants and shall initiate a voluntary negotiation period among the participants.

(ii) *Distribution proceeding.*—Promptly after the date for filing of petitions to participate in a proceeding to determine the distribution of royalties, the Copyright Royalty Judges shall make available to all participants in the proceeding a list of such participants. The initiation of a voluntary negotiation period among the participants shall be set at a time determined by the Copyright Royalty Judges.

(B) *Length of proceedings.* —The voluntary negotiation period initiated under subparagraph (A) shall be 3 months.

(C) *Determination of subsequent of proceedings.* —At the close of the voluntary negotiation proceedings, the Copyright Royalty Judges shall, if further proceedings under this chapter are necessary, determine whether and to what extent paragraphs (4) and (5) will apply to the parties.

(4) *Small claims procedure in distribution proceedings.* —

(A) *In general.* —If, in a proceeding under this chapter to determine the distribution of royalties, the contested amount of a claim is $10,000 or less, the Copyright Royalty Judges shall decide the controversy on the basis of the filing of the written direct statement by the participant, the response by any opposing participant, and 1 additional response by each such party.

(B) *Bad faith inflation of claim.* —If the Copyright Royalty Judges determine that a participant asserts in bad faith an amount in controversy in excess of $10,000 for the purpose of avoiding a determination under the procedure set forth in subparagraph (A), the Copyright Royalty Judges shall impose a fine on that participant in an amount not to exceed the difference between the actual amount distributed and the amount asserted by the participant.

(5) *Paper proceedings.* —The Copyright Royalty Judges in proceedings under this chapter may decide, sua sponte or upon motion of a participant, to determine issues on the basis of the filing of the written direct statement by the participant, the response by any opposing participant, and one additional response by each such participant. Prior to making such decision to proceed on such a paper record only, the Copyright Royalty Judges shall offer to all parties to the proceeding the opportunity to comment on the decision. The procedure under this paragraph—

(A) shall be applied in cases in which there is no genuine issue of material fact, there is no need for evidentiary hearings, and all participants in the proceeding agree in writing to the procedure; and

(B) may be applied under such other circumstances as the Copyright Royalty Judges consider appropriate.

(6) *Regulations.* —

(A) *In general.*—The Copyright Royalty Judges may issue regulations to carry out their functions under this title. All regulations issued by the Copyright Royalty Judges are subject to the approval of the Librarian of Congress and are subject to judicial review pursuant to chapter 7 of title 5, except as set forth in subsection (d). Not later than 120 days after Copyright Royalty Judges or interim Copyright Royalty Judges, as the case may be, are first appointed after the enactment of the Copyright Royalty and Distribution Reform Act of 2004, such judges shall issue regulations to govern proceedings under this chapter.

(B) *Interim regulations.*—Until regulations are adopted under subparagraph (A), the Copyright Royalty Judges shall apply the regulations in effect under this chapter on the day before the effective date of the Copyright Royalty and Distribution Reform Act of 2004, to the extent such regulations are not inconsistent with this chapter, except that functions carried out under such regulations by the Librarian of Congress, the Register of Copyrights, or copyright arbitration royalty panels that, as of such date of enactment, are to be carried out by the Copyright Royalty Judges under this chapter, shall be carried out by the Copyright Royalty Judges under such regulations.

(C) *Requirements.*—Regulations issued under subparagraph (A) shall include the following:

(i) The written direct statements and written rebuttal statements of all participants in a proceeding under paragraph (2) shall be filed by a date specified by the Copyright Royalty Judges, which, in the case of written direct statements, may be not earlier than 4 months, and not later than 5 months, after the end of the voluntary negotiation period under paragraph (3). Notwithstanding the preceding sentence, the Copyright Royalty Judges may allow a participant in a proceeding to file an amended written direct statement based on new information received during the discovery process, within 15 days after the end of the discovery period specified in clause (iv).

(ii) (I) Following the submission to the Copyright Royalty Judges of written direct statements and written rebuttal statements by the participants in a proceeding under paragraph (2), the Copyright Royalty Judges, after taking into consideration the views of the participants in the proceeding, shall determine a schedule for conducting and completing discovery.

(II) In this chapter, the term "written direct statements" means witness statements, testimony, and exhibits to be presented in the proceedings, and such other information that is necessary to establish terms and rates, or the distribution of royalty payments, as the case may be, as set forth in regulations issued by the Copyright Royalty Judges.

(iii) Hearsay may be admitted in proceedings under this chapter to the extent deemed appropriate by the Copyright Royalty Judges.

(iv) Discovery in connection with written direct statements shall be permitted for a period of 60 days, except for discovery ordered by the Copyright Royalty Judges in connection with the resolution of motions, orders, and disputes pending at the end of such period. The Copyright Royalty Judges may order a discovery schedule in connection with written rebuttal statements.

(v) Any participant under paragraph (2) in a proceeding under this chapter to determine royalty rates may request of an opposing participant nonprivileged documents directly related to the written direct statement or written rebuttal statement of that participant. Any objection to such a request shall be resolved by a motion or request to compel production made to the Copyright Royalty Judges in accordance with regulations adopted by the Copyright Royalty Judges. Each motion or request to compel discovery shall be determined by the Copyright Royalty Judges, or by a Copyright Royalty Judge when permitted under subsection (a)(2). Upon such motion, the Copyright Royalty Judges may order discovery pursuant to regulations established under this paragraph.

(vi) (I) Any participant under paragraph (2) in a proceeding under this chapter to determine royalty rates may, by means of written motion or on the record, request of an opposing participant or witness other relevant information and materials if, absent the discovery sought, the Copyright Royalty Judges' resolution of the proceeding would be substantially impaired.

17 U.S.C. § 803

In determining whether discovery will be granted under this clause, the Copyright Royalty Judges may consider—

(aa) whether the burden or expense of producing the requested information or materials outweighs the likely benefit, taking into account the needs and resources of the participants, the importance of the issues at stake, and the probative value of the requested information or materials in resolving such issues;

(bb) whether the requested information or materials would be unreasonably cumulative or duplicative, or are obtainable from another source that is more convenient, less burdensome, or less expensive; and

(cc) whether the participant seeking discovery has had ample opportunity by discovery in the proceeding or by other means to obtain the information sought.

(II) This clause shall not apply to any proceeding scheduled to commence after December 31, 2010.

(vii) In a proceeding under this chapter to determine royalty rates, the participants entitled to receive royalties shall collectively be permitted to take no more than 10 depositions and secure responses to no more than 25 interrogatories, and the participants obligated to pay royalties shall collectively be permitted to take no more than 10 depositions and secure responses to no more than 25 interrogatories. The Copyright Royalty Judges shall resolve any disputes among similarly aligned participants to allocate the number of depositions or interrogatories permitted under this clause.

(viii) The rules and practices in effect on the day before the effective date of the Copyright Royalty and Distribution Reform Act of 2004, relating to discovery in proceedings under this chapter to determine the distribution of royalty fees, shall continue to apply to such proceedings on and after such effective date.

(ix) In proceedings to determine royalty rates, the Copyright Royalty Judges may issue a subpoena commanding a participant or witness to appear and give testimony, or to produce and permit inspection of documents or tangible things, if the Copyright Royalty Judges' resolution of the proceeding would be substantially impaired by the absence of such testimony or production of documents or tangible things. Such subpoena shall specify with reasonable particularity the materials to be produced or the scope and nature of the required testimony. Nothing in this clause shall preclude the Copyright Royalty Judges from requesting the production by a nonparticipant of information or materials relevant to the resolution by the Copyright Royalty Judges of a material issue of fact.

(x) The Copyright Royalty Judges shall order a settlement conference among the participants in the proceeding to facilitate the presentation of offers of settlement among the participants. The settlement conference shall be held during a 21-day period following the 60-day discovery period specified in clause (iv) and shall take place outside the presence of the Copyright Royalty Judges.

(xi) No evidence, including exhibits, may be submitted in the written direct statement or written rebuttal statement of a participant without a sponsoring witness, except where the Copyright Royalty Judges have taken official notice, or in the case of incorporation by reference of past records, or for good cause shown.

(c) *Determination of Copyright Royalty Judges.* —

(1) *Timing.* —The Copyright Royalty Judges shall issue their determination in a proceeding not later than 11 months after the conclusion of the 21-day settlement conference period under subsection (b)(6)(C)(x), but, in the case of a proceeding to determine successors to rates or terms that expire on a specified date, in no event later than 15 days before the expiration of the then current statutory rates and terms.

(2) *Rehearings.* —

(A) *In general.* —The Copyright Royalty Judges may, in exceptional cases, upon motion of a participant in a proceeding under subsection (b)(2), order a rehearing, after the determination in the proceeding is issued under paragraph (1), on such matters as the Copyright Royalty Judges determine to be appropriate.

(B) *Timing for filing motion.* —Any motion for a rehearing under subparagraph (A) may only be filed within 15 days after the date on which the Copyright Royalty Judges deliver to the participants in the proceeding their initial determination.

(C) *Participation by opposing party not required.*—In any case in which a rehearing is ordered, any opposing party shall not be required to participate in the rehearing, except that nonparticipation may give rise to the limitations with respect to judicial review provided for in subsection (d)(1).

(D) *No negative inference.*—No negative inference shall be drawn from lack of participation in a rehearing.

(E) *Continuity of rates and terms.*—

(i) If the decision of the Copyright Royalty Judges on any motion for a rehearing is not rendered before the expiration of the statutory rates and terms that were previously in effect, in the case of a proceeding to determine successors to rates and terms that expire on a specified date, then—

(I) the initial determination of the Copyright Royalty Judges that is the subject of the rehearing motion shall be effective as of the day following the date on which the rates and terms that were previously in effect expire; and

(II) in the case of a proceeding under section 114(f)(1)(C) or 114(f)(2)(C), royalty rates and terms shall, for purposes of section 114(f)(4)(B), be deemed to have been set at those rates and terms contained in the initial determination of the Copyright Royalty Judges that is the subject of the rehearing motion, as of the date of that determination.

(ii) The pendency of a motion for a rehearing under this paragraph shall not relieve persons obligated to make royalty payments who would be affected by the determination on that motion from providing the statements of account and any reports of use, to the extent required, and paying the royalties required under the relevant determination or regulations.

(iii) Notwithstanding clause (ii), whenever royalties described in clause (ii) are paid to a person other than the Copyright Office, the entity designated by the Copyright Royalty Judges to which such royalties are paid by the copyright user (and any successor thereto) shall, within 60 days after the motion for rehearing is resolved or, if the motion is granted, within 60 days after the rehearing is concluded, return any excess amounts previously paid to the extent necessary to comply with the final determination of royalty rates by the Copyright Royalty Judges. Any underpayment of royalties resulting from a rehearing shall be paid within the same period.

(3) *Contents of determination.*—A determination of the Copyright Royalty Judges shall be supported by the written record and shall set forth the findings of fact relied on by the Copyright Royalty Judges. Among other terms adopted in a determination, the Copyright Royalty Judges may specify notice and recordkeeping requirements of users of the copyrights at issue that apply in lieu of those that would otherwise apply under regulations.

(4) *Continuing jurisdiction.*—The Copyright Royalty Judges may issue an amendment to a written determination to correct any technical or clerical errors in the determination or to modify the terms, but not the rates, of royalty payments in response to unforeseen circumstances that would frustrate the proper implementation of such determination. Such amendment shall be set forth in a written addendum to the determination that shall be distributed to the participants of the proceeding and shall be published in the Federal Register.

(5) *Protective order.*—The Copyright Royalty Judges may issue such orders as may be appropriate to protect confidential information, including orders excluding confidential information from the record of the determination that is published or made available to the public, except that any terms or rates of royalty payments or distributions may not be excluded.

(6) *Publication of determination.*—By no later than the end of the 60-day period provided in section 802(f)(1)(D), the Librarian of Congress shall cause the determination, and any corrections thereto, to be published in the Federal Register. The Librarian of Congress shall also publicize the determination and corrections in such other manner as the Librarian considers appropriate, including, but not limited to, publication on the Internet. The Librarian of Congress shall also make the determination, corrections, and the accompanying record available for public inspection and copying.

(7) *Late payment.*—A determination of the Copyright Royalty Judges may include terms with respect to late payment, but in no way shall such terms

17 U.S.C. § 803

prevent the copyright holder from asserting other rights or remedies provided under this title.

(d) *Judicial Review.* —

(1) *Appeal.* —Any determination of the Copyright Royalty Judges under subsection (c) may, within 30 days after the publication of the determination in the Federal Register, be appealed, to the United States Court of Appeals for the District of Columbia Circuit, by any aggrieved participant in the proceeding under subsection (b)(2) who fully participated in the proceeding and who would be bound by the determination. Any participant that did not participate in a rehearing may not raise any issue that was the subject of that rehearing at any stage of judicial review of the hearing determination. If no appeal is brought within that 30-day period, the determination of the Copyright Royalty Judges shall be final, and the royalty fee or determination with respect to the distribution of fees, as the case may be, shall take effect as set forth in paragraph (2).

(2) *Effect of rates.* —

(A) *Expiration on specified date.* —When this title provides that the royalty rates and terms that were previously in effect are to expire on a specified date, any adjustment or determination by the Copyright Royalty Judges of successor rates and terms for an ensuing statutory license period shall be effective as of the day following the date of expiration of the rates and terms that were previously in effect, even if the determination of the Copyright Royalty Judges is rendered on a later date. A licensee shall be obligated to continue making payments under the rates and terms previously in effect until such time as rates and terms for the successor period are established. Whenever royalties pursuant to this section are paid to a person other than the Copyright Office, the entity designated by the Copyright Royalty Judges to which such royalties are paid by the copyright user (and any successor thereto) shall, within 60 days after the final determination of the Copyright Royalty Judges establishing rates and terms for a successor period or the exhaustion of all rehearings or appeals of such determination, if any, return any excess amounts previously paid to the extent necessary to comply with the final determination of royalty rates. Any underpayment of royalties by a copyright user shall be paid to the entity designated by the Copyright Royalty Judges within the same period.

17 U.S.C. § 803

(B) *Other cases.*—In cases where rates and terms have not, prior to the inception of an activity, been established for that particular activity under the relevant license, such rates and terms shall be retroactive to the inception of activity under the relevant license covered by such rates and terms. In other cases where rates and terms do not expire on a specified date, successor rates and terms shall take effect on the first day of the second month that begins after the publication of the determination of the Copyright Royalty Judges in the Federal Register, except as otherwise provided in this title, or by the Copyright Royalty Judges, or as agreed by the participants in a proceeding that would be bound by the rates and terms. Except as otherwise provided in this title, the rates and terms, to the extent applicable, shall remain in effect until such successor rates and terms become effective.

(C) *Obligation to make payments.*—

(i) The pendency of an appeal under this subsection shall not relieve persons obligated to make royalty payments under section 111, 112, 114, 115, 116, 118, 119, or 1003, who would be affected by the determination on appeal, from—

(I) providing the applicable statements of account and reports of use; and

(II) paying the royalties required under the relevant determination or regulations.

(ii) Notwithstanding clause (i), whenever royalties described in clause (i) are paid to a person other than the Copyright Office, the entity designated by the Copyright Royalty Judges to which such royalties are paid by the copyright user (and any successor thereto) shall, within 60 days after the final resolution of the appeal, return any excess amounts previously paid (and interest thereon, if ordered pursuant to paragraph (3)) to the extent necessary to comply with the final determination of royalty rates on appeal. Any underpayment of royalties resulting from an appeal (and interest thereon, if ordered pursuant to paragraph (3)) shall be paid within the same period.

(3) *Jurisdiction of court.*—Section 706 of title 5 shall apply with respect to review by the court of appeals under this subsection. If the court modifies or vacates a determination of the Copyright Royalty Judges, the court may

enter its own determination with respect to the amount or distribution of royalty fees and costs, and order the repayment of any excess fees, the payment of any underpaid fees, and the payment of interest pertaining respectively thereto, in accordance with its final judgment. The court may also vacate the determination of the Copyright Royalty Judges and remand the case to the Copyright Royalty Judges for further proceedings in accordance with subsection (a).

(e) *Administrative Matters.—*

(1) *Deduction of costs of Library of Congress and Copyright Office from filing fees.—*

(A) *Deduction from filing fees.—*The Librarian of Congress may, to the extent not otherwise provided under this title, deduct from the filing fees collected under subsection (b) for a particular proceeding under this chapter the reasonable costs incurred by the Librarian of Congress, the Copyright Office, and the Copyright Royalty Judges in conducting that proceeding, other than the salaries of the Copyright Royalty Judges and the 3 staff members appointed under section 802(b).

(B) *Authorization of appropriations.—*There are authorized to be appropriated such sums as may be necessary to pay the costs incurred under this chapter not covered by the filing fees collected under subsection (b). All funds made available pursuant to this subparagraph shall remain available until expended.

(2) *Positions required for administration of compulsory licensing.—* Section 307 of the Legislative Branch Appropriations Act, 1994, shall not apply to employee positions in the Library of Congress that are required to be filled in order to carry out section 111, 112, 114, 115, 116, 118, or 119 or chapter 10.

(Nov. 30, 2004, Pub. L. 108-419, §3, 118 Stat. 2341; Dec. 8, 2004, Pub. L. 108-447, §112, 118 Stat. 3409, Oct. 9, 2006, Pub. L. 109-303, §3, 120 Stat. 1478; Dec. 9, 2010, Pub. L. 111-295, §5, 124 Stat. 3181.)

§ 804   Institution of proceedings

(a) *Filing of Petition.—*With respect to proceedings referred to in paragraphs (1) and (2) of section 801(b) concerning the determination or adjustment of royalty rates as provided in sections 111, 112, 114, 115, 116, 118, 119, and 1004, during the calendar years specified in the schedule set forth in subsection (b), any owner or user of a copyrighted work whose royalty rates are specified by this title, or are established under this chapter before or after the enactment of the Copyright Royalty and Distribution Reform Act of 2004, may file a petition with the Copyright Royalty Judges declaring that the petitioner requests a determination or adjustment of the rate. The Copyright Royalty Judges shall make a determination as to whether the petitioner has such a significant interest in the royalty rate in which a determination or adjustment is requested. If the Copyright Royalty Judges determine that the petitioner has such a significant interest, the Copyright Royalty Judges shall cause notice of this determination, with the reasons for such determination, to be published in the Federal Register, together with the notice of commencement of proceedings under this chapter. With respect to proceedings under paragraph (1) of section 801(b) concerning the determination or adjustment of royalty rates as provided in sections 112 and 114, during the calendar years specified in the schedule set forth in subsection (b), the Copyright Royalty Judges shall cause notice of commencement of proceedings under this chapter to be published in the Federal Register as provided in section 803(b)(1)(A).

(b) *Timing of Proceedings.* —

(1) *Section 111 proceedings.* —

(A) A petition described in subsection (a) to initiate proceedings under section 801(b)(2) concerning the adjustment of royalty rates under section 111 to which subparagraph (A) or (D) of section 801(b)(2) applies may be filed during the year 2015 and in each subsequent fifth calendar year.

(B) In order to initiate proceedings under section 801(b)(2) concerning the adjustment of royalty rates under section 111 to which subparagraph (B) or (C) of section 801(b)(2) applies, within 12 months after an event described in either of those subsections, any owner or user of a copyrighted work whose royalty rates are specified by section 111, or by a rate established under this chapter before or after the enactment of the Copyright Royalty and Distribution Reform Act of 2004, may file a petition with the Copyright Royalty Judges declaring that the petitioner requests an adjustment of the rate. The Copyright Royalty Judges shall then proceed as set forth in subsection (a) of this section. Any change in royalty rates made under this chapter pursuant to this subparagraph may be reconsidered in the year 2015, and each fifth calendar year thereafter, in accordance with the provisions in section 801(b)(2)(B) or (C), as the case may be. A petition for adjustment of rates established by section 111(d)(1)(B) as a result of a change in the rules and regulations of the Federal Communications Commission shall set forth the change on which the petition is based.

(C) Any adjustment of royalty rates under section 111 shall take effect as of the first accounting period commencing after the publication of the determination of the Copyright Royalty Judges in the Federal Register, or on such other date as is specified in that determination.

(2) *Certain section 112 proceedings.* —Proceedings under this chapter shall be commenced in the year 2007 to determine reasonable terms and rates of royalty payments for the activities described in section 112(e)(1) relating to the limitation on exclusive rights specified by section 114(d)(1)(C)(iv), to become effective on January 1, 2009. Such proceedings shall be repeated in each subsequent fifth calendar year.

(3) *Section 114 and corresponding 112 proceedings.* —

(A) *For eligible nonsubscription services and new subscription services.* — Proceedings under this chapter shall be commenced as soon as practicable after the date of enactment of the Copyright Royalty and Distribution Reform Act of 2004 to determine reasonable terms and rates of royalty payments under sections 114 and 112 for the activities of eligible nonsubscription transmission services and new subscription services, to be effective for the period beginning on January 1, 2006, and ending on December 31, 2010. Such proceedings shall next be commenced in January 2009 to determine reasonable terms and rates of royalty payments, to become effective on January 1, 2011. Thereafter, such proceedings shall be repeated in each subsequent fifth calendar year.

(B) *For preexisting subscription and satellite digital audio radio services.* — Proceedings under this chapter shall be commenced in January 2006 to determine reasonable terms and rates of royalty payments under sections 114 and 112 for the activities of preexisting subscription services, to be effective during the period beginning on January 1, 2008, and ending on December 31, 2012, and preexisting satellite digital audio radio services, to be effective during the period beginning on January 1, 2007, and ending on December 31, 2012. Such proceedings shall next be commenced in 2011 to determine reasonable terms and rates of royalty payments, to become effective on January 1, 2013. Thereafter, such proceedings shall be repeated in each subsequent fifth calendar year.

(C) (i) Notwithstanding any other provision of this chapter, this subparagraph shall govern proceedings commenced pursuant to section 114(f)(1)(C) and 114(f)(2)(C) concerning new types of services.

(ii) Not later than 30 days after a petition to determine rates and terms for a new type of service is filed by any copyright owner of sound recordings, or such new type of service, indicating that such new type of service is or is about to become operational, the Copyright Royalty Judges shall issue a notice for a proceeding to determine rates and terms for such service.

(iii) The proceeding shall follow the schedule set forth in subsections (b), (c), and (d) of section 803, except that—

(I) the determination shall be issued by not later than 24 months after the publication of the notice under clause (ii); and

(II) the decision shall take effect as provided in subsections (c)(2) and (d)(2) of section 803 and section 114(f)(4)(B)(ii) and (C).

(iv) The rates and terms shall remain in effect for the period set forth in section 114(f)(1)(C) or 114(f)(2)(C), as the case may be.

(4) *Section 115 proceedings.*—A petition described in subsection (a) to initiate proceedings under section 801(b)(1) concerning the adjustment or determination of royalty rates as provided in section 115 may be filed in the year 2006 and in each subsequent fifth calendar year, or at such other times as the parties have agreed under section 115(c)(3) (B) and (C).

(5) *Section 116 proceedings.*— (A) A petition described in subsection (a) to initiate proceedings under section 801(b) concerning the determination of royalty rates and terms as provided in section 116 may be filed at any time within 1 year after negotiated licenses authorized by section 116 are terminated or expire and are not replaced by subsequent agreements.

(B) If a negotiated license authorized by section 116 is terminated or expires and is not replaced by another such license agreement which provides permission to use a quantity of musical works not substantially smaller than the quantity of such works performed on coin-operated phonorecord players during the 1- year period ending March 1, 1989, the Copyright Royalty Judges shall, upon petition filed under paragraph (1) within 1 year after such termination or expiration, commence a proceeding to promptly establish an interim royalty rate or rates for the public performance by means of a coin-operated phonorecord player of nondramatic musical works embodied in phonorecords which had been subject to the terminated or expired negotiated license agreement. Such rate or rates shall be the same as the last such rate or rates and shall remain in force until the conclusion of proceedings by the Copyright Royalty Judges, in accordance with section 803, to adjust the royalty rates applicable to such works, or until superseded by a new negotiated license agreement, as provided in section 116(b).

(6) *Section 118 proceedings.* — A petition described in subsection (a) to initiate proceedings under section 801(b)(1) concerning the determination of reasonable terms and rates of royalty payments as provided in section 118 may be filed in the year 2006 and in each subsequent fifth calendar year.

(7) *Section 1004 proceedings.* — A petition described in subsection (a) to initiate proceedings under section 801(b)(1) concerning the adjustment of reasonable royalty rates under section 1004 may be filed as provided in section 1004(a)(3).

(8) *Proceedings concerning distribution of Royalty fees.* — With respect to proceedings under section 801(b)(3) concerning the distribution of royalty fees in certain circumstances under section 111, 119, or 1007, the Copyright Royalty Judges shall, upon a determination that a controversy exists concerning such distribution, cause to be published in the Federal Register notice of commencement of proceedings under this chapter.

(Nov. 30, 2004, Pub. L. 108-419, §3, 118 Stat. 2341; Dec. 8, 2004, Pub. L. 108-447, §112, 118 Stat. 3409, Oct. 9, 2006, Pub. L. 109-303, §3, 120 Stat. 1478; May 27, 2010, Pub. L. 111-175, §103, 124 Stat. 1227.)

§ 805   General rule for voluntarily negotiated agreements

Any rates or terms under this title that —

(1) are agreed to by participants to a proceeding under section 803(b)(3),

(2) are adopted by the Copyright Royalty Judges as part of a determination under this chapter, and

(3) are in effect for a period shorter than would otherwise apply under a determination pursuant to this chapter, shall remain in effect for such period of time as would otherwise apply under such determination, except that the Copyright Royalty Judges shall adjust the rates pursuant to the voluntary negotiations to reflect national monetary inflation during the additional period the rates remain in effect.

(Nov. 30, 2004, Pub. L. 108-419, §3, 118 Stat. 2341; Dec. 8, 2004, Pub. L. 108-447, §112, 118 Stat. 3409.)

CHAPTER 9—PROTECTION OF SEMICONDUCTOR CHIP PRODUCTS

§ 901 Definitions

(a) As used in this chapter—

(1) a "semiconductor chip product" is the final or intermediate form of any product—

(A) having two or more layers of metallic, insulating, or semiconductor material, deposited or otherwise placed on, or etched away or otherwise removed from, a piece of semiconductor material in accordance with a predetermined pattern; and

(B) intended to perform electronic circuitry functions;

(2) a "mask work" is a series of related images, however fixed or encoded—

(A) having or representing the predetermined, three-dimensional pattern of metallic, insulating, or semiconductor material present or removed from the layers of a semiconductor chip product; and

(B) in which series the relation of the images to one another is that each image has the pattern of the surface of one form of the semiconductor chip product;

(3) a mask work is "fixed" in a semiconductor chip product when its embodiment in the product is sufficiently permanent or stable to permit the mask work to be perceived or reproduced from the product for a period of more than transitory duration;

(4) to "distribute" means to sell, or to lease, bail, or otherwise transfer, or to offer to sell, lease, bail, or otherwise transfer;

(5) to "commercially exploit" a mask work is to distribute to the public for commercial purposes a semiconductor chip product embodying the mask work; except that such term includes an offer to sell or transfer a semiconductor chip product only when the offer is in writing and occurs after the mask work is fixed in the semiconductor chip product;

(6) the "owner" of a mask work is the person who created the mask work, the legal representative of that person if that person is deceased or under a legal incapacity, or a party to whom all the rights under this chapter of such person or representative are transferred in accordance with section 903(b); except that, in the case of a work made within the scope of a person's employment, the owner is the employer for whom the person created the mask work or a party to whom all the rights under this chapter of the employer are transferred in accordance with section 903(b);

(7) an "innocent purchaser" is a person who purchases a semiconductor chip product in good faith and without having notice of protection with respect to the semiconductor chip product;

(8) having "notice of protection" means having actual knowledge that, or reasonable grounds to believe that, a mask work is protected under this chapter; and

(9) an "infringing semiconductor chip product" is a semiconductor chip product which is made, imported, or distributed in violation of the exclusive rights of the owner of a mask work under this chapter.

17 U.S.C. § 901

(b) For purposes of this chapter, the distribution or importation of a product incorporating a semiconductor chip product as a part thereof is a distribution or importation of that semiconductor chip product.
(Added Nov. 8, 1984, Pub. L. 98-620, §302, 98 Stat. 3347.)

§ 902 Subject matter of protection

(a) (1) Subject to the provisions of subsection (b), a mask work fixed in a semiconductor chip product, by or under the authority of the owner of the mask work, is eligible for protection under this chapter if—

(A) on the date on which the mask work is registered under section 908, or is first commercially exploited anywhere in the world, whichever occurs first, the owner of the mask work is (i) a national or domiciliary of the United States, (ii) a national, domiciliary, or sovereign authority of a foreign nation that is a party to a treaty affording protection to mask works to which the United States is also a party, or (iii) a stateless person, wherever that person may be domiciled;

(B) the mask work is first commercially exploited in the United States; or

(C) the mask work comes within the scope of a Presidential proclamation issued under paragraph (2).

(2) Whenever the President finds that a foreign nation extends, to mask works of owners who are nationals or domiciliaries of the United States protection (A) on substantially the same basis as that on which the foreign nation extends protection to mask works of its own nationals and domiciliaries and mask works first commercially exploited in that nation, or (B) on substantially the same basis as provided in this chapter, the President may by proclamation extend protection under this chapter to mask works (i) of owners who are, on the date on which the mask works are registered under section 908, or the date on which the mask works are first commercially exploited anywhere in the world, whichever occurs first, nationals, domiciliaries, or sovereign authorities of that nation, or (ii) which are first commercially exploited in that nation. The President may revise, suspend, or revoke any such proclamation or impose any conditions or limitations on protection extended under any such proclamation.

(b) Protection under this chapter shall not be available for a mask work that—

(1) is not original; or

(2) consists of designs that are staple, commonplace, or familiar in the semiconductor industry, or variations of such designs, combined in a way that, considered as a whole, is not original.

(c) In no case does protection under this chapter for a mask work extend to any idea, procedure, process, system, method of operation, concept, principle, or discovery, regardless of the form in which it is described, explained, illustrated, or embodied in such work.

(Nov. 8, 1984, Pub. L. 98-620, §302, 98 Stat. 3348; Nov. 9, 1987, Pub. L. 100-159, §3, 101 Stat. 900.)

§ 903   Ownership, transfer, licensing, and recordation

(a) The exclusive rights in a mask work subject to protection under this chapter belong to the owner of the mask work.

(b) The owner of the exclusive rights in a mask work may transfer all of those rights, or license all or less than all of those rights, by any written instrument signed by such owner or a duly authorized agent of the owner. Such rights may be transferred or licensed by operation of law, may be bequeathed by will, and may pass as personal property by the applicable laws of intestate succession.

(c) (1) Any document pertaining to a mask work may be recorded in the Copyright Office if the document filed for recordation bears the actual signature of the person who executed it, or if it is accompanied by a sworn or official certification that it is a true copy of the original, signed document. The Register of Copyrights shall, upon receipt of the document and the fee specified pursuant to section 908(d), record the document and return it with a certificate of recordation. The recordation of any transfer or license under this paragraph gives all persons constructive notice of the facts stated in the recorded document concerning the transfer or license.

(2) In any case in which conflicting transfers of the exclusive rights in a mask work are made, the transfer first executed shall be void as against a subsequent transfer which is made for a valuable consideration and without notice of the first transfer, unless the first transfer is recorded in accordance with paragraph (1) within three months after the date on which it is executed, but in no case later than the day before the date of such subsequent transfer.

(d) Mask works prepared by an officer or employee of the United States Government as part of that person's official duties are not protected under this chapter, but the United States Government is not precluded from receiving and holding exclusive rights in mask works transferred to the Government under subsection (b).

(Added Nov. 8, 1984, Pub. L. 98-620, §302, 98 Stat. 3349; Nov. 2, 2002, Pub. L. 107-273, §13210, 116 Stat. 1909.)

§ 904   Duration of protection

(a) The protection provided for a mask work under this chapter shall commence on the date on which the mask work is registered under section 908, or the date on which the mask work is first commercially exploited anywhere in the world, whichever occurs first.

(b) Subject to subsection (c) and the provisions of this chapter, the protection provided under this chapter to a mask work shall end ten years after the date on which such protection commences under subsection (a).

(c) All terms of protection provided in this section shall run to the end of the calendar year in which they would otherwise expire.

(Nov. 8, 1984, Pub. L. 98-620, §302, 98 Stat. 3349.)

§ 905   Exclusive rights in mask works

The owner of a mask work provided protection under this chapter has the exclusive rights to do and to authorize any of the following:

(1) to reproduce the mask work by optical, electronic, or any other means;

(2) to import or distribute a semiconductor chip product in which the mask work is embodied; and

(3) to induce or knowingly to cause another person to do any of the acts described in paragraphs (1) and (2).

(Nov. 8, 1984, Pub. L. 98-620, §302, 98 Stat. 3350.)

§ 906   Limitation on exclusive rights: reverse engineering; first sale

(a) Notwithstanding the provisions of section 905, it is not an infringement of the exclusive rights of the owner of a mask work for—

(1) a person to reproduce the mask work solely for the purpose of teaching, analyzing, or evaluating the concepts or techniques embodied in the mask work or the circuitry, logic flow, or organization of components used in the mask work; or

(2) a person who performs the analysis or evaluation described in paragraph (1) to incorporate the results of such conduct in an original mask work which is made to be distributed.

(b) Notwithstanding the provisions of section 905(2), the owner of a particular semiconductor chip product made by the owner of the mask work, or by any person authorized by the owner of the mask work, may import, distribute, or otherwise dispose of or use, but not reproduce, that particular semiconductor chip product without the authority of the owner of the mask work.

(Nov. 8, 1984, Pub. L. 98-620, §302, 98 Stat. 3350.)

§ 907 Limitation on exclusive rights: innocent infringement

(a) Notwithstanding any other provision of this chapter, an innocent purchaser of an infringing semiconductor chip product—

(1) shall incur no liability under this chapter with respect to the importation or distribution of units of the infringing semiconductor chip product that occurs before the innocent purchaser has notice of protection with respect to the mask work embodied in the semiconductor chip product; and

(2) shall be liable only for a reasonable royalty on each unit of the infringing semiconductor chip product that the innocent purchaser imports or distributes after having notice of protection with respect to the mask work embodied in the semiconductor chip product.

(b) The amount of the royalty referred to in subsection (a)(2) shall be determined by the court in a civil action for infringement unless the parties resolve the issue by voluntary negotiation, mediation, or binding arbitration.

(c) The immunity of an innocent purchaser from liability referred to in subsection (a)(1) and the limitation of remedies with respect to an innocent purchaser referred to in subsection (a)(2) shall extend to any person who directly or indirectly purchases an infringing semiconductor chip product from an innocent purchaser.

(d) The provisions of subsections (a), (b), and (c) apply only with respect to those units of an infringing semiconductor chip product that an innocent purchaser purchased before having notice of protection with respect to the mask work embodied in the semiconductor chip product.

(Nov. 8, 1984, Pub. L. 98-620, §302, 98 Stat. 3350.)

17 U.S.C. § 907

§ 908   Registration of claims of protection

(a) The owner of a mask work may apply to the Register of Copyrights for registration of a claim of protection in a mask work. Protection of a mask work under this chapter shall terminate if application for registration of a claim of protection in the mask work is not made as provided in this chapter within two years after the date on which the mask work is first commercially exploited anywhere in the world.

(b) The Register of Copyrights shall be responsible for all administrative functions and duties under this chapter. Except for section 708, the provisions of chapter 7 of this title relating to the general responsibilities, organization, regulatory authority, actions, records, and publications of the Copyright Office shall apply to this chapter, except that the Register of Copyrights may make such changes as may be necessary in applying those provisions to this chapter.

(c) The application for registration of a mask work shall be made on a form prescribed by the Register of Copyrights. Such form may require any information regarded by the Register as bearing upon the preparation or identification of the mask work, the existence or duration of protection of the mask work under this chapter, or ownership of the mask work. The application shall be accompanied by the fee set pursuant to subsection (d) and the identifying material specified pursuant to such subsection.

(d) The Register of Copyrights shall by regulation set reasonable fees for the filing of applications to register claims of protection in mask works under this chapter, and for other services relating to the administration of this chapter or the rights under this chapter, taking into consideration the cost of providing those services, the benefits of a public record, and statutory fee schedules under this title. The Register shall also specify the identifying material to be deposited in connection with the claim for registration.

(e) If the Register of Copyrights, after examining an application for registration, determines, in accordance with the provisions of this chapter, that the application relates to a mask work which is entitled to protection under this chapter, then the Register shall register the claim of protection and issue to the applicant a certificate of registration of the claim of protection under the seal of the Copyright Office. The effective date of registration of a claim of protection shall be the date on which an application, deposit of identifying material, and fee, which are determined by the Register of Copyrights or by a court of competent jurisdiction to be acceptable for registration of the claim, have all been received in the Copyright Office.

(f) In any action for infringement under this chapter, the certificate of registration of a mask work shall constitute prima facie evidence (1) of the facts stated in the certificate, and (2) that the applicant issued the certificate has met the requirements of this chapter, and the regulations issued under this chapter, with respect to the registration of claims.

(g) Any applicant for registration under this section who is dissatisfied with the refusal of the Register of Copyrights to issue a certificate of registration under this section may seek judicial review of that refusal by bringing an action for such review in an appropriate United States district court not later than sixty days after the refusal. The provisions of chapter 7 of title 5 shall apply to such judicial review. The failure of the Register of Copyrights to issue a certificate of registration within four months after an application for registration is filed shall be deemed to be a refusal to issue a certificate of registration for purposes of this subsection and section 910(b)(2), except that, upon a showing of good cause, the district court may shorten such four-month period.

(Nov. 8, 1984, Pub. L. 98-620, §302, 98 Stat. 3351.)

§ 909   Mask work notice

(a) The owner of a mask work provided protection under this chapter may affix notice to the mask work, and to masks and semiconductor chip products embodying the mask work, in such manner and location as to give reasonable notice of such protection. The Register of Copyrights shall prescribe by regulation, as examples, specific methods of affixation and positions of notice for purposes of this section, but these specifications shall not be considered exhaustive. The affixation of such notice is not a condition of protection under this chapter, but shall constitute prima facie evidence of notice of protection.

(b) The notice referred to in subsection (a) shall consist of—

(1) the words ["mask work,"][18] the symbol *M*, or the symbol Ⓜ (the letter M in a circle); and

---

[18] *Ed. Note:* Statute uses "mask force." Probably should be "mask work."

(2) the name of the owner or owners of the mask work or an abbreviation by which the name is recognized or is generally known.

(Nov. 8, 1984, Pub. L. 98-620, §302, 98 Stat. 3352.)

§ 910   Enforcement of exclusive rights

(a) Except as otherwise provided in this chapter, any person who violates any of the exclusive rights of the owner of a mask work under this chapter, by conduct in or affecting commerce, shall be liable as an infringer of such rights. As used in this subsection, the term "any person" includes any State, any instrumentality of a State, and any officer or employee of a State or instrumentality of a State acting in his or her official capacity. Any State, and any such instrumentality, officer, or employee, shall be subject to the provisions of this chapter in the same manner and to the same extent as any nongovernmental entity.

(b) (1) The owner of a mask work protected under this chapter, or the exclusive licensee of all rights under this chapter with respect to the mask work, shall, after a certificate of registration of a claim of protection in that mask work has been issued under section 908, be entitled to institute a civil action for any infringement with respect to the mask work which is committed after the commencement of protection of the mask work under section 904(a).

(2) In any case in which an application for registration of a claim of protection in a mask work and the required deposit of identifying material and fee have been received in the Copyright Office in proper form and registration of the mask work has been refused, the applicant is entitled to institute a civil action for infringement under this chapter with respect to the mask work if notice of the action, together with a copy of the complaint, is served on the Register of Copyrights, in accordance with the Federal Rules of Civil Procedure. The Register may, at his or her option, become a party to the action with respect to the issue of whether the claim of protection is eligible for registration by entering an appearance within sixty days after such service, but the failure of the Register to become a party to the action shall not deprive the court of jurisdiction to determine that issue.

(c) (1) The Secretary of the Treasury and the United States Postal Service shall separately or jointly issue regulations for the enforcement of the rights set forth in section 905 with respect to importation. These regulations may

17 U.S.C. § 910

require, as a condition for the exclusion of articles from the United States, that the person seeking exclusion take any one or more of the following actions:

(A) Obtain a court order enjoining, or an order of the International Trade Commission under section 337 of the Tariff Act of 1930 excluding, importation of the articles.

(B) Furnish proof that the mask work involved is protected under this chapter and that the importation of the articles would infringe the rights in the mask work under this chapter.

(C) Post a surety bond for any injury that may result if the detention or exclusion of the articles proves to be unjustified.

(2) Articles imported in violation of the rights set forth in section 905 are subject to seizure and forfeiture in the same manner as property imported in violation of the customs laws. Any such forfeited articles shall be destroyed as directed by the Secretary of the Treasury or the court, as the case may be, except that the articles may be returned to the country of export whenever it is shown to the satisfaction of the Secretary of the Treasury that the importer had no reasonable grounds for believing that his or her acts constituted a violation of the law.

(Nov. 8, 1984, Pub. L. 98-620, §302, 98 Stat. 3352; Nov. 15, 1990, Pub. L. 101-553, §2, 104 Stat. 2750.)

§ 911   Civil actions

(a) Any court having jurisdiction of a civil action arising under this chapter may grant temporary restraining orders, preliminary injunctions, and permanent injunctions on such terms as the court may deem reasonable to prevent or restrain infringement of the exclusive rights in a mask work under this chapter.

(b) Upon finding an infringer liable, to a person entitled under section 910(b)(1) to institute a civil action, for an infringement of any exclusive right under this chapter, the court shall award such person actual damages suffered by the person as a result of the infringement. The court shall also award such person the infringer's profits that are attributable to the infringement and are not taken into account in computing the award of actual damages. In establishing the infringer's profits, such person is required to present proof only of the infringer's gross revenue, and the infringer is required to prove his or her deductible expenses and the elements of profit attributable to factors other than the mask work.

(c) At any time before final judgment is rendered, a person entitled to institute a civil action for infringement may elect, instead of actual damages and profits as provided by subsection (b), an award of statutory damages for all infringements involved in the action, with respect to any one mask work for which any one infringer is liable individually, or for which any two or more infringers are liable jointly and severally, in an amount not more than $250,000 as the court considers just.

(d) An action for infringement under this chapter shall be barred unless the action is commenced within three years after the claim accrues.

(e) (1) At any time while an action for infringement of the exclusive rights in a mask work under this chapter is pending, the court may order the impounding, on such terms as it may deem reasonable, of all semiconductor chip products, and any drawings, tapes, masks, or other products by means of which such products may be reproduced, that are claimed to have been made, imported, or used in violation of those exclusive rights. Insofar as practicable, applications for orders under this paragraph shall be heard and determined in the same manner as an application for a temporary restraining order or preliminary injunction.

(2) As part of a final judgment or decree, the court may order the destruction or other disposition of any infringing semiconductor chip products, and any masks, tapes, or other articles by means of which such products may be reproduced.

(f) In any civil action arising under this chapter, the court in its discretion may allow the recovery of full costs, including reasonable attorneys' fees, to the prevailing party.

(g) (1) Any State, any instrumentality of a State, and any officer or employee of a State or instrumentality of a State acting in his or her official capacity, shall not be immune, under the Eleventh Amendment of the Constitution of the United States or under any other doctrine of sovereign immunity, from suit in Federal court by any person, including any governmental or nongovernmental entity, for a violation of any of the exclusive rights of the owner of a mask work under this chapter, or for any other violation under this chapter.

17 U.S.C. § 911

(2) In a suit described in paragraph (1) for a violation described in that paragraph, remedies (including remedies both at law and in equity) are available for the violation to the same extent as such remedies are available for such a violation in a suit against any public or private entity other than a State, instrumentality of a State, or officer or employee of a State acting in his or her official capacity. Such remedies include actual damages and profits under subsection (b), statutory damages under subsection (c), impounding and disposition of infringing articles under subsection (e), and costs and attorney's fees under subsection (f).

(Nov. 8, 1984, Pub. L. 98-620, §302, 98 Stat. 3353; Nov. 15, 1990, Pub. L. 101-553, §2, 104 Stat. 2750.)

§ 912   Relation to other laws

(a) Nothing in this chapter shall affect any right or remedy held by any person under chapters 1 through 8 or 10 of this title, or under title 35.

(b) Except as provided in section 908(b) of this title, references to "this title" or "title 17" in chapters 1 through 8 or 10 of this title shall be deemed not to apply to this chapter.

(c) The provisions of this chapter shall preempt the laws of any State to the extent those laws provide any rights or remedies with respect to a mask work which are equivalent to those rights or remedies provided by this chapter, except that such preemption shall be effective only with respect to actions filed on or after January 1, 1986.

(d) Notwithstanding subsection (c), nothing in this chapter shall detract from any rights of a mask work owner, whether under Federal law (exclusive of this chapter) or under the common law or the statutes of a State, heretofore or hereafter declared or enacted, with respect to any mask work first commercially exploited before July 1, 1983.

(Nov. 8, 1984, Pub. L. 98-620, §302, 98 Stat. 3354; Nov. 19, 1988, Pub. L. 100-702, §1020, 102 Stat. 4672; Oct. 29, 1992, Pub. L. 102-563, §3, 106 Stat. 4248.)

§ 913   Transitional provisions

(a) No application for registration under section 908 may be filed, and no civil action under section 910 or other enforcement proceeding under this chapter may be instituted, until sixty days after the date of the enactment of this chapter.

(b) No monetary relief under section 911 may be granted with respect to any conduct that occurred before the date of the enactment of this chapter, except as provided in subsection (d).

(c) Subject to subsection (a), the provisions of this chapter apply to all mask works that are first commercially exploited or are registered under this chapter, or both, on or after the date of the enactment of this chapter.

(d)(1) Subject to subsection (a), protection is available under this chapter to any mask work that was first commercially exploited on or after July 1, 1983, and before the date of the enactment of this chapter, if a claim of protection in the mask work is registered in the Copyright Office before July 1, 1985, under section 908.

(2) In the case of any mask work described in paragraph (1) that is provided protection under this chapter, infringing semiconductor chip product units manufactured before the date of the enactment of this chapter may, without liability under sections 910 and 911, be imported into or distributed in the United States, or both, until two years after the date of registration of the mask work under section 908, but only if the importer or distributor, as the case may be, first pays or offers to pay the reasonable royalty referred to in section 907(a)(2) to the mask work owner, on all such units imported or distributed, or both, after the date of the enactment of this chapter.

(3) In the event that a person imports or distributes infringing semiconductor chip product units described in paragraph (2) of this subsection without first paying or offering to pay the reasonable royalty specified in such paragraph, or if the person refuses or fails to make such payment, the mask work owner shall be entitled to the relief provided in sections 910 and 911.

(Nov. 8, 1984, Pub. L. 98-620, §302, 98 Stat. 3354.)

§ 914   International transitional provisions

(a) Notwithstanding the conditions set forth in subparagraphs (A) and (C) of section 902(a)(1) with respect to the availability of protection under this chapter to nationals, domiciliaries, and sovereign authorities of a foreign nation, the Secretary of Commerce may, upon the petition of any person, or upon the Secretary's own motion, issue an order extending protection under this chapter to such foreign nationals, domiciliaries, and sovereign authorities if the Secretary finds—

(1) that the foreign nation is making good faith efforts and reasonable progress toward—

(A) entering into a treaty described in section 902(a)(1)(A); or

(B) enacting or implementing legislation that would be in compliance with subparagraph (A) or (B) of section 902(a)(2); and

(2) that the nationals, domiciliaries, and sovereign authorities of the foreign nation, and persons controlled by them, are not engaged in the misappropriation, or unauthorized distribution or commercial exploitation, of mask works; and

(3) that issuing the order would promote the purposes of this chapter and international comity with respect to the protection of mask works.

(b) While an order under subsection (a) is in effect with respect to a foreign nation, no application for registration of a claim for protection in a mask work under this chapter may be denied solely because the owner of the mask work is a national, domiciliary, or sovereign authority of that foreign nation, or solely because the mask work was first commercially exploited in that foreign nation.

(c) Any order issued by the Secretary of Commerce under subsection (a) shall be effective for such period as the Secretary designates in the order, except that no such order may be effective after the date on which the authority of the Secretary of Commerce terminates under subsection (e). The effective date of any such order shall also be designated in the order. In the case of an order issued upon the petition of a person, such effective date may be no earlier than the date on which the Secretary receives such petition.

(d) (1) Any order issued under this section shall terminate if—

(A) the Secretary of Commerce finds that any of the conditions set forth in paragraphs (1), (2), and (3) of subsection (a) no longer exist; or

(B) mask works of nationals, domiciliaries, and sovereign authorities of that foreign nation or mask works first commercially exploited in that foreign nation become eligible for protection under subparagraph (A) or (C) of section 902(a)(1).

(2) Upon the termination or expiration of an order issued under this section, registrations of claims of protection in mask works made pursuant to that order shall remain valid for the period specified in section 904.

17 U.S.C. § 914

(e) The authority of the Secretary of Commerce under this section shall commence on the date of the enactment of this chapter, and shall terminate on July 1, 1995.

(f) (1) The Secretary of Commerce shall promptly notify the Register of Copyrights and the Committees on the Judiciary of the Senate and the House of Representatives of the issuance or termination of any order under this section, together with a statement of the reasons for such action. The Secretary shall also publish such notification and statement of reasons in the Federal Register.

(2) Two years after the date of the enactment of this chapter, the Secretary of Commerce, in consultation with the Register of Copyrights, shall transmit to the Committees on the Judiciary of the Senate and the House of Representatives a report on the actions taken under this section and on the current status of international recognition of mask work protection. The report shall include such recommendations for modifications of the protection accorded under this chapter to mask works owned by nationals, domiciliaries, or sovereign authorities of foreign nations as the Secretary, in consultation with the Register of Copyrights, considers would promote the purposes of this chapter and international comity with respect to mask work protection. Not later than July 1, 1994, the Secretary of Commerce, in consultation with the Register of Copyrights, shall transmit to the Committees on the Judiciary of the Senate and the House of Representatives a report updating the matters contained in the report transmitted under the preceding sentence.

(Nov. 8, 1984, Pub. L. 98-620, §302, 98 Stat. 3355; Nov. 9, 1987, Pub. L. 100-159, §2, 4, 101 Stat. 899, 900; June 28, 1991, Pub. L. 102-64, §3, 4, 105 Stat. 320, 321.)

CHAPTER 10 — DIGITAL AUDIO RECORDING DEVICES AND MEDIA

SUBCHAPTER A — DEFINITIONS

§ 1001   Definitions

As used in this chapter, the following terms have the following meanings:

(1) A "digital audio copied recording" is a reproduction in a digital recording format of a digital musical recording, whether that reproduction is made directly from another digital musical recording or indirectly from a transmission.

(2) A "digital audio interface device" is any machine or device that is designed specifically to communicate digital audio information and related interface data to a digital audio recording device through a nonprofessional interface.

(3) A "digital audio recording device" is any machine or device of a type commonly distributed to individuals for use by individuals, whether or not included with or as part of some other machine or device, the digital recording function of which is designed or marketed for the primary purpose of, and that is capable of, making a digital audio copied recording for private use, except for —

(A) professional model products, and

(B) dictation machines, answering machines, and other audio recording equipment that is designed and marketed primarily for the creation of sound recordings resulting from the fixation of nonmusical sounds.

(4) (A) A "digital audio recording medium" is any material object in a form commonly distributed for use by individuals, that is primarily marketed or most commonly used by consumers for the purpose of making digital audio copied recordings by use of a digital audio recording device.

17 U.S.C. § 1001

(B) Such term does not include any material object—

(i) that embodies a sound recording at the time it is first distributed by the importer or manufacturer; or

(ii) that is primarily marketed and most commonly used by consumers either for the purpose of making copies of motion pictures or other audiovisual works or for the purpose of making copies of nonmusical literary works, including computer programs or data bases.

(5) (A) A "digital musical recording" is a material object—

(i) in which are fixed, in a digital recording format, only sounds, and material, statements, or instructions incidental to those fixed sounds, if any, and

(ii) from which the sounds and material can be perceived, reproduced, or otherwise communicated, either directly or with the aid of a machine or device.

(B) A "digital musical recording" does not include a material object—

(i) in which the fixed sounds consist entirely of spoken word recordings, or

(ii) in which one or more computer programs are fixed, except that a digital musical recording may contain statements or instructions constituting the fixed sounds and incidental material, and statements or instructions to be used directly or indirectly in order to bring about the perception, reproduction, or communication of the fixed sounds and incidental material.

(C) For purposes of this paragraph—

(i) a "spoken word recording" is a sound recording in which are fixed only a series of spoken words, except that the spoken words may be accompanied by incidental musical or other sounds, and

(ii) the term "incidental" means related to and relatively minor by comparison.

(6) "Distribute" means to sell, lease, or assign a product to consumers in the United States, or to sell, lease, or assign a product in the United States for ultimate transfer to consumers in the United States.

(7) An "interested copyright party" is—

(A) the owner of the exclusive right under section 106(1) of this title to reproduce a sound recording of a musical work that has been embodied in a digital musical recording or analog musical recording lawfully made under this title that has been distributed;

(B) the legal or beneficial owner of, or the person that controls, the right to reproduce in a digital musical recording or analog musical recording a musical work that has been embodied in a digital musical recording or analog musical recording lawfully made under this title that has been distributed;

(C) a featured recording artist who performs on a sound recording that has been distributed; or

(D) any association or other organization—

(i) representing persons specified in subparagraph (A), (B), or (C), or

(ii) engaged in licensing rights in musical works to music users on behalf of writers and publishers.

(8) To "manufacture" means to produce or assemble a product in the United States. A "manufacturer" is a person who manufactures.

(9) A "music publisher" is a person that is authorized to license the reproduction of a particular musical work in a sound recording.

(10) A "professional model product' is an audio recording device that is designed, manufactured, marketed, and intended for use by recording professionals in the ordinary course of a lawful business, in accordance with such requirements as the Secretary of Commerce shall establish by regulation.

(11) The term "serial copying" means the duplication in a digital format of a copyrighted musical work or sound recording from a digital reproduction of a digital musical recording. The term "digital reproduction of a digital musical recording" does not include a digital musical recording as distributed, by authority of the copyright owner, for ultimate sale to consumers.

(12) The "transfer price" of a digital audio recording device or a digital audio recording medium—

(A) is, subject to subparagraph (B)—

(i) in the case of an imported product, the actual entered value at United States Customs (exclusive of any freight, insurance, and applicable duty), and

(ii) in the case of a domestic product, the manufacturer's transfer price (FOB the manufacturer, and exclusive of any direct sales taxes or excise taxes incurred in connection with the sale); and

(B) shall, in a case in which the transferor and transferee are related entities or within a single entity, not be less than a reasonable arms-length price under the principles of the regulations adopted pursuant to section 482 of the Internal Revenue Code of 1986, or any successor provision to such section.

(13) A "writer" is the composer or lyricist of a particular musical work.

(Oct. 28, 1992, Pub. L. 102-563, §2, 106 Stat. 4237-39.)

Subchapter B—Copying Controls

§ 1002 Incorporation of copying controls

(a) *Prohibition on importation, manufacture, and distribution.*—No person shall import, manufacture, or distribute any digital audio recording device or digital audio interface device that does not conform to—

(1) the Serial Copy Management System;

(2) a system that has the same functional characteristics as the Serial Copy Management System and requires that copyright and generation status information be accurately sent, received, and acted upon between devices using the system's method of serial copying regulation and devices using the Serial Copy Management System; or

(3) any other system certified by the Secretary of Commerce as prohibiting unauthorized serial copying.

(b) *Development of verification procedure.*—The Secretary of Commerce shall establish a procedure to verify, upon the petition of an interested party, that a system meets the standards set forth in subsection (a)(2).

(c) *Prohibition on circumvention of the system.*—No person shall import, manufacture, or distribute any device, or offer or perform any service, the primary purpose or effect of which is to avoid, bypass, remove, deactivate, or otherwise circumvent any program or circuit which implements, in whole or in part, a system described in subsection (a).

17 U.S.C. § 1002

(d) *Encoding of information on digital musical recordings.—*

(1) *Prohibition on encoding inaccurate information.—*No person shall encode a digital musical recording of a sound recording with inaccurate information relating to the category code, copyright status, or generation status of the source material for the recording.

(2) *Encoding of copyright status not required.—*Nothing in this chapter requires any person engaged in the importation or manufacture of digital musical recordings to encode any such digital musical recording with respect to its copyright status.

(e) *Information accompanying transmissions in digital format.—*Any person who transmits or otherwise communicates to the public any sound recording in digital format is not required under this chapter to transmit or otherwise communicate the information relating to the copyright status of the sound recording. Any such person who does transmit or otherwise communicate such copyright status information shall transmit or communicate such information accurately.

(Oct. 28, 1992, Pub. L. 102-563, §2, 106 Stat. 4240.)

SUBCHAPTER C—ROYALTY PAYMENTS

§ 1003   Obligation to make royalty payments

(a) *Prohibition on importation and manufacture.—*No person shall import into and distribute, or manufacture and distribute, any digital audio recording device or digital audio recording medium unless such person records the notice specified by this section and subsequently deposits the statements of account and applicable royalty payments for such device or medium specified in section 1004.

(b) *Filing of notice.—*The importer or manufacturer of any digital audio recording device or digital audio recording medium, within a product category or utilizing a technology with respect to which such manufacturer or importer has not previously filed a notice under this subsection, shall file with the Register of Copyrights a notice with respect to such device or medium, in such form and content as the Register shall prescribe by regulation.

(c) *Filing of quarterly and annual statements of account.* —

(1) *Generally.* —Any importer or manufacturer that distributes any digital audio recording device or digital audio recording medium that it manufactured or imported shall file with the Register of Copyrights, in such form and content as the Register shall prescribe by regulation, such quarterly and annual statements of account with respect to such distribution as the Register shall prescribe by regulation.

(2) *Certification, verification, and confidentiality.* —Each such statement shall be certified as accurate by an authorized officer or principal of the importer or manufacturer. The Register shall issue regulations to provide for the verification and audit of such statements and to protect the confidentiality of the information contained in such statements. Such regulations shall provide for the disclosure, in confidence, of such statements to interested copyright parties.

(3) *Royalty payments.* —Each such statement shall be accompanied by the royalty payments specified in section 1004.

(Oct. 28, 1992, Pub. L. 102-563, §2, 106 Stat. 4240-41.)

§ 1004   Royalty payments

(a) *Digital audio recording devices.* —

(1) *Amount of payment.* —The royalty payment due under section 1003 for each digital audio recording device imported into and distributed in the United States, or manufactured and distributed in the United States, shall be 2 percent of the transfer price. Only the first person to manufacture and distribute or import and distribute such device shall be required to pay the royalty with respect to such device.

(2) *Calculation for devices distributed with other devices.* —With respect to a digital audio recording device first distributed in combination with one or more devices, either as a physically integrated unit or as separate components, the royalty payment shall be calculated as follows:

(A) If the digital audio recording device and such other devices are part of a physically integrated unit, the royalty payment shall be based on the transfer price of the unit, but shall be reduced by any royalty payment made on any digital audio recording device included within the unit that was not first distributed in combination with the unit.

(B) If the digital audio recording device is not part of a physically integrated unit and substantially similar devices have been distributed separately at any time during the preceding 4 calendar quarters, the royalty payment shall be based on the average transfer price of such devices during those 4 quarters.

(C) If the digital audio recording device is not part of a physically integrated unit and substantially similar devices have not been distributed separately at any time during the preceding 4 calendar quarters, the royalty payment shall be based on a constructed price reflecting the proportional value of such device to the combination as a whole.

(3) *Limits on royalties.* — Notwithstanding paragraph (1) or (2), the amount of the royalty payment for each digital audio recording device shall not be less than $1 nor more than the royalty maximum. The royalty maximum shall be $8 per device, except that in the case of a physically integrated unit containing more than 1 digital audio recording device, the royalty maximum for such unit shall be $12. During the 6th year after the effective date of this chapter, and not more than once each year thereafter, any interested copyright party may petition the Copyright Royalty Judges to increase the royalty maximum and, if more than 20 percent of the royalty payments are at the relevant royalty maximum, the Copyright Royalty Judges shall prospectively increase such royalty maximum with the goal of having no more than 10 percent of such payments at the new royalty maximum; however the amount of any such increase as a percentage of the royalty maximum shall in no event exceed the percentage increase in the Consumer Price Index during the period under review.

(b) *Digital audio recording media.* — The royalty payment due under section 1003 for each digital audio recording medium imported into and distributed in the United States, or manufactured and distributed in the United States, shall be 3 percent of the transfer price. Only the first person to manufacture and distribute or import and distribute such medium shall be required to pay the royalty with respect to such medium.

(Oct. 28, 1992, Pub. L. 102-563, §2, 106 Stat. 4241-42; Nov. 30, 2004, Pub. L. 108-419, §5, 118 Stat. 2368.)

§ 1005 Deposit of royalty payments and deduction of expenses

The Register of Copyrights shall receive all royalty payments deposited under this chapter and, after deducting the reasonable costs incurred by the

Copyright Office under this chapter, shall deposit the balance in the Treasury of the United States as offsetting receipts, in such manner as the Secretary of the Treasury directs. All funds held by the Secretary of the Treasury shall be invested in interest-bearing United States securities for later distribution with interest under section 1007. The Register may, in the Register's discretion, 4 years after the close of any calendar year, close out the royalty payments account for that calendar year, and may treat any funds remaining in such account and any subsequent deposits that would otherwise be attributable to that calendar year as attributable to the succeeding calendar year.

(Oct. 28, 1992, Pub. L. 102-563, §2, 106 Stat. 4242; Dec. 17, 1993, Pub. L. 103-198, §6(b), 107 Stat. 2312.)

§ 1006   Entitlement to royalty payments

(a) *Interested copyright parties.*—The royalty payments deposited pursuant to section 1005 shall, in accordance with the procedures specified in section 1007, be distributed to any interested copyright party—

(1) whose musical work or sound recording has been—

(A) embodied in a digital musical recording or an analog musical recording lawfully made under this title that has been distributed, and

(B) distributed in the form of digital musical recordings or analog musical recordings or disseminated to the public in transmissions, during the period to which such payments pertain; and

(2) who has filed a claim under section 1007.

(b) *Allocation of royalty payments to groups.*—The royalty payments shall be divided into 2 funds as follows:

(1) *The sound recordings fund.*—66²/₃ percent of the royalty payments shall be allocated to the Sound Recordings Fund. 2⁵/₈ percent of the royalty payments allocated to the Sound Recordings Fund shall be placed in an escrow account managed by an independent administrator jointly appointed by the interested copyright parties described in section 1001(7)(A) and the American Federation of Musicians (or any successor entity) to be distributed to nonfeatured musicians (whether or not members of the American Federation of Musicians or any successor entity) who have performed on sound recordings distributed in the United States. 1³/₈ percent of the royalty payments allocated to the Sound Recordings Fund shall be placed in an escrow account managed by an independent administrator jointly appointed by the interested copyright parties described in sec-

17 U.S.C. § 1006

tion 1001(7)(A) and the American Federation of Television and Radio Artists (or any successor entity) to be distributed to nonfeatured vocalists (whether or not members of the American Federation [of] Television and Radio Artists or any successor entity) who have performed on sound recordings distributed in the United States. 40 percent of the remaining royalty payments in the Sound Recordings Fund shall be distributed to the interested copyright parties described in section 1001(7)(C), and 60 percent of such remaining royalty payments shall be distributed to the interested copyright parties described in section 1001(7)(A).

(2) *The musical works fund.—*

(A) 33 percent of the royalty payments shall be allocated to the Musical Works Fund for distribution to interested copyright parties described in section 1001(7)(B).

(B) (i) Music publishers shall be entitled to 50 percent of the royalty payments allocated to the Musical Works Fund.

(ii) Writers shall be entitled to the other 50 percent of the royalty payments allocated to the Musical Works Fund.

(c) *Allocation of royalty payments within groups.—*If all interested copyright parties within a group specified in subsection (b) do not agree on a voluntary proposal for the distribution of the royalty payments within each group, the Copyright Royalty Judges shall, pursuant to the procedures specified under section 1007(c), allocate royalty payments under this section based on the extent to which, during the relevant period—

(1) for the Sound Recordings Fund, each sound recording was distributed in the form of digital musical recordings or analog musical recordings; and

(2) for the Musical Works Fund, each musical work was distributed in the form of digital musical recordings or analog musical recordings or disseminated to the public in transmissions.

(Oct. 28, 1992, Pub. L. 102-563, §2, 106 Stat. 4242-44; Dec. 17, 1993, Pub. L. 103-198, §6(b), 107 Stat. 2312; Nov. 30, 2004, Pub. L. 108-419, §5, 118 Stat. 2368.)

§ 1007   Procedures for distributing royalty payments

(a) *Filing of claims and negotiations.—*

(1) *Filing of claims.—*During the first 2 months of each calendar year, every interested copyright party seeking to receive royalty payments to which

such party is entitled under section 1006 shall file with the Copyright Royalty Judges a claim for payments collected during the preceding year in such form and manner as the Copyright Royalty Judges shall prescribe by regulation.

(2) *Negotiations.*—Notwithstanding any provision of the antitrust laws, for purposes of this section interested copyright parties within each group specified in section 1006(b) may agree among themselves to the proportionate division of royalty payments, may lump their claims together and file them jointly or as a single claim, or may designate a common agent, including any organization described in section 1001(7)(D), to negotiate or receive payment on their behalf; except that no agreement under this subsection may modify the allocation of royalties specified in section 1006(b).

(b) *Distribution of payments in the absence of a dispute.*—After the period established for the filing of claims under subsection (a), in each year, the Copyright Royalty Judges shall determine whether there exists a controversy concerning the distribution of royalty payments under section 1006(c). If the Copyright Royalty Judges determine that no such controversy exists, the Copyright Royalty Judges shall, within 30 days after such determination, authorize the distribution of the royalty payments as set forth in the agreements regarding the distribution of royalty payments entered into pursuant to subsection (a). The Librarian of Congress shall, before such royalty payments are distributed, deduct the reasonable administrative costs incurred under this section.

(c) *Resolution of disputes.*—If the Copyright Royalty Judges find the existence of a controversy, the Copyright Royalty Judges shall, pursuant to chapter 8 of this title, conduct a proceeding to determine the distribution of royalty payments. During the pendency of such a proceeding, the Copyright Royalty Judges shall withhold from distribution an amount sufficient to satisfy all claims with respect to which a controversy exists, but shall, to the extent feasible, authorize the distribution of any amounts that are not in controversy. The Librarian of Congress shall, before such royalty payments are distributed, deduct the reasonable administrative costs incurred under this section.

(Oct. 28, 1992, Pub. L. 102-563, §2, 106 Stat. 4244; Dec. 17, 1993, Pub. L. 103-198, §6(b), 107 Stat. 2312; Nov. 13, 1997, Pub. L. 105-80, §9, 12, 111 Stat. 1534, 1536; Nov. 30, 2004, Pub. L. 108-419, §5, 118 Stat. 2368, Oct. 6, 2006, Pub. L. 109-303, §4(a), 120 Stat. 1481.)

17 U.S.C. § 1007

SUBCHAPTER D—PROHIBITION ON CERTAIN INFRINGEMENT ACTIONS, REMEDIES, AND ARBITRATION

§ 1008   Prohibition on certain infringement actions

No action may be brought under this title alleging infringement of copyright based on the manufacture, importation, or distribution of a digital audio recording device, a digital audio recording medium, an analog recording device, or an analog recording medium, or based on the noncommercial use by a consumer of such a device or medium for making digital musical recordings or analog musical recordings.

(Oct. 28, 1992, Pub. L. 102-563, §2, 106 Stat. 4244.)

§ 1009   Civil remedies

(a) *Civil actions.*—Any interested copyright party injured by a violation of section 1002 or 1003 may bring a civil action in an appropriate United States district court against any person for such violation.

(b) *Other civil actions.*—Any person injured by a violation of this chapter may bring a civil action in an appropriate United States district court for actual damages incurred as a result of such violation.

(c) *Powers of the court.*—In an action brought under subsection (a), the court—

(1) may grant temporary and permanent injunctions on such terms as it deems reasonable to prevent or restrain such violation;

(2) in the case of a violation of section 1002, or in the case of an injury resulting from a failure to make royalty payments required by section 1003, shall award damages under subsection (d);

(3) in its discretion may allow the recovery of costs by or against any party other than the United States or an officer thereof; and

(4) in its discretion may award a reasonable attorney's fee to the prevailing party.

(d) *Award of damages.*—

(1) *Damages for section 1002 or 1003 violations.*—

(A) *Actual damages.*—

(i) In an action brought under subsection (a), if the court finds that a violation of section 1002 or 1003 has occurred, the court shall award to the complaining party its actual damages if the complaining party elects such damages at any time before final judgment is entered.

(ii) In the case of section 1003, actual damages shall constitute the royalty payments that should have been paid under section 1004 and deposited under section 1005. In such a case, the court, in its discretion, may award an additional amount of not to exceed 50 percent of the actual damages.

(B) *Statutory damages for section 1002 violations.* —

(i) *Device.*—A complaining party may recover an award of statutory damages for each violation of section 1002 (a) or (c) in the sum of not more than $2,500 per device involved in such violation or per device on which a service prohibited by section 1002(c) has been performed, as the court considers just.

(ii) *Digital musical recording.*—A complaining party may recover an award of statutory damages for each violation of section 1002(d) in the sum of not more than $25 per digital musical recording involved in such violation, as the court considers just.

(iii) *Transmission.* —A complaining party may recover an award of damages for each transmission or communication that violates section 1002(e) in the sum of not more than $10,000, as the court considers just.

(2) *Repeated violations.*—In any case in which the court finds that a person has violated section 1002 or 1003 within 3 years after a final judgment against that person for another such violation was entered, the court may increase the award of damages to not more than double the amounts that would otherwise be awarded under paragraph (1), as the court considers just.

(3) *Innocent violations of section 1002.*—The court in its discretion may reduce the total award of damages against a person violating section 1002 to a sum of not less than $250 in any case in which the court finds that the violator was not aware and had no reason to believe that its acts constituted a violation of section 1002.

(e) *Payment of damages.*—Any award of damages under subsection (d) shall be deposited with the Register pursuant to section 1005 for distribution to interested copyright parties as though such funds were royalty payments made pursuant to section 1003.

17 U.S.C. § 1009

(f) *Impounding of articles.*—At any time while an action under subsection (a) is pending, the court may order the impounding, on such terms as it deems reasonable, of any digital audio recording device, digital musical recording, or device specified in section 1002(c) that is in the custody or control of the alleged violator and that the court has reasonable cause to believe does not comply with, or was involved in a violation of, section 1002.

(g) *Remedial modification and destruction of articles.*—In an action brought under subsection (a), the court may, as part of a final judgment or decree finding a violation of section 1002, order the remedial modification or the destruction of any digital audio recording device, digital musical recording, or device specified in section 1002(c) that—

(1) does not comply with, or was involved in a violation of, section 1002, and

(2) is in the custody or control of the violator or has been impounded under subsection (f).

(Oct. 28, 1992, Pub. L. 102-563, §2, 106 Stat. 4245-46.)

§1010   Determination of certain disputes

(a) *Scope of Determination.*—Before the date of first distribution in the United States of a digital audio recording device or a digital audio interface device, any party manufacturing, importing, or distributing such device, and any interested copyright party may mutually agree to petition the Copyright Royalty Judges to determine whether such device is subject to section 1002, or the basis on which royalty payments for such device are to be made under section 1003.

(b) *Initiation of Proceedings.*—The parties under subsection (a) shall file the petition with the Copyright Royalty Judges requesting the commencement of a proceeding. Within 2 weeks after receiving such a petition, the Chief Copyright Royalty Judge shall cause notice to be published in the Federal Register of the initiation of the proceeding.

(c) *Stay of Judicial Proceedings.*—Any civil action brought under section 1009 against a party to a proceeding under this section shall, on application of one of the parties to the proceeding, be stayed until completion of the proceeding.

(d) *Proceeding.*—The Copyright Royalty Judges shall conduct a proceeding with respect to the matter concerned, in accordance with such procedures as the Copyright Royalty Judges may adopt. The Copyright Royalty Judges shall act on the basis of a fully documented written record. Any party to the proceeding may submit relevant information and proposals to the Copyright Royalty Judges. The parties to the proceeding shall each bear their respective costs of participation.

(e) *Judicial Review.*—Any determination of the Copyright Royalty Judges under subsection (d) may be appealed, by a party to the proceeding, in accordance with section 803(d) of this title. The pendency of an appeal under this subsection shall not stay the determination of the Copyright Royalty Judges. If the court modifies the determination of the Copyright Royalty Judges, the court shall have jurisdiction to enter its own decision in accordance with its final judgment. The court may further vacate the determination of the Copyright Royalty Judges and remand the case for proceedings as provided in this section.

(Nov. 30, 2004, Pub. L. 108-419, §5, 118 Stat. 2368.)

CHAPTER 11—SOUND RECORDINGS AND MUSIC VIDEOS

SEC.
1101.   Unauthorized fixation and trafficking in sound recordings
         and music videos.

§ 1101 Unauthorized fixation and trafficking in sound recordings and music videos

(a) *Unauthorized acts.*—Anyone who, without the consent of the performer or performers involved—

(1) fixes the sounds or sounds and images of a live musical performance in a copy or phonorecord, or reproduces copies or phonorecords of such a performance from an unauthorized fixation,

(2) transmits or otherwise communicates to the public the sounds or sounds and images of a live musical performance, or

(3) distributes or offers to distribute, sells or offers to sell, rents or offers to rent, or traffics in any copy or phonorecord fixed as described in paragraph (1), regardless of whether the fixations occurred in the United States,

shall be subject to the remedies provided in sections 502 through 505, to the same extent as an infringer of copyright.

(b) *Definition.*—In this section, the term "traffic" has the same meaning as in section 2320(e) of title 18.

(c) *Applicability.*—This section shall apply to any act or acts that occur on or after the date of the enactment of the Uruguay Round Agreements Act [Dec. 8, 1994].

(d) *State law not preempted.*—Nothing in this section may be construed to annul or limit any rights or remedies under the common law or statutes of any State.

(Dec. 8, 1994, Pub. L. 103-465, §512, 108 Stat. 4974; Mar. 16, 2006, Pub. L. 109-181, § 2, 120 Stat. 288.)

CHAPTER 12—COPYRIGHT PROTECTION AND MANAGEMENT SYSTEMS

§ 1201   Circumvention of copyright protection systems

(a) Violations regarding circumvention of technological measures—

(1) (A) No person shall circumvent a technological measure that effectively controls access to a work protected under this title. The prohibition contained in the preceding sentence shall take effect at the end of the 2-year period beginning on the date of the enactment of this chapter.

(B) The prohibition contained in subparagraph (A) shall not apply to persons who are users of a copyrighted work which is in a particular class of works, if such persons are, or are likely to be in the succeeding 3-year period, adversely affected by virtue of such prohibition in their ability to make noninfringing uses of that particular class of works under this title, as determined under subparagraph (C).

(C) During the 2-year period described in subparagraph (A), and during each succeeding 3-year period, the Librarian of Congress, upon the recommendation of the Register of Copyrights, who shall consult with the Assistant Secretary for Communications and Information of the Department of Commerce and report and comment on his or her views in making such recommendation, shall make the determination in a rulemaking proceeding for purposes of subparagraph (B) of whether persons who are users of a copyrighted work are, or are likely to be in the succeeding 3-year period, adversely affected by the prohibition under subparagraph (A) in their ability to make noninfringing uses under this title of a particular class of copyrighted works. In conducting such rulemaking, the Librarian shall examine—

(i) the availability for use of copyrighted works;

(ii) the availability for use of works for nonprofit archival, preservation, and educational purposes;

(iii) the impact that the prohibition on the circumvention of technological measures applied to copyrighted works has on criticism, comment, news reporting, teaching, scholarship, or research;

(iv) the effect of circumvention of technological measures on the market for or value of copyrighted works; and

(v) such other factors as the Librarian considers appropriate.

(D) The Librarian shall publish any class of copyrighted works for which the Librarian has determined, pursuant to the rulemaking conducted under subparagraph (C), that noninfringing uses by persons who are users of a copyrighted work are, or are likely to be, adversely affected, and the prohibition contained in subparagraph (A) shall not apply to such users with respect to such class of works for the ensuing 3-year period.

(E) Neither the exception under subparagraph (B) from the applicability of the prohibition contained in subparagraph (A), nor any determination made in a rulemaking conducted under subparagraph (C), may be used as a defense in any action to enforce any provision of this title other than this paragraph.

(2) No person shall manufacture, import, offer to the public, provide, or otherwise traffic in any technology, product, service, device, component, or part thereof, that—

(A) is primarily designed or produced for the purpose of circumventing a technological measure that effectively controls access to a work protected under this title;

(B) has only limited commercially significant purpose or use other than to circumvent a technological measure that effectively controls access to a work protected under this title; or

(C) is marketed by that person or another acting in concert with that person with that person's knowledge for use in circumventing a technological measure that effectively controls access to a work protected under this title.

(3) As used in this subsection—

(A) to "circumvent a technological measure" means to descramble a scrambled work, to decrypt an encrypted work, or otherwise to avoid, bypass, remove, deactivate, or impair a technological measure, without the authority of the copyright owner; and

(B) a technological measure "effectively controls access to a work" if the measure, in the ordinary course of its operation, requires the application of information, or a process or a treatment, with the authority of the copyright owner, to gain access to the work.

(b) *Additional violations.*—

(1) No person shall manufacture, import, offer to the public, provide, or otherwise traffic in any technology, product, service, device, component, or part thereof, that—

(A) is primarily designed or produced for the purpose of circumventing protection afforded by a technological measure that effectively protects a right of a copyright owner under this title in a work or a portion thereof;

(B) has only limited commercially significant purpose or use other than to circumvent protection afforded by a technological measure that effectively protects a right of a copyright owner under this title in a work or a portion thereof; or

(C) is marketed by that person or another acting in concert with that person with that person's knowledge for use in circumventing protection afforded by a technological measure that effectively protects a right of a copyright owner under this title in a work or a portion thereof.

(2) As used in this subsection—

(A) to "circumvent protection afforded by a technological measure" means avoiding, bypassing, removing, deactivating, or otherwise impairing a technological measure; and

(B) a technological measure "effectively protects a right of a copyright owner under this title" if the measure, in the ordinary course of its operation, prevents, restricts, or otherwise limits the exercise of a right of a copyright owner under this title.

(c) *Other rights, etc., not affected.*—

(1) Nothing in this section shall affect rights, remedies, limitations, or defenses to copyright infringement, including fair use, under this title.

(2) Nothing in this section shall enlarge or diminish vicarious or contributory liability for copyright infringement in connection with any technology, product, service, device, component, or part thereof.

(3) Nothing in this section shall require that the design of, or design and selection of parts and components for, a consumer electronics, telecommunications, or computing product provide for a response to any particular technological measure, so long as such part or component, or the product in which such part or component is integrated, does not otherwise fall within the prohibitions of subsection (a)(2) or (b)(1).

(4) Nothing in this section shall enlarge or diminish any rights of free speech or the press for activities using consumer electronics, telecommunications, or computing products.

(d) *Exemption for nonprofit libraries, archives, and educational institutions.*—

(1) A nonprofit library, archives, or educational institution which gains access to a commercially exploited copyrighted work solely in order to make a good faith determination of whether to acquire a copy of that work for the sole purpose of engaging in conduct permitted under this title shall not be in violation of subsection (a)(1)(A). A copy of a work to which access has been gained under this paragraph—

(A) may not be retained longer than necessary to make such good faith determination; and

(B) may not be used for any other purpose.

17 U.S.C. § 1201

(2) The exemption made available under paragraph (1) shall only apply with respect to a work when an identical copy of that work is not reasonably available in another form.

(3) A nonprofit library, archives, or educational institution that willfully for the purpose of commercial advantage or financial gain violates paragraph (1)—

(A) shall, for the first offense, be subject to the civil remedies under section 1203; and

(B) shall, for repeated or subsequent offenses, in addition to the civil remedies under section 1203, forfeit the exemption provided under paragraph (1).

(4) This subsection may not be used as a defense to a claim under subsection (a)(2) or (b), nor may this subsection permit a nonprofit library, archives, or educational institution to manufacture, import, offer to the public, provide, or otherwise traffic in any technology, product, service, component, or part thereof, which circumvents a technological measure.

(5) In order for a library or archives to qualify for the exemption under this subsection, the collections of that library or archives shall be—

(A) open to the public; or

(B) available not only to researchers affiliated with the library or archives or with the institution of which it is a part, but also to other persons doing research in a specialized field.

(e) *Law enforcement, intelligence, and other government activities.*—This section does not prohibit any lawfully authorized investigative, protective, information security, or intelligence activity of an officer, agent, or employee of the United States, a State, or a political subdivision of a State, or a person acting pursuant to a contract with the United States, a State, or a political subdivision of a State. For purposes of this subsection, the term "information security" means activities carried out in order to identify and address the vulnerabilities of a government computer, computer system, or computer network.

(f) *Reverse engineering.*—

(1) Notwithstanding the provisions of subsection (a)(1)(A), a person who has lawfully obtained the right to use a copy of a computer program may circumvent a technological measure that effectively controls access to a

particular portion of that program for the sole purpose of identifying and analyzing those elements of the program that are necessary to achieve interoperability of an independently created computer program with other programs, and that have not previously been readily available to the person engaging in the circumvention, to the extent any such acts of identification and analysis do not constitute infringement under this title.

(2) Notwithstanding the provisions of subsections (a)(2) and (b), a person may develop and employ technological means to circumvent a technological measure, or to circumvent protection afforded by a technological measure, in order to enable the identification and analysis under paragraph (1), or for the purpose of enabling interoperability of an independently created computer program with other programs, if such means are necessary to achieve such interoperability, to the extent that doing so does not constitute infringement under this title.

(3) The information acquired through the acts permitted under paragraph (1), and the means permitted under paragraph (2), may be made available to others if the person referred to in paragraph (1) or (2), as the case may be, provides such information or means solely for the purpose of enabling interoperability of an independently created computer program with other programs, and to the extent that doing so does not constitute infringement under this title or violate applicable law other than this section.

(4) For purposes of this subsection, the term "interoperability" means the ability of computer programs to exchange information, and of such programs mutually to use the information which has been exchanged.

(g) *Encryption research.* —

(1) *Definitions.* —For purposes of this subsection—

(A) the term "encryption research" means activities necessary to identify and analyze flaws and vulnerabilities of encryption technologies applied to copyrighted works, if these activities are conducted to advance the state of knowledge in the field of encryption technology or to assist in the development of encryption products; and

(B) the term "encryption technology" means the scrambling and descrambling of information using mathematical formulas or algorithms.

17 U.S.C. § 1201

(2) *Permissible acts of encryption research.*—Notwithstanding the provisions of subsection (a)(1)(A), it is not a violation of that subsection for a person to circumvent a technological measure as applied to a copy, phonorecord, performance, or display of a published work in the course of an act of good faith encryption research if—

(A) the person lawfully obtained the encrypted copy, phonorecord, performance, or display of the published work;

(B) such act is necessary to conduct such encryption research;

(C) the person made a good faith effort to obtain authorization before the circumvention; and

(D) such act does not constitute infringement under this title or a violation of applicable law other than this section, including section 1030 of title 18 and those provisions of title 18 amended by the Computer Fraud and Abuse Act of 1986.

(3) *Factors in determining exemption.*—In determining whether a person qualifies for the exemption under paragraph (2), the factors to be considered shall include—

(A) whether the information derived from the encryption research was disseminated, and if so, whether it was disseminated in a manner reasonably calculated to advance the state of knowledge or development of encryption technology, versus whether it was disseminated in a manner that facilitates infringement under this title or a violation of applicable law other than this section, including a violation of privacy or breach of security;

(B) whether the person is engaged in a legitimate course of study, is employed, or is appropriately trained or experienced, in the field of encryption technology; and

(C) whether the person provides the copyright owner of the work to which the technological measure is applied with notice of the findings and documentation of the research, and the time when such notice is provided.

(4) *Use of technological means for research activities.*—Notwithstanding the provisions of subsection (a)(2), it is not a violation of that subsection for a person to—

(A) develop and employ technological means to circumvent a technological measure for the sole purpose of that person performing the acts of good faith encryption research described in paragraph (2); and

(B) provide the technological means to another person with whom he or she is working collaboratively for the purpose of conducting the acts of good faith encryption research described in paragraph (2) or for the purpose of having that other person verify his or her acts of good faith encryption research described in paragraph (2).

(5) *Report to Congress.*—Not later than 1 year after the date of the enactment of this chapter, the Register of Copyrights and the Assistant Secretary for Communications and Information of the Department of Commerce shall jointly report to the Congress on the effect this subsection has had on—

(A) encryption research and the development of encryption technology;

(B) the adequacy and effectiveness of technological measures designed to protect copyrighted works; and

(C) protection of copyright owners against the unauthorized access to their encrypted copyrighted works.

The report shall include legislative recommendations, if any.

(h) *Exceptions regarding minors.*—In applying subsection (a) to a component or part, the court may consider the necessity for its intended and actual incorporation in a technology, product, service, or device, which—

(1) does not itself violate the provisions of this title; and

(2) has the sole purpose to prevent the access of minors to material on the Internet.

(i) *Protection of personally identifying information.*—

(1) *Circumvention permitted.*—Notwithstanding the provisions of subsection (a)(1)(A), it is not a violation of that subsection for a person to circumvent a technological measure that effectively controls access to a work protected under this title, if—

(A) the technological measure, or the work it protects, contains the capability of collecting or disseminating personally identifying information reflecting the online activities of a natural person who seeks to gain access to the work protected;

17 U.S.C. § 1201

(B) in the normal course of its operation, the technological measure, or the work it protects, collects or disseminates personally identifying information about the person who seeks to gain access to the work protected, without providing conspicuous notice of such collection or dissemination to such person, and without providing such person with the capability to prevent or restrict such collection or dissemination;

(C) the act of circumvention has the sole effect of identifying and disabling the capability described in subparagraph (A), and has no other effect on the ability of any person to gain access to any work; and

(D) the act of circumvention is carried out solely for the purpose of preventing the collection or dissemination of personally identifying information about a natural person who seeks to gain access to the work protected, and is not in violation of any other law.

(2) *Inapplicability to certain technological measures.*—This subsection does not apply to a technological measure, or a work it protects, that does not collect or disseminate personally identifying information and that is disclosed to a user as not having or using such capability.

(j) *Security testing.*—

(1) *Definition.*—For purposes of this subsection, the term "security testing" means accessing a computer, computer system, or computer network, solely for the purpose of good faith testing, investigating, or correcting, a security flaw or vulnerability, with the authorization of the owner or operator of such computer, computer system, or computer network.

(2) *Permissible acts of security testing.*—Notwithstanding the provisions of subsection (a)(1)(A), it is not a violation of that subsection for a person to engage in an act of security testing, if such act does not constitute infringement under this title or a violation of applicable law other than this section, including section 1030 of title 18 and those provisions of title 18 amended by the Computer Fraud and Abuse Act of 1986.

(3) *Factors in determining exemption.*—In determining whether a person qualifies for the exemption under paragraph (2), the factors to be considered shall include—

(A) whether the information derived from the security testing was used solely to promote the security of the owner or operator of such computer, computer system or computer network, or shared directly with the developer of such computer, computer system, or computer network; and

(B) whether the information derived from the security testing was used or maintained in a manner that does not facilitate infringement under this title or a violation of applicable law other than this section, including a violation of privacy or breach of security.

(4) *Use of technological means for security testing.*—Notwithstanding the provisions of subsection (a)(2), it is not a violation of that subsection for a person to develop, produce, distribute or employ technological means for the sole purpose of performing the acts of security testing described in subsection (2), provided such technological means does not otherwise violate section (a)(2).

(k) *Certain analog devices and certain technological measures.* —

(1) *Certain analog devices.*—

(A) Effective 18 months after the date of the enactment of this chapter, no person shall manufacture, import, offer to the public, provide or otherwise traffic in any—

(i) VHS format analog video cassette recorder unless such recorder conforms to the automatic gain control copy control technology;

(ii) 8mm format analog video cassette camcorder unless such camcorder conforms to the automatic gain control technology;

(iii) Beta format analog video cassette recorder, unless such recorder conforms to the automatic gain control copy control technology, except that this requirement shall not apply until there are 1,000 Beta format analog video cassette recorders sold in the United States in any one calendar year after the date of the enactment of this chapter;

(iv) 8mm format analog video cassette recorder that is not an analog video cassette camcorder, unless such recorder conforms to the automatic gain control copy control technology, except that this requirement shall not apply until there are 20,000 such recorders sold in the United States in any one calendar year after the date of the enactment of this chapter; or

(v) analog video cassette recorder that records using an NTSC format video input and that is not otherwise covered under clauses (i) through (iv), unless such device conforms to the automatic gain control copy control technology.

(B) Effective on the date of the enactment of this chapter, no person shall manufacture, import, offer to the public, provide or otherwise traffic in—

(i) any VHS format analog video cassette recorder or any 8mm format analog video cassette recorder if the design of the model of such recorder has been modified after such date of enactment so that a model of recorder that previously conformed to the automatic gain control copy control technology no longer conforms to such technology; or

(ii) any VHS format analog video cassette recorder, or any 8mm format analog video cassette recorder that is not an 8mm analog video cassette camcorder, if the design of the model of such recorder has been modified after such date of enactment so that a model of recorder that previously conformed to the four-line colorstripe copy control technology no longer conforms to such technology.

Manufacturers that have not previously manufactured or sold a VHS format analog video cassette recorder, or an 8mm format analog cassette recorder, shall be required to conform to the four-line colorstripe copy control technology in the initial model of any such recorder manufactured after the date of the enactment of this chapter, and thereafter to continue conforming to the four-line colorstripe copy control technology. For purposes of this subparagraph, an analog video cassette recorder "conforms to" the four-line colorstripe copy control technology if it records a signal that, when played back by the playback function of that recorder in the normal viewing mode, exhibits, on a reference display device, a display containing distracting visible lines through portions of the viewable picture.

(2) *Certain encoding restrictions.*—No person shall apply the automatic gain control copy control technology or colorstripe copy control technology to prevent or limit consumer copying except such copying—

(A) of a single transmission, or specified group of transmissions, of live events or of audiovisual works for which a member of the public has exercised choice in selecting the transmissions, including the content of the transmissions or the time of receipt of such transmissions, or both, and as to which such member is charged a separate fee for each such transmission or specified group of transmissions;

(B) from a copy of a transmission of a live event or an audiovisual work if such transmission is provided by a channel or service where payment is made by a member of the public for such channel or service in the form of a subscription fee that entitles the member of the public to receive all of the programming contained in such channel or service;

(C) from a physical medium containing one or more prerecorded audiovisual works; or

(D) from a copy of a transmission described in subparagraph (A) or from a copy made from a physical medium described in subparagraph (C).

In the event that a transmission meets both the conditions set forth in subparagraph (A) and those set forth in subparagraph (B), the transmission shall be treated as a transmission described in subparagraph (A).

(3) *Inapplicability.*—This subsection shall not—

(A) require any analog video cassette camcorder to conform to the automatic gain control copy control technology with respect to any video signal received through a camera lens;

(B) apply to the manufacture, importation, offer for sale, provision of, or other trafficking in, any professional analog video cassette recorder; or

(C) apply to the offer for sale or provision of, or other trafficking in, any previously owned analog video cassette recorder, if such recorder was legally manufactured and sold when new and not subsequently modified in violation of paragraph (1)(B).

(4) *Definitions.*—For purposes of this subsection:

(A) An "analog video cassette recorder" means a device that records, or a device that includes a function that records, on electromagnetic tape in an analog format the electronic impulses produced by the vid-

17 U.S.C. § 1201

eo and audio portions of a television program, motion picture, or other form of audiovisual work.

(B) An "analog video cassette camcorder" means an analog video cassette recorder that contains a recording function that operates through a camera lens and through a video input that may be connected with a television or other video playback device.

(C) An analog video cassette recorder "conforms" to the automatic gain control copy control technology if it—

(i) detects one or more of the elements of such technology and does not record the motion picture or transmission protected by such technology; or

(ii) records a signal that, when played back, exhibits a meaningfully distorted or degraded display.

(D) The term "professional analog video cassette recorder" means an analog video cassette recorder that is designed, manufactured, marketed, and intended for use by a person who regularly employs such a device for a lawful business or industrial use, including making, performing, displaying, distributing, or transmitting copies of motion pictures on a commercial scale.

(E) The terms "VHS format" "8mm format", "Beta format", "automatic gain control copy control technology", "colorstripe copy control technology", "four-line version of the colorstripe copy control technology", and "NTSC" have the meanings that are commonly understood in the consumer electronics and motion picture industries as of the date of the enactment of this chapter.

(5) *Violations.*—Any violation of paragraph (1) of this subsection shall be treated as a violation of subsection (b)(1) of this section. Any violation of paragraph (2) of this subsection shall be deemed an "act of circumvention" for the purposes of section 1203(c)(3)(A) of this chapter.

(Oct. 28, 1998, Pub. L. 105-304, §103, 112 Stat. 2863; Nov. 29, 1999, Pub. L. 106-113, §5006, 113 Stat. 1501A-594.)

§ 1202   Integrity of copyright management information

(a) *False copyright management information.*—No person shall knowingly and with the intent to induce, enable, facilitate, or conceal infringement—

(1) provide copyright management information that is false, or

(2) distribute or import for distribution copyright management information that is false.

(b) *Removal or alteration of copyright management information.*—No person shall, without the authority of the copyright owner or the law—

(1) intentionally remove or alter any copyright management information,

(2) distribute or import for distribution copyright management information knowing that the copyright management information has been removed or altered without authority of the copyright owner or the law, or

(3) distribute, import for distribution, or publicly perform works, copies of works, or phonorecords, knowing that copyright management information has been removed or altered without authority of the copyright owner or the law,

knowing, or, with respect to civil remedies under section 1203, having reasonable grounds to know, that it will induce, enable, facilitate, or conceal an infringement of any right under this title.

(c) *Definition.*—As used in this section, the term "copyright management information" means any of the following information conveyed in connection with copies or phonorecords of a work or performances or displays of a work, including in digital form, except that such term does not include any personally identifying information about a user of a work or of a copy, phonorecord, performance, or display of a work:

(1) The title and other information identifying the work, including the information set forth on a notice of copyright.

(2) The name of, and other identifying information about, the author of a work.

(3) The name of, and other identifying information about, the copyright owner of the work, including the information set forth in a notice of copyright.

(4) With the exception of public performances of works by radio and television broadcast stations, the name of, and other identifying information about, a performer whose performance is fixed in a work other than an audiovisual work.

(5) With the exception of public performances of works by radio and television broadcast stations, in the case of an audiovisual work, the name

17 U.S.C. § 1202

of, and other identifying information about, a writer, performer, or director who is credited in the audiovisual work.

(6) Terms and conditions for use of the work.

(7) Identifying numbers or symbols referring to such information or links to such information.

(8) Such other information as the Register of Copyrights may prescribe by regulation, except that the Register of Copyrights may not require the provision of any information concerning the user of a copyrighted work.

(d) *Law enforcement, intelligence, and other government activities.*—This section does not prohibit any lawfully authorized investigative, protective, information security, or intelligence activity of an officer, agent, or employee of the United States, a State, or a political subdivision of a State, or a person acting pursuant to a contract with the United States, a State, or a political subdivision of a State. For purposes of this subsection, the term "information security" means activities carried out in order to identify and address the vulnerabilities of a government computer, computer system, or computer network.

(e) *Limitations on liability.*—

(1) *Analog transmissions.*—In the case of an analog transmission, a person who is making transmissions in its capacity as a broadcast station, or as a cable system, or someone who provides programming to such station or system, shall not be liable for a violation of subsection (b) if—

(A) avoiding the activity that constitutes such violation is not technically feasible or would create an undue financial hardship on such person; and

(B) such person did not intend, by engaging in such activity, to induce, enable, facilitate, or conceal infringement of a right under this title.

(2) *Digital transmissions.*—

(A) If a digital transmission standard for the placement of copyright management information for a category of works is set in a voluntary, consensus standard-setting process involving a representative cross-section of broadcast stations or cable systems and copyright owners of a category of works that are intended for public performance by such stations or systems, a person identified in paragraph (1) shall not be liable for a violation of subsection (b) with respect to the particular copyright management information addressed by such standard if—

(i) the placement of such information by someone other than such person is not in accordance with such standard; and

(ii) the activity that constitutes such violation is not intended to induce, enable, facilitate, or conceal infringement of a right under this title.

(B) Until a digital transmission standard has been set pursuant to subparagraph (A) with respect to the placement of copyright management information for a category of works, a person identified in paragraph (1) shall not be liable for a violation of subsection (b) with respect to such copyright management information, if the activity that constitutes such violation is not intended to induce, enable, facilitate, or conceal infringement of a right under this title, and if—

(i) the transmission of such information by such person would result in a perceptible visual or aural degradation of the digital signal; or

(ii) the transmission of such information by such person would conflict with—

(I) an applicable government regulation relating to transmission of information in a digital signal;

(II) an applicable industry-wide standard relating to the transmission of information in a digital signal that was adopted by a voluntary consensus standards body prior to the effective date of this chapter; or

(III) an applicable industry-wide standard relating to the transmission of information in a digital signal that was adopted in a voluntary, consensus standards-setting process open to participation by a representative cross-section of broadcast stations or cable systems and copyright owners of a category of works that are intended for public performance by such stations or systems.

(3) *Definitions.*—As used in this subsection—

(A) the term "broadcast station" has the meaning given that term in section 3 of the Communications Act of 1934 (47 U.S.C. 153); and

(B) the term "cable system" has the meaning given that term in section 602 of the Communications Act of 1934 (47 U.S.C. 522).

(Oct. 28, 1998, Pub. L. 105-304, §103, 112 Stat. 2863; Aug. 5, 1999, Pub. L. 106-44, §1(e), 113 Stat. 222.)

§ 1203 Civil remedies

(a) *Civil actions.*—Any person injured by a violation of section 1201 or 1202 may bring a civil action in an appropriate United States district court for such violation.

(b) *Powers of the court.*—In an action brought under subsection (a), the court—

(1) may grant temporary and permanent injunctions on such terms as it deems reasonable to prevent or restrain a violation, but in no event shall impose a prior restraint on free speech or the press protected under the 1st amendment to the Constitution;

(2) at any time while an action is pending, may order the impounding, on such terms as it deems reasonable, of any device or product that is in the custody or control of the alleged violator and that the court has reasonable cause to believe was involved in a violation;

(3) may award damages under subsection (c);

(4) in its discretion may allow the recovery of costs by or against any party other than the United States or an officer thereof;

(5) in its discretion may award reasonable attorney's fees to the prevailing party; and

(6) may, as part of a final judgment or decree finding a violation, order the remedial modification or the destruction of any device or product involved in the violation that is in the custody or control of the violator or has been impounded under paragraph (2).

(c) *Award of damages.*—

(1) *In general.*—Except as otherwise provided in this title, a person committing a violation of section 1201 or 1202 is liable for either—

(A) the actual damages and any additional profits of the violator, as provided in paragraph (2), or

(B) statutory damages, as provided in paragraph (3).

(2) *Actual damages.*—The court shall award to the complaining party the actual damages suffered by the party as a result of the violation, and any profits of the violator that are attributable to the violation and are not taken into account in computing the actual damages, if the complaining party elects such damages at any time before final judgment is entered.

(3) *Statutory damages.*—

(A) At any time before final judgment is entered, a complaining party may elect to recover an award of statutory damages for each violation of section 1201 in the sum of not less than $200 or more than $2,500 per act of circumvention, device, product, component, offer, or performance of service, as the court considers just.

(B) At any time before final judgment is entered, a complaining party may elect to recover an award of statutory damages for each violation of section 1202 in the sum of not less than $2,500 or more than $25,000.

(4) *Repeated violations.*—In any case in which the injured party sustains the burden of proving, and the court finds, that a person has violated section 1201 or 1202 within 3 years after a final judgment was entered against the person for another such violation, the court may increase the award of damages up to triple the amount that would otherwise be awarded, as the court considers just.

(5) *Innocent violations.*—

(A) *In general.*—The court in its discretion may reduce or remit the total award of damages in any case in which the violator sustains the burden of proving, and the court finds, that the violator was not aware and had no reason to believe that its acts constituted a violation.

(B) *Nonprofit library, archives, educational institutions, or public broadcasting entities.*—

(i) *Definition.*—In this subparagraph, the term "public broadcasting entity" has the meaning given such term under section 118(f).

(ii) *In general.*—In the case of a nonprofit library, archives, educational institution, or public broadcasting entity, the court shall remit damages in any case in which the library, archives, educational institution, or public broadcasting entity sustains the burden of proving, and the court finds, that the library, archives, educational institution, or public broadcasting entity was not

17 U.S.C. § 1203

aware and had no reason to believe that its acts constituted a violation.

(Oct. 28, 1998, Pub. L. 105-304, §103, 112 Stat. 2863; Nov. 29, 1999, Pub. L. 106-113, §5004, 113 Stat. 1501A-593; Dec. 9, 2010, Pub. L. 111-295, §6, 124 Stat. 3181.)

§ 1204 Criminal offenses and penalties

(a) *In general.*—Any person who violates section 1201 or 1202 willfully and for purposes of commercial advantage or private financial gain—

(1) shall be fined not more than $500,000 or imprisoned for not more than 5 years, or both, for the first offense; and

(2) shall be fined not more than $1,000,000 or imprisoned for not more than 10 years, or both, for any subsequent offense.

(b) *Limitation for nonprofit library, archives, educational institution, or public broadcasting entity.*—Subsection (a) shall not apply to a nonprofit library, archives, educational institution, or public broadcasting entity (as defined under section 118(f).

(c) *Statute of limitations.*—No criminal proceeding shall be brought under this section unless such proceeding is commenced within 5 years after the cause of action arose.

(Oct. 28, 1998, Pub. L. 105-304, §103, 112 Stat. 2863; Nov. 29, 1999, Pub. L. 106-113, §5004, 113 Stat. 1501A-593; Dec. 9, 2010, Pub. L. 111-295, §6, 124 Stat. 3181.)

§ 1205 Savings clause

Nothing in this chapter abrogates, diminishes, or weakens the provisions of, nor provides any defense or element of mitigation in a criminal prosecution or civil action under, any Federal or State law that prevents the violation of the privacy of an individual in connection with the individual's use of the Internet.

(Oct. 28, 1998, Pub. L. 105-304, §103, 112 Stat. 2863.)

CHAPTER 13—PROTECTION OF ORIGINAL DESIGNS

§ 1301   Designs Protected

(a) *Designs protected.* —

(1) *In general.* —The designer or other owner of an original design of a useful article which makes the article attractive or distinctive in appearance to the purchasing or using public may secure the protection provided by this chapter upon complying with and subject to this chapter.

(2) *Vessel features.* —The design of a vessel hull, deck, or combination of a hull and deck, including a plug or mold, is subject to protection under this chapter, notwithstanding section 1302(4).

(3) *Exceptions.* —Department of Defense rights in a registered design under this chapter, including the right to build to such registered design, shall be determined solely by operation of section 2320 of title 10 or by the instru-

17 U.S.C. § 1301

ment under which the design was developed for the United States Government.

(b) *Definitions.*—For the purpose of this chapter, the following terms have the following meanings:

(1) A design is "original" if it is the result of the designer's creative endeavor that provides a distinguishable variation over prior work pertaining to similar articles which is more than merely trivial and has not been copied from another source.

(2) A "useful article" is a vessel hull or deck, including a plug or mold, which in normal use has an intrinsic utilitarian function that is not merely to portray the appearance of the article or to convey information. An article which normally is part of a useful article shall be deemed to be a useful article.

(3) A "vessel" is a craft—

(A) that is designed and capable of independently steering a course on or through water through its own means of propulsion; and

(B) that is designed and capable of carrying and transporting one or more passengers.

(4) A "hull" is the exterior frame or body of a vessel, exclusive of the deck, superstructure, masts, sails, yards, rigging, hardware, fixtures, and other attachments.

(5) A "plug" means a device or model used to make a mold for the purpose of exact duplication, regardless of whether the device or model has an intrinsic utilitarian function that is not only to portray the appearance of the product or to convey information.

(6) A "mold" means a matrix or form in which a substance for material is used, regardless of whether the matrix or form has an intrinsic utilitarian function that is not only to portray the appearance of the product or to convey information.

(7) A "deck" is the horizontal surface of a vessel that covers the hull, including exterior cabin and cockpit surfaces, and exclusive of masts, sails, yards, rigging, hardware, fixtures, and other attachments.

(Oct. 28, 1998, Pub. L. 105-304, §502, 112 Stat. 2905; Nov. 29, 1999, Pub. L. 106-113, §5005, 113 Stat. 1501A-593; Oct. 16, 2008, Pub. L. 110-434, §1, 122 Stat. 4972.)

17 U.S.C. § 1301

§ 1302 Designs not subject to protection

Protection under this chapter shall not be available for a design that is —

(1) not original;

(2) staple or commonplace, such as a standard geometric figure, a familiar symbol, an emblem, or a motif, or another shape, pattern, or configuration which has become standard, common, prevalent, or ordinary;

(3) different from a design excluded by paragraph (2) only in insignificant details or in elements which are variants commonly used in the relevant trades;

(4) dictated solely by a utilitarian function of the article that embodies it; or

(5) embodied in a useful article that was made public by the designer or owner in the United States or a foreign country more than 2 years before the date of the application for registration under this chapter.

(Oct. 28, 1998, Pub. L. 105-304, §502, 112 Stat. 2905; Aug. 5, 1999, Pub. L. 106-44, §1(f), 113 Stat. 222.)

§ 1303 Revisions, adaptations, and rearrangements

Protection for a design under this chapter shall be available notwithstanding the employment in the design of subject matter excluded from protection under section 1302 if the design is a substantial revision, adaptation, or rearrangement of such subject matter. Such protection shall be independent of any subsisting protection in subject matter employed in the design, and shall not be construed as securing any right to subject matter excluded from protection under this chapter or as extending any subsisting protection under this chapter.

(Oct. 28, 1998, Pub. L. 105-304, §502, 112 Stat. 2905.)

§ 1304 Commencement of protection

The protection provided for a design under this chapter shall commence upon the earlier of the date of publication of the registration under section 1313(a) or the date the design is first made public as defined by section 1310(b).

(Oct. 28, 1998, Pub. L. 105-304, §502, 112 Stat. 2905.)

§ 1305   Term of protection

(a) *In general.*—Subject to subsection (b), the protection provided under this chapter for a design shall continue for a term of 10 years beginning on the date of the commencement of protection under section 1304.

(b) *Expiration.*—All terms of protection provided in this section shall run to the end of the calendar year in which they would otherwise expire.

(c) *Termination of rights.*—Upon expiration or termination of protection in a particular design under this chapter, all rights under this chapter in the design shall terminate, regardless of the number of different articles in which the design may have been used during the term of its protection.

(Oct. 28, 1998, Pub. L. 105-304, §502, 112 Stat. 2905.)

§ 1306   Design notice

(a) *Contents of design notice.*—

(1) Whenever any design for which protection is sought under this chapter is made public under section 1310(b), the owner of the design shall, subject to the provisions of section 1307, mark it or have it marked legibly with a design notice consisting of—

(A) the words "Protected Design", the abbreviation "Prot'd Des.", or the letter "D" with a circle, or the symbol *D*;

(B) the year of the date on which protection for the design commenced; and

(C) the name of the owner, an abbreviation by which the name can be recognized, or a generally accepted alternative designation of the owner.

Any distinctive identification of the owner may be used for purposes of subparagraph (C) if it has been recorded by the Administrator before the design marked with such identification is registered.

(2) After registration, the registration number may be used instead of the elements specified in subparagraphs (B) and (C) of paragraph (1).

(b) *Location of notice.*—The design notice shall be so located and applied as to give reasonable notice of design protection while the useful article embodying the design is passing through its normal channels of commerce.

(c) *Subsequent removal of notice.*—When the owner of a design has complied with the provisions of this section, protection under this chapter shall not be affected by the removal, destruction, or obliteration by others of the design notice on an article.

(Oct. 28, 1998, Pub. L. 105-304, §502, 112 Stat. 2905.)

§ 1307   Effect of omission of notice

(a) *Actions with notice.*—Except as provided in subsection (b), the omission of the notice prescribed in section 1306 shall not cause loss of the protection under this chapter or prevent recovery for infringement under this chapter against any person who, after receiving written notice of the design protection, begins an undertaking leading to infringement under this chapter.

(b) *Actions without notice.*—The omission of the notice prescribed in section 1306 shall prevent any recovery under section 1323 against a person who began an undertaking leading to infringement under this chapter before receiving written notice of the design protection. No injunction shall be issued under this chapter with respect to such undertaking unless the owner of the design reimburses that person for any reasonable expenditure or contractual obligation in connection with such undertaking that was incurred before receiving written notice of the design protection, as the court in its discretion directs. The burden of providing written notice of design protection shall be on the owner of the design.

(Oct. 28, 1998, Pub. L. 105-304, §502, 112 Stat. 2905.)

§1308   Exclusive rights

The owner of a design protected under this chapter has the exclusive right to—

(1) make, have made, or import, for sale or for use in trade, any useful article embodying that design; and

(2) sell or distribute for sale or for use in trade any useful article embodying that design.

(Oct. 28, 1998, Pub. L. 105-304, §502, 112 Stat. 2905.)

§ 1309   Infringement

(a) *Acts of infringement.*—Except as provided in subsection (b), it shall be infringement of the exclusive rights in a design protected under this chapter for any person, without the consent of the owner of the design, within the United States and during the term of such protection, to—

(1) make, have made, or import, for sale or for use in trade, any infringing article as defined in subsection (e); or

(2) sell or distribute for sale or for use in trade any such infringing article.

(b) *Acts of sellers and distributors.*—A seller or distributor of an infringing article who did not make or import the article shall be deemed to have infringed on a design protected under this chapter only if that person—

(1) induced or acted in collusion with a manufacturer to make, or an importer to import such article, except that merely purchasing or giving an order to purchase such article in the ordinary course of business shall not of itself constitute such inducement or collusion; or

(2) refused or failed, upon the request of the owner of the design, to make a prompt and full disclosure of that person's source of such article, and that person orders or reorders such article after receiving notice by registered or certified mail of the protection subsisting in the design.

(c) *Acts without knowledge.*—It shall not be infringement under this section to make, have made, import, sell, or distribute, any article embodying a design which was created without knowledge that a design was protected under this chapter and was copied from such protected design.

(d) *Acts in ordinary course of business.*—A person who incorporates into that person's product of manufacture an infringing article acquired from others in the ordinary course of business, or who, without knowledge of the protected design embodied in an infringing article, makes or processes the infringing article for the account of another person in the ordinary course of business, shall not be deemed to have infringed the rights in that design under this chapter except under a condition contained in paragraph (1) or (2) of subsection (b). Accepting an order or reorder from the source of the infringing article shall be deemed ordering or reordering within the meaning of subsection (b)(2).

(e) *Infringing article defined.*—As used in this section, an "infringing article" is any article the design of which has been copied from a design protected under this chapter, without the consent of the owner of the protected design. An infringing article is not an illustration or picture of a protected design in an advertisement, book, periodical, newspaper, photograph, broadcast, motion picture, or similar medium. A design shall not be deemed to have been copied from a protected design if it is original and not substantially similar in appearance to a protected design.

17 U.S.C. § 1309

(f) *Establishing originality.*—The party to any action or proceeding under this chapter who alleges rights under this chapter in a design shall have the burden of establishing the design's originality whenever the opposing party introduces an earlier work which is identical to such design, or so similar as to make prima facie showing that such design was copied from such work.

(g) *Reproduction for teaching or analysis.*—It is not an infringement of the exclusive rights of a design owner for a person to reproduce the design in a useful article or in any other form solely for the purpose of teaching, analyzing, or evaluating the appearance, concepts, or techniques embodied in the design, or the function of the useful article embodying the design.

(Oct. 28, 1998, Pub. L. 105-304, §502, 112 Stat. 2905.)

§ 1310 Application for registration

(a) *Time limit for application for registration.*—Protection under this chapter shall be lost if application for registration of the design is not made within 2 years after the date on which the design is first made public.

(b) *When design is made public.*—A design is made public when an existing useful article embodying the design is anywhere publicly exhibited, publicly distributed, or offered for sale or sold to the public by the owner of the design or with the owner's consent.

(c) *Application by owner of design.*—Application for registration may be made by the owner of the design.

(d) *Contents of application.*—The application for registration shall be made to the Administrator and shall state—

   (1) the name and address of the designer or designers of the design;

   (2) the name and address of the owner if different from the designer;

   (3) the specific name of the useful article embodying the design;

   (4) the date, if any, that the design was first made public, if such date was earlier than the date of the application;

   (5) affirmation that the design has been fixed in a useful article; and

   (6) such other information as may be required by the Administrator.

The application for registration may include a description setting forth the salient features of the design, but the absence of such a description shall not prevent registration under this chapter.

(e) *Sworn statement.*—The application for registration shall be accompanied by a statement under oath by the applicant or the applicant's duly authorized agent or representative, setting forth, to the best of the applicant's knowledge and belief—

(1) that the design is original and was created by the designer or designers named in the application;

(2) that the design has not previously been registered on behalf of the applicant or the applicant's predecessor in title; and

(3) that the applicant is the person entitled to protection and to registration under this chapter.

If the design has been made public with the design notice prescribed in section 1306, the statement shall also describe the exact form and position of the design notice.

(f) *Effect of errors.*—

(1) Error in any statement or assertion as to the utility of the useful article named in the application under this section, the design of which is sought to be registered, shall not affect the protection secured under this chapter.

(2) Errors in omitting a joint designer or in naming an alleged joint designer shall not affect the validity of the registration, or the actual ownership or the protection of the design, unless it is shown that the error occurred with deceptive intent.

(g) *Design made in scope of employment.*—In a case in which the design was made within the regular scope of the designer's employment and individual authorship of the design is difficult or impossible to ascribe and the application so states, the name and address of the employer for whom the design was made may be stated instead of that of the individual designer.

(h) *Pictorial representation of design.*—The application for registration shall be accompanied by two copies of a drawing or other pictorial representation of the useful article embodying the design, having one or more views, adequate to show the design, in a form and style suitable for reproduction, which shall be deemed a part of the application.

(i) *Design in more than one useful article.*—If the distinguishing elements of a design are in substantially the same form in different useful articles, the design shall be protected as to all such useful articles when protected as to one of them, but not more than one registration shall be required for the design.

(j) *Application for more than one design.*—More than one design may be included in the same application under such conditions as may be prescribed by the Administrator. For each design included in an application the fee prescribed for a single design shall be paid.

(Oct. 28, 1998, Pub. L. 105-304, §502, 112 Stat. 2905.)

§ 1311   Benefit of earlier filing date in foreign country

An application for registration of a design filed in the United States by any person who has, or whose legal representative or predecessor or successor in title has, previously filed an application for registration of the same design in a foreign country which extends to designs of owners who are citizens of the United States, or to applications filed under this chapter, similar protection to that provided under this chapter shall have that same effect as if filed in the United States on the date on which the application was first filed in such foreign country, if the application in the United States is filed within 6 months after the earliest date on which any such foreign application was filed.

(Oct. 28, 1998, Pub. L. 105-304, §502, 112 Stat. 2905.)

§ 1312   Oaths and acknowledgments

(a) *In general.*—Oaths and acknowledgments required by this chapter—

(1) may be made—

(A) before any person in the United States authorized by law to administer oaths; or

(B) when made in a foreign country, before any diplomatic or consular officer of the United States authorized to administer oaths, or before any official authorized to administer oaths in the foreign country concerned, whose authority shall be proved by a certificate of a diplomatic or consular officer of the United States; and

(2) shall be valid if they comply with the laws of the State or country where made.

(b) *Written declaration in lieu of oath.—*

(1) The Administrator may by rule prescribe that any document which is to be filed under this chapter in the Office of the Administrator and which is required by any law, rule, or other regulation to be under oath, may be subscribed to by a written declaration in such form as the Administrator may prescribe, and such declaration shall be in lieu of the oath otherwise required.

(2) Whenever a written declaration under paragraph (1) is used, the document containing the declaration shall state that willful false statements are punishable by fine or imprisonment, or both, pursuant to section 1001 of title 18, and may jeopardize the validity of the application or document or a registration resulting therefrom.

(Oct. 28, 1998, Pub. L. 105-304, §502, 112 Stat. 2905.)

§ 1313 Examination of application and issue or refusal of registration

(a) *Determination of registrability of design; registration.—*Upon the filing of an application for registration in proper form under section 1310, and upon payment of the fee prescribed under section 1316, the Administrator shall determine whether or not the application relates to a design which on its face appears to be subject to protection under this chapter, and, if so, the Register shall register the design. Registration under this subsection shall be announced by publication. The date of registration shall be the date of publication.

(b) *Refusal to register; reconsideration.—*If, in the judgment of the Administrator, the application for registration relates to a design which on its face is not subject to protection under this chapter, the Administrator shall send to the applicant a notice of refusal to register and the grounds for the refusal. Within 3 months after the date on which the notice of refusal is sent, the applicant may, by written request, seek reconsideration of the application. After consideration of such a request, the Administrator shall either register the design or send to the applicant a notice of final refusal to register.

(c) *Application to cancel registration.—*Any person who believes he or she is or will be damaged by a registration under this chapter may, upon payment of the prescribed fee, apply to the Administrator at any time to cancel the registration on the ground that the design is not subject to protection under this chapter, stating the reasons for the request. Upon receipt of an application for cancellation, the Administrator shall send to the owner of the design, as shown in the records of the Office of the Administrator, a notice of the application, and the owner shall have a period of 3 months after the date on which such notice is mailed in which to present arguments to the Administrator for support of the validity of the registration. The Administrator shall also have the authority to establish, by regulation, conditions under which the opposing parties may appear and be heard in support of their arguments. If, after the periods provided for the presentation of arguments have expired, the Administrator determines that the applicant for cancellation has established that the design is not subject to protection under this chapter, the Administrator shall order the registration stricken from the record. Cancellation under this subsection shall be announced by publication, and notice of the Administrator's final determination with respect to any application for cancellation shall be sent to the applicant and to the owner of record. Costs of the cancellation procedure under this subsection shall be borne by the nonprevailing party or parties, and the Administrator shall have the authority to assess and collect such costs.

(Oct. 28, 1998, Pub. L. 105-304, §502, 112 Stat. 2905; Nov. 29, 1999, Pub. L. 106-113, §5005, 113 Stat. 1501A-593.)

§ 1314   Certification of registration

Certificates of registration shall be issued in the name of the United States under the seal of the Office of the Administrator and shall be recorded in the official records of the Office. The certificate shall state the name of the useful article, the date of filing of the application, the date of registration, and the date the design was made public, if earlier than the date of filing of the application, and shall contain a reproduction of the drawing or other pictorial representation of the design. If a description of the salient features of the design appears in the application, the description shall also appear in the certificate. A certificate of registration shall be admitted in any court as prima facie evidence of the facts stated in the certificate.

(Oct. 28, 1998, Pub. L. 105-304, §502, 112 Stat. 2905.)

§ 1315   Publication of announcements and indexes

(a) *Publications of the administrator.*—The Administrator shall publish lists and indexes of registered designs and cancellations of designs and may also publish the drawings or other pictorial representations of registered designs for sale or other distribution.

(b) *File of representatives of registered designs.*—The Administrator shall establish and maintain a file of the drawings or other pictorial representations of registered designs. The file shall be available for use by the public under such conditions as the Administrator may prescribe.

(Oct. 28, 1998, Pub. L. 105-304, §502, 112 Stat. 2905.)

§ 1316   Fees

The Administrator shall by regulation set reasonable fees for the filing of applications to register designs under this chapter and for other services relating to the administration of this chapter, taking into consideration the cost of providing these services and the benefit of a public record.

(Oct. 28, 1998, Pub. L. 105-304, §502, 112 Stat. 2905.)

§ 1317   Regulations

The Administrator may establish regulations for the administration of this chapter.

(Oct. 28, 1998, Pub. L. 105-304, §502, 112 Stat. 2905.)

§ 1318   Copies of records

Upon payment of the prescribed fee, any person may obtain a certified copy of any official record of the Office of the Administrator that relates to this chapter. That copy shall be admissible in evidence with the same effect as the original.

(Oct. 28, 1998, Pub. L. 105-304, §502, 112 Stat. 2905.)

§ 1319   Correction of errors in certificates

The Administrator may, by a certificate of correction under seal, correct any error in a registration incurred through the fault of the Office, or, upon payment of the required fee, any error of a clerical or typographical nature occurring in good faith but not through the fault of the Office. Such registration, together with the certificate, shall thereafter have the same effect as if it had been originally issued in such corrected form.

(Oct. 28, 1998, Pub. L. 105-304, §502, 112 Stat. 2905.)

§ 1320   Ownership and transfer

(a) *Property right in design.*—The property right in a design subject to protection under this chapter shall vest in the designer, the legal representatives of a deceased designer or of one under legal incapacity, the employer for whom the designer created the design in the case of a design made within the regular scope of the designer's employment, or a person to whom the rights of the designer or of such employer have been transferred. The person in whom the property right is vested shall be considered the owner of the design.

(b) *Transfer of property right.*—The property right in a registered design, or a design for which an application for registration has been or may be filed, may be assigned, granted, conveyed, or mortgaged by an instrument in writing, signed by the owner, or may be bequeathed by will.

(c) *Oath or acknowledgment of transfer.*—An oath or acknowledgment under section 1312 shall be prima facie evidence of the execution of an assignment, grant, conveyance, or mortgage under subsection (b).

(d) *Recordation of transfer.*—An assignment, grant, conveyance, or mortgage under subsection (b) shall be void as against any subsequent purchaser or mortgagee for a valuable consideration, unless it is recorded in the Office of the Administrator within 3 months after its date of execution or before the date of such subsequent purchase or mortgage.

(Oct. 28, 1998, Pub. L. 105-304, §502, 112 Stat. 2905; Aug. 5, 1999, Pub. L. 106-44, §1(f), 113 Stat. 222.)

§ 1321 Remedy for infringement

(a) *In general.*—The owner of a design is entitled, after issuance of a certificate of registration of the design under this chapter, to institute an action for any infringement of the design.

(b) *Review of refusal to register.*—

(1) Subject to paragraph (2), the owner of a design may seek judicial review of a final refusal of the Administrator to register the design under this chapter by bringing a civil action, and may in the same action, if the court adjudges the design subject to protection under this chapter, enforce the rights in that design under this chapter.

(2) The owner of a design may seek judicial review under this section if—

(A) the owner has previously duly filed and prosecuted to final refusal an application in proper form for registration of the design;

(B) the owner causes a copy of the complaint in the action to be delivered to the Administrator within 10 days after the commencement of the action; and

(C) the defendant has committed acts in respect to the design which would constitute infringement with respect to a design protected under this chapter.

(c) *Administrator as party to action.*—The Administrator may, at the Administrator's option, become a party to the action with respect to the issue of registrability of the design claim by entering an appearance within 60 days after being served with the complaint, but the failure of the Administrator to become a party shall not deprive the court of jurisdiction to determine that issue.

(d) *Use of arbitration to resolve dispute.*—The parties to an infringement dispute under this chapter, within such time as may be specified by the Administrator by regulation, may determine the dispute, or any aspect of the dispute, by arbitration. Arbitration shall be governed by title 9. The parties shall give notice of any arbitration award to the Administrator, and such award shall, as between the parties to the arbitration, be dispositive of the issues to which it relates. The arbitration award shall be unenforceable until such notice is given. Nothing in this subsection shall preclude the Administrator from determining whether a design is subject to registration in a cancellation proceeding under section 1313(c).

(Oct. 28, 1998, Pub. L. 105-304, §502, 112 Stat. 2905.)

§ 1322 Injunctions

(a) *In general.*—A court having jurisdiction over actions under this chapter may grant injunctions in accordance with the principles of equity to prevent infringement of a design under this chapter, including, in its discretion, prompt relief by temporary restraining orders and preliminary injunctions.

(b) *Damages for injunctive relief wrongfully obtained.*—A seller or distributor who suffers damage by reason of injunctive relief wrongfully obtained under this section has a cause of action against the applicant for such injunctive relief and may recover such relief as may be appropriate, including damages for lost profits, cost of materials, loss of good will, and punitive damages in instances where the injunctive relief was sought in bad faith, and, unless the court finds extenuating circumstances, reasonable attorney's fees.

(Oct. 28, 1998, Pub. L. 105-304, §502, 112 Stat. 2905.)

§ 1323 Recovery for infringement

(a) *Damages.*—Upon a finding for the claimant in an action for infringement under this chapter, the court shall award the claimant damages adequate to compensate for the infringement. In addition, the court may increase the damages to such amount, not exceeding $50,000 or $1 per copy, whichever is greater, as the court determines to be just. The damages awarded shall constitute compensation and not a penalty. The court may receive expert testimony as an aid to the determination of damages.

(b) *Infringer's profits.*—As an alternative to the remedies provided in subsection (a), the court may award the claimant the infringer's profits resulting from the sale of the copies if the court finds that the infringer's sales are reasonably related to the use of the claimant's design. In such a case, the claimant shall be required to prove only the amount of the infringer's sales and the infringer shall be required to prove its expenses against such sales.

(c) *Statute of limitations.*—No recovery under subsection (a) or (b) shall be had for any infringement committed more than 3 years before the date on which the complaint is filed.

(d) *Attorney's fees.*—In an action for infringement under this chapter, the court may award reasonable attorney's fees to the prevailing party.

(e) *Disposition of infringing and other articles.*—The court may order that all infringing articles, and any plates, molds, patterns, models, or other means specifically adapted for making the articles, be delivered up for destruction or other disposition as the court may direct.

(Oct. 28, 1998, Pub. L. 105-304, §502, 112 Stat. 2905.)

§ 1324 Power of court over registration

In any action involving the protection of a design under this chapter, the court, when appropriate, may order registration of a design under this chapter or the cancellation of such a registration. Any such order shall be certified by the court to the Administrator, who shall make an appropriate entry upon the record.

(Oct. 28, 1998, Pub. L. 105-304, §502, 112 Stat. 2905.)

§ 1325 Liability for action on registration fraudulently obtained

Any person who brings an action for infringement knowing that registration of the design was obtained by a false or fraudulent representation materially affecting the rights under this chapter, shall be liable in the sum of $10,000, or such part of that amount as the court may determine. That amount shall be to compensate the defendant and shall be charged against the plaintiff and paid to the defendant, in addition to such costs and attorney's fees of the defendant as may be assessed by the court.

(Oct. 28, 1998, Pub. L. 105-304, §502, 112 Stat. 2905.)

§ 1326 Penalty for false marking

(a) *In general.*—Whoever, for the purpose of deceiving the public, marks upon, applies to, or uses in advertising in connection with an article made, used, distributed, or sold, a design which is not protected under this chapter, a design notice specified in section 1306, or any other words or symbols importing that the design is protected under this chapter, knowing that the design is not so protected, shall pay a civil fine of not more than $500 for each such offense.

(b) *Suit by private persons.*—Any person may sue for the penalty established by subsection (a), in which event one-half of the penalty shall be awarded to the person suing and the remainder shall be awarded to the United States.

(Oct. 28, 1998, Pub. L. 105-304, §502, 112 Stat. 2905.)

§ 1327 Penalty for false representation

Whoever knowingly makes a false representation materially affecting the rights obtainable under this chapter for the purpose of obtaining registration of a design under this chapter shall pay a penalty of not less than $500 and not more than $1,000, and any rights or privileges that individual may have in the design under this chapter shall be forfeited.

(Oct. 28, 1998, Pub. L. 105-304, §502, 112 Stat. 2905.)

§ 1328 Enforcement by Treasury and Postal Service

(a) *Regulations.*—The Secretary of the Treasury and the United States Postal Service shall separately or jointly issue regulations for the enforcement of the rights set forth in section 1308 with respect to importation. Such regulations may require, as a condition for the exclusion of articles from the United States, that the person seeking exclusion take any one or more of the following actions:

> (1) Obtain a court order enjoining, or an order of the International Trade Commission under section 337 of the Tariff Act of 1930 excluding, importation of the articles.

(2) Furnish proof that the design involved is protected under this chapter and that the importation of the articles would infringe the rights in the design under this chapter.

(3) Post a surety bond for any injury that may result if the detention or exclusion of the articles proves to be unjustified.

(b) *Seizure and forfeiture.* — Articles imported in violation of the rights set forth in section 1308 are subject to seizure and forfeiture in the same manner as property imported in violation of the customs laws. Any such forfeited articles shall be destroyed as directed by the Secretary of the Treasury or the court, as the case may be, except that the articles may be returned to the country of export whenever it is shown to the satisfaction of the Secretary of the Treasury that the importer had no reasonable grounds for believing that his or her acts constituted a violation of the law.

(Oct. 28, 1998, Pub. L. 105-304, §502, 112 Stat. 2905.)

§ 1329 Relation to design patent law

The issuance of a design patent under title 35, United States Code, for an original design for an article of manufacture shall terminate any protection of the original design under this chapter.

(Oct. 28, 1998, Pub. L. 105-304, §502, 112 Stat. 2905.)

§ 1330 Common law and other rights unaffected

Nothing in this chapter shall annul or limit—

(1) common law or other rights or remedies, if any, available to or held by any person with respect to a design which has not been registered under this chapter; or

(2) any right under the trademark laws or any right protected against unfair competition.

(Oct. 28, 1998, Pub. L. 105-304, §502, 112 Stat. 2905.)

§ 1331 Administrator; Office of the Administrator

In this chapter, the "Administrator" is the Register of Copyrights, and the "Office of the Administrator" and the "Office" refer to the Copyright Office of the Library of Congress.

(Oct. 28, 1998, Pub. L. 105-304, §502, 112 Stat. 2905.)

§ 1332   No retroactive effect

Protection under this chapter shall not be available for any design that has been made public under section 1310(b) before the effective date of this chapter.

(Oct. 28, 1998, Pub. L. 105-304, §502, 112 Stat. 2905.)

UNCODIFIED COPYRIGHT-RELATED PROVISIONS

§ 1.   Short Title.

This Act may be cited as the "Unlocking Consumer Choice and Wireless Competition Act".

§ 2.   Repeal of Existing Rule and Additional Rulemaking by Librarian of Congress.

(a) *Repeal and Replace.*—As of the date of the enactment of this Act, paragraph (3) of section 201.40(b) of title 37, Code of Federal Regulations, as amended and revised by the Librarian of Congress on October 28, 2012, pursuant to the Librarian's authority under section 1201(a) of title 17, United States Code, shall have no force and effect, and such paragraph shall read, and shall be in effect, as such paragraph was in effect on July 27, 2010.

(b) *Rulemaking.*—The Librarian of Congress, upon the recommendation of the Register of Copyrights, who shall consult with the Assistant Secretary for Communications and Information of the Department of Commerce and report and comment on his or her views in making such recommendation, shall determine, consistent with the requirements set forth under section 1201(a)(1) of title 17, United States Code, whether to extend the exemption for the class of works described in section 201.40(b)(3) of title 37, Code of Federal Regulations, as amended by subsection (a), to include any other category of wireless devices in addition to wireless telephone handsets. The determination shall be made in the first rulemaking under section 1201(a)(1)(C) of title 17, United States Code, that begins on or after the date of enactment of this Act.

(c) *Unlocking at Direction of Owner.*—Circumvention of a technological measure that restricts wireless telephone handsets or other wireless devices from connecting to a wireless telecommunications network—

> (1)(A) as authorized by paragraph (3) of section 201.40(b) of title 37, Code of Federal Regulations, as made effective by subsection (a); and

(B) as may be extended to other wireless devices pursuant to a determination in the rulemaking conducted under subsection (b); or

(2) as authorized by an exemption adopted by the Librarian of Congress pursuant to a determination made on or after the date of enactment of this Act under section 1201(a)(1)(C) of title 17, United States Code,

may be initiated by the owner of any such handset or other device, by another person at the direction of the owner, or by a provider of a commercial mobile radio service or a commercial mobile data service at the direction of such owner or other person, solely in order to enable such owner or a family member of such owner to connect to a wireless telecommunications network, when such connection is authorized by the operator of such network.

(d) *Rule of Construction.* —

(1) *In general.* —Except as expressly provided herein, nothing in this Act shall be construed to alter the scope of any party's rights under existing law.

(2) *Librarian of Congress.* —Nothing in this Act alters, or shall be construed to alter, the authority of the Librarian of Congress under section 1201(a)(1) of title 17, United States Code.

(e) *Definitions.* —In this Act:

(1) *Commercial mobile data service; commercial mobile radio service.* —The terms "commercial mobile data service" and "commercial mobile radio service" have the respective meanings given those terms in section 20.3 of title 47, Code of Federal Regulations, as in effect on the date of the enactment of this Act.

(2) *Wireless telecommunications network.* —The term "wireless telecommunications network" means a network used to provide a commercial mobile radio service or a commercial mobile data service.

(3) *Wireless telephone handsets; wireless devices.* —The terms "wireless telephone handset" and "wireless device" mean a handset or other device that operates on a wireless telecommunications network.

(Aug. 1, 2014, Pub. L. 113-144, 128 Stat. 1751.)

Part 5

OTHER STATUTES

UNITED STATES CODE
OTHER STATUTES

OTHER STATUTES

Note.—Some sections, or portions of sections, of other titles of the United States Code and of the District of Columbia Code relating to patents, trademarks, copyrights, trade secrets, or to the Patent and Trademark Office and the Copyright Office, are reprinted or noted here for convenience. This collection does not purport to be complete.

I. REMEDIES FOR INFRINGEMENT OF PATENTS AND TRADEMARKS AND OTHER ACTIONS

A. FEDERAL DISTRICT COURTS—JURISDICTION, VENUE, AND SERVICE OF PROCESS; ITC-RELATED PROVISIONS

28 U.S.C. § 1338   Patents, plant variety protection, copyrights, mask works, designs, trademarks, and unfair competition

(a) The district courts shall have original jurisdiction of any civil action arising under any Act of Congress relating to patents, plant variety protection, copyrights and trademarks. No State court shall have jurisdiction over any claim for relief arising under any Act of Congress relating to patents, plant variety protection, or copyrights. For purposes of this subsection, the term "State" includes any State of the United States, the District of Columbia, the Commonwealth of Puerto Rico, the United States Virgin Islands, American Samoa, Guam, and the Northern Mariana Islands.

(b) The district courts shall have original jurisdiction of any civil action asserting a claim of unfair competition when joined with a substantial and related claim under the copyright, patent, plant variety protection or trademark laws.

(c) Subsections (a) and (b) apply to exclusive rights in mask works under chapter 9 of title 17, and to exclusive rights in designs under chapter 13 of title 17, to the same extent as such subsections apply to copyrights.

(June 25, 1948, ch. 646, §1, 62 Stat. 931; Dec. 24, 1970, Pub. L. 91-577, §143, 84 Stat. 1559; Nov. 19, 1988, Pub. L. 100-702, §1020, 102 Stat. 4671, Oct. 28, 1998, Pub. L. 105-304, §503(b), 112 Stat. 2917; Nov. 29, 1999, Pub. L. 106-113, §3009, 113 Stat. 1501A-551; (Sept. 16, 2011, Pub. L. 112-29, §19, 125 Stat. 331.)

28 U.S.C. § 1368   Counterclaims in unfair practices in international trade

The district courts shall have original jurisdiction of any civil action based on a counterclaim raised pursuant to section 337(c) of the Tariff Act of 1930, to the extent that it arises out of the transaction or occurrence that is the subject matter of the opposing party's claim in the proceeding under section 337(a) of that Act.

(Dec. 8, 1994, Pub. L. 103-465, §321, 108 Stat. 4943.)

28 U.S.C. § 1391   Venue generally

(a) *Applicability of section.* — Except as otherwise provided by law —

(1) this section shall govern the venue of all civil actions brought in district courts of the United States; and

(2) the proper venue for a civil action shall be determined without regard to whether the action is local or transitory in nature.

(b) *Venue in general.* — A civil action may be brought in —

(1) a judicial district in which any defendant resides, if all defendants are residents of the State in which the district is located;

(2) a judicial district in which a substantial part of the events or omissions giving rise to the claim occurred, or a substantial part of property that is the subject of the action is situated; or

(3) if there is no district in which an action may otherwise be brought as provided in this section, any judicial district in which any defendant is subject to the court's personal jurisdiction with respect to such action.

(c) *Residency.* — For all venue purposes —

(1) a natural person, including an alien lawfully admitted for permanent residence in the United States, shall be deemed to reside in the judicial district in which that person is domiciled;

(2) an entity with the capacity to sue and be sued in its common name under applicable law, whether or not incorporated, shall be deemed to reside, if a defendant, in any judicial district in which such defendant is subject to the court's personal jurisdiction with respect to the civil action in question and, if a plaintiff, only in the judicial district in which it maintains its principal place of business; and

(3) a defendant not resident in the United States may be sued in any judicial district, and the joinder of such a defendant shall be disregarded in determining where the action may be brought with respect to other defendants.

(d) *Residency of corporations in states with multiple districts.* — For purposes of venue under this chapter, in a State which has more than one judicial district and in which a defendant that is a corporation is subject to personal jurisdiction at the time an action is commenced, such corporation shall be deemed to reside in any district in that State within which its contacts would be sufficient to subject it to personal jurisdiction if that district were a separate State, and, if there is no such district, the corporation shall be deemed to reside in the district within which it has the most significant contacts.

* * *

(June 25, 1948, ch. 646, §1, 62 Stat. 935; Oct. 5, 1962, Pub. L. 87-748, §2, 76 Stat. 744; Dec. 23, 1963, Pub. L. 88-234, 77 Stat. 473; Nov. 2, 1966, Pub. L. 89-714, §§1, 2, 80 Stat. 1111; Oct. 21, 1976, Pub. L. 94-583, §§3, 5, 90 Stat. 2721, 2897; Nov. 19, 1988, Pub. L. 100-702, §1013, 102 Stat. 4669; Dec. 1, 1990, Pub. L. 101-650, §311, 104 Stat. 5114; Dec. 9, 1991, Pub. L. 102-198, §3, 105 Stat. 1623; Oct. 29, 1992, Pub. L. 102-572, §902(a), 106 Stat. 4516; Oct. 3, 1995, Pub. L. 104-34, §1, 109 Stat. 293; Dec. 7, 2011, Pub. L. 112-63, §202, 125 Stat. 763.)

28 U.S.C. § 1400   Patents and copyrights, mask works, and designs

(a) Civil actions, suits, or proceedings arising under any Act of Congress relating to copyrights or exclusive rights in mask works or designs may be instituted in the district in which the defendant or his agent resides or may be found.

(b) Any civil action for patent infringement may be brought in the judicial district where the defendant resides, or where the defendant has committed acts of infringement and has a regular and established place of business.

(June 25, 1948, ch. 646, §1, 62 Stat. 936; Nov. 19, 1988, Pub. L. 100-702, §1020, 102 Stat. 4671; Oct. 28, 1998, Pub. L. 105-304, §503(c), 112 Stat. 2917.)

28 U.S.C. § 1446   Procedure for removal

* * *

(e) *Counterclaim in 337 proceeding.*—With respect to any counterclaim re-moved to a district court pursuant to section 337(c) of the Tariff Act of 1930, the district court shall resolve such counterclaim in the same manner as an original complaint under the Federal Rules of Civil Procedure, except that the payment of a filing fee shall not be required in such cases and the counter-claim shall relate back to the date of the original complaint in the proceeding before the International Trade Commission under section 337 of that Act.

(Dec. 8, 1994, Pub. L. 103-465, §321, 108 Stat. 4943; Dec. 7, 2011, Pub. L. 112-63, §103(b), 125 Stat. 761.)

28 U.S.C. § 1498   Patent and copyright cases

(a) Whenever an invention described in and covered by a patent of the United States is used or manufactured by or for the United States without license of the owner thereof or lawful right to use or manufacture the same, the owner's remedy shall be by action against the United States in the United States Court of Federal Claims for the recovery of his reasonable and entire compensation for such use and manufacture. Reasonable and entire compensation shall include the owner's reasonable costs, including reasonable fees for expert witnesses and attorneys, in pursuing the action if the owner is an independent inventor, a nonprofit organization, or an entity that had no more than 500 employees at any time during the 5-year period preceding the use or manufacture of the patented invention by or for the United States. Notwithstanding the preceding sentences, unless the action has been pending for more than 10 years from the time of filing to the time that the owner applies for such costs and fees, reasonable and entire compensation shall not include such costs and fees if the court finds that the position of the United States was substantially justified or that special circumstances make an award unjust.[1]

For the purposes of this section, the use or manufacture of an invention described in and covered by a patent of the United States by a contractor, a subcontractor, or any person, firm, or corporation for the Government and with the authorization or consent of the Government, shall be construed as use or manufacture for the United States.

The court shall not award compensation under this section if the claim is based on the use or manufacture by or for the United States of any article owned, leased, used by, or in the possession of the United States prior to July 1, 1918.

A Government employee shall have the right to bring suit against the Government under this section except where he was in a position to order, influence, or induce use of the invention by the Government. This section shall not confer a right of action on any patentee or any assignee of such patentee with respect to any invention discovered or invented by a person while in the employment or service of the United States, where the invention was related to the official functions of the employee, in cases in which such functions included research and development, or in the making of which Government time, materials or facilities were used.

(b) Hereafter, whenever the copyright in any work protected under the copyright laws of the United States shall be infringed by the United States, by a corporation owned or controlled by the United States, or by a contrac-

---

[1] *Ed. Note:* Pursuant to section 1(b) of Public Law 104-308, the amendment made by section 1(a) applies to actions under section 1498(a) of title 28, United States Code, that are pending on, or brought on or after, the date of the enactment, which was October 19, 1996.

28 U.S.C. § 1498

tor, subcontractor, or any person, firm, or corporation acting for the Government and with the authorization or consent of the Government, the exclusive action which may be brought for such infringement shall be an action by the copyright owner against the United States in the Court of Federal Claims for the recovery of his reasonable and entire compensation as damages for such infringement, including the minimum statutory damages as set forth in section 504(c) of title 17, United States Code: *Provided,* That a Government employee shall have a right of action against the Government under this subsection except where he was in a position to order, influence, or induce use of the copyrighted work by the Government. *Provided, however,* That this subsection shall not confer a right of action on any copyright owner or any assignee of such owner with respect to any copyrighted work prepared by a person while in the employment or service of the United States, where the copyrighted work was prepared as a part of the official functions of the employee, or in the preparation of which Government time, material, or facilities were used: *And provided further,* That before such action against the United States has been instituted the appropriate corporation owned or controlled by the United States or the head of the appropriate department or agency of the Government, as the case may be, is authorized to enter into an agreement with the copyright owner in full settlement and compromise for the damages accruing to him by reason of such infringement and to settle the claim administratively out of available appropriations.

Except as otherwise provided by law, no recovery shall be had for any infringement of a copyright covered by this subsection committed more than three years prior to the filing of the complaint or counterclaim for infringement in the action, except that the period between the date of receipt of a written claim for compensation by the department or agency of the Government or corporation owned or controlled by the United States, as the case may be, having authority to settle such claim and the date of mailing by the Government of a notice to the claimant that his claim has been denied shall not be counted as a part of the three years, unless suit is brought before the last-mentioned date.

(c) The provisions of this section shall not apply to any claim arising in a foreign country.

* * *

28 U.S.C. § 1498

(e) Subsections (b) and (c) of this section apply to exclusive rights in mask works under chapter 9 of title 17, and to exclusive rights in designs under chapter 13 of title 17, to the same extent as such subsections apply to copyrights.

(June 25, 1948, ch. 646, §1, 62 Stat. 941; May 24, 1949, ch. 139, §87, 63 Stat. 102; Oct. 31, 1951, ch. 655, §50, 65 Stat. 727; July 17, 1952, ch. 930, 66 Stat. 757; Sept. 8, 1960, Pub. L. 86-726, §§1, 4, 74 Stat. 855, 856; Oct. 19, 1976, Pub. L. 94-553, §105, 90 Stat. 2599; Apr. 2, 1982, Pub. L. 97-164, §133, 96 Stat. 40; Nov. 19, 1988, Pub. L. 100-702, §1020, 102 Stat. 4671; Oct. 29, 1992, Pub. L. 102-572, §902(a), 106 Stat. 4516; Oct. 19, 1996, Pub. L. 104-308 §1(a), 110 Stat. 3814; Dec. 16, 1997, Pub. L. 105-147, §3, 111 Stat. 2680; Oct. 28, 1998, Pub. L. 105-304, §503(d), 112 Stat. 2917.)

28 U.S.C. § 1659 Stay of certain actions pending disposition of related proceedings before the United States International Trade Commission

(a) *Stay.*—In a civil action involving parties that are also parties to a proceeding before the United States International Trade Commission under section 337 of the Tariff Act of 1930, at the request of a party to the civil action that is also a respondent in the proceeding before the Commission, the district court shall stay, until the determination of the Commission becomes final, proceedings in the civil action with respect to any claim that involves the same issues involved in the proceeding before the Commission, but only if such request is made within—

(1) 30 days after the party is named as a respondent in the proceeding before the Commission, or

(2) 30 days after the district court action is filed,

whichever is later.

(b) *Use of Commission record.*—Notwithstanding section 337(n)(l) of the Tariff Act of 1930, after dissolution of a stay under subsection (a), the record of the proceeding before the United States International Trade Commission shall be transmitted to the district court and shall be admissible in the civil action, subject to such protective order as the district court determines necessary, to the extent permitted under the Federal Rules of Evidence and the Federal Rules of Civil Procedure.

(Dec. 8, 1994, Pub. L. 103-465, §321, 108 Stat. 4943.)

28 U.S.C. § 1694   Patent infringement action

In a patent infringement action commenced in a district where the defendant is not a resident but has a regular and established place of business, service of process, summons or subpoena upon such defendant may be made upon his agent or agents conducting such business.

(June 25, 1948, ch. 646, §1, 62 Stat. 945.)

28 U.S.C. § 1928   Patent infringement actions; disclaimer not filed

Whenever a judgment is rendered for the plaintiff in any patent infringement action involving a part of a patent and it appears that the patentee, in his specifications, claimed to be, but was not, the original and first inventor or discoverer of any material or substantial part of the thing patented, no costs shall be included in such judgment, unless the proper disclaimer has been filed in the United States Patent and Trademark Office prior to the commencement of the action.

(June 25, 1948, ch. 646, §1, 62 Stat. 957; Nov. 29, 1999, Pub. L. 106-113, §4732, 113 Stat. 1501A-581.)

B. COURTS OF APPEAL—JURISDICTION—U.S. COURT OF APPEALS FOR THE FEDERAL CIRCUIT

28 U.S.C. § 44   Appointment, tenure, residence and salary of circuit judges

(a) The President shall appoint, by and with the advice and consent of the Senate, circuit judges for the several circuits as follows:

Circuits	Number of judges
District of Columbia	12
First	6
Second	13
Third	14
Fourth	15
Fifth	17
Sixth	16
Seventh	11

* * *

(Apr. 2, 1982, Pub. L. 97-164, §102, 96 Stat. 25; Dec. 1, 1990, Pub. L. 101-650, §201, 104 Stat. 5099.)

Pub. L. 97-164   (Related Provisions)

Ed. Note: Sections 165, 166, and 168 of Pub. L. 97-164 contain miscellaneous provisions regarding the membership of the United States Court of Appeals for the Federal Circuit, as follows:

§165.   *Continued Service of Current Judges.*—The judges of the United States Court of Claims and of the United States Court of Customs and Patent Appeals in regular active service on the effective date of this Act shall continue in office as judges of the United States Court of Appeals for the Federal Circuit. Senior judges of the United States Court of Claims and of the United States Court of Customs and Patent Appeals on the effective date of this Act shall continue in office as senior judges of the United States Court of Appeals for the Federal Circuit.

§166.   *Appointment of Chief Judge of Court of Appeals for the Federal Circuit.*— Notwithstanding the provisions of section 45(a) of title 28, United States Code, the first chief judge of the United States Court of Appeals for the Federal Circuit shall be the Chief Judge of the United States Court of Claims or the Chief Judge of the United States Court of Customs and Patent Appeals, whoever has served longer as chief judge of his court. Notwithstanding section 45 of title 28, United States Code, whichever of the two chief judges does not become the first chief judge of the United States Court of Appeals for the Federal Circuit under the preceding sentence shall, while in active service, have precedence and be deemed senior in commission over all the circuit judges of the United States Court of Appeals for the Federal Circuit (other than the first chief judge of that circuit). When the person who serves as chief judge of the United States Court of Appeals for the Federal Circuit vacates that position, the position shall be filled in accordance with section 45(a) of title 28, United States Code, as modified by the preceding sentence of this section.

§168. *Appointment of Judges by the President.*—The Congress—

(1) takes notice of the fact that the quality of the Federal judiciary is determined by the competence and experience of its judges; and

(2) suggests that the President, in nominating individuals to judgeships on the United States Court of Appeals for the Federal Circuit and the United States Claims Court [now the U.S. Court of Federal Claims—ed.], select from a broad range of qualified individuals.

(Apr. 2, 1982, Pub. L. 97-164, §§165, 166, & 168, 96 Stat. 51.)

28 U.S.C. § 46   Assignment of judges; divisions; hearings; quorum

(a) Circuit judges shall sit on the court and its panel in such order and at such times as the court directs.

(b) In each circuit the court may authorize the hearing and determination of cases and controversies by separate panels, each consisting of three judges, at least a majority of whom shall be judges of that court, unless such judges cannot sit because recused or disqualified, or unless the chief judge of that court certifies that there is an emergency including, but not limited to, the unavailability of a judge of the court because of illness. Such panels shall sit at the times and places and hear the cases and controversies assigned as the court directs. The United States Court of Appeals for the Federal Circuit shall determine by rule a procedure for the rotation of judges from panel to panel to ensure that all of the judges sit on a representative cross section of the cases heard and, notwithstanding the first sentence of this subsection, may determine by rule the number of judges, not less than three, who constitute a panel.

(c) Cases and controversies shall be heard and determined by a court or panel of not more than three judges (except that the United States Court of Appeals for the Federal Circuit may sit in panels of more than three judges if its rules so provide), unless a hearing or rehearing before the court in banc is ordered by a majority of the circuit judges of the circuit who are in regular active service. A court in banc shall consist of all circuit judges in regular active service, or such number of judges as may be prescribed in accordance with section 6 of Public Law 95-486 (92 Stat. 1633), except that any senior circuit judge of the circuit shall be eligible (1) to participate, at his election and upon designation and assignment pursuant to section 294(c) of this title and the rules of the circuit, as a member of an in banc court reviewing a decision of a panel of which such judge was a member, or (2) to continue to participate in the decision of a case or controversy that was heard or reheard by the court in banc at a time when such judge was in regular active service.

(d) A majority of the number of judges authorized to constitute a court or panel thereof, as provided in paragraph (c), shall constitute a quorum.

(June 25, 1948, ch. 646, §1, 62 Stat. 871; Nov. 13, 1963, Pub. L. 88-176, §1, 77 Stat. 331; Oct. 20, 1978, Pub. L. 95-486, §5, 92 Stat. 1633; Apr. 2, 1982, Pub. L. 97-164, §§103, 205, 96 Stat. 25, 53; Aug. 6, 1996, Pub. L. 104-175, §1, 110 Stat. 1556.)

28 U.S.C. § 1291   Final decisions of district courts

The courts of appeals (other than the United States Court of Appeals for the Federal Circuit) shall have jurisdiction of appeals from all final decisions of the district courts of the United States, the United States District Court for the District of the Canal Zone, the District Court of Guam, and the District Court of the Virgin Islands, except where a direct review may be had in the Supreme Court. The jurisdiction of the United States Court of Appeals for the Federal Circuit shall be limited to the jurisdiction described in sections 1292(c) and (d) and 1295 of this title.

(June 25, 1948, ch. 646, §1, 62 Stat. 929; Oct. 31, 1951, ch. 655, §48, 65 Stat. 726; July 7, 1958, Pub. L. 85-508, §12, 72 Stat. 348; Apr. 2, 1982, Pub. L. 97-164, §124, 96 Stat. 36.)

28 U.S.C. § 1292   Interlocutory decisions

(a) Except as provided in subsections (c) and (d) of this section, the courts of appeals shall have jurisdiction of appeals from:

(1) Interlocutory orders of the district courts of the United States, the United States District Court for the District of the Canal Zone, the District Court of Guam, and the District Court of the Virgin Islands, or of the judges thereof, granting, continuing, modifying, refusing or dissolving injunctions, or refusing to dissolve or modify injunctions, except where a direct review may be had in the Supreme Court.

(2) Interlocutory orders appointing receivers, or refusing orders to wind up receiverships or to take steps to accomplish the purposes thereof, such as directing sales or other disposals of property;

(3) Interlocutory decrees of such district courts or the judges thereof determining the rights and liabilities of the parties to admiralty cases in which appeals from final decrees are allowed.

(b) When a district judge, in making in a civil action an order not otherwise appealable under this section, shall be of the opinion that such order involves a controlling question of law as to which there is substantial ground for difference of opinion and that an immediate appeal from the order may materially advance the ultimate termination of the litigation, he shall so state in writing in such order. The Court of Appeals which would have jurisdiction of an appeal of such action may thereupon, in its discretion, permit an appeal to be taken from such order, if application is made to it within ten days after the entry of the order: *Provided, however,* That application for an appeal hereunder shall not stay proceedings in the district court unless the district judge or the Court of Appeals or a judge thereof shall so order.

(c) The United States Court of Appeals for the Federal Circuit shall have exclusive jurisdiction—

   (1) of an appeal from an interlocutory order or decree described in subsection (a) or (b) of this section in any case over which the court would have jurisdiction of an appeal under section 1295 of this title; and

   (2) of an appeal from a judgment in a civil action for patent infringement which would otherwise be appealable to the United States Court of Appeals for the Federal Circuit and is final except for an accounting.

(d) (1) When the chief judge of the Court of International Trade issues an order under the provisions of section 256(b) of this title, or when any judge of the Court of International Trade, in issuing any other interlocutory order, includes in the order a statement that a controlling question of law is involved with respect to which there is a substantial ground for difference of opinion and that an immediate appeal from that order may materially advance the ultimate termination of the litigation, the United States Court of Appeals for the Federal Circuit may, in its discretion, permit an appeal to be taken from such order, if application is made to that Court within ten days after the entry of such order.

   (2) When any judge of the United States Claims Court,[2] in issuing an interlocutory order, includes in the order a statement that a controlling question of law is involved with respect to which there is a substantial ground for difference of opinion and that an immediate appeal from that order may materially advance the ultimate termination of the litigation, the United States Court of Appeals for the Federal Circuit may, in its discretion, permit an appeal to be taken from such order, if application is made to that Court within ten days after the entry of such order.

---

[2] *Ed. Note:* Pursuant to the Court of Federal Claims Technical and Procedural Improvements Act of 1992, §902(b)(2), Pub. L. 102-572, 106 Stat. 4516, statutory references to the U.S. Claims Court are deemed to refer to the U.S. Court of Federal Claims.

(3) Neither the application for nor the granting of an appeal under this subsection shall stay proceedings in the Court of International Trade or in the Claims Court, as the case may be, unless a stay is ordered by a judge of the Court of International Trade or of the Claims Court or by the United States Court of Appeals for the Federal Circuit or a judge of that court.

(4) (A) The United States Court of Appeals for the Federal Circuit shall have exclusive jurisdiction of an appeal from an interlocutory order of a district court of the United States, the District Court of Guam, the District Court of the Virgin Islands, or the District Court for the Northern Mariana Islands, granting or denying, in whole or in part, a motion to transfer an action to the United States Claims Court under section 1631 of this title.

(B) When a motion to transfer an action to the Claims Court is filed in a district court, no further proceedings shall be taken in the district court until 60 days after the court has ruled upon the motion. If an appeal is taken from the district court's grant or denial of the motion, proceedings shall be further stayed until the appeal has been decided by the Court of Appeals for the Federal Circuit. The stay of proceedings in the district court shall not bar the granting of preliminary or injunctive relief, where appropriate and where expedition is reasonably necessary. However, during the period in which proceedings are stayed as provided in this subparagraph, no transfer to the Claims Court pursuant to the motion shall be carried out.

(e) The Supreme Court may prescribe rules, in accordance with section 2072 of this title, to provide for an appeal of an interlocutory decision to the courts of appeals that is not otherwise provided for under subsection (a), (b), (c), or (d).

(June 25, 1948, ch. 646, §1, 62 Stat. 929; Oct. 31, 1951, ch. 655, §49, 65 Stat. 726; July 7, 1958, Pub. L. 85-508, §12(e), 72 Stat. 348; Sept. 2, 1958, Pub. L. 85-919, 72 Stat. 1770; Apr. 2, 1982, Pub. L. 97-164, §125, 96 Stat. 36; Nov. 8, 1984, Pub. L. 98-620, §412, 98 Stat. 3362; Nov. 19, 1988, Pub. L. 100-702, §501, 102 Stat. 4652; Oct. 29, 1992, Pub. L. 102-572, §101, 106 Stat. 4516.)

28 U.S.C. § 1294   Circuits in which decisions reviewable

Except as provided in sections 1292(c), 1292(d), and 1295 of this title, appeals from reviewable decisions of the district and territorial courts shall be taken to the courts of appeals as follows:

(1) From a district court of the United States to the court of appeals for the circuit embracing the district;

(2) From the United States District Court for the District of the Canal Zone, to the Court of Appeals for the Fifth Circuit;

(3) From the District Court of the Virgin Islands, to the Court of Appeals for the Third Circuit;

(4) From the District Court of Guam, to the Court of Appeals for the Ninth Circuit.

(June 25, 1948, ch. 646, 62 Stat. 930; Oct. 31, 1951, ch. 655, §50, 65 Stat. 727; July 7, 1958, Pub. L. 85-508, §12, 72 Stat. 348; Mar. 18, 1959, Pub. L. 86-3, §14, 73 Stat. 10; Aug. 30, 1961, Pub. L. 87-189, §5, 75 Stat. 417; Nov. 6, 1978, Pub. L. 95-598, §237, 92 Stat. 2667; Apr. 2, 1982, Pub. L. 97-164, §126, 96 Stat. 37.)

28 U.S.C. § 1295   Jurisdiction of the United States Court of Appeals for the Federal Circuit

(a) The United States Court of Appeals for the Federal Circuit shall have exclusive jurisdiction—

(1) of an appeal from a final decision of a district court of the United States, the District Court of Guam, the District Court of the Virgin Islands, or the District Court of the Northern Mariana Islands, in any civil action arising under, or in any civil action in which a party has asserted a compulsory counterclaim arising under, any Act of Congress relating to patents or plant variety protection;

(2) of an appeal from a final decision of a district court of the United States, the United States District Court for the District of the Canal Zone, the District Court of Guam, the District Court of the Virgin Islands, or the District Court for the Northern Mariana Islands, if the jurisdiction of that court was based, in whole or in part, on section 1346 of this title, except that jurisdiction of an appeal in a case brought in a district court under section 1346(a)(1), 1346(b), 1346(e), or 1346(f) of this title or under section 1346(a)(2) when the claim is founded upon an Act of Congress or a regulation of an executive department providing for internal revenue shall be governed by sections 1291, 1292, and 1294 of this title;

[3](3) of an appeal from a final decision of the United States Claims Court;

---

[3] *Ed. Note:* Pursuant to the Court of Federal Claims Technical and Procedural Improvements Act of 1992, §902(b)(2), Pub. L. 102-572, 106 Stat. 4516, statutory references to the U.S. Claims Court are deemed to refer to the U.S. Court of Federal Claims.

(4) of an appeal from a decision of—

(A)[4] the Patent Trial and Appeal Board of the United States Patent and Trademark Office with respect to a patent application, derivation proceeding, reexamination, post-grant review, or inter partes review under title 35, at the instance of a party who exercised that party's right to participate in the applicable proceeding before or appeal to the Board, except that an applicant or a party to a derivation proceeding may also have remedy by civil action pursuant to section 145 or 146 of title 35; an appeal under this subparagraph of a decision of the Board with respect to an application or derivation proceeding shall waive the right of such applicant or party to proceed under section 145 or 146 of title 35;

(B) the Under Secretary of Commerce for Intellectual Property and Director of the United States Patent and Trademark Office or the Trademark Trial and Appeal Board with respect to applications for registration of marks and other proceedings as provided in section 21 of the Trademark Act of 1946 (15 U.S.C. 1071); or

(C) a district court to which a case was directed pursuant to section 145, 146, or 154(b) of title 35;

(5) of an appeal from a final decision of the United States Court of International Trade;

(6) to review the final determinations of the United States International Trade Commission relating to unfair practices in import trade, made under section 337 of the Tariff Act of 1930 (19 U.S.C. 1337);

(7) to review, by appeal on questions of law only, findings of the Secretary of Commerce under U.S. note 6 to subchapter X of chapter 98 of the Harmonized Tariff Schedule of the United States (relating to importation of instruments or apparatus);

(8) of an appeal under section 71 of the Plant Variety Protection Act (7 U.S.C. 2461);

---

[4] *Ed. Note:* The provisions of section 1295(a)(4)(A), as in effect on September 15, 2012, shall apply to interference proceedings that are declared after September 15, 2012, under section 135, as in effect before the effective date under section 3(n) of the Leahy-Smith America Intents Act. The Patent Trial and Appeal Board may be deemed to be the Board of Patent Appeals and Interferences for purposes of such interference proceedings. See Pub. L. 112-274, section (k)(3).

(9) of an appeal from a final order or final decision of the Merit Systems Protection Board, pursuant to sections 7703(b)(1) and 7703(d) of title 5;

(10) of an appeal from a final decision of an agency board of contract appeals pursuant to section 7107(a)(1) of title 41;

(11) of an appeal under section 211 of the Economic Stabilization Act of 1970;

(12) of an appeal under section 5 of the Emergency Petroleum Allocation Act of 1973;

(13) of an appeal under section 506(c) of the Natural Gas Policy Act of 1978; and

(14) of an appeal under section 523 of the Energy Policy and Conservation Act.

(b) The head of any executive department or agency may, with the approval of the Attorney General, refer to the Court of Appeals for the Federal Circuit for judicial review any final decision rendered by a board of contract appeals pursuant to the terms of any contract with the United States awarded by that department or agency which the head of such department or agency has concluded is not entitled to finality pursuant to the review standards specified in section 7107(b) of title 41. The head of each executive department or agency shall make any referral under this section within one hundred and twenty days after the receipt of a copy of the final appeal decision.

(c) The Court of Appeals for the Federal Circuit shall review the matter referred in accordance with the standards specified in section 7107(b) of title 41. The court shall proceed with judicial review on the administrative record made before the board of contract appeals on matters so referred as in other cases pending in such court, shall determine the issue of finality of the appeal decision, and shall, if appropriate, render judgment thereon, or remand the matter to any administrative or executive body or official with such direction as it may deem proper and just.

(Apr. 2, 1982, Pub. L. 97-164, §127, 96 Stat. 37; Nov. 8, 1984, Pub. L. 98-622, §205, 98 Stat. 3388; Aug. 23, 1988, Pub. L. 100-418, §1214, 102 Stat. 1156; Nov. 19, 1988, Pub. L. 100-702, §1020, 102 Stat. 4671; Oct. 29, 1992, Pub. L. 102-572, §102(c), 106 Stat. 4506; Nov. 29, 1999, Pub. L. 106-113, §§4402, 4732, 113 Stat. 1501A-557, 581; Jan. 4, 2011, Pub. L. 111-350, §5, 124 Stat. 3841; Sept. 16, 2011, Pub. L. 112-29, §§8, 19, 125 Stat. 331.)

28 U.S.C. § 1295

28 U.S.C. § 1454   Patent, plant variety protection, and copyright cases

(a) *In general.*—A civil action in which any party asserts a claim for relief arising under any Act of Congress relating to patents, plant variety protection, or copyrights may be removed to the district court of the United States for the district and division embracing the place where the action is pending.

(b) *Special rules.*—The removal of an action under this section shall be made in accordance with section 1446, except that if the removal is based solely on this section—

(1) the action may be removed by any party; and

(2) the time limitations contained in section 1446(b) may be extended at any time for cause shown.

(c) *Clarification of jurisdiction in certain cases.*—The court to which a civil action is removed under this section is not precluded from hearing and determining any claim in the civil action because the State court from which the civil action is removed did not have jurisdiction over that claim.

(d) *Remand.*—If a civil action is removed solely under this section, the district court—

(1) shall remand all claims that are neither a basis for removal under subsection (a) nor within the original or supplemental jurisdiction of the district court under any Act of Congress; and

(2) may, under the circumstances specified in section 1367(c), remand any claims within the supplemental jurisdiction of the district court under section 1367.

(Sept. 16, 2011, Pub. L. 112-29, §19, 125 Stat. 331.)

28 U.S.C. § 2201   Creation of remedy

(a) In a case of actual controversy within its jurisdiction, except with respect to Federal taxes other than actions brought under section 7428 of the Internal Revenue Code of 1986, a proceeding under section 505 or 1146 of title 11, or in any civil action involving an antidumping or countervailing duty proceeding regarding a class or kind of merchandise of a free trade area country (as defined in section 516A(f)(10) of the Tariff Act of 1930), as determined by the administering authority, any court of the United States, upon the filing of an appropriate pleading, may declare the rights and other legal relations of any interested party seeking such declaration, whether or not further relief is or could be sought. Any such declaration shall have the force and effect of a final judgment or decree and shall be reviewable as such.

(b) For limitations on actions brought with respect to drug patents see section 505 or 512 of the Federal Food, Drug, and Cosmetic Act, or section 351 of the Public Health Service Act.

(June 25, 1948, ch. 646, 62 Stat. 964; May 24, 1949, ch. 139, §111, 63 Stat. 105; Aug. 28, 1954, ch. 1033, 68 Stat. 890; Pub. L. 85–508, §12(p), July 7, 1958, 72 Stat. 349; Pub. L. 94–455, title XIII, §1306(b)(8), Oct. 4, 1976, 90 Stat. 1719; Pub. L. 95–598, title II, §249, Nov. 6, 1978, 92 Stat. 2672; Pub. L. 98–417, title I, §106, Sept. 24, 1984, 98 Stat. 1597; Pub. L. 100–449, title IV, §402(c), Sept. 28, 1988, 102 Stat. 1884; Pub. L. 100–670, title I, §107(b), Nov. 16, 1988, 102 Stat. 3984; Pub. L. 103–182, title IV, §414(b), Dec. 8, 1993, 107 Stat. 2147; Pub. L. 111–148, title VII, §7002(c)(2), Mar. 23, 2010, 124 Stat. 816.)

C. INTELLECTUAL PROPERTY AND INTERNATIONAL TRADE

19 U.S.C. § 1337   Unfair practices in import trade

(a) *Unlawful activities; covered industries; definitions.*—

(1) Subject to paragraph (2), the following are unlawful, and when found by the Commission to exist shall be dealt with, in addition to any other provision of law, as provided in this section:

(A) Unfair methods of competition and unfair acts in the importation of articles (other than articles provided for in subparagraphs (B), (C), (D), and (E)) into the United States, or in the sale of such articles by the owner, importer, or consignee, the threat or effect of which is—

(i) to destroy or substantially injure an industry, in the United States;

(ii) to prevent the establishment of such an industry; or

(iii) to restrain or monopolize trade and commerce in the United States.

(B) The importation into the United States, the sale for importation, or the sale within the United States after importation by the owner, importer, or consignee, of articles that—

(i) infringe a valid and enforceable United States patent or a valid and enforceable United States copyright registered under title 17, United States Code; or

(ii) are made, produced, processed, or mined under, or by means of, a process covered by the claims of a valid and enforceable United States patent.

(C) The importation into the United States, the sale for importation, or the sale within the United States after importation by the owner, importer, or consignee, of articles that infringe a valid and enforceable United States trademark registered under the Trademark Act of 1946.

(D) The importation into the United States, the sale for importation, or the sale within the Untied States after importation by the owner, importer, or consignee, of a semiconductor chip product in a manner that constitutes infringement of a mask work registered under chapter 9 of title 17, United States Code.

(E) The importation into the United States, the sale for importation, or the sale within the United States after importation by the owner, importer, or consigner, of an article that constitutes infringement of the exclusive rights in a design protected under chapter 13 of title 17, United States Code.

(2) Subparagraphs (B), (C), (D), and (E) of paragraph (1) apply only if an industry in the United States, relating to the articles protected by the patent, copyright, trademark, mask work, or design concerned, exists or is in the process of being established.

(3) For purposes of paragraph (2), an industry in the United States shall be considered to exist if there is in the United States, with respect to the articles protected by the patent, copyright, trademark, mask work, or design concerned—

(A) significant investment in plant and equipment;

(B) significant employment of labor or capital; or

(C) substantial investment in its exploitation, including engineering, research and development, or licensing.

(4) For the purposes of this section, the phrase "owner, importer, or consignee" includes any agent of the owner, importer, or consignee.

(b) *Investigation of violations by Commission.*—

(1) The Commission shall investigate any alleged violation of this section on complaint under oath or upon its initiative. Upon commencing any such investigation, the Commission shall publish notice thereof in the

Federal Register. The Commission shall conclude any such investigation and make its determination under this section at the earliest practicable time after the date of publication of notice of such investigation. To promote expeditious adjudication, the Commission shall, within 45 days after an investigation is initiated, establish a target date for its final determination.

(2) During the course of each investigation under this section, the Commission shall consult with, and seek advice and information from, the Department of Health and Human Services, the Department of Justice, the Federal Trade Commission, and such other departments and agencies as it considers appropriate.

(3) Whenever, in the course of an investigation under this section, the Commission has reason to believe, based on information before it, that a matter, in whole or in part, may come within the purview of this Act or of part II of subtitle IV of this chapter, it shall promptly notify the Secretary of Commerce so that such action may be taken as is otherwise authorized by such subtitle. If the Commission has reason to believe that the matter before it (A) is based solely on alleged acts and effects which are within the purview of section 303, 671, or 673 [§1303, 1671, or 1673], or (B) relates to an alleged copyright infringement with respect to which action is prohibited by section 1008 of title 17, United States Code, the Commission shall terminate, or not institute, any investigation into the matter. If the Commission has reason to believe the matter before it is based in part on alleged acts and effects which are within the purview of section 1303, 1671, or 1673 of this title, and in part on alleged acts and effects which may, independently from or in conjunction with those within the purview of such section, establish a basis for relief under this section, then it may institute or continue an investigation into the matter. If the Commission notifies the Secretary or the administering authority (as defined in section 1677(1) of this title) with respect to a matter under this paragraph, the Commission may suspend its investigation during the time the matter is before the Secretary or administering authority for final decision. Any final decision of the Secretary under section 1303 of this title or by the administering authority under section 1671 or 1673 of this title with respect to the matter within such section 1303, 1671, or 1673 of this title of which the Commission has notified the Secretary or administering authority shall be conclusive upon the Commission with respect to the issue of

19 U.S.C. § 1337

less-than-fair-value sales or subsidization and the matters necessary for such decision.

(c) *Determinations; review.* — The Commission shall determine, with respect to each investigation conducted by it under this section, whether or not there is a violation of this section, except that the Commission may, by issuing a consent order or on the basis of an agreement between the private parties to the investigation, including an agreement to present the matter for arbitration, terminate any such investigation, in whole or in part, without making such a determination. Each determination under subsection (d) or (e) of this section shall be made on the record after notice and opportunity for a hearing in conformity with the provisions of subchapter II of chapter 5 of title 5. All legal and equitable defenses may be presented in all cases. A respondent may raise any counterclaim in a manner prescribed by the Commission. Immediately after a counterclaim is received by the Commission, the respondent raising such counterclaim shall file a notice of removal with a United States district court in which venue for any of the counterclaims raised by the party would exist under section 1391 of title 28, United States Code. Any counterclaim raised pursuant to this section shall relate back to the date of the original complaint in the proceeding before the Commission. Action on such counterclaim shall not delay or affect the proceeding under this section, including the legal and equitable defenses that may be raised under this subsection. Any person adversely affected by a final determination of the Commission under subsection (d), (e), (f), or (g), of this section may appeal such determination within 60 days after the determination becomes final, to the United States Court of Appeals for the Federal Circuit for review in accordance with chapter 7 of title 5. Notwithstanding the foregoing provisions of this subsection, Commission determinations under subsections (d), (e), (f), or (g), of this section with respect to its findings on the public health and welfare, competitive conditions in the United States economy, the production of like or directly competitive articles in the United States, and United States consumers, the amount and nature of bond, or the appropriate remedy shall be reviewable in accordance with section 706 of title 5. Determinations by the Commission under subsections (e), (f), and (j) with respect to forfeiture of bonds and under subsection (h) with respect to the imposition of sanctions for abuse of discovery or abuse of process shall also be reviewable in accordance with section 706 of title 5, United States Code.

19 U.S.C. § 1337

(d) *Exclusion of articles from entry.—*

(1) If the Commission determines, as a result of an investigation under this section, that there is a violation of this section, it shall direct that the articles concerned, imported by any person violating the provision of this section, be excluded from entry into the United States, unless, after considering the effect of such exclusion upon the public health and welfare, competitive conditions in the United States economy, the production of like or directly competitive articles in the United States, and United States consumers, it finds that such articles should not be excluded from entry. The Commission shall notify the Secretary of the Treasury of its action under this subsection directing such exclusion from entry, and upon receipt of such notice, the Secretary shall, through the proper officers, refuse such entry.

(2) The authority of the Commission to order an exclusion from entry of articles shall be limited to persons determined by the Commission to be violating this section unless the Commission determines that—

(A) a general exclusion from entry of articles is necessary to prevent circumvention of an exclusion order limited to products of named persons; or

(B) there is a pattern of violation of this section and it is difficult to identify the source of infringing products.

(e) *Exclusion of articles from entry during investigation except under bond.—*

(1) If, during the course of an investigation under this section, the Commission determines that there is reason to believe that there is a violation of this section, it may direct that the articles concerned, imported by any person with respect to whom there is reason to believe that such person is violating this section, be excluded from entry into the United States, unless, after considering the effect of such exclusion upon the public health and welfare, competitive conditions in the United States economy, the production of like or directly competitive articles in the United States, and United States consumers, it finds that such articles should not be excluded from entry. The Commission shall notify the Secretary of the Treasury of its action under this subsection directing such exclusion from entry, and upon receipt of such notice, the Secretary shall, through the proper officers, refuse such entry, except that such articles shall be entitled to entry under bond prescribed by the Secretary in an amount determined by the

Commission to be sufficient to protect the complainant from any injury. If the Commission later determines that the respondent has violated the provisions of this section, the bond may be forfeited to the complainant.

(2) A complainant may petition the Commission for the issuance of an order under this subsection. The Commission shall make a determination with regard to such petition by not later than the 90th day after the date on which the Commission's notice of investigation is published in the Federal Register. The Commission may extend the 90-day period for an additional 60 days in a case it designates as a more complicated case. The Commission shall publish in the Federal Register its reasons why it designated the case as being more complicated. The Commission may require the complainant to post a bond as a prerequisite to the issuance of an order under this subsection. If the Commission later determines that the respondent has not violated the provisions of this section, the bond may be forfeited to the respondent.

(3) The Commission may grant preliminary relief under this subsection or subsection (f) of this section to the same extent as preliminary injunctions and temporary restraining orders may be granted under the Federal Rules of Civil Procedure.

(4) The Commission shall prescribe the terms and conditions under which bonds may be forfeited under paragraphs (1) and (2).

(f) *Cease and desist orders; civil penalty for violation of orders.* —

(1) In addition to, or in lieu of, taking action under subsection (d) or (e), the Commission may issue and cause to be served on any person violating this section, or believed to be violating this section, as the case may be, an order directing such person to cease and desist from engaging in the unfair methods or acts involved, unless after considering the effect of such order upon the public health and welfare, competitive conditions in the United States economy, the production of like or directly competitive articles in the United States, and United States consumers, it finds that such order should not be issued. The Commission may at any time, upon such notice and in such manner as it deems proper, modify or revoke any such order, and, in the case of a revocation, may take action under subsection (d) or (e) of this section, as the case may be. If a temporary cease and desist order is issued in addition to, or in lieu of, an exclusion order under subsection (e), the Commission may require the complainant to post a bond, in an amount determined by the Commission to be sufficient to

protect the respondent from any injury, as a prerequisite to the issuance of an order under this subsection. If the Commission later determines that the respondent has not violated the provisions of this section, the bond may be forfeited to the respondent. The Commission shall prescribe the terms and conditions under which the bonds may be forfeited under this paragraph.

(2) Any person who violates an order issued by the Commission under paragraph (1) after it has become final shall forfeit and pay to the United States a civil penalty for each day on which an importation of articles, or their sale, occurs in violation of the order of not more than the greater of $100,000 or twice the domestic value of the articles entered or sold on such day in violation of the order. Such penalty shall accrue to the United States and may be recovered for the United States in a civil action brought by the Commission in the Federal District Court for the District of Columbia or for the district in which the violation occurs. In such actions, the United States district courts may issue mandatory injunctions incorporating the relief sought by the Commission as they deem appropriate in the enforcement of such final orders of the Commission.

(g) *Exclusion from entry or cease and desist order; conditions and procedures applicable.* —

(1) If —

(A) a complaint is filed against a person under this section;

(B) the complaint and a notice of investigation are served on the person;

(C) the person fails to respond to the complaint and notice or otherwise fails to appear to answer the complaint and notice;

(D) the person fails to show good cause why the person should not be found in default; and

(E) the complainant seeks relief limited solely to that person;

the Commission shall presume the facts alleged in the complaint to be true and shall, upon request, issue an exclusion from entry or a cease and desist order, or both, limited to that person unless, after considering the effect of such exclusion or order upon the public health and welfare, competitive conditions in the United States economy, the production of like or directly competitive articles in the United States, and United States consumers, the Commission finds that such exclusion or order should not be issued.

19 U.S.C. § 1337

(2) In addition to the authority of the Commission to issue a general exclusion from entry of articles when a respondent appears to contest an investigation concerning a violation of the provisions of this section, a general exclusion from entry of articles, regardless of the source or importer of the articles, may be issued if—

(A) no person appears to contest an investigation concerning a violation of the provisions of this section,

(B) such a violation is established by substantial, reliable, and probative evidence, and

(C) the requirements of subsection (d)(2) are met.

(h) *Sanctions for abuse of discovery and abuse of process.*—The Commission may by rule prescribe sanctions for abuse of discovery and abuse of process to the extent authorized by Rule 11 and Rule 37 of the Federal Rules of Civil Procedure.

(i) *Forfeiture.*—

(1) In addition to taking action under subsection (d), the Commission may issue an order providing that any article imported in violation of the provisions of this section be seized and forfeited to the United States if—

(A) the owner, importer, or consignee of the article previously attempted to import the article into the United States;

(B) the article was previously denied entry into the United States by reason of an order issued under subsection (d); and

(C) upon such previous denial of entry, the Secretary of the Treasury provided the owner, importer, or consignee of the article written notice of—

(i) such order, and

(ii) the seizure and forfeiture that would result from any further attempt to import the article into the United States.

(2) The Commission shall notify the Secretary of the Treasury of any order issued under this subsection and, upon receipt of such notice, the Secretary of the Treasury shall enforce such order in accordance with the provisions of this section.

(3) Upon the attempted entry of articles subject to an order issued under this subsection, the Secretary of the Treasury shall immediately notify all

ports of entry of the attempted importation and shall identify the persons notified under paragraph (1)(C).

(4) The Secretary of the Treasury shall provide—

(A) the written notice described in paragraph (1)(C) to the owner, importer, or consignee of any article that is denied entry into the United States by reason of an order issued under subsection (d); and

(B) a copy of such written notice to the Commission.

(j) *Referral to President.* —

(1) If the Commission determines that there is a violation of this section, or that, for purposes of subsection (e), there is reason to believe that there is such a violation, it shall—

(A) publish such determination in the Federal Register, and

(B) transmit to the President a copy of such determination and the action taken under subsection (d), (e), (f), (g), or (i), with respect thereto, together with the record upon which such determination is based.

(2) If, before the close of the 60-day period beginning on the day after the day on which he receives a copy of such determination, the President, for policy reasons, disapproves such determination and notifies the Commission of his disapproval, then, effective on the date of such notice, such determination and the action taken under subsection (d), (e), (f), (g), or (i) with respect thereto shall have no force or effect.

(3) Subject to the provisions of paragraph (2), such determination shall, except for purposes of subsection (c), be effective upon publication thereof in the Federal Register, and the action taken under subsection (d), (e), (f), (g), or (i), with respect thereto shall be effective as provided in such subsections, except that articles directed to be excluded from entry under subsection (d) or subject to a cease and desist order under subsection (f) shall, until such determination becomes final, be entitled to entry under bond prescribed by the Secretary in an amount determined by the Commission to be sufficient to protect the complainant from any injury. If the determination becomes final, the bond may be forfeited to the complainant. The Commission shall prescribe the terms and conditions under which bonds may be forfeited under this paragraph.

(4) If the President does not disapprove such determination within such 60-day period, or if he notifies the Commission before the close of such period that he approves such determination, then, for purposes of para-

graph (3) and subsection (c) such determination shall become final on the day after the close of such period or the day on which the President notifies the Commission of his approval, as the case may be.

(k) *Period of effectiveness; termination of violation or modification or rescission of exclusion or order.—*

(1) Except as provided in subsections (f) and (j), any exclusion from entry or order under this section shall continue in effect until the Commission finds, and in the case of exclusion from entry notifies the Secretary of the Treasury, that the conditions which led to such exclusion from entry or order no longer exist.

(2) If any person who has previously been found by the Commission to be in violation of this section petitions the Commission for a determination that the petitioner is no longer in violation of this section or for a modification or rescission of an exclusion from entry or order under subsection (d), (e), (f), (g), or (i)—

(A) the burden of proof in any proceeding before the Commission regarding such petition shall be on the petitioner; and

(B) relief may be granted by the Commission with respect to such petition—

(i) on the basis of new evidence or evidence that could not have been presented at the prior proceeding, or

(ii) on grounds which would permit relief from a judgment or order under the Federal Rules of Civil Procedure.

(l) *Importation by or for United States.—*

Any exclusion from entry or order under subsection (d), (e), (f), (g), or (i), in cases based on a proceeding involving a patent, copyright, mask work, or design under subsection (a)(1), shall not apply to any articles imported by and for the use of the United States, or imported for, and to be used for, the United States with the authorization or consent of the Government. Whenever any article would have been excluded from entry or would not have been entered pursuant to the provisions of such subsections but for the operation of this subsection, an owner of the patent, copyright, mask work, or design adversely affected shall be entitled to reasonable and entire compensation in an action before the United States Court of Federal Claims pursuant to the procedures of section 1498 of title 28, United States Code.

19 U.S.C. § 1337

(m) *Definition of "United States".—*

For purposes of this section and sections 1338 and 1340, the term "United States" means the customs territory of the United States as defined in general note 2 of the Harmonized Tariff Schedule of the United States.

(n) *Disclosure of confidential information.—*

(1) Information submitted to the Commission or exchanged among the parties in connection with proceedings under this section which is properly designated as confidential pursuant to Commission rules may not be disclosed (except under a protective order issued under regulations of the Commission which authorizes limited disclosure of such information) to any person (other than a person described in paragraph (2)) without the consent of the person submitting it.

(2) Notwithstanding the prohibition contained in paragraph (1), information referred to in that paragraph may be disclosed to—

(A) an officer or employee of the Commission who is directly concerned with—

(i) carrying out the investigation or related proceeding in connection with which the information is submitted,

(ii) the administration of a bond posted pursuant to subsection (e), (f), or (j),

(iii) the administration or enforcement of an exclusion order issued pursuant to subsection (d), (e), or (g), a cease and desist order issued pursuant to subsection (f), or a consent order issued pursuant to subsection (c),

(iv) proceedings for the modification or rescission of a temporary or permanent order issued under subsection (d), (e), (f), (g), or (i), or a consent order issued under this section, or

(v) maintaining the administrative record of the investigation or related proceeding,

(B) an officer or employee of the United States Government who is directly involved in the review under subsection (j), or

(C) an officer or employee of the United States Customs Service who is directly involved in administering an exclusion from entry under subsection (d), (e), or (g) resulting from the investigation in connection with which the information is submitted.

19 U.S.C. § 1337

(June 17, 1930, ch. 497, §337, 46 Stat. 703; Aug. 20, 1958, Pub. L. 85-686, §9, 72 Stat. 679; Jan. 3, 1975, Pub. L. 93-618, §341, 88 Stat. 2053; July 26, 1979, Pub. L. 96-39, §§106, 1105, 93 Stat. 193, 310; Oct. 10, 1980, Pub. L. 96-417, §604, 94 Stat. 1744; Apr. 2, 1982, Pub. L. 97-164, §§160, 163, 96 Stat. 48, 49; Nov. 8, 1984, Pub. L. 98-620, §413, 98 Stat. 3362; Aug. 23, 1988, Pub. L. 100-418, §§1214, 1342, 102 Stat. 1157, 1212-15; Nov. 10, 1988, Pub. L. 100-647, §9001, 102 Stat. 3807; Oct. 29, 1992, Pub. L. 102-563, §3, 106 Stat. 4248; Dec. 8, 1994, Pub. L. 103-465, §321, 108 Stat. 4943; Oct. 11, 1996, Pub. L. 104-295, Title II(12), 110 Stat. 3527; Nov. 29, 1999, Pub. L. 106-113, §5005, 113 Stat. 1501A-593; Nov. 30, 2004, Pub. L. 108-429, §2004(d)(5), 118 Stat. 2592.)

19 U.S.C. § 1526   Merchandise bearing American trademark

(a) *Importation prohibited.*—Except as provided in subsection (d) of this section, it shall be unlawful to import into the United States any merchandise of foreign manufacture if such merchandise, or the label, sign, print, package, wrapper, or receptacle, bears a trademark owned by a citizen of, or by a corporation or association created or organized within, the United States, and registered in the Patent and Trademark Office by a person domiciled in the United States, under the provisions of sections 81 to 109 of title 15, and if a copy of the certificate of registration of such trademark is filed with the Secretary of the Treasury, in the manner provided in section 106 of said title 15, unless written consent of the owner of such trademark is produced at the time of making entry.

(b) *Seizure and forfeiture.*—Any such merchandise imported into the United States in violation of the provisions of this section shall be subject to seizure and forfeiture for violation of the customs laws.

(c) *Injunction and damages.*—Any person dealing in any such merchandise may be enjoined from dealing therein within the United States or may be required to export or destroy such merchandise or to remove or obliterate such trademark and shall be liable for the same damages and profits provided for wrongful use of a trade-mark, under the provisions of sections 81 to 109 of title 15.

(d) *Exemptions; publication in Federal Register; forfeitures; rules and regulations.*—

(1) The trademark provisions of this section and section 1124 of title 15, do not apply to the importation of articles accompanying any person arriving in the United States when such articles are for his personal use and not for sale if (A) such articles are within the limits of types and quantities determined by the Secretary pursuant to paragraph (2) of this subsection, and (B) such person has not been granted an exemption under this subsection within thirty days immediately preceding his arrival.

(2) The Secretary shall determine and publish in the Federal Register lists of the types of articles and the quantities of each which shall be entitled to the exemption provided by this subsection. In determining such quantities of particular types of trademarked articles, the Secretary shall give such consideration as he deems necessary to the numbers of such articles usually purchased at retail for personal use.

(3) If any article which has been exempted from the restrictions on importation of the trademark laws under this subsection is sold within one year after the date of importation, such article, or its value (to be recovered from the importer), is subject to forfeiture. A sale pursuant to a judicial order or in liquidation of the estate of a decedent is not subject to the provisions of this paragraph.

(4) The Secretary may prescribe such rules and regulations as may be necessary to carry out the provisions of this subsection.

(e) *Merchandise bearing counterfeit mark; seizure and forfeiture; disposition of seized goods.* — Any such merchandise bearing a counterfeit mark (within the meaning of section 1127 of title 15) imported into the United States in violation of the provisions of section 1124 of title 15, shall be seized and, in the absence of the written consent of the trademark owner, forfeited for violations of the customs laws. Upon seizure of such merchandise, the Secretary shall notify the owner of the trademark, and shall, after forfeiture, destroy the merchandise. Alternatively, if the merchandise is not unsafe or a hazard to health, and the Secretary has the consent of the trademark owner, the Secretary may obliterate the trademark where feasible and dispose of the goods seized —

(1) by delivery to such Federal, State, and local government agencies as in the opinion of the Secretary have a need for such merchandise,

(2) by gift to such eleemosynary institutions as in the opinion of the Secretary have a need for such merchandise, or

(3) more than 90 days after the date of forfeiture, by sale by the Customs Service at public auction under such regulations as the Secretary prescribes, except that before making any such sale the Secretary shall determine that no Federal, State, or local government agency or eleemosynary institution has established a need for such merchandise under paragraph (1) or (2).

19 U.S.C. § 1526

(f) *Civil Penalties.* — (1) Any person who directs, assists financially or other-wise, or aids and abets the importation of merchandise for sale or public distribution that is seized under subsection (e) shall be subject to a civil fine.

(2) For the first such seizure, the fine shall be not more than the value that the merchandise would have had if it were genuine, according to the manufacturer's suggested retail price, determined under regulations promulgated by the Secretary.

(3) For the second seizure and thereafter, the fine shall be not more than twice the value that the merchandise would have had if it were genuine, as determined under regulations promulgated by the Secretary.

(4) The imposition of a fine under this subsection shall be within the discretion of the Customs Service, and shall be in addition to any other civil or criminal penalty or other remedy authorized by law.

(June 17, 1930, ch 497, Title IV, Part III, §526, 46 Stat. 741; Oct. 3, 1978, Pub. L. 95-410, Title II, §211 (a), (c), 92 Stat. 903; Dec. 8, 1993, Pub. L. 103 — 182, Title VI, Subtitle C, §663, 107 Stat. 2214; July 2, 1996, Pub. L. 104-153, §§9-10, 110 Stat. 1388.)

19 U.S.C. § 2411   Actions by United States Trade Representative
[Section 301][5]

(a) *Mandatory action.* —

(1) If the United States Trade Representative determines under section 304(a)(1) that —

(A) the rights of the United States under any trade agreement are being denied; or

(B) an act, policy, or practice of a foreign country —

(i) violates, or is inconsistent with, the provisions of, or otherwise denies benefits to the United States under, any trade agreement, or

(ii) is unjustifiable and burdens or restricts United States com-merce;

the Trade Representative shall take action authorized in subsection (c), subject to the specific direction, if any, of the President regarding any such action, and shall take all other appropriate and feasible action within the power of the President that the President may direct the Trade Repre-

---

[5] *Ed. Note:* The bracketed references are to the section designations of the Trade Act of 1974.

sentative to take under this subsection, to enforce such rights or to obtain the elimination of such act, policy, or practice. Actions may be taken that are within the power of the President with respect to trade in any goods or services, or with respect to any other area of pertinent relations with the foreign country.

(2) The Trade Representative is not required to take action under paragraph (1) in any case in which—

(A) the Contracting Parties to the General Agreement on Tariffs and Trade have determined, a panel of experts has reported to the Contracting Parties, or a ruling issued under the formal dispute settlement proceeding provided under any other trade agreement finds, that—

(i) the rights of the United States under a trade agreement are not being denied, or

(ii) the act, policy, or practice—

(I) is not a violation of, or inconsistent with, the rights of the United States, or

(II) does not deny, nullify, or impair benefits to the United States under any trade agreement; or

(B) the Trade Representative finds that—

(i) the foreign country is taking satisfactory measures to grant the rights of the United States under a trade agreement,

(ii) the foreign country has—

(I) agreed to eliminate or phase out the act, policy, or practice, or

(II) agreed to an imminent solution to the burden or restriction on United States commerce that is satisfactory to the Trade Representative,

(iii) it is impossible for the foreign country to achieve the results described in clause (i) or (ii), as appropriate, but the foreign country agrees to provide to the United States compensatory trade benefits that are satisfactory to the Trade Representative,

(iv) in extraordinary cases, where the taking of action under this subsection would have an adverse impact on the United States economy substantially out of proportion to the benefits of such ac-

19 U.S.C. § 2411

tion, taking into account the impact of not taking such action on the credibility of the provisions of this chapter, or

(v) the taking of action under this subsection would cause serious harm to the national security of the United States.

(3) Any action taken under paragraph (1) to eliminate an act, policy, or practice shall be devised so as to affect goods or services of the foreign country in an amount that is equivalent in value to the burden or restriction being imposed by that country on United States commerce.

(b) *Discretionary action.*—If the Trade Representative determines under section 304(a)(1) that—

(1) an act, policy, or practice of a foreign country is unreasonable or discriminatory and burdens or restricts United States commerce, and

(2) action by the United States is appropriate, the Trade Representative shall take all appropriate and feasible action authorized under subsection (c), subject to the specific direction, if any, of the President regarding any such action, and all other appropriate and feasible action within the power of the President that the President may direct the Trade Representative to take under this subsection, to obtain the elimination of that act, policy, or practice. Actions may be taken that are within the power of the President with respect to trade in any goods or services, or with respect to any other area of pertinent relations with the foreign country.

(c) *Scope of authority.*—

(1) For purposes of carrying out the provisions of subsection (a) or (b), the Trade Representative is authorized to—

(A) suspend, withdraw, or prevent the application of, benefits of trade agreement concessions to carry out a trade agreement with the foreign country referred to in such subsection;

(B) impose duties or other import restrictions on the goods of, and, notwithstanding any other provision of law, fees or restrictions on the services of, such foreign country for such time as the Trade Representative determines appropriate;

(C) in a case in which the act, policy, or practice also fails to meet the eligibility criteria for receiving duty-free treatment under subsections (b) and (c) of section 502 of this Act, subsections (b) and (c) of section 212 of the Caribbean Basin Economic Recovery Act (19 U.S.C. 2702(b) and (c)), or subsections (c) and (d) of section 203 of the Andean Trade Preference Act (19 U.S.C. 3202(c) and (d)), withdraw, limit, or suspend such treatment under such provisions, notwithstanding the provisions of subsection (a)(3) of this section; or

(D) enter into binding agreements with such foreign country, that commit such foreign country to—

(i) eliminate, or phase out, the act, policy, or practice that is the subject of the action to be taken under subsection (a) or (b),

(ii) eliminate any burden or restriction on United States commerce resulting from such act, policy, or practice, or

(iii) provide the United States with compensatory trade benefits that—

(I) are satisfactory to the Trade Representative, and

(II) meet the requirements of paragraph (4).

(2) (A) Notwithstanding any other provision of law governing any service sector access authorization, and in addition to the authority conferred in paragraph (1), the Trade Representative may, for purposes of carrying out the provisions of subsection (a) or (b)—

(i) restrict, in the manner and to the extent the Trade Representative determines appropriate, the terms and conditions of any such authorization, or

(ii) deny the issuance of any such authorization.

(B) Actions described in subparagraph (A) may only be taken under this section with respect to service sector access authorizations granted, or applications therefor pending, on or after the date on which—

(i) a petition is filed under section 302(a), or

(ii) a determination to initiate an investigation is made by the Trade Representative under section 302(b).

(C) Before the Trade Representative takes any action under this section involving the imposition of fees or other restrictions on the services of a foreign country, the Trade Representative shall, if the services involved are subject to regulation by any agency of the Federal Government or of any State, consult, as appropriate, with the head of the agency concerned.

19 U.S.C. § 2411

(3) The actions the Trade Representative is authorized to take under subsection (a) or (b) may be taken against any goods or economic sector—

(A) on a nondiscriminatory basis or solely against the foreign country described in such subsection, and

(B) without regard to whether or not such goods or economic sector were involved in the act, policy, or practice that is the subject of such action.

(4) Any trade agreement described in paragraph (1)(D)(iii) shall provide compensatory trade benefits that benefit the economic sector which includes the domestic industry that would benefit from the elimination of the act, policy, or practice that is the subject of the action to be taken under subsection (a) or (b), or benefit the economic sector as closely related as possible to such economic sector, unless—

(A) the provision of such trade benefits is not feasible, or

(B) trade benefits that benefit any other economic sector would be more satisfactory than such trade benefits.

(5) If the Trade Representative determines that actions to be taken under subsection (a) or (b) are to be in the form of import restrictions, the Trade Representative shall—

(A) give preference to the imposition of duties over the imposition of other import restrictions, and

(B) if an import restriction other than a duty is imposed, consider substituting, on an incremental basis, an equivalent duty for such other import restriction.

(6) Any action taken by the Trade Representative under this section with respect to export targeting shall, to the extent possible, reflect the full benefit level of the export targeting to the beneficiary over the period during which the action taken has an effect.

(d) *Definitions and special rules.*—For purposes of this chapter—

(1) The term "commerce" includes, but is not limited to—

(A) services (including transfers of information) associated with international trade, whether or not such services are related to specific goods, and

(B) foreign direct investment by United States persons with implications for trade in goods or services.

(2) An act, policy, or practice of a foreign country that burdens or restricts United States commerce may include the provision, directly or indirectly, by that foreign country of subsidies for the construction of vessels used in the commercial transportation by water of goods between foreign countries and the United States.

(3) (A) An act, policy, or practice is unreasonable if the act, policy, or practice, while not necessarily in violation of, or inconsistent with, the international legal rights of the United States, is otherwise unfair and inequitable.

(B) Acts, policies, and practices that are unreasonable include, but are not limited to, any act, policy, or practice, or any combination of acts, policies, or practices, which—

    (i) denies fair and equitable—

        (I) opportunities for the establishment of an enterprise,

        (II) provision of adequate and effective protection of intellectual property rights notwithstanding the fact that the foreign country may be in compliance with the specific obligations of the Agreement on Trade-Related Aspects of Intellectual Property Rights referred to in section 101(d)(15) of the Uruguay Round Agreements Act,

        (III) nondiscriminatory market access opportunities for United States persons that rely upon intellectual property protection, or

        (IV) market opportunities, including the toleration by a foreign government of systematic anticompetitive activities by enterprises or among enterprises in the foreign country that have the effect of restricting, on a basis that is inconsistent with commercial considerations, access of United States goods or services to a foreign market,

    (ii) constitutes export targeting, or

    (iii) constitutes a persistent pattern of conduct that—

        (I) denies workers the right of association,

19 U.S.C. § 2411

(II) denies workers the right to organize and bargain collectively,

(III) permits any form of forced or compulsory labor,

(IV) fails to provide a minimum age for the employment of children, or

(V) fails to provide standards for minimum wages, hours of work, and occupational safety and health of workers.

(C) (i) Acts, policies, and practices of a foreign country described in subparagraph (B)(iii) shall not be treated as being unreasonable if the Trade Representative determines that—

(I) the foreign country has taken, or is taking, actions that demonstrate a significant and tangible overall advancement in providing throughout the foreign country (including any designated zone within the foreign country) the rights and other standards described in the subclauses of subparagraph (B)(iii), or

(II) such acts, policies, and practices are not inconsistent with the level of economic development of the foreign country.

(ii) The Trade Representative shall publish in the Federal Register any determination made under clause (i), together with a description of the facts on which such determination is based.

(D) For purposes of determining whether any act, policy, or practice is unreasonable, reciprocal opportunities in the United States for foreign nationals and firms shall be taken into account, to the extent appropriate.

(E) The term "export targeting" means any government plan or scheme consisting of a combination of coordinated actions (whether carried out severally or jointly) that are bestowed on a specific enterprise, industry, or group thereof, the effect of which is to assist the enterprise, industry, or group to become more competitive in the export of a class or kind of merchandise.

(F) (i) For the purposes of subparagraph (B)(i)(II), adequate and effective protection of intellectual property rights includes adequate and effective means under the laws of the foreign country for persons who are not citizens or nationals of such country to secure, exercise, and enforce rights and enjoy commercial benefits relating to patents, trademarks, copyrights and related rights, mask works, trade secrets, and plant breeder's rights.

(ii) For purposes of subparagraph (B)(i)(IV), the denial of fair and equitable nondiscriminatory market access opportunities includes restrictions on market access related to the use, exploitation, or enjoyment of commercial benefits derived from exercising intellectual property rights in protected works or fixations or products embodying protected works.

(4) (A) An act, policy, or practice is unjustifiable if the act, policy, or practice is in violation of, or inconsistent with, the international legal rights of the United States.

(B) Acts, policies, and practices that are unjustifiable include, but are not limited to, any act, policy, or practice described in subparagraph (A) which denies national or most-favored-nation treatment or the right of establishment or protection of intellectual property rights.

(5) Acts, policies, and practices that are discriminatory include, when appropriate, any act, policy, and practice which denies national or most-favored-nation treatment to United States goods, services, or investment.

(6) The term "service sector access authorization" means any license, permit, order, or other authorization, issued under the authority of Federal law, that permits a foreign supplier of services access to the United States market in a service sector concerned.

(7) The term "foreign country" includes any foreign instrumentality. Any possession or territory of a foreign country that is administered separately for customs purposes shall be treated as a separate foreign country.

(8) The term "Trade Representative" means the United States Trade Representative.

(9) The term "interested persons", only for purposes of sections 302(a)(4)(B), 304(b)(1)(A), 306(c)(2), and 307(a)(2), includes, but is not limited to, domestic firms and workers, representatives of consumer interests, United States product exporters, and any industrial user of any goods or services that may be affected by actions taken under subsection (a) or (b).

(Jan. 3, 1975, Pub. L. 93-618, §301, as added July 26, 1979, Pub. L. 96-39, §901, 93 Stat. 295; Oct. 30, 1984, Pub. L. 98-573, §304, 98 Stat. 3002, 3005; Aug. 23, 1988, Pub. L. 100-418, §1301, 102 Stat. 1164; Dec. 8, 1994, Pub. L. 103-465, §314, 108 Stat. 4939; Oct. 11, 1996, Pub. L. 104-295, Title III(4), 110 Stat. 3528.)

19 U.S.C. § 2411

19 U.S.C. § 2412   **Initiation of investigations** [Section 302]

(a) *Petitions.* —

(1) Any interested person may file a petition with the Trade Representative requesting that action be taken under section 301 and setting forth the allegations in support of the request.

(2) The Trade Representative shall review the allegations in any petition filed under paragraph (1) and, not later than 45 days after the date on which the Trade Representative received the petition, shall determine whether to initiate an investigation.

(3) If the Trade Representative determines not to initiate an investigation with respect to a petition, the Trade Representative shall inform the petitioner of the reasons therefor and shall publish notice of the determination, together with a summary of such reasons, in the Federal Register.

(4) If the Trade Representative makes an affirmative determination under paragraph (2) with respect to a petition, the Trade Representative shall initiate an investigation regarding the issues raised in the petition. The Trade Representative shall publish a summary of the petition in the Federal Register and shall, as soon as possible, provide opportunity for the presentation of views concerning the issues, including a public hearing —

    (A) within the 30-day period beginning on the date of the affirmative determination (or on a date after such period if agreed to by the petitioner) if a public hearing within such period is requested in the petition, or

    (B) at such other time if a timely request therefor is made by the petitioner or by any interested person.

(b) *Initiation of investigation by means other than petition.* —

    (1) (A) If the Trade Representative determines that an investigation should be initiated under this chapter with respect to any matter in order to determine whether the matter is actionable under section 301, the Trade Representative shall publish such determination in the Federal Register and shall initiate such investigation.

    (B) The Trade Representative shall, before making any determination under subparagraph (A), consult with appropriate committees established pursuant to section 135.

    (2) (A) By no later than the date that is 30 days after the date on which a country is identified under section 182(a)(2), the Trade Representative

shall initiate an investigation under this chapter with respect to any act, policy, or practice of that country that—

(i) was the basis for such identification, and

(ii) is not at that time the subject of any other investigation or action under this chapter.

(B) The Trade Representative is not required under subparagraph (A) to initiate an investigation under this chapter with respect to any act, policy, or practice of a foreign country if the Trade Representative determines that the initiation of the investigation would be detrimental to United States economic interests.

(C) If the Trade Representative makes a determination under subparagraph (B) not to initiate an investigation, the Trade Representative shall submit to the Congress a written report setting forth, in detail—

(i) the reasons for the determination, and

(ii) the United States economic interests that would be adversely affected by the investigation.

(D) The Trade Representative shall, from time to time, consult with the Register of Copyrights, the Under Secretary of Commerce for Intellectual Property and Director of the United States Patent and Trademark Office, and other appropriate officers of the Federal Government, during any investigation initiated under this chapter by reason of subparagraph (A).

(c) *Discretion.*—In determining whether to initiate an investigation under subsection (a) or (b) of any act, policy, or practice that is enumerated in any provision of section 301(d), the Trade Representative shall have discretion to determine whether action under section 301 would be effective in addressing such act, policy, or practice.

(Jan. 3, 1975, Pub. L. 93-618, §302, as added July 26, 1979, Pub. L. 96-39, §901, 93 Stat. 296; Oct. 30, 1984, Pub. L. 98-573, §304, 98 Stat. 3003; Aug. 23, 1988, Pub. L. 100-418, §1301, 102 Stat. 1168; Nov. 29, 1999, Pub. L. 106-113, §4732, 1113 Stat. 1501A-581.)

19 U.S.C. § 2413   Consultation upon initiation of investigation
[Section 303]

(a) *In general.*—

(1) On the date on which an investigation is initiated under section 302, the Trade Representative, on behalf of the United States, shall request

consultations with the foreign country concerned regarding the issues involved in such investigation.

(2) If the investigation initiated under section 302 involves a trade agreement and a mutually acceptable resolution is not reached before the earlier of—

(A) the close of the consultation period, if any, specified in the trade agreement, or

(B) the 150th day after the day on which consultation was commenced,

the Trade Representative shall promptly request proceedings on the matter under the formal dispute settlement procedures provided under such agreement.

(3) The Trade Representative shall seek information and advice from the petitioner (if any) and the appropriate committees established pursuant to section 135 in preparing United States presentations for consultations and dispute settlement proceedings.

(b) *Delay of request for consultations.—*

(1) Notwithstanding the provisions of subsection (a)—

(A) the United States Trade Representative may, after consulting with the petitioner (if any), delay for up to 90 days any request for consultations under subsection (a) for the purpose of verifying or improving the petition to ensure an adequate basis for consultation, and

(B) if such consultations are delayed by reason of subparagraph (A), each time limitation under section 304 shall be extended for the period of such delay.

(2) The Trade Representative shall—

(A) publish notice of any delay under paragraph (1) in the Federal Register, and

(B) report to Congress on the reasons for such delay in the report required under section 309(a)(3).

(Jan. 3, 1975, Pub. L. 93-618, §303, as added July 26, 1979, Pub. L. 96-39, §901, 93 Stat. 297; Oct. 30, 1984, Pub. L. 98-573, §§304, 306, 98 Stat. 3004-05, 3012; Aug. 23, 1988, Pub. L. 100-418, §1301, 102 Stat. 1170.)

19 U.S.C. § 2413

19 U.S.C. § 2414   Determination by the Trade Representative
[Section 304]

(a) *In general.* —

(1) On the basis of the investigation initiated under section 302 and the consultations (and the proceedings, if applicable) under section 303, the Trade Representative shall—

(A) determine whether—

(i) the rights to which the United States is entitled under any trade agreement are being denied, or

(ii) any act, policy, or practice described in subsection (a)(1)(B) or (b)(1) of section 301 exists, and

(B) if the determination made under subparagraph (A) is affirmative, determine what action, if any, the Trade Representative should take under subsection (a) or (b) of section 301.

(2) The Trade Representative shall make the determinations required under paragraph (1) on or before—

(A) in the case of an investigation involving a trade agreement, except an investigation initiated pursuant to section 302(b)(2)(A) involving rights under the Agreement on Trade-Related Aspects of Intellectual Property Rights (referred to in section 101(d)(15) of the Uruguay Round Agreements Act) or the GATT 1994 (as defined in section 2(1)(B) of that Act) relating to products subject to intellectual property protection, the earlier of—

(i) the date that is 30 days after the date on which the dispute settlement procedure is concluded, or

(ii) the date that is 18 months after the date on which the investigation is initiated, or

(B) in all cases not described in subparagraph (A) or paragraph (3), the date that is 12 months after the date on which the investigation is initiated.

(3) (A) If an investigation is initiated under this chapter by reason of section 302(b)(2) and—

(i) the Trade Representative considers that rights under the Agreement on Trade-Related Aspects of Intellectual Property Rights or the GATT 1994 relating to products subject to intellectual property protection are involved, the Trade Representative shall make the determination required under paragraph (1) not later than 30 days after the date on which the dispute settlement procedure is concluded; or

(ii) the Trade Representative does not consider that a trade agreement, including the Agreement on Trade-Related Aspects of Intellectual Property Rights, is involved or does not make a determination described in subparagraph (B) with respect to such investigation, the Trade Representative shall make the determinations required under paragraph (1) with respect to such investigation not later than the date that is 6 months after the date on which such investigation is initiated.

(B) If the Trade Representative determines with respect to an investigation initiated by reason of section 302(b)(2) (other than an investigation involving a trade agreement) that—

(i) complex or complicated issues are involved in the investigation that require additional time,

(ii) the foreign country involved in the investigation is making substantial progress in drafting or implementing legislative or administrative measures that will provide adequate and effective protection of intellectual property rights, or

(iii) such foreign country is undertaking enforcement measures to provide adequate and effective protection of intellectual property rights,

the Trade Representative shall publish in the Federal Register notice of such determination and shall make the determinations required under paragraph (1) with respect to such investigation by no later than the date that is 9 months after the date on which such investigation is initiated.

(4) In any case in which a dispute is not resolved before the close of the minimum dispute settlement period provided for in a trade agreement, the Trade Representative, within 15 days after the close of such dispute settlement period, shall submit a report to Congress setting forth the reasons why the dispute was not resolved within the minimum dispute settlement period, the status of the case at the close of the period, and the prospects for resolution. For purposes of this paragraph, the minimum

dispute settlement period provided for under any such trade agreement is the total period of time that results if all stages of the formal dispute settlement procedures are carried out within the time limitations specified in the agreement, but computed without regard to any extension authorized under the agreement at any stage.

(b) *Consultation before determinations.* —

(1) Before making the determinations required under subsection (a)(1), the Trade Representative, unless expeditious action is required—

(A) shall provide an opportunity (after giving not less than 30 days notice thereof) for the presentation of views by interested persons, including a public hearing if requested by any interested person,

(B) shall obtain advice from the appropriate committees established pursuant to section 135, and

(C) may request the views of the United States International Trade Commission regarding the probable impact on the economy of the United States of the taking of action with respect to any goods or service.

(2) If the Trade Representative does not comply with the requirements of subparagraphs (A) and (B) of paragraph (1) because expeditious action is required, the Trade Representative shall, after making the determinations under subsection (a)(1), comply with such subparagraphs.

(c) *Publication.*—The Trade Representative shall publish in the Federal Register any determination made under subsection (a)(1), together with a description of the facts on which such determination is based.

(Jan. 3, 1975, Pub. L. 93-618, §304, as added July 26, 1979, Pub. L. 96-39, §901, 93 Stat. 297; Oct. 30, 1984, Pub. L. 98-573, §§304, 306, 98 Stat. 3004-05, 3012; Aug. 23, 1988, Pub. L. 100-418, §1301, 102 Stat. 1170; Dec. 8, 1994, Pub. L. 103-465, §314, 108 Stat. 4939; Oct. 11, 1996, Pub. L. 104-295, Title III(6), 110 Stat. 3528; Nov. 30, 2004, Pub. L. 108-429, §2201, 118 Stat. 2598.)

19 U.S.C. § 2415   Implementation of actions [Section 305]

(a) *Actions to be taken under section 301.* —

(1) Except as provided in paragraph (2), the Trade Representative shall implement the action the Trade Representative determines under section 304(a)(1)(B) to take under section 301, subject to the specific direction, if

any, of the President regarding any such action, by no later than the date that is 30 days after the date on which such determination is made.

(2) (A) Except as otherwise provided in this paragraph, the Trade Representative may delay, by not more than 180 days, the implementation of any action that is to be taken under section 301 —

> (i) if —

>> (I) in the case of an investigation initiated under section 302(a), the petitioner requests a delay, or

>> (II) in the case of an investigation initiated under section 302(b)(1) or to which section 304(a)(3)(B) applies, a delay is requested by a majority of the representatives of the domestic industry that would benefit from the action, or

> (ii) if the Trade Representative determines that substantial progress is being made, or that a delay is necessary or desirable, to obtain United States rights or a satisfactory solution with respect to the acts, policies, or practices that are the subject of the action.

(B) The Trade Representative may not delay under subparagraph (A) the implementation of any action that is to be taken under section 301 with respect to any investigation to which section 304(a)(3)(A) (ii) applies.

(C) The Trade Representative may not delay under subparagraph (A) the implementation of any action that is to be taken under section 301 with respect to any investigation to which section 304(a)(3)(B) applies by more than 90 days.

(b) *Alternative actions in certain cases of export targeting.* —

(1) If the Trade Representative makes an affirmative determination under section 304(a)(1)(A) involving export targeting by a foreign country and determines to take no action under section 301 with respect to such affirmation determination, the Trade Representative —

(A) shall establish an advisory panel to recommend measures which will promote the competitiveness of the domestic industry affected by the export targeting,

(B) on the basis of the report of such panel submitted under paragraph (2)(B) and subject to the specific direction, if any, of the President, may take any administrative actions authorized under any other provision of law, and, if necessary, propose legislation to implement any other actions, that would restore or improve the international competitiveness of the domestic industry affected by the export targeting, and

(C) shall, by no later than the date that is 30 days after the date on which the report of such panel is submitted under paragraph (2)(B), submit a report to the Congress on the administrative actions taken, and legislative proposals made, under subparagraph (B) with respect to the domestic industry affected by the export targeting.

(2) (A) The advisory panels established under paragraph (1)(A) shall consist of individuals appointed by the Trade Representative who —

(i) earn their livelihood in the private sector of the economy, including individuals who represent management and labor in the domestic industry affected by the export targeting that is the subject of the affirmative determination made under section 304(a)(1)(A), and

(ii) by education or experience, are qualified to serve on the advisory panel.

(B) By no later than the date that is 6 months after the date on which an advisory panel is established under paragraph (1)(A), the advisory panel shall submit to the Trade Representative and to the Congress a report on measures that the advisory panel recommends be taken by the United States to promote the competitiveness of the domestic industry affected by the export targeting that is the subject of the affirmative determination made under section 304(a)(1)(A).

(Jan. 3, 1975, Pub. L. 93-618, §305, as added July 26, 1979, Pub. L. 96-39, §901, 93 Stat. 299; Oct. 30, 1984, Pub. L. 98-573, §304, 98 Stat. 3006; Aug. 23, 1988, Pub. L. 100-418, §1301, 102 Stat. 1172; Nov. 30, 2004, Pub. L. 108-429, §2201, 118 Stat. 2599.)

19 U.S.C. § 2416   Monitoring of foreign compliance [Section 306]

(a) *In general.* — The Trade Representative shall monitor the implementation of each measure undertaken, or agreement that is entered into, by a foreign country to provide a satisfactory resolution of a matter subject to investigation under this chapter or subject to dispute settlement proceedings to enforce the rights of the United States under a trade agreement providing for such proceedings.

(b) *Further action.*—

(1) *In general.*—If, on the basis of the monitoring carried out under subsection (a), the Trade Representative considers that a foreign country is not satisfactorily implementing a measure or agreement referred to in subsection (a), the Trade Representative shall determine what further action the Trade Representative shall take under section 301(a). For purposes of section 301, any such determination shall be treated as a determination made under section 304(a)(1).

(2) *WTO dispute settlement recommendations.*—

(A) *Failure to implement recommendation.*—If the measure or agreement referred to in subsection (a) concerns the implementation of a recommendation made pursuant to dispute settlement proceedings under the World Trade Organization, and the Trade Representative considers that the foreign country has failed to implement it, the Trade Representative shall make the determination in paragraph (1) no later than 30 days after the expiration of the reasonable period of time provided for such implementation under paragraph 21 of the Understanding on Rules and Procedures Governing the Settlement of Disputes that is referred to in section 101(d)(16) of the Uruguay Round Agreements Act.

(B) *Revision of retaliation list and action.*—

(i) *In general.*—Except as provided in clause (ii), in the event that the United States initiates a retaliation list or takes any other action described in section 301(c)(1)(A) or (B) against the goods of a foreign country or countries because of the failure of such country or countries to implement the recommendation made pursuant to a dispute settlement proceeding under the World Trade Organization, the Trade Representative shall periodically revise the list or action to affect other goods of the country or countries that have failed to implement the recommendation.

(ii) *Exception.*—The Trade Representative is not required to revise the retaliation list or the action described in clause (i) with respect to a country, if—

(I) the Trade Representative determines that implementation of a recommendation made pursuant to a dispute settlement proceeding described in clause (i) by the country is imminent; or

(II) the Trade Representative together with the petitioner involved in the initial investigation under this chapter (or if no petition was filed, the affected United States industry) agree that it is unnecessary to revise the retaliation list.

(C) *Schedule for revising list or action.*—The Trade Representative shall, 120 days after the date the retaliation list or other section 301(a) action is first taken, and every 180 days thereafter, review the list or action taken and revise, in whole or in part, the list or action to affect other goods of the subject country or countries.

(D) *Standards for revising list or action.*—In revising any list or action against a country or countries under this subsection, the Trade Representative shall act in a manner that is most likely to result in the country or countries implementing the recommendations adopted in the dispute settlement proceeding or in achieving a mutually satisfactory solution to the issue that gave rise to the dispute settlement proceeding. The Trade Representative shall consult with the petitioner, if any, involved in the initial investigation under this chapter.

(E) *Retaliation list.*—The term "retaliation list" means the list of products of a foreign country or countries that have failed to comply with the report of the panel or Appellate Body of the WTO and with respect to which the Trade Representative is imposing duties above the level that would otherwise be imposed under the Harmonized Tariff Schedule of the United States.

(F) *Requirement to include reciprocal goods on retaliation list.*—The Trade Representative shall include on the retaliation list, and on any revised lists, reciprocal goods of the industries affected by the failure of the foreign country or countries to implement the recommendation made pursuant to a dispute settlement proceeding under the World Trade Organization, except in cases where existing retaliation and its corresponding preliminary retaliation list do not already meet this requirement.

(c) *Consultations.*—Before making any determination under subsection (b), the Trade Representative shall—

(1) consult with the petitioner, if any, involved in the initial investigation under this chapter and with representatives of the domestic industry concerned; and

(2) provide an opportunity for the presentation of views by interested persons.

(Jan. 3, 1975, Pub. L. 93-618, §306, as added July 26, 1979, Pub. L. 96-39, §901, 93 Stat. 299; Aug. 23, 1988, Pub. L. 100-418, §1301, 102 Stat. 1173; Dec. 8, 1994, Pub. L. 103-465, §314, 108 Stat. 4939; May. 18, 2000, Pub. L. 106-200, §407, 114 Stat. 293.)

19 U.S.C. § 2417   Modification and termination of actions [Section 307]

(a) *In general.* —

(1) The Trade Representative may modify or terminate any action, subject to the specific direction, if any, of the President with respect to such action, that is being taken under section 301 if —

(A) any of the conditions described in section 301(a)(2) exist,

(B) the burden or restriction on United States commerce of the denial rights, or of the acts, policies, and practices, that are the subject of such action has increased or decreased, or

(C) such action is being taken under section 301(b) and is no longer appropriate.

(2) Before taking any action under paragraph (1) to modify or terminate any action taken under section 301, the Trade Representative shall consult with the petitioner, if any, and with representatives of the domestic industry concerned, and shall provide opportunity for the presentation of views by other interested persons affected by the proposed modification or termination concerning the effects of the modification or termination and whether any modification or termination of the action is appropriate.

(b) *Notice; report to Congress.* — The Trade Representative shall promptly publish in the Federal Register notice of, and report in writing to the Congress with respect to, any modification or termination of any action taken under section 301 and the reasons therefor.

(c) *Review of necessity.* —

(1) If —

(A) a particular action has been taken under section 301 during any 4-year period, and

(B) neither the petitioner nor any representative of the domestic industry which benefits from such action has submitted to the Trade

Representative during the last 60 days of such 4-year period a written request for the continuation of such action,

such action shall terminate at the close of such 4-year period.

(2) The Trade Representative shall notify by mail the petitioner and representatives of the domestic industry described in paragraph (1)(B) of any termination of action by reason of paragraph (1) at least 60 days before the date of such termination.

(3) If a request is submitted to the Trade Representative under paragraph (1)(B) to continue taking a particular action under section 301, the Trade Representative shall conduct a review of—

(A) the effectiveness in achieving the objectives of section 301 of—

(i) such action, and

(ii) other actions that could be taken (including actions against other products or services) and

(B) the effects of such actions on the United States economy, including consumers.

(Jan. 3, 1975, Pub. L. 93-618, §307, as added Aug. 23, 1988, Pub. L. 100-418, §1301, 102 Stat. 1174.)

19 U.S.C. § 2418   Request for information [Section 308]

(a) *In general.*—Under receipt of written request therefor from any person, the Trade Representative shall make available to that person information (other than that to which confidentiality applies) concerning—

(1) the nature and extent of a specific trade policy or practice of a foreign country with respect to particular goods, services, investment, or intellectual property rights, to the extent that such information is available to the Trade Representative or other Federal agencies;

(2) United States rights under any trade agreement and the remedies which may be available under that agreement and under the laws of the United States; and

(3) past and present domestic and international proceedings or actions with respect to the policy or practice concerned.

(b) *If information not available.*—If information that is requested by a person under subsection (a) is not available to the Trade Representative or other

Federal agencies, the Trade Representative shall, within 30 days after receipt of the request—

(1) request the information from the foreign government; or

(2) decline to request the information and inform the person in writing of the reasons for refusal.

(c) *Certain business information not made available.*—

(1) Except as provided in paragraph (2), and notwithstanding any other provision of law (including section 552 of title 5, United States Code), no information requested and received by the Trade Representative in aid of any investigation under this chapter shall be made available to any person if—

(A) the person providing such information certifies that—

(i) such information is business confidential,

(ii) the disclosure of such information would endanger trade secrets or profitability, and

(iii) such information is not generally available;

(B) the Trade Representative determines that such certification is well-founded; and

(C) to the extent required in regulations prescribed by the Trade Representative, the person providing such information provides an adequate nonconfidential summary of such information.

(2) The Trade Representative may—

(A) use such information, or make such information available (in his own discretion) to any employee of the Federal Government for use, in any investigation under this chapter, or

(B) may make such information available to any other person in a form which cannot be associated with, or otherwise identify, the person providing the information.

(Jan. 3, 1975, Pub. L. 93-618, §308, as added Aug. 23, 1988, Pub. L. 100-418, §1301, 102 Stat. 1175.)

19 U.S.C. § 2419   Administration [Section 309]

The Trade Representative shall—

(1) issue regulations concerning the filing of petitions and the conduct of investigations and hearings under this subchapter,

(2) keep the petitioner regularly informed of all determinations and developments regarding the investigation conducted with respect to the petition under this chapter, including the reasons for any undue delays, and

(3) submit a report to the House of Representatives and the Senate semiannually describing—

(A) the petitions filed and the determinations made (and reasons therefor) under section 302,

(B) developments in, and the current status of, each investigation or proceeding under this chapter,

(C) the actions taken, or the reasons for no action, by the Trade Representative under section 301 with respect to investigations conducted under this chapter, and

(D) the commercial effects of actions taken under section 301.

(Jan. 3, 1975, Pub. L. 93-618, §309, as added Aug. 23, 1988, Pub. L. 100-418, §1301, 102 Stat. 1175-76.)

19 U.S.C. § 2242   Identification of countries that deny adequate protection, or market access, for intellectual property rights [Section 182]

(a) *In general.*—By no later than the date that is 30 days after the date on which the annual report is submitted to Congressional committees under section 181(b) [19 U.S.C. §2241(b)], the United States Trade Representative (hereafter in this section referred to as the "Trade Representative") shall identify—

(1) those foreign countries that—

(A) deny adequate and effective protection of intellectual property rights, or

(B) deny fair and equitable market access to United States persons that rely upon intellectual property protection, and

(2) those foreign countries identified under paragraph (1) that are determined by the Trade Representative to be priority foreign countries.

(b) *Special rules for identifications.—*

(1) In identifying priority foreign countries under subsection (a)(2), the Trade Representative shall only identify those foreign countries—

(A) that have the most onerous or egregious acts, policies, or practices that—

(i) deny adequate and effective intellectual property rights, or

(ii) deny fair and equitable market access to United States persons that rely upon intellectual property protection,

(B) whose acts, policies, or practices described in subparagraph (A) have the greatest adverse impact (actual or potential) on the relevant United States products, and

(C) that are not—

(i) entering into good faith negotiations, or

(ii) making significant progress in bilateral or multilateral negotiations,

to provide adequate and effective protection of intellectual property rights.

(2) In identifying priority foreign countries under subsection (a)(2), the Trade Representative shall—

(A) consult with the Register of Copyrights, the Under Secretary of Commerce for Intellectual Property and Director of the United States Patent and Trademark Office, other appropriate officers of the Federal Government, and

(B) take into account information from such sources as may be available to the Trade Representative and such information as may be submitted to the Trade Representative by interested persons, including information contained in reports submitted under section 181(b) [19 U.S.C. §224(b)] and petitions submitted under section 302.

(3) The Trade Representative may identify a foreign country under subsection (a)(1)(B) only if the Trade Representative finds that there is a factual basis for the denial of fair and equitable market access as a result of

the violation of international law or agreement, or the existence of barriers, referred to in subsection (d)(3).

(4) In identifying foreign countries under paragraphs (1) and (2) of subsection (a), the Trade Representative shall take into account—

(A) the history of intellectual property laws and practices of the foreign country, including any previous identification under subsection (a)(2), and

(B) the history of efforts of the United States, and the response of the foreign country, to achieve adequate and effective protection and enforcement of intellectual property rights.

(c) *Revocations and additional identifications.* —

(1) The Trade Representative may at any time—

(A) revoke the identification of any foreign country as a priority foreign country under this section, or

(B) identify any foreign country as a priority foreign country under this section,

if information available to the Trade Representative indicates that such action is appropriate.

(2) The Trade Representative shall include in the semiannual report submitted to the Congress under section 309(3) a detailed explanation of the reasons for the revocation under paragraph (1) of the identification of any foreign country as a priority foreign country under this section.

(d) *Definitions.* —For purposes of this section—

(1) The term "persons that rely upon intellectual property protection" means persons involved in—

(A) the creation, production or licensing of works of authorship (within the meaning of sections 102 and 103 of title 17, United States Code) that are copyrighted, or

(B) the manufacture of products that are patented or for which there are process patents.

(2) A foreign country denies adequate and effective protection of intellectual property rights if the foreign country denies adequate and effective means under the laws of the foreign country for persons who are not citizens or nationals of such foreign country to secure, exercise, and enforce

19 U.S.C. § 2242

rights relating to patents, process patents, registered trademarks, copy-rights and mask works.

(3) A foreign country denies fair and equitable market access if the foreign country effectively denies access to a market for a product protected by a copyright or related right, patent, trademark, mask work, trade secret, or plant breeder's right, through the use of laws, procedures, practices, or regulations which—

(A) violate provisions of international law or international agreements to which both the United States and the foreign country are parties, or

(B) constitute discriminatory nontariff trade barriers.

(4) A foreign country may be determined to deny adequate and effective protection of intellectual property rights, notwithstanding the fact that the foreign country may be in compliance with the specific obligations of the Agreement on Trade-Related Aspects of Intellectual Property Rights re-ferred to in section 101(d)(15) of the Uruguay Round Agreements Act.

(e) *Publication.*—The Trade Representative shall publish in the Federal Register a list of foreign countries identified under subsection (a) and shall make such revisions to the list as may be required by reason of action under subsection (c).

(f) *Special rule for actions affecting United States cultural industries.* —

(1) *In general.*—By no later than the date that is 30 days after the date on which the annual report is submitted to Congressional committees under section 2241(b) of this title, the Trade Representative shall identify any act, policy, or practice of Canada which—

(A) affects cultural industries,

(B) is adopted or expanded after December 17, 1992, and

(C) is actionable under article 2106 of the North American Free Trade Agreement.

(2) *Special rules for identifications.*—For purposes of section 2412(b)(2)(A) of this title, an act, policy, or practice identified under this subsection shall be treated as an act, policy, or practice that is the basis for identification of a country under subsection (a)(2) of this section, unless the United States has already taken action pursuant to article 2106 of the North American Free Trade Agreement in response to such act, policy, or practice. In de-

ciding whether to identify an act, policy, or practice under paragraph (1), the Trade Representative shall—

(A) consult with and take into account the views of representatives of the relevant domestic industries, appropriate committees established pursuant to section 2155 of this title, and appropriate officers of the Federal Government, and

(B) take into account the information from such sources as may be available to the Trade Representative and such information as may be submitted to the Trade Representative by interested persons, including information contained in reports submitted under section 2241(b) of this title.

(3) *Cultural industries.*—For purposes of this subsection the term "cultural industries" means persons engaged in any of the following activities:

(A) The publication, distribution, or sale of books, magazines, periodicals, or newspapers in print or machine readable form but not including the sole activity of printing or typesetting any of the foregoing.

(B) The production, distribution, sale, or exhibition of film or video recordings.

(C) The production, distribution, sale, or exhibition of audio or video music recordings.

(D) The publication, distribution, or sale of music in print or machine readable form.

(E) Radio communications in which the transmissions are intended for direct reception by the general public, and all radio, television, and cable broadcasting undertakings and all satellite programming and broadcast network services.

(g) *Annual report.*—The Trade Representative shall, by not later than the date by which countries are identified under subsection (a), transmit to the Committee on Ways and Means of the House of Representatives and the Committee on Finance of the Senate, a report on actions taken under this section during the 12 months preceding such report, and the reasons for such actions, including a description of progress made in achieving improved intellectual property protection and market access for persons relying on intellectual property rights.

19 U.S.C. § 2242

(Jan. 3, 1975, Pub. L. 93-618, §182, as added Aug. 23, 1988, Pub. L. 100-418, §1303, 102 Stat. 1179; Dec. 8, 1994, Pub. L. 103-465, §313, 108 Stat. 4938; Dec. 8, 1994, Pub. L. 103-465, §313, 108 Stat. 4938)

D. DOCUMENTARY EVIDENCE IN PATENT CASES

28 U.S.C. § 1733   Government records and papers; copies

(a) Books or records of account or minutes of proceedings of any department or agency of the United States shall be admissible to prove the act, transaction or occurrence as a memorandum of which the same were made or kept.

(b) Properly authenticated copies or transcripts of any books, records, papers or documents of any department or agency of the United States shall be admitted in evidence equally with the originals thereof.

(c) This section does not apply to cases, actions, and proceedings to which the Federal Rules of Evidence apply.

(June 25, 1948, ch. 646, §1, 62 Stat. 946; Jan. 2, 1975, Pub. L. 93-595, §2, 88 Stat. 1949.)

28 U.S.C. § 1741   Foreign official documents

An official record or document of a foreign country may be evidenced by a copy, summary, or excerpt authenticated as provided in the Federal Rules of Civil Procedure.

(June 25, 1948, ch. 646, §1, 62 Stat. 948; May 24, 1949, ch. 139, §92, 63 Stat. 103; Oct. 3, 1964, Pub. L. 88-619, §5, 78 Stat. 996.)

28 U.S.C. § 1744   Copies of United States Patent and Trademark Office documents, generally

Copies of letters patent or of any records, books, papers, or drawings belonging to the United States Patent and Trademark Office and relating to patents, authenticated under the seal of the United States Patent and Trademark Office and certified by the Under Secretary of Commerce for Intellectual Property and Director of the United States Patent and Trademark Office, or by another officer of the United States Patent and Trademark Office authorized to do so by the Director, shall be admissible in evidence with the same effect as the originals.

Any person making application and paying the required fee may obtain such certified copies.

(June 25, 1948, ch. 646, §1, 62 Stat. 948; May 24, 1949, ch. 139, §92, 63 Stat. 103; Nov. 29, 1999, Pub. L. 106-113, §4732, 113 Stat. 1501A-581.)

28 U.S.C. § 1733

28 U.S.C. § 1745   Copies of foreign patent documents

Copies of specifications and drawings of foreign letters patent, or applications for foreign letters patent, and copies of excerpts of the official journals and other official publications of foreign patent offices belonging to the United States Patent and Trademark Office, certified in the manner provided by section 1744 of this title are prima facie evidence of their contents and of the dates indicated on their face.

(June 25, 1948, ch. 646, §1, 62 Stat. 948; May 24, 1949, ch. 139, §92, 63 Stat. 103; Oct. 3, 1964, Pub. L. 88-619, §7, 78 Stat. 996; Nov. 29, 1999, Pub. L. 106-113, §4732, 113 Stat. 1501A-581.)

28 U.S.C. § 1781   Transmittal of letter rogatory or request

(a) The Department of State has power, directly, or through suitable channels—

(1) to receive a letter rogatory issued, or request made, by a foreign or international tribunal, to transmit it to the tribunal, officer, or agency in the United States to whom it is addressed, and to receive and return it after execution; and

(2) to receive a letter rogatory issued, or request made, by a tribunal in the United States, to transmit it to the foreign or international tribunal, officer, or agency to whom it is addressed, and to receive and return it after execution.

(b) This section does not preclude—

(1) the transmittal of a letter rogatory or request directly from a foreign or international tribunal to the tribunal, officer, or agency in the United States to whom it is addressed and its return in the same manner; or

(2) the transmittal of a letter rogatory or request directly from a tribunal in the United States to the foreign or international tribunal, officer, or agency to whom it is addressed and its return in the same manner.

(June 25, 1945, ch. 646, §1, 62 Stat. 949; Oct. 3, 1964, Pub. L. 88-619, §8, 78 Stat. 996.)

E. PILOT PROGRAM IN CERTAIN DISTRICT COURTS

(a) *Establishment.*—

(1) *In general.*—There is established a program, in each of the United States district courts designated under subsection (b), under which—

Patent Cases Pilot Program

670 • Patent, Trademark, & Copyright Laws, June 2015 Edition

(A) those district judges of that district court who request to hear cases under which 1 or more issues arising under any Act of Congress relating to patents or plant variety protection are required to be decided, are designated by the chief judge of the court to hear those cases;

(B) cases described in subparagraph (A) are randomly assigned to the judges of the district court, regardless of whether the judges are designated under subparagraph (A);

(C) a judge not designated under subparagraph (A) to whom a case is assigned under subparagraph (B) may decline to accept the case; and

(D) a case declined under subparagraph (C) is randomly reassigned to 1 of those judges of the court designated under subparagraph (A).

(2) *Senior judges.*—Senior judges of a district court may be designated under paragraph (1)(A) if at least 1 judge of the court in regular active service is also so designated.

(3) *Right to transfer cases preserved.*—This section shall not be construed to limit the ability of a judge to request the reassignment of or otherwise transfer a case to which the judge is assigned under this section, in accordance with otherwise applicable rules of the court.

(b) *Designation.*—

(1) *In general.*—Not later than 6 months after the date of the enactment of this Act, the Director of the Administrative Office of the United States Courts shall designate not less than 6 United States district courts, in at least 3 different judicial circuits, in which the program established under subsection (a) will be carried out.

(2) *Criteria for designations.*—

(A) *In general.*—The Director shall make designations under paragraph (1) from—

(i) the 15 district courts in which the largest number of patent and plant variety protection cases were filed in the most recent calendar year that has ended; or

(ii) the district courts that have adopted, or certified to the Director the intention to adopt, local rules for patent and plant variety protection cases.

Patent Cases Pilot Program

(B) *Selection of courts.*—From amongst the district courts that satisfy the criteria for designation under this subsection, the Director shall select—

(i) 3 district courts that each have at least 10 district judges authorized to be appointed by the President, whether under section 133(a) of title 28, United States Code, or on a temporary basis under any other provision of law, and at least 3 judges of the court have made the request under subsection (a)(1)(A); and

(ii) 3 district courts that each have fewer than 10 district judges authorized to be appointed by the President, whether under section 133(a) of title 28, United States Code, or on a temporary basis under any other provision of law, and at least 2 judges of the court have made the request under subsection (a)(1)(A).

(c) *Duration.*—The program established under subsection (a) shall terminate 10 years after the end of the 6-month period described in subsection (b).

(d) *Applicability.*—The program established under subsection (a) shall apply in a district court designated under subsection (b) only to cases commenced on or after the date of such designation.

(e) *Reports to Congress.* —

(1) *In general.*—At the times specified in paragraph (2), the Director of the Administrative Office of the United States Courts, in consultation with the chief judge of each of the district courts designated under subsection (b) and the Director of the Federal Judicial Center, shall submit to the Committee on the Judiciary of the House of Representatives and the Committee on the Judiciary of the Senate a report on the pilot program established under subsection (a). The report shall include—

(A) an analysis of the extent to which the program has succeeded in developing expertise in patent and plant variety protection cases among the district judges of the district courts so designated;

(B) an analysis of the extent to which the program has improved the efficiency of the courts involved by reason of such expertise;

(C) with respect to patent cases handled by the judges designated pursuant to subsection (a)(1)(A) and judges not so designated, a comparison between the 2 groups of judges with respect to—

(i) the rate of reversal by the Court of Appeals for the Federal Circuit, of such cases on the issues of claim construction and substantive patent law; and

(ii) the period of time elapsed from the date on which a case is filed to the date on which trial begins or summary judgment is entered;

(D) a discussion of any evidence indicating that litigants select certain of the judicial districts designated under subsection (b) in an attempt to ensure a given outcome; and

(E) an analysis of whether the pilot program should be extended to other district courts, or should be made permanent and apply to all district courts.

(2) *Timetable for reports.*—The times referred to in paragraph (1) are—

(A) not later than the date that is 5 years and 3 months after the end of the 6-month period described in subsection (b); and

(B) not later than 5 years after the date described in subparagraph (A).

(3) *Periodic reports.*—The Director of the Administrative Office of the United States Courts, in consultation with the chief judge of each of the district courts designated under subsection (b) and the Director of the Federal Judicial Center, shall keep the committees referred to in paragraph (1) informed, on a periodic basis while the pilot program is in effect, with respect to the matters referred to in subparagraphs (A) through (E) of paragraph (1).

(Jan. 4, 2011, Pub. L. 111-349, §1, 124 Stat. 3674.)

II. THE PATENT AND TRADEMARK OFFICE

A. ESTABLISHMENT, OFFICERS, AND EMPLOYEES

15 U.S.C. § 1511   Bureaus in Department

The following named bureaus, administrations, services, offices, and programs of the public service, and all that pertains thereto, shall be under the jurisdiction and subject to the control of the Secretary of Commerce: *   *   *

(4) United States Patent and Trademark Office;[6]

* * *

(As amended, Jan. 2, 1975, Pub. L. 93-596, §3, 88 Stat. 1949; Aug. 6, 1981, Pub. L. 97-31, §12, 95 Stat. 154; Nov. 29, 1999, Pub. L. 106-113, §4732, 113 Stat. 1501A-581.)

5 U.S.C. § 3104   Employment of specially qualified scientific and professional personnel

(a) The Director of the Office of Personnel Management may establish, and from time to time revise, the maximum number of scientific or professional positions for carrying out research and development functions which require the services of specially qualified personnel which may be established outside of the General Schedule. Any such position may be established by action of the Director or, under such standards and procedures as the Office prescribes and publishes in such form as the Director may determine (including procedures under which the prior approval of the Director may be required), by agency action.

(b) The provisions of subsection (a) of this section shall not apply to any Senior Executive Service position (as defined in section 3132(a) of this title [5 U.S.C. §3132(a)]).

(c) In addition to the number of positions authorized by subsection (a) of this section, the Librarian of Congress may establish, without regard to the second sentence of subsection (a) of this section, not more than 8 scientific or professional positions to carry out the research and development functions of the Library of Congress which require the services of specially qualified personnel.

(Sept. 6, 1966, Pub. L. 89-554, §1, 80 Stat. 415; Sept. 11, 1967, Pub. L. 90-83, §1, 81 Stat. 196; Aug. 12, 1970, Pub. L. 1-375, §6, 84 Stat. 776; Oct. 13, 1978, Pub. L. 95-454, §§414, 801, 92 Stat. 1178, 1221; Aug. 22, 1986, Pub. L. 99-386, §101, 100 Stat. 821; Oct. 2, 1992, Pub. L. 102-378, §2, 106 Stat. 1346; Oct. 8, 2008, Pub. L. 110-372, §2, 122 Stat. 4044.)

5 U.S.C. § 3325   Appointments to scientific and professional positions

(a) Positions established under section 3104 of this title are in the competitive service. However, appointments to the positions are made without competitive examination on approval of the qualifications of the proposed appointee by the Office of Personnel Management on the basis of standards developed

---

[6] *Ed. Note:* By executive order, the Department of Commerce also has special responsibility in respect of patent protection abroad of inventions resulting from research financed by the government.

by the agency involved in accordance with criteria specified in regulations prescribed by the Director of the Office of Personnel Management. * * *

(Sept. 6, 1966, Pub. L. 89-554, §1, 80 Stat. 423; Oct. 13, 1978, Pub. L. 95-454, §906, 92 Stat. 1224; Oct. 8, 2008, Pub. L. 110-372, §2, 122 Stat. 4044.)

5 U.S.C. § 5102   Definitions; application

* * *

(c) This chapter [5 U.S.C. §§5101 et seq. ("Classification")] does not apply to
* * *

(23) administrative patent judges and designated administrative patent judges in the United States Patent and Trademark Office; * * *

(Sept. 6, 1966, Pub. L. 89-554, §1, 80 Stat. 444; Aug. 14, 1979, Pub. L. 96-54, §2, 93 Stat. 382; Nov. 29, 1999, Pub. L. 106-113, §4732, 113 Stat. 1501A-581.)

* * * * * * *

B. PATENT AND TRADEMARK OFFICE APPROPRIATIONS

Pub. L. 113-235 Patent and Trademark Office Appropriations for Fiscal Year 2015

Salaries and expenses (including transfers of funds)—For necessary expenses of the United States Patent and Trademark Office (USPTO) provided for by law, including defense of suits instituted against the Under Secretary of Commerce for Intellectual Property and Director of the USPTO, $3,458,000,000, to remain available until expended: *Provided,* That the sum herein appropriated from the general fund shall be reduced as offsetting collections of fees and surcharges assessed and collected by the USPTO under any law are received during fiscal year 2015, so as to result in a fiscal year 2015 appropriation from the general fund estimated at $0: *Provided further,* That during fiscal year 2015, should the total amount of such offsetting collections be less than $3,458,000,000 this amount shall be reduced accordingly: *Provided further,* That any amount received in excess of $3,458,000,000 in fiscal year 2015 and deposited in the Patent and Trademark Fee Reserve Fund shall remain available until expended: *Provided further,* That the Director of USPTO shall submit a spending plan to the Committees on Appropriations of the House of Representatives and the Senate for any amounts made available by the preceding proviso and such spending plan shall be treated as a reprogramming under section 505 of this Act and shall not be available for obligation or expenditure except in compliance with the procedures set forth in that section: *Provided further,* That any amounts reprogrammed in accordance with the preceding proviso shall be transferred to the United States Patent and Trademark Office Salaries and Expenses account: *Provided further,* That from amounts provided herein, not to exceed $900 shall be made available in fiscal year 2015 for official reception and representation expenses: *Provided further,* That in fiscal year 2015 from the amounts made available for "Salaries and Expenses" for the USPTO, the amounts necessary to pay (1) the difference between the percentage of basic pay contributed by the USPTO and employees under section 8334(a) of title 5, United States Code, and the normal cost percentage (as defined by section 8331(17) of that title) as provided by the Office of Personnel Management (OPM) for USPTO's specific use, of basic pay, of employees subject to subchapter III of chapter 83 of that title, and (2) the present value of the otherwise unfunded accruing costs, as determined by OPM for USPTO's specific use of post-retirement life insurance and post-retirement health benefits coverage for all USPTO employees who are enrolled in Federal Employees Health Benefits (FEHB) and Federal Employees Group Life Insurance (FEGLI), shall be transferred to the Civil Service Retirement and Disability Fund, the FEGLI Fund, and the FEHB Fund, as appropriate, and shall be available for the authorized purposes of those accounts: *Provided further,* That any differences between the present value factors published in OPM's yearly 300 series benefit letters and the factors that OPM provides for USPTO's specific use shall be recognized as an imputed cost on USPTO's financial statements, where applicable: *Provided further,* That, notwithstanding any other provision of law, all fees and surcharges assessed and collected by USPTO are available for USPTO only pursuant to section 42(c) of title 35, United States Code, as amended by section 22 of the Leahy-Smith America Invents Act (Public Law 112-29): *Provided further,* That within the amounts appropriated, $2,000,000 shall be transferred to the "Office of Inspector General" account for activities associated with carrying out investigations and audits related to the USPTO.

(Dec. 16, 2014, Pub. L. 113-235, 128 Stat. ___.)

C. USPTO LAW SCHOOL CLINIC CERTIFICATION PROGRAM

Pub. L. 113-227 USPTO Law School Certification Program

(a) *Establishment.* — The Law School Clinic Certification Program of the United States Patent and Trademark Office, as implemented by the Office, is established as a program entitled the "Law School Clinic Certification Program". The Program shall allow students enrolled in a participating law school's clinic to practice patent and trademark law before the Office by drafting, filing, and prosecuting patent or trademark applications, or both, on a pro-bono basis for clients that qualify for assistance from the law school's clinic. The Director shall establish regulations and procedures for application to and participation in the Program. All law schools accredited by the American Bar Association are eligible for participation in the Program, and shall be examined for acceptance using identical criteria established by the Director. The Program shall be in effect for the 10-year period beginning on the date of the enactment of this Act.

(b) *Report on the Program.*—The Director shall, not later than the last day of the 2-year period beginning on the date of the enactment of this Act, submit to the Committees on the Judiciary of the House of Representatives and the Senate a report on the Program, describing the number of law schools and law students participating in the Program, the work done through the Program, the benefits of the Program, and any recommendations of the Director for modifications to the Program.

(c) *Definitions.*—In this section:

(1) *Office.*—The term "Office" means the United States Patent and Trademark Office.

(2) *Program.*—The term "Program" means the Law School Clinic Certification Program established in subsection (a).

(3) *Director.*—The term "Director" means the Under Secretary of Commerce for Intellectual Property and Director of the United States Patent and Trademark Office.

(Dec. 16, 2014, Pub. L. 113-227, 128 Stat. 2114.)

III. PROCEEDINGS IN THE PATENT AND TRADEMARK OFFICE

A. HOLIDAYS

5 U.S.C. § 6103   Holidays

(a) The following are legal public holidays:

New Year's Day, January 1.

Birthday of Martin Luther King, Jr., the third Monday in January.

Washington's Birthday, the third Monday in February.

Memorial Day, the last Monday in May.

Independence Day, July 4.

5 U.S.C. § 6103

Labor Day, the first Monday in September.

Columbus Day, the second Monday in October.

Veterans Day, November 11.

Thanksgiving Day, the fourth Thursday in November.

Christmas Day, December 25.

(b) For purposes of statutes relating to pay and leave of employees, with respect to a legal public holiday and any other day declared to be a holiday by Federal statute or Executive order, the following rules apply:

(1) Instead of a holiday that occurs on a Saturday, the Friday immediately before is a legal public holiday for—

(A) Employees whose basic workweek is Monday through Friday; and

(B) the purpose of section 6309 [repealed Dec. 31, 1971, Pub. L. 94-183, §2, 89 Stat. 1058.] of this title.

(2) Instead of a holiday that occurs on a regular weekly nonworkday of an employee whose basic workweek is other than Monday through Friday, except the regular weekly nonworkday administratively scheduled for the employee instead of Sunday, the workday immediately before that regular weekly nonworkday is a legal public holiday for the employee.

This subsection, except subparagraph (B) of paragraph (1), does not apply to an employee whose basic workweek is Monday through Saturday.

*   *   *

(Sept. 6, 1966, Pub. L. 89-554, §1, 80 Stat. 515; June 28, 1968, Pub. L. 90-363, §1, 82 Stat. 250; Sept. 18, 1975, Pub. L. 94-97, 89 Stat. 479; Nov. 2, 1983, Pub. L. 98-144, §1, 97 Stat. 917.)

D.C. Code § 28-2701   Holidays designated—Time for performing acts extended

The following days in each year, namely, New Year's Day, January 1; Dr. Martin Luther King, Jr.'s Birthday, the third Monday in January; Washington's Birthday, the third Monday in February; Memorial Day, the last Monday in May; Independence Day, July 4; Labor Day, the first Monday in September; Columbus Day, the second Monday in October; Veteran's Day, November 11; Thanksgiving Day, the fourth Thursday in November; Christmas Day, December 25; every Saturday, after twelve o'clock noon; any day appointed by the President of the United States as a day of public feasting or thanksgiving; and the day of the inauguration of the President, in every fourth year, are holidays in the District for all purposes. When a day set apart as a legal holiday, other than the day of the inauguration of the President, falls on a Saturday, the next preceding day is a holiday. When a day set apart as a legal holiday falls on a Sunday, the next succeeding day is a holiday. In such cases, when a Sunday and a holiday or holidays fall on successive days, all commercial papers falling due on any of those days shall, for all purposes of presenting for payment or acceptance, be deemed to mature and be presentable for payment or acceptance on the next secular business day succeeding. Every Saturday is a holiday in the District for (1) every bank or banking institution having an office or banking house located within the District, (2) every Federal savings and loan association whose main office is in the District, and (3) every building association, building and loan association, or savings and loan association, incorporated or unincorporated, organized and operating under the laws of and having an office located within the District. An act which would otherwise be required, authorized, or permitted to be performed on Saturday in the District at the office or banking house of, or by, any such bank or bank institution, Federal savings and loan association, building association, building and loan association, or savings and loan association, if Saturday were not a holiday, shall or may be so performed on the next succeeding business day, and liability or loss of rights of any kind may not result from such delay.

(Aug. 30, 1964, Pub. L. 88-509, §1, 78 Stat. 671; Aug. 1, 1975, D.C. Law 1-11, §103, 22 DCR 1804; July 12, 1977, D.C. Law 2-13, §2, 24 DCR 1443; Mar. 16, 1982, D.C. Law 4-77, §2, 29 DCR 46; Mar. 14, 1985, D.C. Law 5-155, §3, 32 DCR 11.)

* * * * * * *

IV. PRACTICE BEFORE THE PATENT AND TRADEMARK OFFICE

A. REGULATIONS FOR AGENTS AND ATTORNEYS

5 U.S.C. § 500   Administrative practice; general provisions

* * *

(b) An individual who is a member in good standing of the bar of the highest court of a State may represent a person before an agency on filing with the agency a written declaration that he is currently qualified as provided by this subsection and is authorized to represent the particular person in whose behalf he acts. *   *   *

5 U.S.C. § 500

(e) Subsections (b)–(d) of this section do not apply to practice before the United States Patent and Trademark Office with respect to patent matters that continue to be covered by chapter 3 (sections 31-33) of title 35. *   *   *

(Sept. 11, 1967, Pub. L. 90-83, §1, 81 Stat. 195; Nov. 29, 1999, Pub. L. 106-113, §4732, 113 Stat. 1501A-581.)

18 U.S.C. § 207   Restrictions on former officers, employees, and elected officials of the executive and legislative branches

(a) *Restrictions on all officers and employees of the executive branch and certain other agencies.—*

(1) *Permanent restrictions on representation on particular matters.—*Any person who is an officer or employee (including any special Government employee) of the executive branch of the United States (including any independent agency of the United States), or of the District of Columbia, and who, after the termination of his or her service or employment with the United States or the District of Columbia, knowingly makes, with the intent to influence, any communication to or appearance before any officer or employee of any department, agency, court, or court-martial of the United States or the District of Columbia, on behalf of any other person (except the United States or the District of Columbia), in connection with a particular matter—

(A) in which the United States or the District of Columbia is a party or has a direct and substantial interest,

(B) in which the person participated personally and substantially as such officer or employee, and

(C) which involved a specific party or specific parties at the time of such participation,

shall be punished as provided in section 216 of this title.

(2) *Two-year restrictions concerning particular matters under official responsibility.—*Any person subject to the restrictions contained in paragraph (1) who, within 2 years after the termination of his or her service or employment with the United States or the District of Columbia knowingly makes, with the intent to influence, any communication to or appearance before any officer or employee of any department, agency, court, or court-martial of the United States or the District of Columbia, on behalf of any other

person (except the United States or the District of Columbia), in connection with a particular matter—

(A) in which the United States or the District of Columbia is a party or has a direct and substantial interest,

(B) which such person knows or reasonably should know was actually pending under his or her official responsibility as such officer or employee within a period of 1 year before the termination of his or her service or employment with the United States or the District of Columbia, and

(C) which involved a specific party or specific parties at the time it was so pending,

shall be punished as provided in section 216 of this title.

(3) *Clarification of restrictions.*—The restrictions contained in paragraphs (1) and (2) shall apply—

(A) in the case of an officer or employee of the executive branch of the United States (including any independent agency), only with respect to communications to or appearances before any officer or employee of any department, agency, court, or court-martial of the United States on behalf of any other person (except the United States), and only with respect to a matter in which the United States is a party or has a direct and substantial interest; and

(B) in the case of an officer or employee of the District of Columbia, only with respect to communications to or appearances before any officer or employee of any department, agency, or court of the District of Columbia on behalf of any other person (except the District of Columbia), and only with respect to a matter in which the District of Columbia is a party or has a direct and substantial interest.

(b) *One-year restrictions on aiding or advising.* —

(1) *In general.*—Any person who is a former officer or employee of the executive branch of the United States (including any independent agency) and is subject to the restrictions contained in subsection (a)(1), or any person who is a former officer or employee of the legislative branch or a former Member of Congress, who personally and substantially participated in any ongoing trade or treaty negotiation on behalf of the United States within the 1-year period preceding the date on which his or her service or employment with the United States terminated, and who had access to

information concerning such trade or treaty negotiation which is exempt from disclosure under section 552 of title 5, which is so designated by the appropriate department or agency, and which the person knew or should have known was so designated, shall not, on the basis of that information, knowingly represent, aid, or advise any other person (except the United States) concerning such ongoing trade or treaty negotiation for a period of 1 year after his or her service or employment with the United States terminates. Any person who violates this subsection shall be punished as provided in section 216 of this title.

(2) *Definition.*—For purposes of this paragraph—

(A) the term "trade negotiation" means negotiations which the President determines to undertake to enter into a trade agreement pursuant to section 1102 of the Omnibus Trade and Competitiveness Act of 1988, and does not include any action taken before that determination is made; and

(B) the term "treaty" means an international agreement made by the President that requires the advice and consent of the Senate.

(c) *One-year restrictions on certain senior personnel of the executive branch and independent agencies.*—

(1) *Restrictions.*—In addition to the restrictions set forth in subsections (a) and (b), any person who is an officer or employee (including any special Government employee) of the executive branch of the United States (including an independent agency), who is referred to in paragraph (2), and who, within 1 year after the termination of his or her service or employment as such officer or employee, knowingly makes, with the intent to influence, any communication to or appearance before any officer or employee of the department or agency in which such person served within 1 year before such termination, on behalf of any other person (except the United States), in connection with any matter on which such person seeks official action by any officer or employee of such department or agency, shall be punished as provided in section 216 of this title.

(2) *Persons to whom restrictions apply.*—

(A) Paragraph (1) shall apply to a person (other than a person subject to the restrictions of subsection (d))—

(i) employed at a rate of pay specified in or fixed according to subchapter II of chapter 53 of title 5,

18 U.S.C. § 207

(ii) employed in a position which is not referred to in clause (i) and for which that person is paid at a rate of basic pay which is equal to or greater than 86.5 percent of the rate of basic pay for level II of the Executive Schedule, or, for a period of 2 years following the enactment of the National Defense Authorization Act for Fiscal Year 2004, a person who, on the day prior to the enactment of that Act, was employed in a position which is not referred to in clause (i) and for which the rate of basic pay, exclusive of any locality-based pay adjustment under section 5304 or section 5304a of title 5, was equal to or greater than the rate of basic pay payable for level 5 of the Senior Executive Service on the day prior to the enactment of that Act;

(iii) appointed by the President to a position under section 105(a)(2)(B) of title 3 or by the Vice President to a position under section 106(a)(1)(B) of title 3,

(iv) employed in a position which is held by an active duty commissioned officer of the uniformed services who is serving in a grade or rank for which the pay grade (as specified in section 201 of title 37) is pay grade 0-7 or above; or

(v) assigned from a private sector organization to an agency under chapter 37 of title 5.

(B) Paragraph (1) shall not apply to a special Government employee who serves less than 60 days in the 1-year period before his or her service or employment as such employee terminates.

(C) At the request of a department or agency, the Director of the Office of Government Ethics may waive the restrictions contained in paragraph (1) with respect to any position, or category of positions, referred to in clause (ii) or (iv) of subparagraph (A), in such department or agency if the Director determines that—

(i) the imposition of the restrictions with respect to such position or positions would create an undue hardship on the department or agency in obtaining qualified personnel to fill such position or positions, and

(ii) granting the waiver would not create the potential for use of undue influence or unfair advantage.

(3) *Members of the Independent Medicare Advisory Board.*—

(A) *In general.*—Paragraph (1) shall apply to a member of the Independent Medicare Advisory Board under section 1899A.

(B) *Agencies and Congress.*—For purposes of paragraph (1), the agency in which the individual described in subparagraph (A) served shall be considered to be the Independent Medicare Advisory Board, the Department of Health and Human Services, and the relevant committees of jurisdiction of Congress, including the Committee on Ways and Means and the Committee on Energy and Commerce of the House of Representatives and the Committee on Finance of the Senate.

(d) *Restrictions on very senior personnel of the executive branch and independent agencies.*—

(1) *Restrictions.*—In addition to the restrictions set forth in subsections (a) and (b), any person who—

(A) serves in the position of Vice President of the United States,

(B) is employed in a position in the executive branch of the United States (including any independent agency) at a rate of pay payable for level I of the Executive Schedule, or employed in a position in the Executive Office of the President at a rate of pay payable for level II of the Executive Schedule, or

(C) is appointed by the President to a position under section 105(a)(2)(A) of title 3 or by the Vice President to a position under section 106(a)(1)(A) of title 3,

and who, within two years after the termination of that person's service in that position, knowingly makes, with the intent to influence, any communication to or appearance before any person described in paragraph (2), on behalf of any other person (except the United States), in connection with any matter on which such person seeks official action by any officer or employee of the executive branch of the United States, shall be punished as provided in section 216 of this title.

(2) *Persons who may not be contacted.*—The persons referred to in paragraph (1) with respect to appearances or communications by a person in a position described in subparagraph (A), (B), or (C) of paragraph (1) are—

(A) any officer or employee of any department or agency in which such person served in such position within a period of 1 year before such person's service or employment with the United States Government terminated, and

(B) any person appointed to a position in the executive branch which is listed in section 5312, 5313, 5314, 5315, or 5316 of title 5.

* * *

(Oct. 23, 1962, Pub. L. 87-849, §1, 76 Stat. 1123; Oct. 26, 1978, Pub. L. 95-521, §501, 92 Stat. 1864; June 22, 1979, Pub. L. 96-28, 93 Stat. 76; Nov. 30, 1989, Pub. L. 101-194, §101, 103 Stat. 1716; May 4, 1990, Pub. L. 101-280, §§2, 5, 104 Stat. 149, 159; Nov. 5, 1990, Pub. L. 101-509, §529, 104 Stat. 1440; Aug. 6, 1996, Pub. L. 104-179, §6, 110 Stat. 1568; Dec. 17, 2002, Pub. L. 107-347, §209, 116 Stat. 2930; Nov. 24, 2003, Pub. L. 108-136, §1125, 117 Stat. 1639; Sept. 14, 2007, Pub. L. 110-81, §101, 121 Stat. 737; Mar. 23, 2010, Pub. L. 111-148, §3403, 124 Stat. 506.)

* * * * * * *

V. THE COPYRIGHT OFFICE

A. COPYRIGHT OFFICE APPROPRIATIONS

Pub. L. 113-235 Copyright Office Appropriations for Fiscal Year 2015

Salaries and expenses.—For all necessary expenses of the Copyright Office, $54,303,000, of which not more than $27,971,000, to remain available until expended, shall be derived from collections credited to this appropriation during fiscal year 2015 under section 708(d) of title 17, United States Code: *Provided*, That the Copyright Office may not obligate or expend any funds derived from collections under such section, in excess of the amount authorized for obligation or expenditure in appropriations Acts: *Provided further*, That not more than $5,611,000 shall be derived from collections during fiscal year 2015 under sections 111(d)(2), 119(b)(2), 803(e), 1005, and 1316 of such title: *Provided further*, That the total amount available for obligation shall be reduced by the amount by which collections are less than $33,582,000: *Provided further*, That not more than $100,000 of the amount appropriated is available for the maintenance of an "International Copyright Institute" in the Copyright Office of the Library of Congress for the purpose of training nationals of developing countries in intellectual property laws and policies: *Provided further*, That not more than $6,500 may be expended, on the certification of the Librarian of Congress, in connection with official representation and reception expenses for activities of the International Copyright Institute and for copyright delegations, visitors, and seminars: *Provided further*, That notwithstanding any provision of chapter 8 of title 17, United States Code, any amounts made available under

Pub. L. 113-235

this heading which are attributable to royalty fees and payments received by the Copyright Office pursuant to sections 111, 119, and chapter 10 of such title may be used for the costs incurred in the administration of the Copyright Royalty Judges program, with the exception of the costs of salaries and benefits for the Copyright Royalty Judges and staff under section 802(e).

(Dec. 16, 2014, Pub. L. 113-235, 128 Stat. ___.)

* * * * * * *

VI. PLANTS

PLANT VARIETY PROTECTION ACT

Ed. Note: The "Plant Variety Protection Act," protecting novel varieties of sexually reproduced plants, comprises Chapter 57 of title 7; sections 1545 and 2353 of title 28; amendments to 7 U.S.C. 1551, 1562 (The Federal Seed Act) and sections 1338 and 1498 of title 28; and enacting provisions. (Pub. L. 91-577, Dec. 24, 1970, 84 Stat. 1542; Pub. L. 103-349, Oct. 6, 1994, 108 Stat 3136.)

The text of the Act and the Regulations and Rules of Practice of the Plant Variety Protection Office are available in pamphlet form from that Office, Room 301 National Agricultural Library, AMS, USDA, Beltsville, Md. 20705.

* * * * * * *

VII. BIOSIMILAR BIOLOGICAL PRODUCTS

42 U.S.C. § 262(k)   Licensure of Biological Products as Biosimilar or Interchangeable

(1) *In general.*—Any person may submit an application for licensure of a biological product under this subsection.

(2) *Content.*—

(A) *In general.*—

(i) *Required information.*—An application submitted under this subsection shall include information demonstrating that—

(I) the biological product is biosimilar to a reference product based upon data derived from—

(aa) analytical studies that demonstrate that the biological product is highly similar to the reference product notwithstanding minor differences in clinically inactive components;

(bb) animal studies (including the assessment of toxicity); and (cc) a clinical study or studies (including the assessment of immunogenicity and pharmacokinetics or pharmacodynamics) that are sufficient to demonstrate safety, purity, and potency in 1 or more appropriate conditions of use for which the reference product is licensed and intended to be used and for which licensure is sought for the biological product;

(II) the biological product and reference product utilize the same mechanism or mechanisms of action for the condition or conditions of use prescribed, recommended, or suggested in the proposed labeling, but only to the extent the mechanism or mechanisms of action are known for the reference product;

(III) the condition or conditions of use prescribed, recommended, or suggested in the labeling proposed for the biological product have been previously approved for the reference product;

(IV) the route of administration, the dosage form, and the strength of the biological product are the same as those of the reference product; and

(V) the facility in which the biological product is manufactured, processed, packed, or held meets standards designed to assure that the biological product continues to be safe, pure, and potent.

(ii) *Determination by Secretary.*—The Secretary may determine, in the Secretary's discretion, that an element described in clause (i)(I) is unnecessary in an application submitted under this subsection.

(iii) *Additional information.*—An application submitted under this subsection—

(I) shall include publicly-available information regarding the Secretary's previous determination that the reference product is safe, pure, and potent; and

(II) may include any additional information in support of the application, including publicly-available information with respect to the reference product or another biological product.

(B) *Interchangeability.*—An application (or a supplement to an application) submitted under this subsection may include information demonstrating that the biological product meets the standards described in paragraph (4).

42 U.S.C. § 262(k)

(3) *Evaluation by Secretary.* —Upon review of an application (or a supplement to an application) submitted under this subsection, the Secretary shall license the biological product under this subsection if—

(A) the Secretary determines that the information submitted in the application (or the supplement) is sufficient to show that the biological product—

(i) is biosimilar to the reference product; or

(ii) meets the standards described in paragraph (4), and therefore is interchangeable with the reference product; and

(B) the applicant (or other appropriate person) consents to the inspection of the facility that is the subject of the application, in accordance with subsection (c).

(4) *Safety standards for determining interchangeability.* —Upon review of an application submitted under this subsection or any supplement to such application, the Secretary shall determine the biological product to be interchangeable with the reference product if the Secretary determines that the information submitted in the application (or a supplement to such application) is sufficient to show that—

(A) the biological product—

(i) is biosimilar to the reference product; and

(ii) can be expected to produce the same clinical result as the reference product in any given patient; and

(B) for a biological product that is administered more than once to an individual, the risk in terms of safety or diminished efficacy of alternating or switching between use of the biological product and the reference product is not greater than the risk of using the reference product without such alternation or switch.

(5) *General rules.* —

(A) *One reference product per application.* —A biological product, in an application submitted under this subsection, may not be evaluated against more than 1 reference product.

(B) *Review.* —An application submitted under this subsection shall be reviewed by the division within the Food and Drug Administration that is responsible for the review and approval of the application under which the reference product is licensed.

42 U.S.C. § 262(k)

(C) *Risk evaluation and mitigation strategies.* —The authority of the Secretary with respect to risk evaluation and mitigation strategies under the Federal Food, Drug, and Cosmetic Act shall apply to biological products licensed under this subsection in the same manner as such authority applies to biological products licensed under subsection (a).

(6) *Exclusivity for first interchangeable biological product.* —Upon review of an application submitted under this subsection relying on the same reference product for which a prior biological product has received a determination of interchangeability for any condition of use, the Secretary shall not make a determination under paragraph (4) that the second or subsequent biological product is interchangeable for any condition of use until the earlier of—

(A) 1 year after the first commercial marketing of the first interchangeable biosimilar biological product to be approved as interchangeable for that reference product;

(B) 18 months after—

(i) a final court decision on all patents in suit in an action instituted under subsection (l)(6) against the applicant that submitted the application for the first approved interchangeable biosimilar biological product; or

(ii) the dismissal with or without prejudice of an action instituted under subsection (l)(6) against the applicant that submitted the application for the first approved interchangeable biosimilar biological product; or

(C) (i) 42 months after approval of the first interchangeable biosimilar biological product if the applicant that submitted such application has been sued under subsection (l)(6) and such litigation is still ongoing within such 42-month period; or

(ii) 18 months after approval of the first interchangeable biosimilar biological product if the applicant that submitted such application has not been sued under subsection (l)(6).

For purposes of this paragraph, the term "final court decision" means a final decision of a court from which no appeal (other than a petition to the United States Supreme Court for a writ of certiorari) has been or can be taken.

(7) *Exclusivity for reference product.* —

(A) *Effective date of biosimilar application approval.* —Approval of an application under this subsection may not be made effective by the Secretary until the date that is 12 years after the date on which the reference product was first licensed under subsection (a).

(B) *Filing period.*—An application under this subsection may not be submitted to the Secretary until the date that is 4 years after the date on which the reference product was first licensed under subsection (a).

(C) *First licensure.*—Subparagraphs (A) and (B) shall not apply to a license for or approval of—

(i) a supplement for the biological product that is the reference product; or

(ii) a subsequent application filed by the same sponsor or manufacturer of the biological product that is the reference product (or a licensor, predecessor in interest, or other related entity) for—

(I) a change (not including a modification to the structure of the biological product) that results in a new indication, route of administration, dosing schedule, dosage form, delivery system, delivery device, or strength; or

(II) a modification to the structure of the biological product that does not result in a change in safety, purity, or potency.

(8) *Guidance documents.*—

(A) *In general.*—The Secretary may, after opportunity for public comment, issue guidance in accordance, except as provided in subparagraph (B)(i), with section 701(h) of the Federal Food, Drug, and Cosmetic Act with respect to the licensure of a biological product under this subsection. Any such guidance may be general or specific.

(B) *Public comment.*—

(i) *In general.*—The Secretary shall provide the public an opportunity to comment on any proposed guidance issued under subparagraph (A) before issuing final guidance.

(ii) *Input regarding most valuable guidance.*—The Secretary shall establish a process through which the public may provide the Secretary with input regarding priorities for issuing guidance.

(C) *No requirement for application consideration.*—The issuance (or non-issuance) of guidance under subparagraph (A) shall not preclude the review of, or action on, an application submitted under this subsection.

42 U.S.C. § 262(k)

(D) *Requirement for product class-specific guidance.*—If the Secretary issues product class-specific guidance under subparagraph (A), such guidance shall include a description of—

(i) the criteria that the Secretary will use to determine whether a biological product is highly similar to a reference product in such product class; and

(ii) the criteria, if available, that the Secretary will use to determine whether a biological product meets the standards described in paragraph (4).

(E) *Certain product classes.*—

(i) *Guidance.*—The Secretary may indicate in a guidance document that the science and experience, as of the date of such guidance, with respect to a product or product class (not including any recombinant protein) does not allow approval of an application for a license as provided under this subsection for such product or product class.

(ii) *Modification or reversal.*—The Secretary may issue a subsequent guidance document under subparagraph (A) to modify or reverse a guidance document under clause (i).

(iii) *No effect on ability to deny license.*—Clause (i) shall not be construed to require the Secretary to approve a product with respect to which the Secretary has not indicated in a guidance document that the science and experience, as described in clause (i), does not allow approval of such an application.

(Mar. 23, 2010, Pub. L. 111-148, Title VII, Subtitle A §7002, 124 Stat. 804.)

42 U.S.C. § 262(l) Patents

(1) *Confidential access to subsection (k) application.*—

(A) *Application of paragraph.*—Unless otherwise agreed to by a person that submits an application under subsection (k) (referred to in this subsection as the "subsection (k) applicant") and the sponsor of the application for the reference product (referred to in this subsection as the "reference product sponsor"), the provisions of this paragraph shall apply to the exchange of information described in this subsection.

(B) *In general.*—

(i) *Provision of confidential information.*—When a subsection (k) applicant submits an application under subsection (k), such applicant shall provide to the persons described in clause (ii), subject to the terms of this paragraph, confidential access to the information required to be produced pursuant to paragraph (2) and any other information that the subsection (k) applicant determines, in its sole discretion, to be appropriate (referred to in this subsection as the "confidential information").

(ii) *Recipients of information.*—The persons described in this clause are the following:

(I) *Outside counsel.*—One or more attorneys designated by the reference product sponsor who are employees of an entity other than the reference product sponsor (referred to in this paragraph as the "outside counsel"), provided that such attorneys do not engage, formally or informally, in patent prosecution relevant or related to the reference product.

(II) *In-house counsel.*—One attorney that represents the reference product sponsor who is an employee of the reference product sponsor, provided that such attorney does not engage, formally or informally, in patent prosecution relevant or related to the reference product.

(iii) *Patent owner access.*—A representative of the owner of a patent exclusively licensed to a reference product sponsor with respect to the reference product and who has retained a right to assert the patent or participate in litigation concerning the patent may be provided the confidential information, provided that the representative informs the reference product sponsor and the subsection (k) applicant of his or her agreement to be subject to the confidentiality provisions set forth in this paragraph, including those under clause (ii).

(C) *Limitation on disclosure.*—No person that receives confidential information pursuant to subparagraph (B) shall disclose any confidential information to any other person or entity, including the reference product sponsor employees, outside scientific consultants, or other outside counsel retained by the reference product sponsor, without the prior written consent of the subsection (k) applicant, which shall not be unreasonably withheld.

(D) *Use of confidential information.*—Confidential information shall be used for the sole and exclusive purpose of determining, with respect to each patent assigned to or exclusively licensed by the reference product sponsor, whether a claim of patent infringement could reasonably be asserted if the subsection (k) applicant engaged in the manufacture, use, offering for sale, sale, or importation into the United States of the biological product that is the subject of the application under subsection (k).

(E) *Ownership of confidential information.*—The confidential information disclosed under this paragraph is, and shall remain, the property of the subsection (k) applicant. By providing the confidential information pursuant to this paragraph, the subsection (k) applicant does not provide the reference product sponsor or the outside counsel any interest in or license to use the confidential information, for purposes other than those specified in subparagraph (D).

(F) *Effect of infringement action.*—In the event that the reference product sponsor files a patent infringement suit, the use of confidential information shall continue to be governed by the terms of this paragraph until such time as a court enters a protective order regarding the information. Upon entry of such order, the subsection (k) applicant may redesignate confidential information in accordance with the terms of that order. No confidential information shall be included in any publicly-available complaint or other pleading. In the event that the reference product sponsor does not file an infringement action by the date specified in paragraph (6), the reference product sponsor shall return or destroy all confidential information received under this paragraph, provided that if the reference product sponsor opts to destroy such information, it will confirm destruction in writing to the subsection (k) applicant.

(G) *Rule of construction.*—Nothing in this paragraph shall be construed—

(i) as an admission by the subsection (k) applicant regarding the validity, enforceability, or infringement of any patent; or

(ii) as an agreement or admission by the subsection (k) applicant with respect to the competency, relevance, or materiality of any confidential information.

(H) *Effect of violation.*—The disclosure of any confidential information in violation of this paragraph shall be deemed to cause the subsection (k) applicant to suffer irreparable harm for which there is no adequate legal remedy and the court shall consider immediate injunctive relief to be an appropriate and necessary remedy for any violation or threatened violation of this paragraph.

(2) *Subsection (k) application information.* —Not later than 20 days after the Secretary notifies the subsection (k) applicant that the application has been accepted for review, the subsection (k) applicant—

(A) shall provide to the reference product sponsor a copy of the application submitted to the Secretary under subsection (k), and such other information that describes the process or processes used to manufacture the biological product that is the subject of such application; and

(B) may provide to the reference product sponsor additional information requested by or on behalf of the reference product sponsor.

(3) *List and description of patents.* —

(A) *List by reference product sponsor.* —Not later than 60 days after the receipt of the application and information under paragraph (2), the reference product sponsor shall provide to the subsection (k) applicant—

(i) a list of patents for which the reference product sponsor believes a claim of patent infringement could reasonably be asserted by the reference product sponsor, or by a patent owner that has granted an exclusive license to the reference product sponsor with respect to the reference product, if a person not licensed by the reference product sponsor engaged in the making, using, offering to sell, selling, or importing into the United States of the biological product that is the subject of the subsection (k) application; and

(ii) an identification of the patents on such list that the reference product sponsor would be prepared to license to the subsection (k) applicant.

(B) *List and description by subsection (k) applicant.* —Not later than 60 days after receipt of the list under subparagraph (A), the subsection (k) applicant—

(i) may provide to the reference product sponsor a list of patents to which the subsection (k) applicant believes a claim of patent infringement could reasonably be asserted by the reference product sponsor if a person not licensed by the reference product sponsor engaged in the making, using, offering to sell, selling, or importing into the United States of the biological product that is the subject of the subsection (k) application;

(ii) shall provide to the reference product sponsor, with respect to each patent listed by the reference product sponsor under subparagraph (A) or listed by the subsection (k) applicant under clause (i)—

(I) a detailed statement that describes, on a claim by claim basis, the factual and legal basis of the opinion of the subsection (k) applicant that such patent is invalid, unenforceable, or will not be infringed by the commercial marketing of the biological product that is the subject of the subsection (k) application; or

(II) a statement that the subsection (k) applicant does not intend to begin commercial marketing of the biological product before the date that such patent expires; and

(iii) shall provide to the reference product sponsor a response regarding each patent identified by the reference product sponsor under subparagraph (A)(ii).

(C) *Description by reference product sponsor.* — Not later than 60 days after receipt of the list and statement under subparagraph (B), the reference product sponsor shall provide to the subsection (k) applicant a detailed statement that describes, with respect to each patent described in subparagraph (B)(ii)(I), on a claim by claim basis, the factual and legal basis of the opinion of the reference product sponsor that such patent will be infringed by the commercial marketing of the biological product that is the subject of the subsection (k) application and a response to the statement concerning validity and enforceability provided under subparagraph (B)(ii)(I).

(4) *Patent resolution negotiations.* —

(A) *In general.* — After receipt by the subsection (k) applicant of the statement under paragraph (3)(C), the reference product sponsor and the subsection (k) applicant shall engage in good faith negotiations to agree on which, if any, patents listed under paragraph (3) by the subsection (k) applicant or the reference product sponsor shall be the subject of an action for patent infringement under paragraph (6).

(B) *Failure to reach agreement.* — If, within 15 days of beginning negotiations under subparagraph (A), the subsection (k) applicant and the reference product sponsor fail to agree on a final and complete list of which, if any, patents listed under paragraph (3) by the subsection (k) applicant or the reference product sponsor shall be the subject of an action for patent infringement under paragraph (6), the provisions of paragraph (5) shall apply to the parties.

(5) *Patent resolution if no agreement.* —

(A) *Number of patents.* —The subsection (k) applicant shall notify the reference product sponsor of the number of patents that such applicant will provide to the reference product sponsor under subparagraph (B)(i)(I).

(B) *Exchange of patent lists.* —

(i) *In general.* —On a date agreed to by the subsection (k) applicant and the reference product sponsor, but in no case later than 5 days after the subsection (k) applicant notifies the reference product sponsor under subparagraph (A), the subsection (k) applicant and the reference product sponsor shall simultaneously exchange—

(I) the list of patents that the subsection (k) applicant believes should be the subject of an action for patent infringement under paragraph (6); and

(II) the list of patents, in accordance with clause (ii), that the reference product sponsor believes should be the subject of an action for patent infringement under paragraph (6).

(ii) *Number of patents listed by reference product sponsor.* —

(I) *In general.* —Subject to subclause (II), the number of patents listed by the reference product sponsor under clause (i)(II) may not exceed the number of patents listed by the subsection (k) applicant under clause (i)(I).

(II) *Exception.* —If a subsection (k) applicant does not list any patent under clause (i)(I), the reference product sponsor may list 1 patent under clause (i)(II).

(6) *Immediate patent infringement action.* —

(A) *Action if agreement on patent list.* —If the subsection (k) applicant and the reference product sponsor agree on patents as described in paragraph (4), not later than 30 days after such agreement, the reference product sponsor shall bring an action for patent infringement with respect to each such patent.

(B) *Action if no agreement on patent list.* —If the provisions of paragraph (5) apply to the parties as described in paragraph (4)(B), not later than 30 days after the exchange of lists under paragraph (5)(B), the reference product sponsor shall bring an action for patent infringement with respect to each patent that is included on such lists.

(C) *Notification and publication of complaint.*—

(i) *Notification to Secretary.*—Not later than 30 days after a complaint is served to a subsection (k) applicant in an action for patent infringement described under this paragraph, the subsection (k) applicant shall provide the Secretary with notice and a copy of such complaint.

(ii) *Publication by Secretary.*—The Secretary shall publish in the Federal Register notice of a complaint received under clause (i).

(7) *Newly issued or licensed patents.*—In the case of a patent that—

(A) is issued to, or exclusively licensed by, the reference product sponsor after the date that the reference product sponsor provided the list to the subsection (k) applicant under paragraph (3)(A); and

(B) the reference product sponsor reasonably believes that, due to the issuance of such patent, a claim of patent infringement could reasonably be asserted by the reference product sponsor if a person not licensed by the reference product sponsor engaged in the making, using, offering to sell, selling, or importing into the United States of the biological product that is the subject of the subsection (k) application,

not later than 30 days after such issuance or licensing, the reference product sponsor shall provide to the subsection (k) applicant a supplement to the list provided by the reference product sponsor under paragraph (3)(A) that includes such patent, not later than 30 days after such supplement is provided, the subsection (k) applicant shall provide a statement to the reference product sponsor in accordance with paragraph (3)(B), and such patent shall be subject to paragraph (8).

(8) *Notice of commercial marketing and preliminary injunction.*—

(A) *Notice of commercial marketing.*—The subsection (k) applicant shall provide notice to the reference product sponsor not later than 180 days before the date of the first commercial marketing of the biological product licensed under subsection (k).

(B) *Preliminary injunction.*—After receiving the notice under subparagraph (A) and before such date of the first commercial marketing of such biological product, the reference product sponsor may seek a preliminary injunction prohibiting the subsection (k) applicant from engaging in the commercial manufacture or sale of such biological product until the court decides the issue of patent validity, enforcement, and infringement with respect to any patent that is—

42 U.S.C. § 262(l)

(i) included in the list provided by the reference product sponsor under paragraph (3)(A) or in the list provided by the subsection (k) applicant under paragraph (3)(B); and

(ii) not included, as applicable, on—

(I) the list of patents described in paragraph (4); or

(II) the lists of patents described in paragraph (5)(B).

(C) *Reasonable cooperation.* —If the reference product sponsor has sought a preliminary injunction under subparagraph (B), the reference product sponsor and the subsection (k) applicant shall reasonably cooperate to expedite such further discovery as is needed in connection with the preliminary injunction motion.

(9) *Limitation on declaratory judgment action.* —

(A) *Subsection (k) application provided.* —If a subsection (k) applicant provides the application and information required under paragraph (2)(A), neither the reference product sponsor nor the subsection (k) applicant may, prior to the date notice is received under paragraph (8)(A), bring any action under section 2201 of title 28, United States Code, for a declaration of infringement, validity, or enforceability of any patent that is described in clauses (i) and (ii) of paragraph (8)(B).

(B) *Subsequent failure to act by subsection (k) applicant.* —If a subsection (k) applicant fails to complete an action required of the subsection (k) applicant under paragraph (3)(B)(ii), paragraph (5), paragraph (6)(C)(i), paragraph (7), or paragraph (8)(A), the reference product sponsor, but not the subsection (k) applicant, may bring an action under section 2201 of title 28, United States Code, for a declaration of infringement, validity, or enforceability of any patent included in the list described in paragraph (3)(A), including as provided under paragraph (7).

(C) *Subsection (k) application not provided.* —If a subsection (k) applicant fails to provide the application and information required under paragraph (2)(A), the reference product sponsor, but not the subsection (k) applicant, may bring an action under section 2201 of title 28, United States Code, for a declaration of infringement, validity, or enforceability of any patent that claims the biological product or a use of the biological product.

[* * *]

(Mar. 23, 2010, Pub. L. 111-148, Title VII, Subtitle A §7002, 124 Stat. 808.)

* * * * * * * *

42 U.S.C. § 262(l)

VIII. GOVERNMENT INTERESTS IN PATENTS

A. DEPARTMENT OF ENERGY/NUCLEAR REGULATORY COMMISSION

1. INVENTIONS RELATING TO ATOMIC WEAPONS [7]

42 U.S.C. § 2014   Definitions

The intent of the Congress in the definitions as given in this section should be construed from the words or phrases used in the definitions. As used in this Act [Atomic Energy Act of 1954]:

* * *

(c) The term "atomic energy" means all forms of energy released in the course of nuclear fission or nuclear transformation.

(d) The term "atomic weapon" means any device utilizing atomic energy, exclusive of the means for transporting or propelling the device (where such means is a separable and divisible part of the device), the principal purpose of which is for use as, for development of, a weapon, a weapon prototype, or a weapon test device.

* * *

(u) The term "produce," when used in relation to special nuclear material, means (1) to manufacture, make, produce, or refine special nuclear material; (2) to separate special nuclear material from other substances in which such material may be contained; or (3) to make or to produce new special nuclear material.

* * *

(z) The term "source material" means (1) uranium, thorium, or any other material which is determined by the Commission pursuant to the provisions of section 61 [42 U.S.C. §2091] to be source material; or (2) ores containing one or more of the foregoing materials, in such concentration as the Commission may by regulation determine from time to time.

(aa) The term "special nuclear material" means (1) plutonium, uranium enriched in the isotope 233 or in the isotope 235, and any other material

---

[7] *Ed. Note:* References to the "Commission" in sections 42 U.S.C. 2014 and 2181–90 incl., no longer mean the Atomic Energy Commission, which has been abolished. See sections 42 U.S.C. 5811, 5814, 5841, and 7151, *infra,* under which its functions have been transferred to the Department of Energy and the Nuclear Regulatory Commission. Under the transitional provisions (42 U.S.C. 5871) a reference to "Commission" in any existing statute may mean either of these new agencies.

which the Commission, pursuant to the provisions of section 51 [42 U.S.C. §2071], determines to be special nuclear material, but does not include source material; or (2) any material artificially enriched by any of the foregoing, but does not include source material. * * *

(Aug. 30, 1954, c. 1073, ch. 2, §11, 68 Stat. 922; Sept. 2, 1957, Pub. L. 85-256, §3, 71 Stat. 576.)

42 U.S.C. § 2181   Inventions relating to atomic weapons, and filing of reports

(a) No patent shall hereafter be granted for any invention or discovery which is useful solely in the utilization of special nuclear material or atomic energy in an atomic weapon. Any patent granted for any such invention or discovery is hereby revoked, and just compensation shall be made therefor.

(b) No patent hereafter granted shall confer any rights with respect to any invention or discovery to the extent that such invention or discovery is used in the utilization of special nuclear material or atomic energy in atomic weapons. Any rights conferred by any patent heretofore granted for any invention or discovery are revoked to the extent that such invention or discovery is so used, and just compensation shall be made therefor.

(c) Any person who has made or hereafter makes any invention or discovery useful in the production or utilization of special nuclear material or atomic energy, shall file with the Commission a report containing a complete description thereof unless such invention or discovery is described in an application for a patent filed with the Under Secretary of Commerce for Intellectual Property and Director of the United States Patent and Trademark Office by such person within the time required for the filing of such report. The report covering any such invention or discovery shall be filed on or before the one hundred and eightieth day after such person first discovers or first has reason to believe that such invention or discovery is useful in such production or utilization.

(d) The Under Secretary of Commerce for Intellectual Property and Director of the United States Patent and Trademark Office shall notify the Commission of all applications for patents heretofore or hereafter filed which, in his opinion, disclose inventions or discoveries required to be reported under subsection (c) of this section, and shall provide the Commission access to all such applications.

(e) Reports filed pursuant to subsection (c) of this section, and applications to which access is provided under subsection (d) of this section, shall be kept in confidence by the Commission, and no information concerning the same given without authority of the inventor or owner unless necessary to carry out the provisions of any Act of Congress or in such special circumstances as may be determined by the Commission.

(Aug. 30, 1954, c. 1073, ch. 13, §151, 68 Stat. 943; Sept. 6, 1961, Pub. L. 87-206, §§7-9, 75 Stat. 477; Nov. 29, 1999, Pub. L. 106-113, §4732, 113 Stat. 1501A-581.)

42 U.S.C. § 2182   Inventions conceived during Commission contracts

Any invention or discovery, useful in the production or utilization of special nuclear material or atomic energy, made or conceived in the course of or under any contract, subcontract, or arrangement entered into with or for the benefit of the Commission, regardless of whether the contract, subcontract, or arrangement involved the expenditure of funds by the Commission, shall be vested in, and be the property of, the Commission, except that the Commission may waive its claim to any such invention or discovery under such circumstances as the Commission may deem appropriate, consistent with the policy of this section. No patent for any invention or discovery, useful in the production or utilization of special nuclear material or atomic energy, shall be issued unless the applicant files with the application, or within thirty days after request therefor by the Under Secretary of Commerce for Intellectual Property and Director of the United States Patent and Trademark Office (unless the Commission advises the Under Secretary of Commerce for Intellectual Property and Director of the United States Patent and Trademark Office that its rights have been determined and that accordingly no statement is necessary) a statement under oath setting forth the full facts surrounding the making or conception of the invention or discovery described in the application and whether the invention or discovery was made or conceived in the course of or under any contract, subcontract, or arrangement entered into with or for the benefit of the Commission, regardless of whether the contract, subcontract, or arrangement involved the expenditure of funds by the Commission. The Under Secretary of Commerce for Intellectual Property and Director of the United States Patent and Trademark Office shall as soon as the application is otherwise in condition for allowance forward copies of the application and the statement to the Commission.

The Under Secretary of Commerce for Intellectual Property and Director of the United States Patent and Trademark Office may proceed with the application and issue the patent to the applicant (if the invention or discovery is otherwise patentable) unless the Commission, within 90 days after receipt of copies of the application and statement, directs the Under Secretary of Commerce for Intellectual Property and Director of the United States Patent and Trademark Office to issue the patent to the Commission (if the invention or discovery is otherwise patentable) to be held by the Commission as the agent of and on behalf of the United States.

If the Commission files such a direction with the Under Secretary of Commerce for Intellectual Property and Director of the United States Patent and Trademark Office, and if the applicant's statement claims, and the applicant still believes, that the invention or discovery was not made or conceived in the course of or under any contract, subcontract, or arrangement entered into with or for the benefit of the Commission entitling the Commission to the title to the application or the patent the applicant may, within 30 days after notification of the filing of such a direction, request a hearing before the Patent Trial and Appeal Board. The Board shall have the power to hear and determine whether the Commission was entitled to the direction filed with the Under Secretary of Commerce for Intellectual Property and Director of the United States Patent and Trademark Office. The Board shall follow the rules and procedures established for interference and derivation cases and an appeal may be taken by either the applicant or the Commission from the final order of the Board to the United States Court of Appeals for the Federal Circuit in accordance with the procedures governing the appeals from the Patent Trial and Appeal Board.

If the statement filed by the applicant should thereafter be found to contain false material statements any notification by the Commission that it has no objections to the issuance of a patent to the applicant shall not be deemed in any respect to constitute a waiver of the provisions of this section or of any applicable civil or criminal statute, and the Commission may have the title to the patent transferred to the Commission on the records of the Under Secretary of Commerce for Intellectual Property and Director of the United States Patent and Trademark Office in accordance with the provisions of this section. A determination of rights by the Director pursuant to a contractual provision or other arrangement prior to the request of the Under Secretary of Commerce for Intellectual Property and Director of the United States Patent and Trademark Office for the statement, shall be final in the absence of false material statements or nondisclosure of material facts by the applicant.

(Aug. 30, 1954, c. 1073, ch. 13, §152, 68 Stat. 944; Sept. 6, 1961, Pub. L. 87-206, §10, 75 Stat. 477; Aug. 29, 1962, Pub. L. 87-615, §11, 76 Stat. 411; Apr. 2, 1982, Pub. L. 97-164,

42 U.S.C. § 2182

§162, 96 Stat. 49; Nov. 8, 1984, Pub. L. 98-622, §205, 98 Stat. 3388; Nov. 29, 1988, Pub. L. 106-113, §4732, 113 Stat. 1501A-581; Sept. 16, 2011, Pub. L. 112-29, §7, 125 Stat. 315.)

42 U.S.C. § 2183   Nonmilitary utilization

(a) The Commission may, after giving the patent owner an opportunity for a hearing, declare any patent to be affected with the public interest if (1) the invention or discovery covered by the patent is of primary importance in the production or utilization of special nuclear material or atomic energy; and (2) the licensing of such invention or discovery under this section is of primary importance to effectuate the policies and purposes of this Act.

(b) Whenever any patent has been declared affected with the public interest, pursuant to subsection (a) of this section—

(1) the Commission is hereby licensed to use the invention or discovery covered by such patent in performing any of its powers under this Act; and

(2) any person may apply to the Commission for a nonexclusive patent license to use the invention or discovery covered by such patent, and the Commission shall grant such patent license to the extent that it finds that the use of the invention or discovery is of primary importance to the conduct of an activity by such person authorized under this Act.

(c) Any person—

(1) who has made application to the Commission for a license under sections 2073, 2092, 2093, 2111, 2133 or 2134 of this title, or a permit or lease under section 2097 of this title;

(2) to whom such license, permit, or lease has been issued by the Commission;

(3) who is authorized to conduct such activities as such applicant is conducting or proposes to conduct under a general license issued by the Commission under sections 2092 or 2111 of this title; or

(4) whose activities or proposed activities are authorized under section 2051 of this title,

may at any time make application to the Commission for a patent license for the use of an invention or discovery useful in the production or utilization of special nuclear material or atomic energy covered by a patent. Each such application shall set forth the nature and purpose of the use which the applicant intends to make of the patent license, the steps taken by the applicant to obtain a patent license from the owner of the patent, and a statement of the effects, as estimated by the applicant, on the authorized activities which will result from failure to obtain such patent license and which will result from the granting of such patent license.

(d) Whenever any person has made an application to the Commission for a patent license pursuant to subsection (c) of this section—

(1) the Commission, within 30 days after the filing of such application, shall make available to the owner of the patent all of the information contained in such application, and shall notify the owner of the patent of the time and place at which a hearing will be held by the Commission;

(2) the Commission shall hold a hearing within 60 days after the filing of such application at a time and place designated by the Commission; and

(3) in the event an applicant for two or more patent licenses, the Commission may, in its discretion, order the consolidation of such applications, and if the patents are owned by more than one owner, such owners may be made parties to one hearing.

(e) If, after any hearing conducted pursuant to subsection (d) of this section, the Commission finds that—

(1) the invention or discovery covered by the patent is of primary importance in the production or utilization of special nuclear material or atomic energy;

(2) the licensing of such invention or discovery is of primary importance to the conduct of the activities of the applicant;

(3) the activities to which the patent license are proposed to be applied by such applicant are of primary importance to the furtherance of policies and purposes of this Act; and

(4) such applicant cannot otherwise obtain a patent license from the owner of the patent on terms which the Commission deems to be reasonable for the intended use of the patent to be made by such applicant,

the Commission shall license the applicant to use the invention or discovery covered by the patent for the purposes stated in such application on terms deemed equitable by the Commission and generally not less fair than those granted by the patentee or by the Commission to similar licensees for comparable use.

42 U.S.C. § 2183

(f) The Commission shall not grant any patent license pursuant to subsection (e) of this section for any other purpose than that stated in the application. Nor shall the Commission grant any patent license to any other applicant for a patent license on the same patent without an application being made by such applicant pursuant to subsection (c) of this section, and without separate notification and hearing as provided in subsection (d) of this section, and without a separate finding as provided in subsection (e) of this section.

(g) The owner of the patent affected by a declaration or a finding made by the Commission pursuant to subsection (b) or (e) of this section shall be entitled to a reasonable royalty fee from the licensee for any use of an invention or discovery licensed by this section. Such royalty fee may be agreed upon by such owner and the patent licensee, or in the absence of such agreement shall be determined for each patent license by the Commission pursuant to section 2187(c) of this title.

(h) The provisions of this section shall apply to any patent the application for which shall have been filed before September 1, 1979.

(Aug. 30, 1954, c. 1073, ch. 13, 68 Stat. 945; amended variously as to the date in (h) the latest being Aug. 17, 1974, Pub. L. 93-377, §6, 88 Stat. 475.)

42 U.S.C. § 2184   Injunctions

No court shall have jurisdiction or power to stay, restrain, or otherwise enjoin the use of any invention or discovery by a patent licensee, to the extent that such use is licensed by section 2183(b) or 2183(e) of this title. If, in any action against such patent licensee, the court shall determine that the defendant is exercising such license, the measure of damages shall be the royalty fee determined pursuant to section 2187(c) of this title, together with such costs, interest, and reasonable attorney's fees as may be fixed by the court. If no royalty fee has been determined, the court shall stay the proceeding until the royalty fee is determined pursuant to section 2187(c) of this title. If any such patent licensee shall fail to pay such royalty fee, the patentee may bring an action in any court of competent jurisdiction for such royalty fee, together with such costs, interest, and reasonable attorney's fees as may be fixed by the court.

(Aug. 30, 1954, c. 1073, ch. 13, §154, 68 Stat. 946.)

42 U.S.C. § 2185   Prior art

In connection with applications for patents covered by this subchapter, the fact that the invention or discovery was known or used before shall be a bar to the patenting of such invention or discovery even though such prior knowledge or use was under secrecy within the atomic energy program of the United States.

(Aug. 30, 1954, c. 1073, ch. 13, §155, 68 Stat. 947.)

42 U.S.C. § 2186   Commission patent licenses

The Commission shall establish standard specifications upon which it may grant a patent license to use any patent declared to be affected with the public interest pursuant to section 2183(a) of this title. Such a patent license shall not waive any of the other provisions of this Act.

(Aug. 30, 1954, c. 1073, ch. 13, 68 Stat. 947; Dec. 12, 1980, Pub. L. 96-517, §7, 94 Stat. 3027.)

42 U.S.C. § 2187   Compensation, awards, and royalties

(a) *Patent Compensation Board.*—The Commission shall designate a Patent Compensation Board to consider applications under this section. The members of the Board shall receive a per diem compensation for each day spent in meetings or conferences, and all members shall receive their necessary traveling or other expenses while engaged in the work of the Board. The members of the Board may serve as such without regard to the provisions of sections 281, 283, or 284 of Title 18 of the United States Code, except in so far as such sections may prohibit any such member from receiving compensation in respect of any particular matter which directly involves the Commission or in which the Commission is directly interested.

(b) *Eligibility.*—

(1) Any owner of a patent licensed under section 2188 or subsections 2183(b) or 2183(e) of this title, or any patent licensee thereunder may make application to the Commission for the determination of a reasonable royalty fee in accordance with such procedures as the Commission by regulation may establish.

(2) Any person seeking to obtain the just compensation provided in section 2181 of this title shall make application therefor to the Commission in accordance with such procedures as the Commission may by regulation establish.

(3) Any person making any invention or discovery useful in the production or utilization of special nuclear material or atomic energy, who is not entitled to compensation or a royalty therefor under this Act and who has

complied with the provisions of section 2181(c) of this title may make application to the Commission for, and the Commission may grant, an award. The Commission may also, after consultation with the General Advisory Committee, and with the approval of the President, grant an award for any especially meritorious contribution to the development, use, or control of atomic energy.

(c) *Standards.* —

(1) In determining a reasonable royalty fee as provided for in section 2183(b) or 2183(e) of this title, the Commission shall take into consideration (A) the advice of the Patent Compensation Board; (B) any defense, general or special, that might be pleaded by a defendant in an action for infringement; (C) the extent to which, if any, such patent was developed through federally financed research; and (D) the degree of utility, novelty, and importance of the invention or discovery, and may consider the cost to the owner of the patent of developing such invention or discovery or acquiring such patent.

(2) In determining what constitutes just compensation as provided for in section 2181 of this title, or in determining the amount of any award under subsection (b)(3) of this section, the Commission shall take into account the considerations set forth in subsection (c)(1) of this subsection and the actual use of such invention or discovery. Such compensation may be paid by the Commission in periodic payments or in a lump sum.

(d) *Limitations.*—Every application under this section shall be barred unless filed within six years after the date on which first accrues the right to such reasonable royalty fee, just compensation, or award for which such application is filed.

(Aug. 30, 1954, c. 1073, ch. 13, §157, 68 Stat. 947; Sept. 6, 1961, Pub. L. 87-206, §11, 75 Stat. 478; May 10, 1974, Pub. L. 93-276, §201, 88 Stat. 119.)

Ed. Note.—The Patent Compensation Board and the General Advisory Committee, referred to above, have been transferred to the Department of Energy. See 42 U.S.C. 5814(d) and 7151, *infra.*

42 U.S.C. § 2188   Monopolistic use of patents

Whenever the owner of any patent hereafter granted for any invention or discovery of primary use in the utilization or production of special nuclear material or atomic energy is found by a court of competent jurisdiction to have intentionally used such patent in a manner so as to violate any of the antitrust laws specified in section 2135(a) of this title, there may be included in the judgment of the court, in its discretion and in addition to any other lawful sanctions, a requirement that such owner license such patent to any other licensee of the Commission who demonstrates a need therefor. If the court, at its discretion, deems that such licensee shall pay a reasonable royalty to the owner of the patent, the reasonable royalty shall be determined in accordance with section 2187 of this title.

(Aug. 30, 1954, c. 1073, ch. 13, §158, 68 Stat. 947; Sept. 6, 1961, Pub. L. 87-206, §12, 75 Stat. 478.)

42 U.S.C. § 2189   Federally financed research

Nothing in this Act shall affect the right of the Commission to require that patents granted on inventions, made or conceived during the course of federally financed research or operations, be assigned to the United States.

(Aug. 30, 1954, c. 1073, ch. 13, §159, 68 Stat. 948.)

42 U.S.C. § 2190   Saving clause

Any patent application on which a patent was denied by the United States Patent Office under sections 11(a)(1), 11(a)(2), or 11(b) of the Atomic Energy Act of 1946, and which is not prohibited by section 2181 or 2185 of this title may be reinstated upon application to the Director of Patents within one year after enactment of this Act [August 30, 1954], and shall then be deemed to have been continuously pending since its original filing date: *Provided, however,* That no patent issued upon any patent application so reinstated shall in any way furnish a basis of claim against the Government of the United States.

(Aug. 30, 1954, c. 1073, ch. 13, §160, 68 Stat. 948.)

*   *   *   *   *   *   *

2. GENERAL PROVISIONS

42 U.S.C. § 2201   General provisions

In the performance of its functions the Commission is authorized to

*   *   *

(g) acquire, purchase, lease, and hold real and personal property, including patents, as agent of and on behalf of the United States, subject to the provisions of section 2224 of this title, and to sell, lease, grant and dispose of such real and personal property as provided in this Act; *   *   *

(Aug. 30, 1954, c. 1073, ch. 14, §161, 68 Stat. 948.)

42 U.S.C. § 5811   Establishment of Energy Research and Development Administration

There is hereby established an independent executive agency to be known as the Energy Research and Development Administration (hereinafter in this Act referred to as the "Administration").

(Oct. 11, 1974, Pub. L. 93-438, §101, 88 Stat. 1234.)

42 U.S.C. § 5814   Abolition and transfers

(a) The Atomic Energy Commission is hereby abolished. * * *

(b) All other functions of the Commission, the Chairman and members of the Commission, and the officers and components of the Commission are hereby transferred or allowed to lapse pursuant to the provisions of this Act.

(c) There are hereby transferred to and vested in the Administrator all functions of the Atomic Energy Commission, the Chairman and members of the Commission, and the officers and components of the Commission, except as otherwise provided in this Act.

(d) The General Advisory Committee established pursuant to section 2036 of this title, the Patent Compensation Board established pursuant to section 2187 of this title * * * are transferred to the Energy Research and Development Administration and the functions of the Commission with respect thereto * * * are transferred to the Administrator.

*   *   *

(Oct. 11, 1974, Pub. L. 93-438, §104, 88 Stat. 1237.)

42 U.S.C. § 5817   Powers of the Administrator [now Secretary of Energy]

(a) *Research and development.*—* * * Such functions of the Administrator under this Act as are applicable to the nuclear activities transferred pursuant to this title shall be subject to the provisions of the Atomic Energy Act of 1954, as amended, and to other authority applicable to such nuclear activities. * * *

*   *   *

(d) *Acquisition of copyrights and patents.*—The administrator is authorized to acquire any of the following described rights if the property acquired thereby is for the use in, or is useful to, the performance of functions vested in him:

(1) Copyrights, patents, and applications for patents, designs, processes, specifications, and data.

(2) Licenses under copyrights, patents, and applications for patents.

42 U.S.C. § 5811

(3) Releases, before suit is brought, for past infringement of patents or copyrights.

* * *

(Pub. L. 93-438, Oct. 11, 1974, 88 Stat. 1240.)

42 U.S.C. § 5841   Establishment and transfers

(a) (1) There is established an independent regulatory Commission to be known as the Nuclear Regulatory Commission which shall be composed of five members * * *

* * *

(f) There are hereby transferred to the Commission all the licensing and related regulatory functions of the Atomic Energy Commission * * * which functions * * * are excepted from the transfer to the Administrator by section 5814(c) of this title. * * *

(Oct. 11, 1974, Pub. L. 93-438, §201, 88 Stat. 1242; Aug. 9, 1975, Pub. L. 94-79, §§201-03, 89 Stat. 413-14.)

42 U.S.C. § 5845   Office of Nuclear Regulatory Research

* * *

(b) Subject to the provisions of this Act, the Director of Nuclear Regulatory Research shall perform such functions as the Commission shall delegate including:

* * *

(2) Engaging in or contracting for research which the Commission deems necessary for the performance of its licensing and related regulatory functions.

* * *

(Oct. 11, 1974, Pub. L. 93-438, §205, 88 Stat. 1246.)

42 U.S.C. § 7151   General transfers

(a) Except as otherwise provided in this Act, there are hereby transferred to, and vested in, the Secretary [of Energy] all of the functions vested by law in the * * * Administrator of the Energy Research and Development Administration or the Energy Research and Development Administration * * *

(Aug. 4, 1977, Pub. L. 95-91, §301, 91 Stat. 577.)

42 U.S.C. § 7261   Acquisition of copyrights, patents etc.

The Secretary is authorized to acquire any of the following described rights if the property acquired thereby is for use by or for, or useful to, the Department:

(1) copyrights, patents, and applications for patents, designs, processes, and manufacturing data;

(2) licenses under copyrights, patents, and applications for patents; and

(3) releases, before suit is brought, for past infringement of patents or copyrights.

(Aug. 4, 1977, Pub. L. 95-91, §651, 91 Stat. 601.)

42 U.S.C. § 7261a   Protection of sensitive technical information

(a) *Property rights in inventions and discoveries.*

(1) Whenever any contractor makes an invention or discovery to which the title vests in the Department of Energy pursuant to exercise of section 202(a)(ii) or (iv) of title 35, United States Code, or pursuant to section 152 of the Atomic Energy Act of 1954 (42 U.S.C. 2182) or section 9 of the Federal Nonnuclear Energy Research and Development Act of 1974 (42 U.S.C. 5908) in the course of or under any Government contract or subcontract of the Naval Nuclear Propulsion Program or the nuclear weapons programs or other atomic energy defense activities of the Department of Energy and the contractor requests waiver of any or all of the Government's property rights, the Secretary of Energy may decide to waive the Government's rights and assign the rights in such invention or discovery.

(2) Such decision shall be made within 150 days after the date on which a complete request for waiver of such rights has been submitted to the Secretary by the contractor. For purposes of this paragraph, a complete request includes such information, in such detail and form, as the Secretary by regulation prescribes as necessary to allow the Secretary to take into consideration the matters described in subsection (b) in making the decision.

(3) If the Secretary fails to make the decision within such 150-day period, the Secretary shall submit to the Committees on Armed Services of the House of Representatives and the Senate, within 10 days after the end of the 150-day period, a report on the reasons for such failure. The submission of such report shall not relieve the Secretary of the requirement to

make the decision under this section. The Secretary shall, at the end of each 30-day period after submission of the first report during which the Secretary continues to fail to make the decision required by this section, submit another report on the reasons for such failure to the committees listed in this paragraph.

(b) *Matters to be considered.* —In making a decision under this section, the Secretary shall consider, in addition to the applicable policies of section 152 of the Atomic Energy Act of 1954 (42 U.S.C. 2182) or subsections (c) and (d) of section 9 of the Federal Nonnuclear Energy Research and Development Act of 1974 (42 U.S.C. 5908)—

(1) whether national security will be compromised;

(2) whether sensitive technical information (whether classified or unclassified) under the Naval Nuclear Propulsion Program or the nuclear weapons programs or other atomic energy defense activities of the department of Energy for which dissemination is controlled under federal statutes and regulations will be released to unauthorized person;

(3) whether an organizational conflict of interest contemplated by Federal statutes and regulations will result; and

(4) whether failure to assert such a claim will adversely affect the operation of the Naval Nuclear Propulsion Program or the nuclear weapons programs or other atomic energy defense activities of the Department of Energy.

(Nov. 14, 1986, Pub. L. 99-661, §3131, 100 Stat. 4062; Dec. 4, 1987, Pub. L. 100-180, §3135, 101 Stat. 1240.)

*   *   *   *   *   *   *

3. RIGHTS TO INVENTIONS ARISING FROM SPONSORED R&D

42 U.S.C. § 5908   Patents and inventions

(a) *Vesting of title to invention and issuance of patents to United States; prerequisites.* —Whenever any invention is made or conceived in the course of or under any contract of the Secretary other than nuclear energy research, development, and demonstration pursuant to the Atomic Energy Act of 1954 (42 U.S.C. 2011 et. seq.) and the Secretary determines that—

(1) the person who made the invention was employed or assigned to perform research, development, or demonstration work and the invention

is related to the work he was employed or assigned to perform, or that it was within the scope of his employment duties, whether or not it was made during working hours, or with a contribution by the Government of the use of Government facilities, equipment, materials, allocated funds, information proprietary to the Government, or services of Government employees during working hours; or

(2) the person who made the invention was not employed or assigned to perform research, development, or demonstration work, but the invention is nevertheless related to the contract or to the work or duties he was employed or assigned to perform, and was made during working hours, or with a contribution from the Government of the sort referred to in clause (1),

title to such invention shall vest in the United States, and if patents on such invention are issued they shall be issued to the United States, unless in particular circumstances the Secretary waives all or any part of the rights of the United States to such invention in conformity with the provisions of this section.

(b) *Contract as requiring report to Secretary of inventions, etc., made in course of contract.*—Each contract entered into by the Secretary with any person shall contain effective provisions under which such person shall furnish promptly to the Secretary a written report containing full and complete technical information concerning any invention, discovery, improvement, or innovation which may be made in the course of or under such contract.

(c) *Waiver by Secretary of rights of United States: regulations prescribing procedures; record of waiver determinations; objectives.*—Under such regulations in conformity with the provisions of this section as the Secretary shall prescribe, the Secretary may waive all or any part of the rights of the United States under this section with respect to any invention or class of inventions made or which may be made by any person or class of persons in the course of or under any contract of the Secretary if he determines that the interests of the United States and the general public will best be served by such waiver. The Secretary shall maintain a publicly available, periodically updated record of waiver determinations. In making such determinations, the Secretary shall have the following objectives:

(1) Making the benefits of the energy research, development, and demonstration program widely available to the public in the shortest practicable time.

42 U.S.C. § 5908

(2) Promoting the commercial utilization of such inventions.

(3) Encouraging participation by private persons in the Secretary's energy research, development, and demonstration program.

(4) Fostering competition and preventing undue market concentration or the creation or maintenance of other situations inconsistent with the anti-trust laws.

(d) *Considerations applicable at time of contracting for waiver determination by Secretary.*—In determining whether a waiver to the contractor at the time of contracting will best serve the interests of the United States and the general public, the Secretary shall specifically include as considerations—

(1) the extent to which the participation of the contractor will expedite the attainment of the purposes of the program;

(2) the extent to which a waiver of all or any part of such rights in any or all fields of technology is needed to secure the participation of the particular contractor;

(3) the extent to which the contractor's commercial position may expedite utilization of the research, development, and demonstration program results;

(4) the extent to which the Government has contributed to the field of technology to be funded under the contract;

(5) the purpose and nature of the contract, including the intended use of the results developed thereunder;

(6) the extent to which the contractor has made or will make substantial investment of financial resources or technology developed at the contractor's private expense which will directly benefit the work to be performed under the contract;

(7) the extent to which the field of technology to be funded under the contract has been developed at the contractor's private expense;

(8) the extent to which the Government intends to further develop to the point of commercial utilization the results of the contract effort;

(9) the extent to which the contract objectives are concerned with the public health, public safety, or public welfare;

(10) the likely effect of the waiver on competition and market concentration; and

42 U.S.C. § 5908

(11) in the case of a nonprofit educational institution, the extent to which such institution has a technology transfer capability and program, approved by the Secretary as being consistent with the applicable policies of this section.

(e) *Considerations applicable to identified invention for waiver determination by Secretary.*—In determining whether a waiver to the contractor or inventor of rights to an identified invention will best serve the interests of the United States and the general public, the Secretary shall specifically include as considerations paragraphs (4) through (11) of subsection (d) of this section as applied to the invention and—

(1) the extent to which such waiver is a reasonable and necessary incentive to call forth private risk capital for the development and commercialization of the invention; and

(2) the extent to which the plans, intentions, and ability of the contractor or inventor will obtain expeditious commercialization of such invention.

(f) *Rights subject to reservation where title to invention vested in United States.*— Whenever title to an invention is vested in the United States there may be reserved to the contractor or inventor—

(1) a revocable or irrevocable nonexclusive, paid-up license for the practice of the invention throughout the world; and

(2) the rights to such invention in any foreign country where the United States has elected not to secure patent rights and the contractor elects to do so, subject to the rights set forth in paragraphs (2), (3), (6), and (7) of subsection (h) of this section: *Provided,* That when specifically requested by the Secretary and three years after issuance of such a patent, the contractor shall submit the report specified in subsection (h)(1) of this section.

(g) – (i) [Repealed].

(j) *Small business status of applicant for waiver or licenses.*—The Secretary shall, in granting waivers or licenses, consider the small business status of the applicant.

(k) *Protection of invention, etc., rights by Secretary.*—The Secretary is authorized to take all suitable and necessary steps to protect any invention or discovery to which the United States holds title, and to require that contractors or persons who acquire rights to inventions under this section protect such inventions.

42 U.S.C. § 5908

(*l*) *Department of Energy as defense agency of United States for purpose of maintaining secrecy of inventions.* — The Department of Energy shall be considered a defense agency of the United States for the purpose of chapter 17 of Title 35.

(m) *Definitions.* — As used in this section —

(1) the term "person" means any individual, partnership, corporation, association, institution, or other entity;

(2) the term "contract" means any contract, grant, agreement, understanding, or other arrangement, which includes research, development, or demonstration work, and includes any assignment, substitution of parties, or subcontract executed or entered into thereunder;

(3) the term "made," when used in relation to any invention, means the conception or first actual reduction to practice of such invention;

(4) the term "invention" means inventions or discoveries, whether patented or unpatented; and

(5) the term "contractor" means any person having a contract with or on behalf of the Administration.

(n) *Report concerning applicability of existing patent policies to energy programs; time for submission to President and appropriate congressional committees.* — Within twelve months after December 31, 1974, the Secretary with the participation of the Attorney General, the Secretary of Commerce, and other officials as the President may designate, shall submit to the President and the appropriate congressional committees a report concerning the applicability of existing patent policies affecting the programs under this chapter, along with his recommendations for amendments or additions to the statutory patent policy, including his recommendations on mandatory licensing, which he deems advisable for carrying out the purposes of this chapter.

(Dec. 31, 1974, Pub. L. 93-577, §9, 88 Stat. 1887; Aug. 4, 1977, Pub. L. 95-91, §§301, 703, 707, 91 Stat. 577, 606, 607; Dec. 12, 1980, Pub. L. 96-517, §7, 94 Stat. 3027.)

B. NATIONAL AERONAUTICS AND SPACE ADMINISTRATION

51 U.S.C. § 20113   Powers of the Administration in performance of functions
* * *

(c) *Property.* — In the performance of its functions, the Administration is authorized —

(1) to acquire (by purchase, lease, condemnation, or otherwise), construct, improve, repair, operate, and maintain laboratories, research and testing sites and facilities, aeronautical and space vehicles, quarters and related accommodations for employees and dependents of employees of the Administration, and such other real and personal property (including patents), or any interest therein, as the Administration deems necessary within and outside the continental United States;

* * *

(4) to sell and otherwise dispose of real and personal property (including patents and rights thereunder) in accordance with the provisions of chapters 1 to 11 of title 40 and in accordance with title III of the Federal Property and Administrative Services Act of 1949 (41 U.S.C. 251 et seq.);

* * *

(Pub. L. 111–314, §3, Dec. 18, 2010, 124 Stat. 3333.)

51 U.S.C. § 20135   Property rights in inventions

(a) *Definitions.* — In this section:

(1) *Contract.* — The term "contract" means any actual or proposed contract, agreement, understanding, or other arrangement, and includes any assignment, substitution of parties, or subcontract executed or entered into thereunder.

(2) *Made.* — The term "made", when used in relation to any invention, means the conception or first actual reduction to practice of such invention.

(3) *Person.* — The term "person" means any individual, partnership, corporation, association, institution, or other entity.

(b) *Exclusive property of United States.* —

(1) *In general.* — An invention shall be the exclusive property of the United States if it is made in the performance of any work under any contract of the Administration, and the Administrator determines that—

(A) the person who made the invention was employed or assigned to perform research, development, or exploration work and the invention is related to the work the person was employed or assigned to perform, or was within the scope of the person's employment duties, whether or not it was made during working hours, or with a contribution by the Government of the use of Government facilities, equipment, materials, allocated funds, information proprietary to the Government, or services of Government employees during working hours; or

(B) the person who made the invention was not employed or assigned to perform research, development, or exploration work, but the invention is nevertheless related to the contract, or to the work or duties the person was employed or assigned to perform, and was made during working hours, or with a contribution from the Government of the sort referred to in subparagraph (A).

(2) *Patent to United States.* — If an invention is the exclusive property of the United States under paragraph (1), and if such invention is patentable, a patent therefor shall be issued to the United States upon application made by the Administrator, unless the Administrator waives all or any part of the rights of the United States to such invention in conformity with the provisions of subsection (g).

(c) *Contract provisions for furnishing reports of inventions, discoveries, improvements, or innovations.* — Each contract entered into by the Administrator with any party for the performance of any work shall contain effective provisions under which the party shall furnish promptly to the Administrator a written report containing full and complete technical information concerning any invention, discovery, improvement, or innovation which may be made in the performance of any such work.

(d) *Patent application.* — No patent may be issued to any applicant other than the Administrator for any invention which appears to the Under Secretary of Commerce for Intellectual Property and Director of the United States Patent and Trademark Office (hereafter in this section referred to as the "Director") to have significant utility in the conduct of aeronautical and space activities unless the applicant files with the Director, with the application or within 30 days after request therefor by the Director, a written statement executed under oath setting forth the full facts concerning the circumstances under which the invention was made and stating the relationship (if any) of the invention to the performance of any work under any contract of the Administration. Copies of each such statement and the application to which it relates shall be transmitted forthwith by the Director to the Administrator.

51 U.S.C. § 20135

(e) *Issuance of patent to applicant.*—Upon any application as to which any such statement has been transmitted to the Administrator, the Director may, if the invention is patentable, issue a patent to the applicant unless the Administrator, within 90 days after receipt of the application and statement, requests that the patent be issued to the Administrator on behalf of the United States. If, within such time, the Administrator files such a request with the Director, the Director shall transmit notice thereof to the applicant, and shall issue such patent to the Administrator unless the applicant within 30 days after receipt of the notice requests a hearing before the Patent Trial and Appeal Board on the question whether the Administrator is entitled under this section to receive the patent. The Board may hear and determine, in accordance with rules and procedures established for interference and derivation cases, the question so presented, and its determination shall be subject to appeal by the applicant or by the Administrator to the United States Court of Appeals for the Federal Circuit in accordance with procedures governing appeals from decisions of the Patent Trial and Appeal Board in other proceedings.

(f) *Subsequent transfer of patent in case of false representations.*—Whenever a patent has been issued to an applicant in conformity with subsection (e), and the Administrator thereafter has reason to believe that the statement filed by the applicant in connection with the patent contained a false representation of a material fact, the Administrator, within 5 years after the date of issuance of the patent, may file with the Director a request for the transfer to the Administrator of title to the patent on the records of the Director. Notice of any such request shall be transmitted by the Director to the owner of record of the patent, and title to the patent shall be so transferred to the Administrator unless, within 30 days after receipt of notice, the owner of record requests a hearing before the Patent Trial and Appeal Board on the question whether any such false representation was contained in the statement filed in connection with the patent. The question shall be heard and determined, and the determination shall be subject to review, in the manner prescribed by subsection (e) for questions arising thereunder. A request made by the Administrator under this subsection for the transfer of title to a patent, and prosecution for the violation of any criminal statute, shall not be barred by the failure of the Administrator to make a request under subsection (e) for the issuance of the patent to the Administrator, or by any notice previously given by the Administrator stating that the Administrator had no objection to the issuance of the patent to the applicant.

51 U.S.C. § 20135

(g) *Waiver of rights to inventions.* — Under such regulations in conformity with this subsection as the Administrator shall prescribe, the Administrator may waive all or any part of the rights of the United States under this section with respect to any invention or class of inventions made or which may be made by any person or class of persons in the performance of any work required by any contract of the Administration if the Administrator determines that the interests of the United States will be served thereby. Any such waiver may be made upon such terms and under such conditions as the Administrator shall determine to be required for the protection of the interests of the United States. Each such waiver made with respect to any invention shall be subject to the reservation by the Administrator of an irrevocable, nonexclusive, nontransferable, royalty-free license for the practice of such invention throughout the world by or on behalf of the United States or any foreign government pursuant to any treaty or agreement with the United States. Each proposal for any waiver under this subsection shall be referred to an Inventions and Contributions Board which shall be established by the Administrator within the Administration. Such Board shall accord to each interested party an opportunity for hearing, and shall transmit to the Administrator its findings of fact with respect to such proposal and its recommendations for action to be taken with respect thereto.

(h) *Protection of title.* — The Administrator is authorized to take all suitable and necessary steps to protect any invention or discovery to which the Administrator has title, and to require contractors or persons who retain title to inventions or discoveries under this section to protect the inventions or discoveries to which the Administration has or may acquire a license of use.

(i) *Administration as defense agency.* — The Administration shall be considered a defense agency of the United States for the purpose of chapter 17 of title 35.

(j) *Objects intended for launch, launched, or assembled in outer space.* — Any object intended for launch, launched, or assembled in outer space shall be considered a vehicle for the purpose of section 272 of title 35.

(k) *Use or manufacture of patented inventions incorporated in space vehicles launched for persons other than United States.* — The use or manufacture of any patented invention incorporated in a space vehicle launched by the United States Government for a person other than the United States shall not be considered to be a use or manufacture by or for the United States within the

51 U.S.C. § 20135

meaning of section 1498(a) of title 28, unless the Administration gives an express authorization or consent for such use or manufacture.

(Pub. L. 111-314, §3, Dec. 18, 2010, 124 Stat. 3339; Pub. L. 112-29, §7(d)(2), Sept. 16, 2011, 125 Stat. 315.)

51 U.S.C. § 20136   Contributions awards

(a) *Applications.* — Subject to the provisions of this section, the Administrator is authorized, on the Administrator's own initiative or on application of any person, to make a monetary award, in an amount and on terms the Administrator determines to be warranted, to any person (as defined by section 20135(a) of this title) for any scientific or technical contribution to the Administration which is determined by the Administrator to have significant value in the conduct of aeronautical and space activities. Each application made for such an award shall be referred to the Inventions and Contributions Board established under section 20135 of this title. Such Board shall accord to each applicant an opportunity for hearing on the application, and shall transmit to the Administrator its recommendation as to the terms of the award, if any, to be made to the applicant for the contribution. In determining the terms and conditions of an award the Administrator shall take into account—

(1) the value of the contribution to the United States;

(2) the aggregate amount of any sums which have been expended by the applicant for the development of the contribution;

(3) the amount of any compensation (other than salary received for services rendered as an officer or employee of the Government) previously received by the applicant for or on account of the use of the contribution by the United States; and

(4) any other factors the Administrator determines to be material.

(b) *Apportionment of awards.* — If more than one applicant under subsection (a) claims an interest in the same contribution, the Administrator shall ascertain and determine the respective interests of the applicants, and shall apportion any award to be made among the applicants in amounts the Administrator determines to be equitable.

(c) *Surrender of other claims.* — No award may be made under subsection (a) unless the applicant surrenders, by means the Administrator determines to be effective, all claims that the applicant may have to receive any compensation (other than the award made under this section) for the use of the contribution or any element thereof at any time by or on behalf of the United States, or by or on behalf of any foreign government pursuant to a treaty or agreement with the United States, within the United States or at any other place.

(d) *Report and waiting period.*—No award may be made under subsection (a) in an amount exceeding $100,000 unless the Administrator transmits to the appropriate committees of Congress a full and complete report concerning the amount and terms of, and the basis for, the proposed award, and a period of 30 calendar days of regular session of Congress expires after receipt of the report by the committees.

(Pub. L. 111–314, §3, Dec. 18, 2010, 124 Stat. 3342.)

* * * * * * *

C. DEPARTMENT OF HEALTH AND HUMAN SERVICES

21 U.S.C. § 355 New drugs

(a) No person shall introduce or deliver for introduction into interstate commerce any new drug, unless an approval of an application filed pursuant to subsection (b) or (j) of this section is effective with respect to such drug.

(b) (1) Any person may file with the Secretary an application with respect to any drug subject to the provisions of subsection (a) of this section. Such person shall submit to the Secretary as a part of the application (A) full reports of investigations which have been made to show whether or not such drug is safe for use and whether such drug is effective in use; (B) a full list of the articles used as components of such drug; (C) a full statement of the composition of such drug; (D) a full description of the methods used in, and the facilities and controls used for, the manufacture, processing, and packing of such drug; (E) such samples of such drug and of the articles used as components thereof as the Secretary may require; and (F) specimens of the labeling proposed to be used for such drug. The applicant shall file with the application the patent number and the expiration date of any patent which claims the drug for which the applicant submitted the application or which claims a method of using such drug and with respect to which a claim of patent infringement could reasonably be asserted if a person not licensed by the owner engaged in the manufacture, use, or sale of the drug. If an application is filed under this subsection for a drug and a patent which claims such drug or a method of using such drug is issued after the filing date but before approval of the application, the applicant shall amend the application to include the information required by the preceding sentence. Upon approval of the application, the Secretary shall publish information submitted under the two preceding sentences.

(2) An application submitted under paragraph (1) for a drug for which the investigations described in clause (A) of such paragraph and relied upon by the applicant for approval of the application were not conducted by or for the applicant and for which the applicant has not obtained a right of reference or use from the person by or for whom the investigations were conducted shall also include—

(A) a certification, in the opinion of the applicant and to the best of his knowledge, with respect to each patent which claims the drug for which such investigations were conducted or which claims a use for such drug for which the applicant is seeking approval under this subsection and for which information is required to be filed under paragraph (1) or subsection (c)—

(i) that such patent information has not been filed,

(ii) that such patent has expired,

(iii) of the date on which such patent will expire, or

(iv) that such patent is invalid or will not be infringed by the manufacture, use, or sale of the new drug for which the application is submitted; and

(B) if with respect to the drug for which investigations described in paragraph (1)(A) were conducted information was filed under paragraph (1) or subsection (c) for a method of use patent which does not claim a use for which the applicant is seeking approval under this subsection, a statement that the method of use patent does not claim such a use.

(3) *Notice of opinion that patent is invalid or will not be infringed.*—

(A) *Agreement to give notice.*—An applicant that makes a certification described in paragraph (2)(A)(iv) shall include in the application a statement that the applicant will give notice as required by this paragraph.

(B) *Timing of notice.* — An applicant that makes a certification described in paragraph (2)(A)(iv) shall give notice as required under this paragraph —

> (i) if the certification is in the application, not later than 20 days after the date of the postmark on the notice with which the Secretary informs the applicant that the application has been filed; or

> (ii) if the certification is in an amendment or supplement to the application, at the time at which the applicant submits the amendment or supplement, regardless of whether the applicant has already given notice with respect to another such certification contained in the application or in an amendment or supplement to the application.

(C) *Recipients of notice.* — An applicant required under this paragraph to give notice shall give notice to —

> (i) each owner of the patent that is the subject of the certification (or a representative of the owner designated to receive such a notice); and

> (ii) the holder of the approved application under this subsection for the drug that is claimed by the patent or a use of which is claimed by the patent (or a representative of the holder designated to receive such a notice).

(D) *Contents of notice.* — A notice required under this paragraph shall —

> (i) state that an application that contains data from bioavailability or bioequivalence studies has been submitted under this subsection for the drug with respect to which the certification is made to obtain approval to engage in the commercial manufacture, use, or sale of the drug before the expiration of the patent referred to in the certification; and

> (ii) include a detailed statement of the factual and legal basis of the opinion of the applicant that the patent is invalid or will not be infringed.

(4) (A) An applicant may not amend or supplement an application referred to in paragraph (2) to seek approval of a drug that is a different drug than the drug identified in the application as submitted to the Secretary.

21 U.S.C. § 355

724 • Patent, Trademark, & Copyright Laws, June 2015 Edition

(B) With respect to the drug for which such an application is submitted, nothing in this subsection or subsection (c)(3) prohibits an applicant from amending or supplementing the application to seek approval of a different strength.

(5) (A) The Secretary shall issue guidance for the individuals who review applications submitted under paragraph (1) or under section 351 of the Public Health Service Act, which shall relate to promptness in conducting the review, technical excellence, lack of bias and conflict of interest, and knowledge of regulatory and scientific standards, and which shall apply equally to all individuals who review such applications.

(B) The Secretary shall meet with a sponsor of an investigation or an applicant for approval for a drug under this subsection or section 351 of the Public Health Service Act if the sponsor or applicant makes a reasonable written request for a meeting for the purpose of reaching agreement on the design and size—

    (i) (I) of clinical trials intended to form the primary basis of an effectiveness claim; or

        (II) in the case where human efficacy studies are not ethical or feasible, of animal and any associated clinical trials which, in combination, are intended to form the primary basis of an effectiveness claim; or

    (ii) with respect to an application for approval of a biological product under section 351(k) of the Public Health Service Act, of any necessary clinical study or studies.

The sponsor or applicant shall provide information necessary for discussion and agreement on the design and size of the clinical trials. Minutes of any such meeting shall be prepared by the Secretary and made available to the sponsor or applicant upon request.

(C) Any agreement regarding the parameters of the design and size of clinical trials of a new drug under this paragraph that is reached between the Secretary and a sponsor or applicant shall be reduced to writing and made part of the administrative record by the Secretary. Such agreement shall not be changed after the testing begins, except—

    (i) with the written agreement of the sponsor or applicant; or

(ii) pursuant to a decision, made in accordance with subparagraph (D) by the director of the reviewing division, that a substantial scientific issue essential to determining the safety or effectiveness of the drug has been identified after the testing has begun.

(D) A decision under subparagraph (C)(ii) by the director shall be in writing and the Secretary shall provide to the sponsor or applicant an opportunity for a meeting at which the director and the sponsor or applicant will be present and at which the director will document the scientific issue involved.

(E) The written decisions of the reviewing division shall be binding upon, and may not directly or indirectly be changed by, the field or compliance division personnel unless such field or compliance division personnel demonstrate to the reviewing division why such decision should be modified.

(F) No action by the reviewing division may be delayed because of the unavailability of information from or action by field personnel unless the reviewing division determines that a delay is necessary to assure the marketing of a safe and effective drug.

(G) For purposes of this paragraph, the reviewing division is the division responsible for the review of an application for approval of a drug under this subsection or section 351 of the Public Health Service Act (including all scientific and medical matters, chemistry, manufacturing, and controls).

(6) An application submitted under this subsection shall be accompanied by the certification required under section 402(j)(5)(B) of the Public Health Service Act. Such certification shall not be considered an element of such application.

(c) (1) Within one hundred and eighty days after the filing of an application under subsection (b), or such additional period as may be agreed upon by the Secretary and the applicant, the Secretary shall either—

(A) approve the application if he then finds that none of the grounds for denying approval specified in subsection (d) of this section applies, or

(B) give the applicant notice of an opportunity for a hearing before the Secretary under subsection (d) of this section on the question whether such application is approvable. If the applicant elects to accept the opportunity for hearing by written request with thirty days after such notice, such hearing shall commence not more than ninety days after the expiration of such thirty days unless the Secretary and the applicant otherwise agree. Any such hearing shall thereafter be conducted on an expedited basis and the Secretary's order thereon shall be issued within ninety days after the date fixed by the Secretary for filing final briefs.

(2) If the patent information described in subsection (b) could not be filed with the submission of an application under subsection (b) because the application was filed before the patent information was required under subsection (b) or a patent was issued after the application was approved under such subsection, the holder of an approved application shall file with the Secretary the patent number and the expiration date of any patent which claims the drug for which the application was submitted or which claims a method of using such drug and with respect to which a claim of patent infringement could reasonably be asserted if a person not licensed by the owner engaged in the manufacture, use, or sale of the drug. If the holder of an approved application could not file patent information under subsection (b) because it was not required at the time the application was approved, the holder shall file such information under this subsection not later than thirty days after the date of the enactment of this sentence, and if the holder of an approved application could not file patent information under subsection (b) because no patent had been issued when an application was filed or approved, the holder shall file such information under this subsection not later than thirty days after the date the patent involved is issued. Upon the submission of patent information under this subsection, the Secretary shall publish it.

(3) The approval of an application filed under subsection (b) which contains a certification required by paragraph (2) of such subsection shall be made effective on the last applicable date determined by applying the following to each certification made under subsection (b)(2)(A):

(A) If the applicant only made a certification described in clause (i) or (ii) of subsection (b)(2)(A) or in both such clauses, the approval may be made effective immediately.

(B) If the applicant made a certification described in clause (iii) of subsection (b)(2)(A), the approval may be made effective on the date certified under clause (iii).

21 U.S.C. § 355

(C) If the applicant made a certification described in clause (iv) of subsection (b)(2)(A), the approval shall be made effective immediately unless, before the expiration of 45 days after the date on which the notice described in subsection (b)(3) is received, an action is brought for infringement of the patent that is the subject of the certification and for which information was submitted to the Secretary under paragraph (2) or subsection (b)(1) before the date on which the application (excluding an amendment or supplement to the application) was submitted. If such an action is brought before the expiration of such days, the approval may be made effective upon the expiration of the thirty-month period beginning on the date of the receipt of the notice provided under subsection (b)(3) or such shorter or longer period as the court may order because either party to the action failed to reasonably cooperate in expediting the action, except that—

(i) if before the expiration of such period the district court decides that the patent is invalid or not infringed (including any substantive determination that there is no cause of action for patent infringement or invalidity), the approval shall be made effective on—

(I) the date on which the court enters judgment reflecting the decision; or

(II) the date of a settlement order or consent decree signed and entered by the court stating that the patent that is the subject of the certification is invalid or not infringed;

(ii) if before the expiration of such period the district court decides that the patent has been infringed—

(I) if the judgment of the district court is appealed, the approval shall be made effective on—

(aa) the date on which the court of appeals decides that the patent is invalid or not infringed (including any substantive determination that there is no cause of action for patent infringement or invalidity); or

(bb) the date of a settlement order or consent decree signed and entered by the court of appeals stating that the patent that is the subject of the certification is invalid or not infringed; or

728 • Patent, Trademark, & Copyright Laws, June 2015 Edition

(II) if the judgment of the district court is not appealed or is affirmed, the approval shall be made effective on the date specified by the district court in a court order under section 271(e)(4)(A) of title 35, United States Code;

(iii) if before the expiration of such period the court grants a preliminary injunction prohibiting the applicant from engaging in the commercial manufacture or sale of the drug until the court decides the issues of patent validity and infringement and if the court decides that such patent is invalid or not infringed, the approval shall be made effective as provided in clause (i); or

(iv) if before the expiration of such period the court grants a preliminary injunction prohibiting the applicant from engaging in the commercial manufacture or sale of the drug until the court decides the issues of patent validity and infringement and if the court decides that such patent has been infringed, the approval shall be made effective as provided in clause (ii).

In such an action, each of the parties shall reasonably cooperate in expediting the action.

(D) *Civil action to obtain patent certainty.—*

(i) *Declaratory judgment absent infringement action.—*

(I) *In general.—*No action may be brought under section 2201 of title 28, United States Code, by an applicant referred to in subsection (b)(2) for a declaratory judgment with respect to a patent which is the subject of the certification referred to in subparagraph (C) unless—

(aa) the 45-day period referred to in such subparagraph has expired;

(bb) neither the owner of such patent nor the holder of the approved application under subsection (b) for the drug that is claimed by the patent or a use of which is claimed by the patent brought a civil action against the applicant for infringement of the patent before the expiration of such period; and

(cc) in any case in which the notice provided under paragraph (2)(B) relates to noninfringement, the notice was accompanied by a document described in subclause (III).

21 U.S.C. § 355

(II) *Filing of civil action.*—If the conditions described in items (aa), (bb), and as applicable, (cc) of subclause (I) have been met, the applicant referred to in such subclause may, in accordance with section 2201 of title 28, United States Code, bring a civil action under such section against the owner or holder referred to in such subclause (but not against any owner or holder that has brought such a civil action against the applicant, unless that civil action was dismissed without prejudice) for a declaratory judgment that the patent is invalid or will not be infringed by the drug for which the applicant seeks approval, except that such civil action may be brought for a declaratory judgment that the patent will not be infringed only in a case in which the condition described in subclause (I)(cc) is applicable. A civil action referred to in this subclause shall be brought in the judicial district where the defendant has its principal place of business or a regular and established place of business.

(III) *Offer of confidential access to application.*—For purposes of subclause (I)(cc), the document described in this subclause is a document providing an offer of confidential access to the application that is in the custody of the applicant referred to in subsection (b)(2) for the purpose of determining whether an action referred to in subparagraph (C) should be brought. The document providing the offer of confidential access shall contain such restrictions as to persons entitled to access, and on the use and disposition of any information accessed, as would apply had a protective order been entered for the purpose of protecting trade secrets and other confidential business information. A request for access to an application under an offer of confidential access shall be considered acceptance of the offer of confidential access with the restrictions as to persons entitled to access, and on the use and disposition of any information accessed, contained in the offer of confidential access, and those restrictions and other terms of the offer of confidential access shall be considered terms of an enforceable contract. Any person provided an offer of confidential access shall review the application for the sole and limited purpose of evaluating possible infringement of the patent that is the subject of the certification under subsection (b)(2)(A)(iv) and for no other purpose, and may not disclose information of no relevance to any issue of patent infringement to any person other than a person provided an offer of confidential access. Further, the application may be redacted by the applicant to remove any information of no relevance to any issue of patent infringement.

(ii) *Counterclaim to infringement action.* —

(I) *In general.* —If an owner of the patent or the holder of the approved application under subsection (b) for the drug that is claimed by the patent or a use of which is claimed by the patent brings a patent infringement action against the applicant, the applicant may assert a counterclaim seeking an order requiring the holder to correct or delete the patent information submitted by the holder under subsection (b) or this subsection on the ground that the patent does not claim either—

(aa) the drug for which the application was approved; or

(bb) an approved method of using the drug.

(II) *No independent cause of action.* —Subclause (I) does not authorize the assertion of a claim described in subclause (I) in any civil action or proceeding other than a counterclaim described in subclause (I).

(iii) *No damages.* —An applicant shall not be entitled to damages in a civil action under clause (i) or a counterclaim under clause (ii).

(E) (i) If an application (other than an abbreviated new drug application) submitted under subsection (b) for a drug, no active ingredient (including any ester or salt of the active ingredient) of which has been approved in any other application under subsection (b), was approved during the period beginning January 1, 1982, and ending on the date of the enactment of this subsection [September 24, 1984], the Secretary may not make the approval of another application for a drug for which the investigations described in clause (A) of subsection (b)(1) and relied upon by the applicant for approval of the application were not conducted by or for the applicant and for which the applicant has not obtained a right of reference or use from the person by or for whom the investigations were conducted effective before the expiration of ten years from the date of the approval of the application previously approved under subsection (b).

(ii) If an application submitted under subsection (b) for a drug, no active ingredient (including any ester or salt of the active ingredient) of which has been approved in any other application under subsection (b), is approved after the date of the enactment of this clause [September 24, 1984], no application which refers to the drug for which the subsection (b) application was submitted and for which the investigations described in clause (A) of subsection (b)(1) and relied upon by the applicant for approval of the application was not conducted by or for the applicant and for which the applicant has not obtained a right of reference or use from the person by or for whom the investigations were conducted may be submitted under subsection (b) before the expiration of five years from the date of the approval of the application under subsection (b), except that such an application may be submitted under subsection (b) after the expiration of four years from the date of the approval of the subsection (b) application if it contains a certification of patent invalidity or noninfringement described in clause (iv) of subsection (b)(2)(A). The approval of such an application shall be made effective in accordance with this paragraph except that, if an action for patent infringement is commenced during the one-year period beginning forty-eight months after the date of the approval of the subsection (b) application, the thirty-month period referred to in subparagraph (C) shall be extended by such amount of time (if any) which is required for seven and one-half years to have elapsed from the date of approval of the subsection (b) application.

(iii) If an application submitted under subsection (b) for a drug, which includes an active ingredient (including any ester or salt of the active ingredient) that has been approved in another application approved under subsection (b), is approved after the date of the enactment of this clause and if such application contains reports of new clinical investigations (other than bioavailability studies) essential to the approval of the application and conducted or sponsored by the applicant, the Secretary may not make the approval of an application submitted under subsection (b) for the

21 U.S.C. § 355

conditions of approval of such drug in the approved subsection (b) application effective before the expiration of three years from the date of the approval of the application under subsection (b) if the investigations described in clause (A) of subsection (b)(1) and relied upon by the applicant for approval of the application were not conducted by or for the applicant and if the applicant has not obtained a right of reference or use from the person by or for whom the investigations were conducted.

(iv) If a supplement to an application approved under subsection (b) is approved after the date of enactment of this clause and the supplement contains reports of new clinical investigations (other than bioavailability studies) essential to the approval of the supplement and conducted or sponsored by the person submitting the supplement, the Secretary may not make the approval of an application submitted under subsection (b) for a change approved in the supplement effective before the expiration of three years from the date of the approval of the supplement under subsection (b) if the investigations described in clause (A) of subsection (b)(1) and relied upon by the applicant for approval of the application were not conducted by or for the applicant and if the applicant has not obtained a right of reference or use from the person by or for whom the investigations were conducted.

(v) If an application (or supplement to an application) submitted under subsection (b) for a drug, which includes an active ingredient (including any ester or salt of the active ingredient) that has been approved in another application under subsection (b), was approved during the period beginning January 1, 1982, and ending on the date of the enactment of this clause, the Secretary may not make the approval of an application submitted under this subsection and for which the investigations described in clause (A) of subsection (b)(1) and relied upon by the applicant for approval of the application were not conducted by or for the applicant and for which the applicant has not obtained a right of reference or use from the person by or for whom the investigations were conducted and which refers to the drug for which the subsection (b) application was submitted effective before the expiration of two years from the date of enactment of this clause.

(4) A drug manufactured in a pilot or other small facility may be used to demonstrate the safety and effectiveness of the drug and to obtain approval for the drug prior to manufacture of the drug in a larger facility, unless the Secretary makes a determination that a full scale production facility is necessary to ensure the safety or effectiveness of the drug.

(d) If the Secretary finds, after due notice to the applicant in accordance with subsection (c) of this section and giving him an opportunity for a hearing, in accordance with said subsection, that (1) the investigations, reports of which are required to be submitted to the Secretary pursuant to subsection (b) of this section, do not include adequate tests by all methods reasonably applicable to show whether or not such drug is safe for use under the conditions prescribed, recommended, or suggested in the proposed labeling thereof; (2) the results of such tests show that such drug is unsafe for use under such conditions or do not show that such drug is safe for use under such conditions; (3) the methods used in, and the facilities and controls used for, the manufacture, processing, and packing of such drug are inadequate to preserve its identity, strength, quality, and purity; (4) upon the basis of the information submitted to him as part of the application, or upon the basis of any other information before him with respect to such drug, he has insufficient information to determine whether such drug is safe for use under such conditions; or (5) evaluated on the basis of the information submitted to him as part of the application and any other information before him with respect to such drug, there is a lack of substantial evidence that the drug will have the effect it purports or is represented to have under the conditions of use prescribed, recommended, or suggested in the proposed labeling thereof; or (6) the application failed to contain the patent information prescribed by subsection (b); or (7) based on a fair evaluation of all material facts, such labeling is false or misleading in any particular; he shall issue an order refusing to approve the application. If, after such notice and opportunity for hearing, the Secretary finds that clauses (1) through (7) do not apply, he shall issue an order approving the application. As used in this subsection and subsection (e) of this section, the term "substantial evidence" means evidence consisting of adequate and well-controlled investigations, including clinical investigations, by experts qualified by scientific training and experience to evaluate the effectiveness of the drug involved, on the basis of which it could fairly and responsibly be concluded by such experts that the drug will have the effect it purports or is represented to have under the conditions of use prescribed, recommended, or suggested in the labeling or proposed labeling

21 U.S.C. § 355

thereof. The Secretary shall implement a structured risk-benefit assessment framework in the new drug approval process to facilitate the balanced consideration of benefits and risks, a consistent and systematic approach to the discussion and regulatory decisionmaking, and the communication of the benefits and risks of new drugs. Nothing in the preceding sentence shall alter the criteria for evaluating an application for premarket approval of a drug.

(e) The Secretary shall, after due notice and opportunity for hearing to the applicant, withdraw approval of an application with respect to any drug under this section if the Secretary finds (1) that clinical or other experience, tests, or other scientific data show that such drug is unsafe for use under the conditions of use upon the basis of which the application was approved; (2) that new evidence of clinical experience, not contained in such application or not available to the Secretary until after such application was approved, or tests by new methods, or tests by methods not deemed reasonably applicable when such application was approved, evaluated together with the evidence available to the Secretary when the application was approved, shows that such drug is not shown to be safe for use under the conditions of use upon the basis of which the application was approved; or (3) on the basis of new information before him with respect to such drug, evaluated together with the evidence available to him when the application was approved, that there is a lack of substantial evidence that the drug will have the effect it purports or is represented to have under the conditions of use prescribed, recommended, or suggested in the labeling thereof; or (4) the patent information prescribed by subsection (c) was not filed within thirty days after the receipt of written notice from the Secretary specifying the failure to file such information; or (5) that the application contains any untrue statement of a material fact: *Provided,* That if the Secretary (or in his absence the officer acting as Secretary) finds that there is an imminent hazard to the public health, he may suspend the approval of such application immediately, and give the applicant prompt notice of his action and afford the applicant the opportunity for an expedited hearing under this subsection; but the authority conferred by this proviso to suspend the approval of an application shall not be delegated. The Secretary may also, after due notice and opportunity for hearing to the applicant, withdraw the approval of an application submitted under subsection (b) or (j) with respect to any drug under this section if the Secretary finds (1) that the applicant has failed to establish a system for maintaining required records, or has repeatedly or deliberately failed to maintain such records or to make required reports, in accordance with a regulation or order under subsection (k) of this section or to comply with the notice requirements of section 360(j)(2) of this title, or the applicant has refused to permit access to, or copying or verification of, such records as required by paragraph (2) of such subsection; or (2) that on the basis of new information before him, evaluated together with the evidence before him when the application was approved, the methods used in, or the facilities and controls used for, the manufacture, processing, and packing of such drug are inadequate to assure and preserve its identity, strength, quality, and purity and were not made adequate within a reasonable time after receipt of written notice from the Secretary specifying the matter complained of; or (3) that on the basis of new information before him, evaluated together with the evidence before him when the application was approved, the labeling of such drug, based on a fair evaluation of all material facts, is false or misleading in any particular and was not corrected within a reasonable time after receipt of written notice from the Secretary specifying the matter complained of. Any order under the subsection shall state the findings upon which it is based. The Secretary may withdraw the approval of an application submitted under this section, or suspend the approval of such an application, as provided under this subsection, without first ordering the applicant to submit an assessment of the approved risk evaluation and mitigation strategy for the drug under section 505-1(g)(2)(D).

(f) Whenever the Secretary finds that the facts so require, he shall revoke any previous order under subsection (d) or (e) of this section refusing, withdrawing, or suspending approval of an application and shall approve such application or reinstate such approval, as may be appropriate.

(g) Orders of the Secretary issued under this section shall be served (1) in person by any officer or employee of the Department designated by the Secretary or (2) by mailing the order by registered mail or by certified mail addressed to the applicant or respondent at his last-known address in the records of the Secretary.

(h) An appeal may be taken by the applicant from an order of the Secretary refusing or withdrawing approval of an application under this section. Such appeal shall be taken by filing in the United States court of appeals for the circuit wherein such applicant resides or has his principal place of business, or in the United States Court of Appeals for the District of Columbia Circuit, within sixty days after the entry of such order, a written petition praying that the order of the Secretary be set aside. A copy of such petition shall be

21 U.S.C. § 355

forthwith transmitted by the clerk of the court to the Secretary, or any officer designated by him for that purpose, and thereupon the Secretary shall certify and file in the court the record upon which the order complained of was entered, as provided in section 2112 of title 28, United States Code. Upon the filing of such petition such court shall have exclusive jurisdiction to affirm or set aside such order, except that until the filing of the record the Secretary may modify or set aside his order. No objection to the order of the Secretary shall be considered by the court unless such objection shall have been urged before the Secretary or unless there were reasonable grounds for failure so to do. The finding of the Secretary as to the facts, if supported by substantial evidence, shall be conclusive. If any person shall apply to the court for leave to adduce additional evidence, and shall show to the satisfaction of the court that such additional evidence is material and that there were reasonable grounds for failure to adduce such evidence in the proceeding before the Secretary, the court may order such additional evidence to be taken before the Secretary and to be adduced upon the hearing in such manner and upon such terms and conditions as to the court may seem proper. The Secretary may modify his findings as to the facts by reason of the additional evidence so taken, and he shall file with the court such modified findings which, if supported by substantial evidence, shall be conclusive, and his recommendation, if any, for the setting aside of the original order. The judgment of the court affirming or setting aside any such order of the Secretary shall be final, subject to review by the Supreme Court of the United States upon certiorari or certification as provided in section 1254 of title 28 of the United States Code. The commencement of proceedings under this subsection shall not, unless specifically ordered by the court to the contrary, operate as a stay of the Secretary's order.

(i) (1) The Secretary shall promulgate regulations for exempting from the operation of the foregoing subsections of this section drugs intended solely for investigational use by experts qualified by scientific training and experience to investigate the safety and effectiveness of drugs. Such regulations may, within the discretion of the Secretary, among other conditions relating to the protection of the public health, provide for conditioning such exemption upon—

(A) the submission to the Secretary, before any clinical testing of a new drug is undertaken, of reports, by the manufacturer or the sponsor of the investigation of such drug, of preclinical tests (including tests on animals) of such drug adequate to justify the proposed clinical testing;

21 U.S.C. § 355

(B) the manufacturer or the sponsor of the investigation of a new drug proposed to be distributed to investigators for clinical testing obtaining a signed agreement from each of such investigators that patients to whom the drug is administered will be under his personal supervision, or under the supervision of investigators responsible to him, and that he will not supply such drug to any other investigator, or to clinics, for administration to human beings; and

(C) the establishment and maintenance of such records, and the making of such reports to the Secretary, by the manufacturer or the sponsor of the investigation of such drug, of data (including but not limited to analytical reports by investigators) obtained as the result of such investigational use of such drug, as the Secretary finds will enable him to evaluate the safety and effectiveness of such drug in the event of the filing of an application pursuant to subsection (b) of this section.

(2) Subject to paragraph (3), a clinical investigation of a new drug may begin 30 days after the Secretary has received from the manufacturer or sponsor of the investigation a submission containing such information about the drug and the clinical investigation, including—

(A) information on design of the investigation and adequate reports of basic information, certified by the applicant to be accurate reports, necessary to assess the safety of the drug for use in clinical investigation; and

(B) adequate information on the chemistry and manufacturing of the drug, controls available for the drug, and primary data tabulations from animal or human studies.

(3) (A) At any time, the Secretary may prohibit the sponsor of an investigation from conducting the investigation (referred to in this paragraph as a "clinical hold") if the Secretary makes a determination described in subparagraph (B). The Secretary shall specify the basis for the clinical hold, including the specific information available to the Secretary which served as the basis for such clinical hold, and confirm such determination in writing.

(B) For purposes of subparagraph (A), a determination described in this subparagraph with respect to a clinical hold is that—

(i) the drug involved represents an unreasonable risk to the safety of the persons who are the subjects of the clinical investigation, taking into account the qualifications of the clinical investigators, information about the drug, the design of the clinical investigation, the condition for which the drug is to be investigated, and the health status of the subjects involved; or

(ii) the clinical hold should be issued for such other reasons as the Secretary may by regulation establish (including reasons established by regulation before the date of the enactment of the Food and Drug Administration Modernization Act of 1997).

(C) Any written request to the Secretary from the sponsor of an investigation that a clinical hold be removed shall receive a decision, in writing and specifying the reasons therefor, within 30 days after receipt of such request. Any such request shall include sufficient information to support the removal of such clinical hold.

(4) Regulations under paragraph (1) shall provide that such exemption shall be conditioned upon the manufacturer, or the sponsor of the investigation, requiring that experts using such drugs for investigational purposes certify to such manufacturer or sponsor that they will inform any human beings to whom such drugs, or any controls used in connection therewith, are being administered, or their representatives, that such drugs are being used for investigational purposes and will obtain the consent of such human beings or their representatives, except where it is not feasible or it is contrary to the best interests of such human beings. Nothing in this subsection shall be construed to require any clinical investigator to submit directly to the Secretary reports on the investigational use of drugs. The Secretary shall update such regulations to require inclusion in the informed consent documents and process a statement that clinical trial information for such clinical investigation has been or will be submitted for inclusion in the registry data bank pursuant to subsection (j) of section 402 of the Public Health Service Act.

(j) (1) Any person may file with the Secretary an abbreviated application for the approval of a new drug.

(2) (A) An abbreviated application for a new drug shall contain—

(i) information to show that the conditions of use prescribed, recommended, or suggested in the labeling proposed for the new drug have been previously approved for a drug listed under paragraph (7) (hereinafter in this subsection referred to as a "listed drug");

(ii) (I) if the listed drug referred to in clause (i) has only one active ingredient, information to show that the active ingredient of the new drug is the same as that of the listed drug;

(II) if the listed drug referred to in clause (i) has more than one active ingredient, information to show that the active ingredients of the new drug are the same as those of the listed drug, or

(III) if the listed drug referred to in clause (i) has more than one active ingredient and if one of the active ingredients of the new drug is different and the application is filed pursuant to the approval of a petition filed under subparagraph (C), information to show that the other active ingredients of the new drug are the same as the active ingredients of the listed drug, information to show that the different active ingredient is an active ingredient of a listed drug or of a drug which does not meet the requirements of section 201(p) [21 U.S.C. §321(p)], and such other information respecting the different active ingredient with respect to which the petition was filed as the Secretary may require;

(iii) information to show that the route of administration, the dosage form, and the strength of the new drug are the same as those of the listed drug referred to in clause (i) or, if the route of administration, the dosage form, or the strength of the new drug is different and the application is filed pursuant to the approval of a petition filed under subparagraph (C), such information respecting the route of administration, dosage form, or strength with respect to which the petition was filed as the Secretary may require;

(iv) information to show that the new drug is bioequivalent to the listed drug referred to in clause (i), except that if the application is filed pursuant to the approval of a petition filed under subparagraph (C), information to show that the active ingredients of the new drug are of the same pharmacological or therapeutic class as those of the listed drug referred to in clause (i) and the new drug can be expected to have the same therapeutic effect as the listed drug when administered to patients for a condition of use referred to in clause (i);

(v) information to show that the labeling proposed for the new drug is the same as the labeling approved for the listed drug referred to in clause (i) except for changes required because of differences approved under a petition filed under subparagraph (C) or because the new drug and the listed drug are produced or distributed by different manufacturers;

(vi) the items specified in clauses (B) through (F) of subsection (b)(1);

(vii) a certification, in the opinion of the applicant and to the best of his knowledge, with respect to each patent which claims the listed drug referred to in clause (i) or which claims a use for such listed drug for which the applicant is seeking approval under this subsection and for which information is required to be filed under subsection (b) or (c)—

(I) that such patent information has not been filed,

(II) that such patent has expired,

(III) of the date on which such patent will expire, or

(IV) that such patent is invalid or will not be infringed by the manufacture, use, or sale of the new drug for which the application is submitted; and

(viii) if with respect to the listed drug referred to in clause (i) information was filed under subsection (b) or (c) for a method of use patent which does not claim a use for which the applicant is seeking approval under this subsection, a statement that the method of use patent does not claim such a use.

The Secretary may not require that an abbreviated application contain information in addition to that required by clauses (i) through (viii).

(B) *Notice of opinion that patent is invalid or will not be infringed.*—

(i) *Agreement to give notice.*—An applicant that makes a certification described in subparagraph (A)(vii)(IV) shall include in the application a statement that the applicant will give notice as required by this subparagraph.

21 U.S.C. § 355

(ii) *Timing of notice.* — An applicant that makes a certification described in subparagraph (A)(vii)(IV) shall give notice as required under this subparagraph —

(I) if the certification is in the application, not later than 20 days after the date of the postmark on the notice with which the Secretary informs the applicant that the application has been filed; or

(II) if the certification is in an amendment or supplement to the application, at the time at which the applicant submits the amendment or supplement, regardless of whether the applicant has already given notice with respect to another such certification contained in the application or in an amendment or supplement to the application.

(iii) *Recipients of notice.* — An applicant required under this subparagraph to give notice shall give notice to —

(I) each owner of the patent that is the subject of the certification (or a representative of the owner designated to receive such a notice); and

(II) the holder of the approved application under subsection (b) for the drug that is claimed by the patent or a use of which is claimed by the patent (or a representative of the holder designated to receive such a notice).

(iv) *Contents of notice.* — A notice required under this subparagraph shall —

(I) state that an application that contains data from bioavailability or bioequivalence studies has been submitted under this subsection for the drug with respect to which the certification is made to obtain approval to engage in the commercial manufacture, use, or sale of the drug before the expiration of the patent referred to in the certification; and

(II) include a detailed statement of the factual and legal basis of the opinion of the applicant that the patent is invalid or will not be infringed.

(C) If a person wants to submit an abbreviated application for a new drug which has a different active ingredient or whose route of administration, dosage form, or strength differ from that of a listed drug,

21 U.S.C. § 355

such person shall submit a petition to the Secretary seeking permission to file such an application. The Secretary shall approve or disapprove a petition submitted under this subparagraph within ninety days of the date the petition is submitted. The Secretary shall approve such a petition unless the Secretary finds—

(i) that investigations must be conducted to show the safety and effectiveness of the drug or of any of its active ingredients, the route of administration, the dosage form, or strength which differ from the listed drug; or

(ii) that any drug with a different active ingredient may not be adequately evaluated for approval as safe and effective on the basis of the information required to be submitted in an abbreviated application.

(D)(i) An applicant may not amend or supplement an application to seek approval of a drug referring to a different listed drug from the listed drug identified in the application as submitted to the Secretary.

(ii) With respect to the drug for which an application is submitted, nothing in this subsection prohibits an applicant from amending or supplementing the application to seek approval of a different strength.

(iii) Within 60 days after the date of the enactment of the Medicare Prescription Drug, Improvement, and Modernization Act of 2003, the Secretary shall issue guidance defining the term "listed drug" for purposes of this subparagraph.

(3) (A) The Secretary shall issue guidance for the individuals who review applications submitted under paragraph (1), which shall relate to promptness in conducting the review, technical excellence, lack of bias and conflict of interest, and knowledge of regulatory and scientific standards, and which shall apply equally to all individuals who review such applications.

(B) The Secretary shall meet with a sponsor of an investigation or an applicant for approval for a drug under this subsection if the sponsor or applicant makes a reasonable written request for a meeting for the purpose of reaching agreement on the design and size of bioavailability and bioequivalence studies needed for approval of such application. The sponsor or applicant shall provide information necessary for discussion and agreement on the design and size of such studies. Minutes of any such meeting shall be prepared by the Secretary and made available to the sponsor or applicant.

(C) Any agreement regarding the parameters of design and size of bioavailability and bioequivalence studies of a drug under this paragraph that is reached between the Secretary and a sponsor or applicant shall be reduced to writing and made part of the administrative record by the Secretary. Such agreement shall not be changed after the testing begins, except—

(i) with the written agreement of the sponsor or applicant; or

(ii) pursuant to a decision, made in accordance with subparagraph (D) by the director of the reviewing division, that a substantial scientific issue essential to determining the safety or effectiveness of the drug has been identified after the testing has begun.

(D) A decision under subparagraph (C)(ii) by the director shall be in writing and the Secretary shall provide to the sponsor or applicant an opportunity for a meeting at which the director and the sponsor or applicant will be present and at which the director will document the scientific issue involved.

(E) The written decisions of the reviewing division shall be binding upon, and may not directly or indirectly be changed by, the field or compliance office personnel unless such field or compliance office personnel demonstrate to the reviewing division why such decision should be modified.

(F) No action by the reviewing division may be delayed because of the unavailability of information from or action by field personnel unless the reviewing division determines that a delay is necessary to assure the marketing of a safe and effective drug.

(G) For purposes of this paragraph, the reviewing division is the division responsible for the review of an application for approval of a drug under this subsection (including scientific matters, chemistry, manufacturing, and controls).

(4) Subject to paragraph (5), the Secretary shall approve an application for a drug unless the Secretary finds—

(A) the methods used in, or the facilities and controls used for, the manufacture, processing, and packing of the drug are inadequate to assure and preserve its identity, strength, quality, and purity;

(B) information submitted with the application is insufficient to show that each of the proposed conditions of use have been previously approved for the listed drug referred to in the application;

(C) (i) if the listed drug has only one active ingredient, information submitted with the application is insufficient to show that the active ingredient is the same as that of the listed drug;

(ii) if the listed drug has more than one active ingredient, information submitted with the application is insufficient to show that the active ingredients are the same as the active ingredients of the listed drug, or

(iii) if the listed drug has more than one active ingredient and if the application is for a drug which has an active ingredient different from the listed drug, information submitted with the application is insufficient to show —

(I) that the other active ingredients are the same as the active ingredients of the listed drug, or

(II) that the different active ingredient is an active ingredient of a listed drug or a drug which does not meet the requirements of section 201(p) [21 U.S.C. §321(p)],

or no petition to file an application for the drug with the different ingredient was approved under paragraph (2)(C);

(D) (i) if the application is for a drug whose route of administration, dosage form, or strength of the drug is the same as the route of administration, dosage form, or strength of the listed drug referred to in the application, information submitted in the application is insufficient to show that the route of administration, dosage form, or strength is the same as that of the listed drug, or

(ii) if the application is for a drug whose route of administration, dosage form, or strength of the drug is different from that of the listed drug referred to in the application, no petition to file an application for the drug with the different route of administration, dosage form, or strength was approved under paragraph (2)(C);

(E) if the application was filed pursuant to the approval of a petition under paragraph (2)(C), the application did not contain the information required by the Secretary respecting the active ingredient, route of administration, dosage form, or strength which is not the same;

(F) information submitted in the application is insufficient to show that the drug is bioequivalent to the listed drug referred to in the application or, if the application was filed pursuant to a petition approved under paragraph (2)(C), information submitted in the application is insufficient to show that the active ingredients of the new drug are of the same pharmacological or therapeutic class as those of the listed drug referred to in paragraph (2)(A)(i) and that the new drug can be expected to have the same therapeutic effect as the listed drug when administered to patients for a condition of use referred to in such paragraph;

(G) information submitted in the application is insufficient to show that the labeling proposed for the drug is the same as the labeling approved for the listed drug referred to in the application except for changes required because of differences approved under a petition filed under paragraph (2)(C) or because the drug and the listed drug are produced or distributed by different manufacturers;

(H) information submitted in the application or any other information available to the Secretary shows that (i) the inactive ingredients of the drug are unsafe for use under the conditions prescribed, recommended, or suggested in the labeling proposed for the drug, or (ii) the composition of the drug is unsafe under such conditions because of the type or quantity of inactive ingredients included or the manner in which the inactive ingredients are included;

(I) the approval under subsection (c) of the listed drug referred to in the application under this subsection has been withdrawn or suspended for grounds described in the first sentence of subsection (e), the Secretary has published a notice of opportunity for hearing to withdraw approval of the listed drug under subsection (c) for grounds described in the first sentence of subsection (e), the approval under this subsection of the listed drug referred to in the application under this subsection has been withdrawn or suspended under paragraph (6), or the Secretary has determined that the listed drug has been withdrawn from sale for safety or effectiveness reasons;

(J) the application does not meet any other requirement of paragraph (2)(A); or

(K) the application contains an untrue statement of material fact.

(5) (A) Within one hundred and eighty days of the initial receipt of an application under paragraph (2) or within such additional period as may be agreed upon by the Secretary and the applicant, the Secretary shall approve or disapprove the application.

(B) The approval of an application submitted under paragraph (2) shall be made effective on the last applicable date determined by applying the following to each certification made under paragraph (2)(A)(vii):

(i) If the applicant only made a certification described in subclause (I) or (II) of paragraph (2)(A)(vii) or in both such subclauses, the approval may be made effective immediately.

(ii) If the applicant made a certification described in subclause (III) of paragraph (2)(A)(vii), the approval may be made effective on the date certified under subclause (III).

(iii) If the applicant made a certification described in subclause (IV) of paragraph (2)(A)(vii), the approval shall be made effective immediately unless, before the expiration of 45 days after the date on which the notice described in paragraph (2)(B) is received, an action is brought for infringement of the patent that is the subject of the certification and for which information was submitted to the Secretary under subsection (b)(1) or (c)(2) before the date on which the application (excluding an amendment or supplement to the application), which the Secretary later determines to be substantially complete, was submitted. If such an action is brought before the expiration of such days, the approval shall be made effective upon the expiration of the thirty-month period beginning on the date of the receipt of the notice provided under paragraph (2)(B)(i) or such shorter or longer period as the court may order because either party to the action failed to reasonably cooperate in expediting the action, except that—

(I) if before the expiration of such period the district court decides that the patent is invalid or not infringed (including any substantive determination that there is no cause of action for patent infringement or invalidity), the approval shall be made effective on—

(aa) the date on which the court enters judgment reflecting the decision; or

(bb) the date of a settlement order or consent decree signed and entered by the court stating that the patent that is the subject of the certification is invalid or not infringed;

(II) if before the expiration of such period the district court decides that the patent has been infringed—

(aa) if the judgment of the district court is appealed, the approval shall be made effective on—

(AA) the date on which the court of appeals decides that the patent is invalid or not infringed (including any substantive determination that there is no cause of action for patent infringement or invalidity); or

(BB) the date of a settlement order or consent decree signed and entered by the court of appeals stating that the patent that is the subject of the certification is invalid or not infringed; or

(bb) if the judgment of the district court is not appealed or is affirmed, the approval shall be made effective on the date specified by the district court in a court order under section 271(e)(4)(A) of title 35, United States Code;

(III) if before the expiration of such period the court grants a preliminary injunction prohibiting the applicant from engaging in the commercial manufacture or sale of the drug until the court decides the issues of patent validity and infringement and if the court decides that such patent is invalid or not infringed, the approval shall be made effective as provided in subclause (I); or

(IV) if before the expiration of such period the court grants a preliminary injunction prohibiting the applicant from engaging in the commercial manufacture or sale of the drug until the court decides the issues of patent validity and infringement and if the court decides that such patent has been infringed, the approval shall be made effective as provided in subclause (II).

In such an action, each of the parties shall reasonably cooperate in expediting the action.

(iv) *180-day exclusivity period.*—

(I) *Effectiveness of application.*—Subject to subparagraph (D), if the application contains a certification described in paragraph (2)(A)(vii)(IV) and is for a drug for which a first applicant has submitted an application containing such a certification, the application shall be made effective on the date that is 180 days after the date of the first commercial marketing of the drug (including the commercial marketing of the listed drug) by any first applicant.

(II) *Definitions.*—In this paragraph:

(aa) *180-day exclusivity period.*—The term "180-day exclusivity period" means the 180-day period ending on the day before the date on which an application submitted by an applicant other than a first applicant could become effective under this clause.

(bb) *First applicant.*—As used in this subsection, the term "first applicant" means an applicant that, on the first day on which a substantially complete application containing a certification described in paragraph (2)(A)(vii)(IV) is submitted for approval of a drug, submits a substantially complete application that contains and lawfully maintains a certification described in paragraph (2)(A)(vii)(IV) for the drug.

(cc) *Substantially complete application.*—As used in this subsection, the term "substantially complete application" means an application under this subsection that on its face is sufficiently complete to permit a substantive review and contains all the information required by paragraph (2)(A).

(dd) *Tentative approval.*—

(AA) *In general.*—The term "tentative approval" means notification to an applicant by the Secretary that an application under this subsection meets the requirements of paragraph (2)(A), but cannot receive effective approval because the application does not meet the requirements of this subparagraph, there is a period of exclusivity for the listed drug under subparagraph (F) or section 505A, or there is a 7-year period of exclusivity for the listed drug under section 527.

(BB) *Limitation.*—A drug that is granted tentative approval by the Secretary is not an approved drug and shall not have an effective approval until the Secretary issues an approval after any necessary additional review of the application.

(C) *Civil action to obtain patent certainty.*—

(i) *Declaratory judgment absent infringement action.*—

(I) *In general.*—No action may be brought under section 2201 of title 28, United States Code, by an applicant under paragraph (2) for a declaratory judgment with respect to a patent which is the subject of the certification referred to in subparagraph (B)(iii) unless—

(aa) the 45-day period referred to in such subparagraph has expired;

(bb) neither the owner of such patent nor the holder of the approved application under subsection (b) for the drug that is claimed by the patent or a use of which is claimed by the patent brought a civil action against the applicant for infringement of the patent before the expiration of such period; and

(cc) in any case in which the notice provided under paragraph (2)(B) relates to noninfringement, the notice was accompanied by a document described in subclause (III).

(II) *Filing of civil action.*—If the conditions described in items (aa), (bb), and as applicable, (cc) of subclause (I) have been met, the applicant referred to in such subclause may, in accordance with section 2201 of title 28, United States Code, bring a civil action under such section against the owner or holder referred to in such subclause (but not against any owner or holder that has brought such a civil action against the applicant, unless that civil action was dismissed without prej-

21 U.S.C. § 355

udice) for a declaratory judgment that the patent is invalid or will not be infringed by the drug for which the applicant seeks approval, except that such civil action may be brought for a declaratory judgment that the patent will not be infringed only in a case in which the condition described in subclause (I)(cc) is applicable. A civil action referred to in this subclause shall be brought in the judicial district where the defendant has its principal place of business or a regular and established place of business.

(III) *Offer of confidential access to application.* — For purposes of subclause (I)(cc), the document described in this subclause is a document providing an offer of confidential access to the application that is in the custody of the applicant under paragraph (2) for the purpose of determining whether an action referred to in subparagraph (B)(iii) should be brought. The document providing the offer of confidential access shall contain such restrictions as to persons entitled to access, and on the use and disposition of any information accessed, as would apply had a protective order been entered for the purpose of protecting trade secrets and other confidential business information. A request for access to an application under an offer of confidential access shall be considered acceptance of the offer of confidential access with the restrictions as to persons entitled to access, and on the use and disposition of any information accessed, contained in the offer of confidential access, and those restrictions and other terms of the offer of confidential access shall be considered terms of an enforceable contract. Any person provided an offer of confidential access shall review the application for the sole and limited purpose of evaluating possible infringement of the patent that is the subject of the certification under paragraph (2)(A)(vii)(IV) and for no other purpose, and may not disclose information of no relevance to any issue of patent infringement to any person other than a person provided an offer of confidential access. Further, the application may be redacted by the applicant to remove any information of no relevance to any issue of patent infringement.

21 U.S.C. § 355

(ii) *Counterclaim to infringement action.* —

(I) *In general.* —If an owner of the patent or the holder of the approved application under subsection (b) for the drug that is claimed by the patent or a use of which is claimed by the patent brings a patent infringement action against the applicant, the applicant may assert a counterclaim seeking an order requiring the holder to correct or delete the patent information submitted by the holder under subsection (b) or (c) on the ground that the patent does not claim either—

(aa) the drug for which the application was approved; or

(bb) an approved method of using the drug.

(II) *No independent cause of action.* —Subclause (I) does not authorize the assertion of a claim described in subclause (I) in any civil action or proceeding other than a counterclaim described in subclause (I).

(iii) *No damages.* —An applicant shall not be entitled to damages in a civil action under clause (i) or a counterclaim under clause (ii).

(D) *Forfeiture of 180-day exclusivity period.* —-

(i) *Definition of forfeiture event.* —In this subparagraph, the term "forfeiture event", with respect to an application under this subsection, means the occurrence of any of the following:

(I) *Failure to market.* —The first applicant fails to market the drug by the later of—

(aa) the earlier of the date that is—

(AA) 75 days after the date on which the approval of the application of the first applicant is made effective under subparagraph (B)(iii); or

(BB) 30 months after the date of submission of the application of the first applicant; or

(bb) with respect to the first applicant or any other applicant (which other applicant has received tentative approval), the date that is 75 days after the date as of which, as to each of the patents with respect to which the first applicant submitted and lawfully maintained a certification qualifying the first applicant for the 180-day exclusivity period under subparagraph (B)(iv), at least 1 of the following has occurred:

(AA) In an infringement action brought against that applicant with respect to the patent or in a declaratory judgment action brought by that applicant with respect to the patent, a court enters a final decision from which no appeal (other than a petition to the Supreme Court for a writ of certiorari) has been or can be taken that the patent is invalid or not infringed.

(BB) In an infringement action or a declaratory judgment action described in subitem (AA), a court signs a settlement order or consent decree that enters a final judgment that includes a finding that the patent is invalid or not infringed.

(CC) The patent information submitted under subsection (b) or (c) is withdrawn by the holder of the application approved under subsection (b).

(II) *Withdrawal of application.*—The first applicant withdraws the application or the Secretary considers the application to have been withdrawn as a result of a determination by the Secretary that the application does not meet the requirements for approval under paragraph (4).

(III) *Amendment of certification.*—The first applicant amends or withdraws the certification for all of the patents with respect to which that applicant submitted a certification qualifying the applicant for the 180-day exclusivity period.

(IV) *Failure to obtain tentative approval.*—The first applicant fails to obtain tentative approval of the application within 30 months after the date on which the application is filed, unless the failure is caused by a change in or a review of the requirements for approval of the application imposed after the date on which the application is filed.

(V) *Agreement with another applicant, the listed drug application holder, or a patent owner.*—The first applicant enters into an agreement with another applicant under this subsection for the drug, the holder of the application for the listed drug, or an owner of the patent that is the subject of the certification under paragraph (2)(A)(vii)(IV), the Federal Trade Commission or the Attorney General files a complaint, and there is a final decision of the Federal Trade Commission or the court with regard to the complaint from which no appeal (other than a petition to the Supreme Court for a writ of certiorari) has been or can be taken that the agreement has violated the antitrust laws (as defined in section 1 of the Clayton Act (15 U.S.C. 12), except that the term includes section 5 of the Federal Trade Commission Act (15 U.S.C. 45) to the extent that that section applies to unfair methods of competition).

(VI) *Expiration of all patents.* — All of the patents as to which the applicant submitted a certification qualifying it for the 180-day exclusivity period have expired.

(ii) *Forfeiture.* — The 180-day exclusivity period described in subparagraph (B)(iv) shall be forfeited by a first applicant if a forfeiture event occurs with respect to that first applicant.

(iii) *Subsequent applicant.* — If all first applicants forfeit the 180-day exclusivity period under clause (ii) —

(I) approval of any application containing a certification described in paragraph (2)(A)(vii)(IV) shall be made effective in accordance with subparagraph (B)(iii); and

(II) no applicant shall be eligible for a 180-day exclusivity period.

(E) If the Secretary decides to disapprove an application, the Secretary shall give the applicant notice of an opportunity for a hearing before the Secretary on the question of whether such application is approvable. If the applicant elects to accept the opportunity for hearing by written request within thirty days after such notice, such hearing shall commence not more than ninety days after the expiration of such thirty days unless the Secretary and the applicant otherwise agree. Any such hearing shall thereafter be conducted on an expedited basis and the Secretary's order thereon shall be issued within ninety days after the date fixed by the Secretary for filing final briefs.

(F) (i) If an application (other than an abbreviated new drug application) submitted under subsection (b) for a drug, no active ingredient (including any ester or salt of the active ingredient) of which has been approved in any other application under subsection (b), was approved during the period beginning January 1, 1982, and ending on the date of the enactment of this subsection [September 24, 1984], the Secretary may not make the approval of an application submitted under this subsection which refers to the drug for which the subsection (b) application was submitted effective before the expiration of ten years from the date of the approval of the application under subsection (b).

(ii) If an application submitted under subsection (b) for a drug, no active ingredient (including any ester or salt of the active ingredient) of which has been approved in any other application under subsection (b), is approved after the date of the enactment of this subsection, no application may be submitted under this subsection which refers to the drug for which the subsection (b) application was submitted before the expiration of five years from the date of the approval of the application under subsection (b), except that such an application may be submitted under this subsection after the expiration of four years from the date of the approval of the subsection (b) application if it contains a certification of patent invalidity or noninfringement described in subclause (IV) of paragraph (2)(A)(vii). The approval of such an application shall be made effective in accordance with subparagraph (B) except that, if an action for patent infringement is commenced during the one-year period beginning forty-eight months after the date of the approval of the subsection (b) application, the thirty-month period referred to in subparagraph (B)(iii) shall be extended by such amount of time (if any) which is required for seven and one-half years to have elapsed from the date of approval of the subsection (b) application.

(iii) If an application submitted under subsection (b) for a drug, which includes an active ingredient (including any ester or salt of the active ingredient) that has been approved in another application approved under subsection (b), is approved after the date of enactment of this subsection and if such application contains reports of new clinical investigations (other than bioavailability studies) essential to the approval of the application and conducted or sponsored by the applicant, the Secretary may not make the approval of an application submitted under this subsection for the conditions of approval of such drug in the subsection (b) application effective before the expiration of three years from the date of the approval of the application under subsection (b) for such drug.

(iv) If a supplement to an application approved under subsection (b) is approved after the date of enactment of this subsection and the supplement contains reports of new clinical investigations (other than bioavailability studies) essential to the approval of the supplement and conducted or sponsored by the person submitting the supplement, the Secretary may not make the approval of an application submitted under this subsection for a change approved in the supplement effective before the expiration of three years from the date of the approval of the supplement under subsection (b).

(v) If an application (or supplement to an application) submitted under subsection (b) for a drug, which includes an active ingredient (including any ester or salt of the active ingredient) that has been approved in another application under subsection (b), was approved during the period beginning January 1, 1982, and ending on the date of the enactment of this subsection, the Secretary may not make the approval of an application submitted under this subsection which refers to the drug for which the subsection (b) application was submitted or which refers to a change approved in a supplement to the subsection (b) application effective before the expiration of two years from the date of enactment of this subsection.

(6) If a drug approved under this subsection refers in its approved application to a drug the approval of which was withdrawn or suspended for grounds described in the first sentence of subsection (e) or was withdrawn or suspended under this paragraph or which, as determined by the Secretary, has been withdrawn from sale for safety or effectiveness reasons, the approval of the drug under this subsection shall be withdrawn or suspended—

(A) for the same period as the withdrawal or suspension under subsection (e) or this paragraph, or

(B) if the listed drug has been withdrawn from sale, for the period of withdrawal from sale or, if earlier, the period ending on the date the

21 U.S.C. § 355

Secretary determines that the withdrawal from sale is not for safety or effectiveness reasons.

(7) (A) (i) Within sixty days of the date of the enactment of this subsection [September 24, 1984], the Secretary shall publish and make available to the public—

(I) a list in alphabetical order of the official and proprietary name of each drug which has been approved for safety and effectiveness under subsection (c) before the date of the enactment of this subsection;

(II) the date of approval if the drug is approved after 1981 and the number of the application which was approved; and

(III) whether in vitro or in vivo bioequivalence studies, or both such studies, are required for applications filed under this subsection which will refer to the drug published.

(ii) Every thirty days after the publication of the first list under clause (i) the Secretary shall revise the list to include each drug which has been approved for safety and effectiveness under subsection (c) or approved under this subsection during the thirty-day period.

(iii) When patent information submitted under subsection (b) or (c) respecting a drug included on the list is to be published by the Secretary the Secretary shall, in revisions made under clause (ii), include such information for such drug.

(B) A drug approved for safety and effectiveness under subsection (c) or approved under this subsection shall, for purposes of this subsection, be considered to have been published under subparagraph (A) on the date of its approval or the date of enactment, whichever is later.

(C) If the approval of a drug was withdrawn or suspended for grounds described in the first sentence of subsection (e) or was withdrawn or suspended under paragraph (6) or if the Secretary determines that a drug has been withdrawn from sale for safety or effectiveness reasons, it may not be published in the list under subparagraph (A) or, if the withdrawal or suspension occurred after its publication in such list, it shall be immediately removed from such list—

(i) for the same period as the withdrawal or suspension under subsection (e) or paragraph (6), or

(ii) if the listed drug has been withdrawn from sale, for the period of withdrawal from sale or, if earlier, the period ending on the date the Secretary determines that the withdrawal from sale is not for safety or effectiveness reasons.

A notice of the removal shall be published in the Federal Register.

(8) For purposes of this subsection:

(A)(i) The term "bioavailability" means the rate and extent to which the active ingredient or therapeutic ingredient is absorbed from a drug and becomes available at the site of drug action.

(ii) For a drug that is not intended to be absorbed into the bloodstream, the Secretary may assess bioavailability by scientifically valid measurements intended to reflect the rate and extent to which the active ingredient or therapeutic ingredient becomes available at the site of drug action.

(B) A drug shall be considered to be bioequivalent to a listed drug if—

(i) the rate and extent of absorption of the drug do not show a significant difference from the rate and extent of absorption of the listed drug when administered at the same molar dose of the therapeutic ingredient under similar experimental conditions in either a single dose or multiple doses; or

(ii) the extent of absorption of the drug does not show a significant difference from the extent of absorption of the listed drug when administered at the same molar dose of the therapeutic ingredient under similar experimental conditions in either a single dose or multiple doses and the difference from the listed drug in the rate of absorption of the drug is intentional, is reflected in its proposed labeling, is not essential to the attainment of effective body drug concentrations on chronic use, and is considered medically insignificant for the drug.

(C) For a drug that is not intended to be absorbed into the bloodstream, the Secretary may establish alternative, scientifically valid methods to show bioequivalence if the alternative methods are expected to detect a significant difference between the drug and the listed drug in safety and therapeutic effect.

(9) The Secretary shall, with respect to each application submitted under this subsection, maintain a record of—

(A) the name of the applicant,

(B) the name of the drug covered by the application,

(C) the name of each person to whom the review of the chemistry of the application was assigned and the date of such assignment, and

(D) the name of each person to whom the bioequivalence review for such application was assigned and the date of such assignment.

The information the Secretary is required to maintain under this paragraph with respect to an application submitted under this subsection shall be made available to the public after the approval of such application.

(10)(A) If the proposed labeling of a drug that is the subject of an application under this subsection differs from the listed drug due to a labeling revision described under clause (i), the drug that is the subject of such application shall, notwithstanding any other provision of this Act, be eligible for approval and shall not be considered misbranded under section 502 if—

(i) the application is otherwise eligible for approval under this subsection but for expiration of patent, an exclusivity period, or of a delay in approval described in paragraph (5)(B)(iii), and a revision to the labeling of the listed drug has been approved by the Secretary within 60 days of such expiration;

(ii) the labeling revision described under clause (i) does not include a change to the "Warnings" section of the labeling;

(iii) the sponsor of the application under this subsection agrees to submit revised labeling of the drug that is the subject of such application not later than 60 days after the notification of any changes to such labeling required by the Secretary; and

(iv) such application otherwise meets the applicable requirements for approval under this subsection.

(B) If, after a labeling revision described in subparagraph (A)(i), the Secretary determines that the continued presence in interstate commerce of the labeling of the listed drug (as in effect before the revision described in subparagraph (A)(i)) adversely impacts the safe use of the drug, no application under this subsection shall be eligible for approval with such labeling.

(k) (1) In the case of any drug for which an approval of an application filed under subsection (b) or (j) is in effect, the applicant shall establish and maintain such records, and make such reports to the Secretary, of data relating to clinical experience and other data or information, received or otherwise obtained by such applicant with respect to such drug, as the Secretary may by general regulation, or by order with respect to such application, prescribe on the basis of a finding that such records and reports are necessary in order to enable the Secretary to determine, or facilitate a determination, whether there is or may be ground for invoking subsection (e) of this section: *Provided, however,* That regulations and orders issued under this subsection and under subsection (i) of this section shall have due regard for the professional ethics of the medical profession and the interests of patients and shall provide, where the Secretary deems it to be appropriate, for the examination, upon request, by the persons to whom such regulations or orders are applicable, of similar information received or otherwise obtained by the Secretary.

(2) Every person required under this section to maintain records, and every person in charge or custody thereof, shall, upon request of an officer or employee designated by the Secretary, permit such officer or employee at all reasonable times to have access to and copy and verify such records.

(3) *Active postmarket risk identification.* —

(A) *Definition.* —In this paragraph, the term "data" refers to information with respect to a drug approved under this section or under section 351 of the Public Health Service Act, including claims data, patient survey data, standardized analytic files that allow for the pooling and analysis of data from disparate data environments, and any other data deemed appropriate by the Secretary.

(B) *Development of postmarket risk identification and analysis methods.* —- The Secretary shall, not later than 2 years after the date of the enactment of the Food and Drug Administration Amendments Act of 2007, in collaboration with public, academic, and private entities—

(i) develop methods to obtain access to disparate data sources including the data sources specified in subparagraph (C);

(ii) develop validated methods for the establishment of a postmarket risk identification and analysis system to link and analyze safety data from multiple sources, with the goals of including, in aggregate—

(I) at least 25,000,000 patients by July 1, 2010; and

(II) at least 100,000,000 patients by July 1, 2012; and

(iii) convene a committee of experts, including individuals who are recognized in the field of protecting data privacy and security, to make recommendations to the Secretary on the development of tools and methods for the ethical and scientific uses for, and communication of, postmarketing data specified under subparagraph (C), including recommendations on the development of effective research methods for the study of drug safety questions.

(C) *Establishment of the postmarket risk identification and analysis system.*—

(i) *In general.*—The Secretary shall, not later than 1 year after the development of the risk identification and analysis methods under subparagraph (B), establish and maintain procedures—

(I) for risk identification and analysis based on electronic health data, in compliance with the regulations promulgated under section 264(c) of the Health Insurance Portability and Accountability Act of 1996, and in a manner that does not disclose individually identifiable health information in violation of paragraph (4)(B);

(II) for the reporting (in a standardized form) of data on all serious adverse drug experiences (as defined in section 505-1(b)) submitted to the Secretary under paragraph (1), and those adverse events submitted by patients, providers, and drug sponsors, when appropriate;

(III) to provide for active adverse event surveillance using the following data sources, as available:

(aa) Federal health-related electronic data (such as data from the Medicare program and the health systems of the Department of Veterans Affairs);

(bb) private sector health-related electronic data (such as pharmaceutical purchase data and health insurance claims data); and (cc) other data as the Secretary deems necessary to create a robust system to identify adverse events and potential drug safety signals;

(IV) to identify certain trends and patterns with respect to data accessed by the system;

(V) to provide regular reports to the Secretary concerning adverse event trends, adverse event patterns, incidence and prevalence of adverse events, and other information the Secretary determines appropriate, which may include data on comparative national adverse event trends; and

VI) to enable the program to export data in a form appropriate for further aggregation, statistical analysis, and reporting.

(ii) *Timeliness of reporting.*—The procedures established under clause (i) shall ensure that such data are accessed, analyzed, and reported in a timely, routine, and systematic manner, taking into consideration the need for data completeness, coding, cleansing, and standardized analysis and transmission.

(iii) *Private sector resources.*—To ensure the establishment of the active postmarket risk identification and analysis system under this subsection not later than 1 year after the development of the risk identification and analysis methods under subparagraph (B), as required under clause (i), the Secretary may, on a temporary or permanent basis, implement systems or products developed by private entities.

(iv) *Complementary approaches.*—To the extent the active postmarket risk identification and analysis system under this subsection is not sufficient to gather data and information relevant to a priority drug safety question, the Secretary shall develop, support, and participate in complementary approaches to gather and analyze such data and information, including—

(I) approaches that are complementary with respect to assessing the safety of use of a drug in domestic populations not included, or underrepresented, in the trials used to approve the drug (such as older people, people with comorbidities, pregnant women, or children); and

21 U.S.C. § 355

(II) existing approaches such as the Vaccine Adverse Event Reporting System and the Vaccine Safety Datalink or successor databases.

(v) *Authority for contracts.* — The Secretary may enter into contracts with public and private entities to fulfill the requirements of this subparagraph.

(4) *Advanced analysis of drug safety data.* —

(A) *Purpose.* — The Secretary shall establish collaborations with public, academic, and private entities, which may include the Centers for Education and Research on Therapeutics under section 912 of the Public Health Service Act, to provide for advanced analysis of drug safety data described in paragraph (3)(C) and other information that is publicly available or is provided by the Secretary, in order to —

(i) improve the quality and efficiency of postmarket drug safety risk-benefit analysis;

(ii) provide the Secretary with routine access to outside expertise to study advanced drug safety questions; and

(iii) enhance the ability of the Secretary to make timely assessments based on drug safety data.

(B) *Privacy.* — Such analysis shall not disclose individually identifiable health information when presenting such drug safety signals and trends or when responding to inquiries regarding such drug safety signals and trends.

(C) *Public process for priority questions.* — At least biannually, the Secretary shall seek recommendations from the Drug Safety and Risk Management Advisory Committee (or any successor committee) and from other advisory committees, as appropriate, to the Food and Drug Administration on —

(i) priority drug safety questions; and

(ii) mechanisms for answering such questions, including through —

(I) active risk identification under paragraph (3); and

(II) when such risk identification is not sufficient, postapproval studies and clinical trials under subsection (o)(3).

(D) *Procedures for the development of drug safety collaborations.—*

    (i) *In general.—*Not later than 180 days after the date of the establishment of the active postmarket risk identification and analysis system under this subsection, the Secretary shall establish and implement procedures under which the Secretary may routinely contract with one or more qualified entities to—

        (I) classify, analyze, or aggregate data described in paragraph (3)(C) and information that is publicly available or is provided by the Secretary;

        (II) allow for prompt investigation of priority drug safety questions, including—

            (aa) unresolved safety questions for drugs or classes of drugs; and

            (bb) for newly-approved drugs, safety signals from clinical trials used to approve the drug and other preapproval trials; are, serious drug side effects; and the safety of use in domestic populations not included, or underrepresented, in the trials used to approve the drug (such as older people, people with comorbidities, pregnant women, or children);

        (III) perform advanced research and analysis on identified drug safety risks;

        (IV) focus postapproval studies and clinical trials under subsection (o)(3) more effectively on cases for which reports under paragraph (1) and other safety signal detection is not sufficient to resolve whether there is an elevated risk of a serious adverse event associated with the use of a drug; and

        (V) carry out other activities as the Secretary deems necessary to carry out the purposes of this paragraph.

    (ii) *Request for specific methodology.—*The procedures described in clause (i) shall permit the Secretary to request that a specific methodology be used by the qualified entity. The qualified entity shall work with the Secretary to finalize the methodology to be used.

(E) *Use of analyses.* — The Secretary shall provide the analyses described in this paragraph, including the methods and results of such analyses, about a drug to the sponsor or sponsors of such drug.

21 U.S.C. § 355

(F) *Qualified entities.* —

(i) *In general.* —The Secretary shall enter into contracts with a sufficient number of qualified entities to develop and provide information to the Secretary in a timely manner.

(ii) *Qualification.* —The Secretary shall enter into a contract with an entity under clause (i) only if the Secretary determines that the entity has a significant presence in the United States and has one or more of the following qualifications:

(I) The research, statistical, epidemiologic, or clinical capability and expertise to conduct and complete the activities under this paragraph, including the capability and expertise to provide the Secretary de-identified data consistent with the requirements of this subsection.

(II) An information technology infrastructure in place to support electronic data and operational standards to provide security for such data.

(III) Experience with, and expertise on, the development of drug safety and effectiveness research using electronic population data.

(IV) An understanding of drug development or risk/benefit balancing in a clinical setting.

(V) Other expertise which the Secretary deems necessary to fulfill the activities under this paragraph.

(G) *Contract requirements.* —Each contract with a qualified entity under subparagraph (F)(i) shall contain the following requirements:

(i) *Ensuring privacy.* —The qualified entity shall ensure that the entity will not use data under this subsection in a manner that—

(I) violates the regulations promulgated under section 264(c) of the Health Insurance Portability and Accountability Act of 1996;

(II) violates sections 552 or 552a of title 5, United States Code, with regard to the privacy of individually-identifiable beneficiary health information; or

(III) discloses individually identifiable health information when presenting drug safety signals and trends or when responding to inquiries regarding drug safety signals and trends. Nothing in this clause prohibits lawful disclosure for other purposes.

(ii) *Component of another organization.* — If a qualified entity is a component of another organization —

(I) the qualified entity shall establish appropriate security measures to maintain the confidentiality and privacy of such data; and

(II) the entity shall not make an unauthorized disclosure of such data to the other components of the organization in breach of such confidentiality and privacy requirement.

(iii) *Termination or nonrenewal.* — If a contract with a qualified entity under this subparagraph is terminated or not renewed, the following requirements shall apply:

(I) *Confidentiality and privacy protections.* — The entity shall continue to comply with the confidentiality and privacy requirements under this paragraph with respect to all data disclosed to the entity.

(II) *Disposition of data.* — The entity shall return any data disclosed to such entity under this subsection to which it would not otherwise have access or, if returning the data is not practicable, destroy the data.

(H) *Competitive procedures.* — The Secretary shall use competitive procedures (as defined in section 4(5) of the Federal Procurement Policy Act) to enter into contracts under subparagraph (G).

(I) *Review of contract in the event of a merger or acquisition.* — The Secretary shall review the contract with a qualified entity under this paragraph in the event of a merger or acquisition of the entity in order to ensure that the requirements under this paragraph will continue to be met.

(J) *Coordination.* — In carrying out this paragraph, the Secretary shall provide for appropriate communications to the public, scientific, public health, and medical communities, and other key stakeholders, and to the extent practicable shall coordinate with the activities of private entities, professional associations, or other entities that may have sources of drug safety data.

21 U.S.C. § 355

(5) The Secretary shall—

(A) conduct regular, bi-weekly screening of the Adverse Event Reporting System database and post a quarterly report on the Adverse Event Reporting System Web site of any new safety information or potential signal of a serious risk identified by Adverse Event Reporting System within the last quarter;

(B) report to Congress not later than 2 year after the date of the enactment of the Food and Drug Administration Amendments Act of 2007 on procedures and processes of the Food and Drug Administration for addressing ongoing post market safety issues identified by the Office of Surveillance and Epidemiology and how recommendations of the Office of Surveillance and Epidemiology are handled within the agency; and

(C) on an annual basis, review the entire backlog of postmarket safety commitments to determine which commitments require revision or should be eliminated, report to the Congress on these determinations, and assign start dates and estimated completion dates for such commitments.

(l) (1) Safety and effectiveness data and information which has been submitted in an application under subsection (b) for a drug and which has not previously been disclosed to the public shall be made available to the public, upon request, unless extraordinary circumstances are shown—

(A) if no work is being or will be undertaken to have the application approved,

(B) if the Secretary has determined that the application is not approvable and all legal appeals have been exhausted,

(C) if approval of the application under subsection (c) is withdrawn and all legal appeals have been exhausted,

(D) if the Secretary has determined that such drug is not a new drug, or

(E) upon the effective date of the approval of the first application under subsection (j) which refers to such drug or upon the date upon which the approval of an application under subsection (j) which refers to such drug could be made effective if such an application had been submitted.

21 U.S.C. § 355

[* * *]

(m) For purposes of this section, the term "patent" means a patent issued by the United States Patent and Trademark Office.

(n) (1) For the purpose of providing expert scientific advice and recommendations to the Secretary regarding a clinical investigation of a drug or the approval for marketing of a drug under section 505 or section 351 of the Public Health Service Act, the Secretary shall establish panels of experts or use panels of experts established before the date of enactment of the Food and Drug Administration Modernization Act of 1997, or both.

(2) The Secretary may delegate the appointment and oversight authority granted under section 1004 to a director of a center or successor entity within the Food and Drug Administration.

(3) The Secretary shall make appointments to each panel established under paragraph (1) so that each panel shall consist of—

(A) members who are qualified by training and experience to evaluate the safety and effectiveness of the drugs to be referred to the panel and who, to the extent feasible, possess skill and experience in the development, manufacture, or utilization of such drugs;

(B) members with diverse expertise in such fields as clinical and administrative medicine, pharmacy, pharmacology, pharmacoeconomics, biological and physical sciences, and other related professions;

(C) a representative of consumer interests, and a representative of interests of the drug manufacturing industry not directly affected by the matter to be brought before the panel; and

(D) two or more members who are specialists or have other expertise in the particular disease or condition for which the drug under review is proposed to be indicated. Scientific, trade, and consumer organizations shall be afforded an opportunity to nominate individuals for appointment to the panels. No individual who is in the regular full-time employ of the United States and engaged in the administration of this Act may be a voting member of any panel. The Secretary shall designate one of the members of each panel to serve as chairman thereof.

21 U.S.C. § 355

(4) Each member of a panel shall publicly disclose all conflicts of interest that member may have with the work to be undertaken by the panel. No member of a panel may vote on any matter where the member or the immediate family of such member could gain financially from the advice given to the Secretary. The Secretary may grant a waiver of any conflict of interest requirement upon public disclosure of such conflict of interest if such waiver is necessary to afford the panel essential expertise, except that the Secretary may not grant a waiver for a member of a panel when the member's own scientific work is involved.

(5) The Secretary shall, as appropriate, provide education and training to each new panel member before such member participates in a panel's activities, including education regarding requirements under this Act and related regulations of the Secretary, and the administrative processes and procedures related to panel meetings.

(6) Panel members (other than officers or employees of the United States), while attending meetings or conferences of a panel or otherwise engaged in its business, shall be entitled to receive compensation for each day so engaged, including traveltime, at rates to be fixed by the Secretary, but not to exceed the daily equivalent of the rate in effect for positions classified above grade GS-15 of the General Schedule. While serving away from their homes or regular places of business, panel members may be allowed travel expenses (including per diem in lieu of subsistence) as authorized by section 5703 of title 5, United States Code, for persons in the Government service employed intermittently.

(7) The Secretary shall ensure that scientific advisory panels meet regularly and at appropriate intervals so that any matter to be reviewed by such a panel can be presented to the panel not more than 60 days after the matter is ready for such review. Meetings of the panel may be held using electronic communication to convene the meetings.

(8) Within 90 days after a scientific advisory panel makes recommendations on any matter under its review, the Food and Drug Administration official responsible for the matter shall review the conclusions and recommendations of the panel, and notify the affected persons of the final decision on the matter, or of the reasons that no such decision has been reached. Each such final decision shall be documented including the rationale for the decision.

[* * *]

21 U.S.C. § 355

(June 25, 1938, ch. 675, §505, 52 Stat. 1052; June 11, 1960, Pub. L. 86-507, §1(18), 74 Stat. 201; Oct. 10, 1962, Pub. L. 87-781, §§102-04, 76 Stat. 781-85; Aug. 16, 1972, Pub. L. 92-387, §4, 86 Stat. 562; Sept. 24, 1984, Pub. L. 98-417, §§101-04, 98 Stat. 1585, 1592-93, 1597; May 13, 1992, Pub. L. 102-282, §5, 106 Stat. 161; Nov. 21, 1997, Pub. L. 105-115, §§117, 119, 120, 124, 111 Stat. 2315; Nov. 29, 1999, Pub. L. 106-113, §4732, 113 Stat. 1501A-581; Dec. 8, 2003, Pub. L. 108-173, §§1101 et seq., 117 Stat. 2448; Sept. 27, 2007, Pub. L. 110-85, §§801, 903, 905, 916, 921, 121 Stat. 921, 943, 944, 959, 962; June 22, 2009, Pub. L. 111-31, §103(e), 123 Stat. 1837; Mar. 23, 2010, Pub. L. 111-148, Title VII, Subtitle A §7002, 124 Stat. 804; Mar. 23, 2010, Pub. L. 111-148, Title VII, Subtitle F §10609, 124 Stat. 1014; July 9, 2012, Pub. L. 112-144, §905, 126 Stat. 1092; Mar. 13, 2013, Pub. L. 113-5, §301, 127 Stat. 179.)

* * * * * * *

IX. TREATMENT OF INTELLECTUAL PROPERTY UNDER FEDERAL TAX LAW

26 U.S.C. § 167   Depreciation

(g) *Depreciation under income forecast method.*

(8)[8] *Special rules for certain musical works and copyrights.* —

(A) *In general.* — If an election is in effect under this paragraph for any taxable year, then, notwithstanding paragraph (1), any expense which—

(i) is paid or incurred by the taxpayer in creating or acquiring any applicable musical property placed in service during the taxable year, and

(ii) is otherwise properly chargeable to capital account,

shall be amortized ratably over the 5-year period beginning with the month in which the property was placed in service. The preceding sentence shall not apply to any expense which, without regard to this paragraph, would not be allowable as a deduction.

(B) *Exclusive method.* — Except as provided in this paragraph, no depreciation or amortization deduction shall be allowed with respect to any expense to which subparagraph (A) applies.

(C) *Applicable musical property.* — For purposes of this paragraph—

(i) *In general.* — The term "applicable musical property" means any musical composition (including any accompanying words), or any copyright with respect to a musical composition, which is proper-

---

[8] *Ed. Note:* This provision shall apply to expenses paid or incurred with respect to property placed in service in taxable years beginning after December 31, 2005.

ty to which this subsection applies without regard to this paragraph.

(ii) *Exceptions.*—Such term shall not include any property—

(I) with respect to which expenses are treated as qualified creative expenses to which section 263A(h) applies,

(II) to which a simplified procedure established under section 263A(i)(2) applies, or

(III) which is an amortizable section 197 intangible (as defined in section 197(c)).

(D) *Election.*—An election under this paragraph shall be made at such time and in such form as the Secretary may prescribe and shall apply to all applicable musical property placed in service during the taxable year for which the election applies.

(E) *Termination.*—An election may not be made under this paragraph for any taxable year beginning after December 31, 2010.

* * *

(May 17, 2006, Pub. L. 109-222, §207, 120 Stat. 350; Dec. 29, 2007, Pub. L. 110-172, §11, 121 Stat. 2485.)

26 U.S.C. § 170 (e)   Certain contributions of ordinary income and capital gain property

(1) *General rule.*—The amount of any charitable contribution of property otherwise taken into account under this section shall be reduced by the sum of—

* * *

(A)[9] the amount of gain which would not have been long-term capital gain (determined without regard to section 1221(b)(3)) if the property contributed had been sold by the taxpayer at its fair market value (determined at the time of such contribution), and

(B) in the case of a charitable contribution—

---

[9] *Ed. Note:* The parenthetical "(determined without regard to section 1221(b)(3))" refers to sales and exchanges in taxable years beginning after May 17, 2006.

26 U.S.C. § 170

(iii)[10] of any patent, copyright (other than a copyright described in section 1221(a)(3) or 1231(b)(1)(C)), trademark, trade name, trade secret, know-how, software (other than software described in section 197(e)(3)(A)(i)), or similar property, or applications or registrations of such property,

* * *

(m)[11] *Certain donee income from intellectual property treated as an additional charitable contribution.* —

(1) *Treatment as additional contribution.* —In the case of a taxpayer who makes a qualified intellectual property contribution, the deduction allowed under subsection (a) for each taxable year of the taxpayer ending on or after the date of such contribution shall be increased (subject to the limitations under subsection (b)) by the applicable percentage of qualified donee income with respect to such contribution which is properly allocable to such year under this subsection.

(2) *Reduction in additional deductions to extent of initial deduction.* —With respect to any qualified intellectual property contribution, the deduction allowed under subsection (a) shall be increased under paragraph (1) only to the extent that the aggregate amount of such increases with respect to such contribution exceed the amount allowed as a deduction under subsection (a) with respect to such contribution determined without regard to this subsection.

(3) *Qualified donee income.* —For purposes of this subsection, the term "qualified donee income" means any net income received by or accrued to the donee which is properly allocable to the qualified intellectual property.

(4) *Allocation of qualified donee income to taxable years of donor.* —For purposes of this subsection, qualified donee income shall be treated as properly allocable to a taxable year of the donor if such income is received by or accrued to the donee for the taxable year of the donee which ends within or with such taxable year of the donor.

---

[10] *Ed. Note:* These provisions are included in "The American Jobs Creation Act of 2003" (H.R. 4520), which was signed into law on Oct. 22, 2004. These provisions apply to contributions made after June 3, 2004. For requirements regarding returns relating to certain donated property, including qualified intellectual property contributions, see 26 U.S.C. 6050L, as amended.

[11] *Ed. Note:* These provisions are included in "The American Jobs Creation Act of 2003" (H.R. 4520), which was signed into law on Oct. 22, 2004. These provisions apply to contributions made after June 3, 2004. For requirements regarding returns relating to certain donated property, including qualified intellectual property contributions, see 26 U.S.C. 6050L, as amended.

26 U.S.C. § 170

(5) *10-year limitation.* —Income shall not be treated as properly allocable to qualified intellectual property for purposes of this subsection if such income is received by or accrued to the donee after the 10-year period beginning on the date of the contribution of such property.

(6) *Benefit limited to life of intellectual property.* —Income shall not be treated as properly allocable to qualified intellectual property for purposes of this subsection if such income is received by or accrued to the donee after the expiration of the legal life of such property.

(7) *Applicable percentage.* —For purposes of this subsection, the term "applicable percentage" means the percentage determined under the following table which corresponds to a taxable year of the donor ending on or after the date of the qualified intellectual property contribution:

Taxable Year of Donor Ending on or After Date of Contribution:	Applicable Percentage:
1st	100
2nd	100
3rd	90
4th	80
5th	70
6th	60
7th	50
8th	40
9th	30
10th	20
11th	10
12th	10.

(8) *Qualified intellectual property contribution.* —For purposes of this subsection, the term "qualified intellectual property contribution" means any charitable contribution of qualified intellectual property—

(A) the amount of which taken into account under this section is reduced by reason of subsection (e)(1), and

(B) with respect to which the donor informs the donee at the time of such contribution that the donor intends to treat such contribution as a qualified intellectual property contribution for purposes of this subsection and section 6050L.

(9) *Qualified intellectual property.* —For purposes of this subsection, the term "qualified intellectual property" means property described in subsection (e)(1)(B)(iii) (other than property contributed to or for the use of an organization described in subsection (e)(1)(B)(ii)).

(10) *Other special rules.* —

(A) *Application of limitations on charitable contributions.* —Any increase under this subsection of the deduction provided under subsection (a) shall be treated for purposes of subsection (b) as a deduction which is attributable to a charitable contribution to the donee to which such increase relates.

(B) *Net income determined by donee.* —The net income taken into account under paragraph (3) shall not exceed the amount of such income reported under section 6050L(b)(1).

(C) *Deduction limited to 12 taxable years.* —Except as may be provided under subparagraph (D)(i), this subsection shall not apply with respect to any qualified intellectual property contribution for any taxable year of the donor after the 12th taxable year of the donor which ends on or after the date of such contribution.

(D) *Regulations.* —The Secretary may issue regulations or other guidance to carry out the purposes of this subsection, including regulations or guidance—

(i) modifying the application of this subsection in the case of a donor or donee with a short taxable year, and

(ii) providing for the determination of an amount to be treated as net income of the donee which is properly allocable to qualified intellectual property in the case of a donee who uses such property to further a purpose or function constituting the basis of the donee's exemption under section 501 (or, in the case of a governmental unit, any purpose described in section 170(c)) and does not possess a right to receive any payment from a third party with respect to such property.

* * *

(May 17, 2006, Pub. L. 109-222, §204, 120 Stat. 1077.)

26 U.S.C. § 170

26 U.S.C. § 174   Research and experimental expenditures

(a) *Treatment as expenses.—*

(1) *In general.—*A taxpayer may treat research or experimental expenditures which are paid or incurred by him during the taxable year in connection with his trade or business as expenses which are not chargeable to capital account. The expenditures so treated shall be allowed as a deduction.

(2) *When method may be adopted.—*

(A) *Without consent.—*A taxpayer may, without the consent of the Secretary, adopt the method provided in this subsection for his first taxable year—

(i) which begins after December 31, 1953, and ends after August 16, 1954, and

(ii) for which expenditures described in paragraph (1) are paid or incurred.

(B) *With consent.—*A taxpayer may, with the consent of the Secretary, adopt at any time the method provided in this subsection.

(3) *Scope.—*the method adopted under this subsection shall apply to all expenditures described in paragraph (1). The method adopted shall be adhered to in computing taxable income for the taxable year and for all subsequent taxable years unless, with the approval of the Secretary, a change to a different method is authorized with respect to part or all of such expenditures.

(b) *Amortization of certain research and experimental expenditures.—*

(1) *In general.—*At the election of the taxpayer, made in accordance with regulations prescribed by the Secretary, research or experimental expenditures which are—

(A) paid or incurred by the taxpayer, in connection with his trade or business,

(B) not treated as expenses under subsection (a), and

(C) chargeable to capital account but not chargeable to property of a character which is subject to the allowance under section 167 (relating to allowance for depreciation, etc.) or section 611 (relating to allowance for depletion),

26 U.S.C. § 174

may be treated as deferred expenses. In computing taxable income, such deferred expenses shall be allowed as a deduction ratably over such period of not less than 60 months as may be selected by the taxpayer (beginning with the month in which the taxpayer first realizes benefits from such expenditures). Such deferred expenses are expenditures properly chargeable to capital account for purposes of section 1016(a)(1) (relating to adjustments to basis of property).

(2) *Time for and scope of election.*—The election provided by paragraph (1) may be made for any taxable year beginning after December 31, 1953, but only if made not later than the time prescribed by law for filing the return for such taxable year (including extensions thereof). The method so elected, and the period selected by the taxpayer, shall be adhered to in computing taxable income for the taxable year for which the election is made and for all subsequent taxable years unless, with the approval of the Secretary, a change to a different method (or to a different period) is authorized with respect to part or all of such expenditures. The election shall not apply to any expenditure paid or incurred during any taxable year before the taxable year for which the taxpayer makes the election.

(c) *Land and other property.*—This section shall not apply to any expenditure for the acquisition or improvement of land, or for the acquisition or improvement of property to be used in connection with the research or experimentation and of a character which is subject to the allowance under section 167 (relating to allowance for depreciation, etc.) or section 611 (relating to allowance for depletion); but for purposes of this section allowances under section 167, and allowances under section 611, shall be considered as expenditures.

(d) *Exploration expenditures.*—This section shall not apply to any expenditure paid or incurred for the purpose of ascertaining the existence, location, extent, or quality of any deposit of ore or other mineral (including oil and gas).

(e) This section shall apply to a research or experimental expenditure only to the extent that the amount thereof is reasonable under the circumstances.

* * *

(Aug. 16, 1954, ch. 736, 68A Stat. 66; Oct. 4, 1976, Pub. L. 94-455, §§1901, 1906, 90 Stat. 1769, 1834; Sept. 3, 1982, Pub. L. 97-248, §201, 96 Stat. 420; Jan. 12, 1983, Pub. L. 97-448, §306, 96 Stat. 2400; Oct. 22, 1986, Pub. L. 99-514, §701, 100 Stat. 2343; Nov. 10, 1988, Pub. L. 100-647, §1007, 102 Stat. 3435; Dec. 19, 1989, Pub. L. 101-239, §7110, 103 Stat. 2325.)

26 U.S.C. § 174

26 U.S.C. § 197   Amortization of Goodwill and Certain Other Intangibles

(a) *General rule.*—A taxpayer shall be entitled to an amortization deduction with respect to any amortizable section 197 intangible. The amount of such deduction shall be determined by amortizing the adjusted basis (for purposes of determining gain) of such intangible ratably over the 15-year period beginning with the month in which such intangible was acquired.

(b) *No other depreciation or amortization deduction allowable.*—Except as provided in subsection (a), no depreciation or amortization deduction shall be allowable with respect to any amortizable section 197 intangible.

(c) *Amortizable Section 197 intangible.*—For purposes of this section—

(1) *In general.*—Except as otherwise provided in this section, the term "amortizable section 197 intangible" means any section 197 intangible—

(A) which is acquired by the taxpayer after the date of the enactment of this section, and

(B) which is held in connection with the conduct of a trade or business or an activity described in section 212.

(2) *Exclusion of self-created intangibles, etc.*—The term "amortizable section 197 intangible" shall not include any section 197 intangible—

(A) which is not described in subparagraph (D), (E), or (F) of subsection (d)(1), and

(B) which is created by the taxpayer.

This paragraph shall not apply if the intangible is created in connection with a transaction (or series of related transactions) involving the acquisition of assets constituting a trade or business or substantial portion thereof.

(3) *Anti-churning rules.*—For exclusion of intangibles acquired in certain transactions, see subsection (f)(9).

(d) *Section 197 intangible.*—For purposes of this section—

(1) *In general.*—Except as otherwise provided in this section, the term "section 197 intangible" means—

(A) goodwill,

(B) going concern value,

(C) any of the following intangible items:

(i) workforce in place including its composition and terms and conditions (contractual or otherwise) of its employment,

(ii) business books and records, operating systems, or any other information base (including lists or other information with respect to current or prospective customers),

(iii) any patent, copyright, formula, process, design, pattern, knowhow, format, or other similar item,

(iv) any customer-based intangible,

(v) any supplier-based intangible, and

(vi) any other similar item,

(D) any license, permit, or other right granted by a governmental unit or an agency or instrumentality thereof,

(E) any covenant not to compete (or other arrangement to the extent such arrangement has substantially the same effect as a covenant not to compete) entered into in connection with an acquisition (directly or indirectly) of an interest in a trade or business or substantial portion thereof, and

(F) any franchise, trademark, or trade name.

(2) *Customer-based intangible.* —

(A) *In general.* —The term "customer-based intangible" means—

(i) composition of market,

(ii) market share, and

(iii) any other value resulting from future provision of goods or services pursuant to relationships (contractual or otherwise) in the ordinary course of business with customers.

(B) *Special rule for financial institutions.* —In the case of a financial institution, the term "customer-based intangible" includes deposit base and similar items.

(3) *Supplier-based intangible.* —The term "supplier-based intangible" means any value resulting from future acquisitions of goods or services pursuant to relationships (contractual or otherwise) in the ordinary course of business with suppliers of goods or services to be used or sold by the taxpayer.

(e) *Exceptions.*—For purposes of this section, the term "section 197 intangible" shall not include any of the following:

(1) *Financial interests.*—Any interest—

(A) in a corporation, partnership, trust, or estate, or

(B) under an existing futures contract, foreign currency contract, notional principal contract, or other similar financial contract.

(2) *Land.*—Any interest in land.

(3) *Computer software.*—

(A) *In general.*—Any—

(i) computer software which is readily available for purchase by the general public, is subject to a nonexclusive license, and has not been substantially modified, and

(ii) other computer software which is not acquired in a transaction (or series of related transactions) involving the acquisition of assets constituting a trade or business or substantial portion thereof.

(B) *Computer software defined.*—For purposes of subparagraph (A), the term "computer software" means any program designed to cause a computer to perform a desired function. Such term shall include any data base or similar item unless the data base or item is in the public domain and is incidental to the operation of otherwise qualifying computer software.

(4) *Certain interests or rights acquired separately.*—Any of the following not acquired in a transaction (or series of related transactions) involving the acquisition of assets constituting a trade business or substantial portion thereof:

(A) Any interest in a film, sound recording, video tape, book, or similar property.

(B) Any right to receive tangible property or services under a contract or granted by a governmental unit or agency or instrumentality thereof.

(C) Any interest in a patent or copyright.

(D) To the extent provided in regulations, any right under a contract (or granted by a governmental unit or an agency or instrumentality thereof) if such right—

(i) has a fixed duration of less than 15 years, or

(ii) is fixed as to amount and, without regard to this section, would be recoverable under a method similar to the unit-of-production method.

(5) *Interests under leases and debt instruments.* — Any interest under —

(A) an existing lease of tangible property, or

(B) except as provided in subsection (d)(2)(B), any existing indebtedness.

(6) *Treatment of sports franchises.* — A franchise to engage in professional football, basketball, baseball, or other professional sport, and any item acquired in connection with such a franchise.

(7) *Mortgage servicing.* — Any right to service indebtedness which is secured by residential real property unless such right is acquired in a transaction (or series of related transactions) involving the acquisition of assets (other than rights described in this paragraph) constituting a trade or business or substantial portion thereof.

(8) *Certain transaction costs.* — Any fees for professional services, and any transaction costs, incurred by parties to a transaction with respect to which any portion of the gain or loss is not recognized under part III of subchapter C.

(f) *Special Rules.* —

(1) *Treatment of certain dispositions, etc.* —

(A) *In general.* — If there is a disposition of any amortizable section 197 intangible acquired in a transaction or series of related transactions (or any such intangible becomes worthless) and one or more other amortizable section 197 intangibles acquired in such transaction or series of related transactions are retained —

(i) no loss shall be recognized by reason of such disposition (or such worthlessness), and

(ii) appropriate adjustments to the adjusted bases of such retained intangibles shall be made for any loss not recognized under clause (i).

(B) *Special rule for covenants not to compete.* — In the case of any section 197 intangible which is a covenant not to compete (or other arrangement) described in subsection (d)(1)(E), in no event shall such covenant or other arrangement be treated as disposed of (or becoming worthless) before the disposition of the entire interest described in such subsection in connection with such covenant (or other arrangement) was entered into.

(C) *Special rule.* — All persons treated as a single taxpayer under section 41(f)(1) shall be so treated for purposes of this paragraph.

(2) *Treatment of certain transfers.* —

(A) *In general.* — In the case of any section 197 intangible transferred in a transaction described in subparagraph (B), the transferee shall be treated as the transferor for purposes of applying this section with respect to so much of the adjusted basis in the hands of the transferee as does not exceed the adjusted basis in the hands of the transferor.

(B) *Transactions covered.* — The transactions described in this subparagraph are —

(i) any transaction described in section 332, 351, 361, 721, 731, 1031, or 1033, and

(ii) any transaction between members of the same affiliated group during any taxable year for which a consolidated return is made by such group.

(3) *Treatment of amounts paid pursuant to covenants not to compete, etc.* — Any amount paid or incurred pursuant to a covenant or arrangement referred to in subsection (d)(1)(E) shall be treated as an amount chargeable to capital account.

(4) *Treatment of franchises, etc.* —

(A) *Franchise.* — The term "franchise" has the meaning given to such term by section 1253(b)(1).

(B) *Treatment of renewals.* — Any renewal of a franchise, trademark, or trade name (or of a license, a permit, or other right referred to in subsection (d)(1)(D)) shall be treated as an acquisition. The preceding sentence shall only apply with respect to costs incurred in connection with such renewal.

(C) *Certain amounts not taken into account.* — Any amount to which section 1253(d)(1) applies shall not be taken into account under this section.

(5) *Treatment of certain reinsurance transactions.* — In the case of any amortizable section 197 intangible resulting from an assumption reinsurance transaction, the amount taken into account as the adjusted basis of such intangible under this section shall be the excess of —

(A) the amount paid or incurred by the acquirer under the assumption reinsurance transaction, over

(B) the amount required to be capitalized under section 848 in connection with such transaction.

Subsection (b) shall not apply to any amount required to be capitalized under section 848.

(6) *Treatment of certain subleases.* — For purposes of this section, a sublease shall be treated in the same manner as a lease of the underlying property involved.

(7) *Treatment as depreciable.* — For purposes of this chapter, any amortizable section 197 intangible shall be treated as property which is of a character subject to the allowance for depreciation provided in section 167.

(8) *Treatment of certain increments in value.* — This section shall not apply to any increment in value if, without regard to this section, such increment is properly taken into account in determining the cost of property which is not a section 197 intangible.

(9) *Anti-churning rules.* — For purposes of this section —

(A) *In general.* — The term "amortizable section 197 intangible" shall not include any section 197 intangible which is described in subparagraph (A) or (B) of subsection (d)(1) (or for which depreciation or amortization would not have been allowable but for this section) and which is acquired by the taxpayer after the date of the enactment of this section, if —

(i) the intangible was held or used at any time on or after July 25, 1991, and on or before such date of enactment by the taxpayer or a related person,

(ii) the intangible was acquired from a person who held such intangible at any time on or after July 25, 1991, and on or before such date of enactment, and, as part of the transaction, the user of such intangible does not change, or

(iii) the taxpayer grants the right to use such intangible to a person (or person related to such person) who held or used such intangible at any time on or after July 25, 1991, and on or before such date of enactment.

For purposes of this subparagraph, the determination of whether the user of property changes as part of a transaction shall be determined in accordance with regulations prescribed by the Secretary. For purposes of this subparagraph, deductions allowable under section 1253(d) shall be treated as deductions allowable for amortization.

(B) *Exception where gain recognized.*—If—

(i) subparagraph (A) would not apply to an intangible acquired by the taxpayer but for the last sentence of subparagraph (C)(i), and

(ii) the person from whom the taxpayer acquired the intangible elects, notwithstanding any other provision of this title—

(I) to recognize gain on the disposition of the intangible, and

(II) to pay as tax on such gain which, when added to any other income tax on such gain under this title, equals such gain multiplied by the highest rate of income applicable to such person under this title,

then subparagraph (A) shall apply to the intangible only to the extent that the taxpayer's adjusted basis in the intangible exceeds the gain recognized under clause (ii)(I).

(C) *Related person defined.*—For purposes of this paragraph—

(i) *Related person.*—A person (hereinafter in this paragraph referred to as the "related person") is related to any person if—

(I) the related person bears a relationship to such person specified in section 267(b) or section 707(b)(1), or

(II) the related person and such person are engaged in trades or businesses under common control (within the meaning of subparagraphs (A) and (B) of section 41(f)(1)).

For purposes of subclause (I), in applying section 267(b) or 707(b)(1), "20 percent" shall be substituted for "50 percent".

(ii) *Time for making determination.*—A person shall be treated as related to another person if such relationship exists immediately before or immediately after the acquisition of the intangible involved.

(D) *Acquisitions by reason of death.*—Subparagraph (A) shall not apply to the acquisition of any property by the taxpayer if the basis of the property in the hands of the taxpayer is determined under section 1014(a).

(E) *Special rule for partnerships.*—With respect to any increase in the basis of partnership property under section 732, 734, or 743, determinations under this paragraph shall be made at the partner level and each partner shall be treated as having owned and used such partner's proportionate share of the partnership assets.

(F) *Anti-abuse rules.*—The term "amortizable section 197 intangible" does not include any section 197 intangible acquired in a transaction, one of the principal purposes of which is to avoid the requirement of subsection (c)(1) that the intangible be acquired after the date of the enactment of this section or to avoid the provisions of subparagraph (A).

(g) *Regulations.*—The Secretary shall prescribe such regulations as may be appropriate to carry out the purposes of this section, including such regulations as may be appropriate to prevent avoidance of the purposes of this section through related persons or otherwise.

(Aug. 10, 1993, Pub. L. 103-66, §13261, 107 Stat. 533.)

26 U.S.C. § 543   Personal Holding Company Income

(a) *General rule.*—For purposes of this subtitle, the term "personal holding company income" means the portion of the adjusted ordinary gross income which consists of:

(1) *Dividends, etc.*—Dividends, interest, royalties (other than mineral, oil, or gas royalties or copyright royalties), and annuities. This paragraph shall not apply to—

(A) interest constituting rent (as defined in subsection (b)(3)),

(B) interest on amounts set aside in a reserve fund under section 511 or 607 of the Merchant Marine Act, 1936 (46 U.S.C. App. 1161 or 1177),

(C) active business computer software royalties (within the meaning of subsection (d)), * * *

* * *

(4) *Copyright royalties.*—Copyright royalties; except that copyright royalties shall not be included if—

(A) such royalties (exclusive of royalties received for the use of, or right to use, copyrights or interests in copyrights on works created in whole, or in part, by any shareholder) constitute 50 percent or more of the ordinary gross income,

(B) the personal holding company income for the taxable year computed—

(i) without regard to copyright royalties, other than royalties received for the use of, or right to use, copyrights or interests in copyrights in works created in whole, or in part, by any shareholder owning more than 10 percent of the total outstanding capital stock of the corporation,

(ii) without regard to dividends from any corporation in which the taxpayer owns at least 50 percent of all classes of stock entitled to vote and at least 50 percent of the total value of all classes of stock and which corporation meets the requirements of this subparagraph and subparagraphs (A) and (C), and

(iii) by including as personal holding company income the adjusted income from rents and the adjusted income from mineral, oil, and gas royalties,

is not more than 10 percent of the ordinary gross income, and

(C) the sum of the deductions which are properly allocable to such royalties and which are allowable under section 162, other than—

(i) deductions for compensation for personal services rendered by the shareholders,

(ii) deductions for royalties, paid or accrued, and

(iii) deductions which are specifically allowable under sections other than section 162,

equals or exceeds 25 percent of the amount by which the ordinary gross income exceeds the sum of the royalties paid or accrued and the amounts allowable as deductions under section 167 (relating to depreciation) with respect to copyright royalties.

For purposes of this subsection, the term "copyright royalties" means compensation, however designated, for the use of, or the right to use, copyrights in works protected by copyright issued under title 17 of the United States Code and to which copyright protection is also extended by the laws of any country other than the United States of America by virtue of any international treaty, convention, or agreement, or interests in any such copyrighted works, and includes payments from any person for performing rights in any such copyrighted work and payments (other than produced film rents as defined in paragraph (5)(B)) received for the use of, or right to use, films. For purposes of this paragraph, the term "shareholder" shall include any person who owns stock within the meaning of section 544. This paragraph shall not apply to active business computer software royalties.

(5) *Produced film rents.* —

(A) Produced film rents; except that such rents shall not be included if such rents constitute 50 percent or more of the ordinary gross income.

(B) For purposes of this section, the term "produced film rents" means payments received with respect to an interest in a film for the use of, or right to use, such film, but only to the extent that such interest was acquired before substantial completion of production of such film. In the case of a producer who actively participates in the production of the film, such term includes an interest in the proceeds or profits from the film, but only to the extent such interest is attributable to such active participation.

*   *   *

(Aug. 16, 1954, ch. 736, 68A Stat. 186; Apr. 22, 1960, Pub. L. 86-435, §1, 74 Stat. 77; Feb. 2, 1962, Pub. L. 87-403, §3, 76 Stat. 6; Feb. 26, 1964, Pub. L. 88-272, §225, 78 Stat. 81, 93; Aug. 22, 1964, Pub. L. 88-484, §3, 78 Stat. 598; Nov. 13, 1966, Pub. L. 89-809, §§104, 206, 80 Stat. 1559, 1578-79; Oct. 4, 1976, Pub. L. 94-455, §§211, 1901, 1906, 2106, 90 Stat. 1544, 1800, 1834, 1902; Oct. 19, 1976, Pub. L. 94-553, §105, 90 Stat. 2599; Sept. 3, 1982, Pub. L. 97-248, §222, 96 Stat. 480; July 18, 1984, Pub. L. 98-369, §712, 98 Stat. 948; Oct. 22, 1986, Pub. L. 99-514, §§645, 1899, 100 Stat. 2289, 2291, 2959; Nov. 10, 1988, Pub. L. 100-647, §§1010, 6279, 102 Stat. 3454, 3754.)

26 U.S.C. § 1221   Capital asset defined

(b) *Definitions and special rules.* —

(3)[12] *Sale or exchange of self-created musical works.* — At the election of the taxpayer, paragraphs (1) and (3) of subsection (a) shall not apply to musi-

---

[12] *Ed. Note:* This provision applies to sales and exchanges in taxable years beginning after the date of the enactment, which is May 17, 2006.

cal compositions or copyrights in musical works sold or exchanged before January 1, 2011, by a taxpayer described in subsection (a)(3).

(May 17, 2006, Pub. L. 109-222, §204, 120 Stat. 350.)

26 U.S.C. § 1235   Sale or exchange of patents

(a) *General.*—A transfer (other than by gift, inheritance, or devise) of property consisting of all substantial rights to a patent, or an undivided interest therein which includes a part of all such rights, by any holder shall be considered the sale or exchange of a capital asset held for more than 1 year,[13] regardless of whether or not payments in consideration of such transfer are—

(1) payable periodically over a period generally coterminous with the transferee's use of the patent, or

(2) contingent on the productivity, use, or disposition of the property transferred.

(b) *"Holder" defined.*—For purposes of this section, the term "holder" means—

(1) any individual whose efforts created such property, or

(2) any other individual who has acquired his interest in such property in exchange for consideration in money or money's worth paid to such creator prior to actual reduction to practice of the invention covered by the patent, if such individual is neither—

(A) the employer of such creator, nor

(B) related to such creator (within the meaning of subsection (d)).

(c) *Effective date.*—This section shall be applicable with regard to any amounts received, or payments made, pursuant to a transfer described in subsection (a) in any taxable year to which this subtitle applies, regardless of the taxable year in which such transfer occurred.

(d) *Related persons.*—Subsection (a) shall not apply to any transfer, directly or indirectly, between persons specified within any one of the paragraphs of section 267(b) or persons described in section 707(b); except that, in applying section 267(b) and (c) and section 707(b) for purposes of this section—

(1) the phrase "25 percent or more" shall be substituted for the phrase "more than 50 percent" each place it appears in section 267(b) or 707(b), and

---

[13] *Ed. Note:* Pub. L. 98-369 temporarily substituted "6 months" for "1 year" applicable to property acquired after June 22, 1984 and before January 1, 1988.

(2) paragraph (4) of section 267(c) shall be treated as providing that the family of an individual shall include only his spouse, ancestors, and lineal descendants.

* * *

(Aug. 16, 1954, ch. 736, 68A Stat. 329; Sept. 2, 1958, Pub. L. 85-866, §54, 72 Stat. 1644; Oct. 4, 1976, Pub. L. 94-455, §1402, 90 Stat. 1732; July 18, 1984, Pub. L. 98-369, §§174, 1001, 98 Stat. 707, 1012.)

26 U.S.C. § 1249   Gain from certain sales or exchanges of patents etc., to foreign corporations

(a) *General rule.* — Gain from the sale or exchange after December 31, 1962, of a patent, an invention, model, or design (whether or not patented), a copyright, a secret formula or process, or any other similar property right to any foreign corporation by any United States person (as defined in section 7701(a)(30)) which controls such foreign corporation shall, if such gain would (but for the provisions of this subsection) be gain from the sale or exchange of a capital asset or of property described in section 1231, be considered as ordinary income.

(b) *Control.* — For purposes of subsection (a), control means, with respect to any foreign corporation, the ownership, directly or indirectly, of stock possessing more than 50 percent of the total combined voting power of all classes of stock entitled to vote. For purposes of this subsection, the rules for determining ownership of stock prescribed by section 958 shall apply.

(Oct. 16, 1962, Pub. L. 87-834, §16, 76 Stat. 1045; Nov. 13, 1966, Pub. L. 89-809, §104, 80 Stat. 1563; Oct. 4, 1976, Pub. L. 94-455, §1901, 90 Stat. 1793.)

26 U.S.C. § 1253   Transfers of franchises, trademarks, and trade names.

(a) *General rule.* — A transfer of a franchise, trademark, or trade name shall not be treated as a sale or exchange of a capital asset if the transferor retains any significant power, right, or continuing interest with respect to the subject matter of the franchise, trademark, or trade name.

(b) *Definitions.* — For purposes of this section —

(1) *Franchise.* — The term "franchise" includes an agreement which gives one of the parties to the agreement the right to distribute, sell, or provide goods, services, or facilities, within a specified area.

(2) *Significant power, right, or continuing interest.*—The term "significant power, right, or continuing interest" includes, but is not limited to, the following rights with respect to the interest transferred:

(A) A right to disapprove any assignment of such interest, or any part thereof.

(B) A right to terminate at will.

(C) A right to prescribe the standards of quality of products used or sold, or of services furnished, and of the equipment and facilities used to promote such products or services.

(D) A right to require that the transferee sell or advertise only products or services of the transferor.

(E) A right to require that the transferee purchase substantially all of his supplies and equipment from the transferor.

(F) A right to payments contingent on the productivity, use, or disposition of the subject matter of the interest transferred, if such payments constitute a substantial element under the transfer agreement.

(3) *Transfer.*—The term "transfer" includes the renewal of a franchise, trademark, or trade name.

(c) *Treatment of contingent payments by transferor.*—Amounts received or accrued on account of a transfer, sale, or other disposition of a franchise, trademark, or trade name which are contingent on the productivity, use, or disposition of the franchise, trademark, or trade name transferred shall be treated as amounts received or accrued from the sale or other disposition of property which is not a capital asset.

(d) *Treatment of payments by transferee.*—

(1) *Contingent serial payments.*—

(A) *In general.*—Any amount described in subparagraph (B) which is paid or incurred during the taxable year on account of a transfer, sale, or other disposition of a franchise, trademark, or trade name shall be allowed as a deduction under section 162(a) (relating to trade or business expenses).

(B) *Amounts to which paragraph applies.*—An amount is described in this subparagraph if it—

(i) is contingent on the productivity, use, or disposition of the franchise, trademark, or trade name, and

(ii) is paid as part of a series of payments—

(I) which are payable not less frequently than annually throughout the entire term of the transfer agreement, and

(II) which are substantially equal in amount (or payable under a fixed formula).

(2) *Other payments.*—Any amount paid or incurred on account of a transfer, sale, or other disposition of a franchise, trademark, or trade name to which paragraph (1) does not apply shall be treated as an amount chargeable to capital account.

(3) *Renewals, etc.*—For purposes of determining the term of a transfer agreement under this section, there shall be taken into account all renewal options (and any other period for which the parties reasonably expect the agreement to be renewed.)

* * *

(Dec. 30, 1969, Pub. L. 91-172, §516, 83 Stat. 647; Oct. 4, 1976, Pub. L. 94-455, §1906, 90 Stat. 1834; Dec. 19, 1989, Pub. L. 101-239, §7622, 103 Stat. 2377; Nov. 5, 1990, Pub. L. 101-508, §1170, 104 Stat. 1388; Aug. 10, 1993, Pub. L. 103-66, §13261(c), 107 Stat. 539.)

X. MISCELLANEOUS

A. INTERNATIONAL

22 U.S.C. § 269f   **International Bureau of Intellectual Property; Authorization of appropriations**

Funds appropriated to the Secretary of State for "International Organizations and Conferences" shall be available for the payment by the United States of its proportionate share of the expenses of the International Bureau for the Protection of Industrial Property for any year after 1981 as determined under article 16(4) of the Paris Convention for the Protection of Industrial Property, as revised, except that in no event shall the payment for any year exceed 6 per centum of all expenses of the Bureau apportioned among countries for that year.

(July 12, 1960, Pub. L. 86-614, 74 Stat. 381; July 19, 1963, Pub. L. 88-69, 77 Stat. 82; Oct. 20, 1972, Pub. L. 92-511, 86 Stat. 918; Nov. 22, 1983, Pub. L. 98-164, §112, 97 Stat. 1019.)

19 U.S.C. § 2435   Commercial agreements

(a) *Presidential authority.*—Subject to the provisions of subsections (b) and (c) of this section, the President may authorize the entry into force of bilateral commercial agreements providing nondiscriminatory treatment to the products of countries heretofore denied such treatment whenever he determines that such agreements with such countries will promote the purposes of this Act [ch. 12—Trade Act of 1974] and are in the national interest.

(b) *Terms of agreements.*—Any such bilateral commercial agreement shall—

* * *

(4) if the other party to the bilateral agreement is not a party to the Paris convention for the Protection of Industrial Property, provide rights for United States nationals with respect to patents and trademarks in such country not less than the rights specified in such convention;

* * *

(Jan. 3, 1975, Pub. L. 93-618, §405, 88 Stat. 2061.)

* * * * * * *

B. BANKRUPTCY

11 U.S.C. § 365   Executory Contracts Licensing Rights to Intellectual Property

* * *

(n) (1) If the trustee rejects an executory contract under which the debtor is a licensor of a right to intellectual property, the licensee under such contract may elect—

(A) to treat such contract as terminated by such rejection if such rejection by the trustee amounts to such a breach as would entitle the licensee to treat such contract as terminated by virtue of its own terms, applicable nonbankruptcy law, or an agreement made by the licensee with another entity; or

(B) to retain its rights (including a right to enforce any exclusivity provision of such contract, but excluding any other right under applicable nonbankruptcy law to specific performance of such contract) under such contract and under any agreement supplementary to such contract, to such intellectual property (including any embodiment of such intellectual property to the extent protected by applicable nonbankruptcy law), as such rights existed immediately before the case commenced, for—

(i) the duration of such contract; and

(ii) any period for which such contract may be extended by the licensee as of right under applicable nonbankruptcy law.

(2) If the licensee elects to retain its rights, as described in paragraph (1)(B) of this subsection, under such contract—

(A) the trustee shall allow the licensee to exercise such rights;

(B) the licensee shall make all royalty payments due under such contract for the duration of such contract and for any period described in paragraph (1)(B) of this subsection for which the licensee extends such contract; and

(C) the licensee shall be deemed to waive—

(i) any right of setoff it may have with respect to such contract under this title or applicable nonbankruptcy law; and

(ii) any claim allowable under section 503(b) of this title arising from the performance of such contract.

(3) If the licensee elects to retain its rights, as described in paragraph (1)(B) of this subsection, then on the written request of the licensee the trustee shall—

(A) to the extent provided in such contract, or any agreement supplementary to such contract, provide to the licensee any intellectual property (including such embodiment) held by the trustee; and

(B) not interfere with the rights of the licensee as provided in such contract, or any agreement supplementary to such contract, to such intellectual property (including such embodiment) including any right to obtain such intellectual property (or such embodiment) from another entity.

(4) Unless and until the trustee rejects such contract, on the written request of the licensee the trustee shall—

(A) to the extent provided in such contract or any agreement supplementary to such contract—

(i) perform such contract; or

(ii) provide to the licensee such intellectual property (including any embodiment of such intellectual property to the extent protected by applicable nonbankruptcy law) held by the trustee; and

(B) not interfere with the rights of the licensee as provided in such contract, or any agreement supplementary to such contract, to such intellectual property (including such embodiment), including any right to obtain such intellectual property (or such embodiment) from another entity.

* * *

(Oct. 18, 1988, Pub. L. 100-506, §1, 102 Stat. 2538.)

C. Assumption of Certain Contractual Obligations

28 U.S.C. § 4001   Assumption of contractual obligations related to transfers of rights in motion pictures

(a) *Assumption of obligations.—*

(1) In the case of a transfer of copyright ownership under United States law in a motion picture (as the terms "transfer of copyright ownership" and "motion picture" are defined in section 101 of title 17) that is produced subject to 1 or more collective bargaining agreements negotiated under the laws of the United States, if the transfer is executed on or after the effective date of this chapter and is not limited to public performance rights, the transfer instrument shall be deemed to incorporate the assumption agreements applicable to the copyright ownership being transferred that are required by the applicable collective bargaining agreement, and the transferee shall be subject to the obligations under each such assumption agreement to make residual payments and provide related notices, accruing after the effective date of the transfer and applicable to the exploitation of the rights transferred, and any remedies under each such assumption agreement for breach of those obligations, as those obligations and remedies are set forth in the applicable collective bargaining agreement, if—

(A) the transferee knows or has reason to know at the time of the transfer that such collective bargaining agreement was or will be applicable to the motion picture; or

(B) in the event of a court order confirming an arbitration award against the transferor under the collective bargaining agreement, the transferor does not have the financial ability to satisfy the award within 90 days after the order is issued.

(2) For purposes of paragraph (1)(A), "knows or has reason to know" means any of the following:

(A) Actual knowledge that the collective bargaining agreement was or will be applicable to the motion picture.

(B)(i) Constructive knowledge that the collective bargaining agreement was or will be applicable to the motion picture, arising from recordation of a document pertaining to copyright in the motion picture under section 205 of title 17 or from publication, at a site available to the public on-line that is operated by the relevant union, of information that identifies the motion picture as subject to a collective bargaining agreement with that union, if the site permits commercially reasonable verification of the date on which the information was available for access.

(ii) Clause (i) applies only if the transfer referred to in subsection (a)(1) occurs —

(I) after the motion picture is completed, or

(II) before the motion picture is completed and —

(aa) within 18 months before the filing of an application for copyright registration for the motion picture under section 408 of title 17, or

(bb) if no such application is filed, within 18 months before the first publication of the motion picture in the United States.

(C) Awareness of other facts and circumstances pertaining to a particular transfer from which it is apparent that the collective bargaining agreement was or will be applicable to the motion picture.

(b) *Scope of exclusion of transfers of public performance rights.*—For purposes of this section, the exclusion under subsection (a) of transfers of copyright ownership in a motion picture that are limited to public performance rights includes transfers to a terrestrial broadcast station, cable system, or programmer to the extent that the station, system, or programmer is functioning as an exhibitor of the motion picture, either by exhibiting the motion picture

28 U.S.C. § 4001

on its own network, system, service, or station, or by initiating the transmission of an exhibition that is carried on another network, system, service, or station. When a terrestrial broadcast station, cable system, or programmer, or other transferee, is also functioning otherwise as a distributor or as a producer of the motion picture, the public performance exclusion does not affect any obligations imposed on the transferee to the extent that it is engaging in such functions.

(c) *Exclusion for grants of security interests.* — Subsection (a) shall not apply to—

(1) a transfer of copyright ownership consisting solely of a mortgage, hypothecation, or other security interest; or

(2) a subsequent transfer of the copyright ownership secured by the security interest described in paragraph (1) by or under the authority of the secured party, including a transfer through the exercise of the secured party's rights or remedies as a secured party, or by a subsequent transferee.

The exclusion under this subsection shall not affect any rights or remedies under law or contract.

(d) *Deferral pending resolution of bona fide dispute.* — A transferee on which obligations are imposed under subsection (a) by virtue of paragraph (1) of that subsection may elect to defer performance of such obligations that are subject to a bona fide dispute between a union and a prior transferor until that dispute is resolved, except that such deferral shall not stay accrual of any union claims due under an applicable collective bargaining agreement.

(e) *Scope of obligations determined by private agreement.* — Nothing in this section shall expand or diminish the rights, obligations, or remedies of any person under the collective bargaining agreements or assumption agreements referred to in this section.

(f) *Failure to notify.* — If the transferor under subsection (a) fails to notify the transferee under subsection (a) of applicable collective bargaining obligations before the execution of the transfer instrument, and subsection (a) is made applicable to the transferee solely by virtue of subsection (a)(1)(B), the transferor shall be liable to the transferee for any damages suffered by the transferee as a result of the failure to notify.

(g) *Determination of disputes and claims.* — Any dispute concerning the application of subsections (a) through (f) shall be determined by an action in United States district court, and the court in its discretion may allow the recovery of

28 U.S.C. § 4001

full costs by or against any party and may also award a reasonable attorney's fee to the prevailing party as part of the costs.

(h) *Study.*—The Comptroller General, in consultation with the Register of Copyrights, shall conduct a study of the conditions in the motion picture industry that gave rise to this section, and the impact of this section on the motion picture industry. The Comptroller General shall report the findings of the study to the Congress within 2 years after the effective date of this chapter.

(Oct. 28, 1998, Pub. L. 105-304, §406, 112 Stat. 2902.)

D. DOMAIN NAMES

Pub. L. 113-235   **Patent and Trademark Office Appropriations for Fiscal Year 2015**

(a) None of the funds made available by this Act may be used to relinquish the responsibility of the National Telecommunications and Information Administration during fiscal year 2015 with respect to Internet domain name system functions, including responsibility with respect to the authoritative root zone file and the Internet Assigned Numbers Authority functions.

(b) Subsection (a) of this section shall expire on September 30, 2015.

(Dec. 16, 2014, Pub. L. 113-235, §540, 128 Stat. ___.)

XI. COPYRIGHT AND CRIMINAL LAW

A. NATIONAL STOLEN PROPERTY ACT

18 U.S.C. § 2314   **Transportation of stolen goods, securities, moneys, fraudulent State tax stamps, or articles used in counterfeiting**

Whoever transports, transmits, or transfers in interstate or foreign commerce any goods, wares, merchandise, securities or money, of the value of $5,000 or more, knowing the same to have been stolen, converted or taken by fraud; or

Whoever, having devised or intending to devise any scheme or artifice to defraud, or for obtaining money or property by means of false or fraudulent pretenses, representations, or promises, transports or causes to be transported, or induces any person or persons to travel in, or to be transported in interstate or foreign commerce in the execution or concealment of a scheme or artifice to defraud that person or those persons of money or property having a value of $5,000 or more; or

Whoever, with unlawful or fraudulent intent, transports in interstate or foreign commerce any falsely made, forged, altered, or counterfeited securities or tax stamps, knowing the same to have been falsely made, forged, altered, or counterfeited; or

Whoever, with unlawful or fraudulent intent, transports in interstate or foreign commerce any traveler's check bearing a forged countersignature; or

Whoever, with unlawful or fraudulent intent, transports in interstate or foreign commerce, any tool, implement, or thing used or fitted to be used in falsely making, forging, altering, or counterfeiting any security or tax stamps, or any part thereof—

Shall be fined not more than $10,000 or imprisoned not more than ten years, or both.

This section shall not apply to any falsely made, forged, altered, counterfeited or spurious representation of an obligation or other security of the United States, or of an obligation, bond, certificate, security, treasury note, bill, promise to pay or bank note issued by any foreign government. This section also shall not apply to any falsely made, forged, altered, counterfeited, or spurious representation of any bank note or bill issued by a bank or corporation of any foreign country which is intended by the laws or usage of such country to circulate as money.

(June 25, 1948, ch. 645, §1, 62 Stat. 806, May 24, 1949, ch. 139, §45, 63 Stat. 96; July 9, 1956, ch. 519, 70 Stat. 507; Oct. 4, 1961, Pub. L. 87-371, §2, 75 Stat. 802; Sept. 28, 1968, Pub. L. 90-535, 82 Stat. 885; Nov. 18, 1988, Pub. L. 100-690, §§7057, 7080, 102 Stat. 4402, 4406; Nov. 29, 1990, Pub. L. 101-647, §1208, 104 Stat. 4832.)

B. PIRACY AND COUNTERFEITING

18 U.S.C. § 2318   Trafficking in counterfeit labels, illicit labels, or counterfeit documentation or packaging

(a)(1) Whoever, in any of the circumstances described in subsection (c), knowingly traffics in—

   (A) a counterfeit label or illicit label affixed to, enclosing, or accompanying, or designed to be affixed to, enclose, or accompany—

      (i) a phonorecord;

      (ii) a copy of a computer program;

      (iii) a copy of a motion picture or other audiovisual work;

(iv) a copy of a literary work;

(v) a copy of a pictorial, graphic, or sculptural work;

(vi) a work of visual art; or

(vii) documentation or packaging; or

(B) counterfeit documentation or packaging, shall be fined under this title or imprisoned for not more than 5 years, or both.

(b) As used in this section—

(1) the term "counterfeit label" means an identifying label or container that appears to be genuine, but is not;

(2) the term "traffic" has the same meaning as in section 2320(e) of this title;

(3) the terms "copy", "phonorecord", "motion picture", "computer program", "audiovisual work", "literary work", "pictorial, graphic, or sculptural work", "sound recording", "work of visual art", and "copyright owner" have, respectively, the meanings given those terms in section 101 (relating to definitions) of title 17;

(4) the term "illicit label" means a genuine certificate, licensing document, registration card, or similar labeling component—

(A) that is used by the copyright owner to verify that a phonorecord, a copy of a computer program, a copy of a motion picture or other audiovisual work, a copy of a literary work, a copy of a pictorial, graphic, or sculptural work, a work of visual art, or documentation or packaging is not counterfeit or infringing of any copyright; and

(B) that is, without the authorization of the copyright owner—

(i) distributed or intended for distribution not in connection with the copy, phonorecord, or work of visual art to which such labeling component was intended to be affixed by the respective copyright owner; or

(ii) in connection with a genuine certificate or licensing document, knowingly falsified in order to designate a higher number of licensed users or copies than authorized by the copyright owner, unless that certificate or document is used by the copyright owner solely for the purpose of monitoring or tracking the copyright owner's distribution channel and not for the purpose of verifying that a copy or phonorecord is noninfringing;

(5) the term "documentation or packaging" means documentation or packaging, in physical form, for a phonorecord, copy of a computer program, copy of a motion picture or other audiovisual work, copy of a literary work, copy of a pictorial, graphic, or sculptural work, or work of visual art; and

(6) the term "counterfeit documentation or packaging" means documentation or packaging that appears to be genuine, but is not.

(c) The circumstances referred to in subsection (a) of this section are—

(1) the offense is committed within the special maritime and territorial jurisdiction of the United States; or within the special aircraft jurisdiction of the United States (as defined in section 101 of the Federal Aviation Act of 1958);

(2) the mail or a facility of interstate or foreign commerce is used or intended to be used in the commission of the offense;

(3) the counterfeit label or illicit label is affixed to, encloses, or accompanies, or is designed to be affixed to, enclose, or accompany—

(A) a phonorecord of a copyrighted sound recording or copyrighted musical work;

(B) a copy of a copyrighted computer program;

(C) a copy of a copyrighted motion picture or other audiovisual work;

(D) a copy of a literary work;

(E) a copy of a pictorial, graphic, or sculptural work;

(F) a work of visual art; or

(G) copyrighted documentation or packaging; or

(4) the counterfeited documentation or packaging is copyrighted.

(d) *Forfeiture and destruction of property; restitution.*—Forfeiture, destruction, and restitution relating to this section shall be subject to section 2323, to the extent provided in that section, in addition to any other similar remedies provided by law.

(e) *Civil remedies.—*

(1) *In general.—*Any copyright owner who is injured, or is threatened with injury, by a violation of subsection (a) may bring a civil action in an appropriate United States district court.

(2) *Discretion of court.—*In any action brought under paragraph (1), the court—

(A) may grant 1 or more temporary or permanent injunctions on such terms as the court determines to be reasonable to prevent or restrain a violation of subsection (a);

(B) at any time while the action is pending, may order the impounding, on such terms as the court determines to be reasonable, of any article that is in the custody or control of the alleged violator and that the court has reasonable cause to believe was involved in a violation of subsection (a); and

(C) may award to the injured party—

(i) reasonable attorney fees and costs; and

(ii) (I) actual damages and any additional profits of the violator, as provided in paragraph (3); or

(II) statutory damages, as provided in paragraph (4).

(3) *Actual damages and profits.—*

(A) *In general.—*The injured party is entitled to recover—

(i) the actual damages suffered by the injured party as a result of a violation of subsection (a), as provided in subparagraph (B) of this paragraph; and

(ii) any profits of the violator that are attributable to a violation of subsection (a) and are not taken into account in computing the actual damages.

(B) *Calculation of damages.—*The court shall calculate actual damages by multiplying—

(i) the value of the phonorecords, copies, or works of visual art which are, or are intended to be, affixed with, enclosed in, or accompanied by any counterfeit labels, illicit labels, or counterfeit documentation or packaging, by

18 U.S.C. § 2318

(ii) the number of phonorecords, copies, or works of visual art which are, or are intended to be, affixed with, enclosed in, or accompanied by any counterfeit labels, illicit labels, or counterfeit documentation or packaging.

(C) *Definition.*—For purposes of this paragraph, the "value" of a phonorecord, copy, or work of visual art is—

(i) in the case of a copyrighted sound recording or copyrighted musical work, the retail value of an authorized phonorecord of that sound recording or musical work;

(ii) in the case of a copyrighted computer program, the retail value of an authorized copy of that computer program;

(iii) in the case of a copyrighted motion picture or other audiovisual work, the retail value of an authorized copy of that motion picture or audiovisual work;

(iv) in the case of a copyrighted literary work, the retail value of an authorized copy of that literary work;

(v) in the case of a pictorial, graphic, or sculptural work, the retail value of an authorized copy of that work; and

(vi) in the case of a work of visual art, the retail value of that work.

(4) *Statutory damages.*—The injured party may elect, at any time before final judgment is rendered, to recover, instead of actual damages and profits, an award of statutory damages for each violation of subsection (a) in a sum of not less than $2,500 or more than $25,000, as the court considers appropriate.

(5) *Subsequent violation.*—The court may increase an award of damages under this subsection by 3 times the amount that would otherwise be awarded, as the court considers appropriate, if the court finds that a person has subsequently violated subsection (a) within 3 years after a final judgment was entered against that person for a violation of that subsection.

(6) *Limitation on actions.*—A civil action may not be commenced under this subsection unless it is commenced within 3 years after the date on which the claimant discovers the violation of subsection (a).

(Oct. 9, 1962, Pub. L. 87-773, §1, 76 Stat. 775; Dec. 31, 1974, Pub. L. 93-573, §103, 88 Stat. 1873; Oct. 19, 1976, Pub. L. 94-553, §111, 90 Stat. 2600; May 24, 1982, Pub. L. 97-180, §2, 96 Stat. 91; Nov. 29, 1990, Pub. L. 101-647, §3567, 104 Stat. 4928; July 2, 1996, Pub. L.

18 U.S.C. § 2318

104-153, §4, 110 Stat. 1386; Dec. 23, 2004, Pub. L. 108-482, §102, 118 Stat. 3912; Mar. 16, 2006, Pub. L. 109-181, §2, 120 Stat. 288; Oct. 13, 2008, Pub. L. 110-403, §202, 122 Stat. 4260; Dec. 9, 2010, Pub. L. 111-295, §6, 124 Stat. 3181.)

18 U.S.C. § 2319   Criminal infringement of a copyright

(a) Any person who violates section 506(a) (relating to criminal offenses) of title 17 shall be punished as provided in subsections (b), (c), and (d) and such penalties shall be in addition to any other provisions of title 17 or any other law.

(b) Any person who commits an offense under section 506(a)(1)(A) of title 17—

(1) shall be imprisoned not more than 5 years, or fined in the amount set forth in this title, or both, if the offense consists of the reproduction or distribution, including by electronic means, during any 180-day period, of at least 10 copies or phonorecords, of 1 or more copyrighted works, which have a total retail value of more than $2,500;

(2) shall be imprisoned not more than 10 years, or fined in the amount set forth in this title, or both, if the offense is a felony and is a second or subsequent offense under subsection (a); and

(3) shall be imprisoned not more than 1 year, or fined in the amount set forth in this title, or both, in any other case.

(c) Any person who commits an offense under section 506(a)(1)(B) of title 17—

(1) shall be imprisoned not more than 3 years, or fined in the amount set forth in this title, or both, if the offense consists of the reproduction or distribution of 10 or more copies or phonorecords of 1 or more copyrighted works, which have a total retail value of $2,500 or more;

(2) shall be imprisoned not more than 6 years, or fined in the amount set forth in this title, or both, if the offense is a felony and is a second or subsequent offense under subsection (a); and

(3) shall be imprisoned not more than 1 year, or fined in the amount set forth in this title, or both, if the offense consists of the reproduction or distribution of 1 or more copies or phonorecords of 1 or more copyrighted works, which have a total retail value of more than $1,000.

(d) Any person who commits an offense under section 506(a)(1)(C) of title 17—

(1) shall be imprisoned not more than 3 years, fined under this title, or both;

(2) shall be imprisoned not more than 5 years, fined under this title, or both, if the offense was committed for purposes of commercial advantage or private financial gain;

(3) shall be imprisoned not more than 6 years, fined under this title, or both, if the offense is a felony and is a second or subsequent offense under subsection (a); and

(4) shall be imprisoned not more than 10 years, fined under this title, or both, if the offense is a felony and is a second or subsequent offense under paragraph (2).

(e) (1) During preparation of the presentence report pursuant to Rule 32(c) of the Federal Rules of Criminal Procedure, victims of the offense shall be permitted to submit, and the probation officer shall receive, a victim impact statement that identifies the victim of the offense and the extent and scope of the injury and loss suffered by the victim, including the estimated economic impact of the offense on that victim.

(2) Persons permitted to submit victim impact statements shall include—

(A) producers and sellers of legitimate works affected by conduct involved in the offense;

(B) holders of intellectual property rights in such works; and

(C) the legal representatives of such producers, sellers, and holders.

(f) As used in this section—

(1) the terms "phonorecord" and "copies" have, respectively, the meanings set forth in section 101 (relating to definitions) of title 17;

(2) the terms "reproduction" and "distribution" refer to the exclusive rights of a copyright owner under clauses (1) and (3) respectively of section 106 (relating to exclusive rights in copyrighted works), as limited by sections 107 through 122, of title 17;

(3) the term "financial gain" has the meaning given the term in section 101 of title 17; and

(4) the term "work being prepared for commercial distribution" has the meaning given the term in section 506(a) of title 17.

18 U.S.C. § 2319

(May 24, 1982, Pub. L. 97-180, §3, 96 Stat. 92; Oct. 28, 1992, Pub. L. 102-561, §§1-2, 106 Stat. 4233; Nov. 13, 1997, Pub. L. 105-80, §12, 111 Stat. 1536; Dec. 16, 1997, Pub. L. 105-147, §2(d), 111 Stat. 2678; Nov. 2, 2002, Pub. L. 107-273, §13211, 116 Stat. 1910; Apr. 27, 2005, Pub. L. 109-9, §103, 119 Stat. 220; Oct. 13, 2008, Pub. L. 110-403, §208, 122 Stat. 4263.)

18 U.S.C. § 2319A   Unauthorized fixation of and trafficking in sound recordings and music videos of live musical performances

(a) *Offense.*—Whoever, without the consent of the performer or performers involved, knowingly and for purposes of commercial advantage or private financial gain—

(1) fixes the sounds or sounds and images of a live musical performance in a copy or phonorecord, or reproduces copies or phonorecords of such a performance from an unauthorized fixation;

(2) transmits or otherwise communicates to the public the sounds or sounds and images of a live musical performance; or

(3) distributes or offers to distribute, sells or offers to sell, rents or offers to rent, or traffics in any copy or phonorecord fixed as described in paragraph (1), regardless of whether the fixations occurred in the United States;

shall be imprisoned for not more than 5 years or fined in the amount set forth in this title, or both, or if the offense is a second or subsequent offense, shall be imprisoned for not more than 10 years or fined in the amount set forth in this title, or both.

(b) *Forfeiture and destruction of property; restitution.*—Forfeiture, destruction, and restitution relating to this section shall be subject to section 2323, to the extent provided in that section, in addition to any other similar remedies provided by law.

(c) *Seizure and forfeiture.*—If copies or phonorecords of sounds or sounds and images of a live musical performance are fixed outside of the United States without the consent of the performer or performers involved, such copies or phonorecords are subject to seizure and forfeiture in the United States in the same manner as property imported in violation of the customs laws. The Secretary of Homeland Security shall issue regulations by which any performer may, upon payment of a specified fee, be entitled to notification by United States Customs and Border Protection of the importation of copies or phonorecords that appear to consist of unauthorized fixations of the sounds or sounds and images of a live musical performance.

(d) *Victim impact statement.*—

(1) During preparation of the presentence report pursuant to Rule 32(c) of the Federal Rules of Criminal Procedure, victims of the offense shall be permitted to submit, and the probation officer shall receive, a victim impact statement that identifies the victim of the offense and the extent and scope of the injury and loss suffered by the victim, including the estimated economic impact of the offense on that victim.

(2) Persons permitted to submit victim impact statements shall include—

(A) producers and sellers of legitimate works affected by conduct involved in the offense;

(B) holders of intellectual property rights in such works; and

(C) the legal representatives of such producers, sellers, and holders.

(e) *Definitions.*—As used in this section—

(1) the terms "copy", "fixed", "musical work", "phonorecord", "reproduce", "sound recordings", and "transmit" mean those terms within the meaning of title 17; and

(2) the term "traffic" has the same meaning as in section 2320(e) of this title.

(f) *Applicability.*—This section shall apply to any Act or Acts that occur on or after the date of the enactment of the Uruguay Round Agreements Act.[14]

(Dec. 8, 1994, Pub. L. 103-465, §513, 108 Stat. 4974; Dec. 16, 1997, Pub. L. 105-147, §2(e), 111 Stat. 2679; Mar. 16, 2006, Pub. L. 109-181, §2, 120 Stat. 288; Oct. 13, 2008, Pub. L. 110-403, §203, 122 Stat. 4261.)

18 U.S.C. § 2319B   Unauthorized recording of motion pictures in a motion picture exhibition facility

(a) *Offense.*—Any person who, without the authorization of the copyright owner, knowingly uses or attempts to use an audiovisual recording device to transmit or make a copy of a motion picture or other audiovisual work protected under title 17, or any part thereof, from a performance of such work in a motion picture exhibition facility, shall—

---

[14] *Ed. Note:* The date of enactment of the Uruguay Round Agreements Act was Dec. 8, 1994.

(1) be imprisoned for not more than 3 years, fined under this title, or both; or

(2) if the offense is a second or subsequent offense, be imprisoned for no more than 6 years, fined under this title, or both.

The possession by a person of an audiovisual recording device in a motion picture exhibition facility may be considered as evidence in any proceeding to determine whether that person committed an offense under this subsection, but shall not, by itself, be sufficient to support a conviction of that person for such offense.

(b) *Forfeiture and destruction of property; restitution.* —Forfeiture, destruction, and restitution relating to this section shall be subject to section 2323, to the extent provided in that section, in addition to any other similar remedies provided by law.

(c) *Authorized activities.* —This section does not prevent any lawfully authorized investigative, protective, or intelligence activity by an officer, agent, or employee of the United States, a State, or a political subdivision of a State, or by a person acting under a contract with the United States, a State, or a political subdivision of a State.

(d) *Immunity for theaters.* —With reasonable cause, the owner or lessee of a motion picture exhibition facility where a motion picture or other audiovisual work is being exhibited, the authorized agent or employee of such owner or lessee, the licensor of the motion picture or other audiovisual work being exhibited, or the agent or employee of such licensor—

(1) may detain, in a reasonable manner and for a reasonable time, any person suspected of a violation of this section with respect to that motion picture or audiovisual work for the purpose of questioning or summoning a law enforcement officer; and

(2) shall not be held liable in any civil or criminal action arising out of a detention under paragraph (1).

(e) *Victim impact statement.* —

(1) *In general.* —During the preparation of the presentence report under rule 32(c) of the Federal Rules of Criminal Procedure, victims of an offense under this section shall be permitted to submit to the probation officer a victim impact statement that identifies the victim of the offense and the extent and scope of the injury and loss suffered by the victim, including the estimated economic impact of the offense on that victim.

18 U.S.C. § 2319B

(2) *Contents.*—A victim impact statement submitted under this subsection shall include—

(A) producers and sellers of legitimate works affected by conduct involved in the offense;

(B) holders of intellectual property rights in the works described in subparagraph (A); and

(C) the legal representatives of such producers, sellers, and holders.

(f) *State law not preempted.*—Nothing in this section may be construed to annul or limit any rights or remedies under the laws of any State.

(g) *Definitions.*—In this section, the following definitions shall apply:

(1) *Title 17 definitions.*—The terms "audiovisual work", "copy", "copyright owner", "motion picture", "motion picture exhibition facility", and "transmit" have, respectively, the meanings given those terms in section 101 of title 17.

(2) *Audiovisual recording device.*—The term "audiovisual recording device" means a digital or analog photographic or video camera, or any other technology or device capable of enabling the recording or transmission of a copyrighted motion picture or other audiovisual work, or any part thereof, regardless of whether audiovisual recording is the sole or primary purpose of the device.

(Apr. 27, 2005, Pub. L. 109-9, §102, 119 Stat. 218; Oct. 13, 2008, Pub. L. 110-403, §204, 122 Stat. 4261.)

C. TRADEMARK COUNTERFEITING

18 U.S.C. § 2320   Trafficking in counterfeit goods or services

(a) *Offenses.*—Whoever intentionally—

(1) traffics in goods or services and knowingly uses a counterfeit mark on or in connection with such goods or services,

(2) traffics in labels, patches, stickers, wrappers, badges, emblems, medallions, charms, boxes, containers, cans, cases, hangtags, documentation, or packaging of any type or nature, knowing that a counterfeit mark has been applied thereto, the use of which is likely to cause confusion, to cause mistake, or to deceive,

(3) traffics in goods or services knowing that such good or service is a counterfeit military good or service the use, malfunction, or failure of which is likely to cause serious bodily injury or death, the disclosure of classified information, impairment of combat operations, or other significant harm to a combat operation, a member of the Armed Forces, or to national security, or attempts or conspires to violate any of paragraphs (1) through (4) shall be punished as provided in subsection (b), or

(4) traffics in a counterfeit drug.

(b) *Penalties.*—

(1) *In general.*—Whoever commits an offense under subsection (a)—

(A) if an individual, shall be fined not more than $2,000,000 or imprisoned not more than 10 years, or both, and, if a person other than an individual, shall be fined not more than $5,000,000; and

(B) for a second or subsequent offense under subsection (a), if an individual, shall be fined not more than $5,000,000 or imprisoned not more than 20 years, or both, and if other than an individual, shall be fined not more than $15,000,000.

(2) *Serious bodily injury or death.*—

(A) *Serious bodily injury.*—Whoever knowingly or recklessly causes or attempts to cause serious bodily injury from conduct in violation of subsection (a), if an individual, shall be fined not more than $5,000,000 or imprisoned for not more than 20 years, or both, and if other than an individual, shall be fined not more than $15,000,000.

(B) Death.—Whoever knowingly or recklessly causes or attempts to cause death from conduct in violation of subsection (a), if an individual, shall be fined not more than $5,000,000 or imprisoned for any term of years or for life, or both, and if other than an individual, shall be fined not more than $15,000,000.

(3) *Counterfeit military goods or services and counterfeit drugs.*—Whoever commits an offense under subsection (a) involving a counterfeit military good or service or counterfeit drug—

(A) if an individual, shall be fined not more than $5,000,000, imprisoned not more than 20 years, or both, and if other than an individual, be fined not more than $15,000,000; and

(B) for a second or subsequent offense, if an individual, shall be fined not more than $15,000,000, imprisoned not more than 30 years, or

18 U.S.C. § 2320

both, and if other than an individual, shall be fined not more than $30,000,000.

(c) *Forfeiture and destruction of property; restitution.*—Forfeiture, destruction, and restitution relating to this section shall be subject to section 2323, to the extent provided in that section, in addition to any other similar remedies provided by law.

(d) *Defenses.*—All defenses, affirmative defenses, and limitations on remedies that would be applicable in an action under the Lanham Act shall be applicable in a prosecution under this section. In a prosecution under this section, the defendant shall have the burden of proof, by a preponderance of the evidence, of any such affirmative defense.

(e) *Presentence report.*—

(1) During preparation of the presentence report pursuant to Rule 32(c) of the Federal Rules of Criminal Procedure, victims of the offense shall be permitted to submit, and the probation officer shall receive, a victim impact statement that identifies the victim of the offense and the extent and scope of the injury and loss suffered by the victim, including the estimated economic impact of the offense on that victim.

(2) Persons permitted to submit victim impact statements shall include—

(A) producers and sellers of legitimate goods or services affected by conduct involved in the offense;

(B) holders of intellectual property rights in such goods or services; and

(C) the legal representatives of such producers, sellers, and holders.

(f) *Definitions.*—For the purposes of this section—

(1) the term "counterfeit mark" means—

(A) a spurious mark—

(i) that is used in connection with trafficking in any goods, services, labels, patches, stickers, wrappers, badges, emblems, medallions, charms, boxes, containers, cans, cases, hangtags, documentation, or packaging of any type or nature;

(ii) that is identical with, or substantially indistinguishable from, a mark registered on the principal register in the United States Patent and Trademark Office and in use, whether or not the defendant knew such mark was so registered;

(iii) that is applied to or used in connection with the goods or services for which the mark is registered with the United States Patent and Trademark Office, or is applied to or consists of a label, patch, sticker, wrapper, badge, emblem, medallion, charm, box, container, can, case, hangtag, documentation, or packaging of any type or nature that is designed, marketed, or otherwise intended to be used on or in connection with the goods or services for which the mark is registered in the United States Patent and Trademark Office; and

(iv) the use of which is likely to cause confusion, to cause mistake, or to deceive; or

(B) a spurious designation that is identical with, or substantially indistinguishable from, a designation as to which the remedies of the Lanham Act are made available by reason of section 220506 of title 36;

but such term does not include any mark or designation used in connection with goods or services, or a mark or designation applied to labels, patches, stickers, wrappers, badges, emblems, medallions, charms, boxes, containers, cans, cases, hangtags, documentation, or packaging of any type or nature used in connection with such goods or services, of which the manufacturer or producer was, at the time of the manufacture or production in question, authorized to use the mark or designation for the type of goods or services so manufactured or produced, by the holder of the right to use such mark or designation;

(2) the term "financial gain" includes the receipt, or expected receipt, of anything of value;

(3) the term "Lanham Act" means the Act entitled "An Act to provide for the registration and protection of trademarks used in commerce, to carry out the provisions of certain international conventions, and for other purposes", approved July 5, 1946 (15 U.S.C. 1051 et seq.);

(4) the term "counterfeit military good or service" means a good or service that uses a counterfeit mark on or in connection with such good or service and that—

(A) is falsely identified or labeled as meeting military specifications, or

(B) is intended for use in a military or national security application;

(5) the term "traffic" means to transport, transfer, or otherwise dispose of, to another, for purposes of commercial advantage or private financial

gain, or to make, import, export, obtain control of, or possess, with intent to so transport, transfer, or otherwise dispose of; and

(6) the term "counterfeit drug" means a drug, as defined by section 201 of the Federal Food, Drug, and Cosmetic Act, that uses a counterfeit mark on or in connection with the drug.

(g) *Limitation on cause of action.*—Nothing in this section shall entitle the United States to bring a criminal cause of action under this section for the repackaging of genuine goods or services not intended to deceive or confuse.

(h) *Report to Congress.*—

(1) Beginning with the first year after the date of enactment of this subsection, the Attorney General shall include in the report of the Attorney General to Congress on the business of the Department of Justice prepared pursuant to section 522 of title 28, an accounting, on a district by district basis, of the following with respect to all actions taken by the Department of Justice that involve trafficking in counterfeit labels for phonorecords, copies of computer programs or computer program documentation or packaging, copies of motion pictures or other audiovisual works (as defined in section 2318 of this title), criminal infringement of copyrights (as defined in section 2319 of this title), unauthorized fixation of and trafficking in sound recordings and music videos of live musical performances (as defined in section 2319A of this title), or trafficking in goods or services bearing counterfeit marks (as defined in section 2320 of this title):

(A) The number of open investigations.

(B) The number of cases referred by the United States Customs Service.

(C) The number of cases referred by other agencies or sources.

(D) The number and outcome, including settlements, sentences, recoveries, and penalties, of all prosecutions brought under sections 2318, 2319, 2319A, and 2320 of title 18.

(2)(A) The report under paragraph (1), with respect to criminal infringement of copyright, shall include the following:

(i) The number of infringement cases in these categories: audiovisual (videos and films); audio (sound recordings); literary works (books and musical compositions); computer programs; video games; and, others.

18 U.S.C. § 2320

(ii) The number of online infringement cases.

(iii) The number and dollar amounts of fines assessed in specific categories of dollar amounts. These categories shall be: no fines ordered; fines under $500; fines from $500 to $1,000; fines from $1,000 to $5,000; fines from $5,000 to $10,000; and fines over $10,000.

(iv) The total amount of restitution ordered in all copyright infringement cases.

(B) In this paragraph, the term "online infringement cases" as used in paragraph (2) means those cases where the infringer—

(i) advertised or publicized the infringing work on the Internet; or

(ii) made the infringing work available on the Internet for download, reproduction, performance, or distribution by other persons.

(C) The information required under subparagraph (A) shall be submitted in the report required in fiscal year 2005 and thereafter.

(i) *Transshipment and exportation.*—No goods or services, the trafficking in of which is prohibited by this section, shall be transshipped through or exported from the United States. Any such transshipment or exportation shall be deemed a violation of section 42 of an Act to provide for the registration of trademarks used in commerce, to carry out the provisions of certain international conventions, and for other purposes, approved July 5, 1946 (commonly referred to as the "Trademark Act of 1946" or the "Lanham Act").

(Oct. 12, 1984, Pub. L. 98-473, §1502, 98 Stat. 2178; Sept. 13, 1994, Pub. L. 103-322, §320104, 108 Stat. 2110; July 2, 1996, Pub. L. 104-153, §5, 110 Stat. 1387; Dec. 16, 1997, Pub. L. 105-147, §2(f), 111 Stat. 2679; August 12, 1998, Pub. L. 105-225, §4, 112 Stat. 1499; Nov. 3, 1998, Pub. L. 105-354, §2(b), 112 Stat. 3244; Nov. 2, 2002, Pub. L. 107-273, §205(e), 116 Stat. 1778; Feb. 8, 2002, Pub. L. 107-140, §1, 116 Stat. 12; Mar. 16, 2006, Pub. L. 109-181, § §1, 2, 120 Stat. 285; Oct. 13, 2008, Pub. L. 110-403, §205, 122 Stat. 4261, 4262; Dec. 31, 2011, Pub. L. 112-81, §818, 125 Stat. 1497; July 9, 2012, Pub. L. 112-144, §717, 126 Stat. 1076.)

D. FORFEITURE, DESTRUCTION, AND RESTITUTION

18 U.S.C. § 2323   Forfeiture, destruction, and restitution

(a) *Civil forfeiture.*—

(1) *Property subject to forfeiture.*—The following property is subject to forfeiture to the United States Government:

(A) Any article, the making or trafficking of which is, prohibited under section 506 of title 17, or section 2318, 2319, 2319A, 2319B, or 2320, or chapter 90, of this title.

(B) Any property used, or intended to be used, in any manner or part to commit or facilitate the commission of an offense referred to in subparagraph (A).

(C) Any property constituting or derived from any proceeds obtained directly or indirectly as a result of the commission of an offense referred to in subparagraph (A).

(2) *Procedures.*—The provisions of chapter 46 relating to civil forfeitures shall extend to any seizure or civil forfeiture under this section. For seizures made under this section, the court shall enter an appropriate protective order with respect to discovery and use of any records or information that has been seized. The protective order shall provide for appropriate procedures to ensure that confidential, private, proprietary, or privileged information contained in such records is not improperly disclosed or used. At the conclusion of the forfeiture proceedings, unless otherwise requested by an agency of the United States, the court shall order that any property forfeited under paragraph (1) be destroyed, or otherwise disposed of according to law.

(b) *Criminal forfeiture.*—

(1) *Property subject to forfeiture.*—The court, in imposing sentence on a person convicted of an offense under section 506 of title 17, or section 2318, 2319, 2319A, 2319B, or 2320, or chapter 90, of this title, shall order, in addition to any other sentence imposed, that the person forfeit to the United States Government any property subject to forfeiture under subsection (a) for that offense.

(2) *Procedures.*—

(A) *In general.*—The forfeiture of property under paragraph (1), including any seizure and disposition of the property and any related judicial or administrative proceeding, shall be governed by the procedures set forth in section 413 of the Comprehensive Drug Abuse Prevention and Control Act of 1970 (21 U.S.C. 853), other than subsection (d) of that section.

(B) *Destruction.*—At the conclusion of the forfeiture proceedings, the court, unless otherwise requested by an agency of the United States shall order that any—

(i) forfeited article or component of an article bearing or consisting of a counterfeit mark be destroyed or otherwise disposed of according to law; and

(ii) infringing items or other property described in subsection (a)(1)(A) and forfeited under paragraph (1) of this subsection be destroyed or otherwise disposed of according to law.

(c) *Restitution.*—When a person is convicted of an offense under section 506 of title 17 or section 2318, 2319, 2319A, 2319B, or 2320, or chapter 90, of this title, the court, pursuant to sections 3556, 3663A, and 3664 of this title, shall order the person to pay restitution to any victim of the offense as an offense against property referred to in section 3663A(c)(1)(A)(ii) of this title.

(Oct. 13, 2008, Pub. L. 110-403, §206, 122 Stat. 4262, 4263.)

E. ECONOMIC ESPIONAGE ACT OF 1996

TITLE I—PROTECTION OF TRADE SECRETS

18 U.S.C. § 1831   Economic espionage

(a) *In general.*—Whoever, intending or knowing that the offense will benefit any foreign government, foreign instrumentality, or foreign agent, knowingly—

(1) steals, or without authorization appropriates, takes, carries away, or conceals, or by fraud, artifice, or deception obtains a trade secret;

(2) without authorization copies, duplicates, sketches, draws, photographs, downloads, uploads, alters, destroys, photocopies, replicates, transmits, delivers, sends, mails, communicates, or conveys a trade secret;

(3) receives, buys, or possesses a trade secret, knowing the same to have been stolen or appropriated, obtained, or converted without authorization;

(4) attempts to commit any offense described in any of paragraphs (1) through (3); or

(5) conspires with one or more other persons to commit any offense described in any of paragraphs (1) through (3), and one or more of such persons do any act to effect the object of the conspiracy,

shall, except as provided in subsection (b), be fined not more than $5,000,000 or imprisoned not more than 15 years, or both.

(b) *Organizations.*—Any organization that commits any offense described in subsection (a) shall be fined not more than the greater of $10,000,000 or 3 times the value of the stolen trade secret to the organization, including expenses for research and design and other costs of reproducing the trade secret that the organization has thereby avoided.

18 U.S.C. § 1832   Theft of trade secrets

(a) Whoever, with intent to convert a trade secret, that is related to a product or service used in or intended for use in interstate or foreign commerce, to the economic benefit of anyone other than the owner thereof, and intending or knowing that the offense will, injure any owner of that trade secret, knowingly—

(1) steals, or without authorization appropriates, takes, carries away, or conceals, or by fraud, artifice, or deception obtains such information;

(2) without authorization copies, duplicates, sketches, draws, photographs, downloads, uploads, alters, destroys, photocopies, replicates, transmits, delivers, sends, mails, communicates, or conveys such information;

(3) receives, buys, or possesses such information, knowing the same to have been stolen or appropriated, obtained, or converted without authorization;

(4) attempts to commit any offense described in paragraphs (1) through (3); or

(5) conspires with one or more other persons to commit any offense described in paragraphs (1) through (3), and one or more of such persons do any act to effect the object of the conspiracy,

shall, except as provided in subsection (b), be fined under this title or imprisoned not more than 10 years, or both.

(b) Any organization that commits any offense described in subsection (a) shall be fined not more than $5,000,000.

18 U.S.C. § 1832

18 U.S.C. § 1833   Exceptions to prohibitions

This chapter does not prohibit—

(1) any otherwise lawful activity conducted by a governmental entity of the United States, a State, or a political subdivision of a State; or

(2) the reporting of a suspected violation of law to any governmental entity of the United States, a State, or a political subdivision of a State, if such entity has lawful authority with respect to that violation.

18 U.S.C. § 1834   Criminal forfeiture

Forfeiture, destruction, and restitution relating to this chapter shall be subject to section 2323, to the extent provided in that section, in addition to any other similar remedies provided by law.

18 U.S.C. § 1835   Orders to preserve confidentiality

In any prosecution or other proceeding under this chapter, the court shall enter such orders and take such other action as may be necessary and appropriate to preserve the confidentiality of trade secrets, consistent with the requirements of the Federal Rules of Criminal and Civil Procedure, the Federal Rules of Evidence, and all other applicable laws. An interlocutory appeal by the United States shall lie from a decision or order of a district court authorizing or directing the disclosure of any trade secret.

18 U.S.C. § 1836   Civil proceedings to enjoin violations

(a) The Attorney General may, in a civil action, obtain appropriate injunctive relief against any violation of this chapter.

(b) The district courts of the United States shall have exclusive original jurisdiction of civil actions under this section.

18 U.S.C. § 1837   Applicability to conduct outside the United States

This chapter also applies to conduct occurring outside the United States if—

(1) the offender is a natural person who is a citizen or permanent resident alien of the United States, or an organization organized under the laws of the United States or a State or political subdivision thereof; or

(2) an act in furtherance of the offense was committed in the United States.

18 U.S.C. § 1838   Construction with other laws

This chapter shall not be construed to preempt or displace any other remedies, whether civil or criminal, provided by United States Federal, State, commonwealth, possession, or territory law for the misappropriation of a trade secret, or to affect the otherwise lawful disclosure of information by any Government employee under section 552 of title 5 (commonly known as the Freedom of Information Act).

18 U.S.C. § 1839   Definitions

As used in this chapter—

(1) the term "foreign instrumentality" means any agency, bureau, ministry, component, institution, association, or any legal, commercial, or business organization, corporation, firm, or entity that is substantially owned, controlled, sponsored, commanded, managed, or dominated by a foreign government;

(2) the term "foreign agent" means any officer, employee, proxy, servant, delegate, or representative of a foreign government;

(3) the term "trade secret" means all forms and types of financial, business, scientific, technical, economic, or engineering information, including patterns, plans, compilations, program devices, formulas, designs, prototypes, methods, techniques, processes, procedures, programs, or codes, whether tangible or intangible, and whether or how stored, compiled, or memorialized physically, electronically, graphically, photographically, or in writing if—

(A) the owner thereof has taken reasonable measures to keep such information secret; and

(B) the information derives independent economic value, actual or potential, from not being generally known to, and not being readily ascertainable through proper means by, the public; and

(4) the term "owner", with respect to a trade secret, means the person or entity in whom or in which rightful legal or equitable title to, or license in, the trade secret is reposed.

(Oct. 11, 1996, Pub. L. 104-294, §101, 110 Stat. 3488; Nov. 2, 2002, Pub. L. 107-273, §4002(e)(9), 116 Stat. 1810; Oct. 13, 2008, Pub. L. 110-403, §207, 122 Stat. 4263; Dec. 28, 2012, Pub. L. 112-236, §2, 126 Stat. 1627; Jan. 14, 2013, Pub. L. 112-269, §2, 126 Stat. 2442.)

XII. UNIFORM TRADE SECRETS ACT

Ed. Note: Drafted by the National Conference of Commissioners on Uniform State Laws, as amended 1985.

§ 1. Definitions

As used in this Act, unless the context requires otherwise:

(1) "Improper means" includes theft, bribery, misrepresentation, breach or inducement of a breach of duty to maintain secrecy, or espionage through electronic or other means.

(2) "Misappropriation" means: (i) acquisition of a trade secret of another by a person who knows or has reason to know that the trade secret was acquired by improper means; or (ii) disclosure or use of a trade secret of another without express or implied consent by a person who (A) used improper means to acquire knowledge of the trade secret; or (B) at the time of disclosure or use knew or had reason to know that his knowledge of the trade secret was (I) derived from or through a person who has utilized improper means to acquire it; (II) acquired under circumstances giving rise to a duty to maintain its secrecy or limit its use; or (III) derived from or through a person who owed a duty to the person seeking relief to maintain its secrecy or limit its use; or (C) before a material change of his position, knew or had reason to know that it was a trade secret and that knowledge of it had been acquired by accident or mistake.

(3) "Person" means a natural person, corporation, business trust, estate, trust, partnership, association, joint venture, government, governmental subdivision or agency, or any other legal or commercial entity.

(4) "Trade secret" means information, including a formula, pattern, compilation, program device, method, technique, or process, that: (i) derives independent economic value, actual or potential, from not being generally known to, and not being readily ascertainable by proper means by, other persons who can obtain economic value from its disclosure or use, and (ii) is the subject of efforts that are reasonable under the circumstances to maintain its secrecy.

§ 2. Injunctive Relief

(a) Actual or threatened misappropriation may be enjoined. Upon application to the court an injunction shall be terminated when the trade secret has ceased to exist, but the injunction may be continued for an additional

818 • Patent, Trademark, & Copyright Laws, June 2015 Edition

reasonable period of time in order to eliminate commercial advantage that otherwise would be derived from the misappropriation.

(b) In exceptional circumstances, an injunction may condition future use upon payment of a reasonable royalty for no longer than the period of time for which use could have been prohibited. Exceptional circumstances include, but are not limited to, a material and prejudicial change of position prior to acquiring knowledge or reason to know of misappropriation that renders a prohibitive injunction inequitable.

(c) In appropriate circumstances, affirmative acts to protect a trade secret may be compelled by court order.

§ 3. Damages

(a) Except to the extent that a material and prejudicial change of position prior to acquiring knowledge or reason to know of misappropriation renders a monetary recovery inequitable, a complainant is entitled to recover damages for misappropriation. Damages can include both the actual loss caused by misappropriation and the unjust enrichment caused by misappropriation that is not taken into account in computing actual loss. In lieu of damages measured by any other methods, the damages caused by misappropriation may be measured by imposition of liability for a reasonable royalty for a misappropriator's unauthorized disclosure or use of a trade secret.

(b) If willful and malicious misappropriation exists, the court may award exemplary damages in the amount not exceeding twice any award made under subsection (a).

§ 4. Attorney's Fees

If (i) a claim of misappropriation is made in bad faith, (ii) a motion to terminate an injunction is made or resisted in bad faith, or (iii) willful and malicious misappropriation exists, the court may award reasonable attorney's fees to the prevailing party.

§ 5. Preservation of Secrecy

In actions under this Act, a court shall preserve the secrecy of an alleged trade secret by reasonable means, which may include granting protective orders in connection with discovery proceedings, holding in-camera hearings, sealing the records of the action, and ordering any person involved in the litigation not to disclose an alleged trade secret without prior court approval.

Uniform Trade Secrets Act

§ 6. Statute of Limitations

An action for misappropriation must be brought within 3 years after the misappropriation is discovered or by the exercise of reasonable diligence should have been discovered. For the purposes of this section, a continuing misappropriation constitutes a single claim.

§ 7. Effect on Other Law

(a) Except as provided in subsection (b), this [Act] displaces conflicting tort, restitutionary, and other law of this State providing civil remedies for misappropriation of a trade secret.

(b) This [Act] does not affect: (1) contractual remedies, whether or not based upon misappropriation of a trade secret; or (2) other civil remedies that are not based upon misappropriation of a trade secret; or (3) criminal remedies, whether or not based upon misappropriation of a trade secret.

§ 8. Uniformity of Application and Construction

This act shall be applied and construed to effectuate its general purpose to make uniform the law with respect to the subject of this Act among states enacting it.

§ 9. Short Title

This Act may be cited as the Uniform Trade Secrets Act.

§ 10. Severability

If any provision of this Act or its application to any person or circumstances is held invalid, the invalidity does not affect other provisions or applications of the Act which can be given effect without the invalid provision or application, and to this end the provisions of this Act are severable.

§ 11. Time of Taking Effect

This [Act] takes effect on _____, and does not apply to misappropriation occurring prior to the effective date. With respect to a continuing misappropriation that began prior to the effective date, the [Act] also does not apply to the continuing misappropriation that occurs after the effective date.

§ 12. Repeal

The following Acts and parts of Acts are repealed:

Uniform Trade Secrets Act

Part 6

INTERNATIONAL TREATIES AND AGREEMENTS

INTERNATIONAL TREATIES AND AGREEMENTS

I. AGREEMENT ON TRADE-RELATED ASPECTS OF INTELLECTUAL PROPERTY RIGHTS [SELECTED PORTIONS]

Done at Marrakesh on April 15, 1994

PART II. STANDARDS CONCERNING THE AVAILABILITY, SCOPE AND USE OF INTELLECTUAL PROPERTY RIGHTS

1. Copyright and Related Rights
2. Trademarks
3. Geographical Indications
4. Industrial Designs
5. Patents
6. Layout-Designs (Topographies) of Integrated Circuits
7. Protection of Undisclosed Information
8. Control of Anti-Competitive Practices in Contractual Licences

SECTION 1: COPYRIGHT AND RELATED RIGHTS

Article 9.   Relation to the Berne Convention

1. Members shall comply with Articles 1 through 21 of the Berne Convention (1971) and the Appendix thereto. However, Members shall not have rights or obligations under this Agreement in respect of the rights conferred under Article 6bis of that Convention or of the rights derived therefrom.

2. Copyright protection shall extend to expressions and not to ideas, procedures, methods of operation or mathematical concepts as such.

Article 10.   Computer Programs and Compilations of Data

1. Computer programs, whether in source or object code, shall be protected as literary works under the Berne Convention (1971).

2. Compilations of data or other material, whether in machine readable or other form, which by reason of the selection or arrangement of their contents constitute intellectual creations shall be protected as such. Such protection, which shall not extend to the data or material itself, shall be without prejudice to any copyright subsisting in the data or material itself.

Article 11. Rental Rights

In respect of at least computer programs and cinematographic works, a Member shall provide authors and their successors in title the right to authorize or to prohibit the commercial rental to the public of originals or copies of their copyright works. A Member shall be excepted from this obligation in respect of cinematographic works unless such rental has led to widespread copying of such works which is materially impairing the exclusive right of reproduction conferred in that Member on authors and their successors in title. In respect of computer programs, this obligation does not apply to rentals where the program itself is not the essential object of the rental.

Article 12. Term of Protection

Whenever the term of protection of a work, other than a photographic work or a work of applied art, is calculated on a basis other than the life of a natural person, such term shall be no less than 50 years from the end of the calendar year of authorized publication, or, failing such authorized publication within 50 years from the making of the work, 50 years from the end of the calendar year of making.

Article 13. Limitations and Exceptions

Members shall confine limitations or exceptions to exclusive rights to certain special cases which do not conflict with a normal exploitation of the work and do not unreasonably prejudice the legitimate interests of the right holder.

Article 14. Protection of Performers, Producers of Phonograms (Sound Recordings) and Broadcasting Organizations

1. In respect of a fixation of their performance on a phonogram, performers shall have the possibility of preventing the following acts when undertaken without their authorization: the fixation of their unfixed performance and the reproduction of such fixation. Performers shall also have the possibility of preventing the following acts when undertaken without their authorization: the broadcasting by wireless means and the communication to the public of their live performance.

2. Producers of phonograms shall enjoy the right to authorize or prohibit the direct or indirect reproduction of their phonograms.

3. Broadcasting organizations shall have the right to prohibit the following acts when undertaken without their authorization: the fixation, the reproduction of fixations, and the rebroadcasting by wireless means of broadcasts, as well as the communication to the public of television broadcasts of the same. Where Members do not grant such rights to broadcasting organizations, they shall provide owners of copyright in the subject matter of broadcasts with the possibility of preventing the above acts, subject to the provisions of the Berne Convention (1971).

4. The provisions of Article 11 in respect of computer programs shall apply *mutatis mutandis* to producers of phonograms and any other right holders in phonograms as determined in a Member's law. If on 15 April 1994 a Member has in force a system of equitable remuneration of right holders in respect of the rental of phonograms, it may maintain such system provided that the commercial rental of phonograms is not giving rise to the material impairment of the exclusive rights of reproduction of right holders.

5. The term of the protection available under this Agreement to performers and producers of phonograms shall last at least until the end of a period of 50 years computed from the end of the calendar year in which the fixation was made or the performance took place. The term of protection granted pursuant to paragraph 3 shall last for at least 20 years from the end of the calendar year in which the broadcast took place.

6. Any Member may, in relation to the rights conferred under paragraphs 1, 2 and 3, provide for conditions, limitations, exceptions and reservations to the extent permitted by the Rome Convention. However, the provisions of Article 18 of the Berne Convention (1971) shall also apply, *mutatis mutandis*, to the rights of performers and producers of phonograms in phonograms.

SECTION 2: TRADEMARKS

Article 15. Protectable Subject Matter

1. Any sign, or any combination of signs, capable of distinguishing the goods or services of one undertaking from those of other undertakings, shall be capable of constituting a trademark. Such signs, in particular words including personal names, letters, numerals, figurative elements and combinations of colours as well as any combination of such signs, shall be eligible for registration as trademarks. Where signs are not inherently capable of distinguishing the relevant goods or services, Members may make registra-

bility depend on distinctiveness acquired through use. Members may require, as a condition of registration, that signs be visually perceptible.

2. Paragraph 1 shall not be understood to prevent a Member from denying registration of a trademark on other grounds, provided that they do not derogate from the provisions of the Paris Convention (1967).

3. Members may make registrability depend on use. However, actual use of a trademark shall not be a condition for filing an application for registration. An application shall not be refused solely on the ground that intended use has not taken place before the expiry of a period of three years from the date of application.

4. The nature of the goods or services to which a trademark is to be applied shall in no case form an obstacle to registration of the trademark.

5. Members shall publish each trademark either before it is registered or promptly after it is registered and shall afford a reasonable opportunity for petitions to cancel the registration. In addition, Members may afford an opportunity for the registration of a trademark to be opposed.

Article 16. Rights Conferred

1. The owner of a registered trademark shall have the exclusive right to prevent all third parties not having the owner's consent from using in the course of trade identical or similar signs for goods or services which are identical or similar to those in respect of which the trademark is registered where such use would result in a likelihood of confusion. In case of the use of an identical sign for identical goods or services, a likelihood of confusion shall be presumed. The rights described above shall not prejudice any existing prior rights, nor shall they affect the possibility of Members making rights available on the basis of use.

2. Article 6bis of the Paris Convention (1967) shall apply, *mutatis mutandis*, to services. In determining whether a trademark is well-known, Members shall take account of the knowledge of the trademark in the relevant sector of the public, including knowledge in the Member concerned which has been obtained as a result of the promotion of the trademark.

3. Article 6bis of the Paris Convention (1967) shall apply, *mutatis mutandis*, to goods or services which are not similar to those in respect of which a trademark is registered, provided that use of that trademark in relation to those goods or services would indicate a connection between those goods or

services and the owner of the registered trademark and provided that the interests of the owner of the registered trademark are likely to be damaged by such use.

Article 17. Exceptions

Members may provide limited exceptions to the rights conferred by a trademark, such as fair use of descriptive terms, provided that such exceptions take account of the legitimate interests of the owner of the trademark and of third parties.

Article 18. Term of Protection

Initial registration, and each renewal of registration, of a trademark shall be for a term of no less than seven years. The registration of a trademark shall be renewable indefinitely.

Article 19. Requirement of Use

1. If use is required to maintain a registration, the registration may be cancelled only after an uninterrupted period of at least three years of non-use, unless valid reasons based on the existence of obstacles to such use are shown by the trademark owner. Circumstances arising independently of the will of the owner of the trademark which constitute an obstacle to the use of the trademark, such as import restrictions on or other government requirements for goods or services protected by the trademark, shall be recognized as valid reasons for non-use.

2. When subject to the control of its owner, use of a trademark by another person shall be recognized as use of the trademark for the purpose of maintaining the registration.

Article 20. Other Requirements

The use of a trademark in the course of trade shall not be unjustifiably encumbered by special requirements, such as use with another trademark, use in a special form or use in a manner detrimental to its capability to distinguish the goods or services of one undertaking from those of other undertakings. This will not preclude a requirement prescribing the use of the trademark identifying the undertaking producing the goods or services along with, but without linking it to, the trademark distinguishing the specific goods or services in question of that undertaking.

Article 21.   Licensing and Assignment

Members may determine conditions on the licensing and assignment of trademarks, it being understood that the compulsory licensing of trademarks shall not be permitted and that the owner of a registered trademark shall have the right to assign the trademark with or without the transfer of the business to which the trademark belongs.

SECTION 3: GEOGRAPHICAL INDICATIONS

Article 22.   Protection of Geographical Indications

1. Geographical indications are, for the purposes of this Agreement, indications which identify a good as originating in the territory of a Member, or a region or locality in that territory, where a given quality, reputation or other characteristic of the good is essentially attributable to its geographical origin.

2. In respect of geographical indications, Members shall provide the legal means for interested parties to prevent:

(a) the use of any means in the designation or presentation of a good that indicates or suggests that the good in question originates in a geographical area other than the true place of origin in a manner which misleads the public as to the geographical origin of the good;

(b) any use which constitutes an act of unfair competition within the meaning of Article 10bis of the Paris Convention (1967).

3. A Member shall, *ex officio* if its legislation so permits or at the request of an interested party, refuse or invalidate the registration of a trademark which contains or consists of a geographical indication with respect to goods not originating in the territory indicated, if use of the indication in the trademark for such goods in that Member is of such a nature as to mislead the public as to the true place of origin.

4. The protection under paragraphs 1, 2 and 3 shall be applicable against a geographical indication which, although literally true as to the territory, region or locality in which the goods originate, falsely represents to the public that the goods originate in another territory.

Article 23. Additional Protection for Geographical Indications for Wines and Spirits

1. Each Member shall provide the legal means for interested parties to prevent use of a geographical indication identifying wines for wines not originating in the place indicated by the geographical indication in question or identifying spirits for spirits not originating in the place indicated by the geographical indication in question, even where the true origin of the goods is indicated or the geographical indication is used in translation or accompanied by expressions such as "kind", "type", "style", "imitation" or the like.[1]

2. The registration of a trademark for wines which contains or consists of a geographical indication identifying wines or for spirits which contains or consists of a geographical indication identifying spirits shall be refused or invalidated, *ex officio* if a Member's legislation so permits or at the request of an interested party, with respect to such wines or spirits not having this origin.

3. In the case of homonymous geographical indications for wines, protection shall be accorded to each indication, subject to the provisions of paragraph 4 of Article 22. Each Member shall determine the practical conditions under which the homonymous indications in question will be differentiated from each other, taking into account the need to ensure equitable treatment of the producers concerned and that consumers are not misled.

4. In order to facilitate the protection of geographical indications for wines, negotiations shall be undertaken in the Council for TRIPS concerning the establishment of a multilateral system of notification and registration of geographical indications for wines eligible for protection in those Members participating in the system.

Article 24. International Negotiations; Exceptions

1. Members agree to enter into negotiations aimed at increasing the protection of individual geographical indications under Article 23. The provisions of paragraphs 4 through 8 below shall not be used by a Member to refuse to conduct negotiations or to conclude bilateral or multilateral agreements. In the context of such negotiations, Members shall be willing to consider the

---

[1] Notwithstanding the first sentence of Article 42, Members may, with respect to these obligations, instead provide for enforcement by administrative action.

continued applicability of these provisions to individual geographical indications whose use was the subject of such negotiations.

2. The Council for TRIPS shall keep under review the application of the provisions of this Section; the first such review shall take place within two years of the entry into force of the WTO Agreement. Any matter affecting the compliance with the obligations under these provisions may be drawn to the attention of the Council, which, at the request of a Member, shall consult with any Member or Members in respect of such matter in respect of which it has not been possible to find a satisfactory solution through bilateral or plurilateral consultations between the Members concerned. The Council shall take such action as may be agreed to facilitate the operation and further the objectives of this Section.

3. In implementing this Section, a Member shall not diminish the protection of geographical indications that existed in that Member immediately prior to the date of entry into force of the WTO Agreement.

4. Nothing in this Section shall require a Member to prevent continued and similar use of a particular geographical indication of another Member identifying wines or spirits in connection with goods or services by any of its nationals or domiciliaries who have used that geographical indication in a continuous manner with regard to the same or related goods or services in the territory of that Member either (a) for at least 10 years preceding 15 April 1994 or (b) in good faith preceding that date.

5. Where a trademark has been applied for or registered in good faith, or where rights to a trademark have been acquired through use in good faith either:

(a) before the date of application of these provisions in that Member as defined in Part VI; or

(b) before the geographical indication is protected in its country of origin;

measures adopted to implement this Section shall not prejudice eligibility for or the validity of the registration of a trademark, or the right to use a trademark, on the basis that such a trademark is identical with, or similar to, a geographical indication.

6. Nothing in this Section shall require a Member to apply its provisions in respect of a geographical indication of any other Member with respect to goods or services for which the relevant indication is identical with the term customary in common language as the common name for such goods or

services in the territory of that Member. Nothing in this Section shall require a Member to apply its provisions in respect of a geographical indication of any other Member with respect to products of the vine for which the relevant indication is identical with the customary name of a grape variety existing in the territory of that Member as of the date of entry into force of the WTO Agreement.

7. A Member may provide that any request made under this Section in connection with the use or registration of a trademark must be presented within five years after the adverse use of the protected indication has become generally known in that Member or after the date of registration of the trademark in that Member provided that the trademark has been published by that date, if such date is earlier than the date on which the adverse use became generally known in that Member, provided that the geographical indication is not used or registered in bad faith.

8. The provisions of this Section shall in no way prejudice the right of any person to use, in the course of trade, that person's name or the name of that person's predecessor in business, except where such name is used in such a manner as to mislead the public.

9. There shall be no obligation under this Agreement to protect geographical indications which are not or cease to be protected in their country of origin, or which have fallen into disuse in that country.

SECTION 4: INDUSTRIAL DESIGNS

Article 25.   Requirements for Protection

1. Members shall provide for the protection of independently created industrial designs that are new or original. Members may provide that designs are not new or original if they do not significantly differ from known designs or combinations of known design features. Members may provide that such protection shall not extend to designs dictated essentially by technical or functional considerations.

2. Each Member shall ensure that requirements for securing protection for textile designs, in particular in regard to any cost, examination or publication, do not unreasonably impair the opportunity to seek and obtain such protection. Members shall be free to meet this obligation through industrial design law or through copyright law.

Article 26.   Protection

1. The owner of a protected industrial design shall have the right to prevent third parties not having the owner's consent from making, selling or importing articles bearing or embodying a design which is a copy, or substantially a copy, of the protected design, when such acts are undertaken for commercial purposes.

2. Members may provide limited exceptions to the protection of industrial designs, provided that such exceptions do not unreasonably conflict with the normal exploitation of protected industrial designs and do not unreasonably prejudice the legitimate interests of the owner of the protected design, taking account of the legitimate interests of third parties.

3. The duration of protection available shall amount to at least 10 years.

SECTION 5: PATENTS

Article 27.   Patentable Subject Matter

1. Subject to the provisions of paragraphs 2 and 3, patents shall be available for any inventions, whether products or processes, in all fields of technology, provided that they are new, involve an inventive step and are capable of industrial application.[2] Subject to paragraph 4 of Article 65, paragraph 8 of Article 70 and paragraph 3 of this Article, patents shall be available and patent rights enjoyable without discrimination as to the place of invention, the field of technology and whether products are imported or locally produced.

2. Members may exclude from patentability inventions, the prevention within their territory of the commercial exploitation of which is necessary to protect *ordre public* or morality, including to protect human, animal or plant life or health or to avoid serious prejudice to the environment, provided that such exclusion is not made merely because the exploitation is prohibited by their law.

3. Members may also exclude from patentability:

(a) diagnostic, therapeutic and surgical methods for the treatment of humans or animals;

---

[2] For the purposes of this Article, the terms "inventive step" and "capable of industrial application" may be deemed by a Member to be synonymous with the terms "non-obvious" and "useful" respectively.

(b) plants and animals other than micro-organisms, and essentially biological processes for the production of plants or animals other than non-biological and microbiological processes. However, Members shall provide for the protection of plant varieties either by patents or by an effective *sui generis* system or by any combination thereof. The provisions of this subparagraph shall be reviewed four years after the date of entry into force of the WTO Agreement.

Article 28. Rights Conferred

1. A patent shall confer on its owner the following exclusive rights:

(a) where the subject matter of a patent is a product, to prevent third parties not having the owner's consent from the acts of: making, using, offering for sale, selling, or importing[3] for these purposes that product;

(b) where the subject matter of a patent is a process, to prevent third parties not having the owner's consent from the act of using the process, and from the acts of: using, offering for sale, selling, or importing for these purposes at least the product obtained directly by that process.

2. Patent owners shall also have the right to assign, or transfer by succession, the patent and to conclude licensing contracts.

Article 29. Conditions on Patent Applicants

1. Members shall require that an applicant for a patent shall disclose the invention in a manner sufficiently clear and complete for the invention to be carried out by a person skilled in the art and may require the applicant to indicate the best mode for carrying out the invention known to the inventor at the filing date or, where priority is claimed, at the priority date of the application.

2. Members may require an applicant for a patent to provide information concerning the applicant's corresponding foreign applications and grants.

Article 30. Exceptions to Rights Conferred

Members may provide limited exceptions to the exclusive rights conferred by a patent, provided that such exceptions do not unreasonably conflict with a normal exploitation of the patent and do not unreasonably prejudice the

---

[3] This right, like all other rights conferred under this Agreement in respect of the use, sale, importation or other distribution of goods, is subject to the provisions of Article 6.

legitimate interests of the patent owner, taking account of the legitimate interests of third parties.

Article 31. Other Use Without Authorization of the Right Holder

Where the law of a Member allows for other use[4] of the subject matter of a patent without the authorization of the right holder, including use by the government or third parties authorized by the government, the following provisions shall be respected:

(a) authorization of such use shall be considered on its individual merits;

(b) such use may only be permitted if, prior to such use, the proposed user has made efforts to obtain authorization from the right holder on reasonable commercial terms and conditions and that such efforts have not been successful within a reasonable period of time. This requirement may be waived by a Member in the case of a national emergency or other circumstances of extreme urgency or in cases of public non-commercial use. In situations of national emergency or other circumstances of extreme urgency, the right holder shall, nevertheless, be notified as soon as reasonably practicable. In the case of public non-commercial use, where the government or contractor, without making a patent search, knows or has demonstrable grounds to know that a valid patent is or will be used by or for the government, the right holder shall be informed promptly;

(c) the scope and duration of such use shall be limited to the purpose for which it was authorized, and in the case of semi-conductor technology shall only be for public non-commercial use or to remedy a practice determined after judicial or administrative process to be anti-competitive;

(d) such use shall be non-exclusive;

(e) such use shall be non-assignable, except with that part of the enterprise or goodwill which enjoys such use;

(f) any such use shall be authorized predominantly for the supply of the domestic market of the Member authorizing such use*;

(g) authorization for such use shall be liable, subject to adequate protection of the legitimate interests of the persons so authorized, to be termi-

---

[4] "Other use" refers to use other than that allowed under Article 30.

* *Ed. Note:* See decision of the General Council of August 30, 2003 regarding waivers from the obligations set out in this paragraph with respect to pharmaceutical products, as reported at http://www.wto.org/english/tratop_e/trips_e/implem_para6_ehtm.

nated if and when the circumstances which led to it cease to exist and are unlikely to recur. The competent authority shall have the authority to review, upon motivated request, the continued existence of these circumstances;

(h) the right holder shall be paid adequate remuneration in the circumstances of each case, taking into account the economic value of the authorization*;

(i) the legal validity of any decision relating to the authorization of such use shall be subject to judicial review or other independent review by a distinct higher authority in that Member;

(j) any decision relating to the remuneration provided in respect of such use shall be subject to judicial review or other independent review by a distinct higher authority in that Member;

(k) Members are not obliged to apply the conditions set forth in subparagraphs (b) and (f) where such use is permitted to remedy a practice determined after judicial or administrative process to be anti-competitive. The need to correct anti-competitive practices may be taken into account in determining the amount of remuneration in such cases. Competent authorities shall have the authority to refuse termination of authorization if and when the conditions which led to such authorization are likely to recur;

(l) where such use is authorized to permit the exploitation of a patent ("the second patent") which cannot be exploited without infringing another patent ("the first patent"), the following additional conditions shall apply:

    (i) the invention claimed in the second patent shall involve an important technical advance of considerable economic significance in relation to the invention claimed in the first patent;

    (ii) the owner of the first patent shall be entitled to a cross-licence on reasonable terms to use the invention claimed in the second patent; and

---

* *Ed. Note:* See decision of the General Council of August 30, 2003 regarding waivers from the obligations set out in this paragraph with respect to pharmaceutical products, as reported at http://www.wto.org/english/tratop_e/trips_e/implem_para6_ehtm.

(iii) the use authorized in respect of the first patent shall be non-assignable except with the assignment of the second patent.

Article 32.   Revocation/Forfeiture

An opportunity for judicial review of any decision to revoke or forfeit a patent shall be available.

Article 33.   Term of Protection

The term of protection available shall not end before the expiration of a period of twenty years counted from the filing date.[5]

Article 34.   Process Patents: Burden of Proof

1. For the purposes of civil proceedings in respect of the infringement of the rights of the owner referred to in paragraph 1(b) of Article 28, if the subject matter of a patent is a process for obtaining a product, the judicial authorities shall have the authority to order the defendant to prove that the process to obtain an identical product is different from the patented process. Therefore, Members shall provide, in at least one of the following circumstances, that any identical product when produced without the consent of the patent owner shall, in the absence of proof to the contrary, be deemed to have been obtained by the patented process:

(a) if the product obtained by the patented process is new;

(b) if there is a substantial likelihood that the identical product was made by the process and the owner of the patent has been unable through reasonable efforts to determine the process actually used.

2. Any Member shall be free to provide that the burden of proof indicated in paragraph 1 shall be on the alleged infringer only if the condition referred to in subparagraph (a) is fulfilled or only if the condition referred to in subparagraph (b) is fulfilled.

3. In the adduction of proof to the contrary, the legitimate interests of defendants in protecting their manufacturing and business secrets shall be taken into account.

---

[5] It is understood that those Members which do not have a system of original grant may provide that the term of protection shall be computed from the filing date in the system of original grant.

SECTION 6: LAYOUT-DESIGNS (TOPOGRAPHIES) OF INTEGRATED CIRCUITS

Article 35. Relation to the IPIC Treaty

Members agree to provide protection to the layout-designs (topographies) of integrated circuits (referred to in this Agreement as "layout-designs") in accordance with Articles 2 through 7 (other than paragraph 3 of Article 6), Article 12 and paragraph 3 of Article 16 of the Treaty on Intellectual Property in Respect of Integrated Circuits and, in addition, to comply with the following provisions.

Article 36. Scope of the Protection

Subject to the provisions of paragraph 1 of Article 37, Members shall consider unlawful the following acts if performed without the authorization of the right holder:[6] importing, selling, or otherwise distributing for commercial purposes a protected layout-design, an integrated circuit in which a protected layout-design is incorporated, or an article incorporating such an integrated circuit only in so far as it continues to contain an unlawfully reproduced layout-design.

Article 37. Acts Not Requiring the Authorization of the Right Holder

1. Notwithstanding Article 36, no Member shall consider unlawful the performance of any of the acts referred to in that Article in respect of an integrated circuit incorporating an unlawfully reproduced layout-design or any article incorporating such an integrated circuit where the person performing or ordering such acts did not know and had no reasonable ground to know, when acquiring the integrated circuit or article incorporating such an integrated circuit, that it incorporated an unlawfully reproduced layout-design. Members shall provide that, after the time that such person has received sufficient notice that the layout-design was unlawfully reproduced, that person may perform any of the acts with respect to the stock on hand or ordered before such time, but shall be liable to pay to the right holder a sum equivalent to a reasonable royalty such as would be payable under a freely negotiated licence in respect of such a layout-design.

2. The conditions set out in subparagraphs (a) through (k) of Article 31 shall apply *mutatis mutandis* in the event of any non-voluntary licensing of a

---

[6] The term "right holder" in this Section shall be understood as having the same meaning as the term "holder of the right" in the IPIC Treaty.

layout-design or of its use by or for the government without the authorization of the right holder.

Article 38.   Term of Protection

1. In Members requiring registration as a condition of protection, the term of protection of layout-designs shall not end before the expiration of a period of 10 years counted from the date of filing an application for registration or from the first commercial exploitation wherever in the world it occurs.

2. In Members not requiring registration as a condition for protection, layout-designs shall be protected for a term of no less than 10 years from the date of the first commercial exploitation wherever in the world it occurs.

3. Notwithstanding paragraphs 1 and 2, a Member may provide that protection shall lapse 15 years after the creation of the layout-design.

SECTION 7: PROTECTION OF UNDISCLOSED INFORMATION

Article 39.

1. In the course of ensuring effective protection against unfair competition as provided in Article 10bis of the Paris Convention (1967), Members shall protect undisclosed information in accordance with paragraph 2 and data submitted to governments or governmental agencies in accordance with paragraph 3.

2. Natural and legal persons shall have the possibility of preventing information lawfully within their control from being disclosed to, acquired by, or used by others without their consent in a manner contrary to honest commercial practices[7] so long as such information:

(a) is secret in the sense that it is not, as a body or in the precise configuration and assembly of its components, generally known among or readily accessible to persons within the circles that normally deal with the kind of information in question;

(b) has commercial value because it is secret; and

---

[7] For the purpose of this provision, "a manner contrary to honest commercial practices" shall mean at least practices such as breach of contract, breach of confidence and inducement to breach, and includes the acquisition of undisclosed information by third parties who knew, or were grossly negligent in failing to know, that such practices were involved in the acquisition.

(c) has been subject to reasonable steps under the circumstances, by the person lawfully in control of the information, to keep it secret.

3. Members, when requiring, as a condition of approving the marketing of pharmaceutical or of agricultural chemical products which utilize new chemical entities, the submission of undisclosed test or other data, the origination of which involves a considerable effort, shall protect such data against unfair commercial use. In addition, Members shall protect such data against disclosure, except where necessary to protect the public, or unless steps are taken to ensure that the data are protected against unfair commercial use.

SECTION 8: CONTROL OF ANTI-COMPETITIVE PRACTICES IN CONTRACTUAL LICENCES

Article 40.

1. Members agree that some licensing practices or conditions pertaining to intellectual property rights which restrain competition may have adverse effects on trade and may impede the transfer and dissemination of technology.

2. Nothing in this Agreement shall prevent Members from specifying in their legislation licensing practices or conditions that may in particular cases constitute an abuse of intellectual property rights having an adverse effect on competition in the relevant market. As provided above, a Member may adopt, consistently with the other provisions of this Agreement, appropriate measures to prevent or control such practices, which may include for example exclusive grantback conditions, conditions preventing challenges to validity and coercive package licensing, in the light of the relevant laws and regulations of that Member.

3. Each Member shall enter, upon request, into consultations with any other Member which has cause to believe that an intellectual property right owner that is a national or domiciliary of the Member to which the request for consultations has been addressed is undertaking practices in violation of the requesting Member's laws and regulations on the subject matter of this Section, and which wishes to secure compliance with such legislation, without prejudice to any action under the law and to the full freedom of an ultimate decision of either Member. The Member addressed shall accord full and sympathetic consideration to, and shall afford adequate opportunity for,

consultations with the requesting Member, and shall cooperate through supply of publicly available non-confidential information of relevance to the matter in question and of other information available to the Member, subject to domestic law and to the conclusion of mutually satisfactory agreements concerning the safeguarding of its confidentiality by the requesting Member.

4. A Member whose nationals or domiciliaries are subject to proceedings in another Member concerning alleged violation of that other Member's laws and regulations on the subject matter of this Section shall, upon request, be granted an opportunity for consultations by the other Member under the same conditions as those foreseen in paragraph 3.

II. PATENT COOPERATION TREATY

PATENT COOPERATION TREATY (PCT)

Done at Washington on June 19, 1970, amended on September 28, 1979, modified on February 3, 1984, and October 3, 2001

The Contracting States,

Desiring to make a contribution to the progress of science and technology,

Desiring to perfect the legal protection of inventions,

Desiring to simplify and render more economical the obtaining of protection for inventions where protection is sought in several countries,

Desiring to facilitate and accelerate access by the public to the technical information contained in documents describing new inventions,

Desiring to foster and accelerate the economic development of developing countries through the adoption of measures designed to increase the efficiency of their legal systems, whether national or regional, instituted for the protection of inventions by providing easily accessible information on the availability of technological solutions applicable to their special needs and by facilitating access to the ever expanding volume of modern technology,

Convinced that cooperation among nations will greatly facilitate the attainment of these aims,

Have concluded the present Treaty.

INTRODUCTORY PROVISIONS

Article 1.   Establishment of a Union

(1) The States party to this Treaty (hereinafter called "the Contracting States") constitute a Union for cooperation in the filing, searching, and examination, of applications for the protection of inventions, and for rendering special technical services. The Union shall be known as the International Patent Cooperation Union.

(2) No provision of this Treaty shall be interpreted as diminishing the rights under the Paris Convention for the Protection of Industrial Property of any national or resident of any country party to that Convention.

PCT Art. 1

Article 2.   Definitions

For the purposes of this Treaty and the Regulations and unless expressly stated otherwise:

(i) "application" means an application for the protection of an invention; references to an "application" shall be construed as references to applications for patents for inventions, inventors' certificates, utility certificates, utility models, patents or certificates of addition, inventors' certificates of addition, and utility certificates of addition;

(ii) references to a "patent" shall be construed as references to patents for inventions, inventors' certificates, utility certificates, utility models, patents or certificates of addition, inventors' certificates of addition, and utility certificates of addition;

(iii) "national patent" means a patent granted by a national authority;

(iv) "regional patent" means a patent granted by a national or an intergovernmental authority having the power to grant patents effective in more than one State;

(v) "regional application" means an application for a regional patent;

(vi) references to a "national application" shall be construed as references to applications for national patents and regional patents, other than applications filed under this Treaty;

(vii) "international application" means an application filed under this Treaty;

(viii) references to an "application" shall be construed as references to international applications and national applications;

(ix) references to a "patent" shall be construed as references to national patents and regional patents;

(x) references to "national law" shall be construed as references to the national law of a Contracting State or, where a regional application or a regional patent is involved, to the treaty providing for the filing of regional applications or the granting of regional patents;

(xi) "priority date," for the purposes of computing time limits, means:

(a) where the international application contains a priority claim under Article 8, the filing date of the application whose priority is so claimed;

(b) where the international application contains several priority claims under Article 8, the filing date of the earliest application whose priority is so claimed;

(c) where the international application does not contain any priority claim under Article 8, the international filing date of such application;

(xii) "national Office" means the government authority of a Contracting State entrusted with the granting of patents; references to a "national Office" shall be construed as referring also to any intergovernmental authority which several States have entrusted with the task of granting regional patents, provided that at least one of those States is a Contracting State, and provided that the said States have authorized that authority to assume the obligations and exercise the powers which this Treaty and the Regulations provide for in respect of national Offices;

(xiii) "designated Office" means the national Office of or acting for the State designated by the applicant under Chapter I of this Treaty;

(xiv) "elected Office" means the national Office of or acting for the State elected by the applicant under Chapter II of this Treaty;

(xv) "receiving Office" means the national Office or the intergovern-mental organization with which the international application has been filed;

(xvi) "Union" means the International Patent Cooperation Union;

(xvii) "Assembly" means the Assembly of the Union;

(xviii) "Organization" means the World Intellectual Property Organization;

(xix) "International Bureau" means the International Bureau of the Organization and, as long as it subsists, the United International Bureaux for the Protection of Intellectual Property (BIRPI);

(xx) "Director General" means the Director General of the Organization and, as long as BIRPI subsists, the Director of BIRPI.

CHAPTER I. INTERNATIONAL APPLICATION AND INTERNATIONAL SEARCH

Article 3. The International Application

(1) Applications for the protection of inventions in any of the Contracting States may be filed as international applications under this Treaty.

(2) An international application shall contain, as specified in this Treaty and the Regulations, a request, a description, one or more claims, one or more drawings (where required), and an abstract.

(3) The abstract merely serves the purpose of technical information and cannot be taken into account for any other purpose, particularly not for the purpose of interpreting the scope of the protection sought.

(4) The international application shall: (i) be in a prescribed language;

(ii) comply with the prescribed physical requirements;

(iii) comply with the prescribed requirement of unity of invention;

(iv) be subject to the payment of the prescribed fees.

Article 4. The Request

(1) The request shall contain:

(i) a petition to the effect that the international application be processed according to this Treaty;

(ii) the designation of the Contracting State or States in which protection for the invention is desired on the basis of the international application ("designated States"); if for any designated State a regional patent is available and the applicant wishes to obtain a regional patent rather than a national patent, the request shall so indicate; if, under a treaty concerning a regional patent, the applicant cannot limit his application to certain of the States party to that treaty, designation of one of those States and the indication of the wish to obtain the regional patent shall be treated as designation of all the States party to that treaty; if, under the national law of the designated State, the designation of that State has the effect of an application for a regional patent, the designation of the said State shall be treated as an indication of the wish to obtain the regional patent;

(iii) the name of and other prescribed data concerning the applicant and the agent (if any);

(iv) the title of the invention;

(v) the name of and other prescribed data concerning the inventor where the national law of at least one of the designated States requires that these indications be furnished at the time of filing a national application. Otherwise, the said indications may be furnished either in the request or in separate notices addressed to each designated Office whose national law requires the furnishing of the said indications but allows that they be furnished at a time later than that of the filing of a national application.

(2) Every designation shall be subject to the payment of the prescribed fee within the prescribed time limit.

(3) Unless the applicant asks for any of the other kinds of protection referred to in Article 43, designation shall mean that the desired protection consists of the grant of a patent by or for the designated State. For the purposes of this paragraph, Article 2(ii) shall not apply.

(4) Failure to indicate in the request the name and other prescribed data concerning the inventor shall have no consequence in any designated State whose national law requires the furnishing of the said indications but allows that they be furnished at a time later than that of the filing of a national application. Failure to furnish the said indications in a separate notice shall have no consequence in any designated State whose national law does not require the furnishing of the said indications.

Article 5.   The Description

The description shall disclose the invention in a manner sufficiently clear and complete for the invention to be carried out by a person skilled in the art.

Article 6.   The Claims

The claim or claims shall define the matter for which protection is sought. Claims shall be clear and concise. They shall be fully supported by the description.

Article 7.   The Drawings

(1) Subject to the provisions of paragraph (2)(ii), drawings shall be required when they are necessary for the understanding of the invention.

(2) Where, without being necessary for the understanding of the invention, the nature of the invention admits of illustration by drawings:

(i) the applicant may include such drawings in the international application when filed,

(ii) any designated Office may require that the applicant file such drawings with it within the prescribed time limit.

Article 8.   Claiming Priority

(1) The international application may contain a declaration, as prescribed in the Regulations, claiming the priority of one or more earlier applications filed in or for any country party to the Paris Convention for the Protection of Industrial Property.

(2) (a) Subject to the provisions of subparagraph (b), the conditions for, and the effect of, any priority claim declared under paragraph (1) shall be as provided in Article 4 of the Stockholm Act of the Paris Convention for the Protection of Industrial Property.

(b) The international application for which the priority of one or more earlier applications filed in or for a Contracting State is claimed may contain the designation of that State. Where, in the international application, the priority of one or more national applications filed in or for a designated State is claimed, or where the priority of an international application having designated only one State is claimed, the conditions for, and the effect of, the priority claim in that State shall be governed by the national law of that State.

Article 9.   The Applicant

(1) Any resident or national of a Contracting State may file an international application.

(2) The Assembly may decide to allow the residents and the nationals of any country party to the Paris Convention for the Protection of Industrial Property which is not party to this Treaty to file international applications.

(3) The concepts of residence and nationality, and the application of those concepts in cases where there are several applicants or where the applicants are not the same for all the designated States, are defined in the Regulations.

Article 10.   The Receiving Office

The international application shall be filed with the prescribed receiving Office, which will check and process it as provided in this Treaty and the Regulations.

Article 11.   Filing Date and Effects of the International Application

(1) The receiving Office shall accord as the international filing date the date of receipt of the international application, provided that that Office has found that, at the time of receipt:

(i) the applicant does not obviously lack, for reasons of residence or nationality, the right to file an international application with the receiving Office,

(ii) the international application is in the prescribed language,

(iii) the international application contains at least the following elements:

(a) an indication that it is intended as an international application,

(b) the designation of at least one Contracting State,

(c) the name of the applicant, as prescribed,

(d) a part which on the face of it appears to be a description,

(e) a part which on the face of it appears to be a claim or claims.

(2) (a) If the receiving Office finds that the international application did not, at the time of receipt, fulfill the requirements listed in paragraph (1), it shall, as provided in the Regulations, invite the applicant to file the required correction.

(b) If the applicant complies with the invitation, as provided in the Regulations, the receiving Office shall accord as the international filing date the date of receipt of the required correction.

(3) Subject to Article 64(4), any international application fulfilling the requirements listed in items (i) to (iii) of paragraph (1) and accorded an international filing date shall have the effect of a regular national application in each designated State as of the international filing date, which date shall be considered to be the actual filing date in each designated State.

(4) Any international application fulfilling the requirements listed in items (i) to (iii) of paragraph (1) shall be equivalent to a regular national filing within the meaning of the Paris Convention for the Protection of Industrial Property.

Article 12.   Transmittal of the International Application to the International Bureau and the International Searching Authority

(1) One copy of the international application shall be kept by the receiving Office ("home copy"), one copy ("record copy") shall be transmitted to the International Bureau, and another copy ("search copy") shall be transmitted to the competent International Searching Authority referred to in Article 16, as provided in the Regulations.

(2) The record copy shall be considered the true copy of the international application.

(3) The international application shall be considered withdrawn if the record copy has not been received by the International Bureau within the prescribed time limit.

Article 13.   Availability of Copy of the International Application to Designated Offices

(1) Any designated Office may ask the International Bureau to transmit to it a copy of the international application prior to the communication provided for in Article 20, and the International Bureau shall transmit such copy to the designated Office as soon as possible after the expiration of one year from the priority date.

(2) (a) The applicant may, at any time, transmit a copy of his international application to any designated Office.

(b) The applicant may, at any time, ask the International Bureau to transmit a copy of his international application to any designated Office, and the International Bureau shall transmit such copy to the designated Office as soon as possible.

(c) Any national Office may notify the International Bureau that it does not wish to receive copies as provided for in subparagraph (b), in which case that subparagraph shall not be applicable in respect of that Office.

Article 14.   Certain Defects in the International Application

(1) (a) The receiving Office shall check whether the international application contains any of the following defects, that is to say:

(i) it is not signed as provided in the Regulations;

(ii) it does not contain the prescribed indications concerning the applicant;

(iii) it does not contain a title;

(iv) it does not contain an abstract;

(v) it does not comply to the extent provided in the Regulations with the prescribed physical requirements.

(b) If the receiving Office finds any of the said defects, it shall invite the applicant to correct the international application within the prescribed time limit, failing which that application shall be considered withdrawn and the receiving Office shall so declare.

(2) If the international application refers to drawings which, in fact, are not included in that application, the receiving Office shall notify the applicant accordingly and he may furnish them within the prescribed time limit and, if he does, the international filing date shall be the date on which the drawings are received by the receiving Office. Otherwise, any reference to the said drawings shall be considered non-existent.

(3) (a) If the receiving Office finds that, within the prescribed time limits, the fees prescribed under Article 3(4)(iv) have not been paid, or no fee prescribed under Article 4(2) has been paid in respect of any of the designated States, the international application shall be considered withdrawn and the receiving Office shall so declare.

(b) If the receiving Office finds that the fee prescribed under Article 4(2) has been paid in respect of one or more (but less than all) designated States within the prescribed time limit, the designation of those States in respect of which it has not been paid within the prescribed time limit shall be considered withdrawn and the receiving Office shall so declare.

(4) If, after having accorded an international filing date to the international application, the receiving Office finds, within the prescribed time limit, that any of the requirements listed in items (i) to (iii) of Article 11(1) was not complied with at that date, the said application shall be considered withdrawn and the receiving Office shall so declare.

Article 15. The International Search

(1) Each international application shall be the subject of international search.

(2) The objective of the international search is to discover relevant prior art.

(3) International search shall be made on the basis of the claims, with due regard to the description and the drawings (if any).

(4) The International Searching Authority referred to in Article 16 shall endeavor to discover as much of the relevant prior art as its facilities permit, and shall, in any case, consult the documentation specified in the Regulations.

(5) (a) If the national law of the Contracting State so permits, the applicant who files a national application with the national Office of or acting for such State may, subject to the conditions provided for in such law, request that a search similar to an international search ("international-type search") be carried out on such application.

(b) If the national law of the Contracting State so permits, the national Office of or acting for such State may subject any national application filed with it to an international-type search.

(c) The international-type search shall be carried out by the International Searching Authority referred to in Article 16 which would be competent for an international search if the national application were an international application and were filed with the Office referred to in subparagraphs (a) and (b). If the national application is in a language which the International Searching Authority considers it is not equipped to handle, the international-type search shall be carried out on a translation prepared by the applicant in a language prescribed for international applications and which the International Searching Authority has undertaken to accept for international applications. The national application and the translation, when required, shall be presented in the form prescribed for international applications.

Article 16.   The International Searching Authority

(1) International search shall be carried out by an International Searching Authority, which may be either a national Office or an intergovernmental organization, such as the International Patent Institute, whose tasks include the establishing of documentary search reports on prior art with respect to inventions which are the subject of applications.

(2) If, pending the establishment of a single International Searching Authority, there are several International Searching Authorities, each receiving Office shall, in accordance with the provisions of the applicable agreement referred to in paragraph (3)(b), specify the International Searching Authority or

Authorities competent for the searching of international applications filed with such Office.

(3) (a) International Searching Authorities shall be appointed by the Assembly. Any national Office and any intergovernmental organization satisfying the requirements referred to in subparagraph (c) may be appointed as International Searching Authority.

(b) Appointment shall be conditional on the consent of the national Office or intergovernmental organization to be appointed and the conclusion of an agreement, subject to approval by the Assembly, between such Office or organization and the International Bureau. The agreement shall specify the rights and obligations of the parties, in particular, the formal undertaking by the said Office or organization to apply and observe all the common rules of international search.

(c) The Regulations prescribe the minimum requirements, particularly as to manpower and documentation, which any Office or organization must satisfy before it can be appointed and must continue to satisfy while it remains appointed.

(d) Appointment shall be for a fixed period of time and may be extended for further periods.

(e) Before the Assembly makes a decision on the appointment of any national Office or intergovernmental organization, or on the extension of its appointment, or before it allows any such appointment to lapse, the Assembly shall hear the interested Office or organization and seek the advice of the Committee for Technical Cooperation referred to in Article 56 once that Committee has been established.

Article 17. Procedure before the International Searching Authority

(1) Procedure before the International Searching Authority shall be governed by the provisions of this Treaty, the Regulations, and the agreement which the International Bureau shall conclude, subject to this Treaty and the Regulations, with the said Authority.

(2) (a) If the International Searching Authority considers

(i) that the international application relates to a subject matter which the International Searching Authority is not required, under the Regulations, to search, and in the particular case decides not to search, or

(ii) that the description, the claims, or the drawings, fail to comply with the prescribed requirements to such an extent that a meaningful search could not be carried out, the said Authority shall so declare and shall notify the applicant and the International Bureau that no international search report will be established.

(b) If any of the situations referred to in subparagraph (a) is found to exist in connection with certain claims only, the international search report shall so indicate in respect of such claims, whereas, for the other claims, the said report shall be established as provided in Article 18.

(3) (a) If the International Searching Authority considers that the international application does not comply with the requirement of unity of invention as set forth in the Regulations, it shall invite the applicant to pay additional fees. The International Searching Authority shall establish the international search report on those parts of the international application which relate to the invention first mentioned in the claims ("main invention") and, provided the required additional fees have been paid within the prescribed time limit, on those parts of the international application which relate to inventions in respect of which the said fees were paid.

(b) The national law of any designated State may provide that, where the national Office of that State finds the invitation, referred to in subparagraph (a), of the International Searching Authority justified and where the applicant has not paid all additional fees, those parts of the international application which consequently have not been searched shall, as far as effects in that State are concerned, be considered withdrawn unless a special fee is paid by the applicant to the national Office of that State.

Article 18.   The International Search Report

(1) The international search report shall be established within the prescribed time limit and in the prescribed form.

(2) The international search report shall, as soon as it has been established, be transmitted by the International Searching Authority to the applicant and the International Bureau.

(3) The international search report or the declaration referred to in Article 17(2)(a) shall be translated as provided in the Regulations. The translations shall be prepared by or under the responsibility of the International Bureau.

Article 19. Amendment of the Claims before the International Bureau

(1) The applicant shall, after having received the international search report, be entitled to one opportunity to amend the claims of the international application by filing amendments with the International Bureau within the prescribed time limit. He may, at the same time, file a brief statement, as provided in the Regulations, explaining the amendments and indicating any impact that such amendments might have on the description and the drawings.

(2) The amendments shall not go beyond the disclosure in the international application as filed.

(3) If the national law of any designated State permits amendments to go beyond the said disclosure, failure to comply with paragraph (2) shall have no consequence in that State.

Article 20. Communication to Designated Offices

(1) (a) The international application, together with the international search report (including any indication referred to in Article 17(2)(b)) or the declaration referred to in Article 17(2)(a), shall be communicated to each designated Office, as provided in the Regulations, unless the designated Office waives such requirement in its entirety or in part.

(b) The communication shall include the translation (as prescribed) of the said report or declaration.

(2) If the claims have been amended by virtue of Article 19(1), the communication shall either contain the full text of the claims both as filed and as amended or shall contain the full text of the claims as filed and specify the amendments, and shall include the statement, if any, referred to in Article 19(1).

(3) At the request of the designated Office or the applicant, the International Searching Authority shall send to the said Office or the applicant, respectively, copies of the documents cited in the international search report, as provided in the Regulations.

Article 21. International Publication

(1) The International Bureau shall publish international applications.

(2) (a) Subject to the exceptions provided for in subparagraph (b) and in Article 64(3), the international publication of the international application

shall be effected promptly after the expiration of 18 months from the priority date of that application.

(b) The applicant may ask the International Bureau to publish his international application any time before the expiration of the time limit referred to in subparagraph (a). The International Bureau shall proceed accordingly, as provided in the Regulations.

(3) The international search report or the declaration referred to in Article 17(2)(a) shall be published as prescribed in the Regulations.

(4) The language and form of the international publication and other details are governed by the Regulations.

(5) There shall be no international publication if the international application is withdrawn or is considered withdrawn before the technical preparations for publication have been completed.

(6) If the international application contains expressions or drawings which, in the opinion of the International Bureau, are contrary to morality or public order, or if, in its opinion, the international application contains disparaging statements as defined in the Regulations, it may omit such expressions, drawings, and statements, from its publications, indicating the place and number of words or drawings omitted, and furnishing, upon request, individual copies of the passages omitted.

Article 22.   Copy, Translation, and Fee, to Designated Offices

(1) The applicant shall furnish a copy of the international application (unless the communication provided for in Article 20 has already taken place) and a translation thereof (as prescribed), and pay the national fee (if any), to each designated Office not later than at the expiration of 30 months from the priority date. Where the national law of the designated State requires the indication of the name of and other prescribed data concerning the inventor but allows that these indications be furnished at a time later than that of the filing of a national application, the applicant shall, unless they were contained in the request, furnish the said indications to the national Office of or acting for the State not later than at the expiration of 30 months from the priority date.

(2) Where the International Searching Authority makes a declaration, under Article 17(2)(a), that no international search report will be established, the

time limit for performing the acts referred to in paragraph (1) of this Article shall be the same as that provided for in paragraph (1).

(3) Any national law may, for performing the acts referred to in paragraphs (1) or (2), fix time limits which expire later than the time limit provided for in those paragraphs.

Article 23.   Delaying of National Procedure

(1) No designated Office shall process or examine the international application prior to the expiration of the applicable time limit under Article 22.

(2) Notwithstanding the provisions of paragraph (1), any designated Office may, on the express request of the applicant, process or examine the international application at any time.

Article 24.   Possible Loss of Effect in Designated States

(1) Subject, in case (ii) below, to the provisions of Article 25, the effect of the international application provided for in Article 11(3) shall cease in any designated State with the same consequences as the withdrawal of any national application in that State:

  (i) if the applicant withdraws his international application or the designation of that State;

  (ii) if the international application is considered withdrawn by virtue of Articles 12(3), 14(1)(b), 14(3)(a), or 14(4), or if the designation of that State is considered withdrawn by virtue of Article 14(3)(b);

  (iii) if the applicant fails to perform the acts referred to in Article 22 within the applicable time limit.

(2) Notwithstanding the provisions of paragraph (1), any designated Office may maintain the effect provided for in Article 11(3) even where such effect is not required to be maintained by virtue of Article 25(2).

Article 25.   Review by Designated Offices

(1) (a) Where the receiving Office has refused to accord an international filing date or has declared that the international application is considered withdrawn, or where the International Bureau has made a finding under Article 12(3), the International Bureau shall promptly send, at the request of the applicant, copies of any document in the file to any of the designated Offices named by the applicant.

(b) Where the receiving Office has declared that the designation of any given State is considered withdrawn, the International Bureau shall promptly send, at the request of the applicant, copies of any document in the file to the national Office of such State.

(c) The request under subparagraphs (a) or (b) shall be presented within the prescribed time limit.

(2) (a) Subject to the provisions of subparagraph (b), each designated Office shall, provided that the national fee (if any) has been paid and the appropriate translation (as prescribed) has been furnished within the prescribed time limit, decide whether the refusal, declaration, or finding, referred to in paragraph (1) was justified under the provisions of this Treaty and the Regulations, and, if it finds that the refusal or declaration was the result of an error or omission on the part of the receiving Office or that the finding was the result of an error or omission on the part of the International Bureau, it shall, as far as effects in the State of the designated Office are concerned, treat the international application as if such error or omission had not occurred.

(b) Where the record copy has reached the International Bureau after the expiration of the time limit prescribed under Article 12(3) on account of any error or omission on the part of the applicant, the provisions of subparagraph (a) shall apply only under the circumstances referred to in Article 48(2).

Article 26.   Opportunity to Correct before Designated Offices

No designated Office shall reject an international application on the grounds of non-compliance with the requirements of this Treaty and the Regulations without first giving the applicant the opportunity to correct the said application to the extent and according to the procedure provided by the national law for the same or comparable situations in respect of national applications.

Article 27.   National Requirements

(1) No national law shall require compliance with requirements relating to the form or contents of the international application different from or additional to those which are provided for in this Treaty and the Regulations.

(2) The provisions of paragraph (1) neither affect the application of the provisions of Article 7(2) nor preclude any national law from requiring, once

the processing of the international application has started in the designated Office, the furnishing:

(i) when the applicant is a legal entity, of the name of an officer entitled to represent such legal entity,

(ii) of documents not part of the international application but which constitute proof of allegations or statements made in that application, including the confirmation of the international application by the signature of the applicant when that application, as filed, was signed by his representative or agent.

(3) Where the applicant, for the purposes of any designated State, is not qualified according to the national law of that State to file a national application because he is not the inventor, the international application may be rejected by the designated Office.

(4) Where the national law provides, in respect of the form or contents of national applications, for requirements which, from the viewpoint of applicants, are more favorable than the requirements provided for by this Treaty and the Regulations in respect of international applications, the national Office, the courts and any other competent organs of or acting for the designated State may apply the former requirements, instead of the latter requirements, to international applications, except where the applicant insists that the requirements provided for by this Treaty and the Regulations be applied to his international application.

(5) Nothing in this Treaty and the Regulations is intended to be construed as prescribing anything that would limit the freedom of each Contracting State to prescribe such substantive conditions of patentability as it desires. In particular, any provision in this Treaty and the Regulations concerning the definition of prior art is exclusively for the purposes of the international procedure and, consequently, any Contracting State is free to apply, when determining the patentability of an invention claimed in an international application, the criteria of its national law in respect of prior art and other conditions of patentability not constituting requirements as to the form and contents of applications.

(6) The national law may require that the applicant furnish evidence in respect of any substantive condition of patentability prescribed by such law.

(7) Any receiving Office or, once the processing of the international application has started in the designated Office, that Office may apply the national

law as far as it relates to any requirement that the applicant be represented by an agent having the right to represent applicants before the said Office and/or that the applicant have an address in the designated State for the purpose of receiving notifications.

(8) Nothing in this Treaty and the Regulations is intended to be construed as limiting the freedom of any Contracting State to apply measures deemed necessary for the preservation of its national security or to limit, for the protection of the general economic interests of that State, the right of its own residents or nationals to file international applications.

Article 28. Amendment of the Claims, the Description, and the Drawings, before Designated Offices

(1) The applicant shall be given the opportunity to amend the claims, the description, and the drawings, before each designated Office within the prescribed time limit. No designated Office shall grant a patent, or refuse the grant of a patent, before such time limit has expired except with the express consent of the applicant.

(2) The amendments shall not go beyond the disclosure in the international application as filed unless the national law of the designated State permits them to go beyond the said disclosure.

(3) The amendments shall be in accordance with the national law of the designated State in all respects not provided for in this Treaty and the Regulations.

(4) Where the designated Office requires a translation of the international application, the amendments shall be in the language of the translation.

Article 29. Effects of the International Publication

(1) As far as the protection of any rights of the applicant in a designated State is concerned, the effects, in that State, of the international publication of an international application shall, subject to the provisions of paragraphs (2) to (4), be the same as those which the national law of the designated State provides for the compulsory national publication of unexamined national applications as such.

(2) If the language in which the international publication has been effected is different from the language in which publications under the national law are effected in the designated State, the said national law may provide that the

effects provided for in paragraph (1) shall be applicable only from such time as:

(i) a translation into the latter language has been published as provided by the national law, or

(ii) a translation into the latter language has been made available to the public, by laying open for public inspection as provided by the national law, or

(iii) a translation into the latter language has been transmitted by the applicant to the actual or prospective unauthorized user of the invention claimed in the international application, or

(iv) both the acts described in (i) and (iii), or both the acts described in (ii) and (iii), have taken place.

(3) The national law of any designated State may provide that, where the international publication has been effected, on the request of the applicant, before the expiration of 18 months from the priority date, the effects provided for in paragraph (1) shall be applicable only from the expiration of 18 months from the priority date.

(4) The national law of any designated State may provide that the effects provided for in paragraph (1) shall be applicable only from the date on which a copy of the international application as published under Article 21 has been received in the national Office of or acting for such State. The said Office shall publish the date of receipt in its gazette as soon as possible.

Article 30.   Confidential Nature of the International Application

(1) (a) Subject to the provisions of subparagraph (b), the International Bureau and the International Searching Authorities shall not allow access by any person or authority to the international application before the international publication of that application, unless requested or authorized by the applicant.

(b) The provisions of subparagraph (a) shall not apply to any transmittal to the competent International Searching Authority, to transmittals provided for under Article 13, and to communications provided for under Article 20.

(2) (a) No national Office shall allow access to the international application by third parties, unless requested or authorized by the applicant, before the earliest of the following dates:

(i) date of the international publication of the international application,

(ii) date of the receipt of the communication of the international application under Article 20,

(iii) date of the receipt of a copy of the international application under Article 22.

(b) The provisions of subparagraph (a) shall not prevent any national Office from informing third parties that it has been designated, or from publishing that fact. Such information or publication may, however, contain only the following data: identification of the receiving Office, name of the applicant, international filing date, international application number, and title of the invention.

(c) The provisions of subparagraph (a) shall not prevent any designated Office from allowing access to the international application for the purposes of the judicial authorities.

(3) The provisions of paragraph (2)(a) shall apply to any receiving Office except as far as transmittals provided for under Article 12(1) are concerned.

(4) For the purposes of this Article, the term "access" covers any means by which third parties may acquire cognizance, including individual communication and general publication, provided, however, that no national Office shall generally publish an international application or its translation before the international publication or, if international publication has not taken place by the expiration of 20 months from the priority date, before the expiration of 20 months from the said priority date.

CHAPTER II. INTERNATIONAL PRELIMINARY EXAMINATION

Article 31. Demand for International Preliminary Examination

(1) On the demand of the applicant, his international application shall be the subject of an international preliminary examination as provided in the following provisions and the Regulations.

(2) (a) Any applicant who is a resident or national, as defined in the Regulations, of a Contracting State bound by Chapter II, and whose international application has been filed with the receiving Office of or acting for such State, may make a demand for international preliminary examination.

(b) The Assembly may decide to allow persons entitled to file international applications to make a demand for international preliminary examination even if they are residents or nationals of a State not party to this Treaty or not bound by Chapter II.

(3) The demand for international preliminary examination shall be made separately from the international application. The demand shall contain the prescribed particulars and shall be in the prescribed language and form.

(4) (a) The demand shall indicate the Contracting State or States in which the applicant intends to use the results of the international preliminary examination ("elected States"). Additional Contracting States may be elected later. Election may relate only to Contracting States already designated under Article 4.

(b) Applicants referred to in paragraph (2)(a) may elect any Contracting State bound by Chapter II. Applicants referred to in paragraph (2)(b) may elect only such Contracting States bound by Chapter II as have declared that they are prepared to be elected by such applicants.

(5) The demand shall be subject to the payment of the prescribed fees within the prescribed time limit.

(6) (a) The demand shall be submitted to the competent International Preliminary Examining Authority referred to in Article 32.

(b) Any later election shall be submitted to the International Bureau.

(7) Each elected Office shall be notified of its election.

Article 32.   The International Preliminary Examining Authority

(1) International preliminary examination shall be carried out by the International Preliminary Examining Authority.

(2) In the case of demands referred to in Article 31(2)(a), the receiving Office, and, in the case of demands referred to in Article 31(2)(b), the Assembly, shall, in accordance with the applicable agreement between the interested International Preliminary Examining Authority or Authorities and the International Bureau, specify the International Preliminary Examining Authority or Authorities competent for the preliminary examination.

(3) The provisions of Article 16(3) shall apply, mutatis mutandis, in respect of International Preliminary Examining Authorities.

Article 33. The International Preliminary Examination

(1) The objective of the international preliminary examination is to formulate a preliminary and non-binding opinion on the questions whether the claimed invention appears to be novel, to involve an inventive step (to be non-obvious), and to be industrially applicable.

(2) For the purposes of the international preliminary examination, a claimed invention shall be considered novel if it is not anticipated by the prior art as defined in the Regulations.

(3) For the purposes of the international preliminary examination, a claimed invention shall be considered to involve an inventive step if, having regard to the prior art as defined in the Regulations, it is not, at the prescribed relevant date, obvious to a person skilled in the art.

(4) For the purposes of the international preliminary examination, a claimed invention shall be considered industrially applicable if, according to its nature, it can be made or used (in the technological sense) in any kind of industry. "Industry" shall be understood in its broadest sense, as in the Paris Convention for the Protection of Industrial Property.

(5) The criteria described above merely serve the purposes of international preliminary examination. Any Contracting State may apply additional or different criteria for the purpose of deciding whether, in that State, the claimed invention is patentable or not.

(6) The international preliminary examination shall take into consideration all the documents cited in the international search report. It may take consideration any additional documents considered to be relevant in the particular case.

Article 34. Procedure before the International Preliminary Examining Authority

(1) Procedure before the International Preliminary Examining Authority shall be governed by the provisions of this Treaty, the Regulations, and the agreement which the International Bureau shall conclude, subject to this Treaty and the Regulations, with the said Authority.

(2) (a) The applicant shall have a right to communicate orally and in writing with the International Preliminary Examining Authority.

(b) The applicant shall have a right to amend the claims, the description, and the drawings, in the prescribed manner and within the prescribed time limit, before the international preliminary examination report is established. The amendment shall not go beyond the disclosure in the international application as filed.

(c) The applicant shall receive at least one written opinion from the International Preliminary Examining Authority unless such Authority considers that all of the following conditions are fulfilled:

(i) the invention satisfies the criteria set forth in Article 33(1),

(ii) the international application complies with the requirements of this Treaty and the Regulations in so far as checked by that Authority, (iii) no observations are intended to be made under Article 35(2), last sentence.

(d) The applicant may respond to the written opinion.

(3) (a) If the International Preliminary Examining Authority considers that the international application does not comply with the requirement of unity of invention as set forth in the Regulations, it may invite the applicant, at his option, to restrict the claims so as to comply with the requirement or to pay additional fees.

(b) The national law of any elected State may provide that, where the applicant chooses to restrict the claims under subparagraph (a), those parts of the international application which, as a consequence of the restriction, are not to be the subject of international preliminary examination shall, as far as effects in that State are concerned, be considered withdrawn unless a special fee is paid by the applicant to the national Office of that State.

(c) If the applicant does not comply with the invitation referred to in subparagraph (a) within the prescribed time limit, the International Preliminary Examining Authority shall establish an international preliminary examination report on those parts of the international application which relate to what appears to be the main invention and shall indicate the relevant facts in the said report. The national law of any elected State may provide that, where its national Office finds the invitation of the International Preliminary Examining Authority justified, those parts of the international application which do not relate to the main invention shall, as far as effects in that State are concerned, be considered withdrawn unless a special fee is paid by the applicant to that Office.

PCT Art. 34

(4) (a) If the International Preliminary Examining Authority considers (i) that the international application relates to a subject matter on which the International Preliminary Examining Authority is not required, under the Regulations, to carry out an international preliminary examination, and in the particular case decides not to carry out such examination, or (ii) that the description, the claims, or the drawings, are so unclear, or the claims are so inadequately supported by the description, that no meaningful opinion can be formed on the novelty, inventive step (non-obviousness), or industrial applicability, of the claimed invention, the said Authority shall not go into the questions referred to in Article 33(1) and shall inform the applicant of this opinion and the reasons therefor. (b) If any of the situations referred to in subparagraph (a) is found to exist in, or in connection with, certain claims only, the provisions of that subparagraph shall apply only to the said claims.

Article 35. The International Preliminary Examination Report

(1) The international preliminary examination report shall be established within the prescribed time limit and in the prescribed form.

(2) The international preliminary examination report shall not contain any statement on the question whether the claimed invention is or seems to be patentable or unpatentable according to any national law. It shall state, subject to the provisions of paragraph (3), in relation to each claim, whether the claim appears to satisfy the criteria of novelty, inventive step (non-obviousness), and industrial applicability, as defined for the purposes of the international preliminary examination in Article 33(1) to (4). The statement shall be accompanied by the citation of the documents believed to support the stated conclusion with such explanations as the circumstances of the case may require. The statement shall also be accompanied by such other observations as the Regulations provide for.

(3) (a) If, at the time of establishing the international preliminary examination report, the International Preliminary Examining Authority considers that any of the situations referred to in Article 34(4)(a) exists, that report shall state this opinion and the reasons therefor. It shall not contain any statement as provided in paragraph (2).

(b) If a situation under Article 34(4)(b) is found to exist, the international preliminary examination report shall, in relation to the claims in question, contain the statement as provided in subparagraph (a), whereas, in relation to the other claims, it shall contain the statement as provided in paragraph (2).

Article 36. Transmittal, Translation, and Communication, of the International Preliminary Examination Report

(1) The international preliminary examination report, together with the prescribed annexes, shall be transmitted to the applicant and to the International Bureau.

(2) (a) The international preliminary examination report and its annexes shall be translated into the prescribed languages.

(b) Any translation of the said report shall be prepared by or under the responsibility of the International Bureau, whereas any translation of the said annexes shall be prepared by the applicant.

(3) (a) The international preliminary examination report, together with its translation (as prescribed) and its annexes (in the original language), shall be communicated by the International Bureau to each elected Office.

(b) The prescribed translation of the annexes shall be transmitted within the prescribed time limit by the applicant to the elected Offices.

(4) The provisions of Article 20(3) shall apply, mutatis mutandis, to copies of any document which is cited in the international preliminary examination report and which was not cited in the international search report.

Article 37. Withdrawal of Demand or Election

(1) The applicant may withdraw any or all elections

(2) If the election of all elected States is withdrawn, the demand shall be considered withdrawn.

(3) (a) Any withdrawal shall be notified to the International Bureau.

(b) The elected Offices concerned and the International Preliminary Examining Authority concerned shall be notified accordingly by the International Bureau.

(4) (a) Subject to the provisions of subparagraph (b), withdrawal of the demand or of the election of a Contracting State shall, unless the national law of that State provides otherwise, be considered to be withdrawal of the international application as far as that State is concerned.

(b) Withdrawal of the demand or of the election shall not be considered to be withdrawal of the international application if such withdrawal is effected prior to the expiration of the applicable time limit under Article 22; however, any Contracting State may provide in its national law that the aforesaid shall apply only if its national Office has received, within the said time limit, a copy of the international application, together with a translation (as prescribed), and the national fee.

Article 38. Confidential Nature of the International Preliminary Examination

(1) Neither the International Bureau nor the International Preliminary Examining Authority shall, unless requested or authorized by the applicant, allow access within the meaning, and with the proviso, of Article 30(4) to the file of the international preliminary examination by any person or authority at any time, except by the elected Offices once the international preliminary examination report has been established.

(2) Subject to the provisions of paragraph (1) and Articles 36(1) and (3) and 37(3)(b), neither the International Bureau nor the International Preliminary Examining Authority shall, unless requested or authorized by the applicant, give information on the issuance or nonissuance of an international preliminary examination report and on the withdrawal or nonwithdrawal of the demand or of any election.

Article 39. Copy, Translation, and Fee, to Elected Offices

(1) (a) If the election of any Contracting State has been effected prior to the expiration of the 19th month from the priority date, the provisions of Article 22 shall not apply to such State and the applicant shall furnish a copy of the international application (unless the communication under Article 20 has already taken place) and a translation thereof (as prescribed), and pay the national fee (if any), to each elected Office not later than at the expiration of 30 months from the priority date.

(b) Any national law may, for performing the acts referred to in subparagraph (a), fix time limits which expire later than the time limit provided for in that subparagraph.

(2) The effect provided for in Article 11(3) shall cease in the elected State with the same consequences as the withdrawal of any national application in that

State if the applicant fails to perform the acts referred to in paragraph (1)(a) within the time limit applicable under paragraph (1)(a) or (b).

(3) Any elected Office may maintain the effect provided for in Article 11(3) even where the applicant does not comply with the requirements provided for in paragraph (1)(a) or (b).

Article 40. Delaying of National Examination and Other Processing

(1) If the election of any Contracting State has been effected prior to the expiration of the 19th month from the priority date, the provisions of Article 23 shall not apply to such State and the national Office of or acting for that State shall not proceed, subject to the provisions of paragraph (2), to the examination and other processing of the international application prior to the expiration of the applicable time limit under Article 39.

(2) Notwithstanding the provisions of paragraph (1), any elected Office may, on the express request of the applicant, proceed to the examination and other processing of the international application at any time.

Article 41. Amendment of the Claims, the Description, and the Drawings, before Elected Offices

(1) The applicant shall be given the opportunity to amend the claims, the description, and the drawings, before each elected Office within the prescribed time limit. No elected Office shall grant a patent, or refuse the grant of a patent, before such time limit has expired, except with the express consent of the applicant.

(2) The amendments shall not go beyond the disclosure in the international application as filed, unless the national law of the elected State permits them to go beyond the said disclosure.

(3) The amendments shall be in accordance with the national law of the elected State in all respects not provided for in this Treaty and the Regulations.

(4) Where an elected Office requires a translation of the international application, the amendments shall be in the language of the translation.

Article 42. Results of National Examination in Elected Offices

No elected Office receiving the international preliminary examination report may require that the applicant furnish copies, or information on the contents, of any papers connected with the examination relating to the same international application in any other elected Office.

CHAPTER III. COMMON PROVISIONS

Article 43. Seeking Certain Kinds of Protection

In respect of any designated or elected State whose law provides for the grant of inventors' certificates, utility certificates, utility models, patents or certificates of addition, inventors' certificates of addition, or utility certificates of addition, the applicant may indicate, as prescribed in the Regulations, that his international application is for the grant, as far as that State is concerned, of an inventor's certificate, a utility certificate, or a utility model, rather than a patent, or that it is for the grant of a patent or certificate of addition, an inventor's certificate of addition, or a utility certificate of addition, and the ensuing effect shall be governed by the applicant's choice. For the purposes of this Article and any Rule thereunder, Article 2(ii) shall not apply.

Article 44. Seeking Two Kinds of Protection

In respect of any designated or elected State whose law permits an application, while being for the grant of a patent or one of the other kinds of protection referred to in Article 43, to be also for the grant of another of the said kinds of protection, the applicant may indicate, as prescribed in the Regulations, the two kinds of protection he is seeking, and the ensuing effect shall be governed by the applicant's indications. For the purposes of this Article, Article 2(ii) shall not apply.

Article 45. Regional Patent Treaties

(1) Any treaty providing for the grant of regional patents ("regional patent treaty"), and giving to all persons who, according to Article 9, are entitled to file international applications the right to file applications for such patents, may provide that international applications designating or electing a State party to both the regional patent treaty and the present Treaty may be filed as applications for such patents.

(2) The national law of the said designated or elected State may provide that any designation or election of such State in the international application shall

have the effect of an indication of the wish to obtain a regional patent under the regional patent treaty.

Article 46. Incorrect Translation of the International Application

If, because of an incorrect translation of the international application, the scope of any patent granted on that application exceeds the scope of the international application in its original language, the competent authorities of the Contracting State concerned may accordingly and retroactively limit the scope of the patent, and declare it null and void to the extent that its scope has exceeded the scope of the international application in its original language.

Article 47. Time Limits

(1) The details for computing time limits referred to in this Treaty are governed by the Regulations.

(2) (a) All time limits fixed in Chapters I and II of this Treaty may, outside any revision under Article 60, be modified by a decision of the Contracting States.

(b) Such decisions shall be made in the Assembly or through voting by correspondence and must be unanimous.

(c) The details of the procedure are governed by the Regulations.

Article 48. Delay in Meeting Certain Time Limits

(1) Where any time limit fixed in this Treaty or the Regulations is not met because of interruption in the mail service or unavoidable loss or delay in the mail, the time limit shall be deemed to be met in the cases and subject to the proof and other conditions prescribed in the Regulations.

(2) (a) Any Contracting State shall, as far as that State is concerned, excuse, for reasons admitted under its national law, any delay in meeting any time limit.

(b) Any Contracting State may, as far as that State is concerned, excuse, for reasons other than those referred to in subparagraph (a), any delay in meeting any time limit.

Article 49. Right to Practice before International Authorities

Any attorney, patent agent, or other person, having the right to practice before the national Office with which the international application was filed, shall be entitled to practice before the International Bureau and the competent International Searching Authority and competent International Preliminary Examining Authority in respect of that application.

CHAPTER IV. TECHNICAL SERVICES

Article 50. Patent Information Services

(1) The International Bureau may furnish services by providing technical and any other pertinent information available to it on the basis of published documents, primarily patents and published applications (referred to in this Article as "the information services").

(2) The International Bureau may provide these information services either directly or through one or more International Searching Authorities or other national or international specialized institutions, with which the International Bureau may reach agreement.

(3) The information services shall be operated in a way particularly facilitating the acquisition by Contracting States which are developing countries of technical knowledge and technology, including available published know-how.

(4) The information services shall be available to Governments of Contracting States and their nationals and residents. The Assembly may decide to make these services available also to others.

(5) (a) Any service to Governments of Contracting States shall be furnished at cost, provided that, when the Government is that of a Contracting State which is a developing country, the service shall be furnished below cost if the difference can be covered from profit made on services furnished to others than Governments of Contracting States or from the sources referred to in Article 51(4).

(b) The cost referred to in subparagraph (a) is to be understood as cost over and above costs normally incident to the performance of the services of a national Office or the obligations of an International Searching Authority.

(6) The details concerning the implementation of the provisions of this Article shall be governed by decisions of the Assembly and, within the limits to be fixed by the Assembly, such working groups as the Assembly may set up for that purpose.

(7) The Assembly shall, when it considers it necessary, recommend methods of providing financing supplementary to those referred to in paragraph (5).

Article 51. Technical Assistance

(1) The Assembly shall establish a Committee for Technical Assistance (referred to in this Article as "the Committee").

(2) (a) The members of the Committee shall be elected among the Contracting States, with due regard to the representation of developing countries.

(b) The Director General shall, on his own initiative or at the request of the Committee, invite representatives of intergovernmental organizations concerned with technical assistance to developing countries to participate in the work of the Committee.

(3) (a) The task of the Committee shall be to organize and supervise technical assistance for Contracting States which are developing countries in developing their patent systems individually or on a regional basis.

(b) The technical assistance shall comprise, among other things, the training of specialists, the loaning of experts, and the supply of equipment both or demonstration and for operational purposes.

(4) The International Bureau shall seek to enter into agreements, on the one hand, with international financing organizations and intergovernmental organizations, particularly the United Nations, the agencies of the United Nations, and the Specialized Agencies connected with the United Nations concerned with technical assistance, and, on the other hand, with the Governments of the States receiving the technical assistance, for the financing of projects pursuant to this Article.

(5) The details concerning the implementation of the provisions of this Article shall be governed by decisions of the Assembly and, within the limits to be fixed by the Assembly, such working groups as the Assembly may set up for that purpose.

Article 52.   Relations with Other Provisions of the Treaty

Nothing in this Chapter shall affect the financial provisions contained in any other Chapter of this Treaty. Such provisions are not applicable to the present Chapter or to its implementation.

CHAPTER V. ADMINISTRATIVE PROVISIONS

Article 53.   Assembly

(1) (a) The Assembly shall, subject to Article 57(8), consist of the Contracting States.

(b) The Government of each Contracting State shall be represented by one delegate, who may be assisted by alternate delegates, advisors, and experts.

(2) (a) The Assembly shall:

(i) deal with all matters concerning the maintenance and development of the Union and the implementation of this Treaty;

(ii) perform such tasks as are specifically assigned to it under other provisions of this Treaty;

(iii) give directions to the International Bureau concerning the preparation for revision conferences;

(iv) review and approve the reports and activities of the Director General concerning the Union, and give him all necessary instructions concerning matters within the competence of the Union;

(v) review and approve the reports and activities of the Executive Committee established under paragraph (9), and give instructions to such Committee;

(vi) determine the program and adopt the triennial2 budget of the Union, and approve its final accounts;

(vii) adopt the financial regulations of the Union;

(viii) establish such committees and working groups as it deems appropriate to achieve the objectives of the Union;

(ix) determine which States other than Contracting States and, subject to the provisions of paragraph (8), which intergovernmental and international non-governmental organizations shall be admitted to its meetings as observers;

(x) take any other appropriate action designed to further the objectives of the Union and perform such other functions as are appropriate under this Treaty.

(b) With respect to matters which are of interest also to other Unions administered by the Organization, the Assembly shall make its decisions after having heard the advice of the Coordination Committee of the Organization.

(3) A delegate may represent, and vote in the name of, one State only.

(4) Each Contracting State shall have one vote.

(5) (a) One-half of the Contracting States shall constitute a quorum.

(b) In the absence of the quorum, the Assembly may make decisions but, with the exception of decisions concerning its own procedure, all such decisions shall take effect only if the quorum and the required majority are attained through voting by correspondence as provided in the Regulations.

(6) (a) Subject to the provisions of Articles 47(2)(b), 58(2)(b), 58(3) and 61(2)(b), the decisions of the Assembly shall require two-thirds of the votes cast.

(b) Abstentions shall not be considered as votes.

(7) In connection with matters of exclusive interest to States bound by Chapter II, any reference to Contracting States in paragraphs (4), (5), and (6), shall be considered as applying only to States bound by Chapter II.

(8) Any intergovernmental organization appointed as International Searching or Preliminary Examining Authority shall be admitted as observer to the Assembly.

(9) When the number of Contracting States exceeds forty, the Assembly shall establish an Executive Committee. Any reference to the Executive Committee in this Treaty and the Regulations shall be construed as references to such Committee once it has been established.

(10) Until the Executive Committee has been established, the Assembly shall approve, within the limits of the program and triennial3 budget, the annual programs and budgets prepared by the Director General.

(11) (a) The Assembly shall meet in every second calendar year in ordinary session upon convocation by the Director General and, in the absence of exceptional circumstances, during the same period and at the same place as the General Assembly of the Organization.

(b) The Assembly shall meet in extraordinary session upon convocation by the Director General, at the request of the Executive Committee, or at the request of one-fourth of the Contracting States.

(12) The Assembly shall adopt its own rules of procedure.

Article 54. Executive Committee

(1) When the Assembly has established an Executive Committee, that Committee shall be subject to the provisions set forth hereinafter.

(2) (a) The Executive Committee shall, subject to Article 57(8), consist of States elected by the Assembly from among States members of the Assembly.

(b) The Government of each State member of the Executive Committee shall be represented by one delegate, who may be assisted by alternate delegates, advisors, and experts.

(3) The number of States members of the Executive Committee shall correspond to one-fourth of the number of States members of the Assembly. In establishing the number of seats to be filled, remainders after division by four shall be disregarded.

(4) In electing the members of the Executive Committee, the Assembly shall have due regard to an equitable geographical distribution.

(5) (a) Each member of the Executive Committee shall serve from the close of the session of the Assembly which elected it to the close of the next ordinary session of the Assembly.

(b) Members of the Executive Committee may be re-elected but only up to a maximum of two-thirds of such members.

(c) The Assembly shall establish the details of the rules governing the election and possible re-election of the members of the Executive Committee.

(6) (a) The Executive Committee shall:

(i) prepare the draft agenda of the Assembly;

(ii) submit proposals to the Assembly in respect of the draft program and biennial budget of the Union prepared by the Director General;

(iii) [deleted]

(iv) submit, with appropriate comments, to the Assembly the periodical reports of the Director General and the yearly audit reports on the accounts;

(v) take all necessary measures to ensure the execution of the program of the Union by the Director General, in accordance with the decisions of the Assembly and having regard to circumstances arising between two ordinary sessions of the Assembly;

(vi) perform such other functions as are allocated to it under this Treaty.

(b) With respect to matters which are of interest also to other Unions administered by the Organization, the Executive Committee shall make its decisions after having heard the advice of the Coordination Committee of the Organization.

(7) (a) The Executive Committee shall meet once a year in ordinary session upon convocation by the Director General, preferably during the same period and at the same place as the Coordination Committee of the Organization.

(b) The Executive Committee shall meet in extraordinary session upon convocation by the Director General, either on his own initiative or at the request of its Chairman or one-fourth of its members.

(8) (a) Each State member of the Executive Committee shall have one vote.

(b) One-half of the members of the Executive Committee shall constitute a quorum.

(c) Decisions shall be made by a simple majority of the votes cast.

(d) Abstentions shall not be considered as votes.

(e) A delegate may represent, and vote in the name of, one State only.

(9) Contracting States not members of the Executive Committee shall be admitted to its meetings as observers, as well as any intergovernmental organization appointed as International Searching or Preliminary Examining Authority.

(10) The Executive Committee shall adopt its own rules of procedure.

Article 55. International Bureau

(1) Administrative tasks concerning the Union shall be performed by the International Bureau.

(2) The International Bureau shall provide the secretariat of the various organs of the Union.

(3) The Director General shall be the chief executive of the Union and shall represent the Union.

(4) The International Bureau shall publish a Gazette and other publications provided for by the Regulations or required by the Assembly.

(5) The Regulations shall specify the services that national Offices shall perform in order to assist the International Bureau and the International Searching and Preliminary Examining Authorities in carrying out their tasks under this Treaty.

(6) The Director General and any staff member designated by him shall participate, without the right to vote, in all meetings of the Assembly, the Executive Committee and any other committee or working group established under this Treaty or the Regulations. The Director General, or a staff member designated by him, shall be ex officio secretary of these bodies.

(7) (a) The International Bureau shall, in accordance with the directions of the Assembly and in cooperation with the Executive Committee, make the preparations for the revision conferences.

(b) The International Bureau may consult with intergovernmental and international non-governmental organizations concerning preparations for revision conferences.

(c) The Director General and persons designated by him shall take part, without the right to vote, in the discussions at revision conferences.

(8) The International Bureau shall carry out any other tasks assigned to it.

Article 56. Committee for Technical Cooperation

(1) The Assembly shall establish a Committee for Technical Cooperation (referred to in this Article as "the Committee").

(2) (a) The Assembly shall determine the composition of the Committee and appoint its members, with due regard to an equitable representation of developing countries.

(b) The International Searching and Preliminary Examining Authorities shall be ex officio members of the Committee. In the case where such an Authority is the national Office of a Contracting State, that State shall not be additionally represented on the Committee.

(c) If the number of Contracting States so allows, the total number of members of the Committee shall be more than double the number of ex officio members.

(d) The Director General shall, on his own initiative or at the request of the Committee, invite representatives of interested organizations to participate in discussions of interest to them.

(3) The aim of the Committee shall be to contribute, by advice and recommendations:

(i) to the constant improvement of the services provided for under this Treaty,

(ii) to the securing, so long as there are several International Searching Authorities and several International Preliminary Examining Authorities, of the maximum degree of uniformity in their documentation and working methods and the maximum degree of uniformly high quality in their reports, and

(iii) on the initiative of the Assembly or the Executive Committee, to the solution of the technical problems specifically involved in the establishment of a single International Searching Authority.

(4) Any Contracting State and any interested international organization may approach the Committee in writing on questions which fall within the competence of the Committee.

(5) The Committee may address its advice and recommendations to the Director General or, through him, to the Assembly, the Executive Committee, all or some of the International Searching and Preliminary Examining Authorities, and all or some of the receiving Offices.

(6) (a) In any case, the Director General shall transmit to the Executive Committee the texts of all the advice and recommendations of the Committee. He may comment on such texts.

(b) The Executive Committee may express its views on any advice, recommendation, or other activity of the Committee, and may invite the Committee to study and report on questions falling within its competence.

The Executive Committee may submit to the Assembly, with appropriate comments, the advice, recommendations and report of the Committee.

(7) Until the Executive Committee has been established, references in paragraph (6) to the Executive Committee shall be construed as references to the Assembly.

(8) The details of the procedure of the Committee shall be governed by the decisions of the Assembly.

Article 57.   Finances

(1) (a) The Union shall have a budget.

(b) The budget of the Union shall include the income and expenses proper to the Union and its contribution to the budget of expenses common to the Unions administered by the Organization.

(c) Expenses not attributable exclusively to the Union but also to one or more other Unions administered by the Organization shall be considered as expenses common to the Unions. The share of the Union in such common expenses shall be in proportion to the interest the Union has in them.

(2) The budget of the Union shall be established with due regard to the requirements of coordination with the budgets of the other Unions administered by the Organization.

(3) Subject to the provisions of paragraph (5), the budget of the Union shall be financed from the following sources:

(i) fees and charges due for services rendered by the International Bureau in relation to the Union;

(ii) sale of, or royalties on, the publications of the International Bureau concerning the Union;

(iii) gifts, bequests, and subventions;

(iv) rents, interests, and other miscellaneous income.

(4) The amounts of fees and charges due to the International Bureau and the prices of its publications shall be so fixed that they should, under normal circumstances, be sufficient to cover all the expenses of the International Bureau connected with the administration of this Treaty.

(5) (a) Should any financial year close with a deficit, the Contracting States shall, subject to the provisions of subparagraphs (b) and (c), pay contributions to cover such deficit.

(b) The amount of the contribution of each Contracting State shall be decided by the Assembly with due regard to the number of international applications which has emanated from each of them in the relevant year.

(c) If other means of provisionally covering any deficit or any part thereof are secured, the Assembly may decide that such deficit be carried forward and that the Contracting States should not be asked to pay contributions.

(d) If the financial situation of the Union so permits, the Assembly may decide that any contributions paid under subparagraph (a) be reimbursed to the Contracting States which have paid them.

(e) A Contracting State which has not paid, within two years of the due date as established by the Assembly, its contribution under subparagraph (b) may not exercise its right to vote in any of the organs of the Union. However, any organ of the Union may allow such a State to continue to exercise its right to vote in that organ so long as it is satisfied that the delay in payment is due to exceptional and unavoidable circumstances.

(6) If the budget is not adopted before the beginning of a new financial period, it shall be at the same level as the budget of the previous year, as provided in the financial regulations.

(7) (a) The Union shall have a working capital fund which shall be constituted by a single payment made by each Contracting State. If the fund becomes insufficient, the Assembly shall arrange to increase it. If part of the fund is no longer needed, it shall be reimbursed.

(b) The amount of the initial payment of each Contracting State to the said fund or of its participation in the increase thereof shall be decided by the Assembly on the basis of principles similar to those provided for under paragraph (5)(b).

(c) The terms of payment shall be fixed by the Assembly on the proposal of the Director General and after it has heard the advice of the Coordination Committee of the Organization.

(d) Any reimbursement shall be proportionate to the amounts paid by each Contracting State, taking into account the dates at which they were paid.

PCT Art. 57

(8) (a) In the headquarters agreement concluded with the State on the territory of which the Organization has its headquarters, it shall be provided that, whenever the working capital fund is insufficient, such State shall grant advances. The amount of these advances and the conditions on which they are granted shall be the subject of separate agreements, in each case, between such State and the Organization. As long as it remains under the obligation to grant advances, such State shall have an ex officio seat in the Assembly and on the Executive Committee.

(b) The State referred to in subparagraph (a) and the Organization shall each have the right to denounce the obligation to grant advances, by written notification. Denunciation shall take effect three years after the end of the year in which it has been notified.

(9) The auditing of the accounts shall be effected by one or more of the Contracting States or by external auditors, as provided in the financial regulations. They shall be designated, with their agreement, by the Assembly.

Article 58. Regulations

(1) The Regulations annexed to this Treaty provide Rules:

(i) concerning matters in respect of which this Treaty expressly refers to the Regulations or expressly provides that they are or shall be prescribed,

(ii) concerning any administrative requirements, matters, or procedures,

(iii) concerning any details useful in the implementation of the provisions of this Treaty.

(2) (a) The Assembly may amend the Regulations.

(b) Subject to the provisions of paragraph (3), amendments shall require three-fourths of the votes cast.

(3) (a) The Regulations specify the Rules which may be amended

(i) only by unanimous consent, or

(ii) only if none of the Contracting States whose national Office acts as an International Searching or Preliminary Examining Authority dissents, and, where such Authority is an intergovernmental organization, if the Contracting State member of that organization authorized for that purpose by the other member States within the competent body of such organization does not dissent.

(b) Exclusion, for the future, of any such Rules from the applicable requirement shall require the fulfillment of the conditions referred to in subparagraph (a)(i) or (a)(ii), respectively.

(c) Inclusion, for the future, of any Rule in one or the other of the requirements referred to in subparagraph (a) shall require unanimous consent.

(4) The Regulations provide for the establishment, under the control of the Assembly, of Administrative Instructions by the Director General.

(5) In the case of conflict between the provisions of the Treaty and those of the Regulations, the provisions of the Treaty shall prevail.

CHAPTER VI. DISPUTES

Article 59. Disputes

Subject to Article 64(5), any dispute between two or more Contracting States concerning the interpretation or application of this Treaty or the Regulations, not settled by negotiation, may, by any one of the States concerned, be brought before the International Court of Justice by application in conformity with the Statute of the Court, unless the States concerned agree on some other method of settlement. The Contracting State bringing the dispute before the Court shall inform the International Bureau; the International Bureau shall bring the matter to the attention of the other Contracting States.

CHAPTER VII. REVISION AND AMENDMENT

Article 60. Revision of the Treaty

(1) This Treaty may be revised from time to time by a special conference of the Contracting States.

(2) The convocation of any revision conference shall be decided by the Assembly.

(3) Any intergovernmental organization appointed as International Searching or Preliminary Examining Authority shall be admitted as observer to any revision conference.

(4) Articles 53(5), (9) and (11), 54, 55(4) to (8), 56, and 57, may be amended either by a revision conference or according to the provisions of Article 61.

Article 61. Amendment of Certain Provisions of the Treaty

(1) (a) Proposals for the amendment of Articles 53(5), (9) and (11), 54, 55(4) to (8), 56, and 57, may be initiated by any State member of the Assembly, by the Executive Committee, or by the Director General.

(b) Such proposals shall be communicated by the Director General to the Contracting States at least six months in advance of their consideration by the Assembly.

(2) (a) Amendments to the Articles referred to in paragraph (1) shall be adopted by the Assembly.

(b) Adoption shall require three-fourths of the votes cast.

(3) (a) Any amendment to the Articles referred to in paragraph (1) shall enter into force one month after written notifications of acceptance, effected in accordance with their respective constitutional processes, have been received by the Director General from three-fourths of the States members of the Assembly at the time it adopted the amendment.

(b) Any amendment to the said Articles thus accepted shall bind all the States which are members of the Assembly at the time the amendment enters into force, provided that any amendment increasing the financial obligations of the Contracting States shall bind only those States which have notified their acceptance of such amendment.

(c) Any amendment accepted in accordance with the provisions of subparagraph (a) shall bind all States which become members of the Assembly after the date on which the amendment entered into force in accordance with the provisions of subparagraph (a).

CHAPTER VIII. FINAL PROVISIONS

Article 62. Becoming Party to the Treaty

(1) Any State member of the International Union for the Protection of Industrial Property may become party to this Treaty by:

(i) signature followed by the deposit of an instrument of ratification, or

(ii) deposit of an instrument of accession.

(2) Instruments of ratification or accession shall be deposited with the Director General.

(3) The provisions of Article 24 of the Stockholm Act of the Paris Convention for the Protection of Industrial Property shall apply to this Treaty.

(4) Paragraph (3) shall in no way be understood as implying the recognition or tacit acceptance by a Contracting State of the factual situation concerning a territory to which this Treaty is made applicable by another Contracting State by virtue of the said paragraph.

Article 63. Entry into Force of the Treaty

(1) (a) Subject to the provisions of paragraph (3), this Treaty shall enter into force three months after eight States have deposited their instruments of ratification or accession, provided that at least four of those States each fulfill any of the following conditions:

  (i) the number of applications filed in the State has exceeded 40,000 according to the most recent annual statistics published by the International Bureau,

  (ii) the nationals or residents of the State have filed at least 1,000 applications in one foreign country according to the most recent annual statistics published by the International Bureau,

  (iii) the national Office of the State has received at least 10,000 applications from nationals or residents of foreign countries according to the most recent annual statistics published by the International Bureau.

(b) For the purposes of this paragraph, the term "applications" does not include applications for utility models.

(2) Subject to the provisions of paragraph (3), any State which does not become party to this Treaty upon entry into force under paragraph (1) shall become bound by this Treaty three months after the date on which such State has deposited its instrument of ratification or accession.

(3) The provisions of Chapter II and the corresponding provisions of the Regulations annexed to this Treaty shall become applicable, however, only on the date on which three States each of which fulfill at least one of the three requirements specified in paragraph (1) have become party to this Treaty without declaring, as provided in Article 64(1), that they do not intend to be bound by the provisions of Chapter II. That date shall not, however, be prior to that of the initial entry into force under paragraph (1).

Article 64.   Reservations

(1) (a) Any State may declare that it shall not be bound by the provisions of Chapter II.

(b) States making a declaration under subparagraph (a) shall not be bound by the provisions of Chapter II and the corresponding provisions of the Regulations.

(2) (a) Any State not having made a declaration under paragraph (1)(a) may declare that:

(i) it shall not be bound by the provisions of Article 39(1) with respect to the furnishing of a copy of the international application and a translation thereof (as prescribed),

(ii) the obligation to delay national processing, as provided for under Article 40, shall not prevent publication, by or through its national Office, of the international application or a translation thereof, it being understood, however, that it is not exempted from the limitations provided for in Articles 30 and 38.

(b) States making such a declaration shall be bound accordingly.

(3) (a) Any State may declare that, as far as it is concerned, international publication of international applications is not required.

(b) Where, at the expiration of 18 months from the priority date, the international application contains the designation only of such States as have made declarations under subparagraph (a), the international application shall not be published by virtue of Article 21(2).

(c) Where the provisions of subparagraph (b) apply, the international application shall nevertheless be published by the International Bureau:

(i) at the request of the applicant, as provided in the Regulations,

(ii) when a national application or a patent based on the international application is published by or on behalf of the national Office of any designated State having made a declaration under subparagraph (a), promptly after such publication but not before the expiration of 18 months from the priority date.

(4) (a) Any State whose national law provides for prior art effect of its patents as from a date before publication, but does not equate for prior art purposes the priority date claimed under the Paris Convention for the Protection of Industrial Property to the actual filing date in that State, may

declare that the filing outside that State of an international application designating that State is not equated to an actual filing in that State for prior art purposes.

(b) Any State making a declaration under subparagraph (a) shall to that extent not be bound by the provisions of Article 11(3).

(c) Any State making a declaration under subparagraph (a) shall, at the same time, state in writing the date from which, and the conditions under which, the prior art effect of any international application designating that State becomes effective in that State. This statement may be modified at any time by notification addressed to the Director General.

(5) Each State may declare that it does not consider itself bound by Article 59. With regard to any dispute between any Contracting State having made such a declaration and any other Contracting State, the provisions of Article 59 shall not apply.

(6) (a) Any declaration made under this Article shall be made in writing. It may be made at the time of signing this Treaty, at the time of depositing the instrument of ratification or accession, or, except in the case referred to in paragraph (5), at any later time by notification addressed to the Director General. In the case of the said notification, the declaration shall take effect six months after the day on which the Director General has received the notification, and shall not affect international applications filed prior to the expiration of the said six-month period.

(b) Any declaration made under this Article may be withdrawn at any time by notification addressed to the Director General. Such withdrawal shall take effect three months after the day on which the Director General has received the notification and, in the case of the withdrawal of a declaration made under paragraph (3), shall not affect international applications filed prior to the expiration of the said three-month period.

(7) No reservations to this Treaty other than the reservations under paragraphs (1) to (5) are permitted.

Article 65. Gradual Application

(1) If the agreement with any International Searching or Preliminary Examining Authority provides, transitionally, for limits on the number or kind of international applications that such Authority undertakes to process, the Assembly shall adopt the measures necessary for the gradual application of

this Treaty and the Regulations in respect of given categories of international applications. This provision shall also apply to requests for an international type search under Article 15(5).

(2) The Assembly shall fix the dates from which, subject to the provision of paragraph (1), international applications may be filed and demands for international preliminary examination may be submitted. Such dates shall not be later than six months after this Treaty has entered into force according to the provisions of Article 63(1), or after Chapter II has become applicable under Article 63(3), respectively.

Article 66. Denunciation

(1) Any Contracting State may denounce this Treaty by notification addressed to the Director General.

(2) Denunciation shall take effect six months after receipt of the said notification by the Director General. It shall not affect the effects of the international application in the denouncing State if the international application was filed, and, where the denouncing State has been elected, the election was made, prior to the expiration of the said six-month period.

Article 67. Signature and Languages

(1) (a) This Treaty shall be signed in a single original in the English and French languages, both texts being equally authentic.

(b) Official texts shall be established by the Director General, after consultation with the interested Governments, in the German, Japanese, Portuguese, Russian and Spanish languages, and such other languages as the Assembly may designate.

(2) This Treaty shall remain open for signature at Washington until December 31, 1970.

Article 68. Depositary Functions

(1) The original of this Treaty, when no longer open for signature, shall be deposited with the Director General.

(2) The Director General shall transmit two copies, certified by him, of this Treaty and the Regulations annexed hereto to the Governments of all States party to the Paris Convention for the Protection of Industrial Property and, on request, to the Government of any other State.

(3) The Director General shall register this Treaty with the Secretariat of the United Nations.

(4) The Director General shall transmit two copies, certified by him, of any amendment to this Treaty and the Regulations to the Governments of all Contracting States and, on request, to the Government of any other State.

Article 69.   Notifications

The Director General shall notify the Governments of all States party to the Paris Convention for the Protection of Industrial Property of:

(i) signatures under Article 62,

(ii) deposits of instruments of ratification or accession under Article 62,

(iii) the date of entry into force of this Treaty and the date from which Chapter II is applicable in accordance with Article 63(3),

(iv) any declarations made under Article 64(1) to (5),

(v) withdrawals of any declarations made under Article 64(6)(b),

(vi) denunciations received under Article 66, and

(vii) any declarations made under Article 31(4).

III. PROTOCOL RELATING TO THE MADRID AGREEMENT CONCERNING THE INTERNATIONAL REGISTRATION OF MARKS

Adopted at Madrid on June 27, 1989

Article 1. Membership in the Madrid Union

The States party to this Protocol (hereinafter referred to as "the Contracting States"), even where they are not party to the Madrid Agreement Concerning the International Registration of Marks as revised at Stockholm in 1967 and as amended in 1979 (hereinafter referred to as "the Madrid (Stockholm) Agreement"), and the organizations referred to in Article 14(1)(b) which are party to this Protocol (hereinafter referred to as "the Contracting Organizations") shall be members of the same Union of which countries party to the Madrid (Stockholm) Agreement are members. Any reference in this Protocol to "Contracting Parties" shall be construed as a reference to both Contracting States and Contracting Organizations.

Article 2. Securing Protection through International Registration

(1) Where an application for the registration of a mark has been filed with the Office of a Contracting Party, or where a mark has been registered in the register of the Office of a Contracting Party, the person in whose name that application (hereinafter referred to as "the basic application") or that registration (hereinafter referred to as "the basic registration") stands may, subject to the provisions of this Protocol, secure protection for his mark in the territory of the Contracting Parties, by obtaining the registration of that mark in the register of the International Bureau of the World Intellectual Property Organization (hereinafter referred to as "the international registration," "the International Register," "the International Bureau" and "the Organization," respectively), provided that,

(i) where the basic application has been filed with the Office of a Contracting State or where the basic registration has been made by such an Office, the person in whose name that application or registration stands is a national of that Contracting State, or is domiciled, or has a real and effective industrial or commercial establishment, in the said Contracting State,

(ii) where the basic application has been filed with the Office of a Contracting Organization or where the basic registration has been made by such an Office, the person in whose name that application or registration stands is a national of a State member of that Contracting Organization, or is domiciled, or has a real and effective industrial or commercial establishment, in the territory of the said Contracting Organization.

(2) The application for international registration (hereinafter referred to as "the international application") shall be filed with the International Bureau through the intermediary of the Office with which the basic application was filed or by which the basic registration was made (hereinafter referred to as "the Office of origin"), as the case may be.

(3) Any reference in this Protocol to an "Office" or an "Office of a Contracting Party" shall be construed as a reference to the office that is in charge, on behalf of a Contracting Party, of the registration of marks, and any reference in this Protocol to "marks" shall be construed as a reference to trademarks and service marks.

(4) For the purposes of this Protocol, "territory of a Contracting Party" means, where the Contracting Party is a State, the territory of that State and, where the Contracting Party is an intergovernmental organization, the territory in which the constituting treaty of that intergovernmental organization applies.

Article 3. International Application

(1) Every international application under this Protocol shall be presented on the form prescribed by the Regulations. The Office of origin shall certify that the particulars appearing in the international application correspond to the particulars appearing, at the time of the certification, in the basic application or basic registration, as the case may be. Furthermore, the said Office shall indicate,

(i) in the case of a basic application, the date and number of that application, (ii) in the case of a basic registration, the date and number of that registration as well as the date and number of the application from which the basic registration resulted. The Office of origin shall also indicate the date of the international application.

(2) The applicant must indicate the goods and services in respect of which protection of the mark is claimed and also, if possible, the corresponding class or classes according to the classification established by the Nice Agreement Concerning the International Classification of Goods and Services for

the Purposes of the Registration of Marks. If the applicant does not give such indication, the International Bureau shall classify the goods and services in the appropriate classes of the said classification. The indication of classes given by the applicant shall be subject to control by the International Bureau, which shall exercise the said control in association with the Office of origin. In the event of disagreement between the said Office and the International Bureau, the opinion of the latter shall prevail.

(3) If the applicant claims color as a distinctive feature of his mark, he shall be required

(i) to state the fact, and to file with his international application a notice specifying the color or the combination of colors claimed;

(ii) to append to his international application copies in color of the said mark, which shall be attached to the notifications given by the International Bureau; the number of such copies shall be fixed by the Regulations.

(4) The International Bureau shall register immediately the marks filed in accordance with Article 2. The international registration shall bear the date on which the international application was received in the Office of origin, provided that the international application has been received by the International Bureau within a period of two months from that date. If the international application has not been received within that period, the international registration shall bear the date on which the said international application was received by the International Bureau. The International Bureau shall notify the international registration without delay to the Offices concerned. Marks registered in the International Register shall be published in a periodical gazette issued by the International Bureau, on the basis of the particulars contained in the international application.

(5) With a view to the publicity to be given to marks registered in the International Register, each Office shall receive from the International Bureau a number of copies of the said gazette free of charge and a number of copies at a reduced price, under the conditions fixed by the Assembly referred to in Article 10 (hereinafter referred to as "the Assembly"). Such publicity shall be deemed to be sufficient for the purposes of all the Contracting Parties, and no other publicity may be required of the holder of the international registration.

Article 3bis. Territorial Effect

The protection resulting from the international registration shall extend to any Contracting Party only at the request of the person who files the international application or who is the holder of the international registration. However, no such request can be made with respect to the Contracting Party whose Office is the Office of origin.

Article 3ter.   Request for "Territorial Extension"

(1) Any request for extension of the protection resulting from the international registration to any Contracting Party shall be specially mentioned in the international application.

(2) A request for territorial extension may also be made subsequently to the international registration. Any such request shall be presented on the form prescribed by the Regulations. It shall be immediately recorded by the International Bureau, which shall notify such recordal without delay to the Office or Offices concerned. Such recordal shall be published in the periodical gazette of the International Bureau. Such territorial extension shall be effective from the date on which it has been recorded in the International Register; it shall cease to be valid on the expiry of the international registration to which it relates.

Article 4.   Effects of International Registration

(1) (a) From the date of the registration or recordal effected in accordance with the provisions of Articles 3 and 3ter, the protection of the mark in each of the Contracting Parties concerned shall be the same as if the mark had been deposited direct with the Office of that Contracting Party. If no refusal has been notified to the International Bureau in accordance with Article 5(1) and (2) or if a refusal notified in accordance with the said Article has been withdrawn subsequently, the protection of the mark in the Contracting Party concerned shall, as from the said date, be the same as if the mark had been registered by the Office of that Contracting Party.

(b) The indication of classes of goods and services provided for in Article 3 shall not bind the Contracting Parties with regard to the determination of the scope of the protection of the mark.

(2) Every international registration shall enjoy the right of priority provided for by Article 4 of the Paris Convention for the Protection of Industrial Property, without it being necessary to comply with the formalities prescribed in Section D of that Article.

Article 4bis. Replacement of a National or Regional Registration by an International Registration

(1) Where a mark that is the subject of a national or regional registration in the Office of a Contracting Party is also the subject of an international registration and both registrations stand in the name of the same person, the international registration is deemed to replace the national or regional registration, without prejudice to any rights acquired by virtue of the latter, provided that

(i) the protection resulting from the international registration extends to the said Contracting Party under Article 3ter(1) or (2),

(ii) all the goods and services listed in the national or regional registration are also listed in the international registration in respect of the said Contracting Party,

(iii) such extension takes effect after the date of the national or regional registration.

(2) The Office referred to in paragraph (1) shall, upon request, be required to take note in its register of the international registration.

Article 5. Refusal and Invalidation of Effects of International Registration in Respect of Certain Contracting Parties

(1) Where the applicable legislation so authorizes, any Office of a Contracting Party which has been notified by the International Bureau of an extension to that Contracting Party, under Article 3ter(1) or (2), of the protection resulting from the international registration shall have the right to declare in a notification of refusal that protection cannot be granted in the said Contracting Party to the mark which is the subject of such extension. Any such refusal can be based only on the grounds which would apply, under the Paris Convention for the Protection of Industrial Property, in the case of a mark deposited direct with the Office which notifies the refusal. However, protection may not be refused, even partially, by reason only that the applicable legislation would permit registration only in a limited number of classes or for a limited number of goods or services.

(2) (a) Any Office wishing to exercise such right shall notify its refusal to the International Bureau, together with a statement of all grounds, within the period prescribed by the law applicable to that Office and at the latest, subject to subparagraphs (b) and (c), before the expiry of one year from

the date on which the notification of the extension referred to in paragraph (1) has been sent to that Office by the International Bureau.

(b) Notwithstanding subparagraph (a), any Contracting Party may declare that, for international registrations made under this Protocol, the time limit of one year referred to in subparagraph (a) is replaced by 18 months.

(c) Such declaration may also specify that, when a refusal of protection may result from an opposition to the granting of protection, such refusal may be notified by the Office of the said Contracting Party to the International Bureau after the expiry of the 18-month time limit. Such an Office may, with respect to any given international registration, notify a refusal of protection after the expiry of the 18-month time limit, but only if (i) it has, before the expiry of the 18-month time limit, informed the International Bureau of the possibility that oppositions may be filed after the expiry of the 18-month time limit, and (ii) the notification of the refusal based on an opposition is made within a time limit of not more than seven months from the date on which the opposition period begins; if the opposition period expires before this time limit of seven months, the notification must be made within a time limit of one month from the expiry of the opposition period.

(d) Any declaration under subparagraphs (b) or (c) may be made in the instruments referred to in Article 14(2), and the effective date of the declaration shall be the same as the date of entry into force of this Protocol with respect to the State or intergovernmental organization having made the declaration. Any such declaration may also be made later, in which case the declaration shall have effect three months after its receipt by the Director General of the Organization (hereinafter referred to as "the Director General"), or at any later date indicated in the declaration, in respect of any international registration whose date is the same as or is later than the effective date of the declaration.

(e) Upon the expiry of a period of ten years from the entry into force of this Protocol, the Assembly shall examine the operation of the system established by subparagraphs (a) to (d). Thereafter, the provisions of the said subparagraphs may be modified by a unanimous decision of the Assembly.

(3) The International Bureau shall, without delay, transmit one of the copies of the notification of refusal to the holder of the international registration. The said holder shall have the same remedies as if the mark had been deposited

Madrid Protocol Art. 5

by him direct with the Office which has notified its refusal. Where the International Bureau has received information under paragraph (2)(c)(i), it shall, without delay, transmit the said information to the holder of the international registration.

(4) The grounds for refusing a mark shall be communicated by the International Bureau to any interested party who may so request.

(5) Any Office which has not notified, with respect to a given international registration, any provisional or final refusal to the International Bureau in accordance with paragraphs (1) and (2) shall, with respect to that international registration, lose the benefit of the right provided for in paragraph (1).

(6) Invalidation, by the competent authorities of a Contracting Party, of the effects, in the territory of that Contracting Party, of an international registration may not be pronounced without the holder of such international registration having, in good time, been afforded the opportunity of defending his rights. Invalidation shall be notified to the International Bureau.

Article 5bis. Documentary Evidence of Legitimacy of Use of Certain Elements of the Mark

Documentary evidence of the legitimacy of the use of certain elements incorporated in a mark, such as armorial bearings, escutcheons, portraits, honorary distinctions, titles, trade names, names of persons other than the name of the applicant, or other like inscriptions, which might be required by the Offices of the Contracting Parties shall be exempt from any legalization as well as from any certification other than that of the Office of origin.

Article 5ter. Copies of Entries in International Register; Searches for Anticipations; Extracts from International Register

(1) The International Bureau shall issue to any person applying therefor, upon the payment of a fee fixed by the Regulations, a copy of the entries in the International Register concerning a specific mark.

(2) The International Bureau may also, upon payment, undertake searches for anticipations among marks that are the subject of international registrations.

(3) Extracts from the International Register requested with a view to their production in one of the Contracting Parties shall be exempt from any legalization.

Article 6.   Period of Validity of International Registration; Dependence and Independence of International Registration

(1) Registration of a mark at the International Bureau is effected for ten years, with the possibility of renewal under the conditions specified in Article 7.

(2) Upon expiry of a period of five years from the date of the international registration, such registration shall become independent of the basic application or the registration resulting therefrom, or of the basic registration, as the case may be, subject to the following provisions.

(3) The protection resulting from the international registration, whether or not it has been the subject of a transfer, may no longer be invoked if, before the expiry of five years from the date of the international registration, the basic application or the registration resulting therefrom, or the basic registration, as the case may be, has been withdrawn, has lapsed, has been renounced or has been the subject of a final decision of rejection, revocation, cancellation or invalidation, in respect of all or some of the goods and services listed in the international registration. The same applies if

(i) an appeal against a decision refusing the effects of the basic application,

(ii) an action requesting the withdrawal of the basic application or the revocation, cancellation or invalidation of the registration resulting from the basic application or of the basic registration, or

(iii) an opposition to the basic application results, after the expiry of the five-year period, in a final decision of rejection, revocation, cancellation or invalidation, or ordering the withdrawal, of the basic application, or the registration resulting therefrom, or the basic registration, as the case may be, provided that such appeal, action or opposition had begun before the expiry of the said period. The same also applies if the basic application is withdrawn, or the registration resulting from the basic application or the basic registration is renounced, after the expiry of the five-year period, provided that, at the time of the withdrawal or renunciation, the said application or registration was the subject of a proceeding referred to in item (i), (ii) or (iii) and that such proceeding had begun before the expiry of the said period.

(4) The Office of origin shall, as prescribed in the Regulations, notify the International Bureau of the facts and decisions relevant under paragraph (3), and the International Bureau shall, as prescribed in the Regulations, notify the interested parties and effect any publication accordingly. The Office of

Madrid Protocol Art. 6

origin shall, where applicable, request the International Bureau to cancel, to the extent applicable, the international registration, and the International Bureau shall proceed accordingly.

Article 7.   Renewal of International Registration

(1) Any international registration may be renewed for a period of ten years from the expiry of the preceding period, by the mere payment of the basic fee and, subject to Article 8(7), of the supplementary and complementary fees provided for in Article 8(2).

(2) Renewal may not bring about any change in the international registration in its latest form.

(3) Six months before the expiry of the term of protection, the International Bureau shall, by sending an unofficial notice, remind the holder of the international registration and his representative, if any, of the exact date of expiry.

(4) Subject to the payment of a surcharge fixed by the Regulations, a period of grace of six months shall be allowed for renewal of the international registration.

Article 8.   Fees for International Application and Registration

(1) The Office of origin may fix, at its own discretion, and collect, for its own benefit, a fee which it may require from the applicant for international registration or from the holder of the international registration in connection with the filing of the international application or the renewal of the international registration.

(2) Registration of a mark at the International Bureau shall be subject to the advance payment of an international fee which shall, subject to the provisions of paragraph (7)(a), include,

(i) a basic fee;

(ii) a supplementary fee for each class of the International Classification, beyond three, into which the goods or services to which the mark is applied will fall;

(iii) a complementary fee for any request for extension of protection under Article 3ter.

(3) However, the supplementary fee specified in paragraph (2)(ii) may, without prejudice to the date of the international registration, be paid within the period fixed by the Regulations if the number of classes of goods or services has been fixed or disputed by the International Bureau. If, upon expiry of the said period, the supplementary fee has not been paid or the list of goods or services has not been reduced to the required extent by the applicant, the international application shall be deemed to have been abandoned.

(4) The annual product of the various receipts from international registration, with the exception of the receipts derived from the fees mentioned in paragraph (2)(ii) and (iii), shall be divided equally among the Contracting Parties by the International Bureau, after deduction of the expenses and charges necessitated by the implementation of this Protocol.

(5) The amounts derived from the supplementary fees provided for in paragraph (2)(ii) shall be divided, at the expiry of each year, among the interested Contracting Parties in proportion to the number of marks for which protection has been applied for in each of them during that year, this number being multiplied, in the case of Contracting Parties which make an examination, by a coefficient which shall be determined by the Regulations.

(6) The amounts derived from the complementary fees provided for in paragraph (2)(iii) shall be divided according to the same rules as those provided for in paragraph (5).

(7) (a) Any Contracting Party may declare that, in connection with each international registration in which it is mentioned under Article 3ter, and in connection with the renewal of any such international registration, it wants to receive, instead of a share in the revenue produced by the supplementary and complementary fees, a fee (hereinafter referred to as "the individual fee") whose amount shall be indicated in the declaration, and can be changed in further declarations, but may not be higher than the equivalent of the amount which the said Contracting Party's Office would be entitled to receive from an applicant for a ten-year registration, or from the holder of a registration for a ten-year renewal of that registration, of the mark in the register of the said Office, the said amount being diminished by the savings resulting from the international procedure. Where such an individual fee is payable,

Madrid Protocol Art. 8

(i) no supplementary fees referred to in paragraph (2)(ii) shall be payable if only Contracting Parties which have made a declaration under this subparagraph are mentioned under Article 3ter, and

(ii) no complementary fee referred to in paragraph (2)(iii) shall be payable in respect of any Contracting Party which has made a declaration under this subparagraph.

(b) Any declaration under subparagraph (a) may be made in the instruments referred to in Article 14(2), and the effective date of the declaration shall be the same as the date of entry into force of this Protocol with respect to the State or intergovernmental organization having made the declaration. Any such declaration may also be made later, in which case the declaration shall have effect three months after its receipt by the Director General, or at any later date indicated in the declaration, in respect of any international registration whose date is the same as or is later than the effective date of the declaration.

Article 9.   Recordal of Change in the Ownership of an International Registration

At the request of the person in whose name the international registration stands, or at the request of an interested Office made ex officio or at the request of an interested person, the International Bureau shall record in the International Register any change in the ownership of that registration, in respect of all or some of the Contracting Parties in whose territories the said registration has effect and in respect of all or some of the goods and services listed in the registration, provided that the new holder is a person who, under Article 2(1), is entitled to file international applications.

Article 9bis.   Recordal of Certain Matters Concerning an International Registration

The International Bureau shall record in the International Register

(i) any change in the name or address of the holder of the international registration,

(ii) the appointment of a representative of the holder of the international registration and any other relevant fact concerning such representative,

(iii) any limitation, in respect of all or some of the Contracting Parties, of the goods and services listed in the international registration,

(iv) any renunciation, cancellation or invalidation of the international registration in respect of all or some of the Contracting Parties,

(v) any other relevant fact, identified in the Regulations, concerning the rights in a mark that is the subject of an international registration.

Article 9ter. Fees for Certain Recordals

Any recordal under Article 9 or under Article 9bis may be subject to the payment of a fee.

Article 9quater. Common Office of Several Contracting States

(1) If several Contracting States agree to effect the unification of their domestic legislations on marks, they may notify the Director General

(i) that a common Office shall be substituted for the national Office of each of them, and

(ii) that the whole of their respective territories shall be deemed to be a single State for the purposes of the application of all or part of the provisions preceding this Article as well as the provisions of Articles 9quinquies and 9sexies.

(2) Such notification shall not take effect until three months after the date of the communication thereof by the Director General to the other Contracting Parties.

Article 9quinquies. Transformation of an International Registration into National or Regional Applications

Where, in the event that the international registration is cancelled at the request of the Office of origin under Article 6(4), in respect of all or some of the goods and services listed in the said registration, the person who was the holder of the international registration files an application for the registration of the same mark with the Office of any of the Contracting Parties in the territory of which the international registration had effect, that application shall be treated as if it had been filed on the date of the international registration according to Article 3(4) or on the date of recordal of the territorial extension according to Article 3ter(2) and, if the international registration enjoyed priority, shall enjoy the same priority, provided that

(i) such application is filed within three months from the date on which the international registration was cancelled,

Madrid Protocol Art. 9quinquies

(ii) the goods and services listed in the application are in fact covered by the list of goods and services contained in the international registration in respect of the Contracting Party concerned, and

(iii) such application complies with all the requirements of the applicable law, including the requirements concerning fees.

Article 9sexies. Relations Between States Party to both this Protocol and the Madrid (Stockholm) Agreement

(1) (a) This Protocol alone shall be applicable as regards the mutual relations of States party to both this Protocol and the Madrid (Stockholm) Agreement.

(b) Notwithstanding subparagraph (a), a declaration made under Article 5(2)(b), Article 5(2)(c) or Article 8(7) of this Protocol, by a State party to both this Protocol and the Madrid (Stockholm) Agreement, shall have no effect in the relations with another State party to both this Protocol and the Madrid (Stockholm) Agreement.

(2) The Assembly shall, after the expiry of a period of three years from September 1, 2008, review the application of paragraph (1)(b) and may, at any time thereafter, either repeal it or restrict its scope, by a three-fourths majority. In the vote of the Assembly, only those States which are party to both the Madrid (Stockholm) Agreement and this Protocol shall have the right to participate.

Article 10. Assembly

(1) (a) The Contracting Parties shall be members of the same Assembly as the countries party to the Madrid (Stockholm) Agreement.

(b) Each Contracting Party shall be represented in that Assembly by one delegate, who may be assisted by alternate delegates, advisors, and experts.

(c) The expenses of each delegation shall be borne by the Contracting Party which has appointed it, except for the travel expenses and the subsistence allowance of one delegate for each Contracting Party, which shall be paid from the funds of the Union.

(2) The Assembly shall, in addition to the functions which it has under the Madrid (Stockholm) Agreement, also

(i) deal with all matters concerning the implementation of this Protocol;

(ii) give directions to the International Bureau concerning the preparation for conferences of revision of this Protocol, due account being taken of any comments made by those countries of the Union which are not party to this Protocol;

(iii) adopt and modify the provisions of the Regulations concerning the implementation of this Protocol;

(iv) perform such other functions as are appropriate under this Protocol.

(3) (a) Each Contracting Party shall have one vote in the Assembly. On matters concerning only countries that are party to the Madrid (Stockholm) Agreement, Contracting Parties that are not party to the said Agreement shall not have the right to vote, whereas, on matters concerning only Contracting Parties, only the latter shall have the right to vote.

(b) One-half of the members of the Assembly which have the right to vote on a given matter shall constitute the quorum for the purposes of the vote on that matter.

(c) Notwithstanding the provisions of subparagraph (b), if, in any session, the number of the members of the Assembly having the right to vote on a given matter which are represented is less than one-half but equal to or more than one-third of the members of the Assembly having the right to vote on that matter, the Assembly may make decisions but, with the exception of decisions concerning its own procedure, all such decisions shall take effect only if the conditions set forth hereinafter are fulfilled. The International Bureau shall communicate the said decisions to the members of the Assembly having the right to vote on the said matter which were not represented and shall invite them to express in writing their vote or abstention within a period of three months from the date of the communication. If, at the expiry of this period, the number of such members having thus expressed their vote or abstention attains the number of the members which was lacking for attaining the quorum in the session itself, such decisions shall take effect provided that at the same time the required majority still obtains.

(d) Subject to the provisions of Articles 5(2)(e), 9sexies(2), 12 and 13(2), the decisions of the Assembly shall require two-thirds of the votes cast.

(e) Abstentions shall not be considered as votes.

Madrid Protocol Art. 10

(f) A delegate may represent, and vote in the name of, one member of the Assembly only.

(4) In addition to meeting in ordinary sessions and extraordinary sessions as provided for by the Madrid (Stockholm) Agreement, the Assembly shall meet in extraordinary session upon convocation by the Director General, at the request of one-fourth of the members of the Assembly having the right to vote on the matters proposed to be included in the agenda of the session. The agenda of such an extraordinary session shall be prepared by the Director General.

Article 11.   International Bureau

(1) International registration and related duties, as well as all other administrative tasks, under or concerning this Protocol, shall be performed by the International Bureau.

(2) (a) The International Bureau shall, in accordance with the directions of the Assembly, make the preparations for the conferences of revision of this Protocol.

(b) The International Bureau may consult with intergovernmental and international non-governmental organizations concerning preparations for such conferences of revision.

(c) The Director General and persons designated by him shall take part, without the right to vote, in the discussions at such conferences of revision.

(3) The International Bureau shall carry out any other tasks assigned to it in relation to this Protocol.

Article 12.   Finances

As far as Contracting Parties are concerned, the finances of the Union shall be governed by the same provisions as those contained in Article 12 of the Madrid (Stockholm) Agreement, provided that any reference to Article 8 of the said Agreement shall be deemed to be a reference to Article 8 of this Protocol. Furthermore, for the purposes of Article 12(6)(b) of the said Agreement, Contracting Organizations shall, subject to a unanimous decision to the contrary by the Assembly, be considered to belong to contribution class I (one) under the Paris Convention for the Protection of Industrial Property.

Article 13. Amendment of Certain Articles of the Protocol

(1) Proposals for the amendment of Articles 10, 11, 12, and the present Article, may be initiated by any Contracting Party, or by the Director General. Such proposals shall be communicated by the Director General to the Contracting Parties at least six months in advance of their consideration by the Assembly.

(2) Amendments to the Articles referred to in paragraph (1) shall be adopted by the Assembly. Adoption shall require three-fourths of the votes cast, provided that any amendment to Article 10, and to the present paragraph, shall require four-fifths of the votes cast.

(3) Any amendment to the Articles referred to in paragraph (1) shall enter into force one month after written notifications of acceptance, effected in accordance with their respective constitutional processes, have been received by the Director General from three fourths of those States and intergovernmental organizations which, at the time the amendment was adopted, were members of the Assembly and had the right to vote on the amendment. Any amendment to the said Articles thus accepted shall bind all the States and intergovernmental organizations which are Contracting Parties at the time the amendment enters into force, or which become Contracting Parties at a subsequent date.

Article 14. Becoming Party to the Protocol; Entry into Force

(1) (a) Any State that is a party to the Paris Convention for the Protection of Industrial Property may become party to this Protocol.

(b) Furthermore, any intergovernmental organization may also become party to this Protocol where the following conditions are fulfilled:

(i) at least one of the member States of that organization is a party to the Paris Convention for the Protection of Industrial Property;

(ii) that organization has a regional Office for the purposes of registering marks with effect in the territory of the organization, provided that such Office is not the subject of a notification under Article 9quater.

(2) Any State or organization referred to in paragraph (1) may sign this Protocol. Any such State or organization may, if it has signed this Protocol, deposit an instrument of ratification, acceptance or approval of this Protocol or, if it has not signed this Protocol, deposit an instrument of accession to this Protocol.

Madrid Protocol Art. 14

(3) The instruments referred to in paragraph (2) shall be deposited with the Director General.

(4) (a) This Protocol shall enter into force three months after four instruments of ratification, acceptance, approval or accession have been deposited, provided that at least one of those instruments has been deposited by a country party to the Madrid (Stockholm) Agreement and at least one other of those instruments has been deposited by a State not party to the Madrid (Stockholm) Agreement or by any of the organizations referred to in paragraph (1)(b).

(b) With respect to any other State or organization referred to in paragraph (1), this Protocol shall enter into force three months after the date on which its ratification, acceptance, approval or accession has been notified by the Director General.

(5) Any State or organization referred to in paragraph (1) may, when depositing its instrument of ratification, acceptance or approval of, or accession to, this Protocol, declare that the protection resulting from any international registration effected under this Protocol before the date of entry into force of this Protocol with respect to it cannot be extended to it.

Article 15. Denunciation

(1) This Protocol shall remain in force without limitation as to time.

(2) Any Contracting Party may denounce this Protocol by notification addressed to the Director General.

(3) Denunciation shall take effect one year after the day on which the Director General has received the notification.

(4) The right of denunciation provided for by this Article shall not be exercised by any Contracting Party before the expiry of five years from the date upon which this Protocol entered into force with respect to that Contracting Party.

(5) (a) Where a mark is the subject of an international registration having effect in the denouncing State or intergovernmental organization at the date on which the denunciation becomes effective, the holder of such registration may file an application for the registration of the same mark with the Office of the denouncing State or intergovernmental organization, which shall be treated as if it had been filed on the date of the international registration according to Article 3(4) or on the date of recordal of

the territorial extension according to Article 3ter(2) and, if the international registration enjoyed priority, enjoy the same priority, provided that

(i) such application is filed within two years from the date on which the denunciation became effective,

(ii) the goods and services listed in the application are in fact covered by the list of goods and services contained in the international registration in respect of the denouncing State or intergovernmental organization, and

(iii) such application complies with all the requirements of the applicable law, including the requirements concerning fees.

(b) The provisions of subparagraph (a) shall also apply in respect of any mark that is the subject of an international registration having effect in Contracting Parties other than the denouncing State or intergovernmental organization at the date on which denunciation becomes effective and whose holder, because of the denunciation, is no longer entitled to file international applications under Article 2(1).

Article 16.   Signature; Languages; Depositary Functions

(1) (a) This Protocol shall be signed in a single copy in the English, French and Spanish languages, and shall be deposited with the Director General when it ceases to be open for signature at Madrid. The texts in the three languages shall be equally authentic.

(b) Official texts of this Protocol shall be established by the Director General, after consultation with the interested governments and organizations, in the Arabic, Chinese, German, Italian, Japanese, Portuguese and Russian languages, and in such other languages as the Assembly may designate.

(2) This Protocol shall remain open for signature at Madrid until December 31, 1989.

(3) The Director General shall transmit two copies, certified by the Government of Spain, of the signed texts of this Protocol to all States and intergovernmental organizations that may become party to this Protocol.

(4) The Director General shall register this Protocol with the Secretariat of the United Nations.

(5) The Director General shall notify all States and international organizations that may become or are party to this Protocol of signatures, deposits of instruments of ratification, acceptance, approval or accession, the entry into force of this Protocol and any amendment thereto, any notification of denunciation and any declaration provided for in this Protocol.

IV. ICANN UNIFORM DOMAIN NAME
DISPUTE RESOLUTION POLICY

ICANN UNIFORM DOMAIN NAME DISPUTE RESOLUTION POLICY*

Policy Adopted: August 26, 1999; Implementation Documents Approved: October 24, 1999

1. *Purpose.*—This Uniform Domain Name Dispute Resolution Policy (the "Policy") has been adopted by the Internet Corporation for Assigned Names and Numbers ("ICANN"), is incorporated by reference into your Registration Agreement, and sets forth the terms and conditions in connection with a dispute between you and any party other than us (the registrar) over the registration and use of an Internet domain name registered by you. Proceedings under Paragraph 4 of this Policy will be conducted according to the Rules for Uniform Domain Name Dispute Resolution Policy (the "Rules of Procedure"), which are available at http://www.icann.org/dndr/udrp/uniform-rules.htm, and the selected administrative-dispute-resolution service provider's supplemental rules.

2. *Your Representations.*—By applying to register a domain name, or by asking us to maintain or renew a domain name registration, you hereby represent and warrant to us that (a) the statements that you made in your Registration Agreement are complete and accurate; (b) to your knowledge, the registration of the domain name will not infringe upon or otherwise violate the rights of any third party; (c) you are not registering the domain name for an unlawful purpose; and (d) you will not knowingly use the domain name in violation of any applicable laws or regulations. It is your responsibility to determine whether your domain name registration infringes or violates someone else's rights.

3. *Cancellations, Transfers, and Changes.*—We will cancel, transfer or otherwise make changes to domain name registrations under the following circumstances:

   a. subject to the provisions of Paragraph 8, our receipt of written or appropriate electronic instructions from you or your authorized agent to take such action;

---

b. our receipt of an order from a court or arbitral tribunal, in each case of competent jurisdiction, requiring such action; and/or

c. our receipt of a decision of an Administrative Panel requiring such action in any administrative proceeding to which you were a party and which was conducted under this Policy or a later version of this Policy adopted by ICANN. (See Paragraph 4(i) and (k) below.) We may also cancel, transfer or otherwise make changes to a domain name registration in accordance with the terms of your Registration Agreement or other legal requirements.

4. *Mandatory Administrative Proceeding.*—This Paragraph sets forth the type of disputes for which you are required to submit to a mandatory administrative proceeding. These proceedings will be conducted before one of the administrative-dispute-resolution service providers listed at http://www.icann.org/dndr/udrp/approved-providers.htm (each, a "Provider").

a. *Applicable Disputes.*—You are required to submit to a mandatory administrative proceeding in the event that a third party (a "complainant") asserts to the applicable Provider, in compliance with the Rules of Procedure, that

(i) your domain name is identical or confusingly similar to a trademark or service mark in which the complainant has rights; and

(ii) you have no rights or legitimate interests in respect of the domain name; and

(iii) your domain name has been registered and is being used in bad faith. In the administrative proceeding, the complainant must prove that each of these three elements are present.

b. *Evidence of Registration and Use in Bad Faith.*—For the purposes of Paragraph 4(a)(iii), the following circumstances, in particular but without limitation, if found by the Panel to be present, shall be evidence of the registration and use of a domain name in bad faith:

(i) circumstances indicating that you have registered or you have acquired the domain name primarily for the purpose of selling, renting, or otherwise transferring the domain name registration to the complainant who is the owner of the trademark or service mark or to a competitor of that complainant, for valuable consideration in excess of your documented out-of-pocket costs directly related to the domain name; or

(ii) you have registered the domain name in order to prevent the owner of the trademark or service mark from reflecting the mark in a corresponding domain name, provided that you have engaged in a pattern of such conduct; or

(iii) you have registered the domain name primarily for the purpose of disrupting the business of a competitor; or

(iv) by using the domain name, you have intentionally attempted to attract, for commercial gain, Internet users to your web site or other on-line location, by creating a likelihood of confusion with the complainant's mark as to the source, sponsorship, affiliation, or endorsement of your web site or location or of a product or service on your web site or location.

c. *How to Demonstrate Your Rights to and Legitimate Interests in the Domain Name in Responding to a Complaint.*—When you receive a complaint, you should refer to Paragraph 5 of the Rules of Procedure in determining how your response should be prepared. Any of the following circumstances, in particular but without limitation, if found by the Panel to be proved based on its evaluation of all evidence presented, shall demonstrate your rights or legitimate interests to the domain name for purposes of Paragraph 4(a)(ii):

(i) before any notice to you of the dispute, your use of, or demonstrable preparations to use, the domain name or a name corresponding to the domain name in connection with a bona fide offering of goods or services; or

(ii) you (as an individual, business, or other organization) have been commonly known by the domain name, even if you have acquired no trademark or service mark rights; or

(iii) you are making a legitimate noncommercial or fair use of the domain name, without intent for commercial gain to misleadingly divert consumers or to tarnish the trademark or service mark at issue.

d. *Selection of Provider.*—The complainant shall select the Provider from among those approved by ICANN by submitting the complaint to that Provider. The selected Provider will administer the proceeding, except in cases of consolidation as described in Paragraph 4(f).

e. *Initiation of Proceeding and Process and Appointment of Administrative Panel.*—The Rules of Procedure state the process for initiating and conducting a proceeding and for appointing the panel that will decide the dispute (the "Administrative Panel").

f. *Consolidation.*—In the event of multiple disputes between you and a complainant, either you or the complainant may petition to consolidate the disputes before a single Administrative Panel. This petition shall be made to the first Administrative Panel appointed to hear a pending dispute between the parties. This Administrative Panel may consolidate before it any or all such disputes in its sole discretion, provided that the disputes being consolidated are governed by this Policy or a later version of this Policy adopted by ICANN.

g. *Fees.*—All fees charged by a Provider in connection with any dispute before an Administrative Panel pursuant to this Policy shall be paid by the complainant, except in cases where you elect to expand the Administrative Panel from one to three panelists as provided in Paragraph 5(b)(iv) of the Rules of Procedure, in which case all fees will be split evenly by you and the complainant.

h. *Our Involvement in Administrative Proceedings.*—We do not, and will not, participate in the administration or conduct of any proceeding before an Administrative Panel. In addition, we will not be liable as a result of any decisions rendered by the Administrative Panel.

i. *Remedies.*—The remedies available to a complainant pursuant to any proceeding before an Administrative Panel shall be limited to requiring the cancellation of your domain name or the transfer of your domain name registration to the complainant.

j. *Notification and Publication.*—The Provider shall notify us of any decision made by an Administrative Panel with respect to a domain name you have registered with us. All decisions under this Policy will be published in full over the Internet, except when an Administrative Panel determines in an exceptional case to redact portions of its decision.

k. *Availability of Court Proceedings.*—The mandatory administrative proceeding requirements set forth in Paragraph 4 shall not prevent either you or the complainant from submitting the dispute to a court of competent jurisdiction for independent resolution before such mandatory administrative proceeding is commenced or after such proceeding is concluded. If an Administrative Panel decides that your domain name registration should be canceled or transferred, we will wait ten (10) business days (as observed in the location of our principal office) after we are informed by the applicable Provider of the Administrative Panel's decision before implementing that decision. We will then implement the decision unless we have received from you during that ten (10) business day period official documentation (such as a copy of a complaint, file-stamped by the clerk of the court) that you have commenced a lawsuit against the complainant in a jurisdiction to which the complainant has submitted under Paragraph 3(b)(xiii) of the Rules of Procedure. (In general, that jurisdiction is either the location of our principal office or of your address as shown in our Whois database. See Paragraphs 1 and 3(b)(xiii) of the Rules of Procedure for details.) If we receive such documentation within the ten (10) business day period, we will not implement the Administrative Panel's decision, and we will take no further action, until we receive (i) evidence satisfactory to us of a resolution between the parties; (ii) evidence satisfactory to us that your lawsuit has been dismissed or withdrawn; or (iii) a copy of an order from such court dismissing your lawsuit or ordering that you do not have the right to continue to use your domain name.

5. *All Other Disputes and Litigation.* — All other disputes between you and any party other than us regarding your domain name registration that are not brought pursuant to the mandatory administrative proceeding provisions of Paragraph 4 shall be resolved between you and such other party through any court, arbitration or other proceeding that may be available.

6. *Our Involvement in Disputes.* — We will not participate in any way in any dispute between you and any party other than us regarding the registration and use of your domain name. You shall not name us as a party or otherwise include us in any such proceeding. In the event that we are named as a party in any such proceeding, we reserve the right to raise any and all defenses deemed appropriate, and to take any other action necessary to defend ourselves.

7. *Maintaining the Status Quo.* — We will not cancel, transfer, activate, deactivate, or otherwise change the status of any domain name registration under this Policy except as provided in Paragraph 3 above.

8. *Transfers During a Dispute.* —

    a. *Transfers of a Domain Name to a New Holder.* — You may not transfer your domain name registration to another holder (i) during a pending administrative proceeding brought pursuant to Paragraph 4 or for a period of fifteen (15) business days (as observed in the location of our principal place of business) after such proceeding is concluded; or (ii) during a pending court proceeding or arbitration commenced regarding your domain name unless the party to whom the domain name registration is being transferred agrees, in writing, to be bound by the decision of the court or arbitrator. We reserve the right to cancel any transfer of a domain name registration to another holder that is made in violation of this subparagraph.

b. *Changing Registrars.* — You may not transfer your domain name registration to another registrar during a pending administrative proceeding brought pursuant to Paragraph 4 or for a period of fifteen (15) business days (as observed in the location of our principal place of business) after such proceeding is concluded. You may transfer administration of your domain name registration to another registrar during a pending court action or arbitration, provided that the domain name you have registered with us shall continue to be subject to the proceedings commenced against you in accordance with the terms of this Policy. In the event that you transfer a domain name registration to us during the pendency of a court action or arbitration, such dispute shall remain subject to the domain name dispute policy of the registrar from which the domain name registration was transferred.

9. *Policy Modifications.* — We reserve the right to modify this Policy at any time with the permission of ICANN. We will post our revised Policy at least thirty (30) calendar days before it becomes effective. Unless this Policy has already been invoked by the submission of a complaint to a Provider, in which event the version of the Policy in effect at the time it was invoked will apply to you until the dispute is over, all such changes will be binding upon you with respect to any domain name registration dispute, whether the dispute arose before, on or after the effective date of our change. In the event that you object to a change in this Policy, your sole remedy is to cancel your domain name registration with us, provided that you will not be entitled to a refund of any fees you paid to us. The revised Policy will apply to you until you cancel your domain name registration.

Part 7

INDEX

INDEX

E

G

N

O

U

PLEASE READ BEFORE USING THIS CD-ROM

This is a legal agreement between you, the individual or entity using this software (the "User"), and The Bureau of National Affairs, Inc. d/b/a Bloomberg BNA ("Bloomberg BNA"). Use of the software files and content included within this CD-ROM (collectively, "Software") is governed by the terms of the following license agreement ("Agreement"). Your use of this CD-ROM will constitute Your acceptance of each of the terms, conditions, and covenants set forth herein. If you do not agree to each of the terms of this Agreement, promptly return the CD-ROM package and the accompanying items (including associated book and packaging) to Bloomberg BNA for a full refund or cancellation of all charges.

BLOOMBERG BNA LICENSE AGREEMENT

1. *Grant of License*. Bloomberg BNA grants You a nonexclusive limited license to use the Software on a single-user computer.

2. *Transfer of License*. You may not rent, loan, or lease the Software, but you may transfer the Software and the accompanying written materials on a permanent basis provided you retain no copies, and the recipient agrees in writing to comply with each of the terms set forth in this Agreement. If the Software is an update, any transfer must include the update and all prior versions.

3. *Other Restrictions*. You may not: reproduce, publish, distribute, sell, or otherwise use any material retrieved from or contained in the CDROM in any manner whatsoever that may infringe any copyright or proprietary interest of Bloomberg BNA; distribute, rent, sublicense, lease, transfer (except as explicitly set forth herein), or assign the product or the License Agreement; decompile, disassemble, or otherwise reverse engineer the CD-ROM. Nothing herein, however, shall prevent You from using the material (electronic or written) in the normal course of business for which the material is intended.

4. *Copyright*. The Software is owned by Bloomberg BNA or its successors, assigns, or suppliers, and is protected by United States copyright laws and international treaty provisions.

Notwithstanding any restrictions provided under applicable copyright law or this Agreement to the contrary, You may either (a) make one copy of the Software solely for backup or archival purposes, or (b) transfer the Software to a single hard disk provided you keep the original solely for backup or archival purposes.

DISCLAIMER

This publication is designed to provide accurate and authoritative information in regard to the subject matter covered. In publishing this book, neither the authors and editors, nor the publisher is engaged in rendering legal, accounting, or other professional service. If legal advice or other expert assistance is required, the services of a competent professional should be sought. Appendix documents may provide links to or refer to material on the Internet. While Bloomberg BNA and the author(s) aim to provide the most current information available, users are cautioned that websites and documents on the Internet are subject to change without notice and their use may be subject to further restrictions; users should consult specific websites identified in this publication for updates and for further information on topics of interest.

LIMITED WARRANTY

Bloomberg BNA warrants the physical media (i.e., CD-ROM) on which the Software is furnished to be free from defects in materials and workmanship under normal use for a period of one year from the date of delivery to you. This limited warranty gives you specific legal rights. You may have others, which vary from state to state. Some states do not allow the limitation or exclusion of some warranties, so the above limitation may not apply to you.

Bloomberg BNA does not warrant that the functions contained in the program will meet your requirements. You assume responsibility for the installation, use, and results obtained from the program.

THE ENCLOSED SOFTWARE IS PROVIDED "AS IS" WITHOUT WARRANTY OF ANY KIND, EITHER EXPRESS OR IMPLIED, INCLUDING BUT NOT LIMITED TO IMPLIED WARRANTIES OF MERCHANTABILITY AND FITNESS FOR A PARTICULAR PURPOSE, WITH RESPECT TO THE SOFTWARE AND ANY OTHER ACCOMPANYING MATERIALS.

LIMITATION OF REMEDIES

If for any reason the limited warranty provided by this Agreement should be determined to be invalid or inapplicable to any claim that is based upon the quality or performance of the licensed Software, the aggregate liability of Bloomberg BNA, its affiliates, and agents shall be limited to the amount paid by You to Bloomberg BNA for the original version of the Software.

IN NO EVENT WILL BLOOMBERG BNA, ITS AFFILIATES, TEHIR RESPECTIVE SUPPLIERS, OR THIRD-PARTY AGENTS BE LIABLE TO YOU FOR ANY DAMAGES, INCLUDING ANY LOST PROFITS, BUSINESS INTERRUPTION, LOST SAVINGS, LOSS OF BUSINESS INFORMATION, OR OTHER INCIDENTAL OR CONSEQUENTIAL DAMAGES ARISING OUT OF THE USE OR INABILITY TO USE SUCH SOFTWARE EVEN IF BLOOMBERG BNA OR AN AUTHORIZED BLOOMBERG BNA DEALER HAS BEEN ADVISED OF THE POSSIBILITY OF SUCH DAMAGES. NOR SHALL BLOOMBERG BNA BE RESPONSIBLE FOR ANY CLAIM BY ANY OTHER PARTY ARISING FROM OR RELATED TO THE SOFTWARE.

SOME STATES DO NOT ALLOW THE LIMITATION OR EXCLUSION OF LIABILITY FOR INCIDENTAL OR CONSEQUENTIAL DAMAGES, SO THE ABOVE LIMITATION OR EXCLUSION MAY NOT APPLY TO YOU.

This Agreement is governed by the laws of the Commonwealth of Virginia. If any provision of this Agreement shall be determined to be invalid or otherwise unenforceable, the enforceability of the remaining provisions shall not be impaired thereby. The failure of Bloomberg BNA to exercise any right provided for herein shall not be deemed a waiver of any right hereunder. This Agreement sets forth the entire understanding of Bloomberg BNA and You with respect to the issues addressed herein and may not be modified except by a writing executed by both parties.

The CD-ROM contains files in HTML and Adobe® Portable Document Format (PDF).